Fromm

Walt Disney World & Orlando

Here's what the critics say about Frommer's:

"Amazingly easy to use. Very portable, very complete."
—*Booklist*

♦

"The only mainstream guide to list specific prices. The Walter Cronkite of guidebooks—with all that implies."
—*Travel & Leisure*

♦

"Complete, concise, and filled with useful information."
—*New York Daily News*

♦

"Hotel information is close to encyclopedic."
—*Des Moines Sunday Register*

Other Great Guides for Your Trip:

Frommer's Florida

Frommer's Florida from $60 a Day

Frommer's Portable Tampa & St. Petersburg

Frommer's Best-Loved Florida's Driving Tours

Frommer's Irreverent Guide to Walt Disney World

The Complete Idiot's Guide to Walt Disney World & Orlando

The Unofficial Guide to Walt Disney World

*Mini Mickey: The Pocket Sized Unofficial Guide
to Walt Disney World*

The Unofficial Disney Companion

Frommer's® 99

Walt Disney World & Orlando

by Mary Meehan

MACMILLAN • USA

ABOUT THE AUTHOR

From opening day at Universal Studios Florida to the first plunge down Tower of Terror, **Mary Meehan** has been on hand as travel options have exploded in Central Florida. As an Orlando-based writer whose award-winning work appears in regional and national publications, Meehan has an insider's view of the best things to see and do in Central Florida—and the best things to avoid.

MACMILLAN TRAVEL

A Simon & Schuster Macmillan Company
1633 Broadway

New York, NY 10019

Find us online at **www.frommers.com**

ISBN 0-02-862241-3
ISSN 1082-2615

Editor: Douglas Stallings
Production Editor: Robyn Burnett
Photo Editor: Richard Fox
Design by Michele Laseau
Digital Cartography by Ortelius Design
Page Creation by Jerry Cole, Stephanie Hammet, Linda Quigley, and David Pruett

SPECIAL SALES

Bulk purchases (10+ copies) of Frommer's and selected Macmillan travel guides are available to corporations, organizations, mail-order catalogs, institutions, and charities at special discounts, and can be customized to suit individual needs. For more information write to: Special Sales, Macmillan General Reference, 1633 Broadway, New York, NY 10019.

Manufactured in the United States of America

Contents

6 Dining 91

7 On Your Mark, Get Set, Go! What to See & Do In & Around Walt Disney World 128

8 What to See & Do Beyond Disney: Universal Studios Florida, Islands of Adventure, Sea World & Other Attractions 184

List of Maps

An Invitation to the Reader

In researching this book, we discovered many wonderful places—hotels, restaurants, shops, and more. We're sure you'll find others. Please tell us about them, so we can share the information with your fellow travelers in upcoming editions. If you were disappointed with a recommendation, We'd love to know that, too. Please write to

Frommer's Walt Disney World & Orlando '99
Macmillan Travel
1633 Broadway
New York, NY 10019

An Additional Note

Please be advised that travel information is subject to change at any time—and this is especially true of prices. We therefore suggest that you write or call ahead for confirmation when making your travel plans. The authors, editors, and publisher cannot be held responsible for the experiences of readers while traveling. Your safety is important to us, however, so we encourage you to stay alert and be aware of your surroundings. Keep a close eye on cameras, purses, and wallets, all favorite targets of thieves and pickpockets.

What the Symbols Mean

❂ Frommer's Favorites

Our favorite places and experiences—outstanding for quality, value, or both.

The following abbreviations are used for credit cards:

AE	American Express	EU	Eurocard
CB	Carte Blanche	JCB	Japan Credit Bank
DC	Diners Club	MC	MasterCard
DISC	Discover	V	Visa

Find Frommer's Online

Arthur Frommer's Outspoken Encyclopedia of Travel (www.frommers.com) offers more than 6,000 pages of up-to-the-minute travel information—including the latest bargains and candid, personal articles updated daily by Arthur Frommer himself. No other Web site offers such comprehensive and timely coverage of the world of travel.

Introducing Walt Disney World & Orlando

The first time you visit Orlando, the urge to do everything in The World and then some can be overwhelming. But, to borrow a phrase from my New York in-laws— fugedaboudit. As your guide, I can promise you that even a two-week stay isn't long enough to hit everything.

With six full-blown theme parks, four nighttime entertainment districts, a thriving downtown, a lively local cultural community, hundreds of smaller attractions, and thousands of restaurants, your focus should be on quality not quantity. But don't panic. I've done it all so you won't have to. Every inch of every park, every restaurant, every hotel. I've inspected them all. (Okay, my husband checked out those theme park men's rooms, and he assures me they are fine.) I provide an insider's view of how to make the most of your time in Orlando. It is, I am proud to say, the place I call home.

Yes, there are enough options to make your head spin like one of those famous Disney teacups. With this book, though, you will have the necessary tools to plan ahead, and you will have enough information about your choices to be flexible. My goal? To help you make the decisions that will make your trip easy and enjoyable. If I've done my job, you'll actually be able to relax before you return to yours.

Such a mind-numbing array of opportunities couldn't have been imagined 30 years ago. In the mid-1960s when Walt Disney started looking for a new home, who knew that Orlando would evolve into such a tourist mecca? Now there are so many theme restaurants that there's actually one with an airline food motif. Seriously: airline seats, tray tables, and meals served in those lovely plastic trays. *YIKES!*

Perhaps that's fitting, though, given how Walt first spotted his new home. Flying over 43 square miles of scrub brush and swampland just south of a sleepy, southern town, Walt Disney had a vision of a whole new world. Orlando, where the biggest tourist draw had previously been a downtown fountain, would never be the same. And, as the millennium approaches and each year brings another full-scale theme park, visitors have never had more options.

There still is an Orlando that most tourists never see, far away from the fairy castles and the splashy whale shows. That Orlando is colored by its deeply southern pioneer roots. Stoked by tourism dollars, however, the Orlando area is looking increasingly to the future. Many national firms, including the American Automobile Association and

Tupperware, have located their headquarters in this thriving Sunbelt region. Orlando has become one of the fastest-growing high-tech centers in the country, with an active downtown. (And I don't mean Downtown Disney—but more about that later.) By the year 2004, the metro Orlando area is expected to lead the nation in the growth of office employment, adding some 65,900 jobs.

While that's impressive to the local chamber of commerce, thinking about the office—any office—is the last thing you want to do when planning your vacation. Not too many people buckle on fanny packs to visit Orlando because it has doubled its high-tech industrial base in 10 years. Ironically, though, much of that high-tech work is in the field of virtual reality. That's something ole Walt began to concoct long ago, and it's a field of expertise in which Disney's competition, often taking tips from the master, is becoming increasingly more adept.

Walt's World now claims four distinct parks, two entertainment districts, more hotel rooms than most small cities, water parks, and a putt-putt golf course. (The Reedy Creek Improvement District, which includes Walt Disney World, has the powers of a small city, and even has a base of voters made up of Disney employees.)

As if that weren't enough, Disney has built its own version of a small-town utopia, Celebration, where tourists slowly drive by houses where real people actually live. (You'll sometimes see signs in the front yards that say THIS HOUSE IS OCCUPIED so people will know it is not the movie set for *Stepford, The Sequel.*) Disney has also opened Animal Kingdom, a zoologically themed park with an emphasis on conservation.

Universal Studios Florida is expanding rapidly, having just added a nighttime entertainment complex—CityWalk, which opens in late 1998—and is in the process of adding a second park complete with stomach-churning thrill rides. Sea World is also growing, though at a slower pace. Chances are if you haven't been to Orlando in 5 years, there's a whole lot you won't recognize.

Disney is still the premiere vacation spot for kids and families, but if you look closely—and standing in those lines you will have plenty of time—you'll notice a lot of singles and seniors. Obviously, Disney and Universal were keeping these markets in mind when they added themed nightclub districts. Grown-ups are coming in increasing numbers and are finding plenty of PG-rated adult entertainment.

That's not to say that Orlando isn't a kid-friendly place. Many hotels, some whimsically themed, have video-game arcades and other child-pleasing features, and just about every restaurant in town has a low-priced children's menu.

In this city, visitors—big or small—are the real VIPs. The major players are vying for your business, as they engage in an ongoing, high-stakes game of one-upmanship. The innovative Disney–MGM Studios theme park, with its movie-magic motif, was countered a year after it opened by Universal Studios Florida, who brought in Steven Spielberg as a creative consultant. Church Street Station, a single-price–admission entertainment complex was followed closely by Disney's Pleasure Island. Wet 'n' Wild in town? Disney has three water parks of its own and provides free transportation to them for its vast numbers of resort guests. Busch Gardens in nearby Tampa has an animal park? Well, by gosh, Disney will have an entire Animal *Kingdom*.

Make no mistake; in this war you are the prize and the stakes, and the roller coasters will continue to rise. The big question for the next few years, after Universal builds its Jurassic Park attraction, is: Will Disney create real dinosaurs from DNA found in amber?

Central Florida

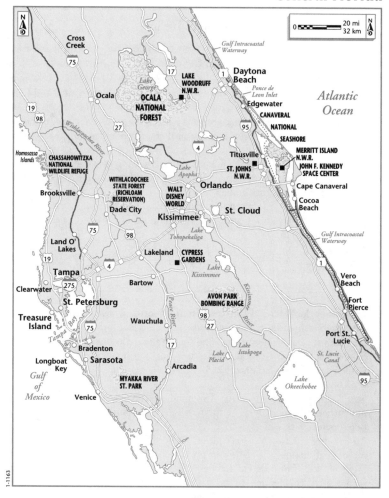

1 Frommer's Favorite Orlando Experiences

From Cinderella's Castle to Space Mountain, everybody loves the Magic Kingdom, but here are some other great things to try, both at Disney and in the greater Orlando area.

- **A Day at EPCOT.** You can travel around the world in an afternoon at the World Showcase pavilions and then have a truly hands-on experience at Innoventions, where rides and a variety of interactive games await you.
- **Visit Disney–MGM Studios.** More grown-up than the Magic Kingdom but still with lots of great activities for the kids. Don't miss The Tower of Terror.
- **Check Out Disney's Wide World of Sports.** From top tennis stars to an NFL "experience," this huge sports complex is worth checking out. There are also numerous other sporting options for the whole family in Orlando—great golfing, tennis, boating, fishing, waterskiing, cycling . . . you name it.

Chills & Thrills

If you are a speed freak who lives for the ups and downs of a good thrill ride, here are the top five stomach churners in Orlando:

- **Bomb Bay** (Wet 'n' Wild). Here you shoot through a tube down a 76-foot nearly vertical slide with only the water between you and the slide. Need I say more?
- **Back to the Future** (Universal Studios Florida). Great special effects combine with a dipping, twisting ride through an alternative universe. You'll want to go again.
- **Space Mountain** (Magic Kingdom). Comets soaring overhead contribute to the nice preshow atmosphere. For a really great ride, get in the first car; you'll feel like you're blasting through space.
- **Terminator 2, 3-D** (Universal Studios Florida). He's back, and this combination of video technology and good old-fashioned fear makes this ride one of the top tickets in town.
- **Tower of Terror** (Disney–MGM Studios). This straight-down drop is more than thrilling; it is truly scary. Once your legs stop shaking, you'll want to ride again.

- **Experience the Movies at Universal Studios Florida.** Universal combines cutting-edge, high-tech effects with great creativity. Adults will find Universal—A Day in the Park with Barney notwithstanding—a hip and sophisticated park, not afraid to poke fun at itself or the Mouse down the road. Not-to-be-missed attractions: Back to the Future, Jaws, Terminator 2: 3-D Battle Across Time, and Earthquake—The Big One.
- **Stroll Around Cypress Gardens.** Two hundred acres of gorgeous botanical gardens punctuated by lakes and lagoons, waterfalls, and sculpture. A very laid-back attraction, popular with seniors.
- **An Evening at Church Street Station.** Dance halls, old-fashioned saloons, dining rooms, and shopping make this the prime non-Disney attraction in Orlando. Top-flight musicians provide entertainment in this downtown renovated train depot spanning real cobblestone streets.
- **An Afternoon at the Orlando Science Center.** Opened in 1997 after a $40-million expansion, this is a wonderful real-world alternative to the go-go pace of the theme parks. It's educational and entertaining fun for both parents and kids. Located in Loch Haven Park near downtown Orlando.
- **Eco-entertainment at Sea World.** With the opening of a major thrill ride, Journey to Atlantis, Sea World has added a little thrill, but it's better to enjoy what this park does best—hands-on encounters with dolphins and stingrays and up-close views of sea animals from polar bears to killer whales. Not to be missed is "Mermaids, Myths & Monsters," a thrilling nighttime multimedia spectacular at Sea World where images appear to dance, hop, and stomp across a 60-foot screen of water.

2 Orlando Today (& Tomorrow)

In the 1990s, Orlando enjoys the best overall business climate in the state of Florida. In addition to tourism, its dynamic economy thrives on diverse industry, thousands of technology-related companies, and agriculture. The only remnant of Orlando's slow-paced, pre-Disney Southern image is its down-home friendliness (but don't look for it during rush-hour traffic on the freeway).

For the observant visitor, this part of Florida is very different from the rest of the state. Indeed, the parts of town most tourists see are unlike any others on the planet. Locals become somewhat immune after a time to the mile after mile of perfectly manicured landscapes courtesy of Disney and other major players here. Aside from the theme parks, the "attractions area" is filled with strip malls, theme restaurants, and resort hotels. This can create a kind of sterile "Twilight Zone" quality. Unfortunately, this plastic presence is only going to increase as Walt Disney World and other parks continue to expand. Disneyesque street signs have even begun to appear downtown within the last few years, and a whole Disney town—Celebration—has opened. Just 20 or so miles in any direction from the tourist mecca, you'll find real towns like anywhere else, where people live, work, play, and send their children to school. But most attractions builders recognize that people coming to Orlando aren't looking for reality.

Recent major developments include:

- **CityWalk** and **Islands of Adventure.** Universal Studios opens its new nighttime entertainment complex in 1998, and its second theme park, Islands of Adventure, will open in the summer of 1999. Built with the help of creative consultant Steven Spielberg, the new park is billed as the most technologically advanced theme park ever constructed. You'll find the Dinosaurs of Jurassic Park and a slew of other attractions based on cartoon heroes and villains as diverse as Spider Man, Popeye, and Dr. Doom. In typical Orlando fashion, press kits called the landlocked Islands of Adventure a "21st-century theme park set among the exotic coastlines of the oceans."

- **New Resorts.** Universal has also announced a multibillion-dollar expansion plan to help keep parkgoers spending their vacation dollars on Universal property (just like the Mouse up the road). Utilizing 600 previously undeveloped acres, the company is creating competition for Disney with five movie- and television-theme resorts, comprising more than 4,300 rooms; a golf-villa community centered on an 18-hole championship course; a top-of-the-line tennis complex; and a series of lakes, winding rivers, canals, and other waterways that will be traversed by water taxis and ferries.

- **Disney's Animal Kingdom.** An exotic "live-animal adventure park," Animal Kingdom is, at 500 acres, five times the size of the Magic Kingdom. "The next best thing to Africa" says head cheese Michael Eisner. Centering on the 14-story "Tree of Life," it combines thrill rides, exotic landscapes, and close encounters with great herds of wild animals, divided into three "regions." Disney has outdone itself on the artistic aspect of this endeavor, even bringing tribal experts from Africa to build the thatched roofs and hiring a team of 12-sculptors who worked for a year to create the "Tree of Life."

- **Disney Cruises.** After a twice-delayed maiden voyage, Disney Cruise Lines will soon offer park vacations in conjunction with Caribbean cruises. On ships reminiscent of classic luxury liners, guests will enjoy a choice of theme restaurants, nightclubs, family entertainment, supervised children's activities, and much more. People tended to flock in the beginning, so now might be a good time to start looking for deals.

- **DisneyQuest.** Disney is touting this attraction as a virtual, high-tech theme park. The 100,000-square-foot, wave-shaped building in Downtown Disney drew a lot of attention during construction, and the contents were kept strictly hush-hush. But soon everyone will be able to experience the kind of three-dimensional virtual reality technology previously available only at research facilities. All this high tech will allow players to compete in hand-to-hand combat with seriously pumped-up Disney villains and to be slammed like a pinball in a virtual game. To keep the games on the cutting edge, 20 to 30% of the content will be changed each year.

- **Safari Lodge.** A jungle-themed hotel adjacent to the Animal Kingdom's 100-acre savannah will open by the end of 2000.

- **Journey to Atlantis.** Sea World's first major roller coaster is a watery adventure, in keeping with the park's aquatic theme. This elaborate "experience" is the park's biggest project to date and its first full-scale thrill ride.

- **Pointe Orlando.** This multimillion-dollar shopping plaza on International Drive near the Orange County Convention Center features a mammoth FAO Schwarz toy store and a Versace boutique along with other upscale, not-found-in-your-average-strip-mall shops.

- **New Performing Arts Center.** Planning is underway for a multimillion-dollar performing arts center in downtown Orlando. Touted as a world-class facility, the joint project between the city of Orlando and the University of Central Florida hopes to draw both locals and tourists by featuring world-class performers and shows.

3 History 101, or How a Sleepy Southern Town Met a Mighty Mouse

Dateline

- **1817–18** The First Seminole War. Aligned with refugee Creeks from Georgia, native Appalachees, and runaway slaves, the Seminoles battle Andrew Jackson's troops while Florida is still a Spanish territory.

- **1843** Mosquito County in central Florida is renamed Orange County.

- **1856** Orlando becomes the official seat of Orange County.

- **1861** Florida secedes from the Union. The demise of slavery sounds the death knell for the area's burgeoning cotton industry.

- **1870** Cattle ranching and citrus growing replace cotton as the bulwark of Orlando's economy.

- **1875** Orlando is officially incorporated as a municipality under state law.

continues

Outsiders, weaned on orange juice commercials and mouse tales, might think the history of the region could be condensed into three terse sentences: (1) There were orange groves; (2) Walt Disney came; (3) You can buy three T-shirts for $10. There is, however, considerably more juice to be squeezed from the story. The modern metropolis of Orlando began as a rough-and-tumble Florida frontier town, where early voters were lured to the polling booths by the promise of a good barbecue dinner.

SETTLERS VS. SEMINOLES: THE ROAD TO STATEHOOD Florida history dates back to 1513—more than a century before the Pilgrims landed at Plymouth Rock—when Ponce de León, in search of the fabled "fountain of youth," spied the beaches and lush greenery of Florida's Atlantic coast. He named it La Florida—"the Flowery Land." After years of alternating Spanish, French, and British rule, the territory was ceded (by Spain) to the United States in 1821. Lost in the international shuffle were the Seminoles, who, after migrating from Georgia and the Carolinas in the late–18th century to some of Florida's richest farmlands, were viewed by the Americans as an obstacle to white settlement. After a series of compromise treaties that left both sides dissatisfied, the federal government threw down the final gauntlet with the Indian Removal Act of 1830, stipulating that all eastern tribes be removed to reservations west of the Mississippi. This cruel edict sparked the Second Seminole War (1835–42). At a treaty conference at Payne's Landing in 1832, a young warrior named Osceola strode up to the bargaining table, slammed his knife into the papers on it, and, pointing to the quivering blade, proclaimed, "The only treaty I will ever make is this!"

Guerrilla warfare thwarted the U.S. army's attempt to remove the Seminoles for almost 8 years, during which time many of the resisters drifted south into the interior of central Florida. In what is today the Orlando area—on a small, triangular parcel of land formed by Lake Gatlin, Lake Gem Mary, and Lake Jennie Jewell—the Americans built Fort Gatlin in 1838 to offer protection to pioneer homesteaders. The fort, sighted near an ancient oak tree where followers of Osceola frequently met to discuss strategies, was the scene of many skirmishes. The Seminoles kept up a fierce rebellion until 1842, when, undefeated, they accepted a treaty whereby their remaining numbers (about 300) were given land and left in peace. The same year, the Armed Occupation Act offered 160 acres to any pioneer willing to settle here for a minimum of 5 years. The land was fertile: Wild turkeys and deer abounded in the woods, grazing land for cattle was equally plentiful, and dozens of lakes provided fish for settlers and water for livestock. In 1843, what had been Mosquito County was more invitingly renamed Orange County. And with the Seminoles more or less out of the way (though sporadic cattle rustling and bloody uprisings still occurred), the Territorial General Legislature petitioned Congress for statehood. On March 3, 1845, President John Tyler signed a bill making Florida the 27th state in the Union.

Settlements and statehood notwithstanding, at the middle of the 19th century the Orlando area (then named Jernigan for one of its first settler families) consisted largely of pristine lakes and pine-forested wilderness. There were no roads, and you could ride all day (if you could find a trail) without meeting a soul. The Jernigans successfully raised cattle, and their home and stockade, which was granted a post office in 1850, became a way stop for travelers and the seat of future development. Farmers and cattle ranchers were drawn to the area's verdant grasslands. Before long, a sawmill went up (on the site of today's Orlando Public Library) and a trading post was opened. Other merchants followed, and farms and ranches—which would grow to vast agricultural dynasties—were carved out of the wilderness. In 1856 the boundaries of Orange County were revised, and,

- **1880** The South Florida Railroad facilitates the expansion of Orlando's agricultural markets.
- **1884** Fire rages out of control, destroying much of Orlando's fledgling business district.
- **1894–95** Freezing temperatures destroy 2 years of citrus crops and wreck orchards. Many growers lose everything.
- **1910–25** A land boom hits Florida. Fortunes are made overnight.
- **1926** The land boom goes bust. Fortunes are lost overnight.
- **1929** An invasion of Mediterranean fruit flies devastates Orlando's citrus industry. Its ruined economy is capped by the stock market crash.
- **1939–45** World War II revives Orlando's ailing economy. The city becomes "Florida's Air Capital."
- **1964** Walt Disney begins surreptitiously buying up central Florida farmland, purchasing more than 28,000 acres at a cost of nearly $5.5 million.
- **1965** Disney announces his plan to build the world's most spectacular theme park in Orlando.
- **1971** The Magic Kingdom opens its gates.
- **1972** A new 1-day attendance mark is set on December 27, when 72,328 people visit the Magic Kingdom. It will be broken almost every year thereafter.
- **1973** Shamu ventures into Orlando waters. Sea World opens.
- **1979** Mickey Mouse welcomes the Magic Kingdom's 100-millionth

continues

visitor, 8-year-old Kurt Miller from Kingsville, Maryland.

- **1982** Epcot opens to the public with vast hoopla. Participating celebrities include everyone from Richard Nixon to George Steinbrenner.

- **1984** Donald Duck's 50th birthday is celebrated with a special parade down Main Street that includes 50 live Peking ducks.

- **1988** Walt Disney World celebrates Mickey Mouse's 60th birthday. A special parade *does not* include 50 live mice!

- **1989** WDW launches Disney–MGM Studios Theme Park (offering a behind-the-scenes look at Tinseltown), Typhoon Lagoon (a 56-acre water theme park), and Pleasure Island (an adult-nightclub theme park).

- **1990** Universal Studios opens, offering visitors thrilling encounters with E.T. and King Kong.

- **1993** Sea World continues a major expansion. Universal Studios unleashes the fearsome *Jaws*.

- **1998** Disney begins its own cruise line and opens Animal Kingdom. Universal Studios opens CityWalk, a vast new entertainment complex.

thanks to the manipulations of resident James Gamble Speer, a member of the Indian Removal Commission, Fort Gatlin (Jernigan) became its official seat.

How the fledgling town came to be named Orlando is a matter of some speculation. Some say Speer renamed the town after a dearly loved friend, whereas other sources say he named it after one of his favorite Shakespearean characters from *As You Like It*. But the most accepted version is that the town was named for plantation owner Orlando Reeves (or Rees), whose homestead had been burned out in the skirmish. For years, it was thought a marker discovered near the shores of Lake Eola, in what is now Downtown, marked his grave. But Reeves died later, in South Carolina. It's assumed the named carved in the tree was a marker for others who were on the Indians' trail. Whatever the origin, Orlando was officially recognized by the U.S. Postmaster in 1857.

THE 1860S: CIVIL WAR/CATTLE WARS

Throughout the early 1860s, cotton plantations and cattle ranches became the hallmarks of central Florida. Orlando was ringed by a vast cotton empire. Log cabins went up along the lakes, and the pioneers eked out a somewhat lonely existence, separated from each other by miles of farmland. But there were troubles brewing in the 31-state nation that would soon devastate Orlando's planters. By 1859 it was obvious that only a war would resolve the slavery issue. In 1861 Florida became the third state to secede from the Union, and the modest progress it had achieved came to a standstill. The Stars and Bars flew from every flagpole, and local men enlisted in the Confederate army, leaving the fledgling town in poverty. A federal blockade made it difficult to obtain necessities, and many slaves fled. In 1866 the Confederate troops of Florida surrendered, the remaining slaves were freed, and a ragtag group of defeated soldiers returned to Orlando. They found a dying cotton industry, unable to function without slave labor or transport to markets. In 1868 Florida was readmitted to the Union.

Its untended cotton fields having gone to seed, Orlando now concentrated on cattle ranching, a business heavily taxed by the occupation government and one that ushered in an era of lawlessness and violence. Back then, messing with another man's cow was serious business, resulting in vicious feuds that clogged courtroom calendars and ignited long-running hostilities between warring parties. A famous battle involving two families, the Barbers and the Mizells, left at least nine men dead in 2 months in a Florida version of the Hatfields and the McCoys.

Like frontier cattle towns out West, post–Civil War Orlando was short on civilized behavior. Gunfights, brawls, and murders were commonplace. But as the 1860s drew to a close, large-herd owners from other parts of the state moved into the area and began organizing the industry in a less chaotic fashion. Branding and penning greatly reduced rustling, though they never totally eliminated the problem. Even a century later—as recently as 1973— soaring beef prices caused a rash of cattle thievery. Some traditions die hard. Even today, an Orange County Sheriff's unit still investigates a number of cattle rustling incidents each year.

AN ORANGE TREE GROWS IN ORLANDO   In the 1870s, articles in national magazines began luring large numbers of Americans to central Florida with promises of arable land and a warm climate. In Orlando, public roads, schools, and churches appeared to serve the newcomers, many of whom replanted defunct cotton fields with citrus groves. Orlando was officially incorporated under state law in 1875, setting up definitive boundaries, a city government complete with a mayor, laws and ordinances, a city hall, a jail, and other adjuncts of a municipality. New settlers poured in from all over the country, businesses flourished, and by the end of the year the town had its first newspaper, the *Orange County Reporter*. The first locomotive of the South Florida Railroad chugged into town in 1880, representing a major step toward growth and prosperity and sparking a building and land boom—the first of many. Orlando got sidewalks and its first bank in 1883—the same year the town voted itself "dry" in hopes of averting the fistfights and brawls that ensued when cowboys crowded into local saloons every Saturday night for rowdy R&R. For many years the city continued to vote itself alternately wet and dry, but in actuality it made very little difference. Legal or not, liquor was always readily available.

FIRE & ICE   In January 1884, a grocery fire that started at 4am wiped out blocks of businesses, including the offices of the *Orange County Reporter*. But 19th-century Orlando was a bit like a Frank Capra movie. The town rallied 'round, providing a new location for the paper and presenting its publisher, Mahlon Gore, with $1,200 in cash to help defray losses and $300 in new subscriptions. The paper not only survived but flourished. And the city, realizing the need, created its first fire brigade. By August 1884, a census revealed that the population had grown to 1,666. That same year 600,000 boxes of oranges were shipped from Florida to points north—most of those boxes originating in Orlando. By 1885 Orlando was a viable town, boasting as many as 50 businesses. It was dubbed the "Phenomenal City," after a South Florida Railroad booklet called the city's growth "phenomenal." This is not to say it was New York. Razorback hogs roamed the streets, and alligator wrestling was a main form of entertainment.

Disaster struck a week after Christmas in 1894, when the temperature plummeted to an unseasonable 24°. Water pipes burst, and orange blossoms froze, blackened, and died. The freeze continued for 3 days, wrecking the citrus crop for the year. Karl H. Abbott, son of the owner of the San Juan Hotel, where Northern buyers met to bid on citrus crops, later described the pandemonium that broke out as the thermometer began dipping shortly after noon:

> *The buyers hurriedly left the lunch tables and went out of doors to view the weather. The big thermometer in front of the hotel indicated unusual cold. By 2pm the San Juan was in an uproar. Prices had dropped to "no sale." Commission merchants were frantically trying to get out of options and heated debates and fistfights started in the lobby . . . . About nine that night a fine-looking gray-haired gentleman in a black coat and Stetson hat walked up the street in front of the hotel and looked at the thermometer, groaned "Oh my God!" and shot himself through the head.*

Many grove owners went bust, and those who remained were hit with a second devastating freeze the following year. Tens of thousands of trees died in the killing frost. Small growers were wiped out, but large conglomerates that could afford to buy up the small growers' properties at bargain prices and to wait for new groves to mature assured the survival of the industry.

SPECULATION FEVER: GOOD DEALS, BAD DEALS . . .   As Orlando entered the 20th century, citrus and agriculture had surpassed cattle ranching as the mainstay of the local economy. Stray cows no longer had to be shooed from the railway tracks. Streets were being paved, and electricity and telephone service installed. The population at the turn of the century was 2,481. In 1902 the city passed its first automobile laws, which included an in-town speed limit of 5 miles per hour. In 1904 the city flooded. And in 1905 it suffered a drought that ended—miraculously or coincidentally—on a day when all faiths united at the local First Baptist Church to pray for rain. By 1910 prosperity had returned, and Orlando, with a population of nearly 4,000, was, in a small way, becoming a tourism and convention center. World War I brought further industrial growth and a real-estate boom, not just to Orlando but to all of Florida. Millions of immigrants, speculators, and builders descended on the state in search of a quick buck. As land speculation reached a fever pitch, and property was bought and resold almost overnight, many citrus groves gave way to urbanization. Preeminent Orlando builder and promoter Carl Dann described the action: "It finally became nothing more than a gambling machine, each man buying on a shoestring, betting dollars a bigger fool would come along and buy his option."

Quite suddenly, the bubble burst. A July 1926 issue of the *Nation* provided the obituary for the Florida land boom: "The world's greatest poker game, played with lots instead of chips, is over. And the players are now . . . paying up." Construction slowed to a trickle, and many newcomers who had arrived in Florida to jump on the bandwagon returned to their homes in the north. Though Orlando was not quite as hard hit as Miami—scene of the greediest land grabs—some belt-tightening was in order. Nevertheless, the city managed to build a municipal airport in 1928. Then came a Mediterranean fruit-fly infestation that crippled the citrus industry. Hundreds of thousands of acres of land in quarantined areas had to be cleared of fruit, and vast quantities of boxed fruit were destroyed. The 1929 stock market crash that precipitated the Great Depression seemed almost an afterthought to Florida's ruined economy.

. . . AND NEW DEALS   President Franklin D. Roosevelt's New Deal helped the state climb back on its feet. The Works Progress Administration (WPA) put 40,000 unemployed Floridians back to work—work that included hundreds of public projects in Orlando. Of these, the most important was the expansion and resurfacing of the city's airport. By 1936 the tourist trade had revived somewhat, construction was up once again, and the state began attracting a broader range of visitors than ever before. But the event that finally lifted Florida—and the nation—out of the depression was World War II.

Orlando had weathered the Great Depression. Now it prepared for war with the construction of army bases, housing for servicemen, and training facilities. Almost all new business was geared toward defense. Enlisted men poured into the city, and the airport was again enlarged and equipped with barracks, a military hospital, administration buildings, and mess halls. By 1944 Orlando had a second airport and was known as "Florida's Air Capital"—home to major aircraft and aviation-parts manufactories. Thousands of U.S. servicemen did part of their hitch in Orlando, and when the war ended, many returned to settle there.

POSTWAR PROSPERITY   By 1950, Orlando, with a population of 51,826, was the financial and transportation hub of central Florida. The city shared the bullish

In the Words of Walt Disney

Why be a governor or a senator when you can be king of Disneyland? You can dream, create, design, and build the most wonderful place in the world . . . but it requires people to make the dream a reality.

economy of the 1950s with the rest of the nation. In the face of the Cold War, the Orlando air force base remained and grew, funneling millions of dollars into the local economy. Florida's population increased by a whopping 78.7% during the decade—making it America's 10th most populous state—and tourists came in droves, nearly 4.5 million in 1950 alone.

One reason for the influx was the advent of the air conditioner, which made life in Florida infinitely more pleasant. Also fueling Orlando's economy was a brand-new industry arriving in nearby Cape Canaveral in 1955—the government-run space program. Cape Canaveral became NASA's headquarters for the Apollo rocket program that eventually blasted Neil Armstrong heavenward toward his famous "giant leap." During the same decade, the Glenn L. Martin Company (later Martin Marietta), builder of the Matador Missile, purchased 10 square miles for a plant site 4 miles south of Orlando. Its advent sparked further industrial growth, and property values soared. More than 60 new industries located in the area in 1959 alone. But even the most optimistic Orlando boosters could not foresee the glorious future that was the city's ultimate destiny.

THE DISNEY DECADES   In 1964 Walt Disney began secretly buying up millions of dollars worth of central Florida farmland. As vast areas of land were purchased in lots of 5,000 acres here, 20,000 there—at remarkably high prices—rumors flew as to who needed so much land and had so much money to acquire it. Some thought it was Howard Hughes; others, the space program. Speculation was rife almost to the very day, November 15, 1965 ("D" Day for Orlando), when Disney himself arrived in town and announced his plans to build the world's most spectacular theme park ("bigger and better than Disneyland"). In a 2-year construction effort, Disney employed 9,000 people. Land speculation reached unprecedented heights, as hotel chains and restaurateurs grabbed up property near the proposed park. Mere swampland sold for millions. Total cost of the project by its October 1971 opening was $400 million. Mickey Mouse personally led the first visitor into the Magic Kingdom, and numerous celebrities, from Bob Hope to Julie Andrews, took part in the opening ceremonies. In Walt Disney World's first 2 years, the attraction drew 20 million visitors and employed 13,000 people. The sleepy citrus-growing town of Orlando had become the "Action Center of Florida" and the fastest-growing city in the state. A 1972 referendum revitalized downtown Orlando, which continues to grow, adding an increasing number of restaurants, bars, and attractions of its own.

Additional attractions multiplied faster than fruit flies, and hundreds of firms relocated their businesses to the area. Sea World, a major theme park, came to town in 1973. All the while, Walt Disney World continued to grow and expand, adding Epcot in 1982 and Disney–MGM Studios in 1989, along with water parks, over a dozen "official" resorts, a shopping/restaurant village, campgrounds, a vast array of recreational facilities, and several other adjuncts that are thoroughly described in this book. Universal Studios, which opened in 1990, continues to expand. In 1998 Disney opened yet another theme park, this one dedicated to zoological entertainment and aptly called Animal Kingdom.

In the Words of Walt Disney

I only hope we never lose sight of one thing . . . that it was all started by a mouse.

At the same time, Universal keeps the stakes high. In 1998 it unveiled a new entertainment district, CityWalk, and in 1999 plans to open Islands of Adventure, a second theme park including, among other things, attractions dedicated to Dr. Seuss, Marvel Comics, and Jurassic Park. Also scheduled to open in 1999 is the Portofino Bay Resort at Universal City Florida, a 750-room Loews hotel. Universal will open three more hotels by 2005.

4 Behind the Scenes

- Forget about partying like it's 1999 at Disney. All the rooms on Disney property—yes *all* the rooms—have been booked for years. One determined, and hopeful, man has reportedly faxed the reservations office for several years reminding them to give him a call if anything opens up for New Year's Eve 1999.
- Talk about a culture clash. The rocking Race Rock cafe on International Drive, known for parking Nascar racers in its lobby and having mini-racers streak across the ceiling, was once the home of a short-lived, opera-themed restaurant with live performances. I guess it really is all over once the fat lady sings.
- Music at Universal's upcoming Islands of Adventure was composed specifically for the theme park, much like a score for a movie. It is the first time such a large-scale musical effort has been mounted for a theme park.
- Known for going to great lengths to protect its image and name—even removing unofficial Disney pictures from murals on the wall of a day-care center—Disney has lost a name game. Originally dubbed "Wild Animal Kingdom," Disney's latest park was renamed after complaints that the moniker too closely mirrored the televised "Wild Kingdom," starring Marlin Perkins and his faithful sidekick Jim Fowler.
- Money really can't buy you love. Denver Bronco's coach Mike Shanahan made news before the 1998 Super Bowl by declining a $30,000 offer to utter the catchphrase "I'm going to Disney World." Shanahan, apparently a Universal man, said "I don't care how much they pay me."
- Just a few months before Universal Studios was to unveil its "Twister" attraction, central Florida was hit by the deadliest tornado in the state's history, killing about 40 people and destroying hundreds of homes. Universal postponed the opening and used the "Twister" locale as a spot to collect donations for storm victims.
- Plenty of shiny coins are dropped into Disney fountains as visitors pick a scenic location and make a wish. To literally squeeze every dime out of its operations, Disney has devised an elaborate mechanized system to retrieve that change from the fountains and put it into the tills of its restaurants and stores—dried, sorted, and rolled—sometimes before the end of the day.
- Disney, who calls its employees "cast members," has continued to create its own lexicon with the opening of its school in the new Disney-designed town of Celebration. Although this is a public school, Disney has imposed a private language. Students are known as "learners," teachers are "specialists," and the principal is called the "director." And Celebration has not a school but "a community of learners."
- It's a story even Disney couldn't make up. The Osbornes of Arkansas apparently took to heart the old hymn that says, "You can't be a beacon if your light don't

shine." Their Christmas-light collection of 2-million-plus blinkers, twinklers, and strands shone so brightly that neighbors complained. There were rumors that even air traffic was disrupted, as well as the flow of faithful in cars, causing mile-long backups in a mostly rural area where a couple of pickups in front of the feed store was considered a major delay. The neighbors, finally seeing the light, went to court in what became a nationally known battle. Disney came to the rescue and in 1995 moved the whole thing to Orlando, adding a million or so bulbs. The display is now known as the Osborne Family Christmas Lights. No complaints, yet.

- Orlando, especially Disney World, is a popular destination for rich Saudi Arabian princes, who routinely rent entire floors of hotels and drop tens of thousands of dollars in local shops. But why do Disney hotels carry Arab TV on their cable network? Well, it seems a Saudi prince, who heavily invested in Disneyland Paris, also owns the network. It is, I think, what Michael Eisner calls "synergy."

- Ever wonder why you never catch a glimpse of, say, Mickey relaxing with his head off or Pluto taking a cigarette break? The people inside the characters at Disney have a very strict code of conduct: Absolutely no talking, and Minnie Mouse must always sign her name in cursive. But, beyond that, the characters and their keepers, along with all the Disney "cast," travel around the park through an intricate system of underground tunnels that are strictly off-limits to the public.

- *BOOOOMMMMM, BOOOOMMMMMM.* Tourists may find themselves occasionally awakened by window-rattling double booms. Don't worry; it's not part of the rumored American crime culture. It's the space shuttle landing. The twin sonic booms are produced as the shuttle reenters the atmosphere. The loud, thunderous sound can be heard from Cape Canaveral on the coast throughout Orange, Seminole, and Osceola counties, including the tourist areas. When skies are clear, the night launches of the shuttles and larger rockets can be seen throughout Central Florida.

2

Planning a Trip to Walt Disney World & Orlando

Orlando is so packed with attractions that advance planning is crucial. In this chapter, I've compiled everything you need to know before you go. In addition to the information below, you'll find tips in chapters 5 (Accommodations), 7 (Walt Disney World), and 8 (Other Attractions in the Orlando Area).

1 Visitor Information You Can Get Before Your Trip

As soon as you know you're going to Orlando, write or call the **Orlando/Orange County Convention & Visitors Bureau,** 8723 International Dr., Suite 101, Orlando, FL 32819 (☎ **407/ 363-5871**). The bureau can answer all your questions and will be happy to send you maps, brochures (including the informative *Official Visitors Guide,* the *African-American Visitors Guide,* the *Area Guide* to local restaurants, and the *Official Accommodations Guide*). The packet, which should arrive in about 3 weeks, includes the "Magicard," good for discounts of 10 to 50% on accommodations, attractions, car rentals, and more.

For general information about **Walt Disney World**—and a copy of the informative *Walt Disney World Vacations* brochure—write or call the Walt Disney World Co., Box 10000, Lake Buena Vista, FL 32830-1000 (☎ **407/934-7639**).

For information about **Universal Studios,** CityWalk, and Islands of Adventure, call (☎ **407/393-8080**). You can also write to **Universal Studios Florida,** 1000 Universal Studios Dr., Orlando, FL 32816.

You might also contact the **Kissimmee–St. Cloud Convention & Visitors Bureau,** 1925 E. Irlo Bronson Memorial Hwy. (U.S. 192), Kissimmee, FL 34744, or P.O. Box 422007, Kissimmee, FL 34742-2007 (☎ **800/327-9159** or 407/847-5000). They'll send maps, brochures, discount coupon books, and the *Kissimmee–St. Cloud Vacation Guide,* which details the area's accommodations and attractions.

For information about the entire state—including Orlando and Kissimmee—write or call the Florida Department of Commerce, **Division of Tourism,** Visitor Inquiry, 126 Van Buren St., Tallahassee, FL 32399-2000. You can also call the **Florida Tourism Industry Marketing Corp.** (☎ **888/735-2872**) for information about the state. Or you can write to **Visit Florida,** P.O. Box 1100, Tallahassee,

FL 32391-1100. They also offer a seasonal visitors guide that includes information on special events and discounts.

For information about the **Winter Park** area, contact the Winter Park Chamber of Commerce, 150 New York Ave., P.O. Box 280, Winter Park, FL 32790 (☎ **407/644-8281**).

ONLINE INFORMATION

If you have Internet access, you can visit Walt Disney World's own Web site at **www.disneyworld.com**, which has extensive, entertaining, and regularly updated information, including a live-action look from video cameras perched throughout the various parks. (This is mostly long-distance shots of tourists walking about, but it is still a chance to see those blue Orlando skies and dream ahead to vacation time.) There are dozens of web pages devoted to Disney, especially Disney trivia. Check out the very informative newsgroup on Usenet called **rec.arts.disney**.

Information about Universal Studios can be found at **www.usf.com**, and Sea World information is available at **www.seaworld.com**. Both sites offer maps and a basic description of rides, shows, and ticket information.

The city newspaper, the *Orlando Sentinel,* also produces *Orlando Sentinel Online* at **www.oso@aol.com**. Once there, click on "Theme Park Central" for a variety of information and updates on happenings at local attractions.

The Orlando/Orange County Convention and Visitors Bureau has a web site at **www.goflorida.com/orlando**. The state has a Web site at **www.flausa.com**.

2 Money

Disney parks, resorts, shops, and restaurants (but not fast-food outlets) accept the three major credit cards—American Express, MasterCard, and Visa. Disney offers some resort guests a debit card that can be used in park shops and restaurants. This is sometimes referred to as a Disney credit card, but you've got to settle the bill when you leave.

You can also purchase **Disney dollars** (currency bearing the images of Mickey, Goofy, and Minnie), available in $1, $5, and $10 denominations. They're good at shops, restaurants, and resorts throughout the Disney realm, as well as Disney stores everywhere. I don't suggest you buy these Disney dollars, because you'll have to cash in any leftover bills for real currency upon leaving, which means another line on your last day.

You can get cash advances on MasterCard and Visa, cash traveler's checks, cash personal checks of $25 or less (drawn on U.S. banks, upon presentation of a valid driver's license and a major credit card), and exchange foreign currency at branches of the **SunTrust** on Main Street in the Magic Kingdom, open from 9am to 4pm daily (☎ **407/828-6102**) and at 1675 Buena Vista Dr., across from the Disney Village Marketplace, open weekdays from 9am to 4pm, until 6pm on Thursday (☎ **407/828-6106**).

ATM machines are conveniently located on Main Street and in Tomorrowland in the Magic Kingdom; at the entrances to Disney–MGM Studios and Epcot; at Pleasure Island; at Disney Village Marketplace; at the All-Star Sports Resort; and at the Crossroads Shopping Center.

There are also ATM machines near the entrance to Sea World and at Universal located in the **First Union National Bank** inside the main entrance, near Guest Services.

What Things Cost in Orlando	U.S. $
Taxi from airport to WDW area	41.00
Bus from airport to WDW area (adult fare)	25.00
Double room at Disney's Grand Floridian Beach Resort (very expensive)	294–545
Double room at Marriott's Orlando World Center (expensive)	152–259
Double room at Disney's Port Orleans Resort (moderate)	95.00–129.00
Double room at Disney's All-Star Music Resort (inexpensive)	74.00–89.00
Double room at Days Inn, Kissimmee (inexpensive)	39–59 double
Seven-course prix-fixe dinner for one at Victoria & Albert's, not including tip or wine (very expensive)	80–160
All-you-can-eat buffet dinner at Akershus in Epcot, not including tip or wine (inexpensive)	18.50
Bottle of beer (restaurant)	2.50
Coca-Cola (restaurant)	1.25
Cup of coffee	1.25
Roll of ASA 100 Kodacolor film, 36 exposures, purchased at Walt Disney World	9.35
Adult 4-Day Value Pass admission to Walt Disney World	149.00
Child 4-Day Value Pass admission to Walt Disney World	119.00
Adult 1-day admission to Sea World	39.95
Child 1-day admission to Sea World	32.80
Adult 1-day admission to Universal Studios	42.14
Child 1-day admission to Universal Studios	33.93

It may come as a surprise to foreign visitors just how prevalent ATM machines are in central Florida. Most malls have at least one ATM, and they can even be found in many convenience stores, namely 7-11s and Circle Ks. They are also increasingly showing up in grocery and drug stores. But there is often an extra charge for using these nonbank machines. Depending on your institution, charges usually range from $1 to $1.50 per transaction. The fee may sometimes be higher in areas with heavy tourist traffic.

Be sure to exercise caution when accessing ATM machines, especially at night and in areas that are not well-lit and heavily traveled. When entering your ATM Personal Identification Number, be sure to shield the keyboard from anyone who may be in line or observing from a distance. Also, keep all doors locked when accessing a drive-through ATM. The common ATM networks are Cirrus, Honor, MasterCard, Plus, and Van.

3 When to Go

Orlando is essentially a theme-park destination, and its busiest seasons are whenever kids are out of school—summer (early June to about August 20), holiday weekends,

Christmas season (mid-December to mid-January), and Easter. Obviously, the whole experience is more enjoyable when the crowds are thinnest and the weather is the most temperate. Hotel rooms are also priced lower off-season. **Best times:** the week after Labor Day until Thanksgiving, the week after Thanksgiving until mid-December, and the 6 weeks before and after school spring vacations. **Worst times:** during the holidays and summer, when many locals haul their families to the parks and many visitors take advantage of breaks from school. Packed parking lots are also the norm during the week before and after Christmas. In summer it's really a double whammy: Crowds are very large, and weather is oppressively hot and humid. I probably shouldn't say this, but I would pull the kids out of school for a few days around an off-season weekend to avoid long lines. But also keep in mind that the large number of international visitors guarantees substantial crowds year round.

Central Florida Average Temperatures

	Jan	Feb	Mar	Apr	May	June	July	Aug	Sept	Oct	Nov	Dec
High °F	71.7	72.9	78.3	83.6	88.3	90.6	91.7	91.6	89.7	84.4	78.2	73.1
°C	22.0	22.7	25.7	28.7	31.3	32.5	33.2	33.1	32.0	29.1	25.7	22.8
Low °F	49.3	50.0	55.3	60.3	66.2	71.2	73.0	73.4	72.5	65.4	56.8	50.9
°C	9.6	10.0	12.5	15.7	19.0	21.8	22.7	23.0	22.5	18.6	13.8	10.5

ORLANDO AREA CALENDAR OF EVENTS

January

✪**CompUSA Florida Citrus Bowl.** January kicks off with this football event, located in downtown Orlando and featuring two of the year's top college teams. Tickets ($28) go on sale in late October or early November. Call ☎ **407/423-2476** for information; 407/839-3900 for tickets. There is also a downtown parade a few days before the game, which features dozens of marching bands, parade units, and a few floats. Seats are free.

✪**Walt Disney World Marathon.** About 90% of the runners finish this 26.2-mile marathon winding through the resort and theme park areas. The race is open to all, including the physically challenged. The $50 entry fee is included in the room price with some Disney resort packages. Preregistration is required. Call ☎ **407/824-4321** for details.

• **The Atlanta Braves.** The Braves began holding Spring Training at Disney's Wide World of Sports Complex in 1998. A three-year contract ensures play through 2001. There are about 18 games during the 1-month season. Tickets are $10.50 and $13.50. For information call TicketMaster ☎ **407/839-3900**.

✪ **The Zora Neale Hurston Festival.** This 4-day celebration in Eatonville, the first incorporated African-American town in America, highlights the life and works of author Zora Neale Hurston and is usually held the last weekend in January. Eatonville is about 25 miles north of the theme parks. Call ☎ **800/352-3865** for details.

February

✪**The Silver Spurs Rodeo.** Featuring real cowboys in contests of calf roping, bull and bronco riding, barrel racing, and more, the rodeo is a celebration of the area's rural, pre-Disney roots. It's held at the Silver Spurs Arena, 1875 E. Irlo Bronson Memorial Hwy. (U.S. 192) in Kissimmee, on the third weekend in February. Call ☎ **407/847-5000** for details. Tickets $15.

- **Mardi Gras at Universal Studios.** Started in the mid-1990s, this evening event has become more elaborate and longer each year. Authentic parade floats from New Orleans, stilt walkers, and traditional doubloons and beads thrown to the crowd add to the fun, and all is included in the regular park admission during this time. Special entertainment is also part of the fun. Mid-February. For information call ☎ **407/363-8000**.
- **Bike Week.** More than 500,000 motorcyclists from across the United States— and increasingly from foreign countries—descend on Daytona Beach each year in late February and early March. People-watching and some street events are free. Prices vary for other special events, including motorcycle races at Daytona Speedway. Since Daytona is only 50 miles northeast of Orlando, many people base themselves here. For information call ☎ **800/854-1234,** or online **www.officialbikeweek.com**.

March

- **Kissimmee Bluegrass Festival.** Major bluegrass and gospel entertainers from all over the country perform at this 4-day event, beginning the first weekend of March at the Silver Spurs Arena, 1875 E. Irlo Bronson Memorial Hwy. Tickets are $12 to $20; multiday packages are available. Call ☎ **800/473-7773** for details.
- **The Central Florida Fair.** During 11 days in early March (some years beginning late February), the fair, held at the Central Florida Fairgrounds, 4603 W. Colonial Dr., features rides, entertainers, 4-H and livestock exhibits, a petting zoo, and food booths. Adults pay $6, children 6 to 10 are charged $3, and children 5 and under enter free. Call ☎ **407/295-3247** for details.
- ❂**Bay Hill Invitational.** Hosted by Arnold Palmer and featuring some Orlando-based golfers like Tiger Woods, this PGA Tour event is held in mid-March at the Bay Hill Club, 9000 Bay Hill Blvd. Daily admission on Tuesday and Wednesday is $18; Thursday to Sunday $28; week-long admission, $50 for grounds-only access; $70 for clubhouse access. Call ☎ **407/876-2888** for details.
- **The Spring Flower Festival.** From March to May at Cypress Gardens, the festival features more than 30,000 brightly colored bedding plants and flowers creating beautiful topiaries shaped as butterflies, birds, and animals. You have to pay admission to the park to get into the festival: adults $29.50, seniors $24.50, children 6–12 $19.50. Call ☎ **941/324-2111** for details.
- **The Sidewalk Art Festival.** Held in Winter Park's Central Park, this exhibition draws artists from all over North America during the third full weekend in March. The festival is consistently named one of the best in the nation by the national magazine *Sunshine Artist.* Call ☎ **407/623-3234** or 407/644-8281 for details. Admission is free, although you may have to pay for parking.

April

- About 100,000 young African Americans descend on nearby Daytona Beach every year in mid-April for a weekend of activities known as the **Black College Reunion.** The town is packed with students and alumni from historically black colleges who come to enjoy concerts, sporting events, and cruising along the beach front. For information, call the Daytona Beach Chamber of Commerce at ☎ **904/255-0981**.
- ❂**Fringe Festival.** Over 100 diverse acts from around the world participate in this eclectic event, held for 10 days at various stages in downtown Orlando. Entertainers perform drama, comedy, political satire, and experimental theater. Everything performed on outdoor stages, from sword swallowing to a 7-minute version of *Hamlet*, is available to Fringegoers free after they purchase a festival button for under $5. Ticket prices vary, but individual performances are generally under $12. Call ☎ **407/648-1333** for details.

- **Orlando Rays Baseball Season.** The Chicago Cubs farm team plays at Tinker Field, 287 Tampa Ave. S., from April to early September. Admission is $3 to $7. Call ☎ **407/245-2827** for details.
- **Easter Sunrise Service.** An interdenominational service, with music, is presented at the Atlantis Theatre at Sea World, 7007 Sea World Dr. It is hosted by a well-known person each year, most recently Elizabeth Dole. Admission is free. Call ☎ **407/351-3600** for details.
- **Easter Sunday** is celebrated in Walt Disney World with an old-fashioned Easter Parade and early opening/late closing throughout the holiday period. Call ☎ **407/824-4321** for details.

May

- **Epcot International Flower and Garden Festival.** A month-long event with theme gardens, topiary characters, special floral displays, speakers, and seminars. The festival is free with regular park admission.

June

- ✪**Gay Weekend.** The first weekend in June has become known for attracting tens of thousands of gay and lesbian travelers to central Florida. In 1997 Universal City Travel offered a "Gay Weekend" tour package including tickets to Universal Studios, Sea World, and Church Street Station. This has all grown out of "Gay Day," which has been held unofficially at Walt Disney World for about 5 years, drawing upwards of 40,000 folks. Special events throughout the weekend cater to gay and lesbian travelers throughout central Florida. Universal City Travel offers special packages (☎ **800/224-3838** for information). You can get online information for the unofficial event at **www.gayday.com**.
- **Walt Disney World Wine Festival.** More than 60 wineries from all over the United States participate. Events include wine tastings, seminars, food, and celebrity-chef cooking demonstrations at Disney's Yacht and Beach Club Convention Center. Call ☎ **407/827-7200** or 407/824-4321 for details.
- **Walt Disney World All-American College Orchestra and College Band.** The best collegiate musical talent in the country performs at Epcot and the Magic Kingdom throughout the summer. Call ☎ **407/824-4321** for details.

July

- **Independence Day.** Walt Disney World's Star-Spangled Spectacular brings bands, singers, dancers, and unbelievable fireworks displays to all the Disney parks, which stay open late. Call ☎ **407/824-4321** for details. Sea World also features a dazzling laser/fireworks spectacular; call ☎ **407/351-3600** for details. There is also a free fireworks display in downtown Orlando at Lake Eola Park. For information call ☎ **407/246-2827**.

September

- **Night of Joy.** One weekend in September, the Magic Kingdom hosts a festival of contemporary Christian music featuring top artists. This is a very popular event; obtain tickets early. Each year performers make a personal appearance at Long's Christian Bookstore in nearby College Park, about 20 minutes north of Disney. Admission to the concert is about $25 to $30 per night. Exclusive use of Magic Kingdom attractions is included. Call ☎ **407/824-4321** for details about the concert. For information about the free appearance at Long's, call ☎ **407/422-0293**.

October

- ✪**Orlando Magic Basketball.** Penny Hardaway and his teammates continue to perform magic long after Shaquille O'Neal opted to go Hollywood with the

Los Angeles Lakers. The Magic does battle against visiting teams between October and April at the Orlando Arena, 600 W. Amelia St. Ticket prices range from about $13 to $50. A few tickets, usually single seats, are often available the day before games involving lesser-known NBA challengers. Call ☎ **407/896-2442** for details, 407/839-3900 for tickets.

✪**Halloween Horror Nights.** Universal Studios Florida transforms its studios and attractions for several weeks before and after Halloween—with haunted attractions, live bands, a psychopath's maze, special shows, and hundreds of ghouls and goblins roaming the studio streets. The studio essentially closes at dusk, reopening in a new macabre form a few hours later. Special admission is charged for this event geared to grown-ups. Call ☎ **407/363-8000** for details.

✪**Walt Disney World Oldsmobile Golf Classic.** Top PGA tour players compete for a total purse of $1 million at WDW golf courses in October's major golf event. Transplanted local golf phenom Tiger Woods is usually among the players. Daily ticket prices range from $8 to $15. The event is preceded by the world's largest golf tournament, the admission-free Oldsmobile Scramble. Call ☎ **407/824-4321** for details.

• **Walt Disney World Village Boat Show.** Central Florida's largest in-the-water boat show, featuring the best of new watercraft. It's held at the Village Marketplace, over a 3-day weekend early in the month. Call ☎ **407/824-4321** for details.

November

• **Mum Festival.** November's month-long flower festival at Cypress Gardens features millions of mums, their colorful flowers displayed in beds, "blooming" gazebos, poodle baskets, and bonsai. Call ☎ **941/324-2111** for details.

✪**The Walt Disney World Festival of the Masters.** One of the largest art shows in the South takes place at Disney's Village Marketplace for 3 days, including the second weekend in November. The exhibition features top artists, photographers, and craftspeople—winners of juried shows throughout the country. Free admission. Call ☎ **407/824-4321** for details.

• **Walt Disney World Doll and Teddy Bear Convention.** The top doll and teddy-bear designers from around the world travel to WDW for this major November event. Call ☎ **407/824-4321** for details.

✪**Jolly Holidays Dinner Shows.** From late November to mid-December these all-you-can-eat events are offered at the Contemporary Resort's Fantasia Ballroom. More than 100 Disney characters, singers, and dancers perform in an old-fashioned Christmas extravaganza. Call ☎ **407/W-DISNEY** (934-7639) for details and ticket prices.

• **Poinsettia Festival.** A spectacular floral showcase of more than 40,000 red, white, and pink poinsettia blooms (including topiary reindeer) highlights this flower festival from late November to mid-January at Cypress Gardens. This is actually one of the best ways to view the park. Call ☎ **941/324-2111** for details.

December

• **Burger King Classic Half-Marathon** and **Hooter's 5K Run.** This annual race, early in December, takes place in downtown Orlando, beginning at Church Street Market, 200 S. Orange Ave. It begins at 8am. Anyone can participate. An entry fee is charged. The event kicks off the Citrus Bowl season. Call ☎ **407/423-2476** for information.

✪**Christmas at Walt Disney World.** During the Walt Disney World Christmas festivities, Main Street is lavishly decked out with lights and holly, and visitors are greeted by carolers. An 80-foot tree is illuminated by thousands of colored lights.

Epcot and MGM Studios also offer special embellishments and entertainment throughout the holiday season, as do all Disney resorts. Some holiday highlights include **Mickey's Very Merry Christmas Party,** an after-dark ticketed event. This takes place weekends at the Magic Kingdom with a traditional Christmas parade and a breathtaking fireworks display. The admission price of $25 includes free cookies and cocoa and a souvenir photo. The best part? Short lines to the rides. The **Candlelight Procession** at Epcot features hundreds of candle-holding carolers, a celebrity narrator telling the Christmas story, and a 450-voice choir. Call ☎ **407/824-4321** for details about all of the above, 407/W-DISNEY (934-7639) to inquire about hotel/events packages. **The Osborne Family Christmas Lights** came to Disney–MGM Studios in 1995 when the Arkansas family ran into trouble with local authorities who claimed their multimillion-light display was too much of a spectacle and interfered with air traffic. In a twinkle, Disney moved the whole thing to central Florida.

- **Christmas at Sea World.** Sea World features a special Shamu show and a luau show called "Christmas in Hawaii." The 400-foot sky tower is lit like a Christmas tree nightly. Call ☎ **407/351-3600** for details.
- **Walt Disney World New Year's Eve Celebration.** For one night the Magic Kingdom is open until 2am for a massive fireworks exhibition. Other New Year's festivities in the WDW parks include a big bash at Pleasure Island featuring music headliners, a special Hoop-Dee-Doo Musical Revue show, and guest performances by well-known musical groups at Disney–MGM Studios and Epcot. Call ☎ **407/824-4321** for details.
- **Church Street Station** in downtown Orlando also offers a New Year's celebration, complete with miniature dropping ball. For information call ☎ **407/422-2434**.
- ✪**The Citrus Bowl Parade.** On an annually selected date in late December, the parade features lavish floats and high-school bands for a nationally televised parade. Reserved seats in the bleachers are $12, but you can watch along the route for free. Call ☎ **407/423-2476** for details.
- **CompUSA Florida Citrus Bowl New Year's.** The official New Year's Eve celebration of the CompUSA Florida Citrus Bowl takes place at Sea World. Events include headliner concerts, a laser and fireworks spectacular, a countdown to midnight, and special shows throughout the park. Admission is charged. Call ☎ **407/423-2476** for details.

4 Tips for Travelers with Special Needs

FOR TRAVELERS WITH DISABILITIES   There is no reason why those with disabilities can't get full enjoyment out of the theme parks—that is, with a little advance planning.

Visitor Information   Call the **Florida Governor's Alliance,** 345 S. Magnolia Dr., Suite D-11, Tallahassee, FL 32301 (☎ **904/487-2223** or 904/487-2222 TTD), for a free copy of *The Florida Planning Companion for People with Disabilities*. It offers valuable information on accessibility at tourist facilities throughout the state.

Accommodations   Every hotel and motel is required by law to have a special room or rooms equipped for wheelchairs. A few, including **Best Western Buena Vista Suites** (☎ **407/239-8588**), **Embassy Suites** (☎ **407/239-1144**), and **Sleep Inn** (☎ **407/396-1600**), have wheel-in showers. Walt Disney World's the **Coronado Springs Resort** (☎ **407/W-DISNEY** (934-7639), 407/934-6632, or 407/824-1000), which opened in 1997, has 99 rooms designed to accommodate guests with disabilities. Make your special needs known when making reservations.

Transportation   All public buses in Orlando have a hydraulic lift and restraining belts for wheelchairs, and they serve Universal Studios, Sea World, the shopping areas, and downtown Orlando. When staying at Disney, you can get a shuttle bus from your hotel that will also accommodate wheelchairs.

If you need to rent a special wheelchair van in Orlando, call **Wheelers Inc.** (☎ **407/826-0616**) or **Vantage Mini Vans** (☎ **407/521-8002**).

Amtrak (☎ **800/872-7245**) provides redcap service, wheelchair assistance, and special seats if you give them 72 hours notice. Travelers with disabilities are also entitled to a discount of 15% off the lowest available adult coach fare. Children ages 2 to 15 with disabilities can also get a 50% discount on already discounted one-way fares for adults with disabilities. Documentation from a doctor or an ID card proving your disability is required. Amtrak also provides wheelchair-accessible sleeping accommodations on long-distance trains. Service dogs are permissible and travel free of charge. For a free booklet called *Amtrak's America,* which has a chapter detailing services for passengers with disabilities, call ☎ **800/872-7245** or write to Amtrak Distribution Center, P.O. Box 7717, Itasca, IL 60143.

Greyhound (☎ **800/752-4841**) allows a passenger with disabilities to travel with a companion for a single fare, and if you call 48 hours in advance, they will arrange help along the way.

Theme Parks   Most attractions at the various theme parks, especially newer ones, are designed to be accessible to a wide variety of people. People with wheelchairs, and their parties, are often given preferential treatment so they can avoid long lines.

The available assistance is outlined by each major park in a brochure, and all the parks offer some parking as close as possible to the park entrance for those with disabilities. Let the booth attendant know your needs, so you will be directed to the appropriate spot. Wheelchair rentals are available at most major attractions, but you will probably be most comfortable with your chair from home. Keep in mind, however, wheelchairs wider than 24.5 inches may be difficult to navigate through some attractions.

At Walt Disney World: Disney does everything possible to facilitate guests with disabilities. Its many services are detailed in the *Guidebook for Guests with Disabilities.* To obtain a copy prior to your visit, write **Guest Letters,** P.O. Box 10040, Lake Buena Vista, FL 32830-0040, or call ☎ **407/824-4321**. Also call that number for answers to any questions regarding special needs. Some examples of Disney services:

- Almost all Disney resorts have rooms for those with disabilities.
- Braille directories are located inside the Magic Kingdom in front of the Main Street train station and in a gazebo in front of the Crystal Palace restaurant, and complimentary guided-tour audiocassette tapes and recorders are available at Guest Services to assist visually impaired guests.
- All parks have special parking lots.
- Personal translator units are available to amplify the audio at selected Epcot attractions (inquire at Earth Station).
- Wheelchairs can be rented at all of the Disney parks.
- Downtown Disney, with its crowded shops and bars, may be hard to navigate in a wheelchair. The movie theater is, however, wheelchair-accessible.
- For information about Telecommunications Devices for the Deaf (TDDs) at Disney World, call ☎ **407/827-5141.**

At Universal Studios: Guests with disabilities should go to Guest Services located just inside the main entrance for a *Disabled Guest Guidebook,* a Telecommunications Device for the Deaf (TDD), or other special assistance. Wheelchairs are for rent.

Universal also provides audio descriptions on cassette for visually impaired guests and has sign-language guides and scripts for all its shows (advance notice is required; ☎ **407/363-8000** for details).

At Sea World: The park has a guide for guests with disabilities, although most of its attractions are easily accessible to those in wheelchairs. Sea World provides a Braille guide for the visually impaired. It also provides a very brief synopsis of shows for the hearing impaired. For information call ☎ **407/351-2600**.

Nationwide Resources   Mobility International USA, P.O. Box 10767, Eugene, OR 97440 (☎ **541/343-1284**), offers accessibility information and has many interesting travel programs for those with disabilities. Membership ($30 a year) includes a quarterly newsletter called *Over the Rainbow.*

Help (accessibility information and more) is also available from the **Society for the Advancement of Travel for the Handicapped** (SATH), 347 Fifth Ave., Suite 610, New York, NY 10016 (☎ **212/447-7284**). It charges $5 to send requested information.

Accessible Journeys (☎ **800/846-4537** or 610/521-0339) and **Flying Wheels Travel** (☎ **800/535-6790** or 507/451-5005) offer tours for people with physical disabilities. Accessible Journeys has a Web site at **www.disabilitytravel.com** and can provide nurse/companions for travelers. **Guided Tour Inc.** (☎ **215/782-1370**) has tours for people with physical or mental disabilities, the visually impaired, and the elderly.

Recommended Books   Twin Peaks Press, Box 129, Vancouver, WA 98666 (☎ **360/694-2462**), specializes in books for people with disabilities. Write for their *Disability Bookshop Catalog,* enclosing $5.

FOR SENIORS   Always carry some form of photo ID so that you can take advantage of discounts wherever they're offered. And it never hurts to ask.

If you haven't already done so, consider joining the **American Association of Retired Persons** (AARP) (☎ **202/434-2277**). Annual membership costs $8 per person or per couple. You must be at least 50 to join. Membership entitles you to many discounts. Write to Purchase Privilege Program, AARP Fulfillment, 601 E St. NW, Washington, DC 20049, to receive a free list of hotels, motels, and car-rental firms nationwide that offer discounts to AARP members.

Elderhostel is a national organization that offers low-priced educational programs for people over 55 (your spouse can be any age; a companion must be at least 50). Programs are generally a week long, and prices average about $335 per person, including room, board, and classes. For information on programs in Florida, call or write Elderhostel Headquarters, 75 Federal St., Boston, MA 02110-1941 (☎ **617/426-7788**) and ask for a free U.S. catalog. Or call the Florida office at ☎ **813/864-8312**.

Amtrak (☎ **800/872-7245**) offers a 15% discount off the lowest available coach fare (with certain travel restrictions) to people 62 or over.

Greyhound also offers discounted fares for senior citizens. Call your local Greyhound office for details.

FOR FAMILIES   No city in the world is more geared to family travel than Orlando. In addition to its theme parks, Orlando's recreational facilities provide abundant opportunities for family fun. Every restaurant in town has a low-priced children's menu, and many hotels maintain children's activity centers (see details in chapter 5). Keep an eye open for coupons. The Friday, Calendar section of the local newspaper, *The Orlando Sentinel,* often has coupons and special deals. Many local restaurants, especially those in tourist areas, offer great discounts that are yours for the clipping. Check the information you receive from the Convention & Visitors Bureau.

Kid-Friendly Tours

Sea World lives up to its reputation for making education fun with a variety of tours. One of the most interesting is the **Polar Expedition Guided Tour.** This hour-long tour provides kids with a chance to visit with Sea World's new stars, Klondike and Snow. It also offers a behind-the-scenes look at penguins. This tour is suitable for children of all ages. It's booked on a first-come, first-serve basis, so make reservations for one of the four daily outings when you enter the park. Go to the Guided Tour Information desk. With the price of admission, the cost is $5 for adults, $4 for children. Tours are offered at 9:30am, 10:30am, 2pm, and 3pm. For more information call ☎ **407/351-2600.** (Also check out tour information by accessing the education department at www.usf.com.

At Walt Disney World, half-day **Disney Day Camp** excursions are for children ages 7 to 10. From exploring special effects at Disney–MGM Studios to experiencing the wonders of China at Epcot, these provide a good opportunity for kids to interact with their peers while providing parents with a little time alone. Disney offers two programs each day, the first from 8am to noon, the second from 1:30 to 5pm. The cost is $75 per child; a box lunch is provided for an additional charge. Theme park admission is not required to take part.

The only tour available at Animal Kingdom is the **Backstage Safari** for those sixteen and older. This three-and-a-half hour tour, which is $60, provides an upclose look at the care and feeding of the Disney wildlife. Tours focus on the animal pens, the nursery, and the feeding areas. The tours are held Monday, Wednesday, and Friday, and advanced registration is required. For information call ☎ **407/939-8687.** Tours are also included in some comprehensive Disney packages.

Central Florida Family magazine and *Black Family Today* both highlight family-friendly—often free—festivals and events in the Orlando area.

Disney–MGM Studios and **Universal Studios** offer parent-swap programs in which parents with children can switch off watching the young ones while the other parents ride. In both parks, ask attendants at the specific attraction what needs to be done.

Here are a few general suggestions to make traveling with kids easier:

Planning Ahead Make reservations for "character breakfasts" at Disney when you make your hotel reservations. Also, in any park, check the daily schedule for character appearances and make sure the kids know when they are going to get to meet their heroes. (This is often a kiddie highlight.) This helps you avoid running after every character you see.

Packing Although your home may be toddler-proof, hotel accommodations are not. Bring blank plugs to cover outlets and whatever else is necessary. Locals can spot tourists by their bright red, just-toasted glow; heed this reminder for parents and children: *Don't forget the sunscreen.*

Accommodations Children under 12, and in many cases even older, stay free in their parents' rooms in most hotels. Look for establishments that have pools and other recreational facilities. If you don't want to rent a car and aren't staying at Disney, International Drive is the place to be. Public buses run frequently, hotels often offer family discounts, and some provide free shuttle service to the homes of the Mouse, the Whale, and King Kong.

Ground Rules   Set up ground rules before leaving home about issues such as bedtime and spending money on souvenirs. Turn the bottom drawer of the dresser into the place to keep toys from home and newly acquired treasures. This keeps the mess down and lets the kids have easy access to their stuff without bothering you.

At the Parks   All park maps explain height restrictions or rides that may unsettle young children. Do yourself and your kids a favor by knowing these restrictions before you get in line. These rules are not bent, no matter how much your child may cry. Also heed those "too intense for children" warnings. One bad trip down a darkened tunnel can make your toddler apprehensive and cranky all day on rides that should be fun.

Take a Break   The Disney parks, Universal Studios, and Sea World all have stylized play areas offering parents and kids a rest. Schedule time to take advantage of these facilities. Since most of these kid zones include toys involving water and all the parks have major water-related attractions, you'd be smart to pack a change of clothes for the kids. Rent a locker and store the spare duds until you need them. Even in summer months the Florida humidity can keep you feeling soggy all day.

Show Time   Schedule an inside, air-conditioned show for mid-afternoon. You might even get the littlest tikes to nap in the darkened theater. For all shows, arrive at least 20 minutes early but not so early that the kids go nuts waiting. Most of the big shows have arena-style seating and huge stages so everyone can see.

Snack Times   When dreaming of your vacation, you probably don't envision hours spent standing in lines and waiting and waiting. It helps to store some lightweight snacks in an easy-to-carry backpack, especially if traveling with small children. This may save you some headaches and will certainly save some money.

Bring Your Own?   Unless you are unusually attached to your stroller or it is specially designed for triplets, it's better to use one provided by the park. That way you avoid hauling yours to and from the car and on and off the trams, trains, or monorails.

FOR PEOPLE IN RECOVERY   Those friends of Bill W. and members of other 12-step programs can call the **Central Florida Intergroup of Alcoholics Anonymous** (☎ **407/521-0012**). This is the local AA hotline and is manned with volunteers 24 hours a day. Please be considerate, however, and don't call at three in the morning just for tourist information. They can provide information, including directions, to meetings in Orange and Seminole counties, as well as those in tourist areas. Disney does not allow meetings on the property, so you will need a car or lots of cash for cab fare to get to a meeting. Hot-line workers can also provide numbers for other local 12-step programs such as Narcotics Anonymous, Al-Anon, and Overeaters Anonymous, groups that also have information hot lines but generally don't operate 24 hours.

Those looking to party away from the sometimes alcohol-drenched tourist areas can have an alcohol-free night at **Club Soda,** 6341 N. Orange Blossom Trail, about 35 miles from the heart of tourist central near the intersection of Clarcona–Ocoee Road and Orange Blossom Trail. For information call ☎ **407/523-1556**. There is sometimes live entertainment or themed nights, such as karaoke.

FOR GAY & LESBIAN TRAVELERS   The popularity of Orlando with gay and lesbian travelers is evidenced by the expansion of the traditional June 6 "Gay Day" celebration at Disney World into a "Gay Weekend," including events at Universal Studios and Sea World. In 1997 Universal City Travel first offered a "Gay Weekend" tour package including tickets to Universal Studios, Sea World, and Church Street Station. ("Gay Day," unofficially held at Walt Disney World since the early 1990s, has

CyberDeals for Net Surfers

It's possible to get some great deals on airfare, hotels, and car rentals via the Internet. So grab your mouse before you visit the *other* Mouse—you could save a bundle on your trip. The Web sites we've highlighted are worth checking out, especially since all services are free (but don't forget that time is money when you're online).

Microsoft Expedia (www.expedia.com) The best part of this multipurpose travel site is the "Fare Tracker": You fill out a form on the screen indicating that you're interested in cheap flights to Orlando from your hometown, and, once a week, they'll e-mail you the best airfare deals. The site's "Travel Agent" will also steer you to bargains on hotels and car rentals, and you can book everything, including flights, right online. This site is even useful once you're booked: Before you go, log on to Expedia for oodles of up-to-date travel information, including weather reports and foreign exchange rates.

Preview Travel (www.reservations.com and www.vacations.com) Another useful travel site, "Reservations.com" has a "Best Fare Finder," which will search the Apollo computer reservations system for the three lowest fares for any route on any days of the year. Say you want to go from Chicago to Orlando and back between December 6th and 13th. Just fill out the form on the screen with times, dates, and destinations, and within minutes, Preview will show you the best deals. If you find an airfare you like, you can book your ticket right online—you can even reserve hotels and car rentals on this site. If you're in the preplanning stage, head to Preview's "Vacations.com" site, where you can check out the latest package deals for Orlando and other destinations around the world by clicking on "Hot Deals."

Travelocity (www.travelocity.com) This is one of the best travel sites out there. In addition to its "Personal Fare Watcher," which notifies you via e-mail of the lowest airfares for up to five different destinations, Travelocity will track the three lowest fares for any routes on any dates in minutes. You can book a flight right then and there, and if you need a rental car or hotel, Travelocity will find you the best deal via the SABRE computer reservations system (a huge database used by travel agents worldwide). Click on "Last Minute Deals" for the latest travel bargains, including a link to "H.O.T. Coupons" (**www.hotcoupons.com**), where you can print out electronic coupons for travel in the U.S. and Canada.

drawn as many as 40,000 folks. On that day parkgoers are supposed to wear red to signify their support of the gay and lesbian community.) For information on tour packages offered by **Universal City Travel,** call ☎ **800/224-3838.** You can also get information on the Internet by accessing **www.gayday.com.**

For information about events for that weekend, or throughout the year, contact **Gay & Lesbian Community Services of Central Florida** by writing 714 E. Colonial Dr., Orlando, FL 32804 or by calling ☎ **407/425-4527.** Ask for a welcome packet. This will include the latest issue of the *Triangle,* a monthly newspaper dedicated to gay and lesbian issues, plus a calendar of events pertaining to the gay and lesbian community. This is not a tourist-specific packet, but it does contain valuable information. Check out the advertisement for nightclubs focused on a gay and lesbian crowd. For information on the *Triangle* specifically—for example, where it can be picked up in tourist areas—call ☎ **407/849-0099.**

Trip.Com (www.thetrip.com)   This site is really geared toward the business traveler, but vacationers-to-be can also use Trip.Com's valuable fare-finding engine, which will e-mail you every week with the best city-to-city airfare deals on your selected route or routes.

Discount Tickets (www.discount-tickets.com)   Operated by the ETN (European Travel Network), this site offers discounts on airfares, accommodations, car rentals, and tours. It deals in flights between the U.S. and other countries, not domestic U.S. flights, so it's most useful for travelers coming to Orlando from abroad.

E-Savers Programs   Several major airlines, most of which service Orlando, offer a free e-mail service known as **E-Savers**, via which they'll send you their best bargain airfares on a weekly basis. Here's how it works: Once a week (usually Wednesday), subscribers receive a list of discounted flights to and from various destinations, both international and domestic. Now here's the catch: These fares are only available if you leave the very next Saturday (or sometimes Friday night) and return on the following Monday or Tuesday. It's really a service for the spontaneously inclined and for travelers looking for a quick getaway (and let's face it, that can be a problem if you're going to Orlando). But the fares are cheap, so it's worth taking a look; you never know. If you have a preference for certain airlines (in other words, the ones you fly most frequently), sign up with them first. Another caveat: You'll get frequent-flier miles if you purchase one of these fares, but you can't use miles to buy the ticket.

Here's a list of airlines and their Web sites, where you can get on the e-mail lists and also book flights directly:

- **American Airlines**: www.americanair.com
- **Continental Airlines**: www.flycontinental.com
- **TWA**: www.twa.com
- **Northwest Airlines**: www.nwa.com
- **US Airways:** www.usairways.com

Epicurious Travel (travel.epicurious.com)   Another good travel site, it allows you to sign up for all these airline e-mail lists at once.

Orlando is a Southern town, but the entertainment industry and theme parks have helped provide the basis for a strong gay and lesbian community. Same-sex dancing is acceptable at most of the clubs at WDW's Pleasure Island, especially the large, crowded Mannequins. (Really, who can tell who is dancing with whom most of the time?) Many of Universal's CityWalk establishments are similarly gender blind. The tenor of crowds can change, depending on what tour is in town, so respect your own intuition.

Same-sex dancing is not expressly forbidden at Church Street Station, but the biggest dance hall is a country honky-tonk frequented by some real, local cowboys, and we are in Dixieland. I've never heard of anyone being asked to leave for dancing, but the crowd probably won't make for your most comfortable two-step. (Lots of line dancing is done, though.)

There are a few exclusively gay or lesbian bars and clubs in Orlando, and they're described in chapter 10.

5 Getting There

BY PLANE

THE MAJOR AIRLINES   There are about 40 scheduled airlines and 38 charter services serving more than 22 million passengers a year. **Delta** (☎ 800/221-1212) has the most flights—over 25%—into Orlando International Airport. It offers service from 200 cities and has a Fantastic Flyer program for kids. **Delta Express** offers direct service from 14 cities and also has the Fantastic Flyer program for kids.

Other carriers include **Air Jamaica** (☎ 800/523-5585), **America West** (☎ 800/235-9292), **American** (☎ 800/433-7300), **American Trans Air** (☎ 800/293-6194), **Canadian Airlines** (☎ 800/426-3838), **Continental** (☎ 800/231-0856), **Midway** (☎ 800/446-4392), **Northwest** (☎ 800/225-2525), **SunJet** (☎ 800/4SUNJET), **Southwest**(☎ 800/435-9792), **TWA** (☎ 800/221-2000), **United** (☎800/241-6522), and **US Airways** (☎ 800/428-4322).

FINDING THE BEST AIRFARE   Here are some tips for discovering the lowest airfares:

- Since advance-purchase fares are almost always the lowest available, it's a good idea to book your flight as far in advance as possible. Advance-purchase fares can be as much as 75% lower than fares booked at the last minute!
- The more flexible you can be about your travel dates and length of stay, the more money you're likely to save.
- Visit a large travel agency to investigate all options. Sometimes a good agent knows about fares you won't find on your own. Major Internet providers, such as AOL, offer travel sections that can provide pricing comparisons. You can book tickets for some airlines via the Internet.
- Check newspaper ads (especially in the travel sections of high-circulation papers like the Sunday *New York Times* Travel section) for announcements of short-term promotional fares.
- Fly at off times (for instance, at night) when planes are less likely to be full.

ORLANDO'S AIRPORT   Orlando International Airport (☎ 407/825-2001) offers direct or nonstop service from 70 U.S. cities and about two dozen international destinations, serving over 26 million passengers each year. It's a thoroughly modern and user-friendly facility with restaurants, shops, a 450-room on-premises Hyatt Regency Hotel, and centrally located information kiosks. All major car-rental companies are located at or near the airport; see "Getting Around" in chapter 4 for more information on rentals.

Airport Transportation   The airport is 25 miles from Walt Disney World and 20 minutes from Downtown. **Mears Transportation Group** (☎ 407/423-5566) has shuttle vans that ply the route from the airport (you board outside the baggage claim) to all Disney resorts and official hotels as well as most other area properties. Their comfortable, air-conditioned vehicles operate around the clock, departing every 15 to 25 minutes in either direction. Rates vary with your destination. Round-trip cost for adults is $21 between the airport and downtown Orlando or International Drive, $25 for Walt Disney World/Lake Buena Vista or Kissimmee/Hwy. 192. Children ages 4 to 11 pay $14 to downtown and $17 to WDW. Children 3 and under ride free.

Driving to Walt Disney World   To get from the airport to the attractions area, take the **North** exit out of the airport to **528 West;** Follow signs to **I-4;** it will take about 20 minutes to get to Walt Disney World if the traffic isn't too heavy. When you get to I-4, head **west** toward the attractions.

Note: It's always a good idea when you make your reservations to ask about transportation options between the airport and your hotel. Also be sure to ask how far you have to travel to pick up and drop off your car. Some lots are located miles from the airport and, with waiting in line and catching shuttles, can result in a half-day trip just to return your car.

BY CAR

Orlando is 436 miles from Atlanta, 1,312 miles from Boston, 1,120 miles from Chicago, 1,009 miles from Cleveland, 1,170 miles from Dallas, 1,114 miles from Detroit, 1,105 miles from New York City, and 1,261 miles from Toronto.

From Atlanta, take I-75 south to the Florida Turnpike to I-4 west.

From points northeast, take I-95 south to I-4 west.

From Chicago, take I-65 south to Nashville and then I-24 south to I-75 south to the Florida Turnpike to I-4 west.

From Cleveland, take I-77 south to Columbia, South Carolina, and then I-26 east to I-95 south to I-4 west.

From Dallas, take I-20 east to I-49 south to I-10 east to I-75 south to the Florida Turnpike to I-4 west.

From Detroit, take I-75 south to the Florida Turnpike to I-4 west.

From Toronto, take Canadian Route 401 south to Queen Elizabeth Way south to I-90 (New York State Thruway) east to I-87 (New York State Thruway) south to I-95 over the George Washington Bridge, and continue south on I-95 to I-4 west.

AAA (☎ **800/222-4357**) members and some other automobile-club members can call local offices for maps and optimum driving directions.

BY TRAIN

Amtrak trains (☎ **800/872-7245**) pull into stations at 1400 Sligh Blvd., between Columbia and Miller streets in downtown Orlando (about 23 miles from Walt Disney World), and 111 Dakin Ave., at Thurman Street in Kissimmee (about 15 miles from Walt Disney World). There are also stops in Winter Park, about 10 miles north of downtown Orlando, at 150 W. Morse Blvd., and in Sanford, about 23 miles northeast of downtown Orlando. The Sanford station, located at 600 Persimmon Ave., is also the end terminal for the Auto Train.

From the Orlando station, you can catch LYNX bus no. 50, which departs weekdays at least once an hour between 6:45am and 8:45pm (weekends, take bus no. 7 or 11 from the stop at the corner of Orange and Columbia avenues, 2 blocks away). All trips involve a transfer at the downtown bus station—not too much of a hassle because the bus will usually be right there when you arrive. This connecting bus (no. 8) makes stops about every 1½ blocks along International Drive, culminating at Sea World, where you can get a taxi (about $28) to Walt Disney World–area hotels.

For further details about bus transportation from the Orlando Amtrak station, call ☎ **407/841-8240**. A taxi from the Orlando Amtrak station to Walt Disney World–area hotels is about $42.

From the Kissimmee Amtrak station, a taxi (about $28 to WDW-area hotels) is your only option.

FARES   As with airline fares, you can sometimes get discounts if you book far in advance. There may be some restrictions on travel dates for discounted fares, mostly around very busy holiday times. Amtrak also offers money-saving packages—including hotel accommodations (some at WDW resorts), car rentals, tours, and more—with your train fare (☎ **800/321-8684**). Zoned fares, available for 45 days to United States residents, range from about $400 during peak season (from Jan to May and from July to mid-Sept) to about $320 during off-peak season (June and from mid-Sept to Dec).

AMTRAK'S AUTO TRAIN   Amtrak's Auto Train offers the convenience of having a car in Florida without driving it there. The Auto Train begins in Lorton, Virginia—about a 4-hour drive from New York, 2 hours from Philadelphia—and ends up at Sanford, Florida, about 23 miles northeast of Orlando. Once again, reserve early for the lowest fares. The Auto Train departs Lorton and Sanford at 4:30pm daily, arriving at its destination at 9am the next morning. *Note:* You have to arrive 1 or 2 hours before departure time so your car can be boarded. Call ☎ **800/872-7245** for details.

BY BUS

Greyhound buses connect the entire country with Orlando. They pull into a terminal at 555 N. Magruder Blvd. (John Young Parkway), between West Colonial Drive and Winter Garden Road, a few miles west of downtown Orlando (☎ **407/292-3422**), or in Kissimmee at 16 N. Orlando Ave., between Emmett and Mabbette streets, about 14 miles from Walt Disney World (☎ **407/847-3911**). There is van transport from the Kissimmee terminal to most area hotels and motels. From Orlando, you can call for a **Mears shuttle** van (☎ **407/423-5566**), which will cost $12 to $13 one-way to a Walt Disney World–area hotel, $8 for children ages 4 to 11, free for those under 4 (round-trip fares are less). For the return trip, call from your hotel 24 hours in advance. A taxi to Walt Disney World–area hotels will cost about $40. Greyhound's fare structure tends to be complex, but the good news is that when you call to make a reservation, the agent will always give you the lowest-fare options. Once again, advance-purchase fares booked 3 to 21 days prior to travel represent vast savings. Check your phone book for a local Greyhound listing or call ☎ **800/231-2222**.

6 Money-Saving Packages

Frankly, the number and the diversity of package tours to Orlando are staggering. But significant savings are available for those willing to do the research. Best bet: Stop at a sizable travel agency and pick up brochures from several companies. Pore over them at home, comparing offerings to find the optimum package for your trip. Also obtain the *Walt Disney World Vacations* brochure (see details at the beginning of this chapter), which lists the company's own packages. Try to find a package that meets rather than exceeds your needs; there's no sense in paying for elements you won't use. Also, read over the advantages accruing to Disney resort guests in chapter 5; some packages list as selling points services that are automatically available to every Walt Disney World guest.

Since 1996, Universal Studios has offered its own packages through **Universal City Travel Company** (☎ **800/224-3838**). These packages highlight Universal Studios and offer special VIP access to the park and rides and discounts to other parks. Universal City Travel also offers trips that include stays at beach hotels before or after the theme-park trips. These excursions are billed as "an alternative resort experience."

Examples of airline-run packages are the **Delta Dream Vacations,** in several price ranges. These packages include round-trip air transport, accommodations (including state and hotel-room tax and baggage gratuities), an air-conditioned intermediate-size rental car with unlimited mileage or round-trip airport transfer, a "Magic Passport" that provides unlimited admission to all Walt Disney World parks for the length of your stay, one breakfast (which can be a character breakfast), and entry into a selected theme park 1 hour before regular opening time. In packages utilizing Walt Disney

World Resorts, you get all the advantages accruing to guests at these properties (see chapter 5 for details). At this writing, 3-night midweek packages begin at $369 to $409 per person (based on double occupancy and New York departure; range reflects season). If you put all of those components together on your own, the cost would be much, much higher. In fact, a Delta Dream Vacation can cost less than airfare alone from certain cities. Delta also has Orlando packages for which WDW tickets and resorts are optional. For details, call ☎ **800/872-7786.**

Additional airline and tour-operator sources for airfare-inclusive packages include **US Airways Vacations** (☎ 800/455-0123), **American Airlines Fly Away Vacations** (☎ 800/321-2121), **American Express Vacations** (☎ 800/241-1700), **Travel Impressions** (☎ 800/941-2639), and **Kingdom Tours** (☎ **800/872-8857**).

7 Weddings at Walt Disney World

Fly down the aisle on Aladdin's magic carpet? Pull up in a glass coach pulled by six white horses? Have Mickey and Minnie greet guests at the reception? Take the plunge, literally and figuratively, on the Twilight Zone Tower of Terror?

If you've always dreamed of meeting Prince Charming and then having a fairy-tale wedding, the folks at Disney are happy to oblige—for a price. Recognizing that Disney World is a popular honeymoon destination, Disney in 1995 cut out the middleman and officially went into the wedding business.

The first step was building a multimillion-dollar nondenominational chapel in the middle of the Seven Seas Lagoon. The next step was letting the world know the Disney wedding chapel was open for business. The first nuptials were televised live on Lifetime television. (Construction was still in progress at the chapel, so the bride and groom wore white hard hats.) About 1,700 couples were married that first year, and now thousands of couples mix matrimony with Disney magic at the pavilion, which resembles a Victorian summer house.

An intimate gathering for two is about $2,000. The average Disney wedding costs $19,000 and is attended by 100 people (Prince Charming not included). People from as far away as the Netherlands have traveled to Orlando for sometimes unusual celebrations to recognize their lifetime commitment to one another. One couple had every guest wear Mickey Mouse ears to the ceremony. Another exchanged Donald and Daisy caps instead of wedding rings. A third walked out of the church to "Zip-a-dee-doo-dah," and one blushing bride topped her veil with Mickey's famous ears. Those are just the examples Disney is willing to promote.

Certainly with the only limits being imagination and money, there have been wackier weddings. From rented coachmen to topiaries in the shape of Pluto, Disney serves up whichever Disney reference or character the couple desires, even if it is "Goofy." For further details on **Disney weddings** (and honeymoons, of course), call ☎ **407/828-3400.**

8 Disney (& Other) Cruise Packages

Can the Disney magic float? The jury was still out in late February 1998. Just as they were getting ready to pack, thousands of vacationers learned their cruise plans had been shipwrecked by construction delays. The first Disney-owned-and-operated cruise ships, the *Disney Magic* and *Disney Wonder,* were originally scheduled to sail in March of 1998 but have been delayed twice. The final date is July 30.

When the ships finally head out to sea, 7-day cruise packages will include 3 or 4 days afloat, with the rest of the week divided among the landlocked properties.

The average cost for a family of four is expected to be about $4,500. Cruises depart from Port Canaveral, about an hour by car from Orlando. Book well in advance. Each ship will hold up to 1,760 passengers, but the cruises are proving popular with the legions of true fans looking for something new. The cruises attempt to create the theme-park magic on water, complete with character visits and entertainment with the Disney touch. For information call ☎ **407/566-3500.**

Premier Cruise Lines (the "Big Red Boat"), previously the official Disney cruise line, continues to offer 3- and 4-night luxury ocean cruises to the Bahamas (Nassau and Port Lucaya) in conjunction with 3- or 4-day Orlando theme-park vacations. Cruises depart from and return to Port Canaveral, 45 minutes from Walt Disney World. You can add the island segment before or after your stay in Orlando. Since Disney began making its own splash, Premier is focusing on other Orlando-area attractions, with better deals likely to be available for those interested in visiting Universal, Sea World, and other non-Disney area attractions. Looney Tunes characters (Bugs Bunny, Tweety, Daffy Duck) are your onboard hosts. Package prices include all meals onboard ship, an Alamo rental car with unlimited mileage for 7 days, round-trip airfare to/from Orlando, and admission to varied attractions. Rates depend on stateroom and hotel category and the season you're traveling in. At this writing, 7-night packages with a New York departure start at about $899 per person, based on double occupancy; $589 for children under 9. For information, call ☎ **407/566-7000.**

All ships are equipped with swimming pools, Jacuzzis, health clubs, jogging tracks, movie theaters, beauty salons, casinos, bars/lounges, video-game arcades, shops, and nightclubs.

Tip: Nothing spoils a cruise vacation quite like a tropical storm and 20-foot swells. You might want to avoid the height of hurricane season, from September through mid-November. Take it from someone who spent 36 hours of her honeymoon in bed—seasick—the lower hurricane season rates are not worth the upheavals. If you do go during hurricane season, be sure to pack the seasickness medicine or check out the seasick remedies, such as a shot, available onboard.

For Foreign Visitors

3

This chapter will provide some specifics about getting to Orlando as economically as possible from overseas, plus some helpful information about how things are done in the United States—from mailing a postcard to making a phone call.

1 Preparing for Your Trip

VISITOR INFORMATION IN THE UNITED KINGDOM

There is an **Orlando Tourism Office** in London. For information from that office, write to 18–24 Westbourne Grove, London, England, W25RH (☎ **44/171-243-8072;** fax 44/171-243-8487). You can also e-mail that office at **06211.1754@compuserve.com**.

ENTRY REQUIREMENTS

DOCUMENT REGULATIONS Canadian citizens may enter the United States without visas; they need only proof of residence.

Citizens of the United Kingdom, New Zealand, Japan, and most other western European countries traveling on valid passports may not need a visa for fewer than 90 days of holiday or business travel to the United States, provided that they hold a round-trip or return ticket and enter the United States on an airline or cruise line that participates in the visa waiver program.

(Note that citizens of these visa-exempt countries who first enter the United States may then visit Mexico, Canada, Bermuda, and/or the Caribbean islands and then re-enter the States, by any mode of transportation, without needing a visa. Further information is available from any U.S. embassy or consulate. See "Fast Facts: For the Foreign Traveler," later in this chapter.)

Citizens of countries other than those stipulated above, including citizens of Australia, must have two documents: a valid **passport,** with an expiration date at least 6 months later than the scheduled end of the visit to the United States; and a **tourist visa,** available without charge from the nearest U.S. consulate. To obtain a visa, the traveler must submit a completed application form (either in person or by mail) with a 1½-inch-square photo and demonstrate binding ties to a residence abroad.

You can usually obtain a visa at once or within 24 hours, but it may take longer during the summer rush from June to August. If you cannot go in person, contact the nearest U.S. embassy or consulate for

Walt Disney World Services for International Visitors

Walt Disney World, which welcomes thousands of foreign visitors each year, has numerous services designed to meet their needs. Unless otherwise indicated, call ☎ **407/W-DISNEY** (934-7639) for details. Services include:

- A special phone number (☎ **407/824-7900**) to speak with someone in French or Spanish (other languages are sometimes available as well).

- Personal translator units (in French, German, and Spanish) to translate narration at some shows and attractions.

- Detailed guidebooks to the three major parks in Spanish, French, German, Portuguese, and Japanese (available at any guest relations location).

- Currency exchange (see "Money," below).

- World Key Terminals at Epcot that offer basic park information and assistance with dining reservations in Spanish.

- Resort phones equipped with software that expedites international calls by allowing guests to dial direct to foreign destinations.

directions on applying by mail. Your travel agent or airline office may also be able to provide you with visa applications and instructions. The U.S. consulate or embassy that issues your visa will determine whether you will be issued a multiple- or single-entry visa and any restrictions regarding the length of your stay.

MEDICAL REQUIREMENTS   No inoculations are needed to enter the United States unless you are coming from, or have stopped over in, areas known to be suffering from epidemics, particularly cholera or yellow fever.

If you have a disease requiring treatment with medications containing narcotics or with drugs requiring a syringe, carry a valid signed prescription from your physician to allay any suspicions that you are smuggling drugs.

CUSTOMS REQUIREMENTS   Every adult visitor may bring in free of duty: 1 liter of wine or hard liquor; 200 cigarettes or 100 cigars (but no cigars from Cuba) or 3 pounds of smoking tobacco; and $100 worth of gifts. These exemptions are offered to travelers who spend at least 72 hours in the United States and who have not claimed them within the preceding 6 months. It is altogether forbidden to bring into the country foodstuffs (particularly cheese, fruit, cooked meats, and canned goods) and plants (vegetables, seeds, tropical plants, and so on). Foreign tourists may bring in or take out up to $10,000 in U.S. or foreign currency with no formalities; larger sums must be declared to Customs upon entering or leaving.

INSURANCE

There is no national health-care system in the United States. Because the cost of medical care is extremely high, we strongly advise every traveler to secure health coverage before setting out.

You may want to take out a comprehensive travel policy that covers (for a relatively low premium) sickness or injury costs (medical, surgical, and hospital); loss or theft of your baggage; trip-cancellation costs; bail guarantee in case you are arrested; and costs of accident, repatriation, or death. Such packages (for example, "Europe Assistance" in Europe) are sold by automobile clubs at attractive rates, as well as by insurance companies and travel agencies.

Walk-in medical clinics are available, with a visit usually costing under $50, not including prescriptions. **Centra-Care,** operated by a locally run Florida Hospital, is a reputable medical facility with more than a dozen locations throughout the Orlando area. For information and the nearest location, call ☎ **407/660-8118.** Prescriptions can be filled at pharmacies such as **Eckerd** or **Walgreens;** many **Kmart** stores also have pharmacies.

MONEY

CURRENCY & EXCHANGE   The U.S. monetary system has a decimal base: one American **dollar ($1)** = 100 **cents (100¢).**

Dollar bills commonly come in $1 ("a buck" in slang), $5, $10, $20, $50, and $100 denominations (the last two are not welcome when paying for small purchases and are not accepted in taxis). There are also $2 bills, but these are not widely circulated.

There are six denominations of coins: 1¢ (one cent or "a penny"), 5¢ (five cents or "a nickel"), 10¢ (ten cents or "a dime"), 25¢ (twenty-five cents or "a quarter"), 50¢ (fifty cents or "a half dollar"), and the rare $1 piece. (These coins are routinely given as change from postage stamp machines at U.S. Post Offices.)

The exchange bureaus so common in Europe are rare even at airports in the United States, and are nonexistent outside major cities. Try to avoid changing foreign money (or traveler's checks that are not denominated in U.S. dollars) at a small-town bank, or even at a branch in a big city.

You can exchange foreign currency at **Guest Services** windows in all three Disney parks, or at **City Hall** in the Magic Kingdom and **Earth Station** at Epcot. Currency can also be exchanged at Walt Disney World resorts and at the **Sun Bank** across from the Village Marketplace. There are also exchange services at the Orlando International Airport.

TRAVELER'S CHECKS   Traveler's checks denominated in U.S. dollars are readily accepted at most hotels, motels, restaurants, and large stores, though they're much less convenient than using cash or a credit card. But the best place to change traveler's checks is at a bank. Do not bring traveler's checks denominated in other currencies.

CREDIT CARDS   Most major credit cards are widely accepted: Visa (BarclayCard in Britain), MasterCard (EuroCard in Europe, Access in Britain, Chargex in Canada), American Express, Diners Club, Discover, and Carte Blanche. Most establishments post near the cash register the credit cards that are accepted. You can save yourself trouble by using plastic rather than cash or traveler's checks in most hotels, motels, restaurants, and retail stores. American Express, MasterCard, and Visa are accepted for admission to the Disney Parks and all restaurants therein. They are also accepted at the other major parks, Sea World, and Universal. You must have a credit card to rent a car. It can also be used as proof of identity (often carrying more weight than a passport), or as a "cash card," enabling you to draw money from banks that accept them.

SAFETY

While the Walt Disney World/Orlando area in general—and the theme parks in particular—are extremely safe, there are some general precautions you can take to minimize your chances of being the victim of crime.`

GENERAL SAFETY   U.S. urban areas tend to be less safe than those in Europe or Japan. Visitors should always stay alert. Orlando is not an especially high-crime area, but as with all U.S. cities visitors should exercise caution. Improved street signage in downtown Orlando has helped to steer visitors away from less-desirable neighborhoods. It is wise to ask the local tourist office if you're in doubt about which neighborhoods are safe. Avoid deserted areas, especially at night. Don't go into any city park at night unless there is an event that attracts crowds. Avoid carrying valuables with you on the street, and don't display expensive cameras or electronic equipment.

Remember also that hotels are open to the public, and in a large hotel, security may not be able to screen everyone entering. Always lock your room door, even if you are simply going to retrieve ice from the machine; take your key or key card. Don't assume that once inside your hotel you are automatically safe and no longer need to be aware of your surroundings. Confirm the identity of the person knocking before answering the door, even if it is hotel staff.

DRIVING

ASSISTANCE   There is a toll-free number that can help visitors by providing general directions. Operators speaking over 100 languages will be available. The number is sponsored by the **Florida Tourism Industry Marketing Corporation,** the state tourism promotions board (☎ **800/647-9284**).

SPEED LIMITS   Obey all posted speed limits. On city highways it is usually 55 or 65 miles per hour. In some rural areas it goes up to 70 miles per hour. In residential areas, 35 miles per hour is generally safe. The corridor between the attractions and downtown Orlando is rumored to be one of the most heavily ticketed stretches of road in the United States. Traffic fines are *doubled* in construction areas, which, because of the building boom in Orlando, are plentiful.

SEAT BELTS   Seat belts for all passengers are required by Florida law. Children under 3 must ride strapped in a car seat, and police will issue tickets to parents who do not put their children in restraints while driving. Rental-car agencies will provide car seats, some for free.

AIR BAG SAFETY   Children, in or out of car seats, should ride only in the backseats of cars that are equipped with air bags. Air bags have been linked to several deaths involving children in the United States. Air bags are a standard feature on most new model cars.

DRINKING & DRIVING   Law enforcement frowns on drunk drivers, and in Florida the rules are strict and strictly enforced. If you are planning to drink alcohol, especially after an exhausting day in the park, designate a sober driver or find an alternative means of transportation. Some nightclubs provide free soft drinks to designated drivers. It doesn't hurt to ask.

DEFENSIVE DRIVING   Drive with extra care in tourist-heavy areas. It's not uncommon for cars to make sudden turns or to slow down unexpectedly when reading road signs. People often come nearly to a stop on the highway while attempting to decipher the Disney signs, and they frequently veer across lanes unexpectedly. The tourist areas in Orlando pack a double traffic punch: workers in a hurry to get to a major employment center and tourists on vacation. Assume that all other drivers have no idea where they are going—which is often close to the truth—and you should do fine.

DRIVING IN THE RAIN   Watch for a hazardous condition called "black ice," where oil on the road creates slick patches when the road is wet. Rainstorms in Florida are intense and frequent, especially in summer. Exercise extreme caution and drive in the slow lane—the far right lane—if you are driving significantly slower than the speed limit. Do not pull off on the shoulder of the road. If the visibility is especially poor, pull off at the first exit and wait out the storm, which seldom lasts more than an hour.

LIGHTS ON   Florida law requires that drivers turn on their lights during rainstorms. These are, at least, a daily occurrence during the summer months.

IF YOU GET LOST   You may have to be content to simply turn around and reenter the highway by accessing the on-ramp near where you just got off. Downtown Orlando is the exception to this rule, but signage has been improved to help direct tourists and visitors from the suburbs. Avoid pulling over to ask directions from people on the street. Instead, stop at a convenience store or gas station and ask the clerk, who should be able to help with basic directions.

SAFETY WHILE DRIVING   Question your rental agency about personal safety, or ask for a brochure of traveler safety tips when you pick up your car. Obtain written directions from the agency, or a map with the route marked in red, showing how to get to your destination. And, if possible, arrive and depart during daylight hours.

Recently, more and more crime has involved cars and drivers. If you drive off a highway into a doubtful neighborhood, leave the area as quickly as possible. If you have an accident, even on the highway, stay in your car with the doors locked until you assess the situation or until the police arrive. If you are bumped from behind on the street or are involved in a minor accident with no injuries and the situation appears to be suspicious, motion to the other driver to follow you. Never get out of your car in such situations. Go directly to the nearest police precinct, well-lighted service station, or all-night store.

If you see someone on the road who indicates a need for help, do not stop. Take note of the location, drive on to a well-lighted area, and telephone the police by dialing ☎ **911.**

Park in well-lighted, well-traveled areas if possible. Always keep your car doors locked, whether attended or unattended. Look around before you get out of your car, and never leave any packages or valuables in sight. Although theme park lots are patrolled, it is best to secure valuables at all times. For extra caution, lock any electronic equipment in the lockers available near all park entrances. If someone attempts to rob you or steal your car, do not try to resist the thief/carjacker. Report the incident to the police department immediately.

2 Getting To & Around the U.S.

Travelers from overseas can take advantage of the **APEX** (Advance Purchase Excursion) fares offered by all the major U.S. and European carriers.

British Airways (☎ **0345/222-111** from within the U.K.) offers direct flights from London to Miami and Orlando, as does Virgin Atlantic (☎ **0129/374-774** from within the U.K.). You might also try Continental (☎ **0293/776-446**).

Canadian readers might book flights with **Air Canada** (☎ **800/361-8620**), which offers service from Toronto and Montréal to Miami and Tampa. Other airlines that fly to Florida from Canada include US Airways (☎ **800/428-4322**); Delta (☎ **800/361-6770**); TWA (☎ **800/892-4141**); American (☎ **800/624-6262**); and Northwest (☎ **800/225-2525**).

Some large American airlines (for example, TWA, American Airlines, Northwest, United, and Delta) offer travelers on their transatlantic or transpacific flights special discount tickets under the name **Visit USA,** allowing travel between U.S. destinations at minimum rates. They are not on sale in the United States and must therefore be purchased before you leave your foreign point of departure. This system is the best, easiest, and fastest way to see the United States at low cost. You should obtain information well in advance from your travel agent or the office of the airline concerned, since the conditions attached to these discount tickets can be changed without advance notice.

The visitor arriving by air, no matter what the port of entry, should cultivate patience and resignation before setting foot on U.S. soil. Getting through Immigration Control may take as long as 2 hours on some days. Add the time it takes to clear Customs, and you'll see that you should make very generous allowances for delays in planning connections between international and domestic flights—an average of 2 to 3 hours, at least.

In contrast, travelers arriving by car or by rail from Canada will find border-crossing formalities streamlined to the vanishing point. And air travelers from Canada, Bermuda, and some places in the Caribbean can sometimes go through Customs and Immigration at the point of departure, which is much quicker and less painful.

GETTING AROUND THE ORLANDO AREA   Though I give some tips on train and bus passes below, you're going to need a car to get around unless you are committed to staying at Disney. Relying on public transportation in the United States is only possible in those few urban areas having comprehensive mass transit systems—and Orlando is not among them.

Renting a Car   To rent a car, you need a major credit card and a valid driver's license (sometimes a hefty cash deposit can be used instead of a credit card). You also must be at least 25 years old. Some companies do rent to younger people but add a daily surcharge. Be sure to return your car with the same amount of gas you started out with; rental companies charge excessive prices for gasoline. All the major car-rental companies are represented in Florida (see "Getting Around" in chapter 4 for a list).

Renting a Motor Home   The following companies rent mobile homes, and all have outlets in Orlando: Cruise America, 613 E. Colonial Dr., Orlando, 32804 (☎ **800/327-7799** or 407/273-5020); Florida RV World, 4260 U.S. 92 E., Plant City, 33566 (☎ **800/330-6171**); Giant Recreation World, 13906 W. Colonial Dr., Winter Garden, 34787 (☎ **407/656-6444**).

Renting a Motorcycle   The increasing popularity of Bike Week, and a growing number of weekend road warriors, has sparked an increase in places specializing in motorcycle rental. The Harley Davidson, in all shapes and sizes, is the most popular. Nearly all the rental agencies are located closer to downtown Orlando or Kissimmee than to the attractions. You must be at least 21 years of age, have a motorcycle license and a major credit card. The average rental fee varies from around $800 to $1,200 for one week and includes helmets, locks, and a brief orientation. You can rent bikes at Cruise America Motorcycle Rentals, 2915 N. Orange Blossom Trail, Kissimee, FL 34744 (☎ **407/931-1409**); and at Eaglerider Motorcycle Rental, 527 W. Miller St., Orlando, FL 32804 (☎ **407/316-1409**). The supply is small, so call ahead. Plan months in advance if visiting during Bike Week, late February and early March, or Biketober Fest in mid-October. (Both events are in Daytona Beach.)

Traveling by Train   International visitors can buy a **USA Railpass,** good for 15 or 30 days of unlimited travel on **Amtrak** trains (☎ **800/872-7245**). The pass is available through many foreign travel agents. You can buy passes for a specific region, for example the Southwest or Southeast, or for the entire United States. Prices in 1998 for a pass to travel the entire country were as follows: a 15-day pass costs $285 off-peak (Jan–May), $425 peak (June–Dec); a 30-day pass costs $375 off-peak, $535 peak.

With a foreign passport, you can also buy passes at some Amtrak offices in the United States, including locations in San Francisco, Los Angeles, Chicago, New York,

Miami, Boston, and Washington, D.C. Reservations are generally required and should be made for each part of your trip as early as possible.

Visitors should be aware of the limitations of long-distance rail travel in the United States. With a few notable exceptions (for instance, the Northeast Corridor line between Boston and Washington, D.C.), service is rarely up to European standards: Delays are common, routes are limited and often infrequently served, and fares are rarely significantly lower than discount airfares. Thus, cross-country train travel should be approached with caution.

Traveling by Bus   Bus travel in the United States can be both slow and uncomfortable, so this option is not for everyone. Although the bus is often the most economical form of public transit for short hops between cities, at this writing bus passes are priced slightly higher than similar train passes. **Greyhound** (☎ **800/231-2222**), the sole nationwide bus line, offers an **Ameripass** for unlimited travel. The 1998 rates were 7 days ($199), 15 days ($299), 30 days ($409), or 60 days ($599).

For further information about travel to Florida, see "Getting There," in chapter 2.

FAST FACTS: For the Foreign Traveler

Automobile Organizations   Auto clubs will supply maps, suggested routes, guidebooks, accident and bail-bond insurance, and emergency road service. The major auto club in the United States, with 983 offices nationwide, is the **American Automobile Association (AAA).** Members of some foreign auto clubs have reciprocal arrangements with AAA and enjoy its services at no charge. If you belong to an auto club, inquire about AAA reciprocity before you leave. AAA can provide you with an International Driving Permit validating your foreign license. You may be able to join AAA even if you are not a member of a reciprocal club. To inquire, call ☎ **800/926-4222.** In addition, some automobile-rental agencies now provide these services, so you should inquire about their availability when you rent your car.

Business Hours   Bank lobby hours are open weekdays from 9am to 5pm. Drive through hours extend until about 6pm. Nearly all branches offer 24-hour access to the automatic teller machines (ATMs) at most banks and other outlets. Some branch offices in Florida are open until noon on Saturday. Generally, business offices are open weekdays from 9am to 5pm. Stores are open 6 days a week, with many open on Sunday, too; department stores usually stay open until 9pm from Monday through Saturday and until about 6pm on Sunday.

Climate   See "When to Go," in chapter 2.

Currency & Exchange   See "Money" in the section "Preparing for Your Trip," earlier in this chapter.

Drinking Laws   See "Liquor Laws" under "Fast Facts," in chapter 4.

Electricity   The United States uses 110 to 120 volts, 60 cycles, compared to 220 to 240 volts, 50 cycles, as in most of Europe. In addition to a 100-volt converter, small appliances of non-American manufacture, such as hair dryers or shavers, will require a plug adapter having two flat, parallel pins.

Embassies & Consulates   All embassies are located in Washington, D.C. Some consulates are located in major cities, and most nations have a mission to the United Nations in New York City. Foreign visitors can obtain telephone numbers for their embassies and consulates by calling "Information" in Washington, D.C. (☎ **202/555-1212**).

The Canadian consulate closest to Orlando is at 200 S. Biscayne Blvd., Suite 1600, Miami, FL 33131 (☎ **305/579-1600**). The British consulate is located at 1001 S. Bayshore Dr., Miami, FL 33131 (☎ **305/374-1522**); the Orlando office for the British consulate is open 9am to 5pm Monday through Friday in the Downtown Orlando SunTrust building, 200 S. Orange Ave., Orlando, FL 32801 (☎ **407/426-7855**). Other consulate offices in Orlando are: Cusulado de Argentino de Orlando, 400 S. Orange Ave., Orlando, 32801 (☎ **407/481-2602**); Consulate of Mexico, 823 E. Colonial Dr., Orlando, 32803 (☎ **407/894-0514**); Consulate of France (☎ **407/294-5844**); Consulate of the Netherlands, 400 S. Orange Ave., Orlando, 32801 (☎ **407/425-8000**).

Emergencies   Call ☎ **911** to report a fire, contact the police, or get an ambulance. This call is free from all public telephones and should be the first call made in case of any serious medical emergency or accident.

Beginning in 1998, another number became available to help visitors. The number is sponsored by the Florida Tourism Industry Marketing Corporation, the state tourism promotions board. It is (☎ **800/647-9284**). With operators speaking over 100 languages, it can provide general directions and can help with lost travel papers and credit cards, medical emergencies, accidents, money transfer, airline confirmation, and much more.

Gasoline (Petrol)   One U.S. gallon equals 3.75 liters, and 1.2 U.S. gallons equal 1 Imperial gallon. There are several grades (and price levels) of gasoline available at most gas stations, and you'll notice that their names change from company to company. The unleaded ones with the highest octane are the most expensive. Most rental cars take the least expensive, "regular" unleaded gas.

Holidays   Banks, government offices, post offices, and many stores, restaurants, and museums are closed on legal national holidays: January 1 (New Year's Day); third Monday in January (Martin Luther King, Jr. Day); third Monday in February (Presidents' Day, Washington's Birthday); last Monday in May (Memorial Day); July 4 (Independence Day); first Monday in September (Labor Day); second Monday in October (Columbus Day); November 11 (Veterans' Day/Armistice Day); fourth Thursday in November (Thanksgiving Day); and December 25 (Christmas). The Tuesday following the first Monday in November is Election Day and is a legal holiday in presidential-election years; the next presidential election is in 2000.

Languages   Major hotels may have multilingual employees. Unless your language is very obscure, they can usually supply a translator on request. Especially in southern Florida and, increasingly, in central Florida, many people are fluent in Spanish. Establishments catering to tourists make a special effort to have bilingual speakers on staff.

Legal Aid   As a foreign tourist, you will probably never become involved with the American legal system. If you are stopped for a minor infraction, such as speeding or some other traffic violation, never attempt to pay the fine directly to a police officer; you may be arrested on the much more serious charge of attempted bribery. Pay fines by mail, or directly into the hands of the clerk of the court. If you are accused of a more serious offense, it's wise to say and do nothing before consulting a lawyer. Under U.S. law, an arrested person is allowed one telephone call to a party of his or her choice. Call your embassy or consulate.

Mail If you want to receive mail on your vacation and you aren't sure of your address, your mail can be sent to you, in your name, ℅ General Delivery at the main post office of the city or region where you expect to be. The addressee must pick it up in person and produce proof of identity (driver's license, credit card, passport, etc.).

Mailboxes Mailboxes are blue with a red-and-white stripe and carry the inscription U.S. MAIL. Make sure you see this inscription. Overnight delivery companies also often have drop-off boxes along the road. Don't forget to add the five-figure postal code, or ZIP code, after the two-letter abbreviation of the state to which the mail is addressed (CA for California, FL for Florida, NY for New York, and so on).

Within the United States, it costs 20¢ to mail a standard-size postcard and 32¢ to send an oversize postcard (larger than 4½ by 6 inches, or 10.8 by 15.4 centimeters). Letters that weigh up to 1 ounce (that's about five pages, 8-by-11-inch paper) cost 32¢, plus 23¢ for each additional ounce. A standard postcard to Mexico costs 30¢, a half-ounce letter 35¢; a postcard to Canada costs 30¢, a 1-ounce letter 40¢. A postcard to Europe, Australia, New Zealand, the Far East, South America, or elsewhere costs 40¢, and a letter is 60¢ for each half-ounce.

Newspapers & Magazines National newspapers include the *New York Times, USA Today,* and the *Wall Street Journal.* National news weeklies include *Newsweek, Time,* and *U.S. News & World Report.* All over Florida, you'll be able to purchase the *Miami Herald,* one of the most highly respected dailies in the country. The local newspaper is the *Orlando Sentinel.*

Many Walgreens and Eckerd drugstores in areas catering to tourists also carry newspapers from the United Kingdom. Since 1997 the *London Daily Mail* is printed in Orlando for distribution along the East Coast. Because of the time difference, British travelers can actually pick up a paper at the airport and read the next day's newspaper on the way home.

Radio & Television Six coast-to-coast networks—ABC, CBS, NBC, Fox, PBS (the Public Broadcasting System), and CNN (Cable News Network), play a major part in American life. Two newer, smaller networks (Paramount and WB) are also available in most major television markets. In Orlando, viewers have a choice of all these. Options on your hotel TV set may be limited, though.

You'll also find a wide choice of local radio stations, each broadcasting particular kinds of talk shows and/or music—classical, country, jazz, pop, gospel—punctuated by news broadcasts and frequent commercials. Most central Florida cable networks also carry at least two Spanish-language stations, and there are numerous Spanish-language radio stations, mostly on the AM dial.

Safety See "Safety" in section 1, earlier in this chapter.

Taxes In the United States, there is no VAT (Value-Added Tax) or other indirect tax at a national level. Every state, and each city in it, has the right to levy its own local tax on all purchases, including hotel and restaurant checks, airline tickets, and so on. In Florida, sales tax is 6%. Hotel tax in Orlando and Kissimmee (which includes sales tax) is 11%.

Telephone, Telegraph & Fax Pay phones can be found in most restaurants, hotels, gas stations, and stores. Local calls in the United States usually cost 35¢.

Most long-distance and international calls can be dialed directly from any phone. For direct overseas calls, dial 011 first, then the country code

(Australia, 61; Republic of Ireland, 353; New Zealand, 64; United Kingdom, 44) followed by the city code, and then the number you wish to call. To place a call to Canada, the Caribbean, or another U.S. state, dial 1 followed by the area code and the seven-digit number.

Generally, hotel surcharges on long-distance and local calls are astronomical. You are usually better off using a public pay telephone. Hotels sometimes even charge a fee if you use your own telephone credit card or call a toll-free number (with an 800, 877, or 888 area code), so ask about surcharges before you dial.

For "collect" (reversed-charge) calls and for "person-to-person" calls, dial 0 (zero, not the letter "O") followed by the area code and number you want. An operator will then come on the line, and you should specify that you are calling collect, or person-to-person, or both. If your operator-assisted call is international, ask for the overseas operator.

Prepaid calling cards, which generally provide a fair per-minute rate— probably lower than that charged by your hotel—are becoming increasingly popular. Calling cards are sold in many convenience stores and drugstores and can generally be purchased in $5 or $10 increments.

For local directory assistance ("Information"), dial ☎ **411;** for long-distance information in Canada or the United States, dial 1, then the appropriate area code and ☎ **555-1212.**

Like the telephone system, telegraph and telex services are provided by private corporations like ITT, MCI, and, above all, Western Union, the most important. You can bring your telegram into the nearest Western Union office (there are hundreds across the country) or dictate it over the phone (a toll-free call, ☎ **800/325-6000**). You can also telegraph money, or have it telegraphed to you, very quickly over the Western Union system.

It's also easy to send a fax. Most hotels have fax service. If yours doesn't, small copy shops found in most neighborhoods provide fax service. Kinko's is a prominent local printing chain that also provides fax service. They are listed in the White Pages of the telephone directory. Faxes are sent for a small fee— usually around $2 per page. If you make arrangements, some places will also receive faxes for you and call you when anything arrives.

Time The United States is divided into four time zones (six, if Alaska and Hawaii are included). From east to west, these are: eastern standard time (EST), central standard time (CST), mountain standard time (MST), Pacific standard time (PST), Alaska standard time (AST), and Hawaii standard time (HST). Orlando, like most of Florida, is on eastern standard time, which is 8 hours behind Greenwich Mean Time. When it is noon in Orlando, it's 11am in New Orleans (CST), 10am in Salt Lake City (MST), 9am in Los Angeles (PST), 8am in Anchorage (AST), and 7am in Honolulu (HST).

Daylight saving time is in effect from the first Sunday in April through 2am on the last Sunday in October, except in Arizona, Hawaii, part of Indiana, and Puerto Rico. Daylight saving time moves the clock 1 hour ahead of standard time.

Tipping Service in the United States tends to be good, but it is rarely included in the price of anything. The amount you should tip does depend on the service you have received. Good service warrants the following tips: Bartenders (do tip them here), 15%; bellhops, at least $2 to $5 depending on the amount of lug-gage they carry for you; cab drivers, 15%; checkroom attendants, $1 per garment (unless there is a charge, then no tip); hairdressers, 15% to 20%; parking valets, $1; redcaps (in airports), at least $1 per piece; restaurants and nightclubs, 15%.

Toilets   Foreign visitors often complain that public toilets are hard to find in most U.S. cities. True, there are none on the streets, but the visitor can usually find one in a bar, restaurant, hotel, museum, department store, convenience store, or service station—and it will probably be clean. In particular, Mobil service stations have made, and kept, a public pledge to provide spic-and-span bathrooms, most decorated with homey touches. Within the theme parks, rest rooms will be clearly marked on the park maps.

THE AMERICAN SYSTEM OF MEASUREMENTS

Length

1 inch (in.)			=	2.54cm			
1 foot (ft.)	=	12 in.	=	30.48cm	=	.305m	
1 yard (yd.)	=	3 ft.			=	.915m	
1 mile	=	5,280 ft.				=	1.609km

To convert miles to kilometers, multiply the number of miles by 1.61 (for example, 50 mi. × 1.61 = 80.5km). Note that this conversion can be used to convert speeds from miles per hour (m.p.h.) to kilometers per hour (kmph).

To convert kilometers to miles, multiply the number of kilometers by .62 (example, 25km × .62 = 15.5 mi.). Note that this same conversion can be used to convert speeds from kilometers per hour to miles per hour.

Capacity

1 fluid ounce (fl. oz.)			=	.03 liter		
1 pint (pt.)	=	16 fl. oz.	=	.47 liter		
1 quart (qt.)	=	2 pints	=	.94 liter		
1 gallon (gal.)	=	4 quarts	=	3.79 liters	=	.83 Imperial gal.

To convert U.S. gallons to liters, multiply the number of gallons by 3.79 (example, 12 gal. × 3.79 = 45.48 liters).

To convert liters to U.S. gallons, multiply the number of liters by .26 (example, 50 liters × .26 = 13 U.S. gal.).

To convert U.S. gallons to Imperial gallons, multiply the number of U.S. gallons by .83 (example, 12 U.S. gal. × .83 = 9.96 Imperial gal.).

To convert Imperial gallons to U.S. gallons, multiply the number of Imperial gallons by 1.2 (example, 8 Imperial gal. × 1.2 = 9.6 U.S. gal.).

Weight

1 ounce (oz.)			=	28.35g			
1 pound (lb.)	=	16 oz.	=	453.6g	=	.45kg	
1 ton	=	2,000 lb.	=		907kg	=	.91 metric ton

To convert pounds to kilograms, multiply the number of pounds by .45 (example, 90 lb. × .45 = 40.5kg).

To convert kilograms to pounds, multiply the number of kilos by 2.2 (example, 75kg × 2.2 = 165 lb.).

Area

1 acre			=	.41ha		
1 square mile	=	640 acres	=	2.59ha	=	2.6 sq. km

To convert acres to hectares, multiply the number of acres by .41 (example, 40 acres × .41 = 16.4ha).

To convert hectares to acres, multiply the number of hectares by 2.47 (example, 20ha × 2.47 = 49.4 acres).

To convert square miles to square kilometers, multiply the number of square miles by 2.6 (example, 80 sq. mi × 2.6 = 208 sq. km).

To convert square kilometers to square miles, multiply the number of square kilometers by .39 (example, 150 sq. km × .39 = 58.5 sq. mi.).

Temperature

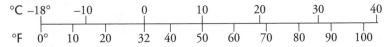

To convert degrees Fahrenheit to degrees Celsius, subtract 32 from °F, multiply by 5, then divide by 9 (example, 85°F − 32 × ⅝ = 29.4°C).

To convert degrees Celsius to degrees Fahrenheit, multiply °C by 9, divide by 5, and add 32 (example, 20°C × ⅝ + 32 = 68°F).

Getting to Know Walt Disney World & Orlando

It's true that 30 years ago there wasn't a whole lot to see outside Walt Disney World except palmetto fronds and orange groves. Orlando was a typical, slow-lane Southern town before Disney World moved this way in 1971. The fancy stores of downtown were giving way to peep shows and tattoo parlors as commerce relocated to the landscaped acres of suburban malls.

Oh, but how success breeds competition. Disney has expanded to include four major parks and two nighttime entertainment districts. Over the years Disney has added everything from water parks to miniature golf to try to keep those tourist dollars from migrating off the very large Disney lot.

No one pretends that Disney isn't King Mouse. The Magic Kingdom is what, at least at first, beckons the masses. But all that unrelenting cheerfulness, days of $3 sodas, and the just-roasted aroma of sweaty, sunburned crowds can make it a small world, after all. You're cheating yourself if you don't plan to spend some time away from Walt Disney's world, visiting Universal Studios Florida, with its new City-Walk and upcoming Islands of Adventure. Also plan to spend at least one night away from the theme parks altogether, going into downtown Orlando to dine and enjoy a little real nightlife, not the kind Imagineered by Disney. Visitors, especially those from other countries, don't really come all this way just to see the theme park version of America. (Heck, for that they could go to Disneyland Paris.)

Because of major renovations, even places you've seen before, such as Sea World or downtown Orlando, are worth another look. Sea World has added a major attraction nearly every year, and downtown Orlando sports an increasing number of fine restaurants and funky clubs where real people mix and mingle. If you do travel, many area hotels offer transportation to the airport and city attractions.

1 Orientation

VISITOR INFORMATION

Once you're in Orlando, stop by the **Orlando/Orange County Convention & Visitors Bureau,** 8723 International Dr., Suite 101, Orlando, FL 32819 (☎ **407/363-5871**). They can answer all your questions and give you maps, brochures, and discount coupons if you haven't sent away for these already. Discount tickets to attractions other than Disney parks are sold on the premises, and the multilingual staff can also make dining reservations and hotel referrals. The bureau is open daily, except Christmas, from 8am to 8pm.

If you're driving, you can stop at the **Disney/AAA Travel Center** in Ocala, Florida, at the intersection of I-75 (exit 68) and Fla. 200, about 90 miles north of Orlando (☎ **904/854-0770**). Here you can purchase tickets and Mickey ears, get help planning your park itinerary, and make hotel reservations. Hours are 9am to 6pm; until 7pm June through August.

The **Kissimmee–St. Cloud Convention & Visitors Bureau** is located at 1925 E. Irlo Bronson Memorial Hwy. (P.O. Box 422007), Kissimmee, FL 34742-2007 (☎ **800/327-9159** or 407/847-5000). They have maps, brochures, and discount coupon books.

If you're looking for state of Florida tourism information, there are five **Florida welcome centers** in the state, located 4 miles north of Jennings on I-75 South; 3 miles north of Campelton on Hwy. 231; 7 miles north of Yulee on I-95; 16 miles west of Pensacola on I-10 East; and another at the Capitol in Tallahassee.

Finally, nearly all hotel lobbies have a rack containing brochures for various area attractions. If this guidebook doesn't convince you of which places to hit, these pamphlets might help you make up your mind. The brochures also often include discount coupons.

INFORMATION AT THE AIRPORTS

At the Orlando International Airport, arriving passengers can stroll over to one of two Disney shops, **The Magic of Disney** (☎ **407/825-2301**) or **Disney's Flight of Fantastic.** They are located in both A and B terminals. This facility sells WDW multiday park tickets, makes dinner show and hotel reservations at Disney hostelries, and provides brochures and assistance. It's open daily from 6am to 9pm.

Also in the airport, you'll find the **Universal Studios Store** (☎ **407/825-2473**), which is open from 6:30am to 10pm daily and sells park tickets and sometimes features special offers such as "Second Day Free." The **Sea World** stores, also located in the A and B terminals are open from 6:30am to 10pm daily. They sell tickets and will be advertising any current discounts or offers.

CITY LAYOUT

Orlando's major artery is **I-4,** which runs diagonally across the state from Tampa to Daytona Beach. Exits from I-4 take you to Walt Disney World, Sea World, International Drive, U.S. 192, Kissimmee, Lake Buena Vista, Church Street Station, downtown Orlando, and Winter Park. Most of the exits are well marked, although you should know that the exit to Universal Studios takes you past the entrance and around the block before you go in. (Watch carefully for the signs, and be aware that a new off-ramp is currently under construction, so the confusion may be cleared up by the time of your visit.) Construction zones, which are plentiful, can complicate finding the exit, so be aware.

The **Florida Turnpike** crosses I-4 and links up with I-75 to the north. **U.S. 192,** a major east-west artery, stretches from Kissimmee (along a major motel strip) to U.S. 27, crossing I-4 near the Walt Disney World entrance road. Farther north, a toll road called the **Bee Line Expressway** (Fla. 528) goes east from I-4 past Orlando International Airport to Cape Canaveral. The **East-West Expressway** (also known as Fla. 408) is a toll road that might be helpful in bypassing surface traffic outside of the main tourist areas.

Walt Disney World is bounded roughly by I-4 and Fla. 535 to the east (the latter also north), World Drive (the entrance road) to the west, and U.S. 192 to the south.

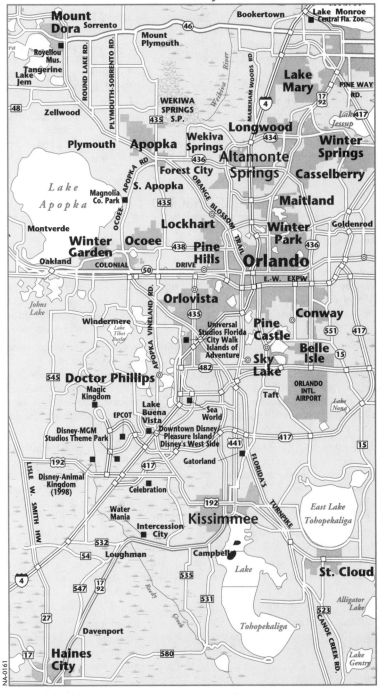

Epcot Center Drive (Hwy. 536/the south end of International Drive) and Buena Vista Drive cut across the complex in a more or less east-west direction; the two roads cross at Bonnet Creek Parkway. In spite of excellent highways and explicit signage, it is relatively easy to get lost. Again, pay close attention and drive carefully because chances are everyone else is lost too. Don't panic or pull across multiple lanes of traffic to make your specific exit once on Disney property. All roads lead to Disney, and you will soon find another sign directing you to the same place on Disney property. Clever landscaping hides the fact that many sections of the Disney parks are actually very close together. (Actually the way some of the roads twist and turn, it makes me wonder if Disney didn't make it purposely convoluted so visitors would drive past other attractions to whet their appetite.) *Note:* Disney parks are actually much closer to Kissimmee than Orlando.

ORLANDO NEIGHBORHOODS IN BRIEF

Walt Disney World   A city unto itself, WDW sprawls over more than 26,000 acres containing theme parks, resorts, hotels, shops, restaurants, and recreational facilities galore. Read on for copious details.

Lake Buena Vista   This area centers on a hotel village/marketplace owned and operated by Walt Disney World on the eastern edge of Disney property. However, while Disney owns all the real estate, many of the hotels, and some shops and restaurants here, are independently owned. Lake Buena Vista is a charming area of manicured lawns and verdant thoroughfares with traffic islands shaded by towering oak trees.

Celebration   Imagine living in a Disney world? Disney tries to re-create its squeaky-clean, completely controlled magic in this town, the first residential area ever to receive the special Disney touch. Located on 4,900 acres in northwest Osceola County, Celebration will eventually have about 8,000 residents living in Disney-designed homes and attending a Disney-run school. The homes start at about $193,000. Celebration's downtown is, however, designed for the tourist trade, being architecturally interesting with some first-rate shops and restaurants.

Downtown Disney   This is more a Disney creation than an actual neighborhood, but with the ever-present signs it is worth explaining. Simply put, Downtown Disney is what WDW has taken to calling its two nighttime entertainment districts, Pleasure Island and Disney's West Side, and the shopping complex, Disney's Village Marketplace. Just so you understand, we consider this area a part of Lake Buena Vista, so you'll find establishments here under that heading.

Kissimmee   South of the Disney parks, Kissimmee centers on U.S. 192/Irlo Bronson Memorial Highway—a somewhat tacky strip, as archetypal of American cities as Main Street. U.S. 192 is lined with budget motels, lesser attractions—like Gatorland—and every fast-food restaurant you can name. Kissimmee is still, in many ways, true to its cowboy roots, and there are some wide open spaces to explore if you are in the mood for a ride in the country.

International Drive Area (Fla. 536)   Can you say tourist mecca? This area extends 7 to 10 miles north of the Disney parks between Fla. 535 and the Florida Turnpike. From bungee jumping to ice skating and dozens of theme restaurants and T-shirt shops, this is the tourist strip in central Florida. It contains numerous hotels, restaurants, shopping centers, and the Orange County Convention Center, and it offers easy access to Sea World and Universal Studios. The place is already packed, but, somehow, developers manage year after year to find space for just one more attraction. *Note:* Locally, this road is always referred to as **I-Drive.**

Downtown Orlando   No, not Downtown Disney, which is not *really* Downtown. To get to the real thing you have to travel on I-4 East, reaching a burgeoning Sunbelt metropolis 17 miles northeast of Walt Disney World. It includes the entertainment/shopping complex Church Street Station and the Orlando Science Center, a recently completed multimillion-dollar complex, which is the largest in the Southeast. Hundreds of clubs, shops, and restaurants are located in the heart of the city, one of the fastest-growing in the country. Dozens of antique shops line "Antique Row" on Orange Avenue near Lake Ivanhoe.

Winter Park   Just north of downtown Orlando, Winter Park is the place many of central Florida's old-money families call home. As the name implies, it began as a haven for Yankees traveling away from the cold. Today, it's home to Park Avenue, a collection of upscale shops and restaurants along an original cobblestoned street that is frequented by local ladies who lunch. With the main attractions being shopping, dining, and several small museums, Winter Park is definitely a grown-up diversion.

2 Getting Around

In a city that thrives on its visitor attractions, you won't find it difficult to get around. If you are traveling outside of the tourist areas, avoid traveling during peak rush-hour times—7 to 9am and 4 to 6pm—so you don't get caught in the daily traffic jams. (Not everybody is on vacation, and thousands of people are coming home from work about the time you're hankering to go to dinner.) International Drive, which has become a prime cruising spot for teens, can get very congested during Spring Break and on weekends. You may get there just as fast by parking and walking along the sidewalks. Signage problems in the downtown area have been corrected through brightly colored signs that have a definite Disney influence. Nearly all hotels offer transport to and from theme parks and other tourist destinations. It's not difficult getting places, but it can be expensive.

BY THE DISNEY TRANSPORTATION SYSTEM

If you plan to stay at a Disney resort and visit mostly Disney parks and attractions, there's a very thorough, free transportation network throughout the complex.

Disney resorts and official hotels offer unlimited complimentary transportation via bus, monorail, ferry, and water taxi to all major parks from 2 hours prior to opening until 2 hours after closing; also to Downtown Disney, Typhoon Lagoon, River Country, Blizzard Beach, Pleasure Island, Fort Wilderness, and other Disney resorts. Disney properties offer transportation to other area attractions as well, though you have to pay.

There are advantages to using this on-property transportation system: It's free, providing a big savings on car rental, insurance, and gas. You don't have to pay for parking ($6 per day in Walt Disney World). You avoid long waits in traffic coming into the parking lots. And if your party wants to split up, you can easily board transport to different areas.

The disadvantages? You are at the mercy of Disney's schedule, and you often have to take a ferry to catch a bus to get the monorail to go to the hotel. Consider this when making your hotel reservations, especially if you are not planning to rent a car. The system makes a complete route, but not necessarily an easy or quick one. You also have to wait as each bus makes multiple stops, loading and unloading a large number of passengers. Schedules, too, often entail long waits for some of these connections.

It can easily take an afternoon to get somewhere that looks as if it is right across the lagoon on the map. Never fear, though, the good part is that the transportation network goes everywhere on the Disney property. The best rule? Ask the bus driver or someone at the hotel information desk to make sure you are heading the right way and getting on the right bus. Keep asking questions along the way. Unlike missing a highway exit, if you miss a stop on the bus route, you will be riding for a while.

BY CAR

To rent or not to rent? First decide exactly how you envision your vacation. If you will happily stay immersed in everything Disney, or you are staying on International Drive, you'll probably do just as well without your own wheels. If you're staying at a Disney property, the question to ask when deciding whether to rent a car is how, exactly, do you get to the major parks? If the Magic Kingdom is accessible by taking a bus, switching to the monorail, and then catching a ferry, you may want to opt for a car. The least expensive properties, the All-Star resorts, are furthest from the parks. Waits between buses can be considerable.

During peak hours in the busiest seasons, you may have trouble getting a seat on the bus, so keep that in mind if you are traveling with someone who is elderly or physically impaired. Also, if you are hauling children and strollers, factor in the frustration factor of loading and unloading strollers and kiddie paraphernalia on and off buses, ferries, and trams. (Although, as in earlier chapters, we suggest you rent strollers at the park.)

A car may drastically cut the commute time between the parks and hotels not directly on the monorail routes. So decide how much your time is worth.

In general, if you will spend all your time at Disney and are laid-back enough to go with the flow of traffic within the transportation network, there's no sense renting a car that will sit in the parking lot between trips to the airport.

But if you're on an extended stay—more than a week—you will probably want to rent a car for at least a day or two to explore beyond the tourist areas. (Yes, there is something beyond the tourist areas.) Discover downtown Orlando, visit museums, the Space Coast, or just hang out for a day at the beach. It will be good for your soul. The tourist areas of Orlando are kind of like Las Vegas: You can't spend too much time in that world of bright lights and make-believe without needing a good dose of reality.

No matter where you are staying, keep in mind where you will be picking up your rental car. If possible, contract with an agency that operates at or near your hotel. This will help to save time—and headaches. Dropping a car off with an airport-based rental service often means riding a shuttle to a lot off-site. That means turning in the car will eat up much of your final day. That is especially true during the holidays or peak season when lots of other folks will be doing the same thing. *Somebody* is renting the miles and miles of rental cars stored in the lots visible from the freeway.

All major rental companies are represented in Orlando and maintain desks at the airport. Many major car-rental agencies provide discount coupons in publications targeted at tourists. When planning your trip and poring over all those brochures, keep an eye out for discounts on car rentals. You may also want to ask your travel agent if he or she has a recommendation or whether a discount is included in any available packages. Also, it never hurts to ask if there is a special available.

I was quoted the lowest rates by **Value Rent-A-Car** (☎ **800/GO-VALUE [46-82583]**), which also turned out to offer excellent service and 24-hour pickup and return. Some other handy phone numbers: **Alamo** (☎ 800/327-9633), **Avis** (☎ 800/331-1212), **Budget** (☎ 800/527-0700), **Dollar** (☎ 800/800-4000), **Hertz** (☎ 800/654-3131), and **Thrifty** (☎ 800/367-2277).

BY BUS

Mears Transportation Group (☎ 407/423-5566) operates buses to all major attractions, including Cypress Gardens, Kennedy Space Center, Universal Studios, Sea World, Busch Gardens (in Tampa), and Church Street Station, among others. Call for details.

BY MOTORCYCLE

The increasing popularity of Bike Week has a growing number of weekend road warriors roaring through central Florida. If you have a motorcycle license, you can join them. The Harley Davidson, in all shapes and sizes, is the most popular bike to rent. Most motorcycle rental agencies are located closer to downtown Orlando than to the attractions. You must be at least 21 years and have a valid motorcycle license and a major credit card. Average rental varies from around $800 to $1,200 for 1 week and includes helmets, locks, and a brief orientation.

You can rent bikes at **Cruise America Motorcycle Rentals** (☎ 407/931-1409), **Eaglerider Motorcycle Rental** (☎ 407/316-1409), or **Saddle Sore Inc.** (☎ 407/872-3115). The supply is small, so call ahead. Plan months in advance if you are visiting during **Bike Week**—late February and early March—or **Biketober Fest** in mid-October. (Both events are in Daytona Beach.)

BY TAXI

Taxis line up in front of major hotels, and at smaller properties the front desk will be happy to call you a cab. Or call **Yellow Cab** (☎ 407/699-9999). The charge is $2.75 for the first mile, $1.50 per mile thereafter.

FAST FACTS: Walt Disney World & Orlando

Ambulances   See "Emergencies," below.

Baby-sitters   Most Orlando hotels offer baby-sitting services. Several Disney properties and several major hotels have marvelous child-care facilities with counselor-supervised activity programs on the premises. Disney properties have used KinderCare sitters since 1980 (☎ 407/827-5444), so you can be sure they've been very carefully checked out, including a criminal background check. If you're not staying at a Disney accommodation, you can call them on your own. You can even have them take your kids to the park or to any of the services at your resort, except swimming. Rates for in-room service are: $11 per hour for one child, $12 per hour for two children, $13 per hour for three children, and $14 per hour for four or more children. There is a 4-hour minimum, the first half hour of which is travel time for the sitter. Advance notice of 24 hours is required.

Car Rentals   See section 2, "Getting Around," in this chapter.

Climate   See "When to Go," in chapter 2.

Convention Center   The Orange County Convention/Civic Center is located at 9800 International Dr. (☎ 407/345-9800).

Crime   See "Safety," below.

Doctors and Dentists   There are basic first-aid centers in all the major parks. Unfortunately, tourists have encountered ill-trained doctors making calls in hotels. You can get a reputable referral from **Ask-A-Nurse**. They will ask whether you have insurance, but that is for information purposes so they can track who uses the system. It is a free service open to everyone. In Kissimmee call ☎ **407/ 870-1700;** in Orlando call ☎ **407/ 897-1700.**

Walk-in medical clinics are also available, with a visit usually costing under $50. Prescriptions are extra. Centra-Care, operated by a locally run Florida Hospital, is a reputable medical facility with more than a dozen locations throughout the Orlando area. Several walk-in clinics have popped up in recent years. Not all are created equal, so we suggest that you opt for Centra-Care. For information, and the nearest location, call ☎ **407/660-8118.**

To find a dentist, call Dental Referral Service (☎ **800/917-6453**). They can tell you the nearest dentist who meets your needs. Phones are manned from 5:30am to 6pm daily. Check the yellow pages for 24-hour emergency services.

Emergencies   Dial ☎ **911** to contact the police or fire department or to call an ambulance. Always call 911 in case of a serious medical emergency or accident. For less urgent requests, another number became available in 1998. The number is sponsored by the Florida Tourism Industry Marketing Corporation, the state tourism promotions board. It is ☎ **800/647-9284.** With operators speaking over 100 languages, it can provide general directions and help with lost travel papers and credit cards, medical emergencies, accidents, money transfer, airline confirmation, and much more.

Florist   Floral and fruit arrangements can be delivered anywhere on Walt Disney World Resort property by calling ☎ **407/827-3505** between 8am and 8pm. Elsewhere in central Florida, try ☎ **1-800-FLOWERS** (800/356-9377) or Flower Star at ☎ **800/311-0404.**

Hospitals   Sand Lake Hospital, 9400 Turkey Lake Rd., is about 2 miles south of Sand Lake Road (☎ **407/351-8550**). From the WDW area, take I-4 east to exit 29, turn left at the exit onto Sand Lake Road, and make a left on Turkey Lake Road. The hospital is 2 miles up on your right.

Kennels   All of the major theme parks offer animal-boarding facilities at reasonable fees. At Walt Disney World, there are kennels at Fort Wilderness, Epcot, the Magic Kingdom, Animal Kingdom, and Disney–MGM Studios. Sea World and Universal also offer kennels where you can leave your animals during the day. If you're traveling with a pet, don't leave it in the car—even with a window cracked—while you enjoy the park. Many pets have perished this way in the hot Florida sun.

Kosher Food   It can be arranged at restaurants at Disney parks and resorts with 24-hour advance notice. Call ☎ **407/WDW-DINE** (939-3463).

Liquor Laws   Minimum drinking age is 21. No liquor is served in the Magic Kingdom at Walt Disney World. However, drinks are available at the other parks and are quite evident at Universal's Mardi Gras celebration and its Halloween Horror Nights. Liquor is not sold on Sunday within the city limits of Orlando.

Lockers   You can rent lockers at all of the Disney parks and at Universal Studios and Sea World. Many other attractions, such as miniature golf courses or water parks, also offer this service. The cost is usually 50¢ or a dollar for the day. Inquire at Guest Relations. For safety purposes it is better to keep valuables, such as camera equipment, in a locker rather than in your car.

Lost Children   Every theme park has a designated spot for parents to meet up with lost children (or lost spouses). Find out where it is when you enter any park and instruct your children to ask park personnel to take them there if they are lost. Point out what park personnel look like. Young children should have name tags.

Newspapers and Magazines   The *Orlando Sentinel* is the major local newspaper, but you can also purchase the Sunday editions of major cities (most notably, the *New York Times*) in most hotel gift shops. Don't count on finding daily editions of west coast papers, such as the *Los Angeles Times* without making special arrangements. The Friday edition of the *Sentinel* includes extensive entertainment and dining listings. The *Orlando Weekly* is a free, alternative paper that has significant entertainment and art listings, most of them focused outside of the tourist areas.

Pharmacies   Walgreens drugstore, 1003 W. Vine St. (Hwy. 192), just east of Bermuda Avenue (☎ **407/847-5252**), operates a 24-hour pharmacy. They can deliver to hotels for a charge ($10 from 7am to 5pm, $15 at all other times). There is an Eckerd drugstore at 7324 International Dr. (☎ **407/345-0491),** open 24 hours a day. There is also a 24-hour Eckerd's store at 1306 Bermuda Ave. (☎ **407/847-5174**).

Photography   Two-hour film processing is available at all major parks. Look for the Photo Express sign. You can also buy film and rent or buy 35mm, disc, and video cameras in all three parks. Many convenience and discount stores, such as Walgreens, Eckerd, Kmart, and Target, also offer next-day photo processing. These discount stores often provide coupons for half-off photo processing, which could save significant money.

Post Office   The main post office in Lake Buena Vista is at 12541 Fla. 535, near TGI Friday's in the Crossroads Shopping Center (☎ **407/828-2606**). It's open Monday through Friday from 9am to 4pm, Saturday from 9am to noon. You can buy stamps and mail letters at nearly all hotels.

Safety   Whenever you're traveling in an unfamiliar city, stay alert. Be aware of your immediate surroundings. It's a good idea to keep your valuables in a safety-deposit box (inquire at the front desk), though some hotels nowadays are equipped with in-room safes. Do keep a close eye on your valuables when you're in a public place—restaurant, theater, even airport terminal. Renting a locker is preferable to leaving your valuables in the trunk of your car, even in the theme park parking lots.

If you are renting a car, read carefully the safety instructions that the rental company provides. Never stop for any reason in an unpopulated area, and remember that children should never ride in the front seat of a car equipped with air bags.

Taxes   Hotel tax in Orlando and Kissimmee is 11%, which includes a state sales tax (6%) that is also charged on all goods except most grocery store items and medicines.

Time   Orlando is in the eastern standard time zone, which is 1 hour later than Chicago and 3 hours later than Los Angeles. Call ☎ **407/646-3131** for the correct time and temperature.

Tourist Information   See section 1, "Orientation," in this chapter.

Weather   Call ☎ **407/851-7510** for a weather recording. Also look for the weather channel on the local cable carrier, Time Warner Cable. Most hotels carry basic cable. The *Orlando Sentinel* also includes a daily forecast. A local 24-hours news station, Channel 13, offers weather forecasts several times an hour.

5 Accommodations

You'll find a wealth of hotel options in the Orlando area, especially in the areas around Walt Disney World, Universal Studios Florida, and Sea World. Beautifully landscaped resorts are the rule when you're talking about Disney properties and those in the immediate area, Lake Buena Vista, but there's something to suit every taste and pocketbook. There are a number of budget motels in the Kissimmee area that provide clean, comfortable rooms at low prices.

For all accommodations, you should reserve as far in advance as possible—really, the minute you've decided on the dates of your trip. This is especially important since Disney and Universal have both opened significant new attractions this spring and summer.

There is good news for the budget-minded. A third **All-Star** resort, Disney's best value, is scheduled to open in 1999. Although the theme had not been decided at press time, the resort will have 1,920 rooms and include a pool and playground. The prices are expected to be the same as those at the other two All-Star resorts, around $74 to $89 a night. The **Safari Lodge,** an African-themed hotel adjacent to Animal Kingdom, will open before 2000.

HOW TO CHOOSE A HOTEL & SAVE MONEY

Many people assume that motels outside the Disney parks cost less than staying on WDW premises, but that isn't always the case. The **average hotel rate** for the Orlando metro area, is about $81, of course that rate is going up at about 10% a year. The lowest room rates for WDW resorts are $74 to $89 (rooms in the All-Star Resorts). Overall room rates are **lowest** in July, August, and September; they are **highest** in January, February, and March.

If you don't have a car, be sure to note the price of **hotel shuttle buses** to and from the theme parks. Compute these charges—which can be as high as $12 per person per day—in determining hotel price value. Or, if you drive your own car, don't forget to count parking fees, usually $6 a day at theme parks. All Disney-owned properties and Disney "official" hotels offer complimentary transportation to and from WDW parks (see details on this, and other advantages of staying at Disney properties, in section 2, "The Perks of Staying with Mickey"). However, the least expensive WDW properties are farther away from the parks, so you have to weigh the value of your time.

In or out of Walt Disney World, if you book your hotel as part of a **package** (see chapter 2 for details), you'll likely enjoy big savings.

Many people don't know that you can bargain with the reservations clerk when booking a hotel. The reason: An unoccupied room nets a hotel zero dollars, and any reasonable offer is better than that. Of course, this works only if you book upon arrival, preferably late in the afternoon when the desk knows there will be empty rooms. It will also work better outside of Walt Disney World; you probably won't have a lot of success for in-park properties.

Another money-saving tip: Reserving via **toll-free numbers** at chain hotels sometimes puts you into the running for lower rates than reserving at individual properties. Ask about special discounts for students, government employees, senior citizens, military, AAA, and/or corporate clients.

Also, Disney does not have an 800 number, so it may be best to review your choices **online** if you have Internet access or can get online at your local library. At the very least, obtain literature and **review your options** before going through the involved reservation process on your dime.

In the descriptions of accommodations, under "Amenities," I have mentioned **concierge levels** whenever they are available. In these "hotels within a hotel," guests enjoy a luxurious private lounge (usually with spectacular views) that is the setting for complimentary continental breakfasts, hot and cold hors d'oeuvres at cocktail hour, and late-night cordials and pastries. Rooms are usually on high floors and room decor is upgraded. Guests are cosseted with special services (private registration and checkout, a personal concierge, nightly bed turndown) and amenities (upgraded toiletries, bathroom scales, terry robes, hair dryers). Ask for specifics when you reserve. Concierge levels are especially attractive to businesspeople traveling on their own.

Also mentioned under "Amenities" in some cases are counselor-supervised **child-care** or **activity centers.** Very popular in Orlando, these are marvelous, creatively run facilities where kids enjoy movies, video games, arts and crafts, storytelling, puppet shows, indoor and outdoor activities, and much more. Some centers provide meals and/or have beds where a child can go to sleep while you're out on the town. Check individual hotel listings for these facilities and call to find out exactly what is offered.

RESERVATION SERVICES

Many of the Kissimmee hotels listed in "Best Bets" can be booked by calling the **Kissimmee–St. Cloud Convention & Visitors Bureau** at ☎ **800/333-KISS (5477).**

Also consider using the services of an Orlando-based organization called **Check-In** (☎ **800/237-1033** or 941/756-4880; fax 941/739-2703). A central booking agency, it has listings for hundreds of condos, resorts, hotels, villas, and luxurious private homes in all price ranges. A minimum stay of 3 nights is required. Check-In doesn't accept credit cards, but it does take personal checks. There's no fee for the service.

You can also get Internet information on Disney hotels at **www.disneyworld.com**. To cruise through the information, click on "Resorts & Spas." To make reservations, click on "Resort Reservations."

HOW TO USE THIS CHAPTER

The hotels listed below are first divided by location, and then by price category alphabetically within a given district. All of the properties I've selected offer easy access to the Walt Disney World parks and other nearby major attractions.

Hotels listed in the **inexpensive** category are those charging $80 or less for a double room (don't blame me, I didn't invent inflation). Properties with $80 to $150 rooms make up the **moderate** category, $150 to $200 I've listed as **expensive,** and anything above that ranks as **very expensive.** Any extras included in the rates (for example, breakfast or other meals) are listed for each property. Categories are approximate because hotel rates do vary considerably, depending on whether you visit in peak or off-seasons.

1 Best Bets

- **Best for Families:** All the Disney properties cater to families, with special menus for kids, character meals, video-game arcades, free transport to the parks, and many, many recreational facilities. Camping at woodsy **Fort Wilderness** (☎ 407/ **W-DISNEY** [934-7639] or 407/824-2900) makes for a special family experience. Bunk beds and a geyser going off in the lobby? What more could kids ask for? Keep in mind the **Wilderness Lodge** (☎ 407/**W-DISNEY** [934-7639] or 407/ 824-3200).

- **Best Moderately Priced Hotels:** Both Disney's **Dixie Landings** (☎ 407/ **W-DISNEY** [934-7639] or 407/934-6000) and **Port Orleans Resort** (☎ 407/ **W-DISNEY** [934-7639] or 407/934-5000) offer magnificently landscaped grounds and extensive facilities, and are worthy of much higher prices.

- **Best Inexpensive Hotels:** That's easy: Disney's **All-Star Music Resort** (☎ 407/ **W-DISNEY** [934-7639] or 407/939-6000) and **All-Star Sports Resort** (☎ 407/ **W-DISNEY** [934-7639] or 407/939-5000). You can't beat 'em with a stick. **Mount Vernon Inn** in Winter Park offers old-fashioned Southern hospitality without airs at a low price (☎ 407/647-1166) but is more distant from the Disney theme parks.

- **Best Budget Motel:** The rooms are clean, it's centrally located, and there is a restaurant right next door. All these things make the **Ramada Inn,** 4559 W. Bronson Memorial Hwy. (☎ 800/544-5712 or 407/396-1212), a great budget choice. Rates range from $29.95–$59.95, and microwaves and refrigerators are available upon request.

- **Best for Business Travelers:** Marriott's **Orlando World Center** (☎ 800/621-0638 or 407/239-4200) offers full concierge service, 24-hour room service, fine restaurants, spacious lounges, and an extensive array of business services, not to mention golf, tennis, and other recreational facilities should you find time to relax.

- **Best for a Romantic Getaway:** The 1,500-acre grounds of the **Hyatt Regency Grand Cypress Resort** (☎ 800/233-1234 or 407/239-1234) are a veritable botanical garden surrounding a swan-inhabited lake. Couples enjoy stunning accommodations, great service, first-rate restaurants, and every imaginable facility. Also consider the luxurious lodgings—with fireplaces and whirlpool tubs—at the adjoining Villas of Grand Cypress (☎ 800/835-7377 or 407/239-4700).

- **Best Location: Disney's Grand Floridian Beach Resort** (☎ 407/W-DISNEY [934-7639] or 407/824-3000), **Polynesian Resort** (☎ 407/W-DISNEY [934-7639] or 407/824-2000), or **Contemporary Resort** (☎ 407/W-DISNEY [934-7639] or 407/824-1000)—all are right on the monorail to whisk you straight to the parks for early opening.

- **Best Service:** The elegant **Peabody Orlando** (☎ 800/PEABODY or 407/ 352-4000) offers 24-hour concierge and room service, nightly bed turndown, and other attentive pampering.

- **Best Pools:** All of the Walt Disney World resorts have terrific swimming pools— generally Olympic-size and often with themes. The pool at the **Caribbean Beach Resort** (☎ 407/W-DISNEY [934-7639] or 407/934-3400), for instance, replicates a Caribbean fort with stone walls and cannons; it also has a water slide. Outside the Disney complex, the **Grand Cypress Resort** (☎ 800/233-1234 or 407/239-1234) also has a notable pool: A half-acre lagoonlike affair, it flows through rock grottos, is spanned by a rope bridge, and has 12 waterfalls and two steep water slides.

- **Best Health Club:** The **Walt Disney World Dolphin** (☎ **800/227-1500** or 407/934-4000) has a fully equipped Body By Jake club complete with a weight room overlooking a lake. It contains a full complement of Polaris, Lifestep, Lifecycle, and Liferower equipment; offers aerobics classes throughout the day, plus personal training, massage, and body wraps; and includes saunas and a large whirlpool.

2 The Perks of Staying with Mickey

Described here are the 15 Disney-owned properties (hotels, resorts, villas, wilderness homes, and campsites) and 9 privately owned properties designated as "official" hotels. All are within the Walt Disney World complex, either in the formal "park" areas or in nearby Lake Buena Vista.

In addition to location (they all offer close proximity to the parks), there are distinct advantages to staying at a Disney property or official hotel, especially the former. The following are included at all Disney resorts and official hotels:

- Unlimited complimentary transportation via bus, monorail, ferry, and water taxi to and from all four Disney World parks from 2 hours prior to opening until 2 hours after closing. Unlimited complimentary transport is also provided to and from Disney Village Marketplace, Typhoon Lagoon, River Country, Blizzard Beach, Downtown Disney, Fort Wilderness, and the other Disney resorts. Three properties—the Polynesian, Contemporary, and Grand Floridian—are stops on the monorail. This free transport can save a lot of money you'd otherwise have to spend on a rental car or expensive hotel shuttle buses. It also means you're guaranteed admission to all parks, even during peak times when parking lots sometimes fill up.
- "Surprise Mornings" where selected rides at different parks are opened early to resort guests.
- Free parking at WDW parking lots (other visitors pay $6 a day).
- Reduced-price children's menus in almost all restaurants.
- Character breakfasts and/or dinners at many restaurants.
- TVs equipped with the Disney channel and Walt Disney World information stations.
- A guest-services desk where you can purchase tickets to all WDW theme parks and attractions and obtain general information.
- Use of—and in some cases, complimentary transport to—the Disney-owned golf courses and preferred tee times (these can be booked up to 30 days in advance).
- Access to most recreational facilities at other Disney resorts.
- Mears airport shuttle service.

Additional perks at Disney-owned hotels, resorts, villas, and campgrounds—as well as at the Walt Disney World Swan and Dolphin, but not at other official hotels—include the following:

- Charge privileges at restaurants and shops throughout Walt Disney World.
- On-premises National Car Rental desk.

WALT DISNEY WORLD CENTRAL RESERVATIONS OFFICE

To reserve a room at Disney hotels, resorts, and villas; official hotels; or Fort Wilderness homes and campsites, contact **Central Reservations Operations (CRO),** P.O. Box 10000, Lake Buena Vista, FL 32830-1000 (☎ **407/W-DISNEY** [934-7639]), open Monday through Friday from 8am to 10pm, Saturday and Sunday from 9am to 6pm. Have your dates and credit card ready when you call. Remember, this is not a toll-free call, so it's best to be prepared.

CRO can recommend accommodations that will suit your specific needs as to price, location (perhaps you wish to be closest to Epcot, Magic Kingdom, or Disney–MGM Studios), and facilities such as counselor-supervised child-care centers, a pool large enough for lap swimming, a state-of-the-art health club, on-premises golf or tennis (or other recreational facilities), a kitchen, and so on.

Be sure to inquire about Disney's numerous package plans, which include meals, tickets, recreation, and other features. The right package plan can save you money and time (more of your vacation is planned in advance), and a comprehensive plan is helpful in computing the cost of your vacation in advance.

CRO can also give you information about various park ticket options and make dinner-show reservations for you at the Hoop-Dee-Doo Musical Revue or the Poly-nesian Luau Dinner Show when you book your room.

OTHER SOURCES FOR PACKAGES

In addition to the CRO, there are other sources for packages utilizing Disney resorts. These include Delta Dream Vacations (☎ **800/872-7786**), US Airways Vacations (☎ **800/455-0123**), American Airlines Fly Away Vacations (☎ **800/321-2121**), American Express Vacations (☎ **800/241-1700**), Travel Impressions (☎ **800/941-2639**), and Kingdom Tours (☎ **800/872-8857**). Best bet: Stop at a sizable travel agency and pick up brochures from all of the above (and others). Pore over them at home, comparing offerings to find the optimum package for your trip.

COMING SOON

Universal Studios Florida is working on an on-site hotel, probably a Loew's hotel, which will offer discounts, perks, and package deals to the Universal Parks. For updates, check out **www.usf.com**. Perk-filled packages, much like the ones offered by Disney, will be offered when the hotel is completed. **Universal City Travel Company** (☎ **800/224-3838**) will handle reservations.

3 Places to Stay in Walt Disney World

The resorts in this section are all either Disney-owned hotels or "official" hotels (affil-iated with but not owned by Disney). More important, all the hotels in this section are on the Disney Transportation system, which means you may not need to rent a car if you stay in one of these choices. Information on all WDW properties can be found at **www.disneyworld.com**; click on "Resorts & Spas." There are large colorful signs directing you to the WDW properties along all major roads within the Disney com-plex. You'll find all these hotels listed on the map "Walt Disney World & Lake Buena Vista Accommodations" found in this section.

VERY EXPENSIVE

✪ **Disney's Beach Club Resort.** 1800 Epcot Resorts Blvd. (off Buena Vista Dr.; P.O. Box 10000), Lake Buena Vista, FL 32830-0100. ☎ **407/W-DISNEY** (934-7639) or 407/934-8000. Fax 407/354-1866. 597 units. A/C MINIBAR TV TEL. $260–$450 double; $415–$1,085 suites. Prices depend on view and season. AE, MC, V. Free self- and valet parking.

From its palm-fringed entranceway and manicured gardens to its plush, sun-dappled lobby, the Beach Club resembles a luxurious Victorian Cape Cod resort. A big draw here—especially for families—is Stormalong Bay, a vast free-form swimming pool/water park that sprawls over 3 acres between the Yacht Club and Beach Club and flows into a lake; it includes a 150-foot serpentine water slide. So posh is the Beach Club—and so extensive are its sports facilities—that you might consider it for an upscale resort vacation even without the draw of the Disney parks nearby. In a similar category are its sister properties, the Yacht Club and the Grand Floridian (described below). The charming rooms, some with balconies, are furnished in bleached woods and equipped with ceiling fans, extra phones in the bathroom, and safes.

Dining: The very elegant Ariel's is open for seafood dinners nightly. Ideal for family dining is the Cape May Café, serving character breakfasts and authentic New England clambake buffet dinners. Other facilities here serve drinks, wine by the glass, light fare, and ice cream.

Amenities: Room service (24 hours), baby-sitting, guest-services desk, complimentary daily newspaper, boat transport to MGM theme park. Large outdoor swimming pool, whirlpool, quarter-mile sand beach, boat rental, fishing, two tennis courts, state-of-the-art health club, volleyball, croquet, bocci ball courts, 2-mile jogging trail, coin-op washers/dryers, unisex hair salon, shops, business center, video-game arcade, Sandcastle Club (a counselor-supervised children's activity center.)

✪ **Disney's BoardWalk.** 2101 N. Epcot Resorts Blvd. (off Buena Vista Dr.; P.O. Box 10000), Lake Buena Vista, FL 32830-1000. ☎ **407/W-DISNEY** (934-7639) or 407/939-5100 (407/939-6200 for villas). Fax 407/354-1866. 378 units, 532 villas. A/C TV TEL. $249–$450 double; $415–$1,200 suites; $210–$780 villa, depending on view and season. Children 17 and under stay free in parents' room. AE, MC, V. Free self- and valet parking.

The BoardWalk—occupying 45 acres along the shores of Lake Crescent—takes its theme from the plush mid-Atlantic Victorian seaside resorts of the 1920s and 1930s. A large deck with rocking chairs overlooks a village green and the lake beyond, and the stunning 70-foot lobby has a working fireplace. With shingled rooftops surrounding private courtyards and New England–style flower gardens, the property connects to a quarter-mile boardwalk complete with shops, restaurants and street performers. There's plenty to do here once the sun goes down, making it a good choice for singles and couples without children. The B&B style accommodations are gorgeous and may include a brass or four-poster bed. All have safes, irons and ironing boards, and hair dryers; refrigerators are available. The villas, though pricey, might be a good choice for large families or groups; they offer kitchenettes or full kitchens and washers/dryers, and some contain whirlpool tubs. This hotel is within walking distance of Epcot and the Yacht and Beach Clubs.

Dining/Diversions: Situated along the boardwalk promenade to provide scenic water views, the dining facilities include the upscale Flying Fish Café for steak and seafood; Spoodle's, a casual spot serving Mediterranean fare; the Big River Grille and Brewing Works (featuring handcrafted beers and ales); ESPN Club, a sports bar; a bakery; and a coffee bar. A 10-piece orchestra plays music from 1940 through Top 40s at the Atlantic Dance, a 1920s-style dance hall. Jellyrolls, a sing-along bar, features dueling pianos. There are also several cocktail lounges and a carousel-themed pool bar.

Amenities: Concierge, room service (24 hours), baby-sitting, boat transport (to MGM, Epcot, and Epcot resorts), guest-services desk, complimentary daily newspaper. Large outdoor swimming pool with water slide, two additional secluded pools, kiddie pool, whirlpool, two tennis courts, croquet, bike rental, 2-mile jogging path, playground, convention center, full business center, shops, extensively equipped health club, two video-game arcades, Community Hall (for games, crafts, recreational equipment rentals, videotapes, and books), Harbour Club (a counselor-supervised child-care activity center).

Walt Disney World & Lake Buena Vista Accommodations

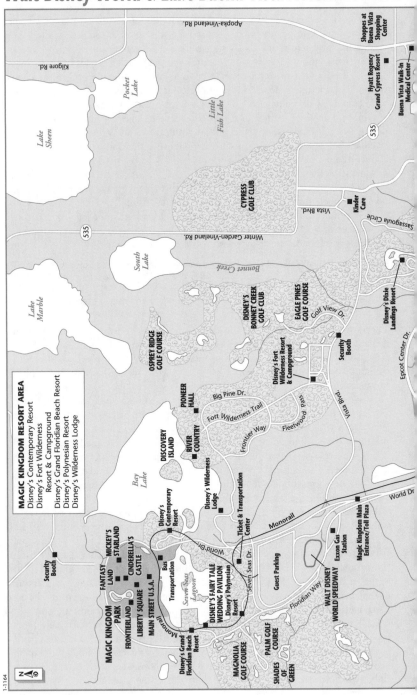

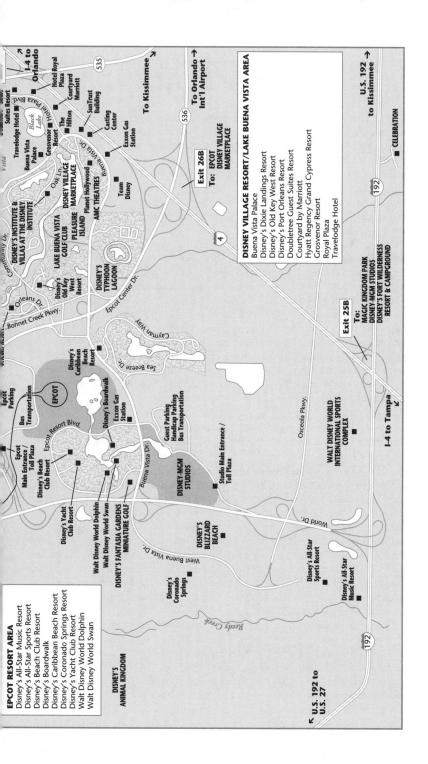

EPCOT RESORT AREA

Disney's All-Star Music Resort
Disney's All-Star Sports Resort
Disney's Beach Club Resort
Disney's Boardwalk
Disney's Caribbean Beach Resort
Disney's Coronado Springs Resort
Disney's Yacht Club Resort
Walt Disney World Dolphin
Walt Disney World Swan

DISNEY VILLAGE RESORT/LAKE BUENA VISTA AREA

Buena Vista Palace
Disney's Dixie Landings Resort
Disney's Old Key West Resort
Disney's Port Orleans Resort
Doubletree Guest Suites Resort
Courtyard by Marriott
Hyatt Regency Grand Cypress Resort
Grosvenor Resort
Royal Plaza
Travelodge Hotel

✪ **Disney's Contemporary Resort.** 4600 N. World Dr. (P.O. Box 10000), Lake Buena Vista, FL 32830-1000. ☎ **407/W-DISNEY** (934-7639) or 407/824-1000. Fax 407/354-1866. 1,121 units. A/C TV TEL. $209–$390 double; $695–$1,150 suites. AE, MC, V. Free self- and valet parking.

When it opened in 1971, the Contemporary's aesthetics were cutting-edge. Today its dramatic angular planes, free-form furnishings, and abstract paintings appear rather charmingly retro-modern. However, a major renovation has spruced up the fading centerpiece of the park. Centering on a sleek, 15-story A-frame tower, the property comprises 26 acres bounded by a natural lake and the Disney-made Seven Seas Lagoon. Kids are thrilled that the monorail whizzes right through the hotel; they also enjoy on-premises character meals. Location is the biggest thing to recommend the Contemporary. Since it is literally on the monorail system, you can zip right to the parks.

Dining: The magnificent 15th-floor California Grill (see chapter 6) provides panoramic vistas of the Magic Kingdom. Other options here are the Concourse Steakhouse, the garden-themed Chef Mickey's Buffet (for character breakfasts and prime rib buffet dinners), and several other spots for drinks and light fare.

Amenities: Room service (24 hours), guest-services desk, daily newspaper delivery, baby-sitting, boat transport (to Fort Wilderness and River Country), monorail to the Polynesian and Grand Floridian resorts. Two swimming pools, kiddie pool, white-sand beach with volleyball court, shuffleboard, boat rental, unisex hair salon, six tennis courts (lessons available), shops, American Express desk, car-rental desk, coin-op washers/dryers, full business center, extensive health club, sauna/massage/tanning rooms, video-game arcade, the Mouseketeer Clubhouse (a counselor-supervised child-care/activity center).

✪ **Disney's Grand Floridian Beach Resort.** 4401 Floridian Way (P.O. Box 10000), Lake Buena Vista, FL 32830-1000. ☎ **407/W-DISNEY** [934-7639] or 407/824-3000). Fax 407/354-1866. 933 units. A/C MINIBAR TV TEL. $294–$545 double, depending on view and season; $729–$1,580 suites. AE, MC, V. Free self- and valet parking.

The Grand Floridian is truly world renowned and magnificent from the moment you step into its opulent, five-story lobby (complete with a Chinese Chippendale aviary) under triple-domed stained-glass skylights. Here a pianist entertains during afternoon tea, and an orchestra plays big-band music every evening. This could be a romantic choice for couples—even honeymooners (the Disney wedding pavilion is here, by the way). And if you're into fitness, you'll appreciate the first-rate health club. The sunny rooms—with private balconies or verandas overlooking either formal gardens, the pool, or a 200-acre lagoon—have two-poster beds dressed with lovely floral-chintz spreads. In-room amenities include safes and ceiling fans; in the bathroom you'll find an extra phone, hair dryer, and terry robe. Great location offers quick access to parks, boating, and water activities.

Dining/Diversions: Victoria & Albert's, Orlando's finest restaurant, is described in chapter 6, section 3, "Places to Dine in Walt Disney World." The lovely Grand Floridian Café, overlooking formal gardens, features Southern specialties. The exposition-themed 1900 Park Fare is the setting for character breakfasts and dinners. Flagler's offers northern Italian fare. At the gazebo-like Narcoossee's, grilled meats and seafood are prepared in an exhibition kitchen. Intimate and very Victorian, Mizner's Lounge features an international selection of ports, brandies, and appetizers. The Garden View Lounge, off the lobby, is the setting for elegant afternoon teas. Other options include the Gasparilla Grill (open 24 hours) and a pool bar.

Amenities: On-premises monorail, boat transport to Magic Kingdom, room service (24 hours), nightly turndown, baby-sitting, free trolley transport around the hotel

The Disney Institute: The Mouse Grows Up

The Disney Institute is an exciting new concept designed for adults and older children (10 and up). Resembling a small town with a village green and architecture evocative of barns, mills, and country houses, it sprawls over 265 acres of lakes, streams, and woodlands.

The Institute enables guests to custom-design Walt Disney World vacations that focus on interactive programs in dozens of diverse areas. This is a great one-day adventure for couples, seniors, or adult children traveling with older parents, and it provides a pleasant physical rest from trekking through the theme parks. Since classes are small, participants spend real face-to-face time with their instructors. My mom and I enjoyed a morning program learning Oriental cooking and an afternoon introduction to animation. We left with the recipes from the cooking class and a tape of our first (and probably last) short film. We even got to eat our (culinary) creations for lunch. The classes tend to be relatively fast-paced because professionals have just a few hours to provide a broad overview, but most are designed with the novice in mind and offer step-by-step instructions.

Gourmets will be especially interested in the programs offered in conjunction with the International Wine Festival in June. During that time you can learn the culinary secrets of prominent chefs. All classes are taught by professionals, and many are enhanced by noted guest artists and speakers. Marshall Brickman, Chris Columbus, Siskel and Ebert, Randy Newman, and Morton Gould are among the dozens of well-known directors, critics, singers, and composers that Disney has tapped to participate in its Entertainment Arts programs. Those programs are augmented by evening concerts and activities. The Institute hasn't caught on with individuals as much as Disney had originally planned, so participants are increasingly part of a group. That narrows your choices a bit, but programs are still available in areas such as Sports and Fitness, Lifestyles, Story Arts, Culinary Arts, Design, the Environment, and Architecture—options are almost limitless. You might opt for golf or tennis clinics, indulge in an array of luxurious spa treatments, learn topiary gardening, canoe on local waterways, or try rock climbing.

Its resort-style public areas and accommodations (bungalows and one- and two-bedroom town houses) are gorgeous. An elegant on-premises restaurant, Seasons, features nightly changing menus and cuisine. There are extensive sporting facilities, an 18-hole/par-72 championship golf course, tennis courts, and swimming pools.

Nightly performances and recitals take place in a 1,150-seat open-air amphitheater and a 250-seat performance center. Films are screened weeknights in a state-of-the-art movie theater. A counselor-supervised youth center, comfortably appointed with couches, videos, and games, offers a full roster of daytime programs and activities for children ages 10 to 12 and teens, as well as evening activities for teens.

The Institute is adjacent to the Disney Village Marketplace at 1960 N. Magnolia Way. Packages rates range from 3-night stays for around $600 to 7-night stays for about $2,000. A good bet for the budget-minded is a single day, at around $100, that includes programs and classes but not accommodations. Single-day visitors should allow plenty of time to find the bungalow classrooms. The signs can be confusing, and we were misdirected several times by employees during our visit. But once you find what you're looking for, you'll be glad you made the effort. For further information on programs and rates, call ☎ **800/ 4-WONDER (966337)** or 407/827-4800.

grounds, shoe shine, massage, guest-services desk, complimentary daily newspaper. Large outside swimming pool with poolside changing area, kiddie pool, whirlpool, two tennis courts, boat rental, waterskiing, croquet, volleyball, playground, jogging trails, fishing excursions, white-sand beach, unisex hair salon, coin-op washers/dryers, shops, car-rental desk, state-of-the-art spa, video-game arcade, organized children's activities in summer and peak seasons, the Mouseketeer Clubhouse (a counselor-supervised child-care activity center).

Disney's Old Key West Resort. 1510 N. Cove Rd. (off Community Dr.; P.O. Box 10000), Lake Buena Vista, FL 32830-1000. ☎ **407/W-DISNEY** (934-7639) or 407/827-7700. Fax 407/354-1866. 709 units. A/C TV TEL. $195–$215 deluxe rooms; $224–$885 villa. Range reflects high and low seasons and 1-, 2-, and 3-bedroom villas. AE, MC, V. Free parking.

An understated theme (at least by Disney standards) makes the Old Key West a good choice for those seeking a quieter environment. Architecturally mirroring Key West at the turn of the century, this is a "vacation ownership" (time-share) property that rents accommodations when they're not in use by the owners. The 156-acre complex is beautifully landscaped: Tree-lined, brick walkways are edged by white picket fences, palms sway softly in the breeze, shorebirds swoop lazily over lagoons, and the air is scented with honeysuckle. Most accommodations are gorgeous homes away from home with living rooms (equipped with large-screen TVs and VCRS, smaller sets and extra phones in the bedroom), fully equipped kitchens, furnished patios (offering water, woodland, or fairway views; the property overlooks the Buena Vista Golf Course), and laundry rooms. Many units contain whirlpool tubs in the master suite, and the Grand Villas have stereo systems.

Dining: The Key West–themed Olivia's Cafe, overlooking a canal, serves all meals. There are a few other spots for drinks and light fare.

Amenities: Guest-services desk, ferry service to Disney Village Marketplace and Downtown Disney, free bus transport around the grounds, food shopping. Two tennis courts, basketball court, white-sand play area, four swimming pools, whirlpool, kiddie pool, bicycle rental, boat rental, playground, extensive health club, sauna, shuffleboard, horseshoes, volleyball, complimentary use of washers/dryers, general store, video-game arcade, video library. The Community Hall, a recreation center, shows Disney movies nightly and offers various activities.

Disney's Polynesian Resort. 1600 Seven Seas Dr. (P.O. Box 10000), Lake Buena Vista, FL 32830-1000. ☎ **407/W-DISNEY** (934-7639) or 407/824-2000. Fax 407/354-1866. 853 units. A/C TV TEL. $275–$395 double, depending on view and season; $335–$395 concierge-floor double; $415–$1,200 suites. AE, MC, V. Free self- and valet parking.

Just below the Magic Kingdom, the 25-acre Polynesian Resort is fronted by lush tropical foliage, waterfalls, and koi ponds. Inside, its skylit lobby is a virtual rain forest of tropical plantings—gorgeous by day but rather depressingly lit for evenings. A private white-sand beach—dotted with canvas cabanas, hammocks, and large swings—overlooks a 200-acre lagoon. Waterfalls, grottoes, and a water slide enhance an immense swimming pool. The large, beautiful rooms—most with balconies or patios—have canopied beds, bamboo and rattan furnishings, and walls hung with Gauguin prints. This is a great choice with kids, who will enjoy the Polynesian theme and child-pleasing eateries.

Dining/Diversions: 'Ohana (see section 3, "Places to Dine in Walt Disney World" in chapter 6) is the setting for character breakfasts and all-you-can-eat island dinners featuring open-pit rock-grilled specialties. Luau Cove hosts Mickey's Tropical Luau and the Polynesian Luau Dinner Show. There are several other restaurants and bars, including a 24-hour ice-cream parlor.

Amenities: Room service, baby-sitting, on-premises monorail, boat transport (to the Magic Kingdom and the Grand Floridian Beach Resort, guest-services desk, complimentary daily newspaper. Two swimming pools, kiddie pool, boat rental, waterskiing, volleyball, playground, 1½-mile jogging trail, fishing excursions, coin-op washers/dryers, shops, video-game arcade, the Neverland Club (a counselor-supervised evening activity center for children).

✪ **Disney's Yacht Club Resort.** 1700 Epcot Resorts Blvd. (off Buena Vista Dr.; P.O. Box 10000), Lake Buena Vista, FL 32830-1000. ☎ **407/W-DISNEY** (934-7639) or 407/934-7000. Fax 407/354-1866. 642 units. A/C MINIBAR TV TEL. $260–$445 double, depending on view and season; $415–$1,085 concierge-level double. AE, MC, V. Free self- and valet parking.

Though first-time visitors to Orlando—who generally spend all their time in the parks—don't require extensive recreational facilities, return visitors will appreciate the extensive sports and entertainment options here. This stunning resort—its main five-story, oyster-gray clapboard building evoking a turn-of-the-century New England yacht club—shares a 25-acre lake, facilities, and gorgeous landscaping with the adjacent Beach Club (described earlier). The nautical theme carries over to the very inviting rooms, decorated in snappy blue and white, with brass sconces, ship lights, and vintage maps on the walls. French doors open onto porches or balconies. Amenities include ceiling fans, extra phones in the bathroom, and safes. The fifth floor is a concierge level, which will especially appeal to business travelers.

Dining/Diversions: The plush Yachtsman Steakhouse grills select cuts of steak, chops, and fresh seafood over oak and hickory. The Yacht Club Galley, a comfortable family restaurant, serves American regional fare. The Crew's Cup Lounge airs sporting events and features international beers. And the cozy Ale and Compass Lounge, a lobby bar with a working fireplace, proffers specialty coffees and cocktails.

Amenities: Room service (24 hours), baby-sitting, guest-services desk, complimentary daily newspaper, boat transport to the MGM theme park, tram and boat transport to Epcot. Yacht Club facilities are identical to those of the Beach Club (described earlier).

Walt Disney World Dolphin. 1500 Epcot Resorts Blvd. (off Buena Vista Dr.; P.O. Box 22653), Lake Buena Vista, FL 32830-2653. ☎ **800/227-1500** or 407/934-4000. Fax 407/934-4884. 1,509 units. A/C MINIBAR TV TEL. $210–$410 double, depending on view and season; $525–$3,050 suites. Up to 2 children under 18 stay free in parents' room. Inquire about packages. AE, CB, DC, DISC, JCB, MC, V. Take 1-4 east to 25B. This is the exit to Epcot/Magic Kingdom. Follow purple and red signs to the resort areas. Free self-parking; valet parking $6.

Though distinctive architecture is its keynote, sports enthusiasts will also appreciate this Sheraton resort's extensive health club, boat rentals, and tennis facilities. Designed by whimsical architect Michael Graves, the property centers on a 27-story pyramid with two 11-story wings crowned by 56-foot twin dolphin sculptures. Graves dubs his more-Disneyesque-than-Disney creations "entertainment architecture." Close to a dozen cascading fountains on the property range from a seven-dolphin extravaganza at the entrance to waters rushing across rock-faced grottoes in a fiber-optic "starlit" foyer. A free-form rock-sculpted grotto pool—with waterfalls, a water slide, rope bridge, and three secluded whirlpools—sprawls over 2 acres between the Dolphin and the adjoining Swan. Both properties also share a white sandy beach on Crescent Lake.

There are thousands of works of art in public areas. In the rooms, walls are hung with art prints (Picasso, Matisse, and others), and painted wood furnishings are stenciled with palm trees and pineapples. Amenities include pay movies, desk and bedside phones, safes, coffeemakers, hair dryers, and irons/ironing boards. The Dolphin Towers comprise a 77-room concierge level.

Dining/Diversions: The elegant Sum Chows serves haute-cuisine pan-Asian dinners. Juan and Only's Bar & Jail offers moderately priced Tex-Mex fare. Harry's Safari Bar & Grille, highlighting steak and seafood, is open for dinner nightly and Sunday character-brunch buffets (details in chapter 6). Other venues are the delightful fish-themed Coral Cafe for American fare, an ice-cream/malt shop, a 24-hour cafeteria, Copa Banana (with a DJ spinning tunes for nightly dancing plus karaoke), a lobby lounge, and a poolside bar.

Amenities: Water-launch transport to Epcot & MGM, concierge, 24-hour room service, guest-services desk (sells tickets and arranges transport to all nearby attractions), baby-sitting, Japanese tour desk. Water volleyball, boat rentals, four hard-surface night-lit tennis courts, tennis pro shop, fully equipped Body by Jake health club, two beach volleyball courts, miniature golf, 3-mile jogging trail, coin-op washers/dryers, unisex hair salon, shops, full business center, Delta Airlines desk, large video-game arcade, Camp Dolphin (a counselor-supervised children's activity center, open daily).

Walt Disney World Swan. 1200 Epcot Resorts Blvd. (off Buena Vista Dr.; P.O. Box 22786), Lake Buena Vista, FL 32830-2786. ☎ **800/248-SWAN** (7926), 800/228-3000, or 407/934-3000. (*Note:* You may get a lower rate by reserving through the second toll-free number for Westin hotels). Fax 407/934-4499. 758 units. A/C MINIBAR TV TEL. $310–$450 double, depending on view and season; $640–$2,050 suites. Children under 18 stay free in parents' room. Inquire about packages. AE, CB, DC, DISC, JCB, MC, V. Free self-parking; valet parking $8.

Operated by Westin Hotels & Resorts, this 12-story hotel—its rooftop flanked by 45-foot swan statues and seashell fountains—is adjacent to the previously mentioned Dolphin and shares with it a white-sand lakeside beach and facilities. The hotels are connected by a canopied walkway. Here Michael Graves has created a festive interior replete with swan fountains, sea horse–motif chandeliers, hallway walls painted with beach scenes, and striped room doors evocative of cabanas. Luxurious accommodations, decorated in cheerful pastels, have furnishings stenciled with parrots and pineapples. Lamps decorated with swans and palm trees and, like the Dolphin, walls hung with fine-art prints carry out the theme. In-room amenities include pay movies, desk and bedside phones, and safes. King-bedded rooms have pullout sleeper sofas. The 11th and 12th floors comprise the Royal Beach Club, a concierge level.

Dining/Diversions: Serving dinner only, the casually elegant Italian-modern Pail has large windows overlooking scenic canals. Strolling musicians entertain while you dine. The delightful Garden Grove Café serves steaks and prime rib, and, in the morning, a traditional Japanese breakfast is an option. Another venue is Kimono's, which serves a wide selection of sushi and becomes a karaoke bar after 8:30pm.

Amenities: Water launch to Epcot & MGM, concierge, 24-hour room service, guest-services desk, complimentary daily newspaper, nightly turndown on request, baby-sitting. Olympic-size lap pool, children's wading pool, fully equipped health club, full business center, children's playground, shops, video-game arcade. See also the earlier description of facilities at the Dolphin.

EXPENSIVE

✪ **Disney's Wilderness Lodge.** 901 West Timberline Dr. (on the southwest shore of Bay Lake just east of the Magic Kingdom; P.O. Box 10000), Lake Buena Vista, FL 32830-1000. ☎ **407/W-DISNEY** (934-7639) or 407/824-3200. Fax 407/354-1866. 728 units. A/C TV TEL. $165–$245 double, depending on view and season; $280–$315 jr suites; $540–$665 suites. AE, MC, V. Free self- and valet parking.

The geyser out back, the bubbling creek and mammoth stone hearth in the lobby, and bunk beds for the kids are just a few reasons this is one of my favorite WDW resorts. The main dining room, with its sweeping view of 340-acre Bay Lake, might even inspire some romance. Reminiscent of rustic turn-of-the-century national park lodges, this 56-acre resort is surrounded by towering oak and pine forests. Wilderness Lodge has the advantage of feeling removed from the rest of WDW and, unfortunately, is one of the more difficult places to access via the WDW transportation system. The 5-minute geyser shows take place in the meadow periodically throughout the day, and nightly electric water pageants can be viewed from the shores of Bay Lake. A lakefront sand beach and an immense serpentine swimming pool seemingly excavated out of the rocks make up for the modest-sized rooms.

The guest rooms—with patios or balconies overlooking lake, woodlands, or meadow scenery—are furnished in Mission style and adorned with tribal friezes and landscape paintings of the Northwest. In-room safes are a plus. To get the lower rooms rates, ask for a "standard view."

Dining: The stunning lodgelike Artist Point, overlooking Bay Lake, is adorned with murals based on the works of Rocky Mountain School painters such as Albert Bierstadt; the menu highlights steak, seafood, and game specialties.

Amenities: Immense swimming pool (see above), kiddie pool with water slide, lakefront sand beach, spa pools, boat rental, bicycle rental, 2-mile jogging/bike trail, video-game arcade, gift shop, Cub's Den (a counselor-supervised activity center for children 4 to 12). Room service; guest-services desk; baby-sitting; boat transport to the Magic Kingdom and Contemporary Resort; bus transport to MGM, Epcot, and other park areas.

MODERATE

Disney's Caribbean Beach Resort. 900 Cayman Way (off Buena Vista Dr.; P.O. Box 10000), Lake Buena Vista, FL 32830-1000. ☎ **407/W-DISNEY** (934-7639) or 407/934-3400. Fax 407/354-1866. 2,112 units. A/C MINIBAR TV TEL. $119–$154 double. Children 16 and under stay free in parents' room. AE, MC, V. Free parking.

Though the facilities here aren't as extensive as those at some other Disney resorts, the Caribbean Beach offers especially good value for families. It occupies 200 lush, palm-fringed tropical acres, with accommodations in five distinct Caribbean "villages" grouped around a large, duck-filled lake. The main swimming pool here replicates a Spanish-style Caribbean fort, complete with water slide, kiddie pool, and whirlpool. There are other pools as well as lakefront white-sand beaches in each village. A 1.4-mile promenade—popular for jogging—circles the lake. An arched wooden bridge leads to Parrot Cay Island where there's a short nature trail, an aviary of tropical birds, and a picnic area. The rooms are charming, with oak furnishings and chintz bedspreads. Amenities include coffeemakers and ceiling fans; refrigerators are available at $5 per night. All rooms have a verandah, many of them overlooking the lake.

Dining: Facilities include a festive food court, the nautically themed Captain's Tavern for American fare, and a pool bar.

Amenities: Room service (pizza only), guest-services desk, baby-sitting, complimentary shuttle around the grounds. Seven swimming pools, video-game arcade, shops, boat rental, bicycle rental, coin-op washers/dryers, playgrounds.

Disney's Coronado Springs Resort. 1000 Buena Vista Dr., near All-Star Resorts and Blizzard Beach, Lake Buena Vista, FL 32830. ☎ **407/W-DISNEY** (934-7639), 407/934-6632, or 407/824-1000. Fax 407/828-5392. 1,967 units. A/C MINIBAR TV TEL. $119–$154 double, depending on view and season; $238–$655 suites. Children under 17 stay free in parents' room. AE, MC, V. Free parking.

Everything here is themed on the American Southwest, with lots of muted pastels, sculptured wolves, and cacti. Its four- and five-story haciendalike buildings have terra-cotta tile roofs and palm-shaded courtyards, and the property itself also houses a major 95,000-square-foot convention center and the largest ballroom in the Southeast. The temple-inspired pool is an interesting addition to the Florida landscape. There are 99 rooms specially designed to accommodate travelers with disabilities, and nearly three-fourths of the rooms are nonsmoking (good news for the very allergic). Since the hotel is new, this means the rooms have always been smoke free.

Dining/Diversions: There is a 420-seat food court, called the Pepper Market, to satisfy the munchies with a variety of fast food. Francisco's is a sit-down, 200-seat Mexican restaurant with the feeling of an outdoor cafe. You won't find a triple-decker burrito here, but rather superbly prepared native dishes such as corn tamales in a spicy green sauce. Siestas offers snacks and light fare.

Amenities: Room service from 6am to 11pm, nightly turndown, lounge, transportation to all WDW parks. White-sand beach, beach volleyball, boat rentals, four large outdoor swimming pools, kiddie pool, arcade, complimentary parking, boutiques, shops, access to golf course, voice-mail system, spa, coin-op laundry.

✪ **Disney's Dixie Landings Resort.** 1251 Dixie Dr. (off Bonnet Creek Pkwy.; P.O. Box 10000), Lake Buena Vista, FL 32830-1000. ☎ **407/W-DISNEY** (934-7639) or 407/934-6000. Fax 407/934-5777. 2,048 units. A/C TV TEL. $119–$154 room for up to 4. AE, MC, V. Free parking.

Low rates, extensive child-oriented facilities, and a food court make the Dixie Landings popular with families, even though the rooms are midsized and the bathrooms rather small. Adults traveling alone might prefer a more sedate setting. Nestled on the banks of the "mighty Sassagoula River" and dotted with bayous, it shares its 325-acre site with the Port Orleans Resort (described next). It includes Ol' Man Island, a woodsy 3½-acre recreation area containing an immense swimming pool with waterfalls cascading from a broken bridge and a water slide, a playground, children's wading pool, whirlpool, and fishin' hole (rent bait and poles and angle for catfish and bass). The accommodations areas, themed after the Louisiana countryside, are divided into "parishes," with rooms housed in stately colonnaded plantation homes or rural Cajun-style dwellings fronted by brick courtyards.

Dining/Diversions: Boatwright's Dining Hall, housed in a replica of an 1800s boat-building factory, serves American/Cajun fare at breakfast and dinner. The Cotton Co-op lounge airs Monday-night football games and offers entertainment (singers and comedians) Tuesday to Saturday nights. A food court and pool bar round out the facilities.

Amenities: Six large swimming pools (one with a water slide), 1.7-mile riverfront jogging/biking path, Fulton's General Store, room service (pizza only), guest-services desk, baby-sitting, boat transport (to Port Orleans, Village Marketplace, and Downtown Disney), coin-op washers/dryers, video-game arcade, car-rental desk, bicycle and boat rental.

✪ **Disney's Port Orleans Resort.** 2201 Orleans Dr. (off Bonnet Creek Pkwy.; P.O. Box 10000), Lake Buena Vista, FL 32830-1000. ☎ **407/W-DISNEY** (934-7639) or 407/934-5000. Fax 407/934-5353. 1,008 units. A/C TV TEL. $95–$129 room for up to 4. AE, MC, V. Free parking.

This beautiful resort, themed after turn-of-the-century New Orleans, shares a site on the banks of the Sassagoula with Dixie Landings, described above. Its identical room rates and comparable facilities make it, too, a good bet for families. The midsized rooms, with small bathrooms, are housed in pastel buildings with shuttered windows and lacy wrought-iron balconies; they're fronted by lovely flower gardens opening onto fountained courtyards. Cherrywood furnishings, swagged draperies, and walls hung with botanical prints and family photographs make for pretty room interiors. And the landscaping throughout the property is especially nice, with stately oaks, formal boxwood hedges, azaleas, and fragrant jasmine.

Dining/Diversions: Bonfamille's Café is open for breakfast and dinner, the latter featuring Creole specialties. Scat Cat's Club, a cocktail lounge off the lobby, airs Monday-night football and features family-oriented live entertainment. A food court and pool bar round out the facilities.

Amenities: Room service (pizza only), guest-services desk, baby-sitting, boat transport (to Dixie Landings, Village Marketplace, and Downtown Disney). The larger-than-Olympic-size Doubloon Lagoon swimming pool has an enormous water slide. Whirlpool, kiddie pool, coin-op washers/dryers, video-game arcade, bicycle rental, car-rental service, boat rental, 1.7-mile riverfront jogging path, shops.

INEXPENSIVE

❂ **Disney's All-Star Music Resort.** 1801 W. Buena Vista Dr. (at World Dr. and Osceola Pkwy.; P.O. Box 10000), Lake Buena Vista, FL 32830-1000. ☎ **407/W-DISNEY** (934-7639) or 407/939-6000. Fax 407/354-1866. 1,920 units. A/C TV TEL. $74–$89 double. Children 17 and under stay free in parents' room. AE, MC, V. Free parking.

Though the unbeatable combination of rock-bottom rates and extensive facilities at Disney's All-Star Music and Sports resorts is very attractive to families, there is one caveat: The rooms are small (a mere 260 square feet). They're all right for single adults or couples traveling with one child; larger families had best be into togetherness. Set amid pristine pine forests, this Disney hostelry is part of a 246-acre complex that also includes the adjacent All-Star Sports Resort (described next) and will soon include a third resort. Its 10 buildings are musically themed around country, jazz, rock, calypso, and Broadway show tunes. The calypso building, for instance, has a palm-fringed roof frieze and balconies adorned with tropical birds and musical notes, while a convoy of 18-wheelers travels around the country building, which is decorated with fiddles and banjos. Oversized icons in the public areas—such as three-story cowboy boots or a walk-through jukebox—are lit by neon and fiber optics at night. The attractive rooms have musically themed bedspreads, paintings, and wallpaper borders. In-room safes are a plus. There's a cheerful food court with an adjoining bar. Room service (pizza only), baby-sitting, guest-services desk. Two vast swimming pools, kiddie pool, playground, coin-op washers/dryers, large retail shop, car-rental desk, video-game arcade.

❂ **Disney's All-Star Sports Resort.** 1701 W. Buena Vista Dr. (at World Dr. and Osceola Pkwy.; P.O. Box 10000), Lake Buena Vista, FL 32830-1000. ☎ **407/W-DISNEY** (934-7639) or 407/939-5000. Fax 407/354-1866. 1,920 units. A/C TV TEL. $74–$89 double. Children 17 and under stay free in parents' room. AE, MC, V. Free parking.

Adjacent to the above-described All-Star Music Resort, this 82-acre hostelry is elaborately sports themed. The rooms are housed in buildings designed around football, baseball, basketball, tennis, and surfing motifs. For instance, the turquoise surf buildings have waves along their rooflines, surfboards mounted on the exterior walls, and pink fish swimming along the balcony railings. The immense public-area icons include tennis ball–can stairways and four-story football helmets and whistles. The cheerful rooms feature sports-action-motif bedspreads, paintings, and wallpaper borders; in-room safes are among your amenities. As noted above, however, the rooms here are small.

There's a brightly decorated food court with an adjoining bar. Room service (pizza only), baby-sitting, guest-services desk. Two vast outdoor swimming pools (one surfing themed with two 38-foot shark fins, the other shaped like a baseball diamond with an "outfield" sundeck), kiddie pool, playground, coin-op washers/ dryers, shops, car-rental service, video-game arcade.

A DISNEY CAMPGROUND

✪ **Disney's Fort Wilderness Resort and Campground.** 3520 N. Fort Wilderness Trail (P.O. Box 10000), Lake Buena Vista, FL 32830-1000. ☎ **407/W-DISNEY** (934-7639) or 407/824-2900. Fax 407/354-1866. 784 campsites, 408 wilderness homes. A/C TV TEL (homes only). $35–$54 campsite (depending on season, location, number of people, size, and extent of hookup); $180–$215 wilderness home. AE, MC, V. Free self-parking.

This woodsy 780-acre camping resort—shaded by towering pines and cypress trees and crossed by fish-filled streams, lakes, and canals—is ideal for family vacations. Though it's a tad less central than other Disney hostelries, its abundance of on-premises facilities more than compensates. Secluded campsites offer 110/220-volt outlets, barbecue grills, picnic tables, and children's play areas. There are also wilderness homes—rustic, one-bedroom cabins with piney interiors that accommodate up to six people. These have cozy living rooms with Murphy beds, fully equipped eat-in kitchens, picnic tables, and barbecue grills. Guests here enjoy extensive recreational facilities ranging from a riding stable to a nightly campfire program hosted by Chip 'n' Dale.

Dining: The rustic log-beamed Trails End offers buffet meals, and the cozy Crockett's Tavern features Texan fare. During summer, guests enjoy a dazzling electrical water pageant from the beach, nightly at 9:45pm. And the rambunctious *Hoop-Dee-Doo Musical Revue* takes place in Pioneer Hall nightly (details in chapter 10).

Amenities: Guest-services desk, baby-sitting, boat transport (to Downtown Disney, the Magic Kingdom, and the Contemporary Resort). Comfort station in each campground area (with rest rooms, private showers, ice machines, phones, and laundry rooms), two large swimming pools, white-sand beach, horseback riding (trail rides), petting farm, pony rides, fishing, three sand volleyball courts, ballfields, tetherball, shuffleboard, bike rentals, boat rental, 1½-mile nature trail, 2.3-mile jogging path, two tennis courts, two 18-hole championship golf courses, shops, kennel, two video-game arcades.

4 "Official Hotels" in Lake Buena Vista

These hostelries, designated "official" Walt Disney World hotels, are located on and around Hotel Plaza Boulevard. Guests at these hotels enjoy many privileges (see section 2, "The Perks of Staying with Mickey" earlier in this chapter), including complimentary transportation to the Disney parks. However, these hotels are *not* on the Disney Transportation System. And the location is a big advantage—close to the Disney parks and within walking distance of Disney Village Marketplace and Crossroads shops and restaurants, as well as Downtown Disney nightlife.

One difference between "official" hotels and actual Disney resorts is that the former (with the exception of the Swan and Dolphin) generally have less relentless themes; decide for yourself if that's a plus or a minus. *Note:* You can also make reservations for all of the below-listed properties through Central Reservations Operations ☎ **407/ W-DISNEY** (934-7639); see the description of this service earlier in the chapter.

You'll find all these hotels located on the map "Walt Disney World & Lake Buena Vista Accommodations" earlier in this chapter.

EXPENSIVE

Buena Vista Palace Resort & Spa. 1900 Buena Vista Dr. (just north of Hotel Plaza Blvd.; P.O. Box 22206), Lake Buena Vista, FL 32830. ☎ **800/327-2990** or 407/827-2727. Fax 407/827-6034. www.bvp-resort.com. 1,014 units. A/C MINIBAR TV TEL. $129–$294 double; $229–$529 1- and 2-bdrm suites; range reflects view and season. Children 17 and under stay free in parents' room. AE, CB, DC, DISC, MC, V. Free self-parking; valet parking $7. From I-4 west, take Exit 27. At end of ramp, turn left. At first light, turn left into Walt Disney World Village. At first stoplight, turn right onto Buena Vista Dr. First hotel on the right.

Complete room renovations in the fall of 1997 added new luster to this already luxurious 27-acre resort. A European-style spa, added in 1996, is just one perk along with extensive boating and recreational facilities. The spacious accommodations—most with lake-view balconies or patios—are appealingly decorated and equipped with Spectravision, safes, bedroom and bathroom phones, and ceiling fans. There are also luxurious one- and two-bedroom suites with living and dining rooms and a 10th-floor concierge level. For those with sensitive systems, or a Howard Hughes inclination toward cleanliness, there are 65 eco-friendly rooms featuring nonallergenic pillows and blankets; nondyed tissue, towels, and linens; filtered water; and extra air-cleaning systems.

Dining/Diversions: Arthur's 27 (perched on the 27th floor) offers haute cuisine and panoramic park views, as well as live jazz, piano-bar entertainment, and dancing in an adjoining lounge. In the Outback Restaurant, complete with a three-story indoor waterfall, an Australian storyteller entertains during dinner; steak and seafood are featured. Character breakfasts take place in the Watercress Cafe. Other venues include pool and snack bars, a pastry shop, and the Laughing Kookaburra Good Time Bar, which offers a selection of 99 beers and nightly hosts happy-hour buffets and live bands for dancing.

Amenities: Free shuttle serves WDW, two large swimming pools, whirlpool, kiddie pool, three tennis courts, boat rental, 2- and 3-mile jogging paths, sand volleyball court, bike rental, playground, car-rental desk. Room service (24 hours), baby-sitting, guest-services desk, complimentary newspaper for crown-level guests, full business center, shops, coin-op washers/dryers, video-game arcade, counselor-supervised child-care program. The spa offers massage, herbal wraps, a fully equipped health club.

Doubletree Guest Suites. 2305 Hotel Plaza Blvd. (just west of Apopka–Vineland Rd./ Fla. 535), Lake Buena Vista, FL 32830. ☎ **800/222-8733** or 407/934-1000. Fax 407/934-1011. 229 units. A/C TV TEL. $149–$263 1-bdrm suites for up to 6; $375–$1,015 2-bdrm suites. Rates depend on view and season. Children 17 and under stay free in parents' room. AE, CB, DC, DISC, JCB, MC, V. From I-4, Exit 27, to Disney Village Marketplace. Left on Hotel Plaza Blvd. Free parking.

Entered via a cheerful, skylit atrium lobby with an aviary of tropical birds and theme-park murals, this seven-story all-suite hotel is a great choice for families. Children have their own check-in desk where they receive a free gift. The large one-bedroom suites—which can sleep up to six—are delightfully decorated and include full living rooms, dining areas, and separate bedrooms. Among your in-room amenities are a wet bar, refrigerator, coffeemaker, microwave oven, TVs with pay-movie options in the living room and bedroom, a smaller black-and-white TV in the bathroom, two phones, and a hair dryer.

Dining/Diversions: The festive Streamers serves buffet and à la carte breakfasts and dinners featuring American fare with Southwestern specialties. A bar/lounge adjoins, as does a theater where kids can watch Disney movies while mom and dad linger over coffee. Another bar serves the pool.

Amenities: Free shuttles to WDW parks. Room service, baby-sitting, guest-services desk (sells tickets and arranges transport to all nearby attractions). Large swimming pool, whirlpool, kiddie pool with fountain, two tennis courts, jogging path, volleyball, playground, car-rental desk, exercise room, shops (including a grocery), coin-op washers/dryers, video-game arcade, boat rental at nearby Disney Village Marina.

○ **Marriott's Orlando World Center.** 8701 World Center Dr. (on Fla. 536 between I-4 and Fla. 535), Orlando, FL 32821. ☎ **800/621-0638** or 407/239-4200. Fax 407/238-8777. www.marriott.com. 1,599 units. A/C MINIBAR TV TEL. $152–$259 room for up to 5 people, range reflects season; $265–$2,400 suites. AE, CB, DC, DISC, JCB, MC, V. Free self-parking; valet parking $8.

Providing the only viable competition for the Grand Cypress Resort (described later), this sprawling 230-acre resort, just 2 miles from WDW parks, is a top convention venue that also offers recreational facilities for the tourist (see the map "Orlando Area Accommodations & Dining," on page 123). These include three swimming pools (one larger than Olympic size with slides and waterfalls), eight tennis courts, and an 18-hole/par-71 Joe Lee–designed championship golf course. A grand palm-lined driveway, flanked by rolling golf greens, leads to the main building—a massive 27-story tower fronted by flower beds and fountains.

Spacious guest rooms are cheerfully decorated in pastel hues with bamboo and rattan furnishings. All have patios or balconies, extensive pay-movie options, irons and ironing boards, safes, and hair dryers. Step outside the tower and you'll find magnificently landscaped grounds, punctuated by rock gardens, shaded groves of pines and magnolias, and cascading waterfalls; swans and ducks inhabit over a dozen lakes and lagoons spanned by arched bridges.

Dining/Diversions: The luxurious Tuscany, Marriott's premier restaurant, offers northern Italian haute cuisine dinners. The Mikado Japanese Steak House is a serene setting for classic teppanyaki dinners. JW's Steakhouse serves breakfasts and lunches on a screened balcony and cozy dinners in a rustic pine interior. Allie's American Grille is a rather elegant family restaurant. Among several smaller eateries and bars are the plush Pagoda Lounge for nightly piano-bar entertainment and Champion's, a first-rate sports bar.

Amenities: Mears transportation/sightseeing desk (sells tickets to all nearby attractions, including WDW parks; also provides transport, by reservation, to WDW, other attractions, and the airport; the round-trip fare to WDW parks is $5 per day, free for children 11 and under), concierge, room service (24 hours), baby-sitting, shoe shine, complimentary newspaper weekdays, 1-hour film developing. Golf and tennis pro shops and instruction, 18-hole miniature golf course, two volleyball courts, four whirlpools, large kiddie pool, car-rental desk, unisex beauty salon, extensive business center, state-of-the-art health club, coin-op washers/dryers, shops, video-game arcade, Lollipop Lounge (a counselor-supervised child-care/activities center). Inquire as well about organized children's activities—games, movies, nature walks, and more.

Summerfield Suites Lake Buena Vista. 8751 Suiteside Dr. (off Apopka–Vineland Rd./Fla. 535), Lake Buena Vista, FL 32836. ☎ **800/833-4353** or 407/238-0777. Fax 407/238-0777. 150 units. A/C TV TEL. $169–$209 1-bedroom suites for up to 4; $199–$249 2-bedroom suites for up to 8. Range reflects season. Rates include continental breakfast. AE, CB, DC, DISC, MC, V. Free parking.

This all-suite property, offering free transport to and from the nearby Disney parks, is an excellent choice for families (see the map "International Drive Area Accommodations & Dining," on page 83). It's notable for its friendliness and immaculate accommodations. The spacious suites—in buildings surrounding a palm-fringed brick courtyard with umbrella tables, fountains, and gazebos—have fully equipped eat-in kitchens, comfortable living rooms, and a bathroom for each bedroom. Amenities include bedroom and kitchen phones (with two lines), TVs in each bedroom and in the living room (with pay-movie options), VCRs (movies can be rented), and irons and ironing boards.

Dining: Guests enjoy continental breakfast in the pleasant dining room or at umbrella tables in the courtyard; omelets and waffles may be purchased. An on-premises lobby deli (which sells light fare and liquor) also serves the pool area. Many local restaurants deliver to the hotel.

Amenities: Free shuttle to the Disney parks, plus a $35 per person round-trip shuttle to the airport and other attractions. Guest-services desk (sells tickets to WDW parks and other nearby attractions, many of them discounted), free daily newspaper, complimentary grocery shopping, baby-sitting. Large swimming pool, whirlpool, kiddie pool, car-rental desk, full business services, exercise room, coin-op washers/dryers, shops, video-game arcade.

MODERATE

Courtyard by Marriott. 1805 Hotel Plaza Blvd. (between Lake Buena Vista Dr. and Apopka–Vineland Rd./Fla. 535), Lake Buena Vista, FL 32830. ☎ **800/223-9930** or 407/828-8888. Fax 407/827-4623. www.marriott.com. 323 units. A/C TV TEL. $110–$169 double, depending on view and season. AE, CB, DC, DISC, JCB, MC, V. Free parking. From I-4, Exit 27 to Walt Disney World Village. Turn left on Hotel Plaza Blvd. On left.

The Courtyard is a moderately priced link in the Marriott chain, with lower prices achieved via limited services. But don't envision a Spartan, no-frills atmosphere. This property was recently renovated to the tune of $4.5 million, and it's looking great. The attractive, standard-sized rooms—most with balconies—have in-room safes, coffeemakers, pay-movie options, and refrigerators available on request. Kids will love in-room Nintendo.

Dining/Diversions: A full-service restaurant serves American fare at all meals and provides room service. There's also a lobby cocktail lounge, a poolside bar (in season), and an on-premises deli featuring pizza and frozen yogurt.

Amenities: Free transportation to WDW parks and attractions. The guest-services desk sells tickets and arranges transport to all nearby attractions. Two outdoor swimming pools, whirlpool, kiddie pool, boat rental at nearby Disney Village Marina, playground, car-rental desk, exercise room, shops, coin-op washers/dryers, and video-game arcade.

Grosvenor Resort. 1850 Hotel Plaza Blvd. (just east of Buena Vista Dr.), Lake Buena Vista, FL 32830. ☎ **800/624-4109** or 407/828-4444. Fax 407/828-8192. 626 units. A/C TV TEL. $99–$175 room for up to 4 people, depending on view and season. AE, CB, DC, DISC, JCB, MC, V. Free self-parking; valet parking $5. From I-4, take Exit 27 to Walt Disney World Village. Turn left.

In the moderately priced category, this is a comfortable choice with a British colonial theme and a few unique entertainment options. Occupying 13 lushly landscaped lakeside acres, it centers on a 19-story peach stucco building fronted by towering palms. The rooms are nicely decorated in an attractive resort motif and are equipped with VCRs (tapes can be rented), coffeemakers, safes, and minibars (stocked on request); refrigerators can be rented.

Dining/Diversions: Baskervilles Restaurant—with a Sherlock Holmes museum on the premises—hosts Saturday-night mystery dinner-theater and buffet breakfasts and dinners, some with Disney characters. Also here: a 24-hour food court, a pool bar, and a lounge where sporting events are aired on a large-screen TV.

Amenities: Free shuttle to WDW parks and attractions, guest-services desk (sells tickets and arranges transport to all nearby attractions), doctor on call, room service, baby-sitting, free daily newspaper. Two swimming pools, whirlpool, kiddie pool, exercise room, two tennis courts, boat rental, playground, lawn games, car-rental desk, coin-op washers/dryers, shops, video-game arcade.

Royal Plaza. 1905 Hotel Plaza Blvd. (between Buena Vista Dr. and Apopka–Vineland Rd./ Fla. 535), Lake Buena Vista, FL 32830. ☎ **800/248-7890** or 407/828-2828. Fax 407/ 827-6338. 394 units. A/C MINIBAR TV TEL. $109–$229 double, depending on view and season. AE, CB, DC, DISC, JCB, MC, V. Free self- and valet parking. From I-4, take Exit 27. Turn into Walt Disney World Village. It's the tall, pink-hued building.

The Royal Plaza recently completed a $24-million renovation and upgrade, including the refurbishment of all accommodations and public areas. Spiffy new rooms—decorated in soft resort hues with bleached oak furnishings—are equipped with VCRs (movies can be rented), safes, coffeemakers, and hair dryers. Pool-view rooms have patios or balconies. Both executive kings and concierge-level rooms, which are among the pricer choices, contain Jacuzzis (the former also offer full living rooms). Every room has a patio or balcony.

Dining/Diversions: The Verandah, a full-service restaurant, specializes in foods with a hint of the islands. Plaza Diner is a full-service family restaurant featuring American foods such as burgers, meat loaf, and daily specials. Intermission, a sports bar with a handful of big-screen televisions, offers a chance to catch that big game—whether hockey, basketball, baseball, or football. A pool bar is set up during the busy season.

Amenities: Free shuttle service to Disney parks. Room service, guest-services desk (sells tickets and arranges transport to all nearby attractions), baby-sitting, foreign-currency exchange. Extensive meeting facilities. Large L-shaped swimming pool, whirlpool, four tennis courts, boat rental, sauna, coin-op washers/dryers, shops, video-game arcade.

Travelodge Hotel. 2000 Hotel Plaza Blvd. (between Buena Vista Dr. and Apopka–Vineland Rd./Fla. 535), Lake Buena Vista, FL 32830. ☎ **800/348-3765** or 407/828-2424. Fax 407/828-8933. www.travelodge.com. 325 units. A/C MINIBAR TV TEL. $103–$179 room for up to 4 people, depending on room size and season. Inquire about packages. AE, CB, DC, DISC, JCB, M, V. Free parking. From I-4, take Exit 27. Go to Walt Disney World Village. Turn left onto Hotel Plaza Blvd. Across from the Doubletree hotel.

This 12-acre lakefront hostelry is spiffy and immaculate, with more upscale rooms and public areas than you might expect at a Travelodge. The rates are also higher than the Travelodge norm but represent good value for your money. The reason: This is the company's flagship hotel. Designed to resemble a Barbados plantation manor house, it has a Caribbean-resort ambience, enhanced by tropical foliage and bright floral-print fabrics. The rooms are particularly inviting, with light bleached-wood furnishings and lovely framed botanical prints and floral friezes. Furnished balconies overlook Lake Buena Vista. In-room perks include Spectravision movies, Nintendo, coffeemakers, safes, hair dryers, and free local phone calls.

Dining/Diversions: Traders, with a wall of windows facing a wooded area, is open for breakfast and steak and seafood dinners. On the 18th floor, Toppers offers magnificent views of Lake Buena Vista, as well as dancing, music videos, pool tables, and dart boards; it's a great vantage point for watching the nightly laser shows and fireworks. There's also a cocktail bar and a casual self-service eatery.

Amenities: Free shuttle to the Disney parks. Room service, baby-sitting, guest-services desk (sells tickets and arranges transport to all nearby attractions), free newspaper weekdays. Large swimming pool, kiddie pool, boat rental, playground, car-rental desk, coin-op washers/dryers, shops, video-game arcade.

5 Other Lake Buena Vista–Area Hotels

All of the below-listed hotels are within a few minutes' drive of WDW parks, in the midst of the "official" hotels. They offer the location, but not the privileges, of staying at an official hotel.

VERY EXPENSIVE

✪ **Hyatt Regency Grand Cypress Resort.** One Grand Cypress Blvd. (off State Rd. 535), Orlando, FL 32836. ☎ **800/233-1234** or 407/239-1234; **800/835-7377** or 407/239-4700 for villas. Fax 407/239-3800, or 407/239-7219 for villas. 750 units, 146 villas. A/C MINIBAR TV TEL. $185–$310 room for up to 5; $305–$410 Regency Club double; $190–$1,400 villas. AE, CB, DC, DISC, JCB, MC, V. Free self-parking; valet parking $9. I-4 Exit 27, right on County Rd. 535, left at second traffic light onto S.R. 535. Two lights on right.

Although only a mile from WDW, this 1,500-acre retreat, ablaze with bougainvillea and hibiscus, is a world away (see the map "Walt Disney World & Lake Buena Vista Accommodations," earlier in this chapter). A romantic getaway, an award-winning golf course, a top-notch equestrian center, and a major renovation in 1997 put this Hyatt resort in a class by itself. Spacious rooms are a welcome respite from the crowded parks—that's if you really find a need to leave. Topping the list of outstanding facilities is a half-acre swimming pool spanned by a rope bridge and flowing through rock grottoes (with 12 waterfalls and 2 steep water slides). Relax on the white-sand beach or play on 12 tennis courts or a Jack Nicklaus–designed golf course.

Deluxe accommodations with wicker furnishings evoke the Southern luxury of a bygone era. The Regency Club, a concierge level, comprises two floors. And especially lavish are the Mediterranean-style Villas of Grand Cypress, all with patios, kitchens, living rooms, and dining rooms; some have working fireplaces and whirlpool baths.

Dining/Diversions: Casual yet elegant, Hemingway's serves Florida seafood at lunch and dinner. The lodgelike Black Swan, overlooking the golf course, features haute American/continental dinners. Similar fare is offered at the plush La Coquina, where a harpist entertains at dinner and the Sunday brunches are exquisite. Other venues include the White Horse Saloon, for prime rib dinners and country music; Trellises, a bar/lounge where a jazz ensemble entertains evenings; the lovely lake-view Cascade, serving American fare at all meals, plus Japanese breakfasts; and several pool-side and snack bars.

Amenities: Free transportation around grounds and to all major attractions except for WDW, hourly shuttle to all WDW parks (round-trip fare $6 per day), concierge (sells tickets to WDW parks and other nearby attractions), room service (24 hours), baby-sitting, Mears airport shuttle. Golf and tennis instruction and pro shops (the golf school here has been called one of the finest in the country); 45-acre Audubon nature walk; 4.7-mile jogging path; and racquetball, volleyball, and shuffleboard courts. Playground, car-rental desk, unisex beauty salon, full business center, state-of-the-art health club, shops, helicopter landing pad, video-game arcade, counselor-supervised child-care center/Camp Hyatt activity center.

MODERATE

✪ **Residence Inn by Marriott.** 8800 Meadow Creek Dr. (just off Fla. 535 between Fla. 536 and I-4), Orlando, FL 32821. ☎ **800/331-3131** or 407/239-7700. Fax 407/239-7605. 688 units. A/C TV TEL. $149–$219 suites; range reflects season. Rates include full breakfast. AE, CB, DC, DISC, JCB, MC, V. Free parking.

This delightful all-suite hostelry occupies 50 acres, alternating wooded grounds with neatly manicured lawns, duck-inhabited ponds, fountains, and flower beds (see the map "International Drive Area Accommodations & Dining," on page 83). Guests, up to four in a single suite and up to six in a double, enjoy a serene environment offering the seclusion and safety of a private community. They can also avail themselves of the extensive facilities at the adjoining Marriott Orlando World Center (see details earlier) with room-charge privileges. The tastefully decorated accommodations—with fully equipped eat-in kitchens, private balconies or patios, and large living rooms—are equipped with Spectravision, VCRs (tapes can be rented), two phones (kitchen and bedroom), ceiling fans, and safes. The two-bedroom units have two bathrooms.

Dining: A full breakfast is available in the gatehouse each morning, a Pizza Hut is on the premises, and local restaurants deliver food.

Amenities: Guest-services desk (sells tickets and provides transport to all nearby theme parks and attractions; round-trip to WDW parks is $8), baby-sitting, complimentary daily newspaper, next-day film developing, free food-shopping service, Mears airport shuttle. Three large swimming pools, two whirlpools, sports court (basketball, badminton, volleyball, paddle tennis, shuffleboard), tennis court, playground, coin-op washers/dryers, shops, two video-game arcades.

✪ **Holiday Inn Sunspree Resort Lake Buena Vista.** 13351 Fla. 535 (between Fla. 536 and I-4), Lake Buena Vista, FL 32821. ☎ **800/FON-MAXX** or 407/239-4500. Fax 407/239-7713. 507 units. A/C TV TEL. $89–$129 for up to 4 people, depending on season. AE, CB, DC, DISC, JCB, MC, V. Free parking.

About a mile from the Disney parks, this Holiday Inn offers the chain's "no surprises" dependability, while catering to children in a big way (see the map "Orlando Area Accommodations & Dining," on page 123). Kids "check in" at their own pint-size desk; receive a free fun bag containing a video-game token coupon, a lollipop, and a small gift; and get a personal welcome from animated raccoon mascots, Max and Maxine. Camp Holiday activities—magic shows, clowns, sing-alongs, arts and crafts, and much more—are available at a minimal charge for kids ages 2 to 12. And parents can arrange (by reservation) for Max to come tuck a child into bed. Pretty rooms have kitchenettes with refrigerators, microwave ovens, and coffeemakers. And if you're renting a second room for the children, "kidsuites" here—themed as igloos, space capsules, Noah's Ark, and others—sleep up to three. Amenities include VCRs (tapes can be rented), hair dryers, and safes.

Dining: Maxine's serves all meals, including steak and seafood dinners. Max's Funtime Parlor offers nightly bingo and karaoke; it also airs sporting events on a large-screen TV. Kids 12 and under eat all meals free, either in a hotel restaurant with parents or in Kid's Kottage, a cheerful facility where movies and cartoons are shown and dinner includes a make-your-own sundae bar.

Amenities: Guest-services desk (sells tickets to all nearby attractions, including WDW parks), free scheduled transport to WDW parks (there's a charge for transport to other nearby attractions). Large swimming pool, two whirlpools, kiddie pool, playground, fitness center, coin-op washers/dryers, shops, car rental, video arcade, Camp Holiday (a counselor-supervised child-care/activity center for ages 2 to 12). Room service.

Riu Orlando Hotel. 8688 Palm Pkwy. (between Fla. 535 and I-4), Lake Buena Vista, FL 32830. ☎ **407/239-8500.** Fax 407/239-8591. 167 units. A/C TV TEL. $80–$175 double, depending on season. Children 17 and under stay free in parents' room. AE, CB, DC, DISC, OPT, MC, V. Free self-parking.

Taken over by new management in 1997, this six-story property still has a location on a pleasant, tree-lined street and overlooks a lake out back—a big plus. The Crossroads

---

⊕ Family-Friendly Hotels

Days Inns at 4104 and 4125 W. Irlo Bronson Memorial Hwy. *(see p. 78)*. Good basic service and a central location make these good bets for families. There is a swimming pool on the property, but, more importantly, there are restaurants, shops, and movie theaters within walking distance.

Disney-Owned Resorts & Official Hotels *(see pp. 58–70)*   These offer many advantages for kids, including proximity to Walt Disney World parks, complimentary transportation between the hotel and the parks, and reduced-price children's menus and Disney character appearances in hotel restaurants. Extensive facilities might include lakefront beaches, boating, waterskiing, bike rentals, playgrounds, video-game arcades, swimming pools with waterfalls and slides, and/or organized children's activities.

Disney's Fort Wilderness Resort and Campground *(see p. 70)*   All of the above perks and more are offered here, including nightly campfire programs with Chip 'n' Dale, trail rides, pony rides, and a petting farm, plus you get to go camping.

Residence Inns *(see pp. 85)*   They not only have swimming pools, children's playgrounds, and other recreational facilities but also have accommodations with fully equipped kitchens—a potential money-saver for families. And rates include breakfast.

Holiday Inn Sunspree Resort Lake Buena Vista *(see p. 76)*   This Holiday Inn has a special check-in desk for kids and on-premises mascots to welcome them. Rooms are equipped with kitchenettes, and themed "kidsuites" are available. Kids under 12 eat free in their own restaurant, where movies and cartoons are shown. Numerous organized children's activities are free.

Shopping Center and Walt Disney World Village Marketplace put dozens of shops, services, and restaurants within easy walking distance. There are free shuttles to all the major attractions, and the in-room coffeemakers are a nice touch and a plus for families. The rooms have cable, Nintendo, hair dryers, irons and ironing boards.

Dining: The Garden Café, serving American fare at breakfast and dinner, has an outdoor poolside seating area and an adjoining bar/lounge.

Amenities: Room service, baby-sitting, and a complimentary daily newspaper are available. The guest-services desk sells tickets (many of them discounted) and arranges transport to all nearby attractions. On the premises are a nice-size swimming pool and whirlpool, coin-op washers/dryers, an exercise room, a business center, and a small video-game arcade.

INEXPENSIVE

Hampton Inn, Orlando Disney Maingate. 3000 Maingate Lane, Kissimmee, FL 34747. ☎ **800/426-7866** or 407/396-6300. Fax 407/396-8989. www.hamptoninn.com. 118 units. A/C TV TEL. $69–$99 double. AE, MC, DISC, V. From I-4 take Exit 25B to U.S. 192 west for about 2 miles. Turn right on Maingate Lane.

Since this is one of the newer low-cost hotels in the Disney World area, rooms show none of the wear of some older properties. The property is clean and nicely, if simply, landscaped. Although the rooms are only average in size, there are connecting rooms and cribs available. Those, along with a coin-operated laundry, make this a good location for a larger family or several families traveling together. Another plus is the free continental breakfast buffet, a pool, and a car rental desk.

6 Places to Stay in the U.S. 192/Kissimmee Area

This very American stretch of highway, dotted with fast-food eateries, isn't what you'd call scenic, but it does contain many inexpensive hotels and motels within 1 to 8 miles of Walt Disney World parks. Almost all provide, or can arrange, for shuttle service to WDW and other attractions. The cost usually runs from $10 to $14 per person. New to this stretch of highway are markers, about 20 feet tall, along the side of the road. Aptly tagged with the word "Marker" and a number, they are a new effort to help tourists find their way along this stretch of road.

You'll find all the places described here on the map "Kissimmee Area Accommodations" in this section.

MODERATE

Comfort Inn Maingate. 7571 W. Irlo Bronson Memorial Hwy. (U.S. 192; between Reedy Creek Blvd. and Sherbeth Rd., markers 15 and 16), Kissimmee, FL 34747. ☎ **800/221-2222** or 407/396-7500. 225 units. AC TV TEL. $69–$199 double. Just 6 miles from WDW parks, and 7 miles from Universal Studios.

Interiors are recently refurbished and include refrigerators, microwaves, and sleep sofas. The rooms are a little small but large enough for a family to be comfortable.

INEXPENSIVE

In addition to the accommodations described here, there are scores of other inexpensive but perfectly serviceable motels within a few miles of the WDW parks. All have swimming pools and arrange transportation to the Disney parks for a fee. Many sell tickets to attractions, but there have been problems with low prices truly being too good to be true. Tourists end up at the gate without a valid ticket. Stick to ordering tickets through the parks themselves.

Days Inn. 4104 and 4125 W. Irlo Bronson Memorial Hwy. (U.S. 192; at Hoagland Blvd. N., markers 15 and 16), Kissimmee, FL 34741. ☎ **800/647-0010,** 800/DAYS-INN, or 407/846-4714. Fax 407/932-2699. 220 units. A/C TV TEL. $39–$59 room for up to 4, depending on season; $37–$63 efficiency; $55–$75 Jacuzzi room (for 1 or 2 people). Rates include continental breakfast. Rates may be higher during major events. AE, CB, DC, DISC, MC, V. Free parking.

Offering good value for your hotel dollar, these two Days Inns—on either side of U.S. 192—share facilities, including two swimming pools, coin-op washers and dryers, and a video-game arcade. Several restaurants (which deliver food), a large shopping mall with a 12-theater movie house, and a supermarket are within close walking distance.

The rooms at both locations are clean and attractive standard motel units. The best bets are the efficiency units with fully equipped kitchenettes at no. 4104. The Jacuzzi rooms are at no. 4125 and also include a refrigerator and a microwave oven. All accommodations offer pay-movie options and in-room safes, and both locations serve free coffee, juice, and doughnuts in their lobbies each morning. The guest services desk at no. 4104 sells tickets (many of them discounted) and arranges transport to all nearby attractions, including WDW parks. A big plus: Round-trip transport to WDW parks is free. Airport transfers can be arranged.

Factoid

U.S. 192 is also known as W. Irlo Bronson Memorial Highway and eventually turns into Vine Street.

Kissimmee Area Accommodations

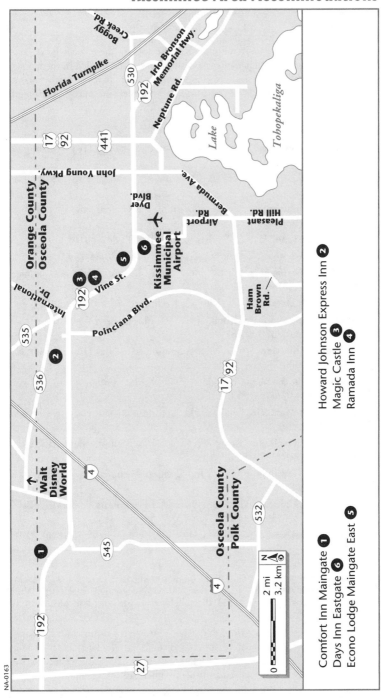

Comfort Inn Maingate ①
Days Inn Eastgate ⑥
Econo Lodge Maingate East ⑤

Howard Johnson Express Inn ②
Magic Castle ③
Ramada Inn ④

NA-0163

So I Didn't Book a Room...

If you're looking for a basic room, you might also try these chain hotels and motels. They are all moderate or inexpensive in price and located in the budget motel corridors of Kissimmee/U.S. 192 or International Drive, all relatively convenient to the attractions. While we can't vouch for these personally, their brand names generally mean reliability:

In Kissimmee

Best Western Eastgate, 5565 W. Irlo Bronson Memorial Hwy., Kissimmee (☎ **407/396-0707**).

Best Western Kissimmee, 2261 E. Irlo Bronson Memorial Hwy., Kissimmee (☎ **407/846-2221**).

Best Western Maingate, 8600 W. Irlo Bronson Memorial Hwy., Kissimmee (☎ **407/396-0100**).

Budget Inn East, 307 E. Vine St., Kissimmee (☎ **407/847-8010**).

Budget Inn West, 4686 W. Vine St., Kissimmee (☎ **407/846-1547**).

Comfort Inn Maingate, 7571 W. Irlo Bronson Memorial Hwy., Kissimmee (☎ **407/396-7500**).

Comfort Suites Hotel, 4018 W. Vine St., Kissimmee (☎ **407/870-2000**).

Comfort Suites Maingate Hotel, 7888 W. Irlo Bronson Memorial Hwy., Kissimmee (☎ **407/390-9888**).

Courtyard by Marriott, 7675 W. Irlo Bronson Memorial Hwy., Kissimmee (☎ **407/396-4000**).

Days Inn East of the Magic Kingdom, 5840 W. Irlo Bronson Memorial Hwy., Kissimmee (☎ **407/396-7969**).

Days Inn West-Maingate, 7980 W. Irlo Bronson Memorial Hwy., Kissimmee (☎ **407/396-1000**).

Doubletree Guest Suites Resort, 4787 W. Irlo Bronson Memorial Hwy., Kissimmee (☎ **407/397-0555**).

Econo Lodge Hawaiian, 7514 W. Irlo Bronson Memorial Hwy., Kissimmee (☎ **407/396-2000**).

Econo Lodge Maingate Central, 4985 W. Irlo Bronson Memorial Hwy., Kissimmee (☎ **407/396-4343**).

Holiday Inn Kissimmee, 2009 W. U.S. Hwy. 192, Kissimmee (☎ **407/826-2713**).

Econo Lodge Maingate East. 4311 W. Irlo Bronson Memorial Hwy. (U.S. 192), Kissimmee, FL 34756. ☎ **800/ENJOY-FL** or 407/396-7100. www.enjoyfloridahotels. A/C TV TEL. $49.95–$54.95. From 1-4, take exit 25A; the motel is across the street from Medieval Times, at marker 15.

This property is set well back from the highway to prevent disturbance from traffic noise (although ask for a room away from the balconies). A new lobby has been added, but the same standard of service and cleanliness continues. A good bargain. Free shuttles to WDW parks. Transportation available to other parks. Heated swimming pool.

Howard Johnson Express Inn. 4836 W. Irlo Bronson Hwy. (U.S. 192), Kissimmee, FL 34746. ☎ **800/952-5464** or 407/396-4762. Fax 407/396-4866. 131 units. A/C TV TEL. $39.95–$66 double. Free parking. Take 1-4 to Exit 25A, 3½ miles on right, between markers 11 and 12.

Howard Johnson, 4643 W. Irlo Bronson Memorial Hwy., Kissimmee (☎ **407/396-1340**).

Motel 6, 7455 W. Irlo Bronson Memorial Hwy., Kissimmee (☎ **407/396-6422**).

Motel 6, 5731 W. Irlo Bronson Memorial Hwy., Kissimmee (☎ **407/ 396-6333**).

Quality Inn on Lake Cecile, 4944 W. Irlo Bronson Memorial Hwy., Kissimmee (☎ **407/396-4455**).

Quality Suites Maingate East, 5876 W. Irlo Bronson Memorial Hwy., Kissimmee (☎ **407/396-4455**).

Ramada Limited, 5055 W. Irlo Bronson Memorial Hwy. (☎ **407/ 396-2212**).

Ramada Plaza Hotel Gateway, 7370 W. Hwy. 192, Kissimmee (☎ **407/ 396-4400**).

In the International Drive Area

Best Western Plaza International, 8738 International Dr., Orlando (☎ **407/345-8195**).

Days Inn, 9990 International Dr., Orlando (☎ **407/352-8700**).

Days Inn, 7200 International Dr., Orlando (☎ **407/351-1200**).

Days Inn/East of Universal Studios, 5827 Caravan Ct., Orlando (☎ **407/ 351-3800**).

Econo Lodge International Dr., 5859 American Way, Orlando (☎ **407/ 345-8880**).

Holiday Inn Express International Dr., 6323 International Dr., Orlando (☎ **407/351-4430**).

Holiday Inn International Drive Resort, 6515 International Dr., Orlando (☎ **407/351-3500**).

Radisson Barcelo Hotel Orlando–International Dr., 8444 International Dr., Orlando (☎ **407/345-0505**).

Ramada Hotel Resort Florida Center, 7400 International Dr., Orlando (☎ **407/351-8400**).

Roadway Inn International, 6327 International Dr., Orlando (☎ **407/ 351-4444**).

As a lakefront property, this is one of the more scenic Kissimmee offerings. You can have picnics by the lake or rent jet skis for about $60 an hour. The pink-and-blue buildings contain clean, comfortable rooms; and some of the suites contain an in-room Jacuzzi, microwave oven, and refrigerator. There is a large, heated swimming pool and a video game room. Another plus is a free shuttle to the WDW parks. Transportation to other attractions can be arranged for a fee.

Magic Castle. 5055 W. Irlo Bronson Memorial Hwy. (U.S. 192), Kissimmee, FL 34746. ☎ **800/446-5669** or 407/396-2212. Fax 407/396-0253. 107 units. A/C TV TEL. $35.95–$61.95 room for up to 4, depending on season. Rates include continental breakfast. AE, DC, DISC, MC, V. Free self-parking. From I-4, take Exit 25A, near marker 11; the motel is about 3½ miles on the left, next to the Olive Garden.

The owner of this property has discontinued his affiliation with Ramada Inn, but this three-story stucco building continues to provide adequate accommodations at a good price. The standard-sized rooms are equipped with cable TV (with Disney Channel and HBO movies), safes, and refrigerators.

Facilities include an outdoor swimming pool and coin-op washers/dryers. Continental breakfast is served in the lobby each morning. Shuttle service to WDW parks is available for $9 per person, round-trip. Service to other parks will cost about $12 or $14. Pets are accepted ($6 per night).

✪ **Ramada Inn.** 4559 W. Irlo Bronson Memorial Hwy. (U.S. 192), Kissimmee, FL 34746. ☎ **800/544-5712** or 407/396-1212. Fax 407/396-7926. 114 units. A/C TV TEL. $29.95–$59.95 for up to 4; range reflects season. AE, DC, DISC, MC, V. Free self-parking. From I-4, between markers 13 and 14, take Exit 25A; the motel is about 5 miles on left, across from Jungleland.

This Ramada offers standard motel rooms, which are a little on the small side, with cable TV and safes; refrigerators and microwaves are available on request for $8 a night. Facilities include coin-op washers/dryers, a swimming pool, a children's playground, and picnic tables. The 1950s-style Hollywood Diner, which has an adjoining bar/lounge, serves American fare at all meals. Shuttle service to WDW parks is available for $10 per person, round-trip. Pets are accepted ($6 per night). Children stay and eat free.

7 Places to Stay in the International Drive Area

The hotels and resorts listed here are 7 to 10 miles north of the Walt Disney World parks (a quick freeway trip) and close to Universal Studios Florida and Sea World. Though you won't get away from rambunctious kids anywhere in this town, International Drive hostelries do tend to be more adult-oriented. You'll find all these places located on the map "International Drive Area Accommodations & Dining" in this section.

VERY EXPENSIVE

✪ **Peabody Orlando.** 9801 International Dr. (between the Bee Line Expwy. and Sand Lake Rd.), Orlando, FL 32819. ☎ **800/PEABODY** (732-3639) or 407/352-4000. www. peabody-orlando.com. Fax 407/351-0073. 891 units. A/C MINIBAR TV TEL. $240–$300 for up to 3 people; $450–$1,350 suites. Children 17 and under stay free in parents' room. Inquire about packages and holiday/summer discounts and senior rate for those over 50. AE, CB, DC, DISC, JCB, MC, V. Free self-parking; valet parking $7.

Okay, let's get the pun out of the way: This property is just ducky, especially those famous avian ambassadors who make their daily march of the mallards through the lobby to John Philip Sousa. There may be a little disarray until 2000, since a second 700-room tower is under construction. But that may translate into better deals. The Peabody's hallmark ambience of sophistication, which extends to its top-rated restaurants, is not found anywhere else and will surely survive the jackhammers.

The luxurious rooms have handsome bamboo and bleached-wood furnishings, two phones, Spectravision, and laser-disc movie setups (there's a vast video library). The bathrooms have cosmetic lights, fine European toiletries, hair dryer, and small TV. The concierge-level Peabody Club occupies the top three floors. Seniors should note the over-50 prices, compensation for wrinkles indeed.

Dining/Diversions: Dux, the Peabody's elegant signature restaurant, and the casual 24-hour B-Line Diner are detailed in chapter 6. Capriccio, for sophisticated Italian fare, is open for dinner and for champagne Sunday brunches. Combos play jazz, blues,

International Drive Area Accommodations & Dining

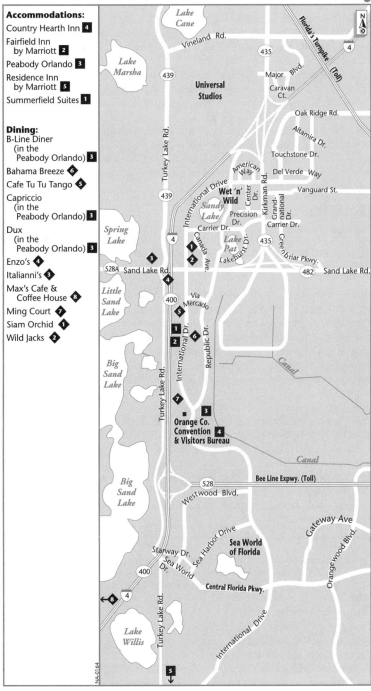

Accommodations:

Country Hearth Inn **4**

Fairfield Inn by Marriott **2**

Peabody Orlando **3**

Residence Inn by Marriott **5**

Summerfield Suites **1**

Dining:

B-Line Diner (in the Peabody Orlando) **3**

Bahama Breeze **6**

Cafe Tu Tu Tango **5**

Capriccio (in the Peabody Orlando) **3**

Dux (in the Peabody Orlando) **3**

Enzo's **4**

Italianni's **3**

Max's Cafe & Coffee House **8**

Ming Court **7**

Siam Orchid **1**

Wild Jacks **2**

and show tunes in the atrium Lobby Bar nightly. The lobby is the setting for exquisite afternoon English teas on weekdays. Sporting events are aired in the cozy duck-themed Mallards Lounge. And alfresco jazz concerts take place on the fourth-floor recreation level in the spring and fall.

Amenities: Concierge (7am to 11pm), room service (24 hours), baby-sitting, nightly bed turndown on request, free daily newspaper, transport between the hotel and all WDW parks throughout the day (unlimited daily round-trips cost $6), Mears transportation/sightseeing desk (sells tickets to all nearby attractions, including WDW parks and dinner shows; also provides transport, by reservation, to attractions and the airport). Olympic-length swimming pool, outdoor whirlpool, kiddie pool, four tennis courts, 7-mile jogging path, car-rental desk, Delta Airlines desk, full-service unisex salon, business center, state-of-the-art health club, shops, video-game arcade, golf privileges at four nearby courses.

EXPENSIVE

Summerfield Suites. 8480 International Dr. (between the Bee Line Expwy. and Sand Lake Rd.), Orlando, FL 32819. ☎ **800/833-4353** or 407/352-2400. Fax 407/238-0778. 146 units. A/C TV TEL. $159–$199 1-bedroom suites for up to 4; $179–$239 2-bedroom suites for up to 8. Range reflects room size and season. Rates include continental breakfast. AE, CB, DC, DISC, MC, V. Free parking.

This delightful hotel—with potted palms on open-air balconies creating a welcoming resort ambience—is built around a nicely landscaped central courtyard. Like its sibling property in Lake Buena Vista, it's notably friendly and well run. The spacious, neat-as-a-pin suites, very attractively decorated, contain fully equipped eat-in kitchens, comfortable living rooms, and large dressing areas. All offer irons and ironing boards, phones in each bedroom and kitchen, and satellite TVs (with pay-movie options) in each bedroom and living room (the latter with a VCR; rent movies downstairs).

Dining: An extensive continental buffet breakfast is served in a charming dining room (waffles and omelets can be purchased), and the cozy lobby bar is a popular gathering place in the evenings. Local restaurants deliver food to the premises.

Amenities: Concierge/tour desk (sells tickets to WDW parks and other nearby attractions), daily newspaper delivery, transport between the hotel and all WDW parks (round-trip fare is $7), shuttle available to the airport and nearby attractions, complimentary grocery shopping. Nice-size swimming pool, whirlpool, kiddie pool, car-rental desk, business services, exercise room, coin-op washers/dryers, 24-hour shop, video-game arcade.

MODERATE

Country Hearth Inn. 9861 International Dr. (between Bee Line Expwy. and Sand Lake Rd.), Orlando, FL 32819. ☎ **800/447-1890** or 407/352-0008. Fax 407/352-5449. 150 units. A/C TV TEL. $59–$139 double, depending on view and season. Extra person $10. Children under 18 stay free in parents' room. Rates include continental breakfast. AE, CB, DC, DISC, MC, V. Free self-parking.

Though it doesn't offer much in the way of resort facilities, the Country Hearth Inn's low rates, great location, and very pretty rooms and restaurant—not to mention wine-and-cheese receptions for guests several times a week—make this an appealing choice. Centered on a white-trimmed, pale-peach octagonal building crowned by a windowed cupola, the inn evokes 19th-century Florida—the leisurely era of riverboat travel and gracious plantations. Ceiling fans whir slowly over verandas and balconies furnished with wicker rocking chairs, and an inviting landscaped courtyard with neat lawns and flower beds encompasses a large free-form swimming pool backed by verdant woodlands and a wide canal. Charming guest rooms, furnished in handsome maple or mahogany pieces, are adorned with floral friezes and 19th-century folk art. French doors open onto patios, balconies, or courtyards, and bathrooms have art-nouveau lighting fixtures. In-room amenities include cable TVs (with HBO and Spectravision movie options), coffeemakers, phones with modem jacks, wood-bladed chandelier ceiling fans, safes, and small refrigerators. Larger deluxe rooms offer sleeper sofas, microwave ovens, and hair dryers.

Dining: The elegant Country Parlor, in the balustraded Victorian lobby, serves moderately priced American fare at all meals; a pianist entertains at Sunday champagne brunches. Equally turn-of-the-century in decor is the Front Porch Lounge, a popular gathering spot for locals. It features happy-hour buffets weekdays from 5:30 to 7pm.

Amenities: Room service, guest-services desk (sells tickets, many of them discounted, and arranges transport to all nearby attractions, including WDW parks), baby-sitting, Mears airport shuttle. Round-trip fare to WDW parks is $10.

Residence Inn by Marriott. 7975 Canada Ave. (just off Sand Lake Rd., a block east of International Dr.), Orlando, FL 32819. ☎ **800/227-3978** or 407/345-0117. Fax 407/352-2689. www.marriott.com. 176 units. A/C TV TEL. $135–$189 for up to 8. Rates include extended continental breakfast. AE, DC, DISC, MC, V. Free parking.

Marriott's Residence Inns were designed to offer home-away-from-home comfort for traveling business people, but the concept also works well for families. The accommodations buildings are surrounded by well-tended lawns, shrubs, and beds of geraniums, and the handsomely decorated suites offer full eat-in kitchens and comfortable living-room areas. All but studio doubles have wood-burning fireplaces, and two-bedroom penthouses (great for families) have full bathrooms upstairs and down. Amenities include irons, ironing boards, and safes.

Dining: The comfortably furnished gatehouse is the setting for an extended continental breakfast daily, and complimentary beer, wine, and hors d'oeuvres Monday to Thursday from 5:30 to 7pm. Local restaurants deliver food (there are menus in each room).

Amenities: Guest-services desk (sells tickets—most of them discounted—and provides transport to all nearby theme parks and attractions), complimentary daily newspaper, free food-shopping service (microwave dinners are sold in the lobby), Mears airport shuttle. Free shuttle to WDW parks. Large swimming pool, whirlpool, basketball court, sand volleyball court, coin-op washers/dryers, food/sundries shop, picnic tables, barbecue grills; free use of nearby health club.

INEXPENSIVE

Fairfield Inn by Marriott. 8342 Jamaican Court (off International Dr. between the Bee Line Expwy. and Sand Lake Rd.), Orlando, FL 32819. ☎ **800/228-2800** or 407/363-1944. Fax 407/363-1944. www.marriott.com 134 units. A/C TV TEL. $45–$79 room for up to 4; range reflects season. Rates include continental breakfast. AE, CB, DC, DISC, JCB, MC, V. Free parking. From I-4 take Exit 29 (Sand Lake Rd.), go east 1 block, turn right on International Drive. Turn right on Jamaican Court. The hotel is on the right.

I love this inn's quiet and safe location in a secluded area off International Drive. It nestles in Jamaican Court, a neatly landscaped complex of hotels and restaurants (that means a number of places are within walking distance). The spiffy-looking rooms offer cable TV with HBO, and the phones are equipped with 25-foot cords and modem jacks. Daily newspapers and local calls are free, as is the continental breakfast served in the lobby each morning.

The guest-services desk sells tickets (most of them discounted) and can arrange transport to all nearby theme parks and attractions and the airport; round-trip to WDW parks is $10. A small outdoor swimming pool and video-game room are on the premises, and the lobby has a microwave oven for guest use.

Amenities: Three swimming pools (one quite large), two kiddie pools, whirlpool, four tennis courts, sand volleyball court, playground, business center, exercise room, 1.4-mile jogging trail, coin-op washers/dryers, car-rental desk, unisex hair salon, shops, two video-game arcades.

8 At the Airport

Hyatt Regency Orlando International Airport. 9300 Airport Blvd., Orlando, FL 32827. ☎ **800/233-1234** or 407/825-1234. Fax 407/856-1672. 469 units. A/C TV TEL. $205 double; $225–$450 suites. Children under 18 stay free in parents' room. AE, CB, DC, DISC, JCB, MC, V. Self-parking $8; valet parking $11.

If you have to catch an early-morning flight out of Orlando, treat yourself to a night at this gorgeous hotel right in the airport's main terminal. It's luxurious from the moment you set foot in the plush, 40,000-square-foot palm court atrium lobby. Large, resort-style rooms—off balconies bordered by planters of bougainvillea or philodendrons—are attractively decorated and equipped with large desks, three phones (desk, bedside, and bathroom), cable TVs (with channels for Spectravision movie, tourism information, and flight arrival/departure), full-size ironing boards/irons, and hair dryers. Rooms are soundproof, so you don't hear planes taking off and landing.

Dining/Diversions: The elegant Hemisphere Restaurant serves sophisticated American fare at lunch and northern Italian specialties at dinner; a pianist entertains weekend nights. McCoy's Bar & Grill centers on a display kitchen with an oak-burning pizza oven. You can also avail yourself of all the airport eateries, including a food court.

Amenities: 24-hour concierge/room service, shoe shine, car rental, baby-sitting, full business center, currency exchange. Airport shopping mall, airline desks, unisex hair salon, swimming pool, sundeck, fully equipped health club, travel agency, business center, game rooms, and shopping arcade.

9 Places to Stay Elsewhere in Orlando

There are two good reasons to stay away from the all the hustle and hassle of the attractions: crowds and money.

If you are traveling in a peak season—during the summer or around Christmas— you will find yourself elbow to elbow with the sweating masses almost everywhere you go. Those theme park crowds spill over into the shops, the restaurants, even the bath-rooms, making it difficult to get a few moments of quiet when you are not in your room. (If you are traveling with kids, not even then.) The world can feel pretty small after several days of very close encounters. Plus, the nearer to the attractions, the higher the cost of just about everything from rooms to soda. The difference might be a nickel here and 50 cents there, but those pennies can add up to serious dollars if you are traveling with your family.

The disadvantages? Well, you will have to travel along I-4 to get back and forth from the parks. But if you travel before 7am or after 10am in the morning, and after 6pm in the evening, you will be able to make the trip in about 20 minutes and encounter minimal traffic congestion. If you have a family, though, it will also be harder to escape back to your hotel's pool for an afternoon swim or to your room for a nap.

The biggest factor in determining whether to stay in or near the parks is how you envision your vacation. If you're the kind of person who explores the Disney parks all day and then spends the night dancing at Pleasure Island, it makes more sense to stay on Disney property or at least close by. If you would like to get away from it all, take a quite stroll along a city sidewalk, see a museum, or experience life in a real American city, try staying in downtown Orlando or Winter Park.

You'll find all the places described here on the map "Orlando Area Accommodations & Dining" in chapter 6, page 123.

IN ORLANDO

All of the following fall within the "Moderate" price category.

The Courtyard at Lake Lucerne. 211 N. Lucerne Circle E., Orlando, FL 32801. ☎ **800/444-5289** or 407/648-5188. Fax 407/246-1368. 24 units. A/C TV TEL. $69 double; $96–$165 suites. Rates include continental breakfast. AE, DC, MC, V. Free self-parking. Take Orange Ave. south, immediately following City Hall (domed building with fountains and glass sculpture) and turn left onto Anderson. After two lights, at Delaney Ave., turn right. Take first right onto Lucerne Circle N. Be aware of one-way streets. Follow brown, "historic inn" signs.

Orlando literally grew around this B&B, which stands incongruously amid a tangle of interstate ramps. Each unit in the three distinct buildings that make up the property was designed by a different artist or decorator. With wide porches and ceiling fans, the I. W. Phillips House (1916) creates an antebellum splendor that never actually flourished this far south. Suites at the Phillips overlook a shared courtyard insulated from the urban hum by old-growth trees. A fountain's gentle trickle is the only sound while strolling the brick walkways. The solitude isn't as complete in the front rooms of Norment–Perry. Traffic sounds there are minimal but audible.

Since opening in 1986, the Courtyard has served mostly business VIPs and locals on weekend getaways. With few amenities, it's a place for simple, private pleasures. Downtown's most famous entertainment district, Church Street Station, is less than 6 blocks north. Walk or take a cab to begin the night, but the urban setting makes riding home the safest choice. The Courtyard is undergoing an expansion as this book goes to press, so more rooms should be available in the future.

Amenities: The staff fulfills most duties of a hotel concierge. Nightly turndown, coffee and refreshments in lobby, complimentary chilled wine with check-in. Suites in the Wellborn include mini-kitchens with refrigerators, microwaves, and coffeemakers. The Courtyard's two honeymoon suites have double whirlpool tubs. Others have claw-foot tubs and sunrooms. The single room has a basic shower and closet-sized toilet.

Hampton Inn at Universal Studios. 5621 Windhover Dr., Orlando, FL 32819. ☎ **800/231-8395.** Fax 407/363-1711. 120 units. A/C TV TEL. $67–$87. Rates include complimentary breakfast buffet. AE, DISC, DC, MC, V. Take I-4 to Exit 30B. Go through 2 traffic lights; turn right at the Shoney's Restaurant. It's a 5-story white building.

There is nothing fancy about this simple hotel, but it's location is ideal if you plan to spend most of your stay at Universal Studios, Sea World, or the rest of Orlando (it's just 2 blocks from Universal Studios). There are no permanent shuttles to Disney parks, and although they can be arranged, the cost ($35 one way) would make it cheaper to rent a car. The rooms themselves are average-sized, and each has an in-room coffeemaker. Some units have microwaves and refrigerators available. There is a small game room, in-room cable, an outdoor heated pool, and valet laundry service. Restaurants are within walking distance.

The Harley of Orlando. 151 E. Washington St., Orlando, FL 32801. ☎ **800/321-2323** or 407/841-3220. Fax 407/849-1839. 264 units. A/C TV TEL. $95–$150 double. AE, MC, V. Free self-parking. Take I-4 to the Anderson St. exit. Turn left on Rosalind. The hotel entrance is located on the left, directly across from the entrance to Lake Eola Park.

Just 15 minutes from the Orlando International Airport and about 25 minutes from the attractions, the Harley of Orlando is an urban alternative to the Disney resorts. Request a balcony room so you can overlook Lake Eola Park, one of the most beautiful spots in the city. The carpet in this five-story structure is a little threadbare in places, but the rooms, done in dark colors, are comfortable and clean. The pictures of Leona Helmsley, the "Queen of Mean," are gone from the elevators.

Dining/Diversions: The Cafe on the Park Restaurant does a competent job on standards such as prime rib. The Sunday brunch, which is buffet-style, is well worth the price. The Monkey Bar Lounge, done up in gilded chrome and leather, isn't the hippest place in town, but the drinks pack a punch and you don't have to drive to get home. The Church Street Station entertainment complex and the nightclubs and restaurants of downtown are just a short walk away. (Or catch a ride on the free city bus, Lymmo, which picks up passengers just up the block.)

Amenities: Room service, nonsmoking rooms, complimentary morning paper (Monday through Friday), free parking. Pool, sundeck, underground parking garage.

Radisson Place Hotel Orlando. 60 S. Ivanhoe Blvd., Orlando, FL 32804. ☎ **800/333-3333** or 407/425-4455. Fax 407/425-7440. 367 units. A/C TV TEL. $104–$129. AE, DISC, MC, V. Take I-4 to Princeton St. (Exit 43). Turn right at the bottom of the ramp. Turn left on Orange Ave. Go through the light, bearing to the right around the landscaping and the miniature Statue of Liberty; the hotel is on the left.

The 15-story Radisson Place Hotel, built in 1985, is really geared more toward the business traveler than the family-leisure crowd. Nevertheless, its location right off I-4, just blocks from downtown and 15 minutes from the airport, make it also a good bet for families. The kids—and adults—might be tempted to play on the escalators rising for two floors in the sun-filled atrium and lobby. But this place has a relatively stuffy air, with all that gleaming brass and marble, and those oversized ferns. The rooms are tastefully appointed with solid bedspreads and carpets. The views of downtown Orlando from the upper floors are impressive, and the suites are a cut above what you will find for the price elsewhere. It is located just across from Lake Ivanhoe, which has a series of exercise stations and a well-lit path for walking or jogging. There is even a small park for the kids less than a mile away. Minibars are available in most rooms, and some rooms are designed to accommodate the physically challenged.

Dining/Diversions: 'Lando Sam's Restaurant offers American cuisine in a casual, colorful setting with a piano player tickling the ivories on a dark-wood baby grand. The decor is heavy on the shiny brass and ferns. The food is what you would expect at any run-of-the-mill hotel eatery. The same goes for 'Lando Sam's Lounge. Daily breakfast and luncheon buffets in the restaurant are, if nothing else, solid values for the price. Your best bets are a few choice eateries within walking distance (under a mile). Try Brian's, just down the street, a non-retro diner with great breakfast food and coffee.

Amenities: Concierge, room service (including late-night room service), valet parking, transportation desk to arrange for taxi or limo service, attraction ticket information available. (Also, right next door is the Greater Orlando Chamber of Commerce, which has plenty of brochures in the lobby on area attractions.) Outdoor swimming pool, Jacuzzi, sundeck, two outdoor tennis courts, well-equipped health club, boutique.

Ramada Inn & Suites by Sea World. 6800 Villa D Costa Dr., Orlando, FL 32821. ☎ **800/272-6232** or 407/239-0707. Fax 407/239-8243. www. marriott.com. A/C TV TEL. 158 units. $129–$209. From the Walt Disney World area, take I-4 east to Exit 27A. AE, DISC, DC, MC, V. At the first traffic light, turn right.

This all-suites resort offers a roomy alternative: double suites including two bedrooms and two bathrooms that are ideal for a larger family or two couples traveling together. Each suite has a complete kitchen, and all rooms have coffeemakers. The recreational facilities aren't as extensive as some locations. But, with a 1996 renovation, this hotel is clean and comfortable and has facilities for nonsmokers and those with disabilities.

Amenities: Limited room services, RV and truck parking, on-site convenience store, outdoor pool, volleyball and basketball court, fishing facilities., baby-sitting, child services.

Renaissance Orlando Hotel. 6677 Sea Harbour Dr., Orlando, FL 32821 (across from Sea World). ☎ **407/351-5555.** Fax 407/351-9991. 780 units. A/C TV TEL. $139–$259, depending on location and season. AE, DISC, DC, MC, V. From I-4 follow signs to Sea World.

On a clear day the Florida sun dances through the sunlit atrium soaring 10 stories and filled with palm trees. This is a quality hotel, with good-sized rooms, fine service, and luxurious surroundings. However, its most valuable feature for recommendation is its location, which is ideal for visitors who will be going to Disney but who also want to explore the other attractions and the rest of Orlando. Located across the street from Sea World, the hotel offers special packages that include tickets to Sea World. It is also only about 10 minutes—in light traffic—from Walt Disney World. Nonsmoking rooms and rooms for travelers with disabilities are available.

Dining/Diversions: There are three lounges and five restaurants, some featuring live entertainment. A small game room and a children's club and day care.

Amenities: Swimming pool, tennis courts, volleyball, small children's play area, health club, massage therapist on-call, laundry services, car rental desk, baby-sitting.

Twin Towers and Convention Center. 5780 Major Blvd., Orlando, FL 32819. ☎ **800/327-2110** or 407/351-1000. Fax 407/363-0106. 761 units. A/C TV TEL. Summer $119–$145 double, depending on the season; $375–$900 suites year-round. AE, DC, DISC, MC, V. Located directly across from the main gate of Universal Studios.

From your balcony you can watch the palms waving at Universal's entrance and the bungee jumpers in the parking lot next door waving on their way down. Built in the 1970s as a convention hotel, the property underwent a makeover in the 1980s as owners realized families would be flocking to Universal right across the street. This location is convenient without being amid the congestion of International Drive proper, and you're just minutes from WDW without being engulfed by the Mouse and the associated higher prices. The hotel still attracts a lot of convention business, but those facilities are in a building separate from the rooms. Aside from occasionally being trapped in the elevator with a herd of human Elk, you hardly notice. *Just a side note:* That red building on the property that looks like an old-fashioned schoolhouse is just that—the Little Red School House, a public school run in cooperation with the local school district for the children of Twin Towers employees.

Dining/Diversions: The Palm Court Restaurant serves three meals a day, and the Everglades Lounge has frequent entertainment and a big-screen TV. Although the Palm Court does an adequate job, there are plenty of other dining options nearby. Most, like the Hard Rock Cafe, are comparable in price but more interesting. The lounge acts are best left alone, although the big-screen TV offers a great respite for sports fans who need a break from quality time with the family.

Amenities: Room service, baby-sitting, children's program, laundry. Deli, pool, whirlpool, sauna, exercise room, playground, game room.

IN WINTER PARK

✪ **Best Western Mount Vernon Inn.** 110 S. Orlando Ave., Winter Park, FL 32789
☎ **407/647-1166.** Fax 407/647-8011. 147 units. A/C TV TEL. $78–$88 double. AE, MC, V. Free self-parking. The Inn is located on U.S. Rte. 17–92, between Fairbanks Ave. and Lee Rd., across from Houston's Steakhouse.

This is one of the best bargains in town, a place where old-money families know their guests will get comfortable accommodations at a reasonable price. Look for lots of late-model Caddies in the parking lot. There are some nice views available overlooking the pool; across the street, about a block away, is a city park the kids will love. But overall, there is nothing too fancy about the Mount Vernon. It is, however, centrally located between the beaches and the theme parks and very close to downtown Winter Park and downtown Orlando.

Dining: The Coach Dining room is open for breakfast and lunch. The food is plentiful and filling, but this is a place for basic dining rather than gourmet. There are many fine restaurants nearby. *One tip:* If you made reservations significantly in advance, save yourself a late-night check-in headache by confirming them before you leave home. The Red Fox Lounge features nightly entertainment that's generally along the lines of a guy with a hair weave and a synthesizer. Unless that sounds really hip to you, it's better to venture to downtown Winter Park or Orlando for entertainment.

Amenities: There is a pool and a Houston's Steakhouse across the street. From there you are pretty much on your own. What do you expect for $72?

✪ **Langford Resort.** 300 E. New England Ave. (at Interlachen Ave.), Winter Park, FL 32789. ☎ **407/644-3400.** Fax 407/628-1952. 220 units. A/C TV TEL. $75–$115 double; $200 suites. Children 17 and under stay free in parents' room. Rooms with kitchenettes $10 extra. AE, DC, MC, V. Free self-parking. I-4 West through downtown Orlando to Winter Park. Take Fairbanks exit, 69. Go east 2 miles to Park Ave. Turn left. Go 2 blocks and turn right on New England. Two blocks on right.

In pre-Disney days, Winter Park was one of central Florida's most-visited resorts, and the Langford was the place to stay. Vaughn Monroe entertained in the lounge, and the guest roster proudly listed Eleanor Roosevelt, Mamie Eisenhower, Lillian Gish, Vincent Price, and Dina Merrill. Ronald and Nancy Reagan celebrated their 25th wedding anniversary here. Stars and just-plain-folk alike came to gawk at the "jungle" and other theme rooms as well as the poolside bathrooms with their wacky paintings of mermaids and mermen.

Today, while kitschy but no longer glamorous, this friendly, family-run resort nevertheless offers extensive facilities at very reasonable rates. The midsized rooms show the wear of the years, but the lobby and hallways have recently been renovated. An on-site spa offers a full range of treatments: sauna, steam, massage (shiatsu, Swedish, and deep athletic), body wraps, seaweed wraps, salt glows, facials, manicures, pedicures, and day-of-beauty packages. And its central location, on a lovely street shaded by tall oaks draped with Spanish moss, is another plus. Room decor varies and it is notably eclectic. Many rooms have balconies and/or fully equipped kitchenettes with two-burner stoves and small refrigerators. The little ones will love the kiddie pool and the small video-game arcade.

Dining 6

Orlando has fast become the theme-restaurant capital of the Planet (Hollywood, anyone?). From souped-up cars to supermodels to superheroes, every category is represented. But there are still some restaurants where the focus is not only the decor but the delicacies.

Since most visitors spend the majority of their time in the Walt Disney World area, I've focused on the best dining choices there. Also listed are some worthwhile restaurants beyond the realm. These "local" eateries often benefit from the high concentration of culinary talent brought to central Florida by the attractions. In the past few years, several high-quality restaurants have opened in downtown Orlando, providing visitors to Church Street Station with more dining options.

Parents will be pleased to note that most mid-priced restaurants offer a children's menu. Many offer kiddie distractions like something to color or a maze to complete.

If you go to a place catering to children, expect the noise level to be high. Kids don't take a vacation from screaming, howling, and tantrums. That's the bad news.

The good news is the higher the average cost of an entree, the less likely you are to find little people. If you're looking for a quiet meal, head for the fancier restaurants further from the Disney parks, on International Drive or on into Orlando. Or patronize the more expensive park offerings. If those howling youngsters belong to you, take advantage of the many in-hotel baby-sitting services for one night while you go out alone.

If kids really get your goat, by all means steer clear of any dining establishment that features "characters." (See the listings for dinner shows in chapter 10.)

Listings are divided by the following price categories: **very expensive** (the average main course at dinner is more than $25), **expensive** ($20 to $25), **moderate** ($10 to $20), and **inexpensive** (under $10). Keep in mind that these categories refer to dinner prices. Also, keep in mind that your complete meal could cost more than twice the main course, especially if you order several courses and wine. Note, however, that some very expensive restaurants offer affordable lunches and/or cheaper early bird dinners. Also, I'm going on the assumption that you're not stinting when you order. Some restaurants, for instance, have main courses ranging from $12 to $20. In most cases, you can dine for less if you order carefully. Especially noteworthy restaurants and those that offer especially good value are marked with a star ✪.

American Express produces a handy, pocket-sized guide that lists basic information about dining and recreational opportunities within WDW. It also lists discounts, which can run about 10%, at selected Disney eateries. The book is available to American Express cardholders only.

You can get a copy if you book a "White Glove" package through American Express, or if you call ☎ **800/528-4802**. (It takes about a month to get the information sent through the mail.) Cardholders can also get a copy at the American Express office at the entrance to Epcot and in the lobby of the Contemporary Resort.

For additional information online about area restaurants, use the keyword **Orlando** on **America Online** to visit **Digital City Orlando.** From there, click on "Entertainment" and you'll find a complete listing of, among other things, Orlando restaurants, A to Z.

PRIORITY SEATING AT WDW RESTAURANTS

Priority seating is similar to a reservation, but less dependable. It means that you get the next table available *after* you arrive at a restaurant, but a table is not kept empty pending your arrival. You can arrange priority seating up to 60 days in advance at almost all full-service restaurants in the Magic Kingdom, Epcot, Disney–MGM Studios, Animal Kingdom, Disney resorts, and Downtown Disney. Priority seating can also be arranged for character meals and shows throughout the complex. To make any of these arrangements, call ☎ **407/WDW-DINE** (939-3463). Nighttime shows can actually be booked as far in advance as you wish.

Note: Since this priority-seating phone number was instituted in 1994, it has become much more difficult to obtain a table by just showing up. I strongly advise you to avoid disappointment by calling ahead.

However, if you don't reserve in advance, you can take your chances by making reservations once you have arrived in the parks themselves:

- **At Epcot:** Make reservations at the Worldkey interactive terminals at Guest Relations in Innoventions East, at Worldkey Information Service Satellites located on the main concourse to World Showcase and at Germany in World Showcase, or at the restaurants themselves.
- **At the Magic Kingdom:** Reserve at the restaurants themselves.
- **At Disney–MGM Studios:** Make reservations at the Hollywood Junction Station on Sunset Boulevard or at the restaurants themselves.
- **At Animal Kingdom:** Make reservations by visiting the guest services desk near the entrance. And good news: You can get priority seating at the RainForest Cafe at Animal Kingdom. You can make that request up to 30 days in advance, and, since this is a very popular place, the sooner you make the call the better.
  You might also keep these restaurant facts in mind:
- All park restaurants have nonsmoking interiors; you can smoke on patios and terraces.
- Magic Kingdom restaurants serve no alcoholic beverages, but liquor is available at Animal Kingdom, Epcot, and Disney–MGM Studios eateries and elsewhere in the WDW complex.
- All sit-down restaurants in Walt Disney World take American Express, MasterCard, Visa, and the Disney Card.
- Guests at Disney resorts and official properties can make restaurant reservations through guest services or concierge desks.
- All WDW restaurants offer low-priced children's menus.

1 Best Bets

- **Best for Kids:** Kids adore the meals with Disney characters offered at almost **all Walt Disney World resorts** and elsewhere in the WDW complex (details follow). Don't forget the jungle-themed **RainForest Cafe** (☎ 407/827-8500) at two locations, Downtown Disney Marketplace and Animal Kingdom, where monkey business is encouraged.
- **Best Spot for a Romantic Dinner:** The elegant candlelit **Dux** at the Peabody Orlando (☎ 407/345-4550) combines a warmly inviting ambience with great food.
- **Best Spot for a Business Lunch:** Generally, **Hemingway's,** an upscale, Key West–style restaurant at the Grand Cypress Resort (☎ 407/239-1234), is kid-free, and its intimate dining areas are perfect for business lunches.
- **Best Spot for a Celebration:** There is no better place than the festive **Bubble Room** (☎ 407/628-3331), located in Maitland, just north of downtown.
- **Best Decor: Victoria & Albert's** takes the prize, with its plush Louis XIII–style furnishings, brocaded walls, and central dome (☎ 407/WDW-DINE [939-3463]).
- **Best View:** Artist Point (☎ 407/WDW-DINE [939-3463]). This carefully crafted resort restaurant offers the illusion that you're dining in a rustically elegant, turn-of-the-century national-park lodge. Large windows overlook a lake and a waterfall. Weather permitting, there's also terrace seating.
- **Best Wine List:** "Sip" for yourself why **Maison et Jardin** (☎ 407/862-4410) in Altamonte Springs was recently honored by *Wine Spectator* magazine for its outstanding wine cellar.
- **Best Value:** At **Romano's Macaroni Grill** (☎ 407/239-6676), the ambience and the northern Italian cuisine are first rate and prices are low, low, low.
- **Best American Cuisine:** Meat loaf and mashed potatoes that would make mama proud are at **B-Line Diner,** in the Peabody Orlando hotel (☎ 407/345-4460).
- **Best Chinese Cuisine: Ming Court** (☎ 407/351-9988) features delicacies from all regions of China.
- **Best California Cuisine:** Waterfalls and animal sounds can't drown out the flood of flavorful dishes at the **RainForest Cafe** (☎ 407/827-8500).
- **Best Barbecue:** You can follow your nose to **Bubbaloo's Bodacious BBQ** (☎ 407/295-1212) by catching a whiff of the tangy hickory smoke. It tastes as good as it smells.
- **Best Italian Cuisine:** I'd pick the northern Italian fare at the charming **Capriccio** in the Peabody Orlando (☎ 407/352-4000) or the sedate and elegant Tuscany at Marriott's Orlando World Center (☎ 407/239-4200).
- **Best Seafood:** The 19th-century-style clambake buffet at the **Cape May Café** at Disney's Beach Club Resort (☎ 407/WDW-DINE [939-3463]) is a feast—seafood stews, clams, mussels, lobster, and more cooked in a rockweed steamer pit.
- **Best Tapas: Cafe Tu Tu Tango** (☎ 407/248-2222) takes the tapas concept international with items ranging from Cajun egg rolls to Thai salad.
- **Best Steak House:** At the **Yachtsman Steakhouse** at Disney's Yacht Club Resort (☎ 407/WDW-DINE [939-3463]), aged prime steaks, chops, and seafood are grilled over oak and hickory.
- **Best Late-Night Dining:** The trendy **B-Line Diner** (☎ 407/345-4460) at the Peabody Orlando is open around the clock for eclectic fare ranging from filet mignon to a falafel sandwich.

- **Best Character Breakfast:** At the revolving **Garden Grill** (☎ 407/WDW-DINE [939-3463]), in the Land Pavilion at Epcot, diners enjoy hearty family-style fare, a just-folks country-style theme, and interesting changes of scenery as the restaurant circles through environments ranging from prairie to rain forest; all this and Minnie and Mickey, too.
- **Best Outdoor Dining:** The terrace at **Artist Point** (☎ 407/WDW-DINE [939-3463]), the premier restaurant at Disney's Wilderness Lodge, overlooks a lake, waterfall, and scenery evocative of America's national parks.
- **Best People-Watching:** The upstairs patio at **Bongo's Cuban Cafe,** Downtown Disney West Side, (☎ **407/828-0999**) is where it's at.
- **Best Afternoon Tea: The Peabody Orlando** (☎ **407/345-4550**) hosts afternoon teas on weekdays from 3 to 4:30pm in its gorgeous skylit atrium lobby. Frolicking in a nearby fountain while you sip your Earl Grey are the Peabody's five resident ducks. The cost is $8.95 per person.
- **Best Brunch: Capriccio** at the Peabody Orlando (☎ **407/352-4000**) offers a lavish buffet of first-rate fare with free-flowing champagne.
- **Best Special Brunch: The House of Blues** (☎ **407/934-2583**) in Disney's West Side has a down-home gospel brunch, $23.99 for adults and $11.99 for kids 4 to 12, featuring foot-stomping music and an awe-inspiring array of Southern fare such as cheese grits and sausage. Foreign visitors might especially enjoy this cultural immersion. Make reservations early since it regularly sells out.

2 Restaurants by Cuisine

AMERICAN

B-Line Diner (International Drive Area, *M*)

The Bubble Room (Maitland, *M*)

Crystal Palace (Magic Kingdom, *M*)

Dexter's at Thorton Park (Orlando, *M*)

Fireworks Factory (Pleasure Island, *M*)

50's Prime Time Cafe (Disney–MGM Studios, *M*)

Hollywood Brown Derby (Disney–MGM Studios, *E*)

Cinderella's Royal Table (Magic Kingdom, *E*)

Liberty Tree Tavern (Magic Kingdom, *E*)

McDonald's Fun House (Disney's West Side, *IE*)

Max's Cafe & Coffee House (Celebration, *IE*)

Planet Hollywood (Pleasure Island, *M*)

Plaza Restaurant (Magic Kingdom, *IE*)

Sci-Fi Dine-In Theater Restaurant (Disney–MGM Studios, *M*)

White Wolf Cafe (Downtown Orlando, *M*)

AMERICAN/CONTINENTAL

Black Swan (Lake Buena Vista, *VE*)

BARBECUE

Bubbaloo's Bodacious BBQ (Winter Park, *IE*)

Wild Jacks (International Drive, *M*)

BRITISH

Rose & Crown (Epcot, *M*)

CALIFORNIA

California Grill (Magic Kingdom Resort Area, *E*)

Pebbles (Lake Buena Vista, *M*)

RainForest Cafe (Downtown Disney Marketplace & Animal Kingdom, *M*)

Wolfgang Puck's Cafe (Disney's West Side, Disney, *M*)

Key to Abbreviations: *IE*=Inexpensive; *M*=Moderate; *E*=Expensive

Canadian

Le Cellier (Epcot, *M*)

Caribbean

Bahama Breeze (International Drive, *M*)

Character Breakfasts & Dinners

Artist Point, (Disney's Wilderness Lodge, *E*)

Cape May Café, (Disney's Beach Club Resort, *E*)

Chef Mickey's, Disney's Contemporary Resort (Breakfast *E*, Dinner *M*)

Cinderella's Royal Table, Cinderella Castle (*E*)

Liberty Tree Tavern, Liberty Square (*M*)

Mickey's Tropical Luau, Disney's Polynesian Resort (*M*)

Minnie's Menehune, Disney's Polynesian Resort (*E*)

1900 Park Fare, Disney's Grand Floridian Beach Resort (Breakfast *E*)

Soundstage Restaurant, Disney-MGM Studios (*E*)

Watercress Café, Buena Vista Palace (*M*)

Chinese

Lotus Blossom Café (Epcot, *IE*)

Ming Court (International Drive, *M*)

Nine Dragons (Epcot, *M*)

Cuban

Bongo (Disney's West Side, *M*)

Rolando's (Casselberry, *IE*)

Food Court

Sunshine Season Food Fair (Epcot, *IE*)

French

Chefs de France (Epcot, *E*)

Le Provence (Downtown Orlando, *E*)

Maison et Jardin (Altamonte Springs, *E*)

German

Biergarten (Epcot, *M*)

Sommerfest (Epcot, *M, IE*)

International

Dux (International Drive, *VE*)

Victoria & Albert's (Magic Kingdom Resort Area, *VE*)

Italian

Capriccio (International Drive, *M*)

Enzo's (International Drive, *IE*)

Italianni's (International Drive, *M*)

N.Y.P.D. (Downtown Orlando, *IE*)

L'Originale Alfredo di Roma (Epcot, *E*)

Portobello Yacht Club (Pleasure Island, *M*)

Romano's Macaroni Grill (Lake Buena Vista, *IE*)

Sergio's (Downtown Orlando, *M*)

Tony's Town Square Restaurant (Magic Kingdom, *E*)

Tuscany (Lake Buena Vista, *E*)

Japanese

Mikado Japanese Steak House (Lake Buena Vista, *E*)

Tempura Kiku Restaurant (Epcot, *E*)

Yakitori House (Epcot, *IE*)

Mexican

Cantina de San Angel (Epcot, *IE*)

San Angel Inn (Epcot, *M*)

Mississippi Delta

House of Blues (Disney's West Side, *M*)

Moroccan

Marrakesh (Epcot, *M*)

New Orleans

Copeland's of New Orleans (International Drive, *M*)

Boatwright's Dining Hall (Lake Buena Vista, *IE*)

Bonfamille's Cafe (Lake Buena Vista, *IE*)

Norwegian

Akershus (Epcot, *M*)

Kringla Bakeri og Kafe (Epcot, *IE*)

PACIFIC RIM
'Ohana (Magic Kingdom Resort
  Area, *M*)

SEAFOOD/STEAKS/CHOPS
Ariel's (Epcot Resort Area, *E*)
Artist Point (Magic Kingdom Resort
  Area, *M*)
Cape May Café (Lake Buena Vista, *IE*)
Coral Reef (Epcot, *M*)
Fulton's Crab House (Pleasure Island, *E*)
Hemingway's (Lake Buena Vista, *E*)

Yachtsman Steakhouse (Epcot Resort
  Area, *E*)

TAPAS
Cafe Tu Tu Tango (International
  Drive, *M*)
Spoodles (Epcot Resort Area, *M*)

THAI
Siam Orchid (International Drive, *M*)

VIETNAMESE
Little Saigon (Orlando, *IE*)

3 Places to Dine in Walt Disney World

The following listings encompass restaurants in the Disney theme parks (Epcot, Magic Kingdom, Disney–MGM Studios, and Animal Kingdom) and the Disney-owned resorts and official hotels. Restaurants in the entertainment and shopping areas (Pleasure Island, Downtown Disney's West Side, and Downtown Disney Marketplace) are in the Lake Buena Vista section.

IN EPCOT

Though an ethnic meal at one of the World Showcase pavilions is a traditional part of the Epcot experience, I find many of the following establishments just a tad pricey for the value received. Unless money is no object, you might want to consider the numerous lower-priced walk-in places at each national pavilion and throughout the park that don't require reservations (for details, check the Epcot Guidemap that you receive upon entering the park). Or go during lunchtime, when entree prices are lower. Almost all of the establishments listed here serve lunch and dinner daily (hours vary with park hours), and, unless otherwise noted, they offer children's meals for under $5. These restaurants are located on the map "Epcot Dining" in this section.

Note: Since the clientele at even the fanciest Epcot World Showcase restaurants are coming directly from the parks, you don't have to dress up for dinner. **Priority seating,** which reserves you a place but not a specific table, is available at all WDW sit-down restaurants, and it is strongly recommended. The chances of getting a table without a long wait are pretty slim. Call ☎ **407/WDW-DINE** (939-3463).

EXPENSIVE

Les Chefs de France Restaurant. France Pavilion, World Showcase. ☎ **407/WDW-DINE** (939-3463). Priority seating. Main courses $9.95–$15.95 at lunch, $17.95–$26.25 at dinner. AE, MC, V. Daily noon until 1 hr. before park closes. FRENCH.

Its art-nouveau/fin-de-siècle interior is agleam with mirrors and brass candelabra chandeliers. Etched-glass and brass dividers create intimate dining areas, and tables are elegantly appointed. I recommend the seafood cream soup with crab dumplings. Main courses at dinner include a superb broiled salmon in sorrel cream sauce (served with ratatouille and new potatoes), braised beef burgundy, and sautéed beef tenderloin with raisins and brandy sauce. The dessert of choice is a sumptuous soufflé Grand-Marnier. There is a substantial wine list, and you may purchase wines on the list at Au Palais du Vin, a wine shop in the pavilion.

Epcot Dining

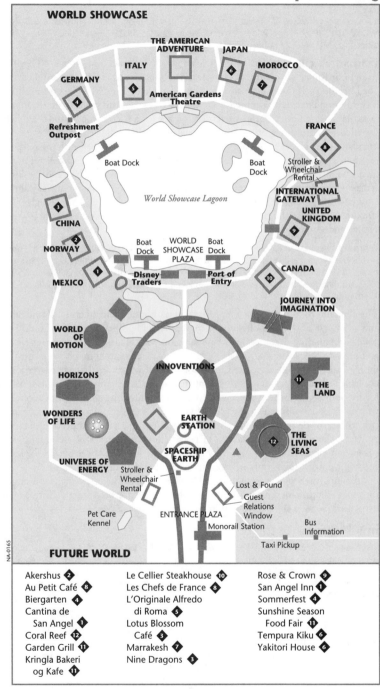

WORLD SHOWCASE

THE AMERICAN ADVENTURE

ITALY

GERMANY

American Gardens Theatre

Refreshment Outpost

Boat Dock

World Showcase Lagoon

Boat Dock

JAPAN

MOROCCO

FRANCE

Stroller & Wheelchair Rental

INTERNATIONAL GATEWAY

UNITED KINGDOM

CHINA

NORWAY

MEXICO

Boat Dock

WORLD SHOWCASE PLAZA

Boat Dock

Disney Traders

Port of Entry

CANADA

JOURNEY INTO IMAGINATION

WORLD OF MOTION

HORIZONS

INNOVENTIONS

THE LAND

WONDERS OF LIFE

EARTH STATION

SPACESHIP EARTH

THE LIVING SEAS

UNIVERSE OF ENERGY

Stroller & Wheelchair Rental

Pet Care Kennel

ENTRANCE PLAZA

Monorail Station

Lost & Found

Guest Relations Window

Bus Information

Taxi Pickup

NA-0165

FUTURE WORLD

Akershus ②
Au Petit Café ⑧
Biergarten ④
Cantina de San Angel ①
Coral Reef ⑫
Garden Grill ⑪
Kringla Bakeri og Kafe ⑪

Le Cellier Steakhouse ⑩
Les Chefs de France ⑧
L'Originale Alfredo di Roma ⑤
Lotus Blossom Café ③
Marrakesh ⑦
Nine Dragons ③

Rose & Crown ⑨
San Angel Inn ①
Sommerfest ④
Sunshine Season Food Fair ⑪
Tempura Kiku ⑥
Yakitori House ⑥

97

L'Originale Alfredo di Roma Ristorante. Italy Pavilion, World Showcase. ☎ **407/ WDW-DINE** (939-3463). Priority seating. Main courses $9.25–$18 at lunch, $11–$27 at dinner. AE, MC, V. Daily noon–park closing. ITALIAN.

Patterned after Alfredo De Lelio's celebrated establishment in Rome, L'Originale Alfredo di Roma Ristorante evokes a seaside Roman palazzo with beautiful trompe l'oeil frescoes of 16th-century patrician villas inspired by Veronese. The theatricality of an exhibition kitchen, charming Italian waiters, and exuberant strolling musicians creates a festive ambience. For a quieter setting, ask for a seat on the veranda. De Lelio invented fettuccine Alfredo—and it remains an excellent choice here. Other recommendations are garlicky linguine al pesto and veal scaloppine served with roasted potatoes and vegetables. And there's a sublime tiramisu for dessert. A special vegetarian menu (with excellent grilled veggies, among other items) is available, and the list of Italian wines is extensive. On your way in or out, note the entrance-room walls; they're covered with photographs of celebrity diners in Rome, most notably Douglas Fairbanks and Mary Pickford, who discovered Alfredo's on their honeymoon and told *tout* Hollywood. A great deal here is a three-course early-bird dinner.

Tempura Kiku. Japan Pavilion, World Showcase. ☎ **407/WDW-DINE** (939-3463). Priority seating for teppanyaki; reservations not accepted at the tempura counter. Teppanyaki main courses $10–$20 at lunch, $15–$30 at dinner; fixed-price menu $39.50 for 2 at lunch, $59.90 for 2 at dinner; tempura $9.25–$11.95 at lunch, $14.75–$22.75 at dinner. AE, MC, V. Daily 11am until 1 hr before park closes. JAPANESE.

The Tempura Kiku centers on a teppanyaki steak house where diners sit at grill tables and white-hatted chefs rapidly dice, slice, stir-fry, and propel cooked food onto your plate with amazing dexterity. Kids especially love watching the chef wield his cleaver and utensils. Since you share a table with strangers, teppanyaki makes for a convivial dining experience. An elaborate dinner for two (of which an abbreviated version is available at lunch) includes a shrimp appetizer, salad with ginger dressing, soup (ask for the *misroshiru*–soybean soup with tofu and mushrooms), grilled fresh vegetables with *udon* noodles, succulent morsels of grilled beef tenderloin and lobster, steamed rice, choice of dessert (perhaps chestnut cake), and green tea. And even à la carte entrees include plenty of extras. Kirin beer, plum wine, and sake are among your beverage options, along with specialty drinks (some of them nonalcoholic, for kids), such as tachibana (light rum, orange curaçao, and mandarin orange juice).

Adjoining the teppanyaki rooms is a U-shaped tempura counter where you can eat shrimp, scallops, chicken, and fresh vegetables that have been lightly battered and deep-fried. Some sushi and sashimi items are served here as well.

MODERATE

Akershus. Norway Pavilion, World Showcase. ☎ **407/WDW-DINE** (939-3463). Priority seating. Lunch buffet $11.95 for adults, $5.25 for children ages 4–9, free for children age 3 and under; dinner buffet $18.50 for adults, $7.95 for children. There are also nonsmorgasbord children's meals for $7.95. AE, MC, V. Daily noon–3:30pm and 4:30pm–park closing. NORWEGIAN.

Akershus re-creates a 14th-century castle fortress that stands in Oslo's harbor and, with a 40-item buffet, shows the definition of smorgasbord. Its pristine white-stone interior, with lofty beamed ceilings and leaded glass windows, features intimate dining niches divided by Gothic archways. The meal is an immense smorgasbord of traditional *småvarmt* (hot) and *koldtbord* (cold) dishes—smoked pork with honey mustard, strips of venison in cream sauce, *gravlax* in mustard sauce, smoked mackerel, Norwegian tomato herring, an array of Norwegian breads and cheeses, potato salad, red cabbage, boiled red potatoes, and much more. Norwegian beer and aquavit complement a list of French and California wines. And do consider the Lillehammer brandy for an after-dinner drink. Desserts, such as a "veiled maiden"—an applesauce and whipped cream concoction—are à la carte.

Biergarten. Germany Pavilion, World Showcase. ☎ **407/WDW-DINE** (939-3463). Priority seating. Lunch buffet $10.95 for adults, $5.50 for children 3–11; dinner buffet $15.75 and $5.99. AE, MC, V. Daily noon–3pm and 4pm–park closing. GERMAN.

Lit by street lamps, the Biergarten simulates a Bavarian village courtyard at Oktoberfest with autumnal trees, a working waterwheel, and geranium-filled flower boxes adorning Tudor-style houses. Entertainment might be an oompah band or a strolling accordionist. Guests are encouraged to dance or sing along. All-you-can-eat buffet meals featuring traditional fare (sauerbraten, spaetzle with gravy, sauerkraut with salads) are offered at lunch and dinner. Beverages and desserts are extra. Wash it all down with a stein of Beck's or a glass of liebfraumilch.

Coral Reef. Living Seas Pavilion, Future World. ☎ **407/WDW-DINE** (939-3463). Main courses $13–$21 at lunch, $13–$25 at dinner—more for lobster or a clambake combination. AE, MC, V. Daily 11:30am–2:45pm and 4pm–park closing. SEAFOOD.

Dine under the sea at the enchanting Coral Reef, where tables ring a 5.6-million-gallon aquarium inhabited by more than 4,000 denizens of the deep. Strains of Debussy's La Mer and Handel's Water Music playing softly in the background help set the tone. This is the most notable restaurant in the front section of Epcot, a favorite of park workers who work around the (Disney) World. Tiered seating—much of it in semicircular booths—ensures everyone a good view, and diners are given "fish-identifier" sheets with labeled pictures so they can put names to the species swimming by. The menu features (what else?) seafood—creamy lobster bisque, sautéed mahimahi in lemon-caper butter, and shrimp satay served atop red-pepper pasta. There are also some steak and chicken dishes. For dessert, choose frangelico-laced white-chocolate mousse cake served on crème anglaise and crowned with dark chocolate Mickey ears. Coral Reef features premium wines by the glass and matches nightly entrees with selected labels.

Le Cellier Steakhouse. Canadian Pavilion, World Showcase. ☎ **407/WDW-DINE** (939-3463). Priority seating. Main courses $8.50–$14.50 at lunch, $11.50–$19.25 at dinner. AE, MC, V. Daily noon–park closing. CANADIAN.

This à la carte family steak house, previously a cafeteria, is a good choice for families. Located in the Victorian Hotel du Canada, with its French Gothic facade and steeply pitched copper roofs, Le Cellier has a castlelike ambience with seating in tapestry-upholstered chairs under vaulted stone arches, and amber light emanating from black, wrought-iron sconces. Regional dishes include cheddar-cheese soup, carved pemeal bacon (a pork loin with a light cornmeal crust), a French-Canadian pork-and-potato-filled pie called *tourtière*, chicken and meatball stew, maple-syrup pie, and Canadian beers.

✪ **Marrakesh. Morocco Pavilion, World Showcase.** ☎ **407/WDW-DINE** (939-3463). Priority seating. Main courses $9.95–$14.95 at lunch, $12.95–$24.95 at dinner; Moroccan diffa $29.95 for two at lunch, $53.90 for two at dinner. AE, MC, V. Daily noon–park closing. MOROCCAN.

The palatial Marrakesh—with its hand-set mosaic tile work, latticed teak shutters, and intricate cut-brass chandeliers suspended from a ceiling painted with elaborate Moorish motifs—represents 12 centuries of Arabic design. Exquisitely carved faux-ivory archways frame the central dining area, where belly dancers perform to oud, kanoun, and darbuka music. Of all Epcot restaurants, this exotic venue best typifies the international-experience spirit of the park. The Moroccan *diffa* (traditional feast) that lets you sample a variety of dishes is recommended. At dinner it includes a hearty saffron-seasoned *harira* soup flavored with onions, tomatoes, lentils, and lamb; beef *brewats* (minced beef seasoned with coriander, ginger, cinnamon, and saffron, rolled in thin pastry layers, and fried); roast lamb served with almond- and raisin-studded rice; braised *tagine* of chicken with green olives and preserved lemon; couscous with seasonal vegetables; Moroccan pastries; and mint tea. Combination appetizer plates are another way to experience culinary diversity. French and Moroccan wines are available to complement your meal.

✪ **Nine Dragons.** China Pavilion, World Showcase. ☎ **407/WDW-DINE** (939-3463). Priority seating. Main courses $8.50–$18.50 at lunch (most are under $15), $10.50–$23.75 at dinner. AE, MC, V. Daily 11:30am–park closing. CHINESE.

One of the most attractive of the World Showcase restaurants, Nine Dragons, with windows overlooking the lagoon, has intricately carved rosewood paneling and furnishings and a beautiful dragon-motif ceiling. Begin your meal here with a selection of dim sum such as honey-glazed spareribs, delicious shrimp toast, pan-fried dumplings (pot stickers) stuffed with pork and vegetables, and ginger-nuanced steamed dumplings stuffed with pork, shrimp, and water chestnuts. Main dishes highlight cooking from four regions of China—**Mandarin, Shanghai, Cantonese,** and **Szechuan.** Examples of these regions are Great Wall duck shredded with green and red peppers and served with pancakes; a saucy stir-fried boneless chicken with onions, carrots, and green peas; tender sliced sirloin and broccoli stir-fried in oyster sauce; deep-fried shrimp ambrosia in a Mao Tai liqueur-spiked fruit sauce respectively. You can order Chinese or California wines with your meal, but I especially love fresh melon juice, either alone or mixed with rum or vodka. For dessert, there's red-bean ice cream with fried banana or Chinese pastries.

Rose & Crown Pub & Dining Room. United Kingdom Pavilion, World Showcase. ☎ **407/WDW-DINE** (939-3463). Priority seating for the Dining Room; reservations not accepted for the pub. Main courses $9–$15 at lunch, $10–$30 at dinner. Traditional afternoon tea is served daily at 3:30pm for $9.95. AE, MC, V. Daily 11am until 1 hr before park closes. BRITISH.

The Rose & Crown, entered via a cozy pub, evokes Victorian England with dark oak wainscoting, beamed Tudor ceilings, and English and Scottish folk music. It also offers outdoor seating at tables overlooking the lagoon—a good place to watch Illumi-Nations. Dinner here might be an appetizer of smoked salmon with Stilton cheese, prime rib with Yorkshire pudding, and a sherry trifle. Wash it all down with a pint of Irish lager, Bass ale, or Guinness stout. Another option is bar fare (sausage rolls, Cornish pasties, a Stilton cheese and fruit plate), all under $10.

San Angel Inn. Mexico Pavilion, World Showcase. ☎ **407/WDW-DINE** (939-3463). Priority seating. Main courses $8.95–$14.95 at lunch, $12.50–$23.25 at dinner. AE, MC, V. Daily 11am–park closing. MEXICAN.

The setting for the San Angel Inn is a hacienda courtyard amid dense jungle foliage in the shadow of a crumbling Yucatán pyramid. It is nighttime: Tables are candlelit (even at lunch), and lighting is very low. The Popocatepetl volcano erupts in the distance, spewing molten lava, and you can hear the sounds of faraway birds. Thunder, lightning, and swiftly moving clouds add a dramatic note, but the overall ambience is soothing. The fare is authentic and prepared from scratch. Order an appetizer of *queso fundido* (melted cheese with Mexican pork sausage, served with homemade corn or flour tortillas). Among entrees, specialties include *mole poblano* (chicken simmered with more than 20 spices and a hint of chocolate) and *filete ranchero* (grilled tenderloin of

---

ⓘ Family-Friendly Restaurants

Keep in mind that almost all Walt Disney World restaurants offer very inexpensive kids' meals (usually $4), as do most restaurants in this very child-oriented town. Themes that appeal to youngsters and place mats with puzzles and pictures to color are also the norm. Of course, all the character meals described in this chapter delight the kids. Some other notables:

Sci-Fi Dine-In Theater Restaurant *(see p. 106)*   A drive-in movie theater at Disney–MGM Studios where you dine in actual convertible cars, eyes glued to a movie screen.

50's Prime Time Cafe *(see p. 106)*   Also at Disney–MGM Studios, this restaurant re-creates the world of 1950s sitcoms. TV sets that air old shows are visible from every table. Homey food, such as meat loaf and mashed potatoes, is also of that era.

Mickey's Tropical Luau *(see p. 126)*   Not just a meal but a Polynesian floor show featuring Minnie, Mickey, Pluto, and Goofy along with a cast of South Sea Islanders. At Disney's Polynesian Resort in Luau Cove. Character breakfasts here, too.

Cape May Café Clambake Buffet *(see p. 111)*   This old-fashioned nightly clambake at Disney's Beach Club Resort is fun for the whole family.

'Ohana *(see p. 110)*   Centering on an 18-foot fire-pit grill, 'Ohana, at Disney's Polynesian Resort, is a sumptuous island feast enhanced by storytellers, hula-hoop contests, and lots of audience participation.

Hoop-Dee-Doo Musical Revue   I've never met anyone who didn't have a great time at this whoopin' and hollerin' country-music dinner show in Fort Wilderness's Pioneer Hall. A less expensive variation on the same theme is the **Diamond Horseshoe Saloon Revue** in the Magic Kingdom's Frontierland.

RainForest Cafe *(see pp. 113)*   Monkeys screech in the background, waterfalls drop near your table, you sit atop zebra or rhinoceros legs. Perfect for kids.

Planet Hollywood *(see p. 112)*   Kids love all the action and excitement—a fiber-optic ceiling, video walls, hundreds of movie costumes and props on display, and the elusive possibility that they'll actually see someone famous. Long waits in line to get in, however.

---

beef served over corn tortillas with sauce ranchero, poblano pepper strips, Monterey Jack cheese, onions, and refried beans). Combination platters are available at both meals. There's chocolate Kahlúa mousse pie for dessert, and drink options include Dos Equis beer and margaritas. A special vegetarian menu is also available.

INEXPENSIVE

Cantina de San Angel. Mexico Pavilion, World Showcase. ☎ **407/827-8570.** Reservations not accepted. Entrees start at $6.50. Children's meal under $5. AE, MC, V. Daily 11am until 1 hr. before park closes. MEXICAN.

Cantina de San Angel, a cafeteria with outdoor seating at umbrella tables overlooking the lagoon, offers affordable tacos, burritos, and combination plates, along with frozen margaritas.

Kringla Bakeri og Kafe. Norway Pavilion, World Showcase. ☎ **407/560-5179.** Reservations not accepted. Most entree prices around $6.50. AE, MC, V. Daily 11am until 1 hr. before park closes. NORWEGIAN.

An informal eatery in the Norway pavilion, Kringla Bakeri og Kafe offers covered outdoor seating and inexpensive light fare. The menu includes open-faced sandwiches (such as smoked salmon stuffed with hard-boiled egg), cheese and fruit platters, waffles sprinkled with powdered sugar, and fresh-baked Norwegian pastries.

Lotus Blossom Café. China Pavilion, World Showcase. ☎ **407/827-5678.** Reservations not accepted. Most entrees around $6; children's meal under $5. AE, MC, V. Daily 11am until 1 hr before park closes. CHINESE.

Try the open-air Lotus Blossom Café, a pleasant (and inexpensive) self-service outlet for light fare—egg rolls, pork-fried rice, and entrees such as stir-fried chicken and vegetables served over noodles. Cooking demonstrations take place near the entrance several times a day.

Sommerfest. Germany Pavilion, World Showcase. ☎ **407/WDW-DINE** (939-3463). Reservations not accepted. All items under $7. AE, MC, V. Hours vary with park hours. GERMAN.

At Sommerfest—a cafeteria with indoor seating backed by a mural of German castles and countryside and courtyard tables overlooking a fountain—you can purchase bratwurst sandwiches with sauerkraut, goulash soup, and desserts such as apple strudel.

Sunshine Season Food Fair. Land Pavilion, Future World. ☎ **407/WDW-DINE** (939-3463). Reservations not accepted. Prices start at $6.95. AE, MC, V. Hours vary with park hours. FOOD COURT.

Located on the lower level of the Land Pavilion, the Sunshine Season Food Fair is a good choice for family dining. Vendors offer an array of low-priced items—barbecued chicken and ribs, homemade soups and fresh salads, immense cinnamon rolls, fresh fruit, pastas, stuffed baked potatoes, sandwiches, oven-fresh cakes and pastries, ice cream, and more. Colorful umbrella tables under a skylit tent-top ring a splashing fountain, and hot-air balloons add to the festive decor.

Yakitori House. Japan Pavilion, World Showcase. ☎ **407/WDW-DINE** (939-3463). Reservations not accepted. All items under $8; children's meal under $5. AE, MC, V. Hours vary with park hours. JAPANESE.

Housed in a replica of the 16th-century Katsura Imperial Villa in Kyoto is Yakitori House, a bamboo-roofed cafeteria serving shrimp tempura over noodles, chicken yakitori, and other Japanese snack fare. Umbrella tables on a terrace overlooking a rock waterfall are a plus.

IN THE MAGIC KINGDOM

In addition to the five places mentioned next, there are plenty of fast-food outlets located throughout the park. I find a quiet sit-down meal an essential respite from theme-park hullabaloo. These restaurants are located on the maps "Walt Disney World & Lake Buena Vista Dining" in this section and (more specifically) "The Magic Kingdom" in chapter 7.

EXPENSIVE

Cinderella's Royal Table. Cinderella's Castle, Fantasyland. ☎ **407/WDW-DINE** (939-3463). Priority seating. Main courses $10–$20 per person at lunch, $21–$40 per person at dinner. AE, MC, V. 11:30am–3pm and 4pm–park closing. AMERICAN.

Cinderella's Royal Table has a Gothic interior with leaded-glass windows and heraldic banners suspended from a vaulted ceiling. The only anachronistic note: Background music is from Disney movies. The menu features hearty cuts of beef such as prime rib and grilled sirloin served with fresh sautéed vegetables and soup. And while you're piling on cholesterol, you might as well opt for an appetizer of almond-breaded brie served with wild-lingonberry relish. Less caloric entrees include grilled swordfish and a vegetarian plate. There's berry and apple cobbler topped with vanilla ice cream for dessert. *Note:* Cinderella often greets guests in the downstairs entrance hall. Cinderella's Royal Table also hosts a daily character breakfast; see details later in this chapter.

MODERATE

Crystal Palace. Main Street, USA. ☎ **407/WDW-DINE** (939-3463). Priority seating. Breakfast buffet $13.95 adults, $7.95 children 3–11; lunch $14.95 adults, $7.95 children 3–11; dinner $19.95 adults, $9.95 children 3–11. AE, MC, V. 8–10:30am, 11:30am–3:15pm, and 4pm–park closing. AMERICAN REGIONAL.

This all-buffet restaurant offers a changing menu of such home-cooked standards as fried chicken, macaroni and cheese, and a variety of vegetables and deserts. The food is filling, if not exactly overwhelming. The real treats here are the characters, Winnie the Pooh and pals, who are on location throughout the day. This is a family restaurant, and the characters are kid-magnets. (*Hint:* It's not exactly the place for romantic getaways.) Also because of the popularity of the characters, priority seating is essential.

Liberty Tree Tavern. Liberty Square. ☎ **407/WDW-DINE** (939-3463). Priority seating. Main courses $10–$17 at lunch; dinners here are all-you-can-eat character meals (discussed in section 7 of this chapter). AE, MC, V. 11:30am–3pm and 4pm–park closing. AMERICAN.

The Liberty Tree Tavern replicates an 18th-century pub, with pegged oak-plank floors, displays of pewterware in oak hutches, and a vast brick fireplace hung with copper pots in its entranceway. Background music is appropriate to the period, and even the windows have panes of hand-pressed glass, a detail typical of Disney thoroughness. Entrees range from New England pot roast braised in burgundy and served with mashed potatoes and vegetables to a traditional roast turkey dinner with all the trimmings. Precede these with a bowl of creamy New England clam chowder. There's apple crisp topped with vanilla ice cream for dessert. I prefer the food here to Cinderella's Royal Table, and this restaurant is also more likely to be able to seat large parties.

Tony's Town Square Restaurant. Main Street. ☎ **407/WDW-DINE** (939-3463). Priority seating. Breakfast items under $10; main courses $10–$20 at lunch, $20–$30 at dinner. AE, MC, V. Daily 8:30–10:45am, noon–3pm, and 3:45pm–park closing. ITALIAN.

Inspired by *Lady and the Tramp*, Tony's Town Square Restaurant is Victorian plush, with rich cherrywood beams and paneling, a central fountain, cut-glass mirrors, and globe lighting fixtures. Walls are hung with original cels from the movie. There's additional seating in a sunny, plant-filled solarium. Tony's opens early for breakfast (you can eat here while waiting for the other lands to open); menu items range from Lady and the Tramp-shaped waffles to French toast tossed in cinnamon sugar and served with warm maple or fruit syrup. The rest of the day, the fare is Italian, featuring appetizers such as a five-cheese vegetable pizza and fried calamari with marinara sauce. The lunch menu lists a variety of pastas, calzones, subs, and salads. Dinner options range from garlicky sautéed shrimp and seasonal vegetables over linguine in a light cream sauce to a 12-ounce strip steak/sautéed lobster combination, also served with linguine in garlic cream sauce.

INEXPENSIVE

The Plaza Restaurant. Main Street. ☎ **407/WDW-DINE** (939-3463). Priority seating. Sandwiches, burgers, and salads. $7.75–$10.75. AE, MC, V. Open 11am–park closing. AMERICAN.

Near the end of Main Street, to your right as you enter the park, is the pretty Plaza Restaurant, with an art-nouveau interior. It serves burgers, salads, and sandwiches

Walt Disney World & Lake Buena Vista Dining

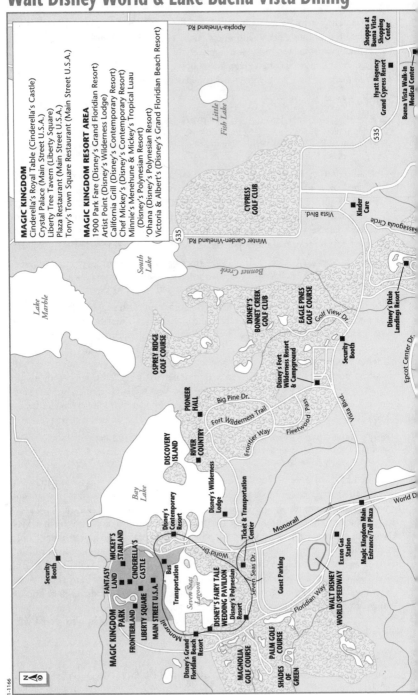

MAGIC KINGDOM

Cinderella's Royal Table (Cinderella's Castle)
Crystal Palace (Main Street U.S.A.)
Liberty Tree Tavern (Liberty Square)
Plaza Restaurant (Main Street U.S.A.)
Tony's Town Square Restaurant (Main Street U.S.A.)

MAGIC KINGDOM RESORT AREA

1900 Park Fare (Disney's Grand Floridian Resort)
Artist Point (Disney's Wilderness Lodge)
California Grill (Disney's Contemporary Resort)
Chef Mickey's (Disney's Contemporary Resort)
Minnie's Menehune & Mickey's Tropical Luau
(Disney's Polynesian Resort)
'Ohana (Disney's Polynesian Resort)
Victoria & Albert's (Disney's Grand Floridian Beach Resort)

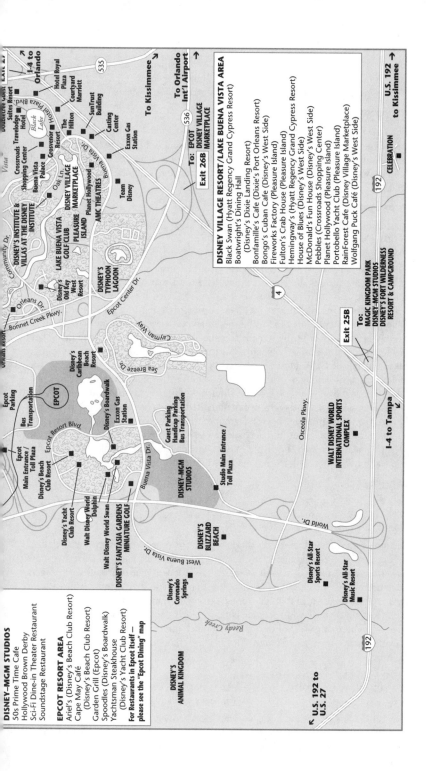

DISNEY-MGM STUDIOS

50s Prime Time Cafe
Hollywood Brown Derby
Sci-Fi Dine-in Theater Restaurant
Soundstage Restaurant

EPCOT RESORT AREA

Ariel's (Disney's Beach Club Resort)
Cape May Café
  (Disney's Beach Club Resort)
Garden Grill (Epcot)
Spoodles (Disney's Boardwalk)
Yachtsman Steakhouse
  (Disney's Yacht Club Resort)
**For Restaurants in Epcot itself —
please see the "Epcot Dining" map**

DISNEY VILLAGE RESORT/LAKE BUENA VISTA AREA

Black Swan (Hyatt Regency Grand Cypress Resort)
Boatwright's Dining Hall
  (Disney's Dixie Landing Resort)
Bonfamille's Cafe (Dixie's Port Orleans Resort)
Bongo's Cuban Cafe (Disney's West Side)
Fireworks Factory (Pleasure Island)
Fulton's Crab House (Pleasure Island)
Hemingway's (Hyatt Regency Grand Cypress Resort)
House of Blues (Disney's West Side)
McDonald's Fun House (Disney's West Side)
Pebbles (Crossroads Shopping Center)
Planet Hollywood (Pleasure Island)
Portobello Yacht Club (Pleasure Island)
RainForest Cafe (Disney Village Marketplace)
Wolfgang Puck Café (Disney's West Side)

105

(tuna and Swiss on whole wheat, a Reuben, hot roast-beef double-deckers) that you can wash down with a vanilla, chocolate, or strawberry shake. Or skip the shake and leave room for a hot-fudge sundae. There's waiter service.

AT DISNEY–MGM STUDIOS

There are more than a dozen places to eat in this Hollywood theme park, with movie-lot monikers like the Studio Commissary and Starring Rolls Bakery. The three listed next are my favorites. These restaurants are located on two maps, "Walt Disney World & Lake Buena Vista Dining" (in this chapter) and, more specifically, "Disney–MGM Studios" (in chapter 7).

EXPENSIVE

Hollywood Brown Derby. Hollywood Blvd. ☎ **407/WDW-DINE** (939-3463). Priority seating. Main courses $9.95–$17.50 at lunch, $17.50–$25 at dinner. AE, MC, V. Hours vary with park hours. AMERICAN.

The Hollywood Brown Derby, modeled after the famed Los Angeles celebrity haunt where Louella Parsons and Hedda Hopper held court, evokes its one-time West Coast counterpart with interior palm trees and roomy, semicircular leather booths lighted by derby-shaded sconces. Mahogany wainscoted walls are hung with 1,600 caricatures of major stars who patronized the California restaurant—everyone from Bette Davis to Sammy Davis. Brown Derby legends abound: It was at the Brown Derby that Clark Gable proposed to Carole Lombard, Wallace Beery poured ketchup over his sponge cake, and Lucille Ball and Jack Haley chucked dinner rolls at each other across the tables! A pianist entertains while you dine. The Derby's signature dish is the Cobb salad, invented by owner Bob Cobb in the 1930s. Dinner entrees come with a choice of soup or salad (select the champagne-nuanced oyster brie, available à la carte at lunch). Go on to an entree of baked grouper meunière, served atop pasta in a light, lemony white-wine cream sauce. Grapefruit cake with cream-cheese frosting is the Derby's signature dessert, but I prefer the white-chocolate cheesecake. There's a full bar, California wines are featured, and after-dinner drinks are a specialty.

MODERATE

50's Prime Time Cafe. Near the Indiana Jones Stunt Spectacular. ☎ **407/WDW-DINE** (939-3463). Priority seating. Main courses $10–$18 at lunch, $13–$22 at dinner. AE, MC, V. Open 11am–park closing. AMERICAN.

The 50's Prime Time Cafe places diners in a 1950s time warp/sitcom psychodrama. Eating areas look like homey 1950s kitchens, wherein black-and-white TV sets show clips from classics like "My Little Margie" and "Topper." The wait staff greets diners like family ("Hi Sis, I'll go tell Mom you're home"), and may threaten you with no dessert if you don't eat your veggies, or tell on you for resting your elbows on the table. The food—meat loaf with mashed potatoes, Granny's pot roast, Dad's chili, and such—isn't all that great, but the place is so much fun, you'll love it anyway. Desserts include banana splits and S'mores. The adjacent Tune-In Lounge serves inexpensive light fare.

Sci-Fi Dine-In Theater Restaurant. Across from the Monster Sound Show. ☎ **407/WDW-DINE** (939-3463). Priority seating. Main courses $8–$13.50 at lunch, $10–$25 at dinner. AE, MC, V. Open 10:30am–park closing. AMERICAN.

The Sci-Fi Dine-In Theater Restaurant replicates an 1950s Los Angeles drive-in movie emporium. Diners are ensconced in flashy, chrome-trimmed convertible cars (complete with fins and whitewalls) under a twinkling, starlit sky with the Hollywood hills as a backdrop. Friendly carhops bring your food order and complimentary popcorn.

While you eat, you can watch the movie screen, where a mix of zany newsreels (for example, News of the Future) is interspersed with cartoons, horror-movie clips (Frankenstein Meets the Space Monster), and coming attractions. The food could be better, but the creative theming is ample compensation. Menu items have names like the Towering Terror (barbecued pork ribs with veggies and fries) and Plucked from Deepest Space (a grilled-chicken sandwich with Cajun remoulade sauce and fries). Finish up with the Cheesecake That Ate New York. Though the restaurant basically appeals to kids (whose menu items are all under $4), beverages include wine and beer (there's a full bar), as well as milk shakes. Your bill is presented as a speeding ticket.

Toy Story Pizza Planet. In the Muppet's Courtyard. ☎ **407/WDW-DINE** (939-3463). No reservations accepted. All main courses under $10. AE, MC, V. Open 10:30am–park closing. PIZZA.

This restaurant offers what the name implies, along with salads, espresso, and cappuccino. The food is not exactly gourmet, but meals are reasonably priced. This is part arcade/part restaurant, and kids of all ages will love the many games and diversions. This boisterous, family eatery, however, is not a quiet place to get away.

IN THE ANIMAL KINGDOM

The RainForest Cafe here, just like the one in Downtown Disney Marketplace, is a big draw for sit-down dining. Other options include **Tuskers House** in Africa, which serves rotisserie, grilled, and fried chicken and salads. The **Restaurantorsaurus**—yup, you guessed it, this one is in DinoLand U.S.A.—serves hamburgers, hot dogs, and authentic McDonald's french fries and Chicken McNuggets.

IN THE WALT DISNEY WORLD RESORTS

These restaurants are located on the map "Walt Disney World & Lake Buena Vista Dining" in this chapter.

VERY EXPENSIVE

✪ **Victoria & Albert's.** In Disney's Grand Floridian Beach Resort, 4401 Floridian Way. ☎ **407/WDW-DINE** (939-3463). Reservations required. Jackets required for men. Prix-fixe meal $80 per person, $30 additional for Royal Wine Pairing; $100–$160 Chef's Table. AE, MC, V. Two dinner seatings daily, 5:45–6:30pm and 9–9:45pm. Free self- and validated valet parking. INTERNATIONAL.

It's not often that I'd ever describe a dining experience as flawless, but Victoria & Albert's, the World's most elite restaurant (in Walt Disney World, that is), managed to win that adjective from me. Its intimate dining room is plush; diners sink into leather-upholstered Louis XIII–style chairs at exquisitely appointed tables lit by silver-shaded Victorian lamps. A maid and butler provide deft and gracious service, and a harpist plays softly while you dine.

Dinner, a seven-course affair, is described in a personalized menu sealed with a gold wax insignia. The fare changes nightly. You might begin with an hors d'oeuvre of Florida lobster tail with aïoli. A more formal appetizer is the vermouth-poached jumbo sea scallops served in a crisp rice-noodle basket on shallot-chive sauce with garnishes of caviar and Chinese tat soi leaves; a shot of peppered vodka adds piquancy to a velvety plum-tomato bisque sprinkled with smoked bacon and lightly topped with pesto cream sauce. For an entree, you could select a fan of pink, juicy sautéed Peking duck breast slices with wild rice and crabapple chutney. A salad of exotic greens in an orange sherry vinaigrette clears the palate for the next course— English Stilton served with pine-nut bread, port wine, and a pear poached in burgundy, cognac, and cinnamon sugar. The conclusion: I would suggest a sumptuous

---

The Chef's Table: The Best Seat in the World

There's a special dining option at **Victoria & Albert's.** Reserve the Chef's Table here, and dine in a charming alcove hung with copper pots and dried flower wreaths at an elegantly appointed candlelit table . . . right in the heart of the kitchen! You'll sip champagne with chef Scott Hunnell while discussing your food preferences for the seven- to nine-course menu he'll be creating especially for you. There's a cooking seminar element to this experience: Diners get to tour the kitchen and observe the artistry of highly skilled chefs at work. The Chef's Table can accommodate up to six people a night. It's a leisurely affair, lasting 3 or 4 hours. The price is $115 without wine, $160 per person including five wines (I strongly recommend the latter). Let me further whet your appetite: There's a surprise during dinner, but I can't tell you what it is or it won't be one. The Chef's Table is immensely popular. Reserve months in advance by calling **407/WDW-DINE** (939-3463) or 407/824-1089.

---

hazelnut-and-Frangelico soufflé, followed by coffee and chocolate truffles. There is, of course, an extensive recherché wine list. I suggest you opt for the Royal Wine Pairing, which provides an appropriate wine with each course and lets you sample a variety of selections from the restaurant's distinguished cellars.

EXPENSIVE

✪ **Ariel's.** In Disney's Beach Club Resort, 1800 Epcot Resorts Blvd. ☎ **407/WDW-DINE** (939-3463). Main courses mostly $17.95–$24. AE, MC, V. Daily 6–10pm. Free self- and valet parking. SEAFOOD.

Named for the Little Mermaid character, this exquisite restaurant overlooking Stormalong Bay is awash in seafoam green, peach, and coral. A 2,000-gallon coral-reef tank is filled with tropical fish, walls are hung with oil paintings of scenes from the movie, and whimsical fish mobiles and glass bubbles dangle from a vaulted ceiling. You'll feel like you're dining in an underwater kingdom.

Appetizers (which supplement a complimentary smoked clam dip) include scrumptious New England silver-dollar crab cakes served with a spicy tartar sauce. Or start off with a Cajun-style shellfish gumbo replete with chunks of shrimp, lobster, and smoky andouille sausage. For your entree, a traditional Spanish paella—an array of fresh lobster, scallops, mussels, calamari, and shrimp inside a ring of saffron rice—is highly recommended. A few nonseafood options are offered as well, among them USDA choice New York strip steak grilled over a hickory and oak fire. Desserts include a rich Chambord raspberry chocolate cake. An extensive award-winning wine list indicates which selections best complement your entree. A children's menu lists items like chicken nuggets and spaghetti with meat sauce in the $4 to $6 range.

✪ **California Grill.** At Disney's Contemporary Resort, 4600 N. World Dr. ☎ **407/WDW-DINE** (939-3463) or 407/824-1576. Reservations recommended. Main courses $14.75–$27.50. AE, MC, V. Daily 5:30–10pm. Lounge open noon–midnight. CALIFORNIA.

You might see Disney CEO Michael Eisner dining here with fellow corporate honchos; it's one of his favorite WDW dining rooms. High above the Magic Kingdom (on the Contemporary Resort's 15th floor), this stunning California-style restaurant offers scenic views of the park and lagoon below. A zig-zaggy Wolfgang Puckish interior incorporates art deco elements (a cove ceiling, curved pear-wood walls, vivid splashes of color, polished black granite surfaces), but the central focus is a dramatic exhibition kitchen with a hearthlike wood-burning oven and rotisserie. Gorgeous flower arrangements and cornucopia-like displays of fruits and vegetables are further embellishments.

Chef Clifford Pleau's menus change seasonally. A sushi sampler makes a good beginning here, as does ravioli filled with goat cheese, shiitake mushrooms, and sun-dried tomatoes. And whole-wheat-crust pizzas might comprise a light entree. Heartier choices include braised lamb shank (with wild chanterelle risotto and orange-nuanced bread topping) or grilled pork tenderloin served atop polenta with crimini mushrooms and a garnish of crispy fried sage. For dessert, it's hard to surpass the butterscotch crème brûlée with almond biscotti. If you like a close-up view of chefs at work, ask to sit at the kitchen counter. There's a good selection of California wines to complement your meal. And light fare (sushi, quesadillas, spring rolls) is available at the plush adjoining bar lounge.

On the Disney Boardwalk, Lake Buena Vista. ☎ **407/939-3463**. Priority seating. Main courses $10–$22. AE, MC. V. Daily 7–11am, noon–2pm, and 5–10pm. TAPAS/MEDITERRANEAN.

The soft, pale colors and clapboard buildings of Disney's Boardwalk evoke the easy living of summer vacations at the seashore and lead to one of Disney's newer, and most acclaimed, restaurants. The food at Spoodles, however, is not for those with a pastel palette. This is true Mediterranean cuisine. It was also recognized in 1997 as one of the nation's top 20 restaurants by *Wine Trader* magazine.

Chef David Reynoso has added spice to traditional Spanish tapas. The barbecued Moroccan beef skewers with raisins, toasted almonds, and couscous are drenched in a hot, tangy sauce. The artichoke ravioli with garlic, cherry tomatoes, and arugula is a vegetarian delight. Those with heartier appetites—or those not inclined to share—can try the "Tapas Grande," such as potato-crusted salmon simmered with wild mushrooms in a veal broth with truffle oil. Disney has gone to great lengths to provide an impressive wine menu, so be sure to indulge. Tableside sangria presentations, where the fruit-laced libation is sliced and spiked before your eyes, also add something special to the evening. There is a kid's menu featuring a "you make it, we bake it" pizza combination. During the height of the summer tourist season, Spoodles can get crowded, and the wait can be long, even with priority seating, so this may not be the best option for famished families coming straight from the parks. It is, however, a nice, relaxed option for adults.

✪ **Yachtsman Steakhouse.** In Disney's Yacht Club Resort, 1700 Epcot Resorts Blvd. ☎ **407/WDW-DINE** (939-3463). Main courses $20–$29. AE, MC, V. Daily 5:30–10pm. Free self- and valet parking. STEAK/CHOPS/SEAFOOD.

The Yacht Club, a gorgeous resort inspired by New England's grand turn-of-the-century summer mansions, houses a fittingly elegant signature restaurant. Lacquered knotty-pine beams, paneling, and plank flooring create a warm, woody feel that is enhanced by burgundy leather-upholstered oak chairs. USDA grain-fed beef—hand-selected to ensure top marbling for natural juices and tenderness—is aged, cured, cut, and ground on the premises. You can see these prime cuts on display in a glass-enclosed beef-aging room, and an exhibition kitchen provides a tantalizing glimpse of sizzling steaks, chops, and seafood being grilled over oak and hickory.

You might begin your meal with an appetizer of garlicky escargots marinated in dry vermouth and served en croûte with rich burgundy sauce. Beef entrees—such as succulent filet mignon, prime rib of beef au jus, or an 18-ounce Kansas City strip steak served on the bone (it's a cattle-drive tradition)—are served with baked potato, a board of fresh-baked bread, and a choice of béarnaise or bordelaise sauce. Side dishes, such as a skillet of fresh mushrooms sautéed in cognac and creamed spinach, are note-worthy. Other dishes run the gamut from lamb chops with apple mint butter and rose-mary gin sauce to crisp-grilled chicken in apricot brandy sauce. And for the truly intrepid, there's a brownie fudge sundae for dessert. An extensive wine list is available, and a children's menu offers full meals for $5 to $10.

MODERATE

Artist Point. In Disney's Wilderness Lodge, 901 W. Timberline Dr. ☎ **407/WDW-DINE** (939-3463). Main courses $17–$26. AE, MC, V. Daily 5:30–10pm. Free self- and valet parking. STEAK & SEAFOOD/GAME SPECIALTIES.

This stunning resort restaurant centers on western-theme murals inspired by Rocky Mountain School artists Albert Bierstadt and Thomas Moran (the theme does deviate a bit, however—look for the hidden Mickeys). The illusion that you're dining in a rustically elegant, turn-of-the-century national park lodge is enhanced by large windows overlooking a lake and waterfall. Weather permitting, there's also terrace seating.

The menu changes seasonally. On a recent visit, I enjoyed a Northwest salmon sampler appetizer (smoked pepperlachs, cured gravlax, and pan-seared salmon served with onion/pepper/caper relish). And entrees ranged from a 16-ounce grilled porterhouse steak (served with red-skin potatoes, fire-roasted onions, garlic, and mushrooms) to grilled, maple-glazed king salmon (served with roasted vegetables, roasted apples, and couscous studded with morsels of sun-dried cherries, pignoli nuts, and smoked onion). Game specials and Pacific Northwestern wines are featured. Desserts—such as chocolate-silk bread pudding topped with vanilla ice cream and chocolate sauce—are immense (consider sharing) and delicious.

'Ohana. At Disney's Polynesian Resort, 1600 Seven Seas Dr. ☎ **407/WDW-DINE** (939-3463). Family-feast $20.95 for adults, $9.95 for children 3–11 (see also "Dining with Disney Characters," later in this chapter). AE, MC, V. Daily 7:30–11am and 5–10pm. Free self- and valet parking. PACIFIC RIM.

You'll be welcomed here with warm island hospitality by a server who addresses you as "cousin." 'Ohana means "family" in Hawaiian, and you're about to enjoy a convivial meal with the extended clan. The setting is South Seas exotic, with thatched roofing and tapa-cloth tenting overhead, carved Polynesian columns, and an open kitchen centering on a wood-burning, 18-foot fire-pit grill. There's lots going on at all times. The blowing of a conch shell summons a storyteller, coconut races take place down the central aisle, couples get up and dance to island music, and people celebrating birthdays participate in hula hoop contests as everyone sings "Happy Birthday" to them in Hawaiian. Kids especially love all the hoopla, but if you're looking for an intimate venue, this isn't it.

Soon after you're seated, a lazy Susan arrives laden with steamed dumplings in soy/sesame oil, Napa cabbage slaw with honey mustard, black-bean and corn relish, and several tangy sauces. And course succeeds course in rapid succession (ask your waiter to slow the pace if it's too fast). The feast includes salad, fresh-baked herbed focaccia bread, grilled chicken, smoky pork sausage, marinated turkey breast, mesquite-seasoned beef, teriyaki ribs, jumbo shrimp, stir-fried noodles and vegetables, fresh pineapple with caramel sauce, soft drinks, and coffee. Passion-fruit crème brûlée is extra, but worth it. A full bar offers tropical drinks, including nonalcoholic ones for kids.

INEXPENSIVE

Boatwright's Dining Hall. In Disney's Dixie Landings Resort, 1251 Dixie Dr. (off Bonnet Creek Pkwy.). ☎ **407/WDW-DINE** (939-3463). Breakfast items $6.25–$9; main courses $11–$19; sandwiches $7.95. AE, MC, V. Daily 7:30–11:30am and 5–10pm. Free self-parking. NEW ORLEANS.

Boatwright's is themed to look like an 1800s boat-building factory, complete with the wooden hull of a Louisiana fishing boat suspended from its lofty beamed ceiling.

An uncommonly pretty factory, it has oak-plank floors and two large working brick fireplaces. Kids will enjoy the wooden toolboxes on every table; each contains a salt shaker that doubles as a level, a wood-clamp sugar dispenser, a pepper-grinder-cum-ruler, a jar of unmatched utensils, shop rags (to be used as napkins), and a little metal pail of crayons.

Cajun breakfasts offer intriguing possibilities. French toast here is made from a sourdough–sweet potato baguette tossed in rich egg custard, deep-fried, and coated with cinnamon sugar. Another option: a pan of sautéed crawfish, mushrooms, green onions, and tomatoes in mustard cream sauce (served with home-style potatoes topped with two eggs and an oven-fresh buttermilk biscuit). Start with deep-fried bacon-wrapped oysters and scallops, then follow with an entree of rich bouillabaisse redolent of oaken cognac or a medley of blackened seafood served over brown-buttered pasta in creamy garlic sauce. For dessert, there's homemade fruit cobbler topped with vanilla ice cream and smothered in whipped cream.

Bonfamille's Cafe. In Disney's Port Orleans Resort, 2201 Orleans Dr. (off Bonnet Creek Pkwy.). ☎ **407/WDW-DINE** (939-3463). Breakfast items $4.25–$6.95; main courses mostly $8.25–$14.95; salads and po'boy sandwiches $6.95. AE, MC, V. Daily 7:30–11:30am and 5–10pm. Free self-parking. NEW ORLEANS.

Named for a character in *The Aristocats,* the charming Bonfamille's is patterned after a French Quarter courtyard with fountains. Exposed-brick walls are hung with paintings of New Orleans, big baskets of flowering plants are suspended from beams overhead, and Dixieland jazz plays softly in the background. During breakfast it's light and sunny; in the evening, candle lamps provide soft lighting.

Louisiana-style breakfasts range from fresh, hot beignets and café au lait to a skillet of crawfish and andouille sausage topped with zesty Creole sauce and melted sharp cheddar. The latter is served with home-style fried potatoes topped with eggs and a hot buttermilk biscuit. A typical dinner here: an appetizer of chicken wings tossed in spicy Louisiana hot sauce served with celery and blue-cheese dip, followed by grilled Atlantic salmon (served with spicy pecan butter, rice, and sautéed vegetables), and a dessert of Bourbon Street pudding with strawberry and caramel bourbon sauces. After dinner, families can head over to the hotel's Scat Cats Lounge, where entertainment—sing-alongs and live music with lots of audience participation—is featured most nights.

✪ **Cape May Cafe.** At Disney's Beach Club Resort, 1800 Epcot Resorts Blvd. ☎ **407/WDW-DINE** (939-3463) for priority seating. Dinner $19.95 for adults, $9.50 for children 3–11; character breakfast $14.95 adults, $8.50 children. AE, MC, V. Daily 5:30–9:30pm. Free valet and self-parking. CLAMBAKE BUFFET.

A hearty 19th-century-style New England clambake is featured here nightly. Sand sculptures and furled striped beach umbrellas create the ambience of an upscale seaside resort. Aromatic New England chowder, steamed clams and mussels, corn on the cob, chicken, lobster, and red-skin potatoes are cooked up in a crackling rockweed steamer pit that serves as the restaurant's centerpiece. And these traditional clambake offerings are supplemented by dozens of salads, hot dishes (barbecued pork ribs, smoked sausage, pastas), and a wide array of oven-fresh breads and desserts. There's a full bar.

4 Places to Dine in Lake Buena Vista

In this section are restaurants located in Downtown Disney and in the Lake Buena Vista area. You can find them on the map "Walt Disney World & Lake Buena Vista Dining" in this chapter.

Located about 2½ miles from Epcot off Buena Vista Drive, Downtown Disney encompasses the Downtown Disney Marketplace, a very pleasant complex of cedar-shingled shops and restaurants overlooking a scenic lagoon; the adjoining Pleasure Island, a nighttime entertainment center; and Downtown Disney's West Side, a slightly more upscale collection of shops, restaurants, and a movie theater opened in 1997.

Note: You don't have to pay the entrance fee to Pleasure Island to dine at any of its restaurants.

AT PLEASURE ISLAND
EXPENSIVE

Fulton's Crab House. Aboard the riverboat docked at Pleasure Island. ☎ **407/934-BOAT** (2628). Reservations recommended, especially during peak season. Main courses $8.95–$15.95 at lunch, $4.95–$50 at dinner. AE, MC, V. Daily 4pm–midnight. SEAFOOD/STEAKS.

Fulton's operates aboard a replica of a 19th-century Mississippi riverboat that is permanently moored on the shores of Lake Buena Vista. An interior decorated with nautical artifacts reflects the seafood menu. There is a deck for outdoor dining. The casual Stone Crab Lounge (open 11:30am–2am) serves light fare. Start with the Florida Stone Crab claws with mustard sauce and lime, or sample the oyster bar. For your main course, try Tuna Filet Mignon, grilled and served with lemon grass dipping sauce. A hearty eater may want to try the steak and lobster dinner, served with asparagus and a tangy house steak sauce. For a tart taste of Florida, try the key lime cheesecake for dessert. Fulton's has one of the area's better wine lists. A character breakfast, 8:30am and 10am daily, is $12.95 for adults, $7.95 for children and features Mickey, Minnie, Pluto, and Goofy. A children's menu available for lunch or dinner.

MODERATE

Fireworks Factory. 1630 Lake Buena Vista Dr., Pleasure Island. ☎ **407/934-8989.** Reservations recommended. Main courses mostly $13.95–$25. AE, MC, V. Daily 11:30am–11:30pm (dinner served from 4pm, light fare and drinks served until 2am). Free self-parking; valet parking $5. AMERICAN REGIONAL.

This exuberant corrugated-tin warehouse has big red pipes overhead and exposed brick or tin walls hung with neon signs and advertisements for fireworks. This is a good choice for family dining. The portions are generous, and kids are encouraged to color on the paper table toppers.

For lunch or dinner, start off with an appetizer sampler (spicy chicken wings, shrimp quesadillas, and applewood-smoked baby back ribs). Dinner entrees range from Cajun shrimp pasta to oak-roasted salmon served with roasted tomato/corn relish and angel-hair sweet potatoes. At lunch opt for a mesquite-smoked barbecued beef sandwich. For dessert: a giant Toll House cookie served warm and topped with vanilla ice cream and hot fudge. The restaurant serves more than 45 varieties of domestic and imported beer, ale, and stout.

Planet Hollywood. Pleasure Island; look for the large, globe-shaped restaurant. ☎ **407/827-7827.** Reservations not accepted. Lines can get long during special events and peak season. Main courses $7.50–$18.95 (most under $13). AE, DC, MC, V. Daily 11am–2am. AMERICAN.

Planet Hollywood was born in 1994 with a lavish opening-night party hosted by Arnold, Sly, Bruce, and Demi. The excitement they generated has started to dim, and the once hours-long lines have thinned. A fiber-optic ceiling creates a planetarium effect, and a veritable show-business museum displays more than 300 items ranging from Peter O'Toole's *Lawrence of Arabia* costume to the front end of the bus from the movie *Speed* (it's suspended from the ceiling). Previews of soon-to-be-released movies and video montages from films and TV are aired while you dine.

The big surprise amid all the special effects is that the food is pretty good. You can opt to nosh on appetizers—hickory-smoked buffalo wings, pot stickers, or nachos. There are also burgers, sandwiches, salads, pizzas, pastas, and platters of grilled steak, ribs, or pork chops. The desserts are worth saving room for.

Portobello Yacht Club. Pleasure Island. ☎ **407/934-8888.** Reservations strongly recommended. Main courses $7.95–$8.95 at lunch, $14.95–$29.95 at dinner; pizzas $6.95–$8.95. AE, MC, V. Daily 11:30am–midnight (dinner served from 4pm). Valet parking $5; free self-parking. REGIONAL ITALIAN.

Occupying a gabled Bermuda-style house, and having undergone extensive recent renovations, Yacht Club is casual, with an interior suggesting a luxury cruise ship. From the lively mahogany-paneled bar, you can watch pizzas being prepared over an oak fire in an exhibition kitchen. Multipaned windows overlook Lake Buena Vista, as do the tables on the awning-covered patios. The pizzas, with thin crisp crusts and toppings such as *quattro formaggi* (mozzarella and provolone) with sun-dried tomatoes, are a tasty deal for lunch or dinner. For the evening meal, try *Costoletta Di MaiAle*, marinated roasted pork loin with fennel, carrots, and roasted garlic whipped potatoes. Also try the Spaghettini Alla Portobello with Alaskan crab and other seafood in a light sauce of olive oil, wine, and herbs. A dessert of *crema bruccioto* (white-chocolate custard with a caramelized sugar glaze) is recommended. There's an extensive wine list.

AT DOWNTOWN DISNEY MARKETPLACE

✪ **RainForest Cafe.** Downtown Disney Marketplace; look for the smoking volcano. ☎ **407/827-8500.** Reservations accepted on-site; expect long waits. Main courses $5.50–$17.95. AE, DISC, MC, V. Sun–Thurs 10:30am–11pm; Fri–Sat 10:30am–midnight. CALIFORNIA.

Don't arrive starving. Waits of 4 hours aren't unheard of, so plan to make reservations and then explore the rest of Downtown Disney. (Lines may shorten as a second Rain-Forest is added near Animal Kingdom, but don't count on it. If the lines stay long, the good news is that you will be able to make priority seating reservations there.) With its lush, dark interiors, calls of the wild, and unique animal-style bar stools, you feel far removed from the rush of the parks. Kids especially love the junglelike setting. This is, after all, one place where monkey business is encouraged. The food is pretty good, too. Try unusual delicacies like Rasta Pasta, bowtie noodles mixed with spinach, roasted red peppers, broccoli, and Parmesan cheese—the whole dish smothered in a garlic-pesto cream sauce. There is an extensive menu, including a reduced-price menu for children. Top off your meal with coconut bread pudding with dried apricots; the lavish garnish of whipped cream, toasted coconut, and chocolate shaving is almost as good as the dessert itself. There is a good selection of beers and wines. The tables are very close together, so those with physical disabilities may find it difficult to maneuver.

DISNEY'S WEST SIDE

Bongo's Cuban Cafe. Disney's West Side. ☎ **407/828-0999.** No reservations. Priority seating for parties of 7 or more. Main courses, $8.95–$24.95. Daily 11am–2am. AE, DISC, DC, V, MC. CUBAN.

Created by Cuban-American songstress Gloria Estefan and husband, Emilio, this cafe is Disney's version of old Havana. The chairs are leopard-spotted, the mosaic bar stools shaped like bongo drums. A Desi Arnaz look-alike might even show up to sing a few tunes. The upbeat salsa music makes this a noisy location, so seek out the patio or the upstairs lounge for some privacy and quiet. A Cuban sandwich—thinly toasted bread with ham and cheese—is done right here (kids also might like it). Start with the thick, slightly spicy, black bean soup and try a dinner of *arroz con pollo* (chicken with rice). Coffee-lovers should sample the thick, dark Cuban coffee.

✪ **House of Blues.** Disney's West Side, under the old-fashioned water tower. ☎ **407/934-2583.** Reservations not accepted (except for Gospel Brunch). AE, DISC, MC, V. $13.95–$18.95. MISSISSIPPI DELTA.

Hearty portions of down-home food served in an atmosphere literally shaking with rock 'n' roll. Exceedingly crowded on days of big concerts, the music in the nightclub next door is as much of a draw as the food. Funky, colorful folk art covers the rustic walls from floor to ceiling. (Take a walk through the small courtyard.) The back patio has seating and a nice view of the bay. Let's not forget the food. The spicy jambalaya and gumbo are good bets. The baby back ribs with garlic mashed potatoes and turnip greens are literally finger-lickin' good. Try the bread pudding for dessert. A children's menu, with staples like grilled cheese and hamburgers, is available. The Sunday Gospel Brunch ($23.99 for adults and $11.99 for children 4–12) features foot-stomping music and an awe-inspiring array of Southern fare such as cheese grits and sausage. Foreign visitors might especially enjoy this cultural immersion. Make reservations early since it regularly sells out.

McDonald's Fun House. Disney's West Side. ☎ **407/WDW-DINE** (939-3463). No reservations. Daily 11am–midnight. Sandwiches and meals $4.95–$9.95. HAMBURGERS.

With over 10,000 square feet, this is one mammoth Mickey D's. This restaurant is equal parts eatery and playground and has such diversions as the Grimace's Game Room, in his signature purple, with wall-mounted toys, tubes, balls, and buzzers. You gotta love the French Fry Organ and the soda cup chandeliers, but know this is a very kid-intensive place except for late in the evening.

Wolfgang Puck Café. Disney's West Side. ☎ **407/WDW-DINE** (939-3463). Reservations recommended. Daily 11am–midnight. $8.95–$18.95. AE, V, MC. CALIFORNIA.

Avante-garde chef Wolfgang Puck brings his West Coast creations to the heart of Florida. You can eat gourmet pizza, with a thin, crisp crust and exotic toppings, either on an outdoor patio or inside. An appetizer of vegetable spring rolls or a sampling from the sushi bar should be followed by the fresh grilled chicken or the Chinois chicken salad.

ELSWHERE IN LAKE BUENA VISTA
VERY EXPENSIVE

Black Swan. In the Hyatt Regency Grand Cypress Resort, 1 Grand Cypress Blvd. (off Fla 535). ☎ **407/239-1999.** Reservations recommended. Main courses $25–$34. AE, CB, DC, DISC, JCB, MC, V. Daily 6–10pm. Free self-parking. AMERICAN/CONTINENTAL.

Overlooking the magnificent emerald fairways of this posh resort's golf course, the Black Swan has a lodgelike, split-level interior with a big working fireplace and a cross-beamed knotty-pine cathedral ceiling. Large, pine-framed windows overlook the 9th hole, and that verdant view is echoed within by lovely floral arrangements and planters of greenery. Golfers make up the majority of the clientele. It's not unusual here to see someone rise up excitedly from a table and demonstrate how he eagled the 17th and birdied the 18th hole to win a match. Barring that, dinner entertainment consists of a pianist at a white baby grand.

A meal here might begin with an appetizer of grilled marinated portobello mushrooms nestled on a bed of wilted arugula and topped with wild mushrooms and Asiago cheese gratinée. A main dish of roast rack of lamb (thick, juicy slices grilled in an herbed honey-Dijon crust) comes with mashed potatoes and rosemary jus. Another choice, corn-tortilla-crusted breast of chicken, is served with black beans and roasted corn relish and cilantro chili fettuccine. A warm, crisp apple tart on caramel sauce topped with honey-vanilla ice cream and whipped cream might provide a fitting finale. The Black Swan has an extensive wine list with many after-dinner libations (cognacs, ports, etc.).

EXPENSIVE

✪ **Hemingway's.** In the Hyatt Regency Grand Cypress Resort, 1 Grand Cypress Blvd. (off Fla. 535). ☎ **407/239-1234.** Reservations recommended. Main courses $7.50–$19.75 at lunch, $20–$28 at dinner. AE, CB, DC, DISC, JCB, MC, V. Tues–Sat 11:30am–2:30pm; daily 6–10:30pm. Free self- and validated valet parking. SEAFOOD.

Fronted by a waterfall that cascades into stone-lined streams, Hemingway's evokes Key West and honors its most famous denizen; walls are hung with sepia photographs of "Papa" and his fishing and hunting trophies. This casually elegant (and generally child-free) restaurant is a good choice for romantic dinners. In a warren of intimate dining areas under a high, weathered-pine ceiling, elegantly appointed tables are lit by gleaming brass hurricane lamps. Weather permitting, you can sit on a screened wooden deck near the waterfall.

Ask not for whom the bell tolls but rather for an appetizer of deep-fried baby squid and grilled eggplant in garlicky herb-seasoned tomato coulis. Follow up with an entree of golden brown beer-battered coconut shrimp; it's served with roasted potatoes, a colorful array of al dente vegetables, and orange marmalade–horseradish sauce. Also recommended are the deliciously light, moist, and fluffy crab cakes; try the Cajun tartar sauce with them. For dessert, key lime pie appropriately reaches its apogee here. The lunch menu offers similar fare, along with paella, sandwiches, and salads. In the adjoining Hurricane Lounge—a most congenial setting with a beautiful oak bar—specialties include a variety of island rums and the Papa Doble, a potent tropical rum and fruit libation invented by Hemingway himself (legend has it he once drank 16 of them at one sitting!).

The restaurants below can be located on the map, "Orlando Area Accommodations & Dining," on page 123.

Mikado Japanese Steak House. In Marriott's Orlando World Center, 8701 World Center Dr. (off Fla. 536). ☎ **407/238-8664.** Reservations recommended. Main courses $12.95–$28.95. AE, CB, DC, DISC, JCB, MC, V. Daily 6–10pm. Free self- and validated valet parking. JAPANESE.

This gorgeous, 230-acre resort houses a beautiful teppanyaki restaurant. Its serene interior, with intimate seating areas created by shoji screens, has windows overlooking rock gardens, reflecting pools, and a palm-fringed pond. Japanese music helps set the tone. Plan to arrive early and enjoy a cocktail at sunset on the wooden deck overlooking the swimming pool.

Meals here are teppanyaki style—which means you're seated with other patrons at a grill-topped table. For businesspeople dining alone, the socializing that happens naturally here can be a plus. A highly trained chef wheels a cart full of raw food to the table and with dazzling dexterity trims, chops, sautés, and flips it onto your waiting plate. Appetizer selections include softshell crab, smoked salmon, cucumber sushi, and assorted tempura vegetables and shrimp. Entrees—offering various combinations of steak and seafood—come with a complimentary hors d'oeuvre of grilled shrimp or scallops, soup (try the tasty miso), salad, steamed rice (yummy fried rice is available for an additional $2.25), an array of stir-fried vegetables, and green tea. A decanter of warm sake is recommended, and green tea or ginger ice cream makes a refreshing dessert. Low-priced meals are available for children.

✪ **Tuscany.** In Marriott's Orlando World Center, 8701 World Center Dr. (off Fla. 536). ☎ **407/239-4200.** Reservations recommended. Main courses $15–$27. AE, CB, DC, DISC, JCB, MC, V. Daily 6–10pm. Free self-parking; valet parking available. TUSCAN.

The showplace restaurant of a luxury resort, Tuscany has rich cherry- and mahogany-paneled walls hung with gilt-framed Michelangelo prints. Tables are set with fresh flowers, and diners are comfortably ensconced in roomy tapestry-upholstered armchairs, booths, and Regency chairs. Soft lighting and opera music complete the ambience.

A pasta appetizer is a good way to begin your meal here—most notably, the gnocchi served with Gorgonzola sauce and a garnish of diced plum tomatoes. Impressive entrees—such as rack of lamb in a light demiglace sauce with roasted eggplant purée, white beans, potato croquette, and *haricots verts*—are aesthetically presented on large, white platters. Herbed focaccia bread served with light, garlicky goat cheese accompanies your meal. An extensive European/California wine list includes many by-the-glass selections. Desserts change nightly; but if it's offered, the exquisite, thin-sliced apple tart served atop crème anglaise and garnished with fresh berries is delicious.

MODERATE

Pebbles. 12551 Fla. 535, in the Crossroads Shopping Center, Lake Buena Vista. ☎ **407/827-1111.** Reservations not accepted. Main courses mostly $9.95–$19.95. AE, DC, DISC, MC, V. Sun–Thurs 11am–11pm; Fri–Sat 11am–midnight. Free self-parking. CALIFORNIA.

Pebbles is one of Orlando's most popular restaurants, especially with a young yuppie crowd. The multilevel dining room centers on a sunken bar under a cross-beamed skylit ceiling, and though it's a large space, white wooden shutters and windowed enclosures create a warren of intimate dining areas. Lush tropical greenery, fountains, and canvas tenting contribute to the garden-party ambience. During the day, sunshine streams in; at night, flickering hurricane lamps provide romantic lighting.

The same menu is offered throughout the day, supplemented by specials. Start off with a "lite bite" of creamy baked chèvre served atop chunky tomato sauce with hot garlic bread. Pebbles offers the option of a casual meal—perhaps a cheddar burger on toasted brioche, honey-roasted spareribs, or a Caesar salad tossed with grilled chicken. Or you can select a more serious entree such as tender leg of smoked duck that has been rubbed with fennel, glazed with triple sec, and slow-roasted to sear in flavorful juices. Dessert of choice: the goldbrick sundae—a scoop of vanilla ice cream encased in a candylike chocolate/almond shell and served atop caramel sauce with fresh strawberries. There's a full bar and a recently updated wine list. Pebbles also has locations in downtown Orlando at 17 W. Church St. (☎ **407/839-0892**) and in Winter Park at 2516 Aloma Ave. (☎ **407/678-7001**).

INEXPENSIVE

✪ **Romano's Macaroni Grill.** 12148 Apopka–Vineland Rd. (just north of Country Road 535/Palm Pkwy.). ☎ **407/239-6676.** Main courses $4.95–$8.25 at lunch, $6.95–$15.95 at dinner (most under $10). AE, CB, DC, DISC, MC, V. Sun–Thurs 11am–10pm and Fri–Sat 11am–11pm. Free self-parking. NORTHERN ITALIAN.

Though friends had raved about the Macaroni Grill, I didn't really expect much from a chain restaurant. Upon entering, I was favorably impressed by its cheerful interior, with arched stone walls, shuttered windows, colorful murals of Venice, and lights festively strung overhead. A welcoming glow emanated from the exhibition kitchen, where white-hatted chefs were tending an oak-burning pizza oven, and foodstuffs, Chianti, flowers, and desserts were aesthetically arranged on counters.

But the big surprise was the food. Everything is made from the freshest ingredients, and the quality of cuisine would have been notable at twice the price. The thin-crust pizzas—such as the Mediterranean topped with fresh tomato sauce, shrimp, and feta and mozzarella cheeses—are scrumptious, as is a dish of bowtie pasta tossed with grilled chicken, pancetta, and red and green onions in Asiago cream sauce. Equally good: an entree of sautéed chicken with mushrooms, artichoke hearts, capers, and pancetta in lemon butter; it comes with spaghettini. There are fresh-baked breads, as well—focaccia and *ciabatta* (a crusty, country loaf) for sopping up sauces or dipping in extra-virgin olive oil. And desserts—especially an apple custard torte with hazelnut crust and caramel topping—keep to the same lofty standard. There's a full bar, premium wines are sold by the glass, and a children's menu offers an entree and beverage for just $3.25. Bravo Romano!

5 Places to Dine in the International Drive Area

Some of the best area restaurants are along International Drive, within about 10 minutes of Walt Disney World parks by car. These restaurants are located on the map "International Drive Area Accommodations & Dining" on page 83.

VERY EXPENSIVE

✪ **Dux.** In the Peabody Orlando, 9801 International Dr. ☎ **407/345-4550.** Reservations recommended. Máin courses $19–$45. AE, CB, DC, DISC, JCB, MC, V. Mon–Thurs 6–10pm; Fri–Sat 6–11pm. Free self- and validated valet parking. INTERNATIONAL.

Named for the hotel's signature ducks that parade ceremoniously into the lobby each morning to "Sousa's King Cotton March," this is one of central Florida's most highly acclaimed restaurants. And since the Peabody is the headquarters hotel for nearby Universal Studios, you might even see a celebrity or two among the diners. Upholstered bamboo chairs and cushioned banquettes provide seating at candlelit tables set with flowers and beautiful ceramic show plates. A lavish dessert display table with a floral centerpiece serves as a visual focus, and the textured gold walls are hung with ornately framed mirrors and watercolors (representing 72 ducks, of course).

The menu varies seasonally. One of the nicest appetizers is a unique version of pot stickers—stuffed with portobello mushrooms, scallions, and creamed goat cheese and garnished with Asiago twigs. An entree of Sonoma lamb chops glazed with Hunan barbecue sauce is accompanied by roasted Chinese mushrooms and green onions, with a small "treasure packet" of Pacific rice concealed under the lamb. Another good choice is a grilled Florida black grouper marinated in fearless (read *hot*) West Indian spices and served with a plantain-yam mash and tropical chutney. Desserts include a sublime hazelnut meringue napoleon topped with homemade frangelico ice cream and a dusting of Brazilian cocoa. Dux has an extensive, award-winning wine list.

MODERATE

✪ **B-Line Diner.** In the Peabody Orlando, 9801 International Dr. ☎ **407/345-4460.** Reservations not accepted. Main courses $2.75–$8.50 at breakfast, $6.50–$10.95 at lunch, $5.95–$29 (most under $15) at dinner. AE, CB, DC, DISC, JCB, MC, V. Daily 24 hours. Free self- and validated valet parking. AMERICAN.

This popular local diner is of the nouvelle art deco genre, which is to say that it's an idealized version of America's ubiquitous roadside establishments. Its interior gleams with chrome edging that adorns everything from a cove ceiling to peach Formica tables, and the jukebox is stocked with oldies tunes. Gorgeous flower arrangements add upscale panache. Though the B-Line is a sophisticated venue, kids get their own

Dining at CityWalk

Universal's answer to Pleasure Island and Disney's West Side opens in the fall of 1998. Although the restaurants were not open at press time, it's clear that this 12-acre entertainment complex could easily be renamed theme-restaurant heaven. Not only will it be home to the world's largest **Hard Rock Cafe**—the grande dame of all theme restaurants—but also the **NASCAR Cafe,** the **Motown Cafe,** and **Marvel Mania,** a theme send-up to villains and superheroes. CityWalk will also contain a hearty dose of Cajun spice with **Pat O'Brien's,** a re-creation of the joint in New Orleans, and **Emeril's of New Orleans,** featuring the Creole-based cuisine of chef Emeril Lagasse. If that's not enough to keep you busy, there is the **Down Beat Jazz Hall of Fame,** a tribute to reggae mon Bob Marley, and a 5,000-seat Cineplex Odeon Megaplex.

low-priced menu, an (ever-present) duck-themed coloring/activities book, and crayons; they can also enjoy ice-cream sundaes for dessert here.

The seasonally varying menu offers haute versions of diner food such as a superior chicken pot pie, pan-seared pork (with grilled apples, sun-dried cherry stuffing, and brandy honey sauce), or a ham-and-cheese sandwich on a baguette. Other items—such as a falafel sandwich on pita bread with mint yogurt sauce—bear no relation to traditional diner fare. Portions are hearty. A glass display case up front is filled with scrumptious fresh-baked desserts: everything from coffee and chocolate eclairs to white-chocolate/Grand Marnier mousse cake. There's a full bar.

✪ **Bahama Breeze.** 8849 International Dr., Orlando. ☎ **407/248-2499.** Reservations not accepted. Main courses $6.95–$15.95; sandwiches and salads $5.95–$6.95. AE, MC, V. Sun–Thurs 4pm–1am; Fri–Sat 4pm–2am. CARIBBEAN.

Traditional Caribbean foods are used to create unusual items such as the moist and tasty "fish in a bag"—strips of mahimahi in a parchment pillow flavored with carrots, sweet peppers, mushrooms, celery, and spices. Also try the paella, a rice dish brimming with shrimp, fish, mussels, chicken, and chunks of sausage. The coconut curry chicken is a light-tasting treat—sautéed chunks of chicken sprinkled with fresh coconut. For dessert try the piña-colada bread pudding, a cube of custard bread in a sweet coconut sauce, or the tart key lime pie. Created by Orlando-based Darden Restaurants, the same folks who brought you Red Lobster and Olive Garden, this Bahama Breeze is essentially a test kitchen for what may soon be a national chain. Unlike Darden's other creations, which serve solid but not necessarily savory offerings, Bahama Breeze is a unique dining experience that challenges the taste buds. You can even watch your entrees being prepared in the open kitchen. The drink menu includes over 50 beers and the expected collection of fruity, pseudo-exotic drinks, such as the Very Berry Daiquiri. Happy-hour prices are featured round-the-clock.

✪ **Cafe Tu Tu Tango.** 8625 International Dr. (just west of the Mercado). ☎ **407/248-2222.** AE, DISC, MC, V. Tapas (small plates) $3.75–$7.95. Sun–Thurs 11:30am–11pm; Fri and Sat 11:30am–1am. Free self- and valet parking. INTERNATIONAL/TAPAS.

Though one might question the need for yet one more theme experience outside the parks, this zany restaurant is a welcome respite from Orlando's predictable "chain gang." For one thing, there's an ongoing performance-art experience taking place while you dine. One evening, an elegantly dressed couple might tango past your table. Another time, a belly dancer might perform, or a magician might do a few tricks tableside. In addition, there are always artists in a studio area creating pottery, paintings, and jewelry.

In case you want to be welcomed there.

We're here to see that you're always welcomed at establishments everywhere. That's why millions of people carry the American Express® Card – for peace of mind, confidence, and security, around the world or just around the corner.

do more

Cards

In case you're running low.

We're here to help with more than 118,000 Express Cash locations around the world. In order to enroll, just call American Express before you start your vacation.

do more

Express Cash

And just in case.

We're here with American Express® Travelers Cheques and Cheques *for Two*.® They're the safest way to carry money on your vacation and the surest way to get a refund, practically anywhere, anytime.

Another way we help you...

do more

Travelers Cheques

Tu Tu's colorful ambience is a lot of fun, but its food is the real draw. The larger your party, the more dishes you can sample; two of the small plates will satisfy most appetites. My favorites include Cajun egg rolls (filled with blackened chicken, corn, and cheddar and goat cheeses, served with chunky tomato salsa and Creole mustard) and pepper-crusted, seared tuna sashimi with crispy rice noodles and cold spinach in a sesame-soy vinaigrette. International wines can be ordered by the glass or bottle. There are great desserts here, too—such as creamy almond/amaretto flan and rich guava cheesecake with strawberry sauce.

✪ **Capriccio.** In the Peabody Orlando, 9801 International Dr. ☎ **407/352-4000.** Reservations recommended. Main courses mostly $12–$22 (with most pizza and pasta dishes priced below $14); Sun champagne brunch buffet $24.95 for adults, $12.95 for children 4–12, under 4 free. AE, CB, DC, DISC, JCB, MC, V. Tues–Sun 6–11pm; Sun brunch 11am–2:30pm. Free self- and validated valet parking. ITALIAN.

Capriccio's striking Italian moderne interior features a gleaming black-and-white checkerboard marble-tile floor and black Italian marble tables elegantly appointed with Tuscan-look Villeroy & Boch show plates. An exhibition kitchen occupying an entire wall showcases chefs tending mesquite-burning pizza ovens and grills.

Seasonally changing menus bring verve and imagination to traditional Italian cookery. The appetizer of fried calamari is served with three aïolis (garlicky Basque mayonnaises) flavored, respectively, with sun-dried tomato, basil, and saffron. Also scrumptious: a pasta dish of bucatini tossed with chunks of mesquite-grilled chicken and mushrooms in a slightly garlicky herbed white-wine/pesto sauce and finished with tomato concasse. The entree of pan-seared tuna with braised fennel and radicchio is served with lentil flan and a buttery citrus sauce. The kitchen also turns out fabulous pizzas, and oven-fresh breads are accompanied by herb-infused extra-virgin olive oil; dip and exult. But save room for Capriccio's desserts, which include the definitive zuppa inglese. An extensive, award-winning wine list is available. *Note:* Capriccio also serves a great champagne Sunday brunch.

Copeland's of New Orleans. 8255 International Dr. ☎ **407/354-2220.** Reservations recommended. Main courses $7–$24. AE, DC, DISC, MC, V. Sun–Thurs 11am–11pm; Fri–Sat 11am–11:30pm. Free self-parking. NEW ORLEANS.

Tucked back in a shopping center, this taste of New Orleans is a pleasant surprise. This is part of a franchise out of New Orleans, but the food is so fresh and spicy, you'd hardly believe it. You can't go wrong with New Orleans staples like jambalaya or gumbo, or try the fresh fish with lacombe sauce. There is a full bar.

Italianni's. 8148 International Dr. ☎ **407/345-8884.** Main courses $7.95–$17.95. AE, DC, DISC, MC, V. Daily 10:30am–11pm. ITALIAN.

This is a chain restaurant from the people who created TGIFriday's. This restaurant shares the same laid-back atmosphere and friendly service. You can't go wrong with the chicken Italianni or one of the many pasta selections. The cheesecake is worth saving room for.

✪ **Ming Court.** 9188 International Dr. (between Sand Lake Rd. and the Bee Line Expwy). ☎ **407/351-9988.** Reservations recommended. Dim sum mostly $1.95–$2.50; main courses $4.50–$7.95 at lunch, $12.50–$19.95 at dinner. AE, CB, DC, DISC, JCB, MC, V. Daily 11am–2:30pm and 4:30pm–midnight. Free self-parking. CHINESE.

At this Chinese restaurant, the clientele includes more local food cognoscenti than tourists. Ming Court is fronted by a serpentine "cloud wall," crowned by engraved sea-green Chinese tiles (it's a celestial symbol; you dine above the clouds here, like the gods). The newly renovated candlelit interior is stunningly decorated in soft earth tones. Glass-walled terrace rooms overlook lotus ponds, filled with colorful koi, and a plant-filled area under a lofty skylight ceiling. A musician plays classical Chinese music on a zheng (a long zither) at dinner.

The innovative menu offers specialties from diverse regions of China and often features fresh Florida seafood. Begin with a variety of appetizers such as wok-charred Mandarin pot stickers, crispy wontons stuffed with vegetables and cream cheese, and wok-smoked shiitake mushrooms topped with sautéed scallions. Entrees will open up new culinary vistas to even the most sophisticated diners. Lightly battered, deep-fried chicken breast is served with a delicate lemon-tangerine sauce. Szechuan charcoal-grilled filet mignon is topped with a toasted onion/garlic/chili sauce and served with stir-fried julienne vegetables. At lunch, you can order dim-sum items in addition to other menu offerings. There's an extensive wine list. As a concession to Western palates, Ming Court features sumptuous desserts such as a moist cake layered with Mandarin oranges, key lime, and fresh whipped cream in an orange-vanilla sauce. Dress is upscale but casual.

Siam Orchid. 7575 Republic Dr. (between Sand Lake Rd. and Carrier Dr.). ☎ **407/ 351-0821.** Reservations recommended. Main courses $10.25–$16.95. AE, DC, DISC, MC, V. Daily 5–11pm. Free self-parking. THAI.

Patterned after a palace in northern Thailand, Siam Orchid centers on a platform used to display wood carvings of angels and musicians representing figures from the *Ramayana,* an ancient Hindu epic poem. The split-level dining room, with a lofty knotty-pine cathedral ceiling on either side, seats diners in cushioned booths and banquettes and bamboo chairs; some tables overlook a lake. For intimate dining, request a *khun toke*—a private carved-teak enclosure that is the Thai answer to Japanese tatami rooms.

Owners Tim and Krissnee Martsching grow many necessary ingredients—fresh chilies, mint, cilantro, lemongrass, and wild lime—in their own garden, and their fare is authentic and delicious. Begin with *tom kha gai* (a savory chicken-and-mushroom soup) and continue with shared appetizers such as *satay* (grilled skewers of pork or chicken, marinated in coconut cream and mild curry, served with hot peanut sauce) and *tod man* (crispy fried chicken patties flavored with lemongrass, basil, and wild lime leaf). Not to be missed (share an order) is an entree of pad Thai (soft rice noodles tossed with ground pork, fresh minced garlic, shrimp, crab claws, crabmeat, crushed peanuts, and bean sprouts in a tangy-sweet sauce). Curries—such as the royal Thai, replete with chunks of chicken, potato, and onion in a yellow curry sauce—are also a specialty. There's a full bar, and beverage choices include sake, plum wine, and Thai beers. Homemade coconut ice cream topped with crushed peanuts makes a refreshing dessert.

Wild Jacks. 7364 International Dr. (between Sand Lake Rd. and Carrier Dr.). ☎ **407/ 352-4407.** Reservations not accepted. AE, CB, DC, DISC, JCB, MC, V. Main courses $9.45–$17.95. Daily 4:30–11pm. Free self-parking. STEAKS AND BARBECUE.

This upscale but exuberantly western steak-and-barbecue restaurant has a whimsical decor, including neon beer signs, mounted buffalo heads, and a longhorn steer poised to jump from a giant horseshoe above the copper bar. Soft lighting emanates from massive, wrought-iron wagon-wheel chandeliers, as well as from fixtures with antler and steer-head motifs. The exhibition kitchen has an open-pit grill. Diners are seated at tables covered with checkered plastic cloths. And the music is country.

Appetizers here are first rate: skewers of tangy barbecued shrimp served over Texas rice (it's studded with corn kernels and red and green peppers), miniature tacos filled with smoked chicken and cheeses, and spicy potato skins topped with melted cheese, chunks of chicken, pico de gallo, sour cream, and guacamole. The best entree choice is the smoked brisket barbecue, served with salad, warm molasses bread and honey, and your choice of two side dishes—I'd recommend the jalapeño mashed potatoes and grilled corn on the cob. Steaks and prime rib are other options, along with pasta dishes. For dessert, there's peach cobbler topped with vanilla ice cream sprinkled with cinnamon. The bar has an iced-beer well.

Wild Jacks also has locations in Altamonte Springs at 108 Markham Woods Rd. (☎ **407/786-5252**), and in Kissimmee at 5817 Irlo Bronson Memorial Hwy. (☎ **407/397-2800**).

INEXPENSIVE

Enzo's. 7600 Dr. Phillips Blvd., Suite 12, in the Marketplace Shopping Center (off Sand Lake Rd., just west of I-4). ☎ **407/351-1187.** Reservations not accepted. Panini $4.75–$5.95; main courses $4.50–$6.95 at lunch, $8.50–$12.75 at dinner. AE, CB, DC, DISC, MC, V. Mon–Thurs 11:30am–10pm; Fri–Sat 11:30am–11pm. Free self-parking. ITALIAN.

Upon entering this charming little restaurant and Italian charcuterie, you'll walk past display cases filled with antipasti, deli meats, pâtés, and cheeses, and shelves stocked with homemade pastas and other fancy foodstuffs. And if that's not enough to whet your appetite, you'll also glimpse chefs tending a pizza oven in an exhibition kitchen. The dining area is cheerful and inviting, with glossy pine-plank floors, peach walls hung with fine-art prints, and tables covered with butcher paper (crayons are provided). Italian music (most of it operatic arias) enhances the atmosphere. Enzo's is a casual kind of place that's very popular locally.

Pretty much the same menu is available throughout the day. Families troop in for pizzas—either the traditional American kind or Napoli pies with more sophisticated toppings and crisp, delicate crusts. Until 4:30pm, you can also opt for panini (sandwiches on crusty Italian bread), with fillings such as Italian sausage, grilled onions, and peppers; they're served with potato salad. A more serious dinner might begin with an appetizer of paper-thin slices of Norwegian salmon and onion served with extra-virgin olive oil, capers, lemon, and red peppers. Homemade pastas include fat bucatini tossed with mushrooms, freshly grated Parmesan, prosciutto, bacon, and peas in a robust sauce. Enzo's most fabulous entree is *pollo alla cecco* (roasted breast of free-range chicken with rosemary potatoes and an Italian version of ratatouille). Beer and wine are available. For dessert try *zuccotto* (Italian sponge cake soaked in Grand Marnier, layered with fresh fruit and crème anglaise, and topped with chocolate shavings). In busy seasons, arrive off-hours to avoid a wait.

Max's Cafe & Coffee House. 701 Front St., Celebration. ☎ **407/566-1144.** Main courses $6.95–$12.95. AE, DC, DISC, MC, V. Free self-parking. Daily 8am–9pm. AMERICAN.

Located in the Disney-created town of Celebration, this is a modern version of the old greasy spoon. The art deco decor is a re-creation of the real thing, but the food offerings are stick-to-your-rib favorites. You get your money's worth here. The sandwiches and meals come in hearty portions. Try the pot roast or fried chicken. The meat loaf, a large slab best sampled with mashed potatoes, is better than Mom used to make. (No offense, Ma.)

6 Places to Dine Elsewhere in Orlando

Visitors wanting a break from themed eating can enjoy some of the local favorites, like great barbecue and authentic Cuban cuisine. There is epicurean life outside of Disney.

For further Orlando eateries, check out the **Church Street Station** listing in chapter 10. All directions assume you are coming from the WDW/International Drive area.

The restaurants in this section are located on the map " Orlando Area Accommo-dations & Dining" in this section.

EXPENSIVE

Maison et Jardin. 430 Wymore Rd., Altamonte Springs, 10 min. north of downtown Orlando. ☎ **407/862-4410.** Main courses $18.50–$28.50. AE, DISC, DC, MC, V. Mon–Sat 6–10pm; Sun 6–9pm; Sun brunch 11am–2pm. Free self-parking. Take I-4 East to Maitland Blvd./East exit. Stay in the far lane, turning right at Lake Destiny Dr. At the next light, turn left onto Wymore Rd. FRENCH.

The succulent beef Wellington served here—a local special-occasion favorite—tastes even better after a diet of theme park burritos. If you're game, try the Elk Medallions sautéed and served with a raspberry sauce. For dessert, the crêpes Suzette. You can order from a full bar, but what really makes Maison et Jardin worth the drive is one of the best wine cellars in the world. The restaurant was recently honored by *Wine Spectator* magazine for its outstanding selection. This is the place for lovers of good wine. (And definitely not the place for children.)

Le Provence. 50 E. Pine St., in downtown Orlando. ☎ **407/843-1320.** Reservations recommended. Main courses $14.95–$26.95. Mon–Fri 5:30–9:30pm; Sat 5:30–10:30pm. Closed Sunday. AE, DC, MC, V. Valet parking available. FRENCH.

This is a local upscale favorite, which features expertly prepared delicacies, including wonderful dishes that star duck and veal. Enjoy a good martini and a cigar at Monaco's, a bar next door, while waiting on your reservation. Dress is casual, but jeans and sneakers may make you feel a bit conspicuous. There is metered street parking available, but it may be hard to find, so opt for the valet.

Sergio's. 355 N. Orange Ave, in downtown Orlando. ☎ **407/428-6162.** Reservations recommended, especially for dinner. Main courses $9–$26. Mon–Fri 11:30am–10:30pm; Sat–Sun 5:30am–11:30pm. Take I-4 to downtown Orlando. Take Exit 41 (Amelia Ave.). Go 1 block, and turn right. Turn right again on Orange Ave. The restaurant is 20 yards ahead on the left, past Livingston St., next to LaBelle's Fur. ITALIAN.

Moving into the heart of the city in 1997 made this old Orlando favorite more accessible to visitors. Careful attention to detail, such as individual lighting adjustments for each table, makes this a nice retreat from the typical tourist fare. The menu is created by the same chef who set the tone for the Bahama Breeze (reviewed earlier). That same Florida flavor is apparent, but here true Italian cooking wins out. Start with the antipasti for an appetizer, and don't miss the spinach pasta with Gorgonzola and pine nuts. The daily specials often highlight the freshest fish available. Heartier eaters should try the veal chop. For dessert, try the tiramisu. You'll find a full wine list.

MODERATE

✪ **The Bubble Room.** 1351 S. Orlando Ave., Maitland (about 10 min. north of downtown Orlando). ☎ **407/628-3331.** Reservations recommended. Main courses $11.95–$18.95. AE, DISC, MC, V. Daily 11:30am–4pm; Sun–Thurs 4–10pm; Fri–Sat 4–11pm. Free self-parking. Take I-4 east to Lee Rd. (Exit 45). Turn right at bottom of ramp. Turn left at Orlando Ave. (17/92). The Bubble Room is on the left, just past the railroad overpass. AMERICAN.

There is nothing subtle about the Bubble Room. You can rock in the Tunnel of Love while a toy train rolls just below the ceiling on a suspended track. Some people might find the hyped-up wait staff—also called Bubble Scouts—a little much. This is a place for celebrations, though, and the Scouts are part of the party. Like the wacky waits, the cutesy entree names are a little over the top. But, like the decor that mixes Christmas lights with vintage movie stills, somehow it all works. At the Bubble Room

Orlando Area Accommodations & Dining

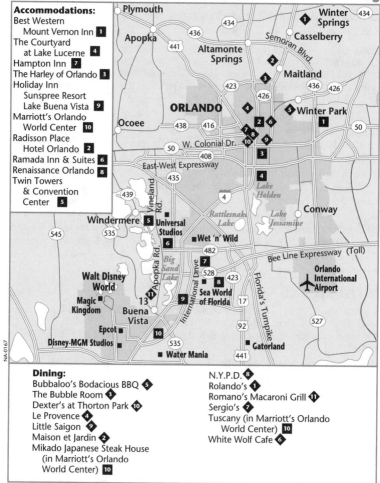

Accommodations:

Best Western
   Mount Vernon Inn **1**
The Courtyard
   at Lake Lucerne **4**
Hampton Inn **7**
The Harley of Orlando **3**
Holiday Inn
   Sunspree Resort
   Lake Buena Vista **9**
Marriott's Orlando
   World Center **10**
Radisson Place
   Hotel Orlando **2**
Ramada Inn & Suites **6**
Renaissance Orlando **8**
Twin Towers
   & Convention
   Center **5**

Dining:

Bubbaloo's Bodacious BBQ **5**
The Bubble Room **3**
Dexter's at Thorton Park **10**
Le Provence **4**
Little Saigon **9**
Maison et Jardin **2**
Mikado Japanese Steak House
   (in Marriott's Orlando
   World Center) **10**

N.Y.P.D. **8**
Rolando's **1**
Romano's Macaroni Grill **11**
Sergio's **7**
Tuscany (in Marriott's Orlando
   World Center) **10**
White Wolf Cafe **6**

everything from the portions to the staff is overwrought, which makes for high-energy fun. The prime rib, in Tarzan and Jane cuts, is a tender favorite that always includes a doggy bag. Also try the Maltese Chicken, roasted and stuffed, served with wild rice, a light gravy, and steamed vegetables. Make up for all those calories you burned trekking through the parks with a huge slab of a Bubble Room specialty, red velvet cake.

Dexter's of Thorton Park. 808 E. Washington St., near downtown Orlando. ☎ **407/ 649-2777.** Reservations not accepted. Main courses $5.99–$16.95. AE, DC, DISC, MC, V. Mon–Sat 11am–midnight; Sun 5–10pm. From I-4, take the Anderson St. exit. Travel to Mills Ave., and take a left. Turn left again on Central Blvd., and continue on Central to Hyer St. Turn left on Hyer; the restaurant is at the corner of Hyer and Washington. AMERICAN.

This popular neighborhood bar/eatery is just a few blocks from Lake Eola in the center of downtown. The fare ranges from basic soups and salads to quiche and more adventurous menu items such as black-and-white sesame grouper and andouille sausages quesadilla. You'll also find tempting daily specials. There is a limited beer and wine menu and varying desert menu. Many of the seats are at high tables, where you sit on bar stools; if you would find these seats uncomfortable, you may have a long wait. This is an upbeat, noisy crowd filled with regulars.

White Wolf Cafe. 1829 N. Orange Ave. (about 1 mile from Loch Haven Park), Orlando. ☎ **407/895-9911.** Reservations not accepted. Main courses $4.25–$6.75 at lunch, $6.95–$12.95 at dinner. AE, MC, V. Mon 10am–6pm; Tues–Thurs 10am–10pm; Fri–Sat 10am–midnight. Free self-parking. Take I-4 east to Princeton St. (Exit 43). Turn right at Orange Ave. Look for striped awnings on the left. AMERICAN.

Even White Wolf's often clueless and notoriously slow servers can't overshadow the first-rate food. No mass-producing theme machine for tourists, this restaurant creates fresh meals from a tiny, deli-style kitchen. With rough-cut marble tables, a furry mascot panting near the door, and an eclectic, handwritten menu, it seems like you're eating in the crowded, funky, and slightly pretentious downtown loft of friends.

For lunch, you could even share the meaty Caribbean chicken salad, lightly accented with tangy apricot vinaigrette (just get extra dressing). For an appetizer pick black bean soup kissed with onion. Three-cheese lasagna, firm pasta slathered in a lightly spiced marinara, is a dinner favorite served with a warm hunk of French bread. Avoid the salmon lavosh. Regulars warn that the slow service rules out firm post-dinner plans. Fortunately, peanut-butter-and-brownie ice cream pie, a lush sugar rush dripping with hot fudge, is the perfect reward for patience.

INEXPENSIVE

N.Y.P.D. 373 N. Orange Ave., in downtown Orlando. ☎ **407/481-8680.** Main courses $4.25–$13.95. No credit cards. Mon–Fri 11:30am–9pm; Sat 12:30–8pm. Take I-4 to downtown and take the Robinson exit. Turn right on Livingston; take it to Orange Ave. and turn left. PIZZA.

N.Y.P.D. stands for New York Pizza Delivery, and this restaurant has become well-known to downtowners for it's bicycle delivery carts. With a husband whose last name is Campagna, I can vouch for the authentic Italian cuisine here. There is a selection of Italian basics such as eggplant parmagiana and lasagna, but the New York–style pies are the real standouts. The white pizza, with a gooey and spicy selection of cheese toppings is to be recommended. There is also deep-dish Sicilian style pizza. But there is no smoking.

✪ **Bubbaloo's Bodacious BBQ.** 1471 Lee Rd., Winter Park (about 5 min. from downtown Orlando). ☎ **407/295-1212.** Reservations not accepted. Main courses $4.95–$7.95. Mon–Thurs 10am–9pm; Fri–Sat 10am–10:30pm; Sun 11am–9pm. AE, MC, V. Free self-parking. Take I-4 east to Lee Rd. (Exit 45). Follow your nose; Bubbaloo's is on the left, next to a dry cleaners. BARBECUE.

You can smell the hickory smoke for blocks, the tangy scent cutting through the humid Florida air. This is, hands down, some of the best barbecue you'll find anywhere. And, if nothing else, you gotta love the name. There are other things on the menu, such as fried clams, but go for the full pork platter with a heaping helping of pork and all the fixin's. The uninitiated should stay away from the "Killer" sauce, which produces a tongue buzz likely to last for hours; you might even taste test the mild before moving up to the hot. The beans are the perfect side dish. Only the some-times-soggy garlic bread brings the meal down, but not too far. Beer is available.

Little Saigon. 1106 E. Colonial Dr. (Colonial is also called Hwy. 50.), near downtown Orlando. ☎ **407/423-8539.** Reservations not accepted. Main courses under $5 at lunch, $4.95–$10.95 at dinner. AE, DISC, MC, V. Daily 10am–9pm. Free self-parking. Take the Colonial Dr. (Hwy. 50) exit; head east. Located between Mills and Thorton aves. Look for the fish mural. Turn right onto Thorton. Lot is immediately to the left. VIETNAMESE.

Few would expect to find a Little Saigon, a bustling enclave of Asian immigrants, in the midst of Orlando. But both the community and the first-class restaurant of the same name make their home near downtown. For an appetizer, don't miss the unfried summer rolls, a soft wrap filled with rice, shrimp, and pork served with a delicious peanut sauce. At $2.50 for two, you could easily make a meal of these sumptuous rolls. Don't. Go on to sample some of the healthy, light dishes in the dozens of menu selections. Try one of the traditional soups with noodles, rice, vegetables, and either chicken, beef, or seafood. The numbered menu is in badly translated English—"soup serve aside"—so don't be afraid to ask your servers exactly what goes into No. 86. Little Saigon's one drawback is the scarcity of English-speaking servers, so don't hesitate to ask for the manager. As far as being authentic, the tables are usually filled with members of the local Vietnamese community, with the owner working the tables like a good ole boy at the corner diner. Stay away from the weak, slightly bitter iced tea. Stick with hot tea, soda, or some of the limited beer and wine options available.

✪ **Rolando's.** 870 E. Fla. 436 (Semoran Blvd., between Red Bug Rd. and U.S. 17/92), in Casselberry. ☎ **407/767-9677.** Reservations not accepted. Main courses $3.25–$4.75 at lunch, $5.75–$11.50 at dinner. AE, DISC, MC, V. Tues–Sat 11am–10pm; Sun 1–8pm. Free self-parking. Take I-4 east to the East-West Expwy., head east, and make a left on Fla. 436. CUBAN.

About 40 minutes from Walt Disney World, this inexpensive mom-and-pop place serves up huge portions of authentic Cuban fare. Its two dining rooms are pleasant but plain, with Formica tables, stucco walls hung with photographs of Cuba, and pots of philodendrons suspended from the ceiling. Soft lighting adds a smidge of ambience.

I recommend ordering up a bunch of appetizers to share: deep-fried ripe plantains, *papas rellenas*—breaded, deep-fried balls of mashed potato stuffed with spicy picadillos (garlicky ground beef cooked with onions, olives, raisins, and green peppers in a tomato sauce)—flavorful Cuban tamales topped with picadillos, and slightly sweet batter-fried corn fritters that are light as air. An entree of roast chicken is brushed with crushed garlic, white-wine vinegar, cumin, and oregano, then briefly deep-fried just before serving. Tender, shredded beef is simmered in a richly seasoned, tomato-based sauce with potatoes, olives, peas, pimentos, onions, green peppers, and sweet red peppers. Paella is an option if you call a few hours in advance to order it. Entrees are served with freshly baked hot rolls, house salad, rice, and plantains or yucca (a chewy root plant); take the plantains. For dessert, try the *dulce de tres leche* (a meringue-topped yellow cake mixed with condensed milk, evaporated milk, and cream). At lunch a hearty sandwich of hot Cuban bread stuffed with slices of ham, roast pork, Swiss cheese, and pickles is served with black bean soup. Beer and wine are available.

7 Only in Orlando: Dining with Disney Characters

Especially for the 10-and-under set, it's a thrill to dine in a restaurant where costumed Disney characters show up to greet the customers, sign autographs, pose in family photos, and interact with little kids. Make reservations as far in advance as possible for these very popular meals. It's best to make reservations when you book your hotel.

The prices for all these character meals are pretty much the same, no matter where you are dining. The **breakfast** prices are all around **$15 for adults** and **$8 for children**; at **dinner $20 for adults, $9 for children** 3–11, free for children 2 and under. The prices do vary a bit, though, from location to location, the character luau at the Polynesian Resort being more expensive than the others.

To make **reservations** for any WDW character meal, call ☎ **407/WDW-DINE** (939-3463). AE, MC, V are accepted at all character meals.

You'll find all the restaurants mentioned in this section on the map "Walt Disney World & Lake Buena Vista Dining" earlier in this chapter.

Note: On selected days, Disney resort guests can arrive earlier at some of the character breakfasts listed here. At press time **Pocahontas** had been pushed out of Artist Point by Pooh & Friends, but they are planning to relocate. If you have a big Pocahontas fan, ask where—and if—she can be found.

Artist Point. At Disney's Wilderness Lodge, 901 Timberline Dr. Breakfast with Winnie the Pooh, Tigger, and the other inhabitants of the Hundred Acre Woods. Daily 7:30–11am.

In a rustic lodgelike dining room with a beamed ceiling supported by tree-trunk beams and large windows providing scenic lake views, **Pooh** and **Tigger** host an all-you-can-eat buffet breakfast.

Cape May Café. At Disney's Beach Club Resort, 1800 Epcot Resorts Blvd. Daily 7:30–11am.

The Cape May Café, a delightful New England–themed dining room, serves lavish buffet character breakfasts hosted by Admiral **Goofy** and his crew—**Chip 'n' Dale** and **Pluto** (exact characters may vary).

Chef Mickey's. At Disney's Contemporary Resort, 4600 N. World Dr. Daily 7:30–11:30am and 5–9:30pm.

The whimsical Chef Mickey's is the setting for buffet character breakfasts and dinners. On hand to meet, greet, and mingle with guests are **Mickey** and various pals. Chef Mickey's character prime-rib buffet dinners include a make-your-own-sundae bar.

✪ **Garden Grill.** In The Land Pavilion at Epcot. Daily 8:30–11:30am, 11:30am–3:30pm, and 3:30–8pm.

This revolving restaurant has comfortable, semicircular booths. As you dine, your table travels past desert, prairie, farmland, and rain-forest environments. There's a "momma's-in-the-kitchen" theme here: You'll be given a straw hat at the entrance, and the just-folks service staff speaks in country lingo. Hearty family-style meals are hosted by **Mickey, Minnie,** and **Chip 'n' Dale**. (Boy that Mickey sure gets around.) American breakfast and lunch choices are extensive. Dinners include several entrees (roast chicken, farm-raised fish, and hickory-smoked steak), mashed potatoes, vegetables, squaw bread and biscuits, salad, beverage, and dessert.

Cinderella's Royal Table. In Cinderella's Castle in the Magic Kingdom. Daily 8–10am.

This Gothic castle—the focal point of the park—serves up character-breakfast buffets daily. Hosts vary, but **Cinderella** always puts in an appearance. This is one of the most popular character meals in the park, so reserve far in advance. It's a great way to start your day in the Magic Kingdom.

Liberty Tree Tavern. In Liberty Square in the Magic Kingdom. Daily 4pm to park closing.

This Williamsburg-like 18th-century pub offers character dinners hosted by **Mickey, Goofy, Pluto, Chip 'n' Dale,** and **Tigger** (some or all of them). Meals, served family style, consist of salad, roast chicken, marinated flank steak, trail sausages, mashed potatoes, rice pilaf, vegetables, and a dessert of warm apple crisp with vanilla ice cream.

Note: In the Magic Kingdom you can also find Pooh and friends at the Crystal Palace in Main Street all day.

Minnie's Menehune & Mickey's Tropical Luau. At Disney's Polynesian Resort, 1600 Seven Seas Dr. $38 adults, $19.50 children 3–11, free for children 2 and under; taxes and gratuities extra. Daily 6:45 and 9:30pm. Free self- and valet parking. No characters at the regular luau dinner show.

Luau Cove, an exotic open-air facility, is the setting for an island-themed character show called Mickey's Tropical Luau. It's an abbreviated version of the Polynesian Luau Dinner Show described in chapter 10 and features Polynesian dancers along with **Mickey, Minnie, Pluto,** and **Goofy**. Your prix-fixe meal includes honey-roasted chicken, vegetables, glazed cinnamon bread, and an ice-cream sundae. Guests are presented with shell leis on entering.

The Polynesian also hosts Minnie's Menehune Character Breakfast in the Polynesian-themed 'Ohana (described earlier in the section "In the Walt Disney Resorts"). Traditional breakfast foods are prepared on an 18-foot fire pit and served family-style. **Minnie, Goofy,** and **Chip 'n' Dale** appear, and there are children's parades with Polynesian musical instruments.

1900 Park Fare. At Disney's Grand Floridian Beach Resort, 4401 Floridian Way. Daily 7:30–11:30am and 5:30–9pm.

This exquisitely elegant Disney resort hosts character meals in the festive exposition-themed 1900 Park Fare. Big Bertha—a French band organ that plays pipes, drums, bells, cymbals, castanets, and xylophone—provides music. **Mary Poppins, Winnie the Pooh, Goofy, Pluto, Chip 'n' Dale,** and **Minnie** appear at the elaborate buffet breakfasts. **Mickey and Minnie** appear at nightly buffets featuring prime rib, stuffed pork loin, fresh fish, and more.

Soundstage Restaurant. At Disney–MGM Studios, adjacent to the Magic of Disney Animation. Daily 8:30–10:30am and 11:30am–3:30pm.

A vast buffet meal is set out in this warehouse-motif restaurant decorated with movie props and posters. Selected characters from the movies **Aladdin, Hercules,** and **Pocahontas** sign autographs as favorite tunes from Disney hits play in the background.

Watercress Café. At the Buena Vista Palace, 1900 Buena Vista Dr. ☎ **407/827-2727.** Reservations not accepted. Sun 8–10:30am.

This breakfast is not at a Disney-owned property but rather at one of the "official" Disney hotels in the Lake Buena Vista area. Prices are similar. The plant-filled Watercress Café—with large windows overlooking Lake Buena Vista—is the setting for Sunday-morning character breakfasts featuring **Minnie, Goofy,** and **Pluto.** Both à la carte and buffet meals are offered. Since reservations are not accepted, arrive early to avoid a wait.

7

On Your Mark, Get Set, Go! What to See & Do In & Around Walt Disney World

We all know what the big attraction is here—the one that put Orlando on the map. With the exception of conventioneers (and I'm sure many of them sneak off to the parks, as well), most people who come to Orlando have come to meet—or become reacquainted with—the Mouse.

Walt Disney World, attracting more than 13 million visitors annually, is one of the world's most popular travel destinations. All of the Disney parks make the industry's top 10 list for attendance. And why not? They provide a welcome retreat in a star-spangled, all-American fantasyland where wonderment, human progress, and old-fashioned family fun are the major themes. And these themes are presented in spectacular parades and fireworks displays; 3-D, 4-D, and 360° Circle-Vision movies; and adventure-filled journeys through time and space. Though it's not inexpensive, you'll seldom hear people complain about not getting their money's worth. Disney delivers!

The Magic Kingdom opened in 1971. Disney's West Side, a collection of shops, restaurants, and nightclubs opened in 1997, joining with Pleasure Island and Disney Village Marketplace to become what WDW is calling Downtown Disney. In 1998, the fourth major park, Animal Kingdom, dedicated to wildlife, opened. But those are just the latest additions. Walt's World includes Epcot, where guests take exhilarating voyages around the world and into the future; Disney–MGM Studios, centered on "Hollywood Boulevard" and providing a thrilling behind-the-scenes look at motion-picture and TV studios; Pleasure Island, an ongoing street festival in a 6-acre complex of nightclubs and shops, featuring live concerts nightly as well as Planet Hollywood; Disney Village Marketplace, a charming lakeside enclave of shops and restaurants; Typhoon Lagoon, a 56-acre water park where you can catch the world's largest man-made waves or plummet down steep water flumes; River Country, another water park; Blizzard Beach, even another water park that's meant to be "a ski resort in the tropics".

1 Essentials

GETTING INFORMATION IN ADVANCE

Before leaving home, call or write the Walt Disney World Co., Box 10000, Lake Buena Vista, FL 32830-1000 (☎ **407/934-7639**), for a copy of the very informative *Walt Disney World Vacations*

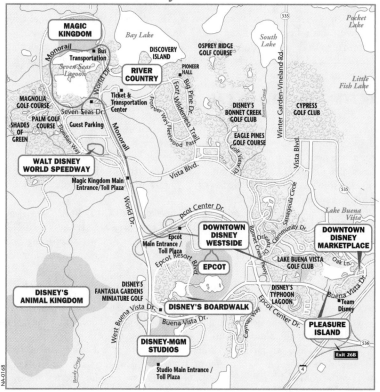

brochure—an invaluable planning aid. When you call, also ask about special events that will be on during your stay (see also "When to Go," in chapter 2 of this book).

Once you've arrived in town, guest services and concierge desks in all the area hotels—especially Disney properties and "official" hotels—have up-to-the-minute information about happenings in the parks. Stop by to ask questions and pick up literature, including a schedule of park hours and special events. If you have questions your hotel can't answer, call ☎ **407/824-4321.**

A very handy pocket-sized guidebook is produced by American Express and lists basic recreational and dining opportunities within WDW. It also details discounts available with American Express.

There are also information locations in each park—at City Hall in the Magic Kingdom, at Innoventions East near the WorldKey terminals in Epcot, and the Guest Services building in Disney–MGM Studios.

If you are hooked up to the Internet, or have access to a library with Internet access, there is a World Wide Web site at **www.disneyworld.com**, which has extensive, entertaining, and regularly updated information, including a live-action look from video cameras perched throughout the various parks. (This is mostly long-distance shots of tourists walking about, but it's still a chance to see those blue Orlando skies and dream ahead to vacation time.) There are dozens of web pages devoted to Disney, especially Disney trivia. Check out the very informative newsgroup on Usenet called **rec.arts.disney**.

The city newspaper, the *Orlando Sentinel,* also produces **Orlando Sentinel Online** at **www.oso@aol.com**. Once there, click on "Theme Park Central" for a variety of information and updates on activities at local attractions. During the peak tourist season, the *Orlando Sentinel* also has special tourist information, including park hours and weather, on the front page of the "Local & State" section.

GETTING TO WDW BY CAR

The exits to all the Disney parks are well marked. From Interstate 4, exits 25, 26, and 27 lead to the Disney parks. Once inside, colorful signs will direct you to your destination. If you miss the exit marked for your specific park, don't panic. Simply get off at the next one. It may take more time, but it's safer than slashing through five lanes of traffic to make the off-ramp. Drive with extra caution. Disney drivers are divided into two categories: workers (in a hurry to make their shift) and tourists (driving and looking at a map).

Upon entering WDW grounds, you can tune your radio to 1030 AM when you're approaching the Magic Kingdom, or 850 AM when approaching Epcot. Tune to 1200 AM when departing from the Magic Kingdom, or 910 AM when departing Epcot. TVs in all Disney resorts and official Disney hotels also have park information stations.

PARKING

All of the WDW lots are tightly controlled; the Disney folks have parking cars down to a science. You park where those nice young people in their yellow-striped shirts tell you to park—or else. Remember to note your parking place. Those nice young people won't be there to direct you to your car when you leave the park.

Visitors are also encouraged to ride the trams. Do this if you're parked in the massive Magic Kingdom lot or at Animal Kingdom. Skip waiting for the trams in lots at Epcot and MGM Studios and walk on up. The parking lots are not necessarily designed for pedestrians, so watch out for those trams.

Parking generally costs $6. There are special lots at each park for travelers with disabilities (☎ **407/824-4321** for details).

TICKETS

There are several ticket options, ranging from 1- to 7-day passes. Most people get the best value from 4- and 5-day passes. All passes offer unlimited use of the WDW transportation system. *Note:* The prices quoted here do not include sales tax, and they are, of course, subject to change. Unless you are especially restless, or an old hand who knows exactly what you want to see, skip the park-hopper option. Getting to and from the various parks can eat up a considerable part of your day.

Adult prices are paid by anyone over 10 years of age. Children's rates are for ages 3 to 9. Children 2 and under are admitted free.

- The **4-Day Value Pass** provides admission for 1 day at the Magic Kingdom, 1 day at Epcot, 1 day at Disney–MGM Studios, and 1 day at Animal Kingdom; you can use it on any 4 days following purchase, but you cannot visit more than one park on any given day. Adults pay $149; children, $119.
- The **5-Day Park-Hopper Pass** provides unlimited admission to the Magic Kingdom, Epcot, and Disney–MGM Studios, and Animal Kingdom on any 5 days; you can visit any combination of parks on any given day. It also includes admission to Typhoon Lagoon, River Country, Blizzard Beach, and Pleasure Island for a period of 7 days beginning the first date stamped. Adults pay $189; children, $151.

- The new **All-in-One Hopper Pass** gives you 6 days of admission to the parks and cost $249 for adults and $199 for children.
- A **1-day, one-park ticket** for the Magic Kingdom, Epcot, Disney–MGM Studios, or Animal Kingdom is $42 for adults, $34 for children.
- A **1-day ticket to Typhoon Lagoon** or **Blizzard Beach** is $25.95 for adults, $20.50 for children.
- A **1-day ticket to River Country** is $15.95 for adults, $12.50 for children.
- A **1-day ticket to Pleasure Island** is $18.95.

If you're staying at any Walt Disney World resort or "official" hotel (see chapter 5, "Accommodations"), you're also eligible for a money-saving **Be Our Guest Pass** priced according to length of stay. It also offers special perks.

If you plan on visiting Walt Disney World more than one time during the year, inquire about a money-saving **annual pass** ($299 adults, $254 children).

OPERATING HOURS

Hours of operation vary somewhat throughout the year and can be influenced by special events, so it is generally a good idea to call during your visit to check opening/closing times.

The **Magic Kingdom, Animal Kingdom,** and **Disney–MGM Studios** are generally open from 9am to 7pm, with extended hours—sometimes as late as midnight—during major holidays and the summer months.

Epcot is generally open from 9am to 9pm, with **Future World** open from 9am to 9pm and **World Showcase** from 11am to 9pm—once again with extended holiday hours.

Typhoon Lagoon and **Blizzard Beach** are open from 10am to 5pm most of the year (with extended hours during some holidays), and 9am to 8pm in summer.

River Country is open from 10am to 5pm most of the year (with extended hours during some holidays), and 10am to 7pm in summer.

Note: Epcot and MGM sometimes open a half hour or more before the posted time. Keep in mind, too, that Disney-resort guests enjoy early admission to all three major parks on designated days.

2 Making Your Visit More Enjoyable

HOW WE'VE MADE THIS CHAPTER USEFUL TO PARENTS

Before every listing in the four major parks, you'll note the "Recommended Ages" entry that tells the appropriate ages that will most appreciate each ride. Though most families will want to do everything, you may find this guideline helpful in planning your daily itinerary. In our ride ratings, we've indicated whether a ride will be more enjoyable for children than for adults.

BEST TIME OF YEAR TO VISIT

Because of the large number of international visitors, there is really no "off" season for Disney, but during the winter months, usually from January through April, the park crowds are smallest, the weather coolest, and the air least humid. The crowds also thin after September until the week before Thanksgiving. The summer months, when the masses throng to the park, are not only crowded but hot, hot, hot, sticky, and humid. During the cooler months, you also don't have to worry about the daily summer storms.

BEST DAYS TO VISIT

The busiest days at the Magic Kingdom, Animal Kingdom, and Epcot are Monday to Wednesday; at Disney–MGM Studios, they're Thursday and Friday. Surprisingly, weekends are the least busy at all parks. Sunday is generally a slow day. Major holidays, such as Christmas, Easter, and Thanksgiving are also generally slow. In peak seasons especially, arrange your visits accordingly. Crowds also tend to thin later in the day.

PLAN YOUR VISIT

How you plan your time at Walt Disney World will depend on a number of factors, including the ages of children in your party, what you've seen on previous visits, your specific interests, and whether you're traveling at a peak time or off-season (when lines are shorter and you can cram more in). Planning, however, is essential. So is choosing age-appropriate activities.

Nothing can spoil a day in the parks more than a child devastated because he or she can't do something promised. Before you get to the park, review this book and the **suggested ages** for children, especially **height restrictions.** The WDW staff does not bend those rules, no matter how loud your little one may wail.

Unless you're staying for considerably more than a week, you can't possibly experience all the rides, shows, and attractions here—not to mention the vast array of recreational facilities. And you'll only wear yourself to a frazzle trying. It's far better to follow a relaxed itinerary, including leisurely meals and some recreation, than to make a demanding job out of trying to see everything.

Note: Many of these suggestions are also applicable at non-Disney theme parks.

CREATE AN ITINERARY FOR EACH DAY

Read the previously mentioned *Walt Disney World Vacations* brochure and the detailed descriptions in this book, and plan your visit to include all shows and attractions that pique your interest and excitement. It's a good idea to make a daily itinerary, putting these in some kind of sensible geographical sequence, so you're not zigzagging all over the place. Familiarize yourself in advance with the layout of each park.

I repeat this advice—schedule sit-down shows, recreational activities (a boat ride or swim late in the afternoon can be wonderfully refreshing), and at least some unhurried meals. My suggested itineraries are below.

SUGGESTED ITINERARIES

A Day in the Magic Kingdom

The key to getting the most out of your theme-park experience is going **against the crowd.** Do arrive with everyone else a little before opening time, having already purchased tickets. When the gates open, don't make a dash for Fantasyland, which is where everyone else will go. Start in one of the lesser realms to avoid the crowds.

While the families are still going loco over the Lion King, hightail it to **Frontierland** and ride **Splash Mountain**—another biggie—before long lines form there. There is little shade near this ride, so you definitely don't want to be waiting there in the middle of the day. When you come off, it will still be early enough to beat the lines at another major attraction; head over to **Adventureland** and do **Pirates of the Caribbean.**

Complete whatever else interests you in Adventureland. Or eat a heavy snack, like a turkey leg from one of the vendor carts, and keep riding during lunch to take advantage of shorter lunchtime lines. Have lunch while taking in the early-afternoon

In the Words of Walt Disney

Family fun is as necessary to modern living as a kitchen refrigerator.

Part of the Disney success is our ability to create a believable world of dreams that appeals to all age groups.

shows in the **Diamond Horseshoe Saloon Revue show** (they don't take reservations, so arrive early).

By 2:30pm (earlier in peak seasons), you should start looking for a seat along the **parade** route. Liberty Square is where most people settle, so look at the map and pick a spot further down the route, which winds through the park.

If you are a ride junkie, skip the parade and hit **Alien Encounters** and other high-volume rides while the rest of the crowd concentrates along the curb.

This is an especially good idea if **SpectroMagic** is on during your stay. That is the parade to see. After the parade, it should be safe to venture into **Fantasyland,** although there is never a truly good time since it contains the heart of what most adults remember from their first Disney visit.

If you have little kids (8 and under) in your party, start your day instead by taking the **WDW Railroad** from Main Street to Mickey's Toontown Fair. That should provide a sufficient Mickey fix so you can work your way through Adventureland and Tomorrowland. Save Fantasyland for after lunch. Take an air-conditioned break at the **Country Bear Jamboree** in Frontierland.

That's a long enough day for most young children, and your best plan is to go back to your hotel for a nap or swim.

If You Can Spend Only 1 Day at Epcot

Epcot really requires at least 2 days, so this is a highlight tour. As suggested for the Magic Kingdom itinerary, arrive early, tickets in hand. If you haven't already made lunch reservations by calling ☎ **407/WDW-DINE** (939-3463) (see chapter 6, "Dining"), make your first stop at the WorldKey terminals in Innoventions East. I suggest a 1pm lunch at the San Angel Inn Restaurant in Mexico. If you don't like Mexican food, move up one pavilion to Norway and reserve for the buffet at Akershus. You can make dinner reservations at the same time. Plan dinner for about 7pm, which will allow you time to eat and find a good viewing spot for IllumiNations (usually at 9pm, but check your schedule).

Spend no more than an hour exploring **Innoventions East.** Then move on to the **Universe of Energy** show, **Ellen's Energy Adventure.** Continue to the **Wonders of Life Pavilion,** where must-sees include **Body Wars, Cranium Command,** and **The Making of Me.**

If time allows—it will depend on line waits at attractions—take in the show at Horizons before heading into World Showcase for lunch. Over lunch, check your show schedule and decide which shows to incorporate into your day.

Then walk around the lagoon, visiting highlight attractions such as Wonders of China, The American Adventure, Impressions de France, and O Canada!, allowing yourself some time for browsing and shopping. After dinner, stay on for Illumi-Nations.

If You Can Spend 2 Days at Epcot

Ignore the 1-day itinerary just described, but do begin your day by making all necessary restaurant reservations—once again for lunch in Mexico or Norway at about 1pm. Make reservations for Day 2 at the same time.

Skip Innoventions East for now and work your way thoroughly through the **Universe of Energy, Wonders of Life, Horizons,** and **Test Track** pavilions, keeping your lunch reservation time in mind.

After lunch, walk clockwise around the lagoon, visiting each pavilion and taking in as many shows as you like (consult your show schedule and try to keep pace as well as possible). Leave IllumiNations for your second day's visit.

Begin your **second day** exploring **Innoventions East** and proceed counterclockwise, taking in **Spaceship Earth, Innoventions West, The Living Seas** (its Coral Reef restaurant is a good choice for lunch), and all the other pavilions on the west side of the park. Cap off your Epcot visit with **IllumiNations.**

A Day at Disney–MGM Studios Theme Park

Since show times change frequently here, it's impossible to really give you a workable itinerary. Upon entering the park, if you haven't already made dining arrangements, stop at the Hollywood Brown Derby (details in chapter 6) and make reservations for lunch. Or you might want to conserve park-touring time by having a light lunch at a casual eatery and saving the Derby for a relaxing dinner.

Nutritional needs accounted for, make a beeline for the **Twilight Zone Tower of Terror 2.** While you're waiting in line, plan the rest of your schedule, being sure to include these not-to-be-missed attractions: the **Magic of Disney Animation,** the **Indiana Jones Epic Stunt Spectacular, Jim Henson's Muppet*Vision 4D,** and the **Goosebumps HorrorLand Fright Show.**

If you have girls under 11 in your party, "The Voyage of the Little Mermaid" and "Beauty and the Beast" will probably be major priorities; for the latter shows, get in line 45 minutes prior to show time.

The **afternoon parades** are generally themed to coincide with a recent Disney movie release. The latest, *Hercules,* was frankly a disappointment. Perhaps the new parade based on the new Disney animated feature *Mulan* will be better. If your child is wild about Flubber, or whatever the theme, you may have to go. If so, snag good seats on the parade route 30 minutes ahead of time. Keep in mind that people tend to congregate along the route near the back of the park, so go where everyone else is not. If there is not a special interest in the parade theme, skip it, especially if you will be viewing the far superior parade at the Magic Kingdom. Enjoy the shorter lines at the major rides.

Time for more? Do Superstar Television, the Indiana Jones Epic Stunt Spectacular, Star Tours, Inside the Magic, and the Backstage Studio Tour. In peak seasons, stay on for fireworks. A new show debuted in the fall of 1998. Fantasmic is a 25-minute combination of dancing waters, lasers, and a real-life cast of 50.

A Day at Animal Kingdom

If you have one day in Animal Kingdom, try to arrive early and be there when the gates open at 8am. This will give you the best chance of actually seeing animals. If you want to eat at the RainForest Cafe, make your reservations early. The size of the park (500 acres) means a considerable amount of travel time once you pass through those opening gates. Don't linger in the Oasis area or around the Tree of Life; instead, head directly to the back of the park to be first in line for the **Kilimanjaro Safari.** This will allow you to see more animals before the heat of the day and before the lines become impossibly long. Work your way back through Africa, visiting **Gorilla Falls,** and if you have children, take the **train to Conservation Station.** (If not, go back to the Safari Village.) Tour the **Tree of Life,** watch **"It's Tough to Be a Bug,"** and then have lunch. You may want to buy snacks from a cart vendor and enjoy some of the street performers or African storytellers. If you want a sit-down lunch, try Tuskers Restaurant. If you have children, head over to **Camp Minnie-Mickey** after lunch to greet some characters, visit **Grandmother Willow's cove,** and then catch a showing of the **Lion King show**. After that, head to **Dinoland** to play in the Boneyard, watch **"Journey into the Jungle Book,"** and, if the kids are tall enough, ride **Countdown to Extinction.** Adults will want to skip Camp Minnie-Mickey and go straight to Dinoland, ending the day with the last Lion King show before heading out through the Gate. A nice way to end the day is with a leisurely stroll through the animal habitats in the Oasis. If you are having dinner at the RainForest Cafe, save time to explore the oasis while you wait for your table to be ready.

SERVICES & FACILITIES IN THE PARKS

ATMs   Money machines are available near the entrances to all parks and usually one other place inside the park. These machines honor cards from banks using the Cirrus, Honor, and Plus systems, and they are marked on the park guide map.

Baby Care   All parks have a Baby Care Center equipped with rocking chairs and selling basic supplies such as disposable diapers. Disposable diapers are also available at Guest Services. All women's rest rooms and some men's rest rooms are equipped with changing tables.

Cameras & Film   Film and Kodak disposable cameras are sold at various locations in all parks. Camcorders are available for rent in Epcot and MGM but not in the Magic Kingdom or Animal Kingdom.

First Aid   All parks have manned first-aid stations near the entrances.

Lost Children   Every park has a designated spot for lost children and also keeps written records of those children. In the Magic Kingdom, it's usually City Hall or the Baby Care Center; in Epcot, the Earth Center or the Baby Care Center; in Disney–MGM Studios, Guest Services; in Animal Kingdom, the Safari Village. Children under 7 should have name tags.

Package Pickup   Clerks at nearly all WDW stores can arrange for large packages to be taken to the front of the park. Allow at least 3 hours for delivery.

Pets   Don't leave your pet in a parked car, even with a window cracked open. The interior of a car becomes incredibly hot baking in the Florida sun. (A dead pet will not enhance your trip.) Only service animals are permitted in the parks, but there are five kennels in the WDW complex. Those at the Transportation and Ticket Center in the Magic Kingdom and near the entrance to Fort Wilderness board animals overnight. Day accommodations are offered at kennels just outside the Entrance Plaza at Epcot and at the entrances to Disney–MGM Studios and Animal Kingdom.

Stroller Rental   Strollers are available for rent near the entrances of all the parks. The cost is $6. Deposits, usually $1 or $2, may vary.

Wheelchair Rental   Both electric and regular wheelchairs are available at all the parks. A regular wheelchair costs about $6. Electric wheelchairs rent for $32 to $35. The deposit, usually only a few dollars, may vary.

FOR TRAVELERS WITH SPECIAL NEEDS

WDW does everything possible to facilitate guests with disabilities. Its many services are detailed in the *Guidebook for Guests with Disabilities.* To obtain a copy prior to your

visit, write **Guest Letters,** P.O. Box 10040, Lake Buena Vista, FL 32830-0040, or call
☎ **407/824-4321.** Also call that number for answers to any questions regarding special needs. Some examples of Disney services: Almost all Disney resorts have rooms for
those with disabilities; there are braille directories inside the Magic Kingdom—in
front of the Main Street train station and in a gazebo in front of the Crystal Palace
restaurant; there are special parking lots at all three parks; complimentary guided-tour
audiocassette tapes and recorders are available at Guest Services to assist visually
impaired guests; personal translator units are available to amplify the audio at selected
Epcot attractions (inquire at Earth Station); and wheelchairs can be rented at all of the
Disney parks. For information about Telecommunications Devices for the Deaf
(TDDs), call ☎ **407/827-5141.**

3 The Magic Kingdom

Centered around Cinderella's Castle—its Gothic spires are Walt Disney World's most
recognizable symbol, after Mickey Mouse—the Magic Kingdom occupies about 100
acres, with numerous attractions, restaurants, and shops in **seven theme sections,** or
"Lands."

ARRIVING   From the parking lot, you have to take a short monorail or ferry ride
to the Magic Kingdom entrance. During peak attendance times, arrive at the
Magic Kingdom no later than an hour before opening time to avoid long lines at
these conveyances. Sections of the parking lot are named for Disney characters
(Goofy, Pluto, Minnie, and so on), and aisles are numbered. Be sure to write down
where you parked.

Upon entering the park, consult your *Magic Kingdom Guidemap* to get your
bearings. It details every shop, restaurant, and attraction in every Land. Also consult
your **entertainment schedule** to see what's on for the day. There are parades, musical
extravaganzas featuring Disney characters, fireworks, band concerts, barbershop
quartets, Disney-character appearances, and more.

If you have questions, all park employees are very knowledgeable, and City Hall, on
your left as you enter, is both an information center and, along with Toontown
Fair (details in the section on Fantasyland), a likely place to meet up with costumed
characters.

HOURS   Generally 9am to 7pm with extended hours—sometimes as late as
midnight—during major holidays and the summer months.

TICKETS & PRICES $42 for adults, $34 for children, children under 4 are free.
See "Tickets" earlier in this chapter for information on 4- and 5-day passes.

SERVICES & FACILITIES IN THE MAGIC KINGDOM

ATMs   These machines honor cards from banks using the Cirrus, Honor, and
Plus systems and are located at the main entrance, the SunTrust Bank on Main
Street, and in Tomorrowland.

Baby Care   Located next to the Crystal Palace at the end of Main Street, the Baby
Care Center is furnished with rocking chairs and toddler-size toilets.
Disposable diapers, formula, baby food, and pacifiers are for sale. There are
changing tables here as well as in all women's rest rooms and some men's rest rooms.
Disposable diapers are also sold at Guest Services.

Cameras & Film   Film and Kodak's disposable Fun Saver cameras are available throughout the park. Although once available, 35mm cameras and camcorders are no longer for rent at the Magic Kingdom.

First Aid   The First Aid Center, staffed by registered nurses, is located alongside the Crystal Palace.

Lockers   Lockers can be found in an arcade underneath the Main Street Railroad Station. The cost is $6, including a $2 refundable deposit.

Lost Children   Lost children in the Magic Kingdom are usually taken to City Hall or the Baby Care Center where lost children logbooks are kept. Children under 7 should wear name tags.

Package Pickup   Any large package you purchase can be sent by the shop clerk to Guest Relations in the Entrance Plaza. Allow 3 hours for delivery.

Pet Care   The Transportation and Ticket Center at Magic Kingdom boards animals overnight for $8 a day. There are also four other kennels in the WDW complex.

Strollers   These can be rented at the Stroller Shop near the entrance to the Magic Kingdom. The cost is $6 a day, including a $1 deposit.

Wheelchair Rental   For wheelchairs, go to the gift shop to the left of the ticket booths at the Transportation and Ticket Center or to the Stroller and Wheelchair Shop inside the main entrance to your right. Cost is $6 regular and $32 electric, including a $2 deposit.

FROMMER'S RATES THE RIDES

Because there is so much to do, here's a guide to help you decide quickly which options might be best for you. You'll notice most of the grades are *A*s, *B*s, and *C*s. All that research and development Disney park designers put into their job hasn't gone to waste. There are few options that rate a *D* for Dud. Here's what the Frommer's ratings mean:

A+	=	Your trip wouldn't be complete with out it.
A	=	Put at the top of "to do" list.
B+	=	Make a real effort to see or do.
B	=	Fun but not a "must see."
C+	=	A nice diversion; see if you have time.
C	=	Go if lines are short.
D	=	Dud. Don't waste your time.

MAIN STREET, U.S.A.

Designed to replicate an archetypal turn-of-the-century American street (okay, so it culminates in a 13th-century European castle), this is the gateway to the Kingdom. Don't dawdle on Main Street when you enter the park; leave it for the end of the day when you're heading back to your hotel.

Main Street Cinema
Frommer's Rating: C
Recommended Ages: all ages
A mannequin is in charge of the ticket booth here, so you can sneak right in without paying. Just kidding—there's no charge for admission. Main Street Cinema is an air-conditioned hexagonal theater where vintage black-and-white Disney cartoons (including the 1928 Steamboat Willie, in which Mickey and Minnie debuted) are aired continually on two screens. You have to watch these standing up; there are no seats.

The Magic Kingdom

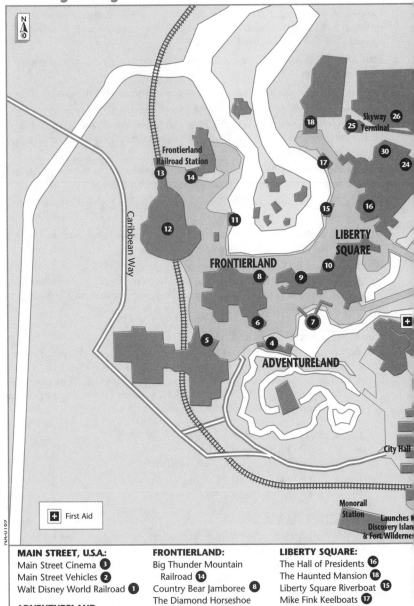

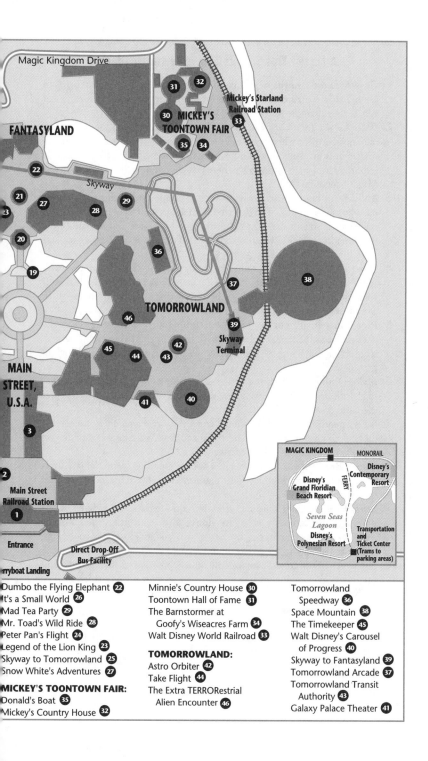

Magic Kingdom Drive

FANTASYLAND

Skyway

MICKEY'S
TOONTOWN FAIR

Mickey's Starland
Railroad Station

TOMORROWLAND

Skyway
Terminal

**MAIN
STREET,
U.S.A.**

Main Street
Railroad Station

Entrance

Direct Drop-Off
Bus Facility

Ferryboat Landing

MAGIC KINGDOM | MONORAIL

Disney's
Grand Floridian
Beach Resort

Disney's
Contemporary
Resort

FERRY

Seven Seas
Lagoon

Disney's
Polynesian Resort

Transportation
and
Ticket Center
(Trams to
parking areas)

Dumbo the Flying Elephant ㉒	
It's a Small World ㉖	
Mad Tea Party ㉙	
Mr. Toad's Wild Ride ㉘	
Peter Pan's Flight ㉔	
Legend of the Lion King ㉓	
Skyway to Tomorrowland ㉕	
Snow White's Adventures ㉗	

MICKEY'S TOONTOWN FAIR:
Donald's Boat ㉟
Mickey's Country House ㉜

Minnie's Country House ㉚
Toontown Hall of Fame ㉛
The Barnstormer at
   Goofy's Wiseacres Farm ㉞
Walt Disney World Railroad ㉝

TOMORROWLAND:
Astro Orbiter ㊷
Take Flight ㊹
The Extra TERRORestrial
   Alien Encounter ㊺

Tomorrowland
   Speedway ㊱
Space Mountain ㊳
The Timekeeper ㊺
Walt Disney's Carousel
   of Progress ㊵
Skyway to Fantasyland ㊴
Tomorrowland Arcade ㊲
Tomorrowland Transit
   Authority ㊸
Galaxy Palace Theater ㊶

A Dozen Tips So You'll Have Fewer Headaches

1. Go Where the Crowds Aren't: Head to the left when the rush is moving to the right. Save the major attractions for late in the day. Eat a little earlier or a little later than the rest of the crowd.

2. Write Down Your Car's Location: That purple minivan in the next space may not be there when you get out. Write down where your car is or do what ever is necessary to commit the location to memory. This is especially important at Epcot and MGM where lots are not as well marked as in the Magic Kingdom.

3. Avoid Rush Hour: I-4 is woefully over capacity, so avoid being on the roads during rush hour, from 8 to 9am and from about 4:30 to 6pm. This is especially true if you are driving toward the downtown area. But remember, the theme parks are also serviced by thousands of office workers keeping bankers hours.

4. Don't Overplan: Face it, you aren't going to do everything in any park. Agree as a group to a list of three "must-do" activities for each day. If your children are old enough to be responsible, split and reunite at an agreed-upon time.

5. Pace Yourself: It's not unusual to see people literally running across the parking lot to the trams. Relax, the park isn't going anywhere. Once inside, stagger long lines with air-conditioned shows or even breaks on a bench in the shade.

6. Make Dining Reservations: If a sit-down dinner is important, make sure to get priority-seating reservations either before your visit or when you enter the park.

7. Set a Spending Limit: Kids should know they have a set amount to spend on take-home trinkets. So should Mom and Dad. Set a budget, building in a small contingency fund for emergencies.

8. Take a Break: If you are staying at a WDW property, spend the late afternoon napping or unwinding. Return to parks for a few more attractions and the closing shows.

9. Dress Comfortably: This may seem like a no-brainer, but judging by the limping, blistered crowds, some don't understand that they will be walking—a lot. This is not the place to break in those way-cool clogs. Comfortable walking shoes are a must.

10. Sunscreen, Sunscreen, Sunscreen: Locals spot tourists by their painful bright-red glow. The Florida sun can bake you, even in the shade and even in the cooler months. A bad first-day burn can ruin the whole trip. Protect yourself and your kids.

11. Travel Light: Don't carry large amounts of cash. The Pirates of the Caribbean aren't the only thieves in WDW. There are ATM machines in all the parks if you begin to run short of cash.

12. Get a Little Goofy: Relax, put on those Mickey Mouse ears, eat that extra piece of fudge, even sing along at the shows. Don't worry about what the staff thinks; they've seen just about everything. Everyone else is on vacation, too.

> ## ❷ Did You Know?
>
> - The movie portion of Universal Studios' *Back to the Future* attraction took 2 years to make and was the most expensive film per minute ever made.
> - Mickey Mouse has more than 80 different outfits, ranging from a scuba suit to a tuxedo. Minnie has only 50.
> - There are enough Mickey Mouse–ear hats sold each year to cover the head of every man, woman, and child in Pittsburgh.
> - You could fit New York's Empire State Building into the Vehicle Assembly Building at the Kennedy Space Center 3¾ times.
> - Shamu, the killer whale at Sea World, eats more than 65,000 pounds of fish a year.
> - Every day an average of 100 pairs of sunglasses are turned in to the Lost and Found at the Magic Kingdom.
> - Since Walt Disney World opened in 1971, the total miles logged by monorail trains is equal to more than 24 trips to the moon.
> - During launch, it takes just 8 minutes for the space shuttle to reach its orbiting speed of 17,500 miles per hour.
> - Both Disneyland and Walt Disney World were built on former citrus groves in counties named Orange.

Walt Disney World Railroad & Other Main Street Vehicles

Frommer's Rating: C+
Recommended Ages: 2–8
You can board an authentic 1928 steam-powered train here for a 15-minute journey clockwise around the perimeter of the park. There are stations in Frontierland and Mickey's Toontown. There are also horse-drawn trolleys, horseless carriages, jitneys, omnibuses, and fire engines plying the short route along Main Street from Town Square to Cinderella Castle.

SHOPPING ON MAIN STREET

The vast Disneyana Collectibles carries limited-edition movie cels, antique Disney clocks and porcelain figures, and collectible dolls and items such as a 1947 Donald Duck cookie jar that today is worth $2,000! Why did I ever let Mom throw out my old toys?

The Emporium, in Town Square, houses the park's largest selection of Disneyana, everything from Mickey-logo golf balls to Dumbo cookie jars. Note the Animatronic window displays.

Basically an old-fashioned candy store, the **Market House** also has an interesting line of pipes and tobaccos, as well as Disney-theme kitchenware—Mickey cupcake papers, ice-cube molds, and cookie cutters.

Over at the **Harmony Barber Shop,** where nostalgic men's grooming items are sold (mustache wax, spice colognes, shaving mugs), a barbershop quartet called The Dapper Dans performs on the hour all day (except at 3pm).

Autographed sports memorabilia and team clothing—Joe Namath–signed footballs, Pittsburgh Steeler T-shirts, Bulls jerseys, a Babe Ruth–autographed 1936 World Series program, and the like—are available at the **Main Street Athletic Club.**

At **Crystal Arts,** you can watch craftspeople create the intricate animals, cut-glass vases and bowls, and other glittering items sold here. And at the adjoining **Shadow Box,** silhouette artists create cut-out portraits of customers on black paper.

At the end of Main Street, the **King's Gallery,** inside Cinderella's Castle, is cluttered with family crests, tapestries, suits of armor, and other medieval wares, as well as miniature carousels. An artisan demonstrates damascening, a form of metal engraving that originated in Damascus circa A.D. 600.

ADVENTURELAND

Cross a bridge to your left and stroll into an exotic jungle of lush tropical foliage, thatch-roofed huts, and carved totems. Amid dense vines and stands of palm and bamboo, drums are beating, and swashbuckling adventures are taking place.

Note: If you're heading toward Adventureland or Frontierland first thing in the morning, wait for the gates to open at the bridge in front of the Crystal Palace, to your left as you enter.

Jungle Cruise

Frommer's Rating: B+
Recommended Ages: 4–14

What a cruise! In the course of about 10 minutes, your boat sails through an African veldt in the Congo, an Amazon rain forest, the Mekong River in Southeast Asia, and along the Nile. Amidst the lavish scenery, with ropes of hanging vines, cascading waterfalls, and lush tropical and subtropical foliage (most of it real), are dozens of audio-animatronic birds and animals—elephants, zebras, lions, giraffes, crocodiles, tigers, even fluttering butterflies. On the shore, you'll pass a Raiders-like Cambodian temple cave fronted by a Buddha and guarded by snakes, a rhino and jackal chasing terrified African beaters up a tree, and a jungle camp taken over by apes. But the adventures aren't all on shore. Passengers are menaced by everything from water-spouting elephants to fierce warriors who attack with spears. The guide keeps up an amusing patter.

Pirates of the Caribbean

Frommer's Rating: B+
Recommended Ages: 6–adult

Although the Disneyland version of this ride has been adapted to be more politically correct, the pirates still chase the wenches in Florida. You'll proceed through a long grotto-like passageway to board a boat into a pitch-black cave. Therein, elaborate scenery and hundreds of audio-animatronic figures (including lifelike dogs, cats, chickens, pigs, and donkeys) depict a rambunctious pirate raid on a Caribbean town. To a background of cheerful "yo-ho-yo-ho" music, the sound of rushing waterfalls, squawking seagulls, and screams of terror, passengers pass through the line of fire in a

In the Words of Walt Disney

Sheer animated fantasy is still my first and deepest production impulse. The fable is the best storytelling device ever conceived . . . . And, of course, animal characters have always been the personnel of fable—animals through which the foibles as well as the virtues of humans can best and most hilariously be reflected.

Never get bored or cynical. Yesterday is a thing of the past.

raging pirate battle and view tableaux of fierce-looking pirates swigging rum, looting, and plundering. This might be scary for kids under 5.

Swiss Family Treehouse

Frommer's Rating: C
Recommended Ages: 4–12

This attraction is based on the 1960 Disney movie version of Johann Wyss's *Swiss Family Robinson,* about a shipwrecked family of five who created an ingenious dwelling for themselves in the branches of a sprawling banyan tree. Using materials and furnishings salvaged from their downed ship, the Robinsons created bedrooms, a kitchen, a library, and a living room. Visitors traverse a rope-suspended bridge and ascend the 50-foot tree for a close-up look into these rooms. Note the Rube Goldberg rope-and-bucket device with bamboo chutes that dips water from a stream and carries it to treetop chambers. The "tree" itself, designed by Disney "Imagineers," has 330,000 polyethylene leaves sprouting from a 90-foot span of branches; although it isn't real, it is draped with actual Spanish moss.

Tropical Serenade

Frommer's Rating: C
Recommended Ages: 2–10

A large hexagonal Polynesian-style dwelling, with a thatched roof, bamboo beams, and tapa-bark murals, is home to 250 tropical birds, chanting totem poles, and singing flowers who whistle, tweet, and warble. The audience is encouraged to sing along. The show is hosted by four feathered friends named José, Michael, Pierre, and Fritz—all with appropriate national accents—who perch atop an "enchanted" fountain. Highlights include a thunderstorm in the dark (The gods are angry!), a light show over the fountain, and, of course, the famous "in the tiki, tiki, tiki, tiki, tiki room" song. Like it or not, you'll find yourself singing it all day. This is a must for young children.

SHOPPING IN ADVENTURELAND

The exotic **Traders of Timbuktu** carries carved wooden and soapstone animals, masks, and cowhide drums from Kenya, among other ethnic wares.

Plaza del Sol Caribe, a Mexican mercado, has piñatas, baskets, straw hats, stuffed and papier-mâché toucans and parrots, and much more.

For the Indiana Jones look, check out the clothing and accessories at **Elephant Tales.** The little **Tiki Tropic Shop** carries surfer-theme merchandise.

Shell mobiles and hangings, plus a wide selection of straw hats, are sold at the **Zanzibar Shell Shop. Island Supply,** a Disney version of The Nature Company, offers nature-theme books, posters, toys, bird feeders, and more.

And both the **House of Treasure** and the adjoining **Lafitte's Portrait Deck** retail pirate merchandise: hats, Captain Hook T-shirts, ships in bottles, and toy muskets and daggers; the latter has a pirate ship photo setup.

FRONTIERLAND

From Adventureland, step into the wild and woolly past of the American frontier, where Disney employees (they're called "cast members") are clad in denim and calico, sidewalks are wooden, rough-and-tumble architecture runs to log cabins and rustic saloons, and the landscape is Southwestern scrubby with mesquite, saguaro cactus, yucca, and prickly pear. Across the river is Tom Sawyer Island, reachable via log rafts.

Big Thunder Mountain Railroad
Frommer's Rating: A
Recommended Ages: 10–adult

This mining disaster–theme roller coaster—its thrills deriving from hairpin turns and descents in the dark, rather than sudden steep drops—is situated in a 200-foot-high red-stone mountain with 2,780 feet of track winding through windswept canyons and bat-filled caves. You enter the ride via the ramshackle headquarters of the Big Thunder Mining Company and board a runaway train that careens through the ribs of a dinosaur, under a thundering waterfall, past spewing geysers and bubbling mud pots, and over a bottomless volcanic pool. Riders are threatened by flash floods, earthquakes, rickety bridges, and avalanches. audio-animatronic characters (such as the long john–clad fellow navigating the floodwaters in a bathtub) and animals (goats, chickens, donkeys, possums) enhance the scenic backdrop, and several-hundred-thousand dollars' worth of authentic antique mining equipment adds verisimilitude. *Note:* You must be 40 inches tall to ride.

Country Bear Jamboree
Frommer's Rating: A (A+ for kids)
Recommended Ages: 4–adult

I've always loved the Country Bear Jamboree, a 15-minute show featuring a troupe of fiddlin', banjo strummin', harmonica playin' audio-animatronic bears belting out rollicking country tunes and crooning plaintive love songs. The chubby Trixie, decked out in a satiny skirt, laments lost love as she sings "Tears Will Be the Chaser for Your Wine." Teddi Barra descends from the ceiling in a swing to perform "Heart We Did All That We Could." Other star performers include a country-western group called the Five Bear Rugs, Liver Lips McGrowl, and the 7-foot-tall master of ceremonies, Henry. In the rousing show finale, the entire cast joins in a foot-stompin' sing-along. Wisecracking commentary comes from a mounted buffalo, moose, and deer on the wall. A special holiday show plays throughout the Christmas season each year.

Diamond Horseshoe Saloon Revue & Medicine Show
Frommer's Rating: B+
Recommended Ages: 6–adult

Sit yourself down in air-conditioned comfort and enjoy a rousing western revue at Dr. Bill U. Later's turn-of-the-century saloon. Marshall John Charles sings and banters with the audience, Jingles the Piano Man plays honky-tonk tunes, there's a magic act, and Miss Lucille L'Amour and her troupe of dance-hall girls do a spirited cancan—all with lots of humor and audience participation. There are seven shows daily; plan on going around lunchtime, so you can eat during the show. The menu features deli or peanut-butter-and-jelly sandwiches served with chips.

Frontierland Shootin' Arcade
Frommer's Rating: C+
Recommended Ages: 8–adult

Combining state-of-the-art electronics with a traditional shooting-gallery format, this vast arcade presents an array of 97 targets (slow-moving ore cars, buzzards, and gravediggers) in a three-dimensional 1850s gold-mining town scenario. Fog creeps across the graveyard, and the setting changes as a calm, starlit night turns stormy with flashes of lightning and claps of thunder. Coyotes howl, bridges creak, and skeletal arms reach out from the grave. If you hit a tombstone, it might spin around and mysteriously change its epitaph. To keep the western ambience authentic, newfangled electronic firing mechanisms loaded with infrared bullets are concealed in genuine Hawkins 54-caliber buffalo rifles. When you hit a target, elaborate sound and motion gags are set off. Fifty cents buys you 25 shots.

Splash Mountain
Frommer's Rating: A+
Recommended Ages: 10–adult
Themed after Walt Disney's 1946 film, *Song of the South,* Splash Mountain takes you on an enchanting journey in a hollowed-out log craft along the canals of a flooded mountain, past 26 brilliantly colored tableaux of backwoods swamps, bayous, spooky caves, and waterfalls. Riders are caught up in the bumbling schemes of Brer Fox and Brer Bear as they pursue the ever-wily Brer Rabbit, who, against the advice of Mr. Bluebird, has left his briar-patch home in search of adventure and the "laughing place." The music from the film forms a delightful audio backdrop. Your log craft twists, turns, and splashes—sometimes plummeting in total darkness— all leading up to a thrilling five-story, 45°-angle splashdown from mountaintop to briar-filled pond at 40 miles per hour! And that's not the end. The ride continues, and finally it's a Zip-A-Dee-Doo-Dah kind of day. *Note:* You must be 44 inches tall to ride.

Tom Sawyer Island
Frommer's Rating: C for adults, B+ for antsy children who need a break from lines.
Recommended Ages: 4–14
Board Huck Finn's raft for a 1-minute float across the river to the densely forested Tom Sawyer Island, where kids can explore the narrow passages of Injun Joe's cave (complete with scary sound effects, like whistling wind), a walk-through windmill, a serpentine abandoned mine, or Fort Sam Clemens, where an audio-animatronic drunk is snoring-off a bender. Maintaining one's balance while crossing rickety swing and barrel bridges is also fun. Narrow, winding dirt paths lined with oaks, pines, and sycamores create an authentic backwoods island feel. It's easy to get briefly lost and stumble upon some unexpected adventure. You might combine this attraction with lunch at Aunt Polly's restaurant, which serves light fare (fried chicken, sandwiches, and the like) and has outdoor tables on a porch overlooking the river. Adults can rest weary feet over coffee, while the kids explore the island.

SHOPPING IN FRONTIERLAND
Mosey into the **Frontier Trading Post** for western-look leather items, cowboy boots and hats, western shirts, coonskin caps, turquoise jewelry, belts, and toy rifles. **Prairie Outpost & Supply** sells Native American items such as drums, headdresses, and bows and arrows, many of them related to Pocahontas.

Visit the **Briar Patch,** under Splash Mountain, for Uncle Remus and Winnie the Pooh merchandise.

LIBERTY SQUARE
Serving as a transitional area between Frontierland and Fantasyland, Liberty Square evokes 18th-century America with Federal and Georgian architecture, Colonial Williamsburg–type shops, and neat flower beds bordering manicured lawns. Thirteen lanterns, symbolizing the colonies, are suspended from the Liberty Tree, an immense live oak. You might encounter a fife and drum corps marching along Liberty Square's cobblestone streets. The Liberty Tree Tavern here (details in chapter 6) is my favorite Magic Kingdom restaurant.

Boat Rides

Frommer's Rating: C
Recommended Ages: 6–adult
A steam-powered sternwheeler called the *Liberty Belle* and two Mike Fink Keelboats (the *Bertha Mae* and the *Gullywhumper*) depart (the latter, summers and holidays only) from Liberty Square for scenic cruises along the Rivers of America. The passing landscape evokes the Wild West. Both ply the same route and make a restful interlude for foot-weary parkgoers.

Hall of Presidents

Frommer's Rating: B
Recommended Ages: 10–adult
In this redbrick colonial hall with a giant bell suspended in its tower, all American presidents—from George Washington to Bill Clinton (whose actual voice was recorded for this attraction)—are represented by audio-animatronic figures who act out important events in the nation's history, from the signing of the Declaration of Independence through the space age. The show begins with a film, projected on a 180°, 70mm screen, about the importance of the Constitution. The curtain then rises on the 42 assembled American leaders, and, as each is spotlighted, he nods or waves with presidential dignity. Lincoln then rises and speaks, occasionally even referring to his notes. In a stunning example of Disney thoroughness, painstaking research was done in creating the figures and scenery, with each president's costume reflecting not only period fashion but period fabrics and tailoring techniques! Poet and author Maya Angelou narrates.

Haunted Mansion

Frommer's Rating: A+
Recommended Ages: 6–adult
What better way to exhibit Disney special-effects wizardry than a haunted mansion? Macabre attendants harry groups of visitors past a graveyard, turning them over to a ghost host who encloses them in a windowless, doorless portrait gallery (are those eyes following you around?) where the floor seems to be descending. Its ambience enhanced by inky darkness, spooky music, eerie howling, and mysterious screams and rappings, this mansion is replete with bizarre scenes and objects: a ghostly banquet and ball, a graveyard band, a suit of armor that comes alive, cobweb-covered chandeliers, luminous spiders, a talking head in a crystal ball, weird flying objects, and much more. At the end of the ride, a ghost joins you in your car. The experience is more amusing than terrifying, so you can take small children inside.

SHOPPING IN LIBERTY SQUARE

Olde World Antiques' high-quality inventory might range from an 18th-century pine hutch to 19th-century Staffordshire Chinoiserie willow-pattern platters. The adjoining **Silversmith** carries Revere-style silver and pewter butter dishes, candlesticks, bowls, trays, jewelry, and picture frames.

The Yankee Trader is a charming country store, its shelves stocked with Lion King and Winnie the Pooh cookie jars, Mickey cookie cutters, and fancy food items.

Over at **Heritage House,** you can purchase parchment copies of famous American documents as well as actual historic framed letters (one signed by President Andrew Johnson in 1864 was priced at $2,350). Old campaign buttons, Civil War hats, and presidential signatures are here, too. A craftsperson on the premises makes jewelry cut from coins.

FANTASYLAND

The attractions in this happy land—themed after Disney film classics such as *Snow White, Peter Pan,* and *Dumbo*—are especially popular with young visitors. If your kids are 8 or under, you might want to make it (and Mickey's Toontown; details later in this section) your first stop in the Magic Kingdom. *Note:* Mr. Toad's Wild Ride is a bit scary. If your under-5 frightens easily, skip it.

Cinderella's Castle

Frommer's Rating: A
Recommended Ages: 2–10

There's not a lot to see here, but its place as the Magic Kingdom icon makes it a must-see. At the end of Main Street, in the center of the park, you'll come to a fairyland castle, 185 feet high and housing a restaurant (King Stefan's Banquet Hall) and shops. Mosaic murals inside depict the Cinderella story, and Disney family coats of arms are displayed over a fireplace. Cinderella herself, dressed for the ball, often makes appearances in the lobby area. You'll be able to see shows on the Castle Forecourt Stage.

Cinderella's Golden Carousel

Frommer's Rating: B+
Recommended Ages: all ages

It's a beauty, built by Italian wood-carvers in the Victorian tradition in 1917 and refurbished by Disney artists who added 18 hand-painted scenes from the Cinderella story on the wooden canopy above the horses. The carousel organ plays Disney classics such as "When You Wish Upon a Star."

Dumbo, the Flying Elephant

Frommer's Rating: A for parents with kids, B for others
Recommended Ages: 2–10

This is a very tame kiddie ride in which the cars—large-eared baby elephants (Dumbos)—go around and around in a circle gently rising and dipping. But it's very exciting for wee ones.

It's a Small World

Frommer's Rating: A
Recommended Ages: 2–14

It rates an A because—love it or hate it—it's something that you have to do. You know the song—and if you don't, you will. It plays continually as you sail "around the world" through vast rooms designed to represent different countries. They're inhabited by appropriately costumed audio-animatronic dolls and animals—all singing "It's a small world after all . . ." in tiny, doll-like voices. This cast of thousands includes Chinese acrobats, Russian kazatski dancers, Indian snake charmers in front of the Taj Mahal, French cancan dancers, Irish leprechauns, singing geese and windmills in Holland, Arabs on magic carpets, mountain goats in the Swiss Alps, African drummers and lunging hyenas in the jungle, a Venetian gondolier, and Australian koala bears. Cute. Very cute. But it just wouldn't be a visit to Disney without it.

Legend of the Lion King

Frommer's Rating: A+
Recommended Ages: 4–12

This stage spectacular based on Disney's blockbuster motion-picture musical combines animation, movie footage, sophisticated puppetry, and high-tech special effects. The show is enhanced by the Academy Award–winning music of Elton John and Tim Rice. Other voices are provided by Whoopi Goldberg and Cheech Marin as laughing hyenas.

Mad Tea Party

Frommer's Rating: C
Recommended Ages: 4–16

This is a traditional amusement park ride à la Disney, with an Alice in Wonderland theme. Riders sit in oversized pastel-hued teacups on saucers that careen around a circular platform while tilting and spinning. In the center of the platform is a big teapot, out from which pops a mouse. Believe it or not, this can be a pretty wild ride— or a tame one. It depends on how much you spin, a factor under your control via a wheel in the cup.

Mr. Toad's Wild Ride

Frommer's Rating: C+
Recommended Ages: 6–16

This ride is based on the 1949 Disney film, *The Adventures of Ichabod and Mr. Toad*, which was itself based on an enduring children's classic, the divine *Wind in the Willows*. In colorful cars named for characters (Weasel, Toady, Moley), riders navigate a series of dark rooms, hurtling into solid objects—a fireplace, a bookcase, a haystack—and through barn doors into a coop of squawking chickens. They're menaced by falling suits of armor, snorting bulls, and an oncoming locomotive in a pitch-black tunnel, and are sent to jail (for car theft), to hell (complete with pitchfork-wielding demons), and through a fiery volcano. The ride's interior space is illuminated   by invisible ultraviolet light, which makes whites and neons in the scenery glow.

Peter Pan's Flight

Frommer's Rating: B+ for kids, C+ for others
Recommended Ages: 4–10

Riding in airborne versions of Captain Hook's ship, passengers careen through dark passages while experiencing the story of Peter Pan. The adventure begins in the Darlings' nursery and includes a flight over nighttime London to Never-Never Land, where riders encounter mermaids, Indians, a ticking crocodile, the lost boys, Princess Tiger Lilly, Tinker Bell, Hook, Smee, and the rest—all to the movie music "You Can Fly, You Can Fly, You Can Fly." It's fun.

Skyway

Frommer's Rating: A
Recommended Ages: all ages

This is another one of the experiences that is signature Disney, so it rates a high mark. Its entrance close to Peter Pan's Flight, the Skyway is an aerial tramway to Tomorrow-land that makes continuous trips throughout the day. A good chance to let those tired feet rest and catch one of the rare Florida breezes.

Snow White's Adventures

Frommer's Rating: D
Recommended Ages: 6–14

My rating may be influenced by the fact that this ride made my favorite 3-year-old bawl, but I still think that there are more worthy ways to spend your time. This attraction once focused only on the more sinister elements of Grimm's fairy tale—most notably the evil queen and the cackling, toothless witch—leaving small children screaming in terror. Since it was the first ride most people hit when entering Fantasyland, it seemed kind of a cruel trick from the same team that killed off Bambi's mother. It's been toned down now, with Snow White appearing in a number of pleasant scenes—at the castle-courtyard wishing well, in the dwarfs' cottage, and riding off with the prince to live "happily ever

In the Words of Walt Disney

Fantasy, if it's really convincing, can't become dated, for the simple reason that it represents a flight into a dimension that lies beyond the reach of time . . . nothing corrodes or gets run down . . . . And nobody gets any older.

We have never lost our faith in family entertainment—stories that make people laugh, stories about warm and human things, stories about historic characters and events, and stories about animals.

after." There are new audio-animatronic dwarfs, and the interior colors have also been brightened up and made less menacing. Even so, this could be scary for kids under 7.

SHOPPING IN FANTASYLAND

It's always the holiday season at **Mickey's Christmas Carol,** supply central for Disney-motif ornaments, caroler dolls, Mickey Christmas stockings, and charming Christmas-theme music boxes.

And little girls will adore **Tinker Bell's Treasures,** its wares comprising Peter Pan merchandise, costumes (Tinker Bell, Snow White, Cinderella, Pocahontas, and others), and collector dolls.

Mickey's Toontown Fair

Frommer's Rating: A+
Recommended Ages: All ages, but great for kids under 10
Head off those cries of "Where's Mickey?" by taking the kids to this 2-acre replacement for Mickey's Starland, which was unveiled during the 25th Anniversary celebration in 1996. Toontown Fair offers kids a chance to meet their favorite Disney characters including Mickey, Minnie, Donald Duck, and Goofy. Set in a whimsical collection of candy-striped tents harking back to those turn-of-the-century county fairs, highlights include the **Toontown Hall of Fame,** animated shorts hosted by the stars, and both **Mickey's and Minnie's country houses.** Everything is brightly colored and kid-friendly in the best Disney tradition. There is even a kid-sized roller coaster. Toontown Fair has its own stop on the WDW Railroad.

TOMORROWLAND

This land focuses on the future—most notably, space travel and exploration. In 1994, the Disney people decided that Tomorrowland (originally designed in the 1970s) was beginning to look like "Yesterdayland." (Although something looking suspiciously like some of the old polyester ride uniforms can be found hanging in The Gap.)

It's now been revamped to reflect the future as a galactic, science fiction–inspired community inhabited by humans, aliens, and robots. A vast state-of-the-art video-game arcade has also been added.

Alien Encounter

Frommer's Rating: A+
Recommended Ages: 10–adult
Director George Lucas, of *Star Wars* fame, contributed his space-age vision to this major Tomorrowland attraction. The action begins at the Interplanetary Convention Center where a mysterious corporation called X-S Tech—a company from a distant planet—is marketing a "teletransporter" to Earthlings. The device is capable of beaming living beings between planets light-years apart. After a slick corporate presentation, S.I.R., a rather sinister robot, demonstrates the product on Skippy, a cute and fuzzy alien, though not with total success. Skippy ends up discombobulated

and with singed fur! Despite this dubious beginning, X-S technicians try to teleport their sinister corporation head, Chairman Clench, to Earth. But the machine malfunctions, sending Clench instead to a distant planet and, inadvertently, teleporting a fearsome extraterrestrial to earth. Dark and truly scary, it is not your typical thrill ride. It's no fantasy that your heart is racing as you work your way through lots of high-tech effects—from the alien's breath on your neck to a mist of alien slime. *Note:* You must be 48 inches tall to ride.

Astro Orbiter
Frommer's Rating: C
Recommended Ages: 8 and under
This is a tame, typical amusement-park ride. The "rockets" are on arms attached to "the center of the galaxy," and they move up and down while orbiting spinning planets.

Skyway
Frommer's Rating: A
Recommended Ages: all ages
Located near the Tomorrowland entrance just west of Space Mountain, this aerial tramway to Fantasyland makes continuous round-trips throughout the day.

Space Mountain
Frommer's Rating: A+
Recommended Ages: 10–adult
Space Mountain entertains visitors on its long lines with space-age music, exhibits, and meteorites, shooting stars, and space debris whizzing about overhead. These "illusioneering" effects, enhanced by appropriate audio, continue during the ride itself, which is a cosmic roller coaster in the inky, starlit blackness of outer space. Your rocket climbs high into the universe before racing through a serpentine complex of aerial galaxies, making thrilling hairpin turns and rapid plunges. (Though it feels as if you're going at breakneck speed, your car actually never goes faster than 28 miles per hour.) Nab the front seat of the train for the best ride. Now that Alien Encounters has come on line, the queues to Space Mountain, which accommodates 3,000 people an hour, are usually relatively short. *Note:* You must be 44 inches tall to ride.

Take Flight
Frommer's Rating: C
Recommended Ages: 6–adult
A breezy look through the story of flight. High-tech special effects and 70mm live-action film footage add dramatic 3-D-style verisimilitude. Guests travel from a futuristic airport up a hillside to witness a flying circus, parachutists, stunt flyers, wing walkers, crop dusters, and aerial acrobats. The action moves on to the ocean-hopping age of commercial flight, as passengers are transported to a Japanese tea garden, Mount Fuji, and Paris at sunset. Finally, your vehicle is pulled into a giant jet engine and sent into hypersonic flight through psychedelic tunnels of light for a journey to outer space at a simulated speed of 300 miles per hour.

The Timekeeper
Frommer's Rating: C+
Recommended Ages: 10–adult
This Jules Verne/H. G. Wells–inspired multimedia presentation combines Circle-Vision™ and IMAX footage with audio-animatronics. It's hosted by Timekeeper, a mad-scientist robot and his assistant, 9-EYE, a flying female camera-headed droid and

time machine test pilot. In an unpredictable jet-speed escapade, the audience hears Mozart as a young prodigy playing his music to French royalty, visits medieval battlefields in Scotland, watches Leonardo at work, and floats in a hot-air balloon above Moscow's Red Square. Can you pick out the famous voices of Jeremy Irons, Robin Williams, Michael Piccoli, and Rhea Perlman?

Tomorrowland Speedway
Frommer's Rating: A+ for kids, C for single adults
Recommended Ages: 6–16
This is a great thrill for kids (including teens still waiting to get their driver's licenses) who get to put the pedal to the metal, steer, and vroom down a speedway in an actual gas-powered sports car. Maximum speed on the 4-minute drive around the track is about 7 miles per hour, and kids have to be 52 inches tall to drive alone.

Tomorrowland Transit Authority
Frommer's Rating: C
Recommended Ages: all ages
A futuristic means of transportation, these small five-car trains have no engines. They work by electromagnets, emit no pollution, and use little power. Narrated by a computer guide named Horack I, TTA offers an overhead look at Tomorrowland, including a pretty good preview of Space Mountain. If you're in the Magic Kingdom for only 1 day, skip this.

Walt Disney's Carousel of Progress
Frommer's Rating: D
Recommended Ages: all ages
Sorry to all the fans of this ride, but this 22-minute show takes up too much time and space, for its limited "wow factor." A revolving theater features an audio-animatronic family in various tableaux demonstrating a century of development (beginning in 1900) in electric gadgetry and contraptions from Victrolas to virtual reality.

SHOPPING IN TOMORROWLAND

Kids love browsing over **Merchant of Venus's** space-themed *Alien Encounter* and *Star Wars* merchandise. Also here: **Mickey's Star Traders,** a large Disneyana shop.

PARADES, FIREWORKS & MORE

You'll get an **Entertainment Show Schedule** when you enter the park, which lists all kinds of special goings-on for the day. These include concerts (everything from steel drums to barbershop quartets), encounters with Disney characters, holiday events, and the three major happenings listed next.

　　During the fireworks and the parades, there are designated viewing spots roped off for those with disabilities and their parties. Consult your park map or a park employee at least an hour before the parade. Like all space along the parade route, the spaces for those with disabilities also fill up quickly.

Fireworks
Frommer's Rating: A+
Recommended Ages: all ages
It's the Fourth of July every night with Fantasy in the Sky Fireworks, probably the most explosive display you have ever seen. Pyrotechnics is a Disney art. Although the water-walking creatures in the Sea World closing show are certainly worth seeing, this is clearly the best way to end your day. It is preceded by Tinker Bell's magical flight from Cinderella's Castle, and takes place nightly in summer, on selected nights during Christmas and Easter vacation times, and during other special celebrations. Consult

Top 10 Orlando-Area Attractions for Grown-Ups

1. **Innoventions** Epcot, generally, is more geared to adults than the other Disney parks, but this display of future technologies is especially intriguing, providing a cogent preview of life in the 21st century.

2. **Sea World** With its lush landscaping and laid-back pace, Sea World is a nice change from the go-go world of the other attractions. Mixing education with entertainment and lots of hands-on animal interaction, this is one of Orlando's most adult attractions, although kids love it too.

3. **World Showcase Pavilions** Experience a 'round-the-world journey visiting 11 nations in microcosm—with authentically reproduced architectural highlights, restaurants, shops, and cultural performances.

4. **Universal Studios** Okay, I'm an adult, but sometimes this really is a great place to play. The thrill rides can't be beat, the shows are fast-paced and funny, and now even the Terminator is back.

5. **Islands of Adventure** Comic book fans and anyone who knows about *Green Eggs and Ham,* will love the Marvel comics and Dr. Seuss themed areas. Plus the thrill rides offer some serious scares.

6. **Cypress Gardens** Stroll 200 acres of gorgeous botanical gardens—roses, bougainvillea, crape myrtles, and magnolias—amid ponds, lagoons, waterfalls, Italian fountains, and manicured lawns.

7. **Kennedy Space Center** Acquaint yourself with the history, present state, and future of America's space program. The kids will like this, too.

8. **A Day in Winter Park** This charming town has a recently expanded museum filled with masterpieces by Louis Comfort Tiffany and other noted 19th-century artists, great upscale shopping, and fine restaurants. Stay overnight at the Langford and arrange a day of beauty at its multifacility spa. Stroll through the shops on Park Avenue and lunch at one of the sidewalk bistros.

9. **A Resort Vacation** Top-of-the-line accommodations, fine restaurants, magnificent grounds, golf, tennis, swimming, first-rate health clubs, and other elements of a plush resort vacation are available at the Hyatt Regency Grand Cypress, Marriott's Orlando World Center, the Peabody Orlando, and Disney's Grand Floridian.

10. **A Night on the Town** Visit an Orlando restaurant and enjoy a night on the town, a carriage ride through downtown Orlando, a few hours at a club, or at Church Street Station. This is the other Orlando, the one for grown-ups.

your *Entertainment Show Schedule* for details. Suggested viewing areas are Liberty Square, Frontierland, and Mickey's Toontown Fair. Many of the Disney hotels close to the park also offer excellent views.

✪ SpectroMagic

Frommer's Rating: A+

Recommended Ages: all ages

If you have time to see only one parade, see this one. Along a darkened parade route (the same one as for "Remember the Magic," described next), 72,000 watts of dazzling high-tech lighting effects (including holography) create a glowing array of pixies and peacocks, sea horses and winged horses, flower gardens and fountains. Roger Rabbit is the eccentric conductor of an orchestra producing a rainbow of musical notes that waft magically into the night air. There are dancing ostriches from Fantasia, whirling electric butterflies, flowers that evoke Tiffany glass, bejeweled coaches, luminescent ElectroMen atop spinning whirlyballs, and, of course, Mickey, surrounded by a sparkling confetti of light. Remember the suit in the *Electric Horseman?* Multiply that by 1,000 and you've got SpectroMagic. It's unlike anything you've ever seen. The music and choreography are on a par with the technology.

Once again, very early arrival is essential to get a seat on the curb. SpectroMagic takes place nightly in summer, on selected nights during Christmas and Easter vacation times, and during other special celebrations. Consult your *Entertainment Show Schedule* for details.

The 3 O'Clock Parade "Remember the Magic"
Frommer's Rating: A
Recommended Ages: all ages

You haven't really seen a parade until you've seen one at Walt Disney World. This spectacular daily event kicks off at 3pm year-round on Main Street and meanders through Liberty Square and Frontierland. The route is outlined in your *Entertainment Show Schedule.*

The only problem: Even in slow seasons, you have to snag a seat along the curb a good half hour before it begins—earlier during peak travel times. That's a long time to sit on a hard curb. You might want to consider bringing along an inflatable pillow. And remember, stay off the grass, or the Disney lawn police will shoo you away from what you thought was a prime viewing spot.

In addition to Mickey and all his Disney pals—everyone from Minnie to Winnie (the Pooh)—there are elaborate floats, stunning costumes, special effects, and a captivating cavalcade of dancers, singers, and other talented performers. Great music, too.

WHERE TO FIND CHARACTERS
Mickey's Toontown Fair was designed as a place where kids can meet and mingle with their favorite characters all day. This is a sure thing, and it doesn't hurt that it's air-conditioned. Mickey, Minnie, Goofy, and Donald Duck are stars in residence. In **Fantasyland** up to eight Disney characters, including Chip 'n' Dale, are available for autographs in a covered area across from Mr. Toad's Wild Ride. Ariel from *The Little Mermaid* can be found in Ariel's Grotto.

4 Epcot

In 1982, Walt Disney World opened its second major theme park, the world's fair–like Epcot (Experimental Prototype Community of Tomorrow). Its aims are described in a dedication plaque: "May Epcot entertain, inform and inspire. And, above all . . . instill a new sense of belief and pride in man's ability to shape a world that offers hope to people everywhere." Ever growing and changing, Epcot today occupies 260 acres so stunningly landscaped as to be worth visiting for botanical beauty alone—so stop and smell the roses. There are two major sections, Future World and World Showcase.

Epcot is huge, and walking around it can be exhausting (some people say its acronym stands for "Every Person Comes Out Tired"). Don't try to do it all in 1 day. And conserve your energy by taking launches across the lagoon from the edge of Future World to Germany or Morocco. There are also double-decker buses circling the World Showcase Promenade and making stops at Norway, Italy, France, and Canada.

Unlike the Magic Kingdom, Epcot's parking lot is right at the gate. Sections of the parking lot are named for Epcot themes (Harvest, Energy, etc.), and aisles are numbered.

Stop by the Guest Relations lobby to the left of Spaceship Earth to pick up an *Epcot Guidemap* and entertainment schedule, and, if you so desire (and haven't already done so by calling ☎ **407/WDW-DINE** [939-3463]), make reservations for lunch or dinner at WorldKey terminals just outside the lobby. (Many Epcot restaurants are described in chapter 6.) Then check out your show schedule and incorporate shows you want to see into your itinerary.

HOURS   Generally 9am to 9pm with extended hours—sometimes as late as midnight—during major holidays and the summer months.

TICKET PRICES $42 for adults, $34 for children, free for children under 4. See "Tickets," earlier in this chapter, for 4- and 5-day passes.

SERVICES & FACILITIES IN EPCOT

ATMs   These machines accept cards issued by banks using the Cirrus, Honor, and Plus systems and are located at the front of the park, in Germany, and on the bridge between World Showcase and Future World.

Baby Care   Epcot's Baby Care Center is located near the Odyssey Restaurant in Future World. It is furnished with rocking chairs, and disposable diapers, formula, baby food, and pacifiers are for sale. There are also changing tables in all women's rest rooms, as well as in some of the men's rest rooms. Disposable diapers are available at Guest Services.

Cameras & Film   Kodak's disposable Fun Saver cameras are available throughout the park. Video camcorders are available for rent from the Kodak Camera Center at the Entrance Plaza. You can also rent from the Lagoon's Edge World Traveler, at the end of the promenade between Future World and the World Showcase, and at Cameras and Film at Journey into Imagination. Cost for camcorder rental is $25, plus a $300 deposit.

First Aid   The First Aid Center, staffed by registered nurses, is located near the Odyssey Restaurant in Future World.

Lockers   Lockers can be found to the west of Spaceship Earth, outside the Entrance Plaza, and in the Bus Information Center by the bus parking lot. The cost is $3 a day, plus a $2 deposit.

Lost Children   Lost children in Epcot are usually taken to Earth Center or the Baby Care Center where lost children logbooks are kept. Children under 7 should wear name tags.

Package Pickup   Any large package you purchase can be sent by the shop clerk to Guest Relations in the Entrance Plaza. Allow 3 hours for delivery.

Pet Care   Day accommodations are offered at kennels just outside the Entrance Plaza at Epcot for $6. Proof of vaccination is required. There are also four other kennels in the WDW complex.

Strollers   These can be rented from special stands on the east side of the Entrance Plaza and at World Showcase's International Gateway. The cost is $6, including a $1 refundable deposit.

Wheelchair Rental   Rent wheelchairs inside the Entrance Plaza to your left, to the right of ticket booths at the Gift Shop, and at World Showcase's International Gateway. The cost for regular chairs is $6, including a $1 refundable deposit. Electric chairs cost $32 a day, including a $2 refundable deposit.

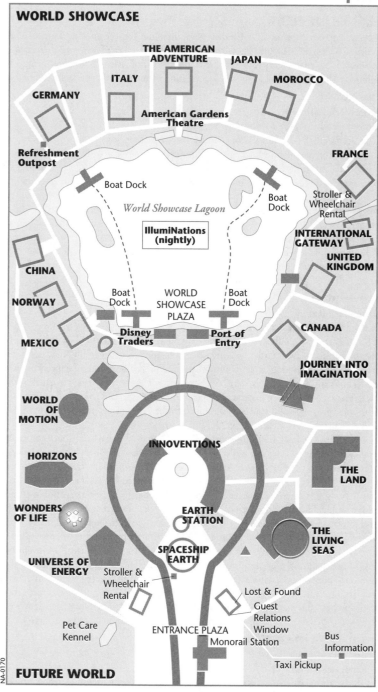

WORLD SHOWCASE

THE AMERICAN ADVENTURE

JAPAN

ITALY

MOROCCO

GERMANY

American Gardens Theatre

Refreshment Outpost

FRANCE

Boat Dock

World Showcase Lagoon

Boat Dock

IllumiNations (nightly)

Stroller & Wheelchair Rental

INTERNATIONAL GATEWAY

CHINA

Boat Dock

WORLD SHOWCASE PLAZA

Boat Dock

UNITED KINGDOM

NORWAY

Disney Traders

Port of Entry

CANADA

MEXICO

JOURNEY INTO IMAGINATION

WORLD OF MOTION

INNOVENTIONS

HORIZONS

THE LAND

WONDERS OF LIFE

EARTH STATION

THE LIVING SEAS

UNIVERSE OF ENERGY

Stroller & Wheelchair Rental

SPACESHIP EARTH

Lost & Found

Guest Relations Window

Pet Care Kennel

ENTRANCE PLAZA

Bus Information

Monorail Station

FUTURE WORLD

Taxi Pickup

NA-0170

FUTURE WORLD

The northern section of Epcot (where you enter the park) comprises Future World, centered on a giant geosphere known as Spaceship Earth. Future World's 10 themed areas, sponsored by major corporations, focus on discovery, scientific achievements, and tomorrow's technologies in areas running the gamut from energy to undersea exploration.

Horizons

Frommer's Rating: B+

Recommended Ages: 8–adult

The theme of this pavilion is the future, which presents an unending series of new horizons. You board gondolas for a 15-minute journey into the next millennium. The first tableau honors visionaries of past centuries (like Jules Verne) and looks at outdated visions of the future and classic sci-fi movies. You ascend to an area where an IMAX film projected on two 80-foot–high screens presents a kaleidoscope of brilliant micro and macro images—growing crystals, colonies in space, a space shuttle launching, DNA molecules, and a computer chip. You then travel to 21st-century cityscapes, desert farms, floating cities under the ocean's surface, and outer-space colonies populated by audio-animatronic denizens. For the return to 20th-century earth, you can select one of three futuristic transportation systems: a personal space-craft, a desert Hovercraft, or a minisubmarine.

Innoventions

Frommer's Rating: A

Recommended Ages: 8–adult

The pair of crescent-shaped buildings to your right and left just beyond Spaceship Earth house a constantly evolving 100,000-square–foot exhibit that showcases cutting-edge technologies and future products. Leading manufacturers sponsor ever-changing exhibit areas here. Visitors get a chance to preview virtual reality, electric cars, experience interactive television, and try out more than 200 new computer programs and games. Kids will be thrilled to preview new Sega video games. It is a chance to feel, hear, and see the future, hands-on.

The virtual-reality offerings—from swimming with the sharks at the Vivid Group pod or a walking tour of St. Peter's Basilica by ENEL—are the latest high-tech wonders and a chance to experience what you have been reading about in science magazines.

There are several show areas: You can be interviewed by Jay Leno on TV, or let Sky Cyberguy take you on a tour of the future of wireless communication. At the Honeywell's Home Automation at the House of Innoventions Tour, visit the computer-controlled abode of the future. The computer literate will find this a fascinating place to play. The technologically challenged will find it less rewarding.

The two-story **Discovery Center,** located on the right side of Innoventions, includes an information resource area where guests can get answers to all their questions about Epcot attractions, in particular, and Walt Disney World, in general. For instance, if after visiting The Land, you would like to learn more about hydroponics, they can print out an information sheet on it. The Discovery Center also houses a shop called Field Trips, featuring educational products and software.

Journey Into Imagination

Frommer's Rating: B

Recommended Ages: 6–adult

In this terrific pavilion, even the fountains are magical, with arching streams of water that leap into the air like glass rods.

Honey I Shrunk the Audience is a 3-D attraction based on the Disney hit *Honey I Shrunk the Kids* film. The audience, after being menaced by hundreds of mice and a

---

Behind the Scenes: Special Tours in Walt Disney World

In addition to the greenhouse tour in Epcot's Land pavilion, the Disney parks offer a number of walking tours and learning programs.

- **Family Magic Tour** explores the nooks and crannies of the Magic Kingdom in the form of a 2-hour scavenger hunt. You meet and greet characters at the end. Children 3–9, $15; adults, $25. You must also buy admission tickets to the park.

The following tours are for those 16 and older.

- The 2-hour **Hidden Treasures of World Showcase,** and the 5-hour Hidden Treasures of World Showcase, both explore the architectural and entertainment offerings of Epcot. The 5-hour tour on Wednesday only is $75 and includes lunch. Park admission is not required if you don't intend to stay in the park after the tour. The 2-hour tour is $35 per person, and park admission is required. Call ☎ **407/939-8687** for information.

- **Gardens of the World,** a 3-hour tour of the extraordinary landscaping at Epcot led by a Disney horticulturist ($45 per person; ☎ **407/939-8687** for information).

- The 4-hour **Keys to the Kingdom** provides an orientation to the Magic Kingdom and a glimpse into the high-tech operational systems behind the magic ($45 per person; ☎ **407/WDW-TOUR** [939-8687]).

There are also learning programs on subjects ranging from animation to international cultures. For details, call ☎ **407/363-6000.**

3-D cat, is shrunk and given a good shaking by a gigantic 5-year-old. Dramatic 3-D action is enhanced by vibrating seats and creepy tactile effects. Finally, everyone returns to proper size—everyone but the family dog, which creates the final, not altogether pleasant, special effect (I won't reveal it).

Visitors board slow-moving cars for a **Journey Into Imagination Ride.** The 14-minute excursion (recommended for ages 6 to adult), is hosted by a red-bearded adventurer named Dreamfinder and his sidekick, Figment—a mischievous baby dragon with a childlike ability to dream. After a simulated flight across the nighttime sky, you enter the "Imaginarium," where a dream-catching machine is vacuuming up "sparks of imagination, ideas, and natural elements" into a giant storage bag. You then ride past whimsical tableaux in which audio-animatronic characters explore the creative worlds of the fine arts, literature, the performing arts (complete with laser-light dancers), science (Dreamfinder's lab is filled with magical gadgetry), and image technology (a.k.a. movies). The ride culminates at Image Works.

At **Image Works** you can activate musical instruments by stepping on hexagons of colored light (remember Tom Hanks in *Big?*), participate in a TV drama, paint on a magic palette, draw patterns with laser beams, operate a giant kaleidoscope, wend your way through the Rainbow Corridor of a sensor maze, and conduct an electronic philharmonic orchestra.

The Land
Frommer's Rating: B
Recommended Ages: 8–adult

This largest of Future World's pavilions highlights humankind's relation to food and nature.

Living with the Land is a 13-minute boat ride through three ecological environments (a rain forest, an African desert, and the windswept American plains), each populated by appropriate audio-animatronic denizens. New farming methods and experiments—ranging from hydroponics to plants growing in simulated Martian soil!—are showcased in real gardens. If you'd like a more serious overview, take a 45-minute guided walking tour of the growing areas, offered daily. Sign up at the Green Thumb Emporium shop near the entrance to Food Rocks. The cost is $5 for adults, $3 for children 3 to 9, free for children 2 and under. It's not, by the way, really geared to children.

Circle of Life combines spectacular live-action footage with animation in a 15-minute, 70mm motion picture based on *The Lion King*. In this cautionary environmental tale, Timon and Pumbaa are building a monument to the good life called Hakuna Matata Lakeside Village, but their project, as Simba points out, is damaging the savannah for other animals. The message: Everything is connected in the great circle of life. Recommended age group: 6 to 16.

In **Food Rocks,** audio-animatronic mock rock performers deliver an entertaining message about nutrition. Neil Moussaka sings "Don't Take My Squash Away from Me," the Refrigerator Police perform "Every Bite You Take," and the Peach Boys harmonize a rendition of "Good Vibrations" ("Good, good, good, good nutrition . . ."), while Excess, a trio of disheveled, obnoxious hard rockers, counters by extolling the virtues of junk food. Rapper Tone Loc (as Füd Wrapper, the show's host), Chubby Checker, Neil Sedaka, Little Richard, and the Pointer Sisters perform the actual voice-over parodies of their music. Recommended age group: 6 to 14.

The Living Seas
Frommer's Rating: B
Recommended Ages: 12–adult
This United Technologies–sponsored pavilion contains the world's sixth "ocean," a 5.7-million-gallon saltwater aquarium (including a complete coral reef) inhabited by more than 4,000 sea creatures—sharks, barracudas, parrot fish, rays, and dolphins among them. While waiting in line, visitors pass exhibits tracing the history of undersea exploration, including a glass diving barrel used by Alexander the Great in 332 B.C. and Sir Edmund Halley's first diving bell (1697).

A 2½-minute multimedia preshow about today's ocean technology is followed by a 7-minute film demonstrating the formation of the earth and seas as a means to support life.

After the films, visitors enter hydrolators for a rapid descent to the sunlit ocean floor. Upon arrival, they board Seacabs that wind around a 400-foot-long tunnel to enjoy stunning close-up views (through acrylic windows) of ocean denizens in a natural coral-reef habitat. The ride concludes in the Seabase Concourse, which is the visitor center of Seabase Alpha, a prototype ocean-research facility of the future. Here exhibits include a 22½-foot scuba tube used by Seabase Alpha scientists to enter and leave the waters. And seven informational modules contain numerous exhibits focusing on ocean ecosystems, harvestable resources grown in controlled undersea environments, marine mammals (dolphins, sea lions, manatees), earth systems (the relationship between the planet's seas and its land masses), the study of ocean-ography from space, undersea exploration (featuring an audio-animatronic deep-sea submersible robot), and life in a coral-reef community. Many of these exhibits are hands-on. You can step into a diver's JIM Suit and use controls to complete diving tasks and expand your knowledge of oceanography via interactive computers. *Note:* Via a program called Epcot DiveQuest, certified divers can participate in a program that includes a 30- to 40-minute scuba dive in the Living Seas aquarium; for details, call ☎ 407/WDW-TOUR (937-8687).

Spaceship Earth

Frommer's Rating: B

Recommended Ages: all ages

This massive, silvery geosphere symbolizes Epcot, so it is a must-do. But long lines can be avoided by saving it until later in the day when you can, more than likely, simply walk on in. The show/ride takes visitors on a 15-minute journey through the history of communications. You board time-machine vehicles to the distant past, where an audio-animatronic Cro-Magnon shaman recounts the story of a hunt while others record it on cave walls. You advance thousands of years to ancient Egypt, where hiero-glyphics adorn temple walls and writing is recorded on papyrus scrolls. You'll progress through the Phoenician and Greek alphabets, and the Gutenberg printing press and the Renaissance (trying not to notice that several of these guys look an awful lot like Barbie's dream date Ken). Technologies develop at a rapid pace, through the telegraph, telephone, radio, movies, and TV. It's but a short step to the age of electronic communications. You are catapulted into outer space to see "spaceship earth" from a new perspective, returning for a finale that places the audience amid interactive global networks. High-tech special effects, animated sets, and laser beams create an exciting experience.

At the end of this journey through time, AT&T invites guests to sample an interactive computer-video wonderland that includes a motion-simulator ride through the company's electronic network. This exhibit complements Innoventions, detailed earlier.

Test Track

Frommer's Rating: A

Recommended Ages: 8–adult

Called a mix of General Motors engineering and Disney imagineering, the newest Epcot attraction has guests in the driver's seat to experience the rigors of automobile testing. During a preshow—essentially a GM commercial—guests will learn how the company works to promote automotive safety, reliability, and performance. Then they'll board full-scale, six-passenger test cars and travel upon what appears to be an actual roadway, accelerating on long straightaways, hugging hairpin turns, climbing steep hills, and braking abruptly—often on less-than-perfect road conditions. The ride will culminate with a terrifying high-speed outdoor run along the track's steeply banked "speed loop," which extends far beyond the pavilion facility. Cars will go at a top speed of 65 miles per hour. This was formerly World of Motion.

Universe of Energy

Frommer's Rating: B

Recommended Ages: 8–adult

Sponsored by Exxon, this pavilion—its roof glistening with solar panels—aims to better our understanding of America's energy problems and potential solutions via a 32-minute ride-through attraction. Recently refurbished, it's called **Ellen's Energy Adventure** and features comedian and television sitcom star Ellen DeGeneres as an energy expert tutored by Bill Nye the Science Guy to be a *"Jeopardy"* contestant. On a massive screen in Theater I, an animated motion picture depicts the earth's molten beginnings, its cooling process, and the formation of fossil fuels. You move from Theater I to travel back 275 million years into an eerie, storm-wracked landscape of the Mesozoic era, a time of violent geological activity. Here, you're menaced by giant audio-animatronic dragonflies, pterodactyls, dinosaurs, earthquakes, and streams of molten lava before entering a steam-filled tunnel deep through the bowels of the volcano, finally emerging back in the 20th century in Theatre II. In this new setting, which looks like a NASA Mission Control room, a 70mm film projected on a massive 210-foot wraparound screen depicts the challenges of the world's increasing energy demands and the emerging technologies that will help meet them. Your moving seats now return to Theatre I, where swirling special effects herald a film about how energy

---

Find the Hidden Mickeys

Hiding Mickeys in designs began as an inside joke with early Walt Disney World "Imagineers" and became a park tradition. Today, dozens of subtle hidden Mickeys—the world-famous set of ears, profiles, and full figures—are concealed in attractions and resorts throughout Walt Disney World. No one even knows their exact number. See how many *HMs* (Hidden Mickeys) you can locate during your visit. A few to look for include the following:

In the Magic Kingdom
In the Haunted Mansion banquet scene, check out the arrangement of plate and adjoining saucers on the table.

In the Africa scene of It's a Small World, note the purple flowers on a vine on the elephant's left side.

While riding Splash Mountain, look for Mickey lying on his back in the pink clouds to the right of the steamboat.

Hint: There are four HMs in The Timekeeper and five in the Carousel of Progress.

At Epcot
In Journey into Imagination, check out the little girl's dress in the lobby film of *Honey I Shrunk the Audience,* one of five HMs in this pavilion.

In The Land pavilion, don't miss the small stones in front of the Native American man on a horse and the baseball cap of the man driving a harvester in the *Circle of Life* film.

As your boat cruises through the Mexico pavilion on the El Rio del Tiempo attraction, notice the arrangement of three clay pots in the marketplace scene.
In Maelstrom, in the Norway pavilion, a Viking wears Mickey ears in the wall mural facing the loading dock.

There are four HMs in Spaceship Earth, one of them in the Renaissance scene, on the page of a book behind the sleeping monk. Try to find the other three.

At Disney–MGM Studios
On the Great Movie Ride, there's an HM on the window above the bank in the gangster scene, and four familiar characters are included in the hieroglyphics wall opposite Indiana Jones.

At Jim Henson's Muppet*Vision 4D, take a good look at the TOP FIVE REASONS FOR TURNING IN YOUR 4-D GLASSES sign, and note the balloons in the film's final scene.

In the Twilight Zone Tower of Terror, note the bell for the elevator behind Rod Serling in the film. There are five other HMs in this attraction.

There are also HMs at many Disney resorts. The best place to look for them is at Wilderness Lodge, which has over a dozen that I know about.

impacts our lives. It ends on a dramatically upbeat note—with a vision of an energy-abundant future and Ellen as a new "Jeopardy" champion.

Wonders of Life
Frommer's Rating: B
Recommended Ages: 8–adult
Housed in a vast geodesic dome fronted by a 75-foot replica of a DNA molecule, this pavilion offers some of Future World's most engaging shows and attractions.

The **Making of Me,** starring Martin Short, is a captivating 15-minute motion picture combining live action with animation and spectacular inutero photography to create the sweetest introduction imaginable to the facts of life. Don't miss it, although the presentation may prompt some questions from young children (recommended for ages 10 and up). Short travels back in time to witness his parents as children, their meeting at a college dance, their wedding, and their decision to have a baby. Along with him, we view his development inside his mother's womb and witness his birth.

You're miniaturized to the size of a single cell for a medical rescue mission inside the immune system of a human body during **Body Wars**. Your objective: to save a miniaturized immunologist who has been accidentally swept into the bloodstream. This motion-simulator ride takes you on a wild journey through gale-force winds (in the lungs) and pounding heart chambers (recommended for ages 6 and up). Although you know they are part of the Disney show, if you've ever seen the movie *Outbreak*, it is a little eerie passing through dermatopic purification stations in order to undergo miniaturization. Leonard Nimoy directed.

In the hilarious, multimedia **Cranium Command**, Buzzy, an audio-animatronic brain-pilot-in-training, is charged with the seemingly impossible task of controlling the brain of a typical 12-year-old boy. The boy's body parts are played by Charles Grodin, Jon Lovitz, Bob Goldthwait, Kevin Nealon and Dana Carvey (as Hans and Franz), and George Wendt. It's another must-see attraction (recommended for ages 8 and up). The audience is seated inside Bobby's head as Buzzy guides him through a day of typical preadolescent traumas—running for the school bus, meeting a girl, fighting bullies, and a run-in with the school principal.

There are large areas filled with fitness-related shows, exhibits, and participatory activities, including a film called **Goofy About Health,** and **Coach's Corner,** where your tennis, golf, or baseball swing is analyzed by experts, and the **Sensory Funhouse** where you can test your perceptions. Grown-ups and kids will enjoy playing here, in air-conditioned comfort. Try working out on a video-enhanced exercise bike, get a computer-generated evaluation of your health habits, and take a video voyage to investigate the effects of drugs on your heart. There's much, much more. You could easily spend hours here.

WORLD SHOWCASE
Surrounding a 40-acre lagoon at the park's southern end is World Showcase—a permanent community of 11 miniaturized nations, all with authentically indigenous landmark architecture, landscaping, background music, restaurants, and shops. The cultural facets of each nation are explored in art exhibits, dance performances, and innovative rides, films, and attractions. And all of the employees in each pavilion are natives of the country represented.

The American Adventure
Frommer's Rating: B+
Recommended Ages: 10–adult
Housed in a vast, Georgian-style structure, **The American Adventure** is a 29-minute dramatization of U.S. history, utilizing a 72-foot rear-projection screen, rousing music, and a large cast of lifelike audio-animatronic figures, including narrators

In the Words of Walt Disney

In my view, wholesome pleasure, sport, and recreation are as vital to this nation as productive work and should have a large share in the national budget.

Mark Twain and Ben Franklin. The "adventure" begins with the voyage of the *Mayflower* and encompasses major historic events. You view Jefferson writing the Declaration of Independence, the expansion of the frontier, Mathew Brady photographing a family about to be divided by the Civil War, the stock market crash of 1929, Pearl Harbor, and the *Eagle* heading toward the moon. John Muir and Teddy Roosevelt discuss the need for national parks. Susan B. Anthony speaks out on women's rights; Frederick Douglass, on slavery; Chief Joseph, on the situation of Native Americans. While waiting for the show to begin, you'll be entertained by the wonderful Voices of Liberty Singers performing American folk songs in the Main Hall. Note the quotes from famous Americans on the walls here.

Formal gardens shaded by live oaks, sycamores, elms, and holly complement the pavilion's 18th-century architecture. A shop called Heritage Manor Gifts sells signed presidential photographs, needlepoint samplers, afghans and quilts, pottery, candles, Davy Crockett hats, books on American history, historically costumed dolls, classic political campaign buttons, and vintage newspapers with banner headlines like "Nixon Resigns!" An artisan at the shop makes jewelry out of coins.

Note: International cultural performances take place here in the **America Gardens Theater.**

Canada

Frommer's Rating: A
Recommended Ages: 8–adult
Our neighbors to the north are represented by diverse architecture ranging from a mansard-roofed replica of Ottawa's 19th-century French-style Château Laurier (here called the Hôtel du Canada) to a British-influenced rustic stone building modeled after a famous landmark near Niagara Falls.

An Indian village—complete with rough-hewn log trading post and 30-foot replicas of Ojibwa totem poles—signifies the culture of the Northwest, while the Canadian wilderness is reflected by a steep mountain (a Canadian Rocky), a waterfall cascading into a whitewater stream, and a "forest" of evergreens, stately cedars, maples, and birch trees. Don't miss the stunning floral displays of azaleas, roses, zinnias, chrysanthemums, petunias, and patches of wildflowers inspired by the Butchart Gardens in Victoria, British Columbia.

The pavilion's highlight attraction is **O Canada!**—a dazzling, 18-minute, 360° Circle-Vision™ film that reveals Canada's scenic splendor from sophisticated Montréal to the thundering flight of thousands of snow geese departing an autumn stopover near the St. Lawrence River.

Canada pavilion shops carry sandstone and soapstone carvings, fringed leather vests, duck decoys, moccasins, a vast array of Eskimo stuffed animals and Native American dolls, Native American spirit stones, rabbit-skin caps, heavy knitted sweaters, and, of course, maple syrup.

China

Frommer's Rating: B
Recommended Ages: 10–adult
Bounded by a serpentine wall that snakes around its perimeter, the China pavilion is entered via a vast, triple-arched ceremonial gate inspired by the Temple of Heaven in

Beijing, a summer retreat for Chinese emperors. Passing through the gate, you'll see a half-size replica of this ornately embellished red-and-gold circular temple, built in 1420 during the Ming dynasty. Gardens simulate those in Suzhou, with miniature waterfalls, fragrant lotus ponds, groves of bamboo, corkscrew willows, and weeping mulberry trees.

The highlight here is **Wonders of China,** a 20-minute, 360° Circle-Vision™ film that explores 6,000 years of dynastic and communist rule and the breathtaking diversity of the Chinese landscape. Narrated by 8th-century Tang dynasty poet Li Bai, it includes scenes of the Great Wall (begun 24 centuries ago!), a performance by the Beijing Opera, the Forbidden City in Beijing, rice terraces of Hunan Province, the Gobi Desert, and tropical rain forests of Hainan Island. Adjacent to the theater, an art gallery houses changing exhibits of Chinese art.

A bustling marketplace—the **Yong Feng Shangdian Shopping Gallery**—offers an array of merchandise including silk robes, lacquer and inlaid mother-of-pearl furniture, jade figures, cloisonné vases, tea sets, silk rugs and embroideries, dolls, fans, wind chimes, and Chinese clothing. Artisans here demonstrate calligraphy.

France
Frommer's Rating: C
Recommended Ages: 8–adult

Focusing on La Belle Epoque—a period from 1870 to 1910 in which French art, literature, and architecture flourished—this pavilion is entered via a replica of the beautiful cast-iron Pont des Arts footbridge over the "Seine." It leads to a park with bleached sycamores, Bradford pear trees, flowering crape myrtle, and sculptured parterre flower gardens inspired by Seurat's painting *A Sunday Afternoon on the Island of La Grande Jatte.* A one-tenth replica of the Eiffel Tower constructed from Gustave Eiffel's original blueprints looms above *les grands boulevards,* and period buildings feature copper mansard roofs and casement windows.

The highlight is **Impressions de France.** Shown in a palatial (mercifully sit-down) theater à la Fontainebleau, this 18-minute film is a breathtakingly scenic journey through diverse French landscapes projected on a vast, 200°-view wraparound screen and enhanced by music of French composers.

Emporia in the covered shopping arcade, with art-nouveau Métro facades at either end, have interiors ranging from a turn-of-the-century bibliothèque to a French château. Merchandise includes French art prints and original art, cookbooks, cookware, wines (there's a tasting counter), fancy French foodstuffs, Madeline and Babar books and dolls, perfumes, and original letters of famous Frenchmen ranging from Jean Cocteau to Napoleon. Another marketplace/tourism center revives the defunct Les Halles, where Parisians used to sip onion soup in the wee hours. The heavenly aroma of a *boulangerie* (bakery) penetrates the atmosphere, and mimes, jugglers, and strolling *chanteurs* (singers) entertain.

Germany
Frommer's Rating: B
Recommended Ages: 8–adult

Enclosed by castle walls and towers, this festive pavilion is centered on a cobblestoned *Platz* (square) with pots of colorful flowers girding a fountain statue of St. George and the Dragon. An adjacent clock tower is embellished with whimsical glockenspiel figures that herald each hour with quaint melodies. The pavilion's outdoor **Biergarten**—where it's Oktoberfest all year long—was inspired by medieval Rothenberg. And 16th-century building facades replicate a merchant's hall in the Black Forest and the town hall in Frankfurt's Römerberg Square.

Shops here carry Hummel figurines, crystal, glassware, cookware, cuckoo clocks, cowbells, Alpine hats, German wines (there's a tasting counter) and specialty foods, toys (German Disneyana, teddy bears, dolls, and puppets), and books. An artisan demonstrates molding and painting Hummel figures; another paints detailed scenes on eggs. Background music runs from oom-pah bands to Mozart symphonies.

Italy
Frommer's Rating: C+
Recommended Ages: 10–adult
One of the prettiest World Showcase pavilions, Italy lures visitors over an arched stone footbridge to a replica of Venice's intricately ornamented pink-and-white Doge's Palace. Other architectural highlights include the 83-foot Campanile (bell tower) of St. Mark's Square, Venetian bridges, and a central piazza enclosing a version of Bernini's Neptune Fountain. A garden wall suggests a backdrop of provincial countryside, and Mediterranean citrus, olive trees, cypress, and pine frame a formal garden. Gondolas are moored on the lagoon.

Shops here carry cameo and filigree jewelry, Armani figurines, kitchenware, Italian wines and foods, Murano and other Venetian glass, alabaster figurines, and inlaid wooden music boxes. A troupe of street actors performs a contemporary version of 16th-century *commedia dell'arte* in the piazza.

Japan
Frommer's Rating: A
Recommended Ages: 8–adult
Heralded by a flaming red *torii* (gate of honor) on the banks of the lagoon and the graceful, blue-roofed Goju No To pagoda (inspired by a shrine built at Nara in A.D. 700), this pavilion focuses on Japan's ancient culture. In a traditional Japanese garden, cedars, yew trees, bamboo, "cloud-pruned" evergreens, willows, and flowering shrubs frame a contemplative setting of pebbled footpaths, rustic bridges, waterfalls, exquisite rock landscaping, and a pond of golden koi. The Yakitori House is based on the renowned 16th-century Katsura Imperial Villa in Kyoto, designed as a royal summer residence and considered by many to be the crowning achievement of Japanese architecture. Exhibits ranging from 18th-century Bunraki puppets to samurai armor take place in the moated **White Heron Castle,** a replica of the Shirasagi-Jo, a 17th-century fortress overlooking the city of Himeji.

And the **Mitsukoshi Department Store** (Japan's answer to Macy's) is housed in a replica of the Shishinden (Hall of Ceremonies) of the Gosho Imperial Palace, built in Kyoto in A.D. 794. It sells lacquerware, kimonos, kites, fans, dolls in traditional costumes, origami books, samurai swords, Japanese Disneyana, bonsai trees, Japanese foods, Netsuke carvings, and pottery—even modern electronics. In the courtyard, artisans demonstrate the ancient arts of *anesaiku* (shaping brown rice candy into dragons, unicorns, and dolphins), *sumi-e* (calligraphy), and *origami* (paper folding).

Be sure to include a show of traditional Japanese music and dance at this pavilion in your schedule. It's one of the best in the World Showcase.

Mexico
Frommer's Rating: A
Recommended Ages: 8–adult
You'll hear the music of marimbas and mariachi bands as you approach the festive showcase of Mexico, fronted by a towering Mayan pyramid modeled on the Aztec temple of Quetzalcoatl (God of Life) and surrounded by dense Yucatán jungle landscaping. Upon entering the pavilion, you'll find yourself in a museum of pre-Colombian art and artifacts.

Down a ramp is a small lagoon, the setting for **El Rio del Tiempo** (River of Time), where visitors board boats for an 8-minute cruise through Mexico's past and present. Passengers get a close-up look at the Mayan pyramid and the erupting Popocatepetl volcano. Dance performances focusing on the cultures of Mayan, Toltec, Aztec, and colonial Mexico are presented in film segments and by an audio-animatronic cast in vignettes ranging from a Day of the Dead skeleton band to children breaking a piñata. Additional film footage focuses on Mexican tourist spots. The show culminates in a Mexico City fiesta with exploding fiber-optic fireworks.

Shops in and around the **Plaza de Los Amigos** (a "moonlit" Mexican *mercado* with a tiered fountain and street lamps) display an array of leather goods, baskets, sombreros, piñatas, pottery, embroidered dresses and blouses, maracas, jewelry, serapes, paper flowers, colorful papier-màché birds, and blown-glass objects (an artisan gives demonstrations). La Casa de, sponsored by the Mexican Tourist Office, provides travel information.

Morocco

Frommer's Rating: B+
Recommended Ages: 10–adult

This exotic pavilion—its architecture embellished with intricate geometrically patterned tile work, minarets, hand-painted wood ceilings, and brass lighting fixtures—is heralded by a replica of the Koutoubia Minaret, the prayer tower of a 12th-century mosque in Marrakesh.

The **Medina** (old city), entered via a replica of an arched gateway in Fez, leads to Fez House (a traditional Moroccan home) and the narrow, winding streets of the *souk,* a bustling marketplace where all manner of authentic handcrafted merchandise is on display. Here you can peruse or purchase pottery, brassware, hand-knotted Berber carpets, colorful Rabat carpets, ornate silver and camel-bone boxes, straw baskets, and prayer rugs. There are weaving demonstrations in the souk throughout the day. The Medina's rectangular courtyard centers on a replica of the ornately tiled Najjarine Fountain in Fez, the setting for musical entertainment.

The pavilion's **Royal Gallery** contains an ever-changing exhibit of Moroccan art, and the Center of Tourism offers a continuous three-screen slide show. Morocco's landscaping includes a formal garden, citrus and olive trees, date palms, and banana plants.

Norway

Frommer's Rating: B
Recommended Ages: 10–adult

Centered on a picturesque cobblestone courtyard, this pavilion evokes ancient Norway. A *stavekirke* (stave church), styled after the 13th-century Gol Church of Hallingdal, its eaves embellished with wooden dragon heads, houses changing exhibits. A replica of Oslo's 14th-century **Akershus Castle,** next to a cascading woodland waterfall, is the setting for the pavilion's featured restaurant. Other buildings simulate the red-roofed cottages of Bergen and the timber-sided farm buildings of the Nordic woodlands.

There's a two-part attraction here. **Maelstrom,** a boat ride in a dragon-headed Viking vessel, traverses Norway's fjords and mythical forests to the music of Peer Gynt—an exciting journey during which you'll be menaced by polar bears prowling the shore and trolls who cast a spell on the boat. The watercraft crashes through a narrow gorge and spins into the North Sea, where a violent storm is in progress. But the storm abates, and passengers disembark safely in a 10th-century Viking village to view the 70mm film *Norway,* which documents a thousand years of history. Featured images include *Oseberg bat* (a 1,000-year-old Viking ship), a small fishing village, festive national-holiday celebrations in Oslo, and soaring jumps at the Holmenkollen ski resort.

Shops feature hand-knit wool hats and sweaters, toys (there's a Lego table where kids can play while you shop), wood carvings, Scandinavian foods, pewterware, and jewelry.

United Kingdom

Frommer's Rating: C+
Recommended Ages: 10–adult
Centered on **Britannia Square**—a formal London-style park, complete with copper-roofed gazebo bandstand and a statue of the Bard—the U.K. pavilion evokes Merry Olde England. Four centuries of architecture are represented along quaint cobblestoned streets; troubadours and minstrels entertain in front of a traditional British pub; and a formal garden with low box hedges in geometric patterns, flagstone paths, and a stone fountain replicates the landscaping of 16th- and 17th-century palaces.

High Street and Tudor Lane shops display a broad sampling of British merchandise— toy soldiers, Paddington bears, personalized coats of arms, tobaccos and pipes, Scottish clothing (cashmere and Shetland sweaters, golf wear, tams, knits, and tartans), fine English china, Waterford crystal, and pub items (tankards, dartboards, and the like). A tea shop occupies a replica of Anne Hathaway's thatch-roofed 16th-century cottage in Stratford-upon-Avon. Other emporia represent the Georgian, Victorian, Queen Anne, and Tudor periods. Background music ranges from "Greensleeves" to the Beatles.

IllumiNations

Frommer's Rating: A
Recommended Ages: 3–adult
IllumiNations, a 16½-minute spectacular using high-tech lighting effects, darting laser beams, fireworks, strobes, and rainbow-lit dancing fountains, takes place nightly. A backdrop of classical music by international composers (representing World Showcase nations) enhances the drama. Each nation is highlighted in turn. Colorful kites fly over Japan, the giant Rockies loom over Canada, a gingerbread house rises in Germany, and so on. Find a seat around the lagoon about a half hour before show time.

OTHER SHOWS

Live shows, especially those in World Showcase, make up an important part of the Epcot experience. Among others, these might include Chinese lion dancers and acro-bats, German oom-pah bands, Caledonian bagpipers, Mexican mariachi bands, Moroccan storytellers and belly dancers, Italian "living statues" and stilt walkers, colonial fife and drum groups, and much more. Two especially good shows are the Voices of Liberty singers at the American Adventure pavilion and the traditional music and dance displays in Japan. Check your show schedule when you come in and plan your day to include some of them.

SHOPPING AT EPCOT

The most fascinating shops are found in World Showcase pavilions, which comprise an international bazaar selling everything from Berber rugs to Japanese kimonos. Noshing and shopping is the only reason to walk around the World Showcase. You'll find descriptions of merchandise available in these pavilions in the World Showcase listings, described earlier.

5 Disney–MGM Studios

Disney–MGM Studios offers exciting movie- and TV-themed shows and behind-the-scenes "reel-life" adventures. You see the eerie Tower of Terror and the Earrfel Tower, a water tower with mouse ears, off in the distance. Once inside, its main streets include Hollywood Boulevard and Sunset Boulevard, with art deco movie sets evoking Hollywood's glamorous golden age. There's also a New York Street lined with Gotham landmarks (the Empire State, Flatiron, and Chrysler buildings) and typical New York characters including peddlers hawking knock-off watches. This is some of the best street performing you'll find in any of the Disney parks. More important, this is a working movie-and-TV studio, where shows are in production even as you tour the premises.

Arrive at the park early, tickets in hand. Unlike the Magic Kingdom and Epcot, MGM's 110 acres of attractions can pretty much be seen in 1 day. The parking lot is right at the gate, although trams do run. Pay attention to your parking location, which is not as distinctly marked as in the Magic Kingdom.

If you don't get a *Disney–MGM Studios Guidemap* and entertainment schedule when you enter the park, you can pick it up at Guest Services (MGM's information center). First thing to do is check show times and work out an entertainment schedule based on highlight attractions and geographical proximity. My favorite MGM restaurants are described in chapter 6.

ESSENTIALS
HOURS   Generally 9am to 7pm with extended hours—sometimes as late as midnight—during major holidays and the summer months.

TICKET PRICES   A 1-day park ticket is $42 for adults, $34 for children, free for children under 4.

SERVICES & FACILITIES IN DISNEY–MGM STUDIOS

ATMs   ATM machines accepting cards from banks using the Cirrus, Honor, and Plus systems are located at the main entrance.

Baby Care   MGM has a small Baby Care Center where you'll find facilities for nursing and changing. Disposable diapers, formula, baby food, and pacifiers are for sale. Changing tables are also in all women's rest rooms and some men's rest rooms. Disposable diapers are also available at the Guest Services building.

Cameras & Film   Kodak's disposable Fun Saver cameras are available throughout the park. Video camcorders are available for rent at Hollywood Boulevard for $30 a day, plus a $450 deposit.

First Aid   The First Aid Center, staffed by registered nurses, is in the Entrance Plaza adjoining Guest Services.

Lockers   Lockers are alongside Oscar's Classic Car Souvenirs, to the right of the Entrance Plaza after you pass through the turnstiles. The cost is $3 to $5 a day, depending on the size.

Lost Children   Lost children at Disney–MGM Studios are taken to Guest Services where lost children logbooks are kept. Children under 7 should wear name tags.

Package Pickup   Any large package you purchase can be sent by the shop clerk to Guest Services in the Entrance Plaza. Allow 3 hours for delivery.

Pet Care   Day accommodations are offered at kennels just outside the entrance for $6 a day. There are also four other kennels in the WDW complex.

Strollers   Strollers can be rented at Oscar's Super Service, inside the main entrance, for $6.

Wheelchair Rental   Wheelchairs are rented at Oscar's Super Service inside the main entrance. The cost for regular chairs is $6 a day. Electric chairs rent for $35.

MAJOR ATTRACTIONS & SHOWS

ABC Sound

Frommer's Rating: B
Recommended Ages: all ages

Scream. Wave your hands. Making a little noise is likely to help get you from the audience onto the stage where you will then take part in creating the sound effects for a short film starring Chevy Chase and Martin Short. The rumble includes thunder, rain, and creaking doors, but the real stars are the tourists trying to make it all happen like the professionals. Volunteer. You're on vacation. You'll probably never see these people again. If you can't muster the gumption to go on stage, the postshow, Soundworks, provides the opportunity of a little joyful noise on interactive computers and away from the maddening crowd.

Four "Foley artists" (Foley is the Hollywood sound-effects system named for its creator, Jack Foley) are chosen from the audience to create sound effects for the 2-minute comic Gothic thriller starring Chevy Chase and Martin Short. You see the film three times, first with professional sound, then without sound as volunteers frantically try to create an appropriate track, and finally with the sound effects they've provided. The show features some of the 20,000-plus ingenious gadgets created by sound master Jimmy Macdonald during his 45 years with Disney Studios. In a postshow area called **Soundworks,** guests can attempt to reproduce flying-saucer sounds from the film *Forbidden Planet,* dub the voice of Roger Rabbit, and create the gallop of the Headless Horseman in *Legend of Sleepy Hollow.*

The American Film Institute Showcase

Frommer's Rating: C
Recommended Ages: 10–adult

This exhibit brings into focus the efforts of all those folks—editors, cinematographers, producers, and directors—whose names blur by as the credits roll. Created in 1996 in partnership with the Los Angeles–based American Film Institute, this walk-through tour also highlights some of the organization's winners of the Lifetime Achievement Award. They include Bette Davis, Jack Nicholson, and Elizabeth Taylor.

Backstage Pass to 101 Dalmatians

Frommer's Rating: B
Recommended Ages: all ages

Have a De Vil of a good time spotting Cruella and the other stars of Disney's live-action remake of the animated classic. The stark, eerie sets from Cruella's movie are among the top attractions during this short tour. Wizzer, the most fluid of the canine actors, is featured in a film about the life of a four-pawed star. Taking a cue from Universal, where you Ride the Movies, the special-effects show allows one lucky—usually tall and male—spectator to ride in the movies by re-creating Jeff Daniels' runaway-bike scene. Real Dalmatians are also on display. But don't call PETA yet. The pups pull only 2-hour shifts and are treated better, one employee grumbled, than most two-legged "cast members."

Disney-MGM Studios Theme Park

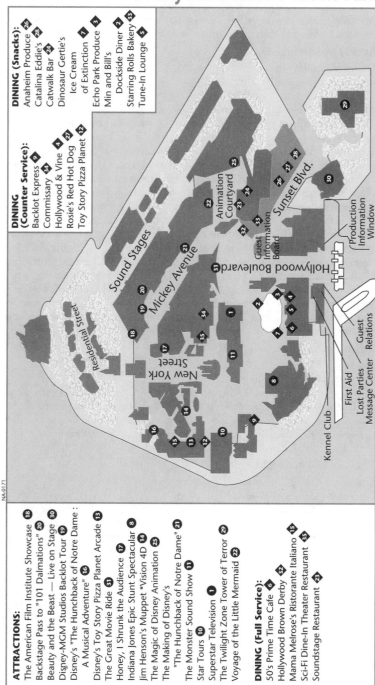

DINING (Snacks):
Anaheim Produce 26
Catalina Eddie's 28
Catwalk Bar 24
Dinosaur Gertie's
  Ice Cream
  of Extinction 7
Echo Park Produce 3
Min and Bill's
Dockside Diner 2
Starring Rolls Bakery 33
Tune-In Lounge 5

DINING (Counter Service):
Backlot Express 9
Commissary 34
Hollywood & Vine 4
Rosie's Red Hot Dog 27
Toy Story Pizza Planet 12

ATTRACTIONS:
The American Film Institute Showcase 18
Backstage Pass to "101 Dalmations" 20
Beauty and the Beast — Live on Stage 30
Disney-MGM Studios Backlot Tour 19
Disney's "The Hunchback of Notre Dame :
  A Musical Adventure" 16
Disney's Toy Story Pizza Planet Arcade 13
The Great Movie Ride 31
Honey, I Shrunk the Audience 17
Indiana Jones Epic Stunt Spectacular 8
Jim Henson's Muppet *Vision 4D 14
The Magic of Disney Animation 25
The Making of Disney's
  "The Hunchback of Notre Dame" 21
The Monster Sound Show 11
Star Tours 10
Superstar Television 1
The Twilight Zone Tower of Terror 29
Voyage of the Little Mermaid 22

DINING (Full Service):
50's Prime Time Cafe 6
Hollywood Brown Derby 32
Mama Melrose's Ristorante Italiano 15
Sci-Fi Dine-In Theater Restaurant 35
Soundstage Restaurant 23

NA-0171

169

Note: The nearby "Making of" exhibits are tied to the latest Disney movie release. At press time it featured *Flubber,* but that is likely to change by the time of your visit.

Backstage Studio Tour

Frommer's Rating: B

Recommended Ages: 10–adult

This 25-minute tram tour takes you behind the scenes for a close-up look at the vehicles, props, costumes, sets, and special effects used in your favorite movies and TV shows. You'll see costumers at work in the wardrobe department (Disney has the world's largest costume collection—more than 2 million garments), house facades of "The Golden Girls" and "Empty Nest" on Residential Street, and carpenters building sets. Most of the props are from short-lived series that you've never heard of, but it's still interesting. The real fun begins once the tram ventures into Catastrophe Canyon, where an earthquake in the heart of desert oil country causes canyon walls to rumble, and riders are threatened by a raging oil fire, massive explosions, torrents of rain, and flash floods! Then you're taken behind the scenes to see how filmmakers use special effects to create such disasters. Almost as interesting as the ride is the preshow. While waiting in line, you can watch entertaining videos—hosted by Tom Selleck and Carol Burnett—of well-known actors and directors on overhead monitors: Penny Marshall talking about the piano scene in *Big,* Richard Dreyfuss sharing how he landed the role in *Jaws* that launched his movie career, Mel Brooks on why he was "forced" to become a director/producer, and many more. After the tram tour, visit Studio Showcase, a changing walk-through display of sets and props from popular and classic movies.

Goosebumps Horrorland FunHouse

Frommer's Rating: B

Recommended Ages: 6–adult

This is probably the Haunted Mansion of the next generation. A spooky trip through the dark passages of the *Goosebumps* books helps the scary characters in the R. L. Stine book series come to life. While it might be too intense for young children, it's just scary enough for most. There are shows on an outdoor stage throughout the day from around 9:30am to 4pm Monday through Saturday.

The Great Movie Ride

Frommer's Rating: C+ for kids, B for older adults

Recommended Ages: 10–adult

Film footage and audio-animatronic replicas of movie stars are used to re-create some of the most famous scenes in filmdom on this thrilling ride through movie history. You'll relive magic moments from the 1930s through the present—Bergman and Bogart's classic airport farewell in *Casablanca,* Rhett carrying Scarlett up the stairs of Tara for a night of passion, Brando bellowing "Stellllaaaa," Sigourney Weaver fending off slimy *Alien* foes, Gene Kelly singin' in the rain, Johnny Weissmuller's trademark Tarzan yell and vine-swing across the jungle, and many more. Action is enhanced by dramatic special effects, and your tram is always highjacked en route by outlaws or gangsters. "Fasten your seat belts. It's going to be a bumpy night." The setting for this attraction is a full-scale reproduction of Hollywood's famous Mann's Chinese Theatre, complete with handprints of the stars out front.

Indiana Jones Epic Stunt Spectacular

Frommer's Rating: A+

Recommended Ages: 6–adult

Visitors get a glimpse into the world of movie stunts in this dramatic 30-minute show, which re-creates major scenes from the Indiana Jones series. The show opens on an elaborate Mayan temple backdrop. Indiana Jones crashes dramatically onto the set via a rope, and, as he searches with a torch for the golden idol, he encounters booby traps, fire and steam, and spears popping up from the ground, before being chased by a vast rolling boulder! The set is dismantled to reveal a colorful Cairo marketplace where a sword fight ensues and the action includes virtuoso bullwhip maneuvers, lots of gunfire, and a truck bursting into flame. An explosive finale takes place in a desert scenario. The action is enhanced by movie theme music and entertaining narrative, and, throughout, guests get to see how elaborate stunts are pulled off. (Here it is, another opportunity to be part of the fun. Arrive early and sit near the stage for your shot at short-lived stardom. Go ahead, you're running out of chances—*this time you get to wear a turban.*)

Inside the Magic

Frommer's Rating: B

Recommended Ages: 10–adult

Movie and TV special effects and production facets are the focus of this behind-the-scenes walking tour of studio facilities. You'll see how a naval battle—complete with burning ships, torpedoes, and undersea explosions—is created and then view the results on videotape. Two young volunteers from the audience help demonstrate how miniaturization was achieved in *Honey, I Shrunk the Kids*. You'll visit three studio soundstages (on some tours, you'll get to see movies or TV shows being filmed from a soundproof catwalk); view a short comedy called *The Lottery* starring Bette Midler and learn how its special effects were achieved; and head to the Walt Disney Theater where, blessed relief, you'll get to sit down and enjoy a behind-the-scenes look at the company's latest animation feature. To find the entrance to this attraction, follow the big pink footsteps of Roger Rabbit.

Jim Henson's Muppet*Vision 4D

Frommer's Rating: A+

Recommended Ages: 4–adult

They added an additional "D" and some more zany effects to this delightful film starring Kermit and Miss Piggy. The film combines Jim Henson's puppets with Disney AudioAnimatronics and special-effects wizardry, 70mm film, and cutting-edge 4D technology. Wow! The coming-right-at-you action includes flying Muppets, cream pies, cannonballs, high winds, fiber-optic fireworks, bubble showers, even an actual spray of water. Kermit is the host, Miss Piggy sings "Dream a Little Dream of Me," Statler and Waldorf critique the action (which includes numerous mishaps and disasters) from a mezzanine balcony, and Nicki Napoleon and his Emperor Penguins (a full Muppet orchestra) provide music from the pit. Kids in the first row get to interact with the characters. In the preshow area, guests view an entertaining Muppet video on overhead monitors and see movie props belonging to Muppet superstars. Note the cute Muppet fountain out front and the Muppet version of a Rousseau painting inside.

The Magic of Disney Animation

Frommer's Rating: A

Recommended Ages: 8–adult

You'll see Disney characters come alive at the stroke of a brush or pencil as you tour actual, glass-walled animation studios and watch artists at work. Walter Cronkite and Robin Williams (guess who plays straight man?) explain what's going on via video monitors, and they also star in a very funny 8-minute Peter Pan–themed film about the basics of animation. It's painstaking work: To produce an 80-minute film, the animation team must complete more than a million individual *cels* (drawings/paintings on clear celluloid sheets) of characters and scenery! Original cels from famous Disney movies, and some of the many Oscars won by Disney artists, are on display here. The tour also includes very entertaining video talks by animators and a grand finale of magical moments from Disney classics such as *Pinocchio, Snow White, Bambi, Beauty and the Beast,* and *The Hunchback of Notre Dame.*

Star Tours

Frommer's Rating: B+
Recommended Ages: 8–adult

A wild galactic journey based on the *Star Wars* trilogy (George Lucas collaborated on its conception), this action-packed adventure uses dramatic film footage and flight-simulator technology to transform the theater into a vehicle careening through space. You enter a preshow area—where R2-D2 and C-3PO are running an intergalactic travel agency—and board a 40-passenger "spacecraft" for a voyage to the Moon of Endor. En route, you encounter robots, aliens, and droids, among them our inexperienced pilot, RX-24. No sooner has he extricated your spaceship from an asteroid-like tunnel of frozen ice fragments than he's drawn into combat with a massive Imperial Star Destroyer. The ship lurches out of control, and passengers experience sudden drops, violent crashes, and oncoming laser blasts. The harrowing ride ends safely, and you exit into a *Star Wars* merchandise shop. It's not a bad thrill ride for a Disney park, and because it has been around a while the lines are usually short.

Superstar Television

Frommer's Rating: B+
Recommended Ages: 10–adult

This 30-minute show takes guests through a broadcast day that spans TV history. During the preshow, "casting directors" choose volunteers from the audience to reenact 15 famous television scenes (arrive early if you want to snag a role, and *wave that hand!*). The broadcast day begins with a 1955 black-and-white "Today" show featuring Dave Garroway and continues through "Late Night with David Letterman," including scenes from a classic "I Love Lucy" episode (the candy factory), "General Hospital," "Bonanza," "Gilligan's Island," "Cheers," and "The Golden Girls," among others. Real footage is mixed with live action, and though occasionally a star is born, there's plenty of fun watching amateur actors freeze up, flub lines, and otherwise deviate from the script.

Theater of the Stars

Frommer's Rating: A
Recommended Ages: 4–adult

This 1,500-seat, covered amphitheater is currently presenting a 25-minute live Broadway-style production, *Beauty and the Beast,* adapted from the movie version. Musical highlights from the show range from the rousing "Be Our Guest" opening number to the poignant title song featured in a romantic waltz-scene finale complete with the release of white doves. A highlight is "The Mob Song" scene in a dark forest, in which villagers led by Gaston (the beast's rival for Belle) and armed with axes, hoes, and pitchforks set out on a rampage to "kill the beast," setting up the emotional climax. Sets and costumes are lavish, production numbers spectacular. Consider going to the last show; it makes for a feel-good (and sit-down) ending to your day. (But when is someone going to do a version of this tale in which the beast is a woman, and the man loves her for her inner qualities?) Arrive early to get a good seat.

Note: Beauty and the Beast has been enjoying a long run here; a new show, based on a more recent Disney hit, may be in progress by the time you visit. *Hunchback of Notre*

In the Words of Walt Disney

A family picture is one the kids can take their parents to see and not be embarrassed.

I don't like downbeat pictures, and I cannot believe that the average family does either . . . when I go to the theater, I don't want to come out depressed.

Dame: A Musical Adventure will probably be a major priority; for the latter, get in line 30 minutes early at the Backlot Theater.

The Twilight Zone Tower of Terror

Frommer's Rating: A+
Recommended Ages: 10–adult

Legend has it that during a violent storm on Halloween night of 1939, lightning struck the Hollywood Tower Hotel, causing an entire wing—along with an elevator full of people—to disappear. And you're about to meet them as you become the star in a special episode of . . . *The Twilight Zone.* En route to this formerly grand hotel, guests walk past overgrown landscaping and faded signs that once directed them to stables and tennis courts; the vines over the entrance trellis are dead, and the hotel itself is a crumbling ruin. Eerie corridors lead to a dimly lit library, where you can hear a storm raging outside. After various spooky adventures, the ride ends in a dramatic climax: a terrifying 13-story fitful, free-fall plunge into *The Twilight Zone!* This is the best thrill ride at Disney, with a "preshow" so authentic that maintenance crews kept fixing leaking pipes designed to drip as part of the ambience. *Note:* You must be 40 inches tall to ride.

Voyage of the Little Mermaid

Frommer's Rating: A
Recommended Ages: 4–adult

Hazy lighting, creating an underwater effect in a reef-walled theater, helps set the mood for this charming musical spectacular based on the Disney feature film. The show combines live performers with more than 100 puppets, movie clips, and innovative special effects. Sebastian sings the movie's Academy Award–winning song, "Under the Sea"; the ethereal Ariel shares her dream of becoming human in a live performance of "Part of Your World"; and the evil, tentacled Ursula, 12 feet tall and 10 feet wide, belts out "Poor Unfortunate Soul." It all has a happy ending, as most of the young audience knows it will; they've seen the movie.

PARADES, SHOWS, FIREWORKS & MORE

A parade celebrating *Mulan,* Disney's 36th full-length animated feature, has replaced the *Hercules* parade in Disney–MGM Studios. The short parade is based on the story of a young, high-spirited girl who saves her father's life by disguising herself as a man and joining the Chinese army in his place. It will be performed daily along Hollywood Boulevard. This parade in no way matches the size and scope of the parades in the Magic Kingdom, so unless you're a big fan of the movie, this might be a good time to drop in on the Tower of Terror while the lines are shorter. The parade takes place daily; check your entertainment schedule for routes and times.

The **Sorcery in the Sky** fireworks show is presented nightly during summer and peak seasons. Check your entertainment schedule to see if it's on.

The **Visiting Celebrity** program features frequent appearances by stars such as Betty White, Burt Reynolds, Joan Collins, Leonard Nimoy, and Billy Dee Williams. They appear at attractions, record their handprints in front of the Chinese Theatre, and appear at question-and-answer sessions with park guests. Check your entertainment schedule to see if it's on. Kids ages 10 and up will enjoy it.

The **Honey, I Shrunk the Kids Movie Set**, an 11,000-square-foot playground based on the film, is located near New York Street. Everything in it is larger than life and will appeal to kids ages 2 to 10. A thicket of grass is 30 feet tall, mushroom caps are three stories high, and a friendly "ant" makes a suitable seat. Play areas—enhanced by sounds such as the buzzing of giant crickets and bees—include a massive cream cookie, a 52-foot garden hose (with leaks), cereal loops 9 feet in diameter (cushioned for jumping), a waterfall cascading from a leaf to a dell of fern sprouts (the sprouts form a musical stairway, activated when guests step from sprout to sprout), a root maze with a flower-petal slide, a "filmstrip" slide in a giant Kodak film can, and a huge spider web with 11 levels to climb.

Centering on a gleaming 14½-foot-tall bronze Emmy, the **Academy of Television Arts & Sciences Hall of Fame Plaza,** adjacent to SuperStar Television, honors TV legends. Bronze statues of television luminaries Carol Burnett, Sid Caesar, James Garner, Andy Griffith, Barbara Walters, Rod Serling, Bill Cosby, Mary Tyler Moore, Red Skelton, Danny Thomas, and Milton Berle are displayed, along with one of Walt Disney. This is really for adults; kids may not know all these names yet. Additional statues will be added each year. ATAS holds its annual Hall of Fame induction ceremonies at the Disney–MGM Studios.

Ace Ventura—When Nature Calls is a 20-minute show featuring a Jim Carrey look-alike who roars onto the set in an old jalopy, coming to a crashing halt. He performs his typically zany antics, does stunts, and gives wiseass answers to an interviewer. After the show, he poses for photos and signs autographs. For ages 6 to 14.

SHOPPING AT DISNEY–MGM STUDIOS

There's some really interesting shopping here. The **Animation Gallery** carries collectible cels, books about animation, arts-and-crafts kits for future animators, and collector figurines.

Sid Cahuenga's One-of-a-Kind sells autographed photos of the stars, original movie posters, and star-touched items such as a bracelet that once belonged to Joan Rivers.

Over at **Cover Story,** you can have your photograph put on the cover of your favorite magazine, anything from *Forbes* to *Psychology Today* to *Golf Digest*. Costumes are available.

Celebrity 5 & 10, modeled after a 1940s Woolworth's, has movie-related merchandise: *Gone With the Wind* memorabilia, MGM Studio T-shirts, movie posters, Elvis mugs, and more.

And major park attractions all have complementary merchandise outlets selling Indiana Jones adventure clothing, *Little Mermaid* stuffed characters and logo-wear, *Star Wars* souvenirs, and so on. There is a package pickup system that allows purchases to be delivered to the front of the park so you can pick them up as you leave. Take advantage of this free service.

6　Animal Kingdom

Disney's fourth major park combines animals, elaborate landscapes, and a handful of rides to create yet another reason not to venture outside of the Disney World. Michael Eisner says it's the next best thing to going to Africa, but don't cancel that safari vacation yet. Although things may improve as the animals adapt to their new habitats, Disney doesn't fare well in this attempt to re-create the zoo. Shortly after the park opened, the animals were hard to find amid the lush landscapes, and the few rides and shows don't provide you with your money's worth. There is also something jarring about the way the ecological lessons hit you over the head, unlike Sea World where they are more a part of the show.

After an opening preview, I'd suggest you postpone your visit until after Asia, the last "land" in the park, opens in 1999, especially if you have less than a week in Orlando, or especially if this is your first visit to Disney and the Orlando area. There are more worthy ways to spend your time and money—either at one of the other Disney Parks, Universal, or Sea World.

Animal Kingdom is divided into five "regions": **The Oasis,** a main entry way; **Safari Village,** a shopping/entertainment area; **Africa,** the main animal-viewing area, which is dedicated to the wildlife in Africa today; **Dinoland,** focusing on issues of extinction; and **Camp Minnie-Mickey,** the Animal Kingdom equivalent of Mickey's Toontown in the Magic Kingdom. The park covers more than 500 acres—nearly twice the size of Epcot—and your feet will tell you that you have covered the territory at the end of the day.

Most of the rides are accessible to guests with disabilities, but the hilly terrain, large crowds, narrow passages, and long hikes can make for a strenuous day if there is someone in a wheelchair in your party. Anyone with heart, neck, or back problems will not be able to enjoy the major attraction, Kilimanjaro Safaris. Also remember that the animals will be most active early in the morning and late in the afternoon.

At the heart of it all is a purportedly 14-story **Tree of Life,** which Disney must have measured from the lowest root stock to the tallest leaf. It is an intricately carved free-form representation of animals, handcrafted by a team of artists over the period of a year. It is not nearly as tall or imposing as the silver golf-ball dome, also known as Spaceship Earth, that has come to best symbolize Epcot or Cinderella's Castle. The art-work is impressive, though, with new animals seemingly appearing at every glance. Parents, however, may have some trouble keeping kids from wanting to climb. It is, after all, a tree, and there are lots of handy footholds.

The **Asia** section of the park is expected to open late in 1999 and will include a tiger exhibit, a water flume ride, displays of giant fruit bats, along with other animals, and an elaborate series of buildings that are supposed to be ruins of an ancient city.

ARRIVING   Once in the parking lot, you can take a tram to the park. If you park in the Peacock section, you can easily walk. But watch out for the trams, since the parking lots are not designed for pedestrians. Also make certain to mark your location. The parking lot signs are not as prominent as in the Magic Kingdom, and all the rows look alike when you come back out. Upon entering the park, consult your guide map as to any special events or entertainment. If you have questions, ask the park personnel, who are dressed in various, wildly colored "native" costumes.

HOURS   Animal Kingdom is open from 8am–5pm.

TICKETS & PRICES $42 for adults, $34 for children, children under 4 are free. See "Tickets" earlier in this chapter for information on 4- and 5-day passes.

SERVICES & FACILITIES IN ANIMAL KINGDOM

ATMs   There is one ATM in Animal Kingdom, located near Garden Gates Gifts just inside the park entrances. It accepts cards from banks using the Cirrus, Honor, and Plus systems.

Baby Care   The Baby Care Center is located near Creature Comforts in Safari Village, but as in the other Disney parks, you'll find changing tables in both men's and women's rest rooms, and you'll be able to buy disposable diapers at Guest Services.

Cameras & Film   You can drop film off for same-day developing at the Kodak Kiosk and in Africa and Garden Gate Gifts near the park entrances. Single-use cameras and film are available in Disney Outfitters in Safari Village; the Kodak Kiosk in Africa, near the entrance to the Kilimanjaro Safari; and Garden Gate Gifts.

First Aid   The First Aid Center, which is staffed by registered nurses, is located near Creature Comforts in Safari Village.

Lockers   Lockers are located in Garden Gate Gifts to your right as you enter the park. They are also located to the left, near RainForest Cafe.

Lost Children   A center for lost children is located near Creature Comforts in Safari Village. This is also the site of same-day lost and found.

Package Pickup   Any large packages can be sent to the front of the park at Garden Gate Gifts. You can send packages back to Disney resort rooms or send them home through Federal Express from here as well.

Pet Care   Pet facilities are located just outside the park entrance. There are four other kennels located in the WDW complex.

Strollers   Stroller rentals are available at the Garden Gates Gifts shop to the right as you enter the park. There are also satellite locations throughout the park. Ask a Disney employee for those locations.

Wheelchair Rentals   You can rent wheelchairs at the Garden Gates Gifts shop to the right as you enter the park. There are also satellite locations throughout the park. Ask a Disney employee for those locations.

THE OASIS

With the taped sounds of birds chirping and its garden entrance, this painstakingly designed landscape of streams, grottoes, and waterfalls sets the tone for the rest of the park. A misty fog provides a jungle tone but makes seeing the animals sometimes difficult. This is one of the key places to see animals such as wallabies, sloths, and several different kinds of birds. Those traveling with children, who are likely to be excited to see the rest of the park, will probably have more time to enjoy these exhibits on the way out.

SAFARI VILLAGE

Like Cinderella's Castle in the Magic Kingdom and the silver, golf-ball dome in Epcot, the 14-story **Tree of Life** located here has been designed to be the park's central landmark. It is an intricately carved, free-form representation of animals, the handcrafted work of Disney artists. Teams of artists worked for months creating the various sculptures, and it is worth a leisurely stroll through the roots. The intricate design makes it appear as if a different animal appears from every angle. One of the creators says he expects it to become one of the most photographed works of art in the world. (Watch out *Mona Lisa.*) There is a wading pond directly in front of the tree that often features flamingos.

It's Tough to Be a Bug!
Frommer's Rating: B-
Recommended Ages: all ages
The creepy (crawly) special effects of this tour of a bug's life will keep you on the edge of your seat. It's fun for the family but not for the arachnaphobic. Located inside the Tree of Life in a 430-seat theater.

Animal Kingdom

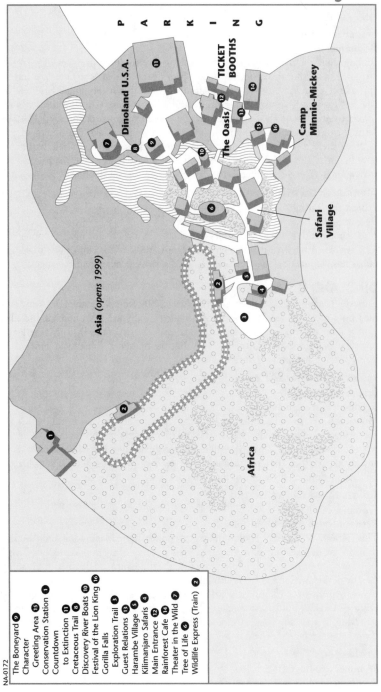

PARKING

Asia (*opens 1999*)

Dinoland U.S.A.

TICKET BOOTHS

The Oasis

Camp Minnie-Mickey

Safari Village

Africa

The Boneyard ❾
Character
  Greeting Area ⓯
Conservation Station ❶
Countdown
  to Extinction ⓫
Cretaceous Trail ❽
Discovery River Boats ❿
Festival of the Lion King ⓰
Gorilla Falls
Exploration Trail ❸
Guest Relations ⓭
Harambe Village ❺
Kilimanjaro Safaris ❹
Main Entrance ⓬
Rainforest Cafe ⓮
Theater in the Wild ❼
Tree of Life ❻
Wildlife Express (Train) ❷

NA-0172

177

Discovery River Boats

Frommer's Rating: C

Recommended Ages: all ages

Rolling along the river may be just the thing to give adults an overview of what they are going to see, but this short ride doesn't provide much of a view. There is a surprise appearance by a very old—let's say prehistoric—friend, but the Jungle Cruise in the Magic Kingdom has much better banter and a better view. (I'm sure the views will improve once Asia opens, but until then you cruise by a construction site.) These are "critter cruises," where an animal handler and his charge take the tour with you. Unfortunately, this is more of a distraction than it is entertainment on the short cruise. Children may also find it hard to keep still if they have just entered the park, so you may want to save this for later in the day when your feet need a rest.

The Garden Path

Frommer's Rating: C

Recommended Ages: all ages

The Garden Path is a leisurely stroll—are you detecting a theme here?—through the root system of the Tree of Life. This soft landscape is filled with otters, flamingos, tamarinds, lemurs, tortoises, and colorful ducks, storks, cranes, and cockatoos.

DINOLAND U.S.A.

Enter by passing under "Olden Gate Bridge," a 40-foot-tall Brachiosaurus reassembled from excavated fossils. Pre-opening publicity said you would find a world filled with a series of wooden cabins and national-parklike structures that give the land a nostalgic look from the 1950s and 1960s, but the buildings didn't make much of an impact on me.

Journey into Jungle Book

Frommer's Rating: B

Recommended Ages: all ages

Mowgli, the man-child abandoned as a baby and raised by wolves, is still the King of the Swingers and the Jungle VIP. Mowgli and friends party in Theater in the Wild and relive their adventures. When Mowgli's life is threatened by a fierce Bengal tiger, a wise and caring panther attempts to guide the boy back to the "man-village" where he rightfully belongs. This is one of the better attractions in the park.

Countdown to Extinction

Frommer's Rating: C

Recommended Ages: 8 and older

This ride is reminiscent of Snow White's Adventures in the Magic Kingdom. You hurl through the darkness in "time machines" past an array of snarling dinosaurs. This is far from a smooth ride, and children may find the dinosaurs and darkness frightening. As a thrill ride, well, it's not very thrilling. The snarling dinos are interesting, but you speed by them so quickly there's little time to appreciate them. In a weird glitch in Disney's usually faultless storytelling, the dinosaur that you are supposed to be retrieving by traveling back in time never appears anywhere at the end of the ride. *Note:* You must be 46 inches tall to ride.

Cretaceous Trail

Frommer's Rating: C

Recommended Ages: all ages

Wander leisurely—there's that theme again—back in time as you stroll down a path filled with living plants and animal species that have survived since the age of the dinosaur. You'll encounter a Chinese alligator, a Florida soft-shelled turtle, and red-legged seriama. The animals are interesting, but skip the re-creation of the dig site.

The Boneyard

Frommer's Rating: B for children, D for adults
Recommended Ages: all ages

Kids love the chance to slip, slither, slide, and crawl through this giant playground and dig site where they can discover the remains of triceratops, T-rex, and other vanished giants. You can even dig up the bones of a woolly mammoth in the dig site. Contained within a latticework of metal bars and netting, this children's play area reminds me of a prisoner of war camp, but the kids still like it. This area is fun, but isn't nearly as inviting at the *Honey I Shrunk the Kids* play area in Disney–MGM Studios.

CONSERVATION STATION

This offers a behind-the-scenes look at how Disney cares for animals inside the park. You walk past a series of nurseries and vet stations. The problem is that these facilities have to be staffed in order to be interesting, and that is not always the case. (I did spy a rare *biologist humanus* sitting at his computer.)

Conservation Station includes the **Affection Section,** where you can cuddle with some friendly animals, explore their private habitats, and learn how they are cared for and fed. The coolest thing here, however, is the pair of elephant sculptures that serve as hand washer and blow dryer.

Check out **Eco Heroes,** interactive videos that connect you to endangered animal information and world-famous biologists and conservationists, and **Song of the Rainforest,** which surrounds you with the sounds of the endangered wildlife in a deep jungle. This lecture/audio adventure is kind of interesting, but skip it if there is a long wait. You can get jungle-sounds CD at the local music store without the annoying whir of a chain saw. Unless you are into doing a little research on your vacation, skip **Eco Web,** a computer link to conservation organizations worldwide.

CAMP MINNIE-MICKEY

Join your favorite Disney characters "on vacation" in Camp Minnie-Mickey, an entire land that re-creates a kid-friendly Adirondack resort.

Grandma Willow's Cove

Frommer's Rating: B
Recommended Ages: all ages

Pocahontas and Grandmother Willow, as well as some new creatures from the forest, perform in a stage show at Grandmother Willow's Grove, a cozy 350-seat theater.

Festival of the Lion King

Frommer's Rating: A
Recommended Ages: all ages

Arrive early for this popular attraction that regularly draws enough people to fill the 1,000-seat pavilion. Based loosely on the animated movie, this stage show combines the pageantry of a parade with a tribal celebration. In an interesting switch, the audience is seated in the center of the theater as the action moves around them. This is definitely the best show in the park.

Character Greeting Pavilions

Frommer's Rating: A for children (C for adults)
Recommended Ages: all ages

This is a must-do for people traveling with children. A variety of Disney characters, from Winnie the Pooh to Timon and Baloo, greet you. Mickey, in recognition of his star status, can be found in his own pavilion.

AFRICA

Enter through the town of Harambe, a run-down representation of an African coastal village poised on the edge of the 21st century. Costumed employees will greet you with cries of "Jumbo" as you enter the buildings. The whitewashed structures, built of coral stone and thatched with reed by craftsmen brought over from Africa, surround a central marketplace rich with local wares and colors.

Gorilla Falls Exploration Trail

Frommer's Rating: C+

Recommended Ages: all ages

You can get a pretty good look at birds and the ever active mole rats, but the gorillas are hard to spy and difficult to track. Small viewing areas give you a glimpse into various parts of the habitat, but because the animals are elusive, lines get three or four people deep when you can actually catch a glimpse. Children—okay, adults too—may find this frustrating. Also the swaying rope bridge you must traverse to reach the compound may be a little tricky for those in wheelchairs and their companions.

Kilimanjaro Safaris

Frommer's Rating: C+

Recommended Ages: all ages

This is one of the few "rides" in Animal Kingdom. Essentially, you board a very big truck for a very bumpy ride through the faux African landscape. The vehicle is open, so open you can get thwacked in the face with foliage, and the animals sometimes wander in very close. But this is hit or miss, depending on how much wildlife you actually get to spot. The lions are difficult to see, and a poacher-fighting story line doesn't add much to the whole experience. (In an early version of the ride, Disney killed off a mother elephant; there was even a fake carcass visible from the cars. This plan was, wisely, changed after Imagineers discovered that the dead mother upset young children.) The poacher looks like a refugee from an old Tommorrowland exhibit. If you have small children, you will need to wrangle a seat on the end so they will be able to look out the sides of the car. The ride gets bumpy, so those with heart, back, and neck problems, as well as expectant mothers, should skip it.

7 Other WDW Attractions

TYPHOON LAGOON

> *Ahoy swimmers, floaters, run-aground boaters!*
> *A furious storm once roared 'cross the sea*
> *Catching ships in its path, helpless to flee . . .*
> *Instead of a certain and watery doom*
> *The winds swept them here to TYPHOON LAGOON.*

Such is the Disney legend relating to Typhoon Lagoon, which you'll see posted on consecutive signs as you enter the park. Located off Lake Buena Vista Drive, halfway between the Disney Village Marketplace and Disney–MGM Studios, this is the ultimate in water-theme parks. Its fantasy setting is a palm-fringed tropical island village of ramshackle, tin-roofed structures, strewn with cargo, surfboards, and other marine wreckage left by the "great typhoon." A storm-stranded fishing boat dangles precariously atop the 95-foot-high Mount Mayday, the steep setting for several major park attractions. Every half hour the boat's smokestack erupts, shooting a 50-foot geyser of water into the air.

ESSENTIALS

HOURS   The park is open from 10am to 5pm most of the year (with extended hours during some holiday periods), 9am to 8pm in the summer.

ENTRANCE FEES   A 1-day ticket to Typhoon Lagoon is $25.95 for adults, $20.50 for children.

HELPFUL HINTS   In summer, arrive no later than 9am to avoid long lines. The park is often filled to capacity by 10am and then closed to later arrivals. Beach towels and lockers can be obtained for a minimal fee, and all beach accessories can be purchased at **Singapore Sal's.** Light fare is available at two eateries, **Leaning Palms** and **Typhoon Tillie's Galley and Grog.** A beach bar called **Let's Go Slurpin'** sells beer and soft drinks, and there are also picnic tables (consider bringing picnic fare; you can keep it in your locker until lunchtime). Guests are not permitted to bring their own flotation devices into the park.

ATTRACTIONS IN THE PARK

Castaway Creek

Hop onto a raft or inner tube and meander along this 2,100-foot lazy river. Circling the lagoon, Castaway Creek tumbles through a misty rain forest, past caves and secluded grottoes. It has a theme area called Water Works, where jets of water spew from shipwrecked boats and a Rube Goldberg assemblage of broken bamboo pipes and buckets sprays and dumps water on passersby. There are exits along the route where you can leave the creek; if you do the whole thing, it takes about a half hour. Tubes are complimentary.

Ketchakiddie Creek

Many of the other attractions require guests to be at least 4 feet tall. This section of the park is a kiddie area exclusively for those under 4 feet. An innovative water playground, it has bubbling fountains to frolic in, mini–water slides, a pint-size whitewater tubing adventure, spouting whales and squirting seals, rubbery crocodiles to climb on, grottoes to explore, and waterfalls to loll under.

Shark Reef

Guests are given free snorkel equipment (and instruction) for a 15-minute swim through this 362,000-gallon simulated coral-reef tank populated by about 4,000 rainbow parrot fish, queen angelfish, yellowtail damselfish, rock beauties, blue tang, puddingwife fish, and other colorful denizens of the deep. Underwater scenery includes shipwrecked boats, and there's a rock waterfall at one end. If you don't want to get in the water, you can observe the fish via portholes in a walk-through area. Shark Reef is housed in a sunken upside-down tanker.

Typhoon Lagoon

This large and lovely lagoon, the size of two football fields and surrounded by white sandy beach (complete with volleyball setup), is the park's main swimming area. The chlorinated water's turquoise hue evokes the Caribbean. Large waves for surfing and bobbing crash against the shore every 90 seconds. A foghorn sounds to warn you when a wave is coming. Young children can wade in the lagoon's more peaceful tidal pools—Blustery Bay or Whitecap Cove.

Water Slides

Humunga Kowabunga consists of two 214-foot Mount Mayday water slides that drop you down the mountain before rushing into a cave and out again at 30 miles per hour. Three longer (about 300 feet each) but less steep slides—Jib Jammer, Rudder Buster, and Stern Burner—take you on a serpentine route through waterfalls and bat caves, past nautical wreckage at about 20 miles per hour before depositing you in a bubbling catch pool; each offers slightly different views and thrills. There's seating for non-participatory parents whose kids have commissioned them to "watch me."

White-Water Rides

Mount Mayday is the setting for three white-water rafting adventures—Keelhaul Falls, Mayday Falls, and Gangplank Falls—all of them offering steep drops, coursing through caves, and passing lush scenery. Keelhaul Falls has the most winding spiral route, Mayday Falls the steepest drops and fastest water, and the slightly tamer Gangplank Falls uses large tubes so the whole family can ride together.

BLIZZARD BEACH

Blizzard Beach is Disney's newest water park—a 66-acre "ski resort" in the midst of a tropical lagoon. The park centers on a 90-foot snowcapped mountain (Mount Gushmore), which swimmers ascend via chairlifts, and the on-premises restaurant resembles a ski lodge. At the base of Mount Gushmore is a sandy beach with several other attractions, including a wave pool and a scaled-down version of Mount Gushmore for younger children. The park is located on World Drive, just north of the All-Star Sports and Music resorts.

ESSENTIALS

HOURS   The park is open from 10am to 5pm most of the year (with extended hours during some holiday periods), 9am to 8pm in the summer.

ENTRANCE FEES   A 1-day ticket to Blizzard Beach is $25.95 for adults, $20.50 for children.

HELPFUL HINTS   Arrive at or before park opening to avoid long lines and to be sure you get in. Beach towels and lockers are available for a small charge, and you can buy beach accessories at the Beach Haus.

MAJOR ATTRACTIONS IN THE PARK
CROSS COUNTRY CREEK

Inner-tubers can float lazily along this meandering 2,900-foot creek, which circles the entire park, but beware: It will take you inside a mysterious cave.

Runoff Rapids

Another inner-tube run, where guests can careen down four different twisting, turning flumes—sometimes in total darkness.

Ski-Patrol Training Camp

Designed for preteens, it features a rope swing, a T-bar drop over water, slides (including the wet and slippery Mogul Mania), and a challenging ice-floe walk along slippery floating icebergs.

Slush Gusher

Another Mount Gushmore–speed slide (a bit tamer than Mogul Mania) that travels along a snowbanked mountain gully.

Snow Stormers

Three flumes descend from the top of Mount Gushmore and follow a switchback course through ski-type slalom gates.

Summit Plummet

Starting 120 feet up, this is a speed slide/thrill ride that makes a 55-mile-per-hour plunge straight down to a splash landing at the base of the mountain.

Steamboat Springs

On the world's longest white-water raft ride, your six-passenger raft twists down a 1,200-foot series of rushing waterfalls.

Toboggan Racers

An eight-lane water slide that sends guests racing head first over exhilarating dips as they descend a snowy slope.

RIVER COUNTRY

One of the many recreational facilities at the Fort Wilderness Resort campground, this mini–water park is themed after Tom Sawyer's swimming hole. Kids can scramble over boulders that double as diving platforms for a 330,000-gallon pool. Two 16-foot water slides also provide access to the pool. Attractions on the adjacent **Bay Lake,** which is equipped with ropes and ships' booms for climbing, include a pair of flumes—one 260 feet long, the other 100 feet—that corkscrew through Whoop-N-Holler Hollow; **White Water Rapids,** which carries inner-tubers along a winding, 230-foot creek with a series of chutes and pools; and **The Ol' Wading Pool,** a smaller version of the swimming hole designed for young children.

There are pool and beachside areas for sunning and picnicking, plus a 350-yard boardwalk nature trail through a cypress swamp. Beach towels and lockers can be obtained for a minimal fee. Light fare is available at **Pop's Place.** To get here without a car, take a launch from the dock near the entrance to the Magic Kingdom or a bus from its Transportation and Ticket Center. River Country is generally open from 10am to 5pm most of the year (with extended hours during holidays), 10am to 7pm during the summer. A 1-day admission to River Country is $15.95 for adults, $12.50 for children.

8

What to See & Do Beyond Disney: Universal Studios Florida, Islands of Adventure, Sea World & Other Orlando Attractions

Locals call it the theme-park wars, the ongoing "anything-you-can-do-I-can-do-better" tussle between the Walt Disney properties and the many other Orlando-area attractions. Universal Studios Florida is the biggest challenger to Disney, opening its own nighttime entertainment complex and (soon) its first on-property resort and Islands of Adventure, its second theme park. But, recognizing that there is strength in numbers, Universal, Sea World, and several other major attractions each now offer their own multiday passes to compete with WDW.

And while the wars rage on in the traditional tourist areas, it has dawned—finally—on the rest of Orlando that central Florida is one of the world's favorite vacation destinations.

Downtown Orlando has in the last decade undergone a major resurgence, with thousands regularly crowding its streets, nightclubs, and restaurants. Recent multimillion-dollar expansions at the Orlando Museum of Art and the Orlando Science Center show that the city is stepping up to compete. A multimillion-dollar performing arts center, to be built in downtown Orlando, is in the works by the city of Orlando. This all means that visitors can enjoy the spoils: more variety, greater opportunities, and a world beyond Disney.

THE FLEX PASS The most economical way to see the various "other than Disney" parks is through a **Flex Pass.** Universal Studios Florida, Sea World, and Wet 'n' Wild have joined together to fight Disney's multipark pass system. Here's how it works. You pay one price to visit any of the participating parks during either a 7- or 10-day period. A 7-day, three-park pass to Universal Studios Florida, Wet 'n' Wild, and Sea World is $99.95 for ages 10 to adult or $82.95 for children under 10. A 10-day, four-park pass, which also includes **Busch Gardens** in Tampa, sells for $129.99 for adults and $107 for children. (Children under 2 are free.) The Flex Pass can be ordered through Universal at ☎ **407/363-8000**, Sea World at ☎ **407/351-3600**, or Wet 'n' Wild at ☎ **800/992-WILD** or 407/351-WILD.

Orlando Area Attractions

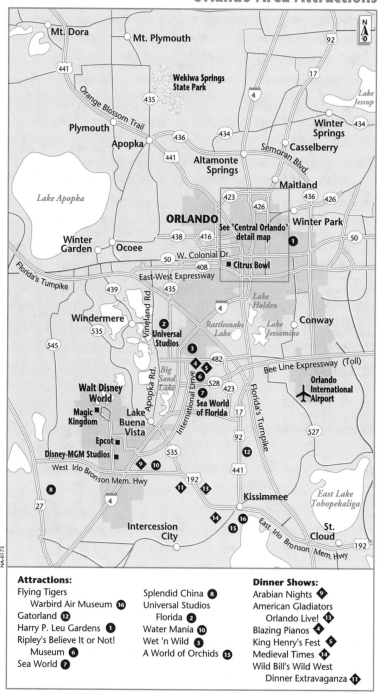

Attractions:

Flying Tigers
  Warbird Air Museum **16**
Gatorland **12**
Harry P. Leu Gardens **1**
Ripley's Believe It or Not!
  Museum **6**
Sea World **7**

Splendid China **8**
Universal Studios
  Florida **2**
Water Mania **10**
Wet 'n Wild **3**
A World of Orchids **15**

Dinner Shows:

Arabian Nights **9**
American Gladiators
  Orlando Live! **13**
Blazing Pianos **4**
King Henry's Fest **5**
Medieval Times **14**
Wild Bill's Wild West
  Dinner Extravaganza **11**

NA-0173

1 Universal Studios Florida

Universal Studios Florida bills itself as the "No. 1 Movie Studio and Theme Park in the World." While it is a working motion-picture and television production studio, most of the production goes on inside the Nickelodeon soundstages, so for all intents and purposes, this is a theme park. Remember cable's "The Swamp Thing," "Clarissa Explains It All," or the short-lived "SeaQuest"? Those television series were shot on the property. Occasionally, visitors will come upon an actual working shoot. But every day you will amble amid reel history displayed in the form of some 40 actual sets displayed along "Hollywood Boulevard" and "Rodeo Drive." On hand to greet visitors are **Hanna-Barbera characters** (Yogi Bear, Scooby Doo, Fred Flintstone, and others) and a talented group of actors representing Universal stars from Harpo Marx to the Blues Brothers.

The long-running Ghostbusters attraction has been closed. (Now who we gonna call?) Blowing into its place is **Twister, the Ride,** an attraction based on the 1996 blockbuster movie *Twister,* which brought Universal more than $245 million at the box office. (Its grand opening in April of 1998 was delayed after a real killer twister roared through Central Florida killing nearly 40 people.)

A more impressive expansion continues in 1999 as Universal opens its second theme park, **Islands of Adventure.** It will also go head-to-head with the competition with its first on-site resort property, à la Disney, reportedly a Loews hotel. Islands of Adventure, with areas to be dedicated to Dr. Seuss and Marvel comic characters, may give Disney real competition with the kiddie crowd, especially those bringing along their Baby Boomer parents.

ESSENTIALS

GETTING TO UNIVERSAL BY CAR Universal is about half a mile north of I-4 exit 30B, Kirkman Road or Route 435. This is the exit leading to the main entrance, but it is very confusing because you follow the signs past the entrance, turn right, and continue to follow the signs around the block.

After getting off the interstate, get into the far right lane and, although you are correct in feeling that you are going in the wrong direction, follow the signs. (A more direct route may be in place at the time of your visit. A new off-ramp is currently being constructed.)

PARKING If you park in the multilevel garage, remember the theme and music on your floor to help you later identify your car. Or, do it the old-fashioned way: Write it down. Parking costs $6 for cars, $7 for RVs and trailers. Valet parking is available for $12. (By the way, this garage is one of the largest in the country, holding nearly 20,000 cars; a second will open along with the new theme park in 1999.)

TICKET PRICES A **1-day ticket** costs $42.14 for ages 10 and over, $33.93 for children 3 to 9; a **2-day ticket** is $63.93 for ages 10 and over, $52.73 for children 3 to 9.

See the beginning of this chapter for information on the **Flex Pass,** which provides multiple-day admission to Universal, Sea World, and Wet 'n' Wild.

There is also a **VIP tour** available, which includes line-cutting privileges, for about $110 per person.

HOURS The park is open 365 days a year, generally from 9am to 7pm. Closing hours vary seasonally and depending on special activities within the park. For example, during Halloween Horror Nights the park closes around 5pm, reopens at 7pm, and

---

Universal Has Character(s), Too

Yogi Bear might say that the Universal character breakfast offers up more than just your "ordinary pic-a-nic basket." The kidlets get a chance to have their picture taken with the Universal characters who are, by the way, Woody Woodpecker, Yogi Bear, BooBoo Bear, Scooby Do, Fred Flintstone, Barney Rubble, Fievel Mouskewitz, George Jetson, and Rocky and Bullwinkle. (A rotating collection comes to each breakfast so don't promise a specific character unless you confirm it through the reservation office.) The menu is your basic breakfast fare of scrambled eggs, danish, cereal, and, for the adults, coffee and tea. These breakfasts are usually less crowded than the ones at WDW, so the kids get more one-on-one time with each character. A nice touch: The children get special cards and crayons so they can get autographs. The character breakfasts are held from 8 to 9am, Tuesday and Thursday. The cost is $13.50 for adults; $8.75 for children ages 3–11. For information call ☎ **407/224-6339.** You can make reservations up to 60 days in advance.

---

remains open until at least midnight. The best bet is to call before you go so you are not caught by surprise.

TIPS FOR MAKING YOUR VISIT MORE ENJOYABLE
PLANNING YOUR VISIT

Get information before you leave by calling **Guest Relations** (☎ **407/363-8000**). Request information about the new travel packages, as well as theme-park information. Universal often offers a "second-day free" promotion. Ask about details.

ON-LINE   Information about Universal Studios can be found at **www.usf.com**. Orlando's daily newspaper, the *Orlando Sentinel,* also produces *Orlando Sentinel Online* at **www.oso@aol.com**. Once there, click on "Theme Park Central" for a variety of information and for updates on what is going on at local attractions. If you are planning a trip during late February or March, keep in mind that a raucous Mardi Gras celebration is going on. Halloween Horror Nights, which usually runs weekends throughout October, is a very grown-up event.

INFORMATION FOR VISITORS WITH SPECIAL NEEDS

Guests with disabilities should go to **Guest Services** located just inside the main entrance for a *Disabled Guest Guidebook,* a Telecommunications Device for the Deaf (TDD), or other special assistance. Wheelchairs are for rent at the park.

BEST TIME OF YEAR TO VISIT

As with Walt Disney World, there is really no "off " season for Universal, but during the winter months, usually from January through April, the park crowds are smallest, the weather coolest, and the air least humid. The summer months, when the masses throng to the park, are not only crowded but uncomfortably hot, sticky, and humid. During the cooler months, you also don't have to worry about the daily summer storms. Avoid spring-break months.

THE BEST DAYS TO VISIT

Go near the end of the week, on Thursday or Friday. The pace is somewhat faster between Monday and Wednesday, with heavy crowds on weekends.

Universal Studios Florida

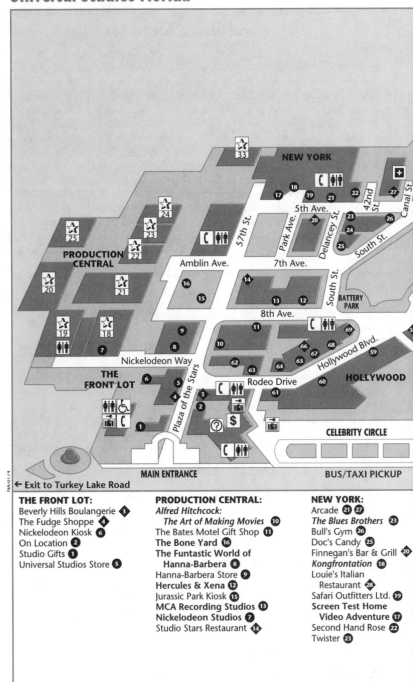

THE FRONT LOT:
Beverly Hills Boulangerie **3**
The Fudge Shoppe **4**
Nickelodeon Kiosk **6**
On Location **2**
Studio Gifts **1**
Universal Studios Store **5**

PRODUCTION CENTRAL:
Alfred Hitchcock:
The Art of Making Movies **10**
The Bates Motel Gift Shop **11**
The Bone Yard **16**
The Funtastic World of
Hanna-Barbera **8**
Hanna-Barbera Store **9**
Hercules & Xena **12**
Jurassic Park Kiosk **15**
MCA Recording Studios **13**
Nickelodeon Studios **7**
Studio Stars Restaurant **14**

NEW YORK:
Arcade **21** **27**
The Blues Brothers **23**
Bull's Gym **26**
Doc's Candy **25**
Finnegan's Bar & Grill **20**
Kongfrontation **18**
Louie's Italian
Restaurant **28**
Safari Outfitters Ltd. **19**
Screen Test Home
Video Adventure **17**
Second Hand Rose **22**
Twister **23**

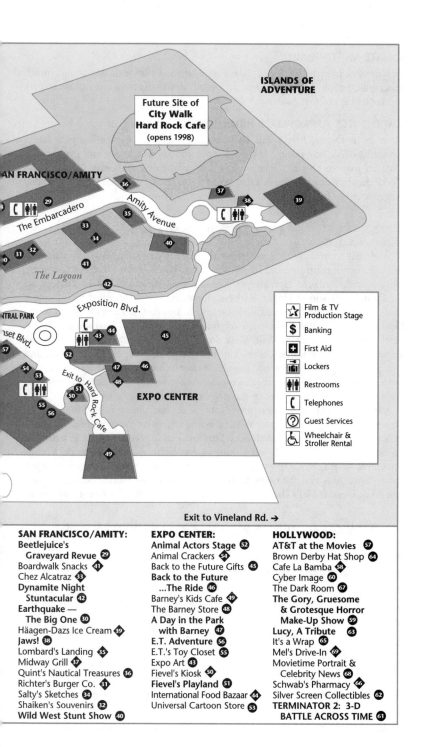

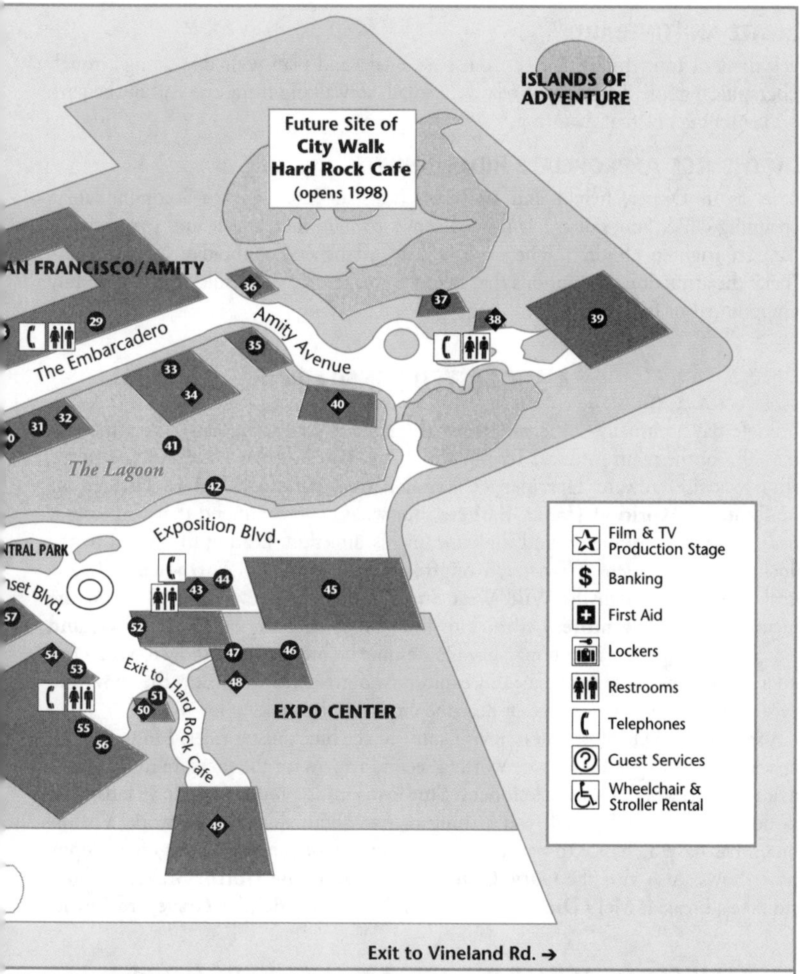
ISLANDS OF ADVENTURE
Future Site of
City Walk
Hard Rock Cafe
(opens 1998)
AN FRANCISCO/AMITY
The Embarcadero
Amity Avenue
The Lagoon
Exposition Blvd.
NTRAL PARK
nset Blvd.
Exit to Hard Rock Cafe
EXPO CENTER
Film & TV Production Stage
Banking
First Aid
Lockers
Restrooms
Telephones
Guest Services
Wheelchair & Stroller Rental
Exit to Vineland Rd. →

SAN FRANCISCO/AMITY:
Beetlejuice's Graveyard Revue (29)
Boardwalk Snacks (41)
Chez Alcatraz (33)
Dynamite Night Stuntacular (42)
Earthquake — The Big One (30)
Häagen-Dazs Ice Cream (39)
Jaws! (38)
Lombard's Landing (35)
Midway Grill (37)
Quint's Nautical Treasures (36)
Richter's Burger Co. (31)
Salty's Sketches (34)
Shaiken's Souvenirs (32)
Wild West Stunt Show (40)

EXPO CENTER:
Animal Actors Stage (52)
Animal Crackers (54)
Back to the Future Gifts (45)
Back to the Future ...The Ride (46)
Barney's Kids Cafe (49)
The Barney Store (48)
A Day in the Park with Barney (47)
E.T. Adventure (56)
E.T.'s Toy Closet (55)
Expo Art (43)
Fievel's Kiosk (50)
Fievel's Playland (51)
International Food Bazaar (44)
Universal Cartoon Store (53)

HOLLYWOOD:
AT&T at the Movies (57)
Brown Derby Hat Shop (64)
Cafe La Bamba (58)
Cyber Image (60)
The Dark Room (67)
The Gory, Gruesome & Grotesque Horror Make-Up Show (59)
Lucy, A Tribute (63)
It's a Wrap (65)
Mel's Drive-In (69)
Movietime Portrait & Celebrity News (68)
Schwab's Pharmacy (66)
Silver Screen Collectibles (62)
TERMINATOR 2: 3-D BATTLE ACROSS TIME (61)

CREATE AN ITINERARY

Pick three or four things that you must see or do and plan your day, along a rough geographical guide. Universal is relatively small, so walking from one end of the park to the other is not that daunting.

CHOOSE AGE-APPROPRIATE RIDES/SHOWS

Here, as in Disney, height and age restrictions are not bent to accommodate a screaming child. Some of the Universal shows contain loud music and pyrotechnics that can frighten children. The same is true of the end-of-the-day "Stuntacular." Check the attraction descriptions that follow to make sure your child won't be unduly disappointed or frightened.

A SUGGESTED ITINERARY

A single day is usually sufficient to see the park if you arrive early. Skip the city sidewalks of the main gate and Terminator 2: 3-D Battle Across Time and veer to the left (clockwise) toward **Hercules & Xena, Alfred Hitchcock's 3-D Theatre,** or the **Funtastic World of Hanna-Barbera,** but we don't recommend that you stop at these. Instead, continue around the park in this direction, beating the crowd to the blockbuster rides such as **Twister, Kongfrontation, Jaws,** and **Earthquake.** Take a break for lunch, watch the **Wild West Stunt Show,** and move on to **Back to the Future** and **ET Adventure.** Let the kids burn off some energy in **Fievel's Playland** and go to **Terminator 2.** You may have some time before the stunt show to visit a few other attractions. If speed boats and explosions don't excite you, skip the show and revisit your favorite attractions, or beat the crowd to the parking lot.

A second day will allow you to revisit some of the blockbuster rides. Most of them, especially Back to the Future, are worth a second trip. With the pressure to hit all the major rides lessened, tour **Nickelodeon Studios.** This is a must if you have kids, who no doubt will be able to tell you a thing or two about this kids' network. Visitors sometimes have a chance to participate in the taping of some of Nick's often sloppy game shows. Also visit the **Gory, Gruesome & Grotesque Horror-Makeup Show,** and take a break at **Mel's Diner** and shows such as the **Beetlejuice Graveyard Revue.**

SERVICES & FACILITIES IN UNIVERSAL STUDIOS FLORIDA

ATMs Machines accepting cards from banks using the Cirrus, Honor, and Plus systems are located outside of the main entrance and just inside the main entrance.

Baby Care Changing tables are in both men's and women's rest rooms; there are nursing facilities at Guest Relations just inside the main entrance and to the right. No diapers are sold on the premises, but complimentary diapers are available to guests in need at the Animal House, Doc's Candy Store, and the Universal Studios Store.

Cameras & Film Camcorders are for rent, and film and disposable cameras are available at the Lights, Camera, Action shop in the Front Lot, just inside the main entrance. One-hour photo developing is available in the Darkroom.

First Aid The First Aid Center is located between New York and San Francisco, next to Louie's Italian Restaurant.

Lockers Lockers are across from Guest Relations near the main entrance and cost $1 a day.

Lost Children   If you lose a child, go to Guest Relations near the main entrance or to Security (behind Louie's, between New York and San Francisco). Children under 7 should wear name tags.

Pet Care   An indoor/outdoor kennel is available for $5 a day near the newest parking lot. Ask the attendant for directions upon entering the toll plaza.

Stroller Rental   Strollers can be rented in Amity and at Guest Relations just inside the entrance to the right. The cost is $6 for a single, $12 for a double.

Wheelchair Rental   Regular wheelchairs can be rented for $6 in Amity and at Guest Relations just inside the main gate. Electric wheelchairs are $30, with a $25 deposit.

MAJOR ATTRACTIONS AT UNIVERSAL STUDIOS FLORIDA

Rides and attractions utilize cutting-edge technology—such as OMNIMAX 70mm film projected on seven-story screens—to create terrific special effects. While waiting in line, you'll be entertained by excellent preshows, better even than those at that other theme park. Universal, as a whole, takes itself less seriously than the Mouse That Roared, and the atmosphere is peppered by subtle reminders that in the competitive 1990s it is not a small world after all.

Back to the Future: The Ride

Frommer's Rating: A+
Recommended Ages: 8–adult
Visitors blast through the space-time continuum, plummeting into volcanic tunnels ablaze with molten lava, colliding with Ice Age glaciers, thundering through caves and canyons, and briefly being swallowed by a dinosaur in a spectacular multisensory adventure. You twist, you turn, you dip and dive, and feel like you are really flying. Stick to seats in the back of the car to avoid ruining the illusion by glimpsing your neighbors careening hydraulically in the next bay. This is a very bumpy ride and might not be appropriate for those with certain health problems. *Note:* Pay heed to the posted warnings displayed at the ride, and remember that children must be 40 inches tall.

The Beetlejuice Graveyard Revue

Frommer's Rating: A
Recommended Ages: 6–adult
Dracula, Wolfman, the Phantom of the Opera, Frankenstein and his bride, and Beetlejuice put on a funky—and very funny—rock musical with pyrotechnic special effects and MTV-style choreography. Loud and lively enough to scare some small children.

A Day in the Park with Barney

Frommer's Rating: A+ for kids and their parents, D for singles
Recommended Ages: all ages
Set in a parklike theater-in-the-round, this musical show—starring the popular Purple One, Baby Bop, and BJ—uses song, dance, and interactive play to deliver an environmental message. For young children, this could be the highlight of the day.

Earthquake—The Big One

Frommer's Rating: B
Recommended Ages: 6–adult
You board a BART train in San Francisco for a peaceful subway ride, but just as you pull into the Embarcadero station there's an earthquake—the big one, 8.3 on the

Richter scale! As you sit helplessly trapped, vast slabs of concrete collapse around you, a propane truck bursts into flames, a runaway train comes hurtling at you, and the station floods (60,000 gallons of water cascade down the steps). *Note:* Children must be 40 inches tall and must ride with an adult.

E.T. Adventure

Frommer's Rating: A
Recommended Ages: all ages

Visitors are given a passport to E.T.'s planet, which needs his healing powers to rejuvenate it. You'll soar with E.T. on a mission to save his ailing planet, through the forest and into space, aboard a star-bound bicycle—all to the accompaniment of that familiar movie theme music. A cool, wooded forest serves to create one of the most pleasant waits for any ride in central Florida. This is a wait worth the ride, a pleasure for kids of all ages.

The Funtastic World of Hanna-Barbera

Frommer's Rating: B+
Recommended Ages: 5–adult

This motion-simulator ride takes guests careening through the universe in a spaceship piloted by Yogi Bear to rescue Elroy Jetson. Prior to this wild ride, you'll learn about how cartoons are created. After it, in an interactive area, you can experiment with animation sound effects—*boing! plop! splash!*—and color in your own cartoons. This is a great place for kids of all ages to take some time and play. Although it doesn't make a lot of sense (since this is the park's most blatant kiddie ride), children must be 40 inches tall.

Twister

Frommer's Rating: A
Recommended Ages: 5–adult

Visitors from the twister-prone Midwest may find this re-creation a little too close to the real thing. An ominous funnel cloud, five-stories tall, is created by 2 million cubic feet of air per minute. And the sound of a freight train fills the theater, as cars, signs, and trucks fly about while the audience watches just 20 feet away. It's the windy version of Earthquake.

Jaws

Frommer's Rating: A
Recommended Ages: 8–adult

Did you really think it was safe to go back into the water? As your boat heads out to the open seas, an ominous dorsal fin appears on the horizon. What follows is a series of terrifying attacks from a 3-ton, 32-foot-long great white shark that tries to sink its teeth into passengers. And there's more trouble ahead. The boat is surrounded by a 30-foot wall of flame from burning fuel that lets you truly feel the heat. I won't tell you how it ends, but let's just say, blackened shark, anyone? (The effects are more startling after dark.)

Kongfrontation

Frommer's Rating: B
Recommended Ages: 6–adult

It's the last thing the Big Apple needed: King Kong is back! As you stand in line in a replica of a grungy, graffiti-scarred New York subway station, CBS newsman Roland Smith reports on Kong's terrifying rampage. Everyone must evacuate to Roosevelt Island, so it's all aboard the tram. Cars collide and hydrants explode below, police helicopters hover overhead putting you directly in the line of fire, the tram malfunctions, and, of course, you encounter Kong—32 feet tall and 13,000 pounds. He emits banana breath in your face and menaces passengers, dangling the tram over the East River. A great thrill—or just another day in New York. *Note:* Children must be 40 inches tall to ride alone. Younger children may be frightened by the dark waiting area.

Nickelodeon Studios Tour
Frommer's Rating: B
Recommended Ages: all ages
You'll tour the soundstages where Nick shows are produced, view concept pilots, visit the kitchen where Gak and green slime are made, play typical show games, and try out new Sega video games. There's lots of audience participation, and a volunteer will get slimed.

Terminator 2: 3-D Battle Across Time
Frommer's Rating: A+
Recommended Ages: 8–adult
He's back…at least in Orlando. This is billed as "the quintessential sight and sound experience for the 21st century!" The same director who made the movie, Jim Cameron, has overseen this production. It features the Big Man himself, along with other original cast members, and combines 70mm 3-D film (utilizing three 23- by 50-foot screens) with live stage action and thrilling technical effects. This ride would probably be rated PG for violence and loud noise. Small children may find it to be too much.

Wild, Wild, Wild West Show
Frommer's Rating: A+
Recommended Ages: all ages
Stunt people demonstrate falls from three-story balconies, gun and whip fights, dynamite explosions, and other wild west staples. This is a well-performed, lively show that is especially popular with foreign visitors who have celluloid visions of the American West. Kids, do not try this at home. *Warning:* Heed the splash zone or you will get very wet.

ADDITIONAL ATTRACTIONS
Hercules & Xena: Wizards of the Screen puts you on the set with scantily-clad gladiators, as the audience battles to make the sound effects match the videos. **Alfred Hitchcock's 3-D Theatre** is a tribute to the "master of suspense," in which Tony Perkins narrates a reenactment of the famous shower scene from *Psycho,* and where *The Birds*—as if the movie weren't scary enough—becomes an in-your-face 3-D movie.

Other park attractions include the **Gory, Gruesome & Grotesque Horror-Makeup Show** for a behind-the-scenes look at the transformation scenes from movies like *The Fly* and *The Exorcist.* **"I Love Lucy," A Tribute,** is a remembrance of America's queen of comedy; and **Fievel's Playland,** is an innovative western-themed playground based on the Spielberg movie *An American Tail.* You might also catch the **Blues Brothers show** or take a look at old movie props in the **Bone Yard.**

Descendants of Lassie, Benji, Mr. Ed, and other animal superstars perform their famous pet tricks in the **Animal Actors Show.** During **Screen Test Home Video Adventure,** a director, crew, and team of "cinemagicians" put visitors on the screen in an exciting video production. And **Dynamite Nights Stuntacular,** a nightly show, combines death-defying stunts with a breathtaking display of fireworks.

CityWalk

While not yet open at press time, this 12-acre entertainment complex could easily be renamed theme-restaurant heaven. Not only is it home to the world's largest **Hard Rock Cafe**—the grande dame of all theme restaurants—but also the **NASCAR Cafe,** the **Motown Cafe,** and **Marvel Mania,** a theme send-up to villains and superheroes. CityWalk, which will open in late 1998, also contains a hearty dose of Cajun spice with **Pat O'Brien's,** a re-creation of the joint in New Orleans, and **Emeril's of New Orleans,** featuring the Creole-based cuisine of chef Emeril Lagasse. If that's not enough to keep you busy, there is the **Down Beat Jazz Hall of Fame,** a tribute to *reggae mon* Bob Marley, and a 5,000-seat **Cineplex Odeon Megaplex.**

Finally, celebrity hounds may catch a live taping involving one of their favorite stars at the **E! Entertainment Television Production Center.**

Detailed reviews of all these establishments will appear in the next edition of *Frommer's Walt Disney World & Orlando.*

SHOPPING AT UNIVERSAL

Every major attraction here (thoughtfully) has a themed store attached. Although the prices are relatively high when you consider you are just buying a T-shirt, the **Hard Rock Cafe** shop is extremely popular and has a small but diverse selection of Hard Rock everything. If you've often longed for a pair of Fred Flintstone boxer shorts or, perhaps, some plastic Scooby snacks, visit the **Hanna-Barbera Shop.**

More than 25 other shops in the park sell everything from Lucy collectibles to Bates Motel towels, and restaurants run the gamut from **Mel's Drive-In** (of *American Graffiti* fame) to the **Hard Rock Cafe,** to **Schwab's.** Be warned, unlike WDW where Mickey is everywhere, these shops are specific to the individual attractions. If you see something you like, buy it. You probably won't find it in another store.

ISLANDS OF ADVENTURE

Universal's second park opens in 1999 with a vibrantly colored, cleverly themed collection of fast, fun rides for kids of all ages.

Divided into four areas, **Seuss Landing, Toon Lagoon, Jurassic Park,** and the **Lost Continent,** this park will offer the biggest concentration of thrill rides and coasters of any park in the area. Park hours and ticket prices had not been released at press time but should be similar to Universal Studios Florida (see the preceding section.) For information on-line, go to **www.usf.com.**

The essentials, from baby care to strollers, weren't available at press time either, but they will be included in the next edition of this guide, along with complete reviews of all the rides and attractions and a suggested itinerary. Also keep in mind that the coaster rides will have height restrictions that will exclude some children.

The following descriptions offer a rundown of the information that was available at press time for all the major rides and attractions. It is likely that some of this information will change before the park actually opens. *Note:* Since these attractions are not yet open and we haven't been able to actually try them, there is no Frommer's Rating.

SEUSS LANDING

This area will be a 10-acre island where those wonderful Dr. Seuss characters come to life. Needless to say, the main attractions here will be aimed at the younger set, though anyone who loved the good Dr. as a child will enjoy some nostaglic fun on these rides.

The Cat in the Hat

Recommended Ages: all ages

This ride will probably remind you of It's A Small World, and like that ride at WDW, The Cat in the Hat will surely become one of the signature experiences of Islands of Adventure. Love it or hate it, you'll just have to do it. Six-passenger couches travel through 18 show scenes including such characters as Thing 1 and Thing 2. The highlight is a revolving 24-foot tunnel that alters your perceptions and leaves your head spinning.

One Fish, Two Fish, Red Fish, Blue Fish

Recommended Ages: all ages, but small children will probably love it best

You ride around in a fish that moves up and down at your control, and a mechanism allows you to spray water at those around you. Of course, if the kids are driving, bring a raincoat. Special adaptations are available for guests with disabilities so that they can enjoy the ride from their chair.

Caro-Seuss-el

Recommended Ages: all ages

This is your basic merry-go-round with a Seussian twist—interactive animation. Go in and out, and up and down on one of seven characters from the world of Seuss, including the elephant birds from *Horton Hatches an Egg*. A special wheelchair-loading system will make it accessible to guests with disabilities.

Sylvester McMonkey McBean's Very Unusual Driving Machines

Recommended Ages: all ages (but more for kids)

The name is almost as long as the ride, but children steer along an elevated track through Seuss Landing. A nice touch to the regular mini-car experience will be honking horns and sound effects if you—*oops!*—just happen to bump the folks ahead of you.

If I Ran the Zoo

Recommended Ages: all ages

An interactive playland for kids of all ages, this attraction includes everything from flying water snakes to a chance to tickle the toes of a Seussian animal. A nice place to let the kids burn off some excited energy.

MARVEL SUPER HERO ISLAND

Thrill junkies will love the twisting, turning, and stomach-churning rides based on characters from Marvel Comics.

The Spider-Man Adventure

Recommended Ages: 8–adult

Combining a moving ride with 3-D action and special effects, the Spider-Man Adventure takes guests on a tour of the Daily Bugle where Peter Parker suddenly encounters evil villains and becomes Spider-Man. This high-tech ride, similar to Back to the Future, includes a simulated 400-foot drop that feels an awful lot like the real thing.

Incredible Hulk Coaster

Recommended Ages: 8–adult

Blasting from zero to 40 miles per hour in 2 seconds, you spin upside down 100 feet from the ground, feeling weightless. Coaster-lovers will be pleased to know that this ride, which will last 2 minutes and 15 seconds, includes seven rollovers and two deep drops.

Dr. Doom's Fearfall
Recommended Ages: 8–adult
You are in for a rush as you drop, with feet dangling, down one of two 200-foot steel towers. The drop will remind you of the Tower of Terror at Disney–MGM Studios but with the added thrill of feeling as if you are hanging free.

TOON LAGOON

More than 150 life-sized sculpted cartoon images let visitors know they have entered this section dedicated to your favorites from the Sunday funnies.

Dudley Do-Right's Ripsaw Falls
Recommended Ages: 6–adult
This water ride, touted as the farthest, fastest drop in the history of flume rides, takes you around a 400,000-gallon lagoon culminating in a 75-foot drop at 50 miles per hour. *Note:* You will get wet. Very wet.

Popeye & Bluto's Bilge Rat Barges
Recommended Ages: 6–adult
Twelve-person rafts bump and churn their way through a white-water ride encountering some scary creatures along the way, including a twirling octopus boat wash. *Note:* Here's another chance to get completely soaked.

Comic Strip Lane
Recommended Ages: all ages
Beetle Baily, Hagar the Horrible, and Dagwood & Blondie are highlighted in this lively jaunt through some of the best-loved comic strips of all times.

JURASSIC PARK

Okay, stay with me here. This is the theme park creation based on a movie featuring a theme park creation that might become a movie. Yes, all the basics from Stephen Spielberg's wildly successful films—and some of the high-tech wizardry—are incorporated in the lushly landscaped tropical locale. Expect hordes.

Jurassic Park River Adventure
Recommended Ages: 6–up
Planned to be the major thrill ride in the Jurassic Park section, this will probably be like the Kongfrontation ride, only better. You'll come face to face with the living, breathing inhabitants of Jurassic Park. Five-story dinosaurs come within inches of the ride; Tyrannosaurus Rex decides you look like a tasty morsel. To escape, you take a 85-foot plunge.

Triceratops Encounter
Recommended Ages: all ages
Meet a "living" dinosaur and learn from the trainers about the care and feeding of the 24-foot-long, 10-foot-high Triceratops. The creature's responses to touch include realistic blinks and muscle flinches.

Jurassic Park Visitors Center
Recommended Ages: all ages
An interactive discovery center within the celebrated gates of Jurassic Park's Visitors Center. Guests will find a variety of entertaining and educational opportunities. This is likely to be a good place to play in air-conditioned comfort with lot of stuff kids of all ages can touch and enjoy.

Pteranodon Flyers
Recommended Ages: All ages
Get a bird's eye view of the Jurassic park compound soaring on the backs of these flying creatures.

Camp Jurassic
Recommended Ages: All ages
A play area with everything from lava pits with dinosaur bones to a rainforest. Watch out for the spitters.

THE LOST CONTINENT
Although they have kind of mixed their millennia—ancient Greece and medieval forest—Universal seems to have done a good job creating a foreboding mood in this section of the park.

Escape from The Lost City
Recommended Ages: 6–adult
Similar to the Earthquake attraction in the other Universal park, this ride exposes you to torrents of water and blasts of heat and fire. The idea is that you are trapped in the midst of a battle between Poseidon, the god of the sea, and Zeus, the king of gods, who hurls fire. It may prove to be more interesting than frightening but should still offer a thrill.

Dueling Dragons
Recommended Ages: 10–adult
This ride consists of two independent but intertwined sets of souped-up swings that move along tracks; the dueling "dragons" are the dueling swing-coasters. Because your legs will dangle freely beneath you, this ride will not be for the fainthearted. Riders zip through the air at speeds of up to 60 miles per hour, at times coming within 12 inches of each other. Get in the very first seat for the feeling that you are really flying through the air.

The 8th Voyage of Sinbad
Recommended Ages: 6–adult
The mythical sailor is showcased in this stunt demonstration that takes place in a 1,700-seat theater. Relying heavily on pyrotechnics for special effects, this will prove to be a hot show, especially if you are in the first few rows. It might be too intense for young children.

2 Sea World

This popular, 200-plus–acre marine-life park explores the mysteries of the deep in a format that combines entertainment with wildlife-conservation awareness. While this is exactly what Disney is attempting with its latest park, Animal Kingdom, the message here is more subtle and is a more inherent part of the experience.

Bell-bottoms and Marcia Brady prints may be all the rage in fashion, but Sea World of Florida has updated its 1970s look. A 55-foot lighthouse topped with a rotating white light in the middle of a harbor decorated with a painting of Shamu anchors the nautically themed renovation. To get to the beacon, visitors will walk underneath a sea of blue and aquamarine "metal waves" and cross wooden bridges nestled amid a rocky shore complete with lapping water and splashing waves.

A new gift shop and upgrades of the ticket booths, turnstiles, guest relations windows, and tram stops make this a world to see.

Sea World's beautifully landscaped grounds, centering on a 17-acre lagoon, include flamingo and pelican ponds and a lush tropical rain forest. Shamu, a killer whale, is the star of the park along with his expanding family, which includes several baby whales. The pace is much more laid-back than either Universal or Disney, and it's a good way to end a long week of trudging through other parks. Be sure to budget some extra money to buy smelt to feed the animals. The close encounters offered at many wading and feeding pools are the real attraction here and more than half the fun. Sea World can't compete with the high-tech wonders abounding elsewhere, but where else can you discover that a stingray feels like crushed velvet or learn the song of a seal?

During 1998 Sea World opened its first major thrill ride, **Journey to Atlantis**, a themed roller coaster with record-breaking twists and turns. If you wonder what Shamu's keepers know about thrill rides remember that Sea World, owned by Anheuser-Busch, is put together by the same folks who operate Busch Gardens where there are wonderful, gut-wrenching thrill rides such as Kumba and Montu.

Sea World is definitely worth a visit, especially if you haven't been here in several years. I have no official word here, but an unofficial poll of friends shows this is a favorite among Floridians—a place you can visit again and again for a lifetime of leisurely afternoons.

ESSENTIALS

GETTING TO SEA WORLD BY CAR   Take I-4 to the Bee Line Expressway (Fla. 528) and follow the signs. It may look like you are going the wrong way, but don't despair, as long as you see the signs.

PARKING   Parking costs $6 per car, $7 for RVs and trailers. The lots are not huge, and you can walk into the park. Trams also run. Note the location of your car. Sections are marked by Sea World characters like Wally Walrus, but it is easy to forget where you parked.

TICKET PRICES   A **1-day ticket** costs $39.95 for ages 10 and over, $32.80 for children 3 to 9; a **2-day ticket** is $44.95 for ages 10 and over, $37.40 for children 3 to 9; children 2 and under enter free.

See the beginning of this chapter for information on the **Flex Pass,** a multiple-day admission ticket for Sea World, Universal Studios Florida, and Wet 'n' Wild.

HOURS   The park is open from 9am to 7pm, 365 days a year, and later during summer and holidays when there are additional shows at night. Call before you go.

TIPS FOR MAKING YOUR VISIT MORE ENJOYABLE
PLAN YOUR VISIT

Get information before you leave by writing to **Sea World Guest Services** at 7007 Sea World Dr., Orlando, FL 32801, or call ☎ **407/351-3600.**

ON-LINE   Sea World information is available at **www.seaworld.com**. The Orlando daily newspaper, the *Orlando Sentinel,* also produces *Orlando Sentinel Online* at **www.oso@aol.com**. Once there, click on "Theme Park Central" for a variety of information and for updates on what is going on at local attractions.

INFORMATION FOR VISITORS WITH SPECIAL NEEDS

The park publishes a guide for guests with disabilities, although most of its attractions are easily accessible to those in wheelchairs. Sea World also provides a Braille guide for the visually impaired. For the hearing impaired, there is a very brief synopsis of shows. For information call ☎ **407/351-2600.**

BEST TIME OF YEAR TO VISIT

Since this is a mostly outdoor, water-related park, you might want to keep in mind that even in Florida it can get a tad nippy during February and March. Like the other parks, Sea World has smaller crowds during the winter months; usually from January through April the park crowds are smallest, the weather coolest, and the air least humid.

BEST DAYS TO VISIT

Monday and Wednesday are busy days at this park. Thursday and Sunday are the best days to visit if you want to avoid crowds.

CHOOSE AGE-APPROPRIATE ACTIVITIES

Since it has few thrill rides, Sea World has few restrictions, but you may want to check out special tour programs offered through the education department.

Sea World lives up to its reputation for making education fun with a variety of tours. One of the newest, and most interesting, is the **Polar Expedition Guided Tour.** For information call ☎ **407/351-2600.**

BUDGET YOUR TIME

Sea World has a naturally leisurely pace, since the major attraction here is taking time to enjoy up-close encounters with the animals. Don't be in a rush. Sea World's many attractions can easily be enjoyed in a single day. The layout of the park amplifies a feeling of space, and the many outdoor exhibits give it an open feel. Because of the large capacity and walk-through nature of many attractions, crowds are generally not a concern. Although you do need to be in Shamu stadium in plenty of time for the show, and Wild Arctic also draws a sizable crowd, lines seldom reach Disney proportions. So, relax. Isn't that what a vacation is supposed to be about?

SERVICES & FACILITIES IN SEA WORLD

ATMs   An ATM machine is located at the front of the park. It accepts Cirrus, Honor, and Plus.

Baby Care   Changing tables are in or near most women's rest rooms and at the men's rest room at the front entrance near Shamu's Emporium. You can buy diapers in machines located near all changing areas and at Shamu's Emporium. There is a special area for nursing mothers near the women's rest room at Friends of the Wild gift shop, near the center of the park.

Cameras & Film   Disposable cameras are available at stores throughout the park.

First Aid   First Aid Centers staffed with registered nurses are behind Stingray Lagoon and near Shamu's Happy Harbour.

Lockers   Lockers are located next to Shamu's Emporium, just inside the park entrance. The cost is $1 a day.

Lost Children   Lost children are taken to the Information Center. A parkwide paging system helps reunite guests. Children under 7 should wear name tags.

Pet Care   A kennel is available between the parking lot and the main gate. The cost is $4 a day.

Strollers   Strollers, in the shape of dolphins, can be rented at the Information Center near the entrance. The cost is $5 for a single, $10 for a double.

Wheelchair Rental   Regular wheelchairs are available at the Information Center. Regular chairs cost $5, electric $25 with a $25 deposit and a driver's license.

MAJOR ATTRACTIONS

Baywatch Nights

Frommer's Rating: A

Recommended Ages: all ages

Actors and stunt drivers re-create some of the high-powered drama of the most popular syndicated television show in the world. Sorry, no Pamela Anderson look-alikes, but plenty of zooming motor boats. It's appropriate for everyone, but the thrill may be lost on very young children, who may also find the noise unsettling. You may have read about a 1996 accident during this show at one of the other Sea World parks. Following that incident, Baywatch shows in all the Sea World parks were closed while an investigation was undertaken. Some minor safety adjustments were made, and the shows have continued without any further problems.

Hotel Clyde & Seamore

Frommer's Rating: A+

Recommended Ages: all ages

Two sea lions, along with a cast of otters and walruses, appear in this fishy "Fawlty Towers" comedy with a conservation theme. Arrive early to catch the mime doing the preshow.

Journey to Atlantis

Frommer's Rating: A

Recommended Ages: 8 and up

This is the park's only true thrill ride. Taking a cue from Disney Imagineers, Sea World has created a storyline to go with a loopy water coaster, something about a Greek fisherman and ancient Sirens in a battle over good and evil. (A "media horde" is somehow involved.) But what really matters is the promise of "two of the steepest, wettest, fastest drops to be found in any theme park." The bottom line is that it's a wild ride down with 60-foot drops and "luge-like curves." Journey to Atlantis breaks from Sea World's edu-tainment formula that stresses equal measures of learning and fun. You'll find no hidden lesson here, just a splashy thrill.

Key West at Sea World

Frommer's Rating: C

Recommended Ages: all ages

It's not quite the way Ernest Hemingway saw it, but this 5-acre paved paradise dotted with palms, hibiscus, and bougainvillea is set in a Caribbean village offering island cuisine, street vendors, and entertainers. The attraction comprises three naturalistic animal habitats: Stingray Lagoon, where visitors enjoy hands-on encounters with harmless southern diamond and cownose rays; Dolphin Cove, a massive habitat for bottlenose dolphins set up for visitor interaction; and Sea Turtle Point, home to threatened and endangered species such as green, loggerhead, and hawksbill sea turtles. Shortly after opening, dolphins showed their intelligence by realizing how easy humans are to tease; they'd routinely swim just out of arm's reach. But they soon discovered that there are advantages to coming in a little closer, namely smelt.

Key West Dolphin Fest

Frommer's Rating: C+

Recommended Ages: all ages

At the Whale and Dolphin Stadium—a big, partially covered open-air stadium—whales and Atlantic bottlenose dolphins perform flips and high jumps, swim at high speeds, twirl, swim on their backs, and give rides to trainers—all to the accompaniment of calypso music. The tricks are impressive, but go before the show-stopping behemoth, Shamu, puts these little mammals to shame.

Manatees: The Last Generation
Frommer's Rating: B+
Recommended Ages: all ages
Today the Florida manatee is in danger of extinction, with as few as 2,000 remaining. Underwater viewing stations, innovative cinema techniques, and interactive displays combine to create an exciting format for teaching visitors about the manatee and its fragile ecosystem. Also on display here are hundreds of other native fish, as well as alligators, turtles, and shore birds. It's amazing to watch the huge beasts move effortlessly through the water. There is something about this mammoth, slow-moving vegetarian that really appeals to children.

Mermaids, Myths & Monsters
Frommer's Rating: A+
Recommended Ages: 3–adult
This nighttime multimedia spectacular is a must-see, featuring fireworks and hologram-like imagery against a towering, 60-foot screen of illuminated water. King Neptune rises majestically from the deep, as do terrifying sea serpents, storm-tossed ships, and frolicking mermaids. It is one of the most innovative closing shows in recent years. While it doesn't have the explosive power of the Disney fireworks, its quieter grace is in keeping with the overall laid-back Sea World theme. Small children may be frightened by the large, moving figures (which appear quite real) walking over the water.

Penguin Encounter
Frommer's Rating: B+
Recommended Ages: all ages
This display of hundreds of penguins and alcids (another species of aquatic bird, including adorable babies), native to the Antarctic and Arctic regions, also serves as a living laboratory for protecting and preserving polar life. On a moving walkway, you'll view six different penguin species congregating on rocks, nesting, and swimming underwater. There's an additional area for puffins and murres (flying Arctic cousins of penguins).

Shamu's Happy Harbor
Frommer's Rating: A+ (for kids)
Recommended Ages: children of all ages
This 3-acre play area has a four-story net tower with a 35-foot crow's-nest lookout, water cannons, remote-controlled vehicles, and a water maze. It's one of the most extensive play areas at any park and a great place for kids to burn off some energy between sitting in shows. Bring extra clothes for the tots (or for yourself) because this place isn't designed to keep you dry.

Shamu: World Focus
Frommer's Rating: A+
Recommended Ages: all ages
Sea World trainers develop close relationships with killer whales, and in this partly covered open-air stadium, they direct performances that are extensions of natural cetacean behaviors—twirling, waving tails and fins, rotating while swimming, and splashing the audience. Splash zones are clearly marked. Sit in the upper tiers if you don't want to get soaked. The evening show here, called "Shamu: Night Magic," utilizes rock music and special lighting effects. There is no reason to attend both shows unless you really like whales. The tricks are much the same. I'd opt for the evening show, taking advantage of shorter lines as others flock to the stadium in the afternoon. If you decide on the afternoon show, arrive at least 30 minutes early. The stadium does fill up.

Shamu: Close Up!, an adjoining exhibit, lets you get close up to killer whales and talk to trainers; don't miss the underwater viewing area here and a chance to see a mother whale with her offspring. Talk about a big baby.

Swim with the Dolphins

Frommer's Rating: A+
Recommended Ages: adults

Since late 1996 a few lucky visitors have been able to don wet suits and join some of Flipper's cousins for an up-close encounter. This effort is modeled after a similar program started in Sea World San Diego in 1995. Animal-rights activists have voiced some concerns, but Sea World argues that the health and well-being of the dolphins is of the utmost importance and is maintained. Guests pay about $125 for a chance to interact with the dolphins under the watchful eyes of their trainers. (Annual-pass holders pay less.) Call ahead for information since this experience must be arranged in advance.

Terrors of the Deep

Frommer's Rating: B
Recommended Ages: 3–adult

This exhibit houses 220 specimens of venomous and otherwise scary sea creatures in a tropical-reef habitat. Immense acrylic tunnels provide close encounters with slithery eels, three dozen sharks, barracudas, lionfish, and poisonous puffer fish. A theatrical presentation focusing on sharks puts across the message that pollution and uncontrolled commercial fishing make humankind the ultimate "terror of the deep." This is not the ride for the claustrophobic, since you walk under a Plexiglas tube beneath hundreds of millions of gallons of water. Also, small children may find the glowing eels and swimming sharks a little too much to handle.

Wild Arctic

Frommer's Rating: B
Recommended Ages: exhibit, all ages; ride, 6–adult

Enveloping guests in the beauty, exhilaration, and danger of a polar expedition, Wild Arctic combines a high-definition adventure film with flight-simulator technology to evoke breathtaking Arctic panoramas. After a hazardous flight over the frozen north, visitors emerge at a remote research base—home to four polar bears (including star residents and polar twins Klondike and Snow), seals, walruses, and white beluga whales. Kids may find the bumpy ride a little much. There is a separate line for those who want to skip the thrill-ride section.

Window to the Sea

Frommer's Rating: C
Recommended Ages: all ages

A multimedia presentation takes visitors behind the scenes at Sea World and explores a variety of marine subjects. These include an ocean dive in search of the rare six-gilled shark, a killer whale giving birth, babies born at Sea World (dolphins, penguins, walruses), dolphin anatomy, and underwater geology.

ADDITIONAL ATTRACTIONS

The park's other attractions include: **Pacific Point Preserve,** a 2½-acre naturalistic setting that duplicates the rocky northern Pacific Coast home of California sea lions and harbor and fur seals; and **Tropical Reef,** a tide pool of touchables, such as sea anemones, starfish, sea cucumbers, and sea urchins, plus a 160,000-gallon manmade coral-reef aquarium, home to 1,000 brightly hued tropical fish displayed in 17 vignettes of undersea life.

A **Hawaiian dance troupe** entertains in an outdoor facility at Hawaiian Village; if you care to join in, grass skirts and leis are available. You can ascend 400 feet to the top of the **Sea World Sky Tower** for a revolving 360° panorama of the park and beyond (there's an extra charge of $3 per person for this activity). And at the 5½-acre **Anheuser-Busch Hospitality Center** you can try free samples of Anheuser-Busch beers and snacks, and stroll through the stables to watch the famous Budweiser Clydesdale horses being groomed. (Remember, the Bud-men of Anheuser-Busch own Sea World.)

The **Aloha! Polynesian Luau Dinner and Show,** a full-scale dinner show featuring South Seas food, song, and fire dancing, takes place nightly at 6:30pm. Park admission is not required. The cost is $35.95 for adults, $25.95 for children 8–12, $15.95 for children 3–7, and free for children 2 and under. Reservations are required (☎ **800/227-8048** or 407/363-2559).

Visitors can take 90-minute **behind-the-scenes tours** of the park's breeding, research, and training facilities and/or attend a 45-minute presentation about Sea World's animal behavior and training techniques. The cost for either tour is $5 for ages 10 and over, $4 for children 3–9, and free for children 2 and under. While there are several tours throughout the day, you should make a reservation when you enter the park.

SHOPPING AT SEA WORLD

This is one area where Sea World really knows better than to compete with Universal and the WDW parks. There aren't nearly as many shops, but there are lots of surprisingly cuddly aquatic-based sea creatures. Where else can you get a stuffed manatee but **Manatee Cove**? The **Friends of the Wild** gift shop near Penguin Encounters is also nice, as is the shop attached to **Wild Arctic**. And, because of the Anheuser-Busch connection, the gift shop outside the entrance to the park offers a staggering array of Budweiser-related items.

3 Other Area Attractions

IN KISSIMMEE

Kissimmee sights are close to the Walt Disney World area—about a 10- to 15-minute drive. Kissimmee has a sign system in place to better help tourists navigate U.S. 192. The large roadside signs say "Marker" along with a number. That information is included where appropriate in the following descriptions.

China Town & Florida Splendid China. Formosa Gardens Blvd., off W. Irlo Bronson Memorial Hwy. (U.S. 192, between Entry Point Blvd./Sherbeth Rd. and Black Lake Rd.). ☎ **407/396-7111.** Admission $26.99 adults, $16.99 children 5–12, free for children 4 and under. Daily from 9:30am; closing hours vary seasonally (call ahead). Free parking. From I-4 take exit 25A, stay left and follow U.S. 192 west; turn left at the Florida Splendid China dragons.

This 76-acre outdoor attraction features more than 60 miniaturized replicas of China's most noted man-made and natural wonders, spanning 5,000 years of history and culture. Park highlights include a half-mile-long copy of the 4,200-mile Great Wall, the Forbidden City's 9,999-room Imperial Palace, Tibet's sacred Potala Palace, the massive Leshan Buddha—which was originally carved out of a mountainside between A.D. 713 and A.D. 803, the Stone Forest of Yunan, and the Mongolian mausoleum of Genghis Khan. Live shows (acrobats, martial-arts demonstrations, storytelling, dance, puppetry, and more) take place throughout the day; check your entertainment schedule. There's recorded commentary at each attraction.

Free trams circle the park, stopping at major attractions for pickup and drop-off. This attraction can be explored in several hours.

Flying Tigers Warbird Air Museum. 231 N. Hoagland Blvd. (off U.S. 192, 1 traffic light west of Armstrong Blvd. and Yates Rd.). ☎ **407/933-1942.** Admission $8 adults, $6 seniors over 60 and children 6–12, under 6 free. Daily 9am–5 or 6pm (hours vary seasonally). Traveling west on I-4, exit to U.S. 192 and go about 10 miles, to the Medieval Times castle; turn right at the second stoplight (Hoagland) past the castle, just beyond Marker 15. The museum is 3/4-mile on left. The building says "Reily Aviation."

Flying Tigers is actually a World War II aircraft restoration facility where vintage planes are rebuilt and test-flown. Seventy-five percent of the displays—which run the gamut from 1920s antiques to 1970s fighter jets—are permanent; the rest are in the shop on a temporary basis. On guided tours, which depart at intervals throughout the day, you'll visit the rebuilding facility where planes in various stages of assemblage are being restored. Exhibits include a U.S. Navy pilot trainer, many World War II bombers (including B-17s), Navy helicopters, torpedo bombers, cargo planes, and a rare World War II Paisacki Hup 1, as well as actual bombs, military jeeps and command cars from World War II and the Korean War, a large display of World War II memorabilia, and much, much more.

Visitors can sit in the cockpit of a jet-fighter simulator, or—for a more realistic Red Baron fantasy experience—arrange to go up in a 1935 three-seat open biplane (call ahead for information on the latter, as well as other flight and piloting opportunities, some for families).

Gatorland. 14501 S. Orange Blossom Trail (U.S. 441; between Osceola Pkwy. and Hunter's Creek Blvd.). ☎ **800/393-JAWS** or 407/855-5496. Admission $14.79 adults, $11.83 seniors over 55, $9.49 children 10–12. For each paying adult, one child 3–9 is admitted free. Daily 8am–dusk. Free parking. From I-4 take exit 26A to 417 north. Take exit 11 to 441 south. Gatorland is 1 mile further on the left.

Founded in 1949 with a handful of alligators living in huts and pens, Gatorland today features thousands of alligators and crocodiles on a 70-acre spread. Breeding pens, nurseries, and rearing ponds are situated throughout the park, which also displays monkeys, snakes, deer, goats, birds, sheep, Florida lake turtles, a Galápagos tortoise, and a bear. A 2,000-foot boardwalk winds through a cypress swamp and a 10-acre breeding marsh with an observation tower. Or you can take the free Gatorland Express Train around the park.

There are three shows scheduled throughout the day—Gator Wrestlin', the Gator Jumparoo, and Snakes of Florida. Facilities include an open-air restaurant (where you can try smoked gator ribs and nuggets), a shop (Gatorland also functions as an alligator-breeding farm for meat and hides; you'll find a wide array of alligator leather products here, not to mention canned gator chowder), and a picnic area.

Water Mania. 6073 W. Irlo Bronson Memorial Hwy. (U.S. 192), just east of I-4. ☎ **407/396-2626.** Admission $23.95 adults, $17.95 children 3–9, under 2 free. Nov–Feb daily 11am–5pm; other times daily 9:30am–7pm with extended hours on some weekends and during spring break. Nov–Feb admission is half-price after 3pm. Parking $4. From I-4, take exit 25A, ½ mile. Across from the old-fashioned water tower that marks the entrance to Celebration.

This conveniently located 36-acre water park offers a variety of aquatic thrill rides and attractions. You can boogie-board or bodysurf in continuous-wave pools, float lazily along an 850-foot river, enjoy a white-water tubing adventure, or plummet down spiraling water slides and steep flumes. Or dare to ride the Abyss, an enclosed tube slide that corkscrews through 300 feet of darkness, exiting into a splash pool. There's a rain forest–themed water playground for children. A miniature golf course and wooded picnic area—with arcade games, a beach, and volleyball—adjoin. Water Mania, smaller than many similar parks, lives up to its billing as being family-friendly. There are lots of opportunities for smaller children, and there tend to be fewer rowdy teenagers and young adults than at parks such as Wet 'n' Wild. You can take in coolers, but glass bottles and alcoholic beverages are not allowed.

A World of Orchids. 2501 Old Lake Wilson Rd. (C.R. 545), off U.S. 192. ☎ **407/ 396-1887.** Admission $8.95 adults, $7.95 seniors, 15 and under free with paid adult. Daily 9:30am–5:30pm. Closed New Year's Day, July 4, Thanksgiving, and Christmas. From I-4 take exit 25B, head west on U.S. 192; after 2 miles turn left on Old Lake Wilson Rd., or CR 545. (There is a tall blue sign here saying "West Gate Towers.") The conservatory is 1 mile ahead on the left.

Lovers of horticulture will enjoy touring this conservatory filled with tropical trees (including 64 varieties of palms and 21 of bamboo), ferns, lush tropical foliage, and, most notably, thousands of orchids—many of them rare—magnificently abloom at all times. Streams, waterfalls, koi ponds, and birds enhance this little enchanted garden. Also on the premises: a nature walk through a wooded area, aquariums of exotic fish, and a small aviary. Free guided tours are given by resident horticulturists at 11am and 3pm weekdays; 11am, 1pm, and 3pm on weekends.

Note: If this is the kind of attraction you enjoy, be sure to also visit Harry P. Leu Gardens in Orlando (see "Elsewhere in Orlando," later in this chapter).

ON INTERNATIONAL DRIVE

Like Kissimmee attractions, these are about a 10- to 15-minute drive from the Disney area.

Ripley's Believe It or Not! Museum. 8201 International Dr. (1½ blocks south of Sand Lake Rd.). ☎ **407/345-0501.** Admission $9.95 adults, $6.95 children 4–12, under 4 free. Daily 9am–11pm. From I-4 west, take exit 29, Sand Lake Rd. Turn right on International Dr.

It's always fun to peruse a Ripley collection of oddities, curiosities, and fascinating artifacts from faraway places. Among the hundreds of items and mannequins on display here are a 1,069-pound man, a two-headed kitten, a five-legged cow, a three-quarter–scale model of a 1907 Rolls-Royce made from a million matchsticks, a mosaic of the Mona Lisa created from 1,426 pieces of toast, torture devices from the Spanish Inquisition, a Tibetan flute made from human bones, an Ecuadorean shrunken head, a painting on a grain of rice, a "disappearing" nude bather (they do it with mirrors), Ubangi women with wooden plates in their lips, and Burmese Padaung women who stretch their necks up to 15 inches long by wearing heavy brass rings around them. There are exhibits on Houdini and Florida sinkholes, and a film documents people swallowing unusual items . . . coat hangers, a lightbulb, and, most notably, a padlock, ring, and keys (when the latter three items were—*ahem!*—evacuated, the ring was locked into the padlock!). Museum visitors are greeted by a hologram of Robert Ripley. *Warning:* A few years back there was a mini–baby boom among employees that was attributed to the statue of a fertility god on display.

Wet 'n' Wild. 6200 International Dr. (at Republic Dr.). ☎ **800/992-WILD** or 407/ 351-WILD (9453). Admission $25.95 adults, $20.95 children 3–9, under 3 free. Age 55 and older always half price; half-price admission for all after 3pm. Daily 10am–5pm. Parking: cars $4, RVs $6. Take I-4 east to exit 30A and follow the signs.

Who knew people came in such a variety of shapes and sizes? Stacked or stubby, tan or terribly white, all kinds of people come to Wet 'n' Wild. According to industry polls, Wet 'n' Wild is one of the hottest tourist attractions in the country. When temperatures soar, head for this 25-acre water park and cool off by jumping waves, careening down steep flumes, and running rapids. When temps aren't soaring, you'll be pleased to know that all the pools are heated. Among the highlights: Fuji Flyer, a six-story, four-passenger toboggan ride through 450 feet of banked curves; The Surge, one of the longest, fastest multipassenger tube rides anywhere in the Southeast, with 580 feet of exciting banked curves; Bomb Bay (enter a bomb-like casing 76 feet in the air for a speedy vertical flight straight down to a target pool); Black Hole (step into a spaceship and board a two-person raft for a 30-second, 500-foot, twisting, turning, space-themed reentry through total darkness propelled by a 1,000-gallon-a-minute blast of water!); Raging Rapids, a simulated white-water tubing adventure with a waterfall plunge; and Lazy River, a leisurely float trip. This is the park that really started it all. Disney built its own water parks to compete with Wet 'n' Wild, and the originator still has plenty to offer. Bomb Bay ranks among one of the best thrill rides in central Florida.

There are additional flumes, a vast wave pool, a large and innovative children's water playground where the preceding rides are re-created in miniature, a sunbathing area, and a picnic area. Food concessions are located throughout the park, lockers and towels can be rented, and you can purchase beach accessories at the gift shop. Bring or buy sunscreen.

You can now purchase a mulitple-day **Flex Pass** that allows admission to Universal Studios Florida, Sea World, and Wet 'n' Wild. See the beginning of this chapter for more information.

ELSEWHERE IN ORLANDO

The rest of the sights and attractions are spread out around Orlando. Loch Haven Park—the location of the Orange County Historical Museum, Orlando Museum of Art, and Orlando Science Center—is about 35 minutes by car from the Disney area. You might also wish to incorporate a trip to Winter Park in the same day (see chapter 11 for details).

✪ **Harry P. Leu Gardens.** 1920 N. Forest Ave. (between Nebraska St. and Corrine Dr.). ☎ **407/246-2620.** Fax 407/246-2849. Admission $5 adults, $1 children 6–16, under 6 free. Daily 9am–5pm. Leu House tours Tues–Sat 10am–3:30pm; Sun–Mon 1–3:30pm. Closed Christmas. Take I-4 east to exit 43 (Princeton St.), follow Princeton St. east, making a right on Mills Ave. and a left on Virginia Dr. Look for the gardens on your left, just after you go around the curve in the road.

This delightful, 50-acre botanical garden on the shores of Lake Rowena offers a serene respite from theme-park razzle-dazzle. Meandering paths lead through forests of giant camphors, moss-draped oaks, palms, cycads, and camellias. (The latter is one of the world's largest collections, comprising some 2,000 plants in 50 species; they bloom October through March.) Exquisite formal rose gardens (the largest in Florida, displaying 75 varieties) are enhanced by Italian fountains, a gazebo, and statuary. Other highlights include orchids, azaleas, desert plants, beds of colorful annuals and perennials, and a 50-foot floral clock. The gardens were created by Orlando businessman Harry P. Leu, who donated his 49-acre estate to the city in the 1960s.

Free 20-minute tours of the Leu House, built in 1888 and restored to reflect the period between 1910 and 1930, take place on the hour and half hour. The house is a decorative arts museum filled with Victorian, Chippendale, and Empire pieces and other furnishings and objets d'art. It takes about 2 hours to see the house and gardens. Inquire about lectures and workshops, including some for children. A new visitor center was added a few years ago, expanding the gift shop and adding a little luster to this laid-back attraction.

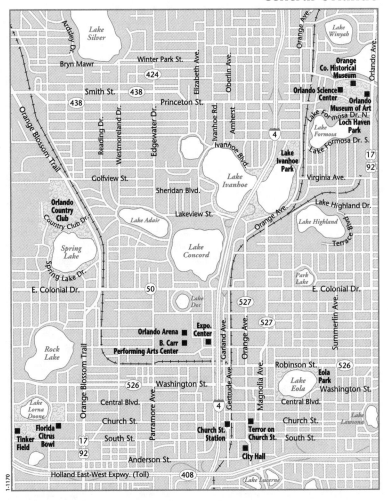

Orange County Historical Museum. 812 E. Rollins St. (between Orange and Mills aves.), in Loch Haven Park. ☎ **407/897-6350.** Fax 407/897-6409. Admission $2 adults, $1.50 seniors 65 and over, $1 children 6–12, under 6 free. Monday admission is by donation. Mon–Sat 9am–5pm; Sun noon–5pm. Closed Martin Luther King, Jr. Day, Memorial Day, July 4, Labor Day, Thanksgiving, Christmas, and New Year's Day. Take I-4 east to exit 43 (Princeton St.) and follow the signs to Loch Haven Park.

Like everything else in Orlando, this museum is soon to get a lift and a make over. It focuses mainly on central Florida history, beginning with prehistoric projectile points, a Timucuan canoe, and tooled animal bones from hunting cultures that existed here 12,000 years ago.

Other exhibits include displays of Seminole pottery and clothing; items from a pioneer kitchen; artifacts from an 1892 courthouse; a chronicle of the citrus industry and the role it played in the development of central Florida; and re-creations of a turn-of-the-century country store, a Victorian parlor, and the old *Orlando Sentinel* composing room. Also on the premises is Fire Station No. 3, a restored 1926 firehouse containing historic fire trucks, equipment, and memorabilia. The permanent collection is supplemented by changing exhibits of local, national, and international significance. It's best enjoyed by true history buffs. (A museum three times larger is in the works, but it won't open until the year 2000.)

✪ Orlando Museum of Art. 2416 N. Mills Ave. (in Loch Haven Park off Hwy. 17/92). **☎ 407/896-4231.** Admission $4 adults, $2 children 4–11, under 4 free. Tues–Sat 9am–5pm; Sun noon–5pm. Art Encounter hours are Tues–Fri and Sun noon–5pm; Sat 10am–5pm. Free parking. Closed New Year's Day, Memorial Day, July 4, Labor Day, Thanksgiving, and Christmas. Take I-4 east to exit 43 (Princeton St.) and follow the signs to Loch Haven Park.

After closing for a 4-month, multimillion-dollar makeover, the Orlando Museum of Art opened in 1997 ready to handle some of the most prestigious exhibits traveling the nation. The improved and expanded museum is worth a look, especially if it is hosting a traveling exhibit, such as the "Imperial Tombs of China," which had an extended stay in the 31,000-square-foot expansion during 1997.

Founded in 1924, the Orlando Museum of Art displays on a rotating basis its permanent collection of 19th- and 20th-century American art, pre-Colombian art dating from 1200 B.C. to A.D. 1500, and African art. These holdings are augmented by long-term loans focusing on Mayan archaeology and art of the African sub-Saharan region. Art Encounter is an interactive hands-on area for young children, where they might weave on a giant loom, piece together a pre-Colombian pot, or play African instruments. Temporary exhibits here range from Hudson River School landscapes to works of Andy Warhol. Inquire about guided tours, workshops for adults and children, gallery talks, and other activities.

From Diego Rivera refrigerator magnets to Georgia O'Keefe cards, and original jewelry and pottery by local artists, the gift shop alone is worth visiting the museum. Where else could you find Mark Harding birth announcements?

✪ Orlando Science Center. 777 E. Princeton St. (between Orange and Mills aves.), in Loch Haven Park. **☎ 407/514-2000** or **888/672-4386.** Admission for all exhibits: $8 for adults, $6 for seniors, $5.50 for children 3–11, under 3 free. For exhibits and either a CineDome film or planetarium show: $12 for adults, $11 seniors, $9.50 children 3–11. For all exhibits and both a CineDome film and planetarium show: $14 for adults, $13 for seniors, $11.50 for children 3–11. Open Mon–Thurs 9am–5pm; Fri and Sat 9am–9pm; Sun noon–5pm. Closed Thanksgiving and Christmas. Parking is available in a garage across the street from the new building and costs $3.50. Take I-4 east to exit 43 (Princeton St.), and cross Orange Ave.

Dan Rather and the CBS evening news gave America a peek at the newly renovated Orlando Science Center when it was unveiled in February 1997 after a $44-million renovation. It drew Dan's attention because the facility is the largest of its kind in the Southeast. (It probably didn't hurt that the show meant a trip to Florida in February.) Those familiar with the Orlando Science Center's previous incarnation as stepsister sharing a building with the Orange County Historical Society will be amazed at the Cinderella that has evolved. The new center provides 10 exhibit halls that allow visitors to spend the whole day exploring everything from the swamplands of Florida to the arid plains of Mars.

One of the major additions is actually just beneath that Trojan helmet–shaped silver dome that has loomed over Orlando for months. The Dr. Phillips CineDome, a 310-seat theater, uses the latest technology to present large-format films, planetarium shows, and laser light shows

In KidsTown, little folks wander around in exhibits representing a miniature version of the big world around them. In one section is a pint-sized community including a construction site, park, and wellness center. Nearby is Science City, which includes a power plant, suspension bridge, and the Inventor's Workshop, a garagelike station for creative play. Children stopping by at 123 Math Avenue work on puzzles and play with math-based toys that teach while entertaining.

Both the Virtual Reality Theater and the New Media Living Room show the real advances that will soon become as commonplace as the once-exotic VCR.

4 Staying Active

Recreational facilities of every description abound in Walt Disney World and the surrounding area. These are especially accessible to guests at Disney-owned resorts, official hotels, and the Fort Wilderness Resort and Campground, though many other large resort hotels also offer comprehensive facilities (see details in chapter 5). The Disney facilities described here are all open to the public, no matter where you're staying. For further information about WDW recreational facilities, call ☎ **407/824-4321.**

Guests at Disney properties can inquire when making hotel reservations or at guest services/concierge desks.

BICYCLING

Bike rentals (single and multispeed bikes for adults, tandems, and children's bikes) are available from the **Bike Barn** (☎ **407/824-2742**) at Fort Wilderness Resort and Campground. Rates are $5 per hour, $12 per day; overnight rentals are $15. Both Fort Wilderness and Disney's Village Resort offer good bike trails. There are even bicycles with training wheels and baby seats. Helmets are available at no additional charge. You must be 12 to rent.

Most of the best biking, though, is done in Lake County, north of the Disney Area. *Florida Backroads* by Robert Howard (under $20 in the bookstore) offers detailed descriptions of favorite biking paths throughout Florida.

BOATING

Walt Disney World, with its many man-made lakes and lagoons, owns the nation's largest fleet of pleasure boats. At the **Walt Disney World Village Marina,** you can rent Water Sprites, canopy boats, and 20-foot pontoon boats. For information call ☎ **407/828-2204.**

The **Bike Barn** at Fort Wilderness (☎ **407/824-2742**) rents canoes ($6 per hour, $10 per day) and paddleboats ($6 per half hour, $10 per hour).You must be 12-years old to rent a boat.

See hotel facilities listings in chapter 5 for additional boating options.

FISHING

WDW offers a variety of fishing excursions on the various Disney lakes, including Bay Lake and Seven Seas Lagoon. These lakes are stocked, so you might actually catch something, but true fishermen will probably not find it a great challenge. The excursions can be arranged 2 to 14 days in advance by calling the **Walt Disney World Village Marina** (☎ **407/824-2621**). No license is required. The fee is $148.40 for up to 5 people for 2 hours; those rates include refreshments, gear, guide, and tax. Bait must be purchased.

The **Dixie Landings** and **Port Orleans** resorts offer early morning and evening sunset fishing trips for $50 per person. The price includes refreshments, guide, equipment, and artificial bait. These trips are available to non-Disney guests. To get information, call ☎ **407/939-7529.** Press "0" to avoid a lengthy menu and speak directly to an operator.

A less expensive alternative: Rent fishing poles at the **Bike Barn** (☎ **407/ 824-2742**) to fish in Fort Wilderness canals. No license is required.

FLYING

The **Flying Tigers Warbird Air Museum** offers rides in a 1934 open-cockpit barn-stormer, and hands-on dual-instruction adventures in a historic World War II fighter trainer. Call ☎ **407/933-1942** for details.

A slightly more offbeat experience is offered by **Fighter Pilots USA.** Ever dreamed of suiting up, jumping into a fighter plane, and engaging in high-speed one-on-one dogfighting? This is your chance to experience the excitement of aerial combat. Actual F-16 pilots are your instructors. To schedule a "mission," call ☎ **800/56-TOPGUN** or 407/931-4333. No license is required, only a very thick wallet. The cost is $795 per person.

See Orlando from a different perspective. Hover over tourist hot spots on a ride with **Falcon Helicopter Service.** Located at 8990 International Dr., the service offers nine different aerial tour packages ranging from $15 to $395. (You get 4 minutes for $15.) For information call ☎ **407/396-7222.**

GOLF

Walt Disney World operates five championship 18-hole, par-72 golf courses and one 9-hole, par-36 walking course. All are open to the general public and offer pro shops, equipment rentals, and instruction. For tee times and information, call ☎ **407/ 824-2270** up to 7 days in advance (up to 30 days for Disney-resort and official-property guests). Call ☎ **407/W-DISNEY** (934-7639) for information about golf packages.

Also consider calling **Golfpac** (☎ **800/327-0878** or 407/260-2288), an organiza-tion that packages golf vacations (with accommodations and other features) and pre-arranges tee times at over 40 Orlando-area courses. The further in advance you call (I'm talking months here), the better your options.

Nick Faldo, three-time winner of the British Open, shares his skills with the average duffer at the new **Faldo Golf Institute by Marriott.** The "institute," as those involved like to call it, features a 9-hole course, a 27-hole putting course, and one of the largest learning centers in the country. Prices begin at $40 for 30-minute private instruction to $195 for a half day and $950 for a 5-day swing-a-thon. You will mostly be dealing with pros trained in the Faldo method, although you may occasionally glimpse the man himself. The school is located **at Marriott's Grande Vista Resort,** 11301 Inter-national Dr., Orlando, FL 32821 (☎ **407/238-6800**).

Golf magazine recognized the 45-holes designed by Jack Nicklaus at **Grand Cypress Resort** among the best in the nation. Tee times begin at 8am daily. Special rates avail-able for children under 18. For information call ☎ **407/239-1909.** The course is gen-erally restricted to guests or guests of guests, but there is limited play available to those not staying at the resort. Those fees begin at $200.

HAYRIDES

The hay wagon departs from **Pioneer Hall** at Fort Wilderness nightly at 7 and 9:15pm for hour-long, old-fashioned hayrides with singing, jokes, and games. Cost is $6 for adults, $4 for children ages 3 to 10, free for children under 3. Children under 12 must be accompanied by an adult. No reservations; it's first-come, first-served.

Hot Links: Orlando's Top Golf Courses

Like most of Florida, Orlando is a golfer's paradise, with 123 courses within a 45-minute drive of downtown . . . courses designed by Arnold Palmer, Jack Nicklaus, Tom Fazio, Pete Dye, Robert Trent Jones, and other major players. Its most famous courses include the following:

- The legendary Arnold Palmer's **Bay Hill Club,** 9000 Bay Hill Blvd. ☎ **800/523-5999** or 407/876-2429. Its 18th hole, nicknamed the Devil's Bathtub, is supposed to be the toughest par-4 on the tour. Site of the Bay Hill Invitational.
- **Falcon's Fire Golf Club,** 3200 Seralago Blvd., in Kissimmee. ☎ **407/239-5445.** A challenging Ree Jones course with 136 bunkers and water on 10 holes.
- **Walt Disney Resorts** facilities (see details earlier) comprising 99 holes. Their most famous hazard is a sand trap on Magnolia Course's 6th hole in the shape of Mickey Mouse.

Also notable are two beautifully landscaped facilities: the award-winning 45-hole/par-72 Jack Nicklaus–designed course at the **Villas of Grand Cypress** (☎ **800/835-7377** or 407/239-4700) and the 18-hole/par-71 Joe Lee–designed championship course at **Marriott's Orlando World Center** (☎ **800/621-0638** or 407/239-4200). See details on both properties in chapter 5.

HORSEBACK RIDING

Disney's Fort Wilderness Resort and Campground offers 45-minute scenic guided-tour trail rides daily, with four to six rides per day. Cost is $23 per person. Children must be at least 9 years old. Maximum weight limit is 250 pounds. For information and reservations up to 30 days in advance, call ☎ **407/824-2832.**

The **Grand Cypress Resort** opens its equestrian center to outsiders. Trail rides, about 50 minutes, are $30. A 30-minute private lesson is $45. For information call ☎ **407/239-4700**. Ask for the equestrian center.

ICE-SKATING

Rock on Ice! Skating Arena, in the Dowdy Pavilion, 7500 Canada Ave., between Sand Lake Road and Carrier Drive (☎ **407/352-9878**), is a gorgeous, Olympic-size indoor rink with high-tech lighting and sound systems. A DJ spins Top 40 tunes. There are ice-skating games with prizes throughout the day. Facilities include video games, a snack bar, and a complete skate shop offering a large selection of figure-skating and hockey equipment. Rental skates are $2. Admission is $4.50 to $6, depending on the season. Hours vary seasonally; call ahead.

To get here from the Disney World area, take International Drive north, turn right at Sand Lake Road and left on Canada Avenue. It's about a 10-minute drive.

JOGGING

Many of the Disney resorts have scenic jogging trails. For instance, the **Yacht** and **Beach Club** resorts share a 2-mile trail, the **Disney Institute** has a 3.4-mile course with 32 exercise stations, the **Caribbean Beach Resort's** 1.4-mile promenade circles a lake, **Dixie Landings** has a 1.7-mile riverfront trail, and **Fort Wilderness's** tree-shaded 2.3-mile jogging path has exercise stations about every quarter mile. Pick up a jogging trail map at any Disney property's guest-services desk.

SWIMMING

The **YMCA Aquatic Center,** 8422 International Dr. Take I-4 to exit 29. Turn right at the end of the ramp. Turn right on International Drive. Turn right at second light. This YMCA has a full-fitness center, racquetball courts and an indoor Olympic-sized pool. $10 for individuals, both children and adults; $15 for families. For information call ☎ **407/363-1911.**

SWIMMING WITH THE MANATEES

An organization called **Oceanic Society Expeditions** (☎ **800/326-7491** or 415/441-1106) offers a "Swim with the Manatees" program in the Crystal River area, 2 hours east of Orlando. A manatee biologist leads 5-day Monday-to-Friday trips aboard a 12-person skiff. The program includes swimming with manatees, bird watching, snorkeling, slide presentations, and an excursion to a facility for the care of injured and orphaned wildlife. Cost is $985, including accommodations, excursions, and most meals. Reserve as far in advance as possible.

TENNIS

Seventeen lighted tennis courts are located throughout the Disney properties. Most are free and available on a first-come, first-served basis. If you're willing to pay, courts can be reserved up to several months in advance at two Disney resorts: the **Contemporary** (☎ **407/824-3578**) and the **Grand Floridian** (☎ **407/824-2435**). Both charge $12 per hour; you can also reserve lesson times with resident pros. The Contemporary offers a large pro shop, a ball machine, rebound walls, and equipment rentals.

WATERSKIING

Waterskiing trips (including boats, drivers, equipment, and instruction) can be arranged at **Walt Disney World** by calling ☎ **407/824-2621.** Make reservations up to 14 days in advance. Cost is $82 per hour for up to 5 people.

You can get some time behind a boat at **Ski World** near downtown Orlando. Lessons are $25 for 20 minutes. For information call ☎ **407/894-5012**. To get there take I-4 to Downtown, then exit 43, Princeton Street. Turn right at the bottom of the ramp. Turn right at the first light. About a mile on your left. The lake will be on your right.

5 Spectator Sports

Disney doesn't want to give the competition a sporting chance. In May 1997, it branched out with a multimillion-dollar **Disney's Wide World of Sports Complex,** a 200-acre facility. The Mouse hopes to hit a home run with a 7,500-seat baseball stadium that will be home to perpetual almost–World Champs, the Atlanta Braves. The Braves began a 3-year stay in 1998. In addition, there is a 5,000-seat field house featuring six basketball courts, a fitness center, and training rooms; major-league practice fields and pitcher mounds; four softball fields; 12 tennis courts, including a 2,000-seat stadium center court; a track-and-field complex; a golf driving range; and much more. A variety of sporting events from tennis tournaments to band competitions have been held there since the center opened. For information about events during your stay, call ☎ **407/363-6262** or 407/363-6100.

The NFL Experience

Even if your days of gridiron glory have long faded, or never actually materialized, you can practice like the big, really big, guys of the NFL at this attraction located at Disney's Wide World of Sports.

There are 10 drills here that test your running, punting, passing, and receiving skills. Among other activities, you can dodge cardboard defensemen to run a pass pattern while a machine shoots you a pass. (A much safer way than actually risking life and limbs.) Depending on your stamina, interest and the size of the crowds, the NFL Experience can last anywhere from 45 minutes to several hours.

Football fans know that a similar traveling exhibit is usually set up in Super Bowl cities during the Big Game. This is the first time a permanent exhibit has been put into place. Kids, and weekend warriors, will love this chance to grapple with the pigskin. Plus, at $8 for adults and $6.75 for children 10 and under, the price is right. For information call ☎ **407/939-1500.** No reservations are needed.

If you are true sports fan, you would be well advised to write and get a package of information about facilities and a calendar of events at **Disney's Wide World of Sports.** Write to Disney's Wide World of Sports, P.O. Box 10,000, Lake Buena Vista, FL 32830-1000, or call ☎ **407/363-6600.**

There are three major sporting arenas in downtown Orlando: the **Florida Citrus Bowl,** the **Orlando Arena,** and **Tinker Field,** which together host six major sporting teams.

ARENA FOOTBALL

Orlando is home to the **Orlando Predators,** who play from April until August. For the uninitiated, arena football is an indoor cross between rugby and football played by 8-man teams on a much-abbreviated field. You don't necessarily need to know the rules to enjoy the up-close crunching and beer-fest atmosphere. The Predators are the Buffalo Bills of arena football, coming close but never quite winning a championship. They have a loyal and rowdy following. Sold-out games are common, but single tickets are often available the day of the game at the Orlando Arena box office. For information call ☎ **407/648-4444.**

BASEBALL

From April to September, the **Orlando Rays**—the Tampa Devil Rays' Class AA Southern league affiliate—play at Tinker Field, 287 S. Tampa Ave., between Colonial Drive (Highway 50) and Gore Street. Call ☎ **407/649-7297** for information and to charge tickets. Tickets are $3 to $7. To get there, take I-4 east to the East-West Expressway and head west to Highway 441. Make a left on Church Street and follow the signs. Tinker Field adjoins the Citrus Bowl. Parking is $2.

The **Atlanta Braves** began Spring Training at Disney's Wide World of Sports Complex in 1998. A 3-year contract ensures play through 2001. There are about 18 games during the 1-month season. Tickets are $10.50 and $13.50. For information call ☎ **407/363-6600.** You can get tickets through **TicketMaster** (☎ **407/839-3900**), or they can be purchased at the Wide World of Sports Complex in person.

BASKETBALL

The 17,500-seat Orlando Arena (the "O-rena"), 600 W. Amelia St., between I-4 and Parramore Avenue (☎ **407/896-2442** for information, 407/839-3900 to charge tickets), is home to the **Orlando Magic** during their October-to-April season. Some of the Magic dimmed when the team was left by star center (and marketing phenomenon) Shaquille O'Neal, but it's still the NBA and, unless he's jumped ship for a better deal, we still have Penny Hardaway. Tickets to games (about $13 to $50) have to be acquired far in advance; they usually sell out by September before the season starts. Several hundred individual seats, sometimes in the nosebleed sections, can often be obtained before games against some of the league's lesser-known teams, like the Timberwolves.

To get there, take I-4 east to Amelia Avenue, turn left at the traffic light at the bottom of the off-ramp, and follow signs. For up-to-the-minute parking information, turn your car radio to 1620 AM.

FOOTBALL

The Florida Citrus Bowl, 1 Citrus Bowl Place, at West Church and Tampa streets (☎ **407/473-2476** for information, 407/839-3900 to charge tickets), hosts the annual **CompUSA Florida Citrus Bowl** game, college football games, and NFL preseason games. Tickets to all football events are hard to come by, but you may have some luck if you try far enough in advance. To get there, take I-4 east to the East-West Expressway and head west to Highway 441. Make a left on Church Street, and follow the signs. Parking is $5.

HOCKEY

Ice Hockey? Orlando? Well, sure, why not? There is an ice rink under the floor at the downtown Orlando Arena; the regular floor is replaced for Orlando Magic games. An International Hockey League team, the **Orlando Solar Bears,** plays from October through April, longer if they do well in the playoffs. Ticket prices are a professional sports bargain beginning at $6 and topping out at $26 for prime lower-bowl seats. For information call ☎ **407/872-7825.**

JAI ALAI

Orlando Jai Alai, 6405 S. U.S. 17/92, at S.R. 436 in Fern Park (☎ **407/339-6221**), offers the action-packed Basque sport of jai alai (it's the world's fastest game). On a 180-foot court with three walls, the ball is hurled at speeds of up to 150 miles an hour from baskets strapped to the players' wrists, and the object of the game is to throw the ball with such force, spin, and/or placement that the opponent is unable to return it before it bounces twice. A score of seven points wins. There are two opposing singles or doubles teams on the court at all times.

Your program offers extensive information about how the game is played and how to wager, and the public-address announcer explains what is happening on the court.

Best bet is to watch the action from the moderately priced, and very attractive, open-air Terrace Restaurant, with some tables as close as 20 feet from the court. There's a color TV monitor at every table. Fare is American/continental; there's a full bar; reservations are suggested. Children 39 inches and taller are admitted into the fronton with parents, but are not allowed in the betting area.

Note: The fronton also features intertrack wagering; you can place bets here on thoroughbred and harness races as well as Miami jai alai.

Admission is $1, reserved seats are $2, restaurant seating is $3, and box seats are $3 to $5. Seniors 55 and older get free admission to matinees. Parking is free; valet parking is $1.50. Open year-round Wednesday to Sunday. Evening games are held at 7:30pm Wednesday to Saturday; matinees at noon Thursday and Saturday and at 1pm Sunday. From the Walt Disney World area, take I-4 east, make a right at exit 47A (Maitland Exchange), a right at U.S. 17/92, and look for the fronton 2 miles along on your right. It's about a 40-minute drive.

9

Shopping

What is a vacation without a little shopping . . . okay, without a lot of shopping. Not only do you really *need* a few extra (bags of) souvenirs, who knows what native Florida treasures you may find?

Of course, the theme parks carry just about everything you can imagine embossed with their name. (Even quite a few things you'd never imagine.) And, we all know, you are really paying more than you should. When searching for deals at home, do you hightail it to the tourist areas? I didn't think so. Although I'm not knocking the staggering number of ways Mickey Mouse can be merchandised, there are plenty of other places to shop and plenty of things to purchase in Orlando that don't carry the initials M.M. (although as Mary Meehan, it works to *my* advantage). The shopping opportunities at the theme parks are outlined in chapters 7 and 8.

Get out and explore some of them, especially if you're making a repeat visit to the theme parks or your first trip to the United States.

One word of advice: If you are traveling during the Christmas holiday season, from the end of November to December 25, it is best to avoid local shopping malls on the weekends.

Most stores are open from 9 or 10am until 9 or 10pm Monday through Saturday and from 10am to 6pm on Sunday.

1 Orlando-Area Malls

FACTORY OUTLETS

Belz Factory Outlet World. 5401 W. Oak Ridge Rd. (at the north end of International Dr.). ☎ **407/354-0126** or 407/352-9600.

This is the largest of the factory outlet centers in town, with 180 stores in two huge, enclosed malls and four shopping annexes. It offers an immense range of merchandise at savings up to 75% off retail prices. There's even an old-fashioned carousel for the kids (and adults).

At its emporia: 18 shoe stores (including Bass, Bally, and Capezio); 14 housewares shops (including Fieldcrest/Cannon, Corning, Oneida, and Mikasa); and more than 60 clothing shops for men, women, and children (including London Fog, Van Heusen, Jonathan Logan, Guess Jeans, Aileen, Danskin, Jordache, Leslie Fay, Carole Little, Harvé Benard, Calvin Klein, and Anne Klein). You can also shop for books and records, electronics, sporting goods, health and beauty aids, jewelry, toys, gifts, accessories, lingerie, and hosiery here.

Tip: There is a lot of great shopping here, but don't kill yourself trying to get to every building. Many of the manufacturers have more than one location, with much the same selection, within the complex. Also, unless you are from out of the country, most of the brand sportswear stores, such as Nike and Reebok, don't offer much of a deal, especially on shoes.

Quality Outlet Center. 5527 International Dr. (1 block east of Kirkman Rd.). ☎ **407/ 423-5885.**

About 20 outlets, including Arrow, American Tourister, Corning-Revere (glassware and cookware), Florsheim shoes, Magnavox, Laura Ashley, Adidas, Great Western Boots, Totes, Le Creuset (cookware), Linens 'n' Things, Mikasa, Royal Doulton, and Villeroy & Boch. Once again, big savings.

Continuing a quarter of a mile north on International Drive, you'll come to the International Drive Value Center, under the same auspices as the Quality Outlet Center (same phone, same hours). Its 15 stores include T.J. Maxx; other women's clothing stores; Old Navy Clothing Company (a Gap concept); Lane Bryant; Linea Garbo (Italian shoes); Converse; Perfumania; Books A Million; and Bed, Bath & Beyond.

Manufacturer's Outlet Mall. (U.S. 192, a mile east of Fla. 535 in Kissimmee). ☎ **407/ 396-8900.**

You'll find about 35 stores here, including Van Heusen, Bugle Boy, Fieldcrest/Cannon, Bass Apparel, Westport (women's fashions), and Acme Boot.

INTERNATIONAL DRIVE–AREA MALLS

The Mercado. 8445 International Dr. (south of Sand Lake Rd.). ☎ **407/345-9337.**

A Mediterranean-style shopping center with brick and cobblestone streets, terra-cotta–roofed buildings, brightly colored awnings, and splashing fountains is home to the Orlando/Orange County Visitor Information Center. A video-game arcade here keeps the kids amused while you shop, and there's live entertainment evenings (jazz, country rock, and reggae bands) in the central courtyard.

More than 60 specialty shops include Swings 'N' Things (everything from hammocks to wind chimes), Kandlestix (handcrafted candles), American Cola Company (Coca-Cola and Anheuser-Busch memorabilia), House of Ireland (china, crystal, claddagh jewelry), Historic Families (find your family's coat of arms), Earth Matters (conservation/ecology-themed merchandise), Lady Bug (needlecrafts), The Magic Shop (novelties, tricks, and pranks), and The Looking Glass (blown glass). It makes good browsing, and there are over a dozen restaurants and bars on the premises.

Stop by Guest Services to get a free "Privilege Card" for discounts at mall stores. Guest Services also offers airline ticketing, discounted attraction tickets (including Disney parks), car rental, help with accommodations, and more.

SUBURBAN MALLS

Florida Mall. 8001 S. Orange Blossom Trail (at Sand Lake Rd.). ☎ **407/851-6255.**

Aside from Saks Fifth Avenue, the more than 200 shops, restaurants, and services here are those in your basic massive American shopping mall. The Florida Mall is a little unusual because of the 500-room Sheraton Hotel plopped in its center. Anchored by six department stores—Saks Fifth Avenue, two Dillard's stores, JCPenney, Gayfers, and Sears—the mall has more than 10 jewelry shops, about 50 clothing and accessory shops (including mall regulars such as Benetton, Warner Bros. Studio Store, Gap/ Gap Kids, The Limited, and Victoria's Secret), over a dozen shoe stores, bookstores, electronics stores, eateries (among them, a food court), and much, much more.

Going Upscale

Orlando, dubbed by city founders as "The City Beautiful," is beginning to attract more upscale retailers catering to the beautiful people.

Saks Fifth Avenue, Versace, and FAO Schwarz aren't exactly names usually associated with the cow-town Orlando once was, but all three have opened in the last few years. Saks Fifth Avenue, one of the nation's premier retailers, carries a variety of exclusive designer labels. It opened in the Florida Mall in late 1996 and, although there were plenty of people predicting it would fail, expanded in early 1998. With only 4,200 square feet of space, Saks is much smaller than the mall's main department store, which is 105,000 square feet, but there's still plenty of shopping and gawking.

FAO Schwarz, which some call the Saks Fifth Avenue of the toy business, opened its 35,600-square-foot flagship store in 1997. With a huge three-story Raggedy Ann and Teddy Bear adorning the outside, this store on International Drive is hard to miss. Inside, toys are stacked to the ceiling, and there's even a copy of those 3-foot piano keys that Tom Hanks danced upon in the movie *Big*. Just so you don't have to worry about explaining that awkwardly shaped carry-on package, you can arrange to mail your purchases home for an additional fee.

FAO Schwartz is part of a development called **Pointe Orlando,** located at the corner of International and Republic drives along the I-Drive tourist corridor, across from the Orlando/Orange County Convention Center.

After much negotiation, Pointe Orlando also landed a Versace boutique that will showcase the line produced by the late Italian fashion designer's company. It is one of the first boutiques opened outside of New York.

Crossroads of Lake Buena Vista. Exit 27 off I-4. ☎ **407/827-7300.**

Anchored by a 24-hour Goodings supermarket with a full-service pharmacy, this shopping center also features sportswear, electronics, books, cards, gifts, shoes, and Disney merchandise. There's also a post office. Restaurants/fast-food outlets include, among others, T.G.I. Friday's, Johnny Rockets, Pebbles (see chapter 6), Pizzeria Uno, and Red Lobster. It's just like a shopping center in the real world.

Orlando Fashion Square Mall. 3201 E. Colonial Dr. ☎ **407/896-1131.** Take I-4 east to exit 41, the Colonial Dr./Hwy. 50 exit. Take Colonial about 3 miles east; the main entrance is just past Maquire Blvd.

This mall underwent a major renovation in the mid-1990s, and with marblelike walkways, indoor palm trees, and high ceilings, it's a comfortable place to shop. Major stores include Burdines, Gayfers, JC Penney, and Sears. There are 165 stores, plus an extensive food court. You'll also find several arcades for the kiddies, and there are two multiplex theaters nearby. Easily accessible, the mall is about 5 miles from downtown Orlando.

Altamonte Mall. 451 E. Altamonte Dr. (about 15 miles north of downtown Orlando). ☎ **407/830-4400.**

Disney brought new life to Orlando, and this mall brought new life to the little one-stoplight town of Altamonte Springs. The mall, built in the early 1970s, underwent a major renovation in 1989 and added a food court in 1990. It is the area's second largest mall, just behind the newly expanded Florida Mall. It includes major department stores such as Gayfers, Burdines, and JC Penney as well as 175 specialty shops. This multilevel mall has a light, airy feel, and benches and indoor palm trees make for a relaxing atmosphere (except during the Christmas holiday shopping rush).

2 Other Shopping in Orlando

IN DOWNTOWN ORLANDO

If you can think of nothing better than a relaxing afternoon of bargain hunting or scouring thrift and antiques shops, check out **Antique Row** in downtown Orlando. This collection of two dozen shops and a couple of restaurants is about as far away as you can get from the manufactured fun of Disney. The shops are an interesting assortment of the old, the new, and the unusual.

Stores such as **Fee Fi Faux** offer colorful, hand-painted furniture or other funky, original works of art. **Flo's Attic, Inc.** and **Pieces of Eight Emporium** sell more-traditional antiques.

Down the road is a handful of shops selling upscale clothing, cigars, or traditional works of art such as wildlife sculptures. **Art's Cigars** is a two-story leather-and-tweed kind of place where patrons are encouraged to light up and enjoy the view of Lake Ivanhoe across the street. **Wildlife Gallery** sells pricey, original works of wildlife art, including sculpture.

The Fly Fisherman sells—guess what?—fly-fishing equipment. You can sometimes see people taking lessons in the park across the street.

All these stores are spread out for about 3 miles along Orange Avenue. The heaviest concentration is along Orange Avenue between Princeton Street and New Hampshire Avenue, although Fee Fi Faux and a few others are scattered between New Hampshire and Virginia avenues. The more upscale shops extend a few blocks beyond Virginia. To get there from the theme parks, take I-4 east to Princeton Street (exit 43). Turn right on Orange Avenue. Parking is limited, so stop wherever you find a space along the street.

These downtown shops are usually open from about 8am to 6pm, Monday to Saturday. (The owners usually run these shops, so hours can vary. A small number of stores are open on Sunday, but it is probably not worth the trip from the resort areas just to shop.)

Built in an ornate Victorian style with hardwood oak floors and hand-painted tin ceilings, **The Exchange Shopping Emporium** is part of Church Street Station. The Exchange offers 50 specialty shops spread over several floors. Although there are some American mall standards such as **Victoria's Secret,** most stores offer more unusual wares. Places to visit include **Black Market Minerals,** which sells an infinite variety of things made from stone—polished semiprecious gems and beads and even big slabs of quartz in a variety of colors. **The Gothic Shop** sells everything plaster, concentrating on angel figures, gargoyles, and Greek and Roman images. **Udderly Country**—you guess the theme.

Just across the tracks is **Church Street Market,** a collection of another 30 shops and restaurants. The Market includes **Behr's Chocolates,** which sells a variety of home-made confections, along with retailers like **Hit or Miss,** a woman's clothing store, and **Brookstone,** an upscale shop specializing in electronic equipment like massage chairs and computerized toys of all sorts. All of the merchandise is on display for you to play with, um, try out. Restaurants include **The Olive Garden, Pizzeria Uno,** and **Hooter's,** a restaurant known for scantily clad, shapely waitresses serving up hot wings, curly fries, and suds. (The name, company officials claim with a straight face, in no way refers to a slang term for a certain part of the female anatomy.)

To get to the shopping complexes from the attractions, take I-4 east to downtown Orlando. Get off at Anderson Street (exit 38). Turn left on Boone Avenue, then left on South Street. Turn right on Garland Avenue. Parking is available in a city-owned lot between South Street and Garland Avenue. Note your parking space and pay at the machines located at the end of the lot.

A FLEA MARKET

Flea World. U.S. 17/92 in Sanford. ☎ **407/321-1792.** Take I-4 to exit 50, Lake Mary Blvd. Go about 3 miles to U.S. 17/92 and turn left. Continue for about 1 mile. Flea World will be on your right.

The largest flea market in the world, that's what you'll find in Sanford, about 40 minutes north of the attractions. Flea World is pretty much exactly what the name implies, a huge flea market with everything from dentists' and lawyers' offices to lingerie and lamps. Although some folks have affectionately called the place the "white-trash mall," the politically correct term would be "economically challenged shopping emporium." Car tires, plants, ginsu knives, gourmet coffee, fresh produce, leather chaps . . . the array of merchandise is impressive even if the surroundings aren't. Unlike flea markets in some regions, this one sells mostly new merchandise in its nearly 2,000 booths. (A couple of folks set up booths to sell old auto parts or garage-style finds.) Among this babble of bargains are many shops selling Florida T-shirts and souvenir-worthy knick-knacks. Entertainment as diverse as live demonstrations by lions and tigers to Elvis impersonators and bingo games is regularly featured on the Flea World stage.

Nearby **Fun World** offers miniature golf courses, a miniature race track with gas-powered cars for the kiddies, a video arcade, and a small collection of carnival rides.

Although it is about 40 minutes from the theme parks, Flea World is more American than apple pie and a good place for bargains. *Be warned:* Some of the barnlike buildings are not air-conditioned, so this is not the best place to shop in the hot summer months.

A MORE HOMESPUN ALTERNATIVE

Mount Dora is a haven for artists and retirees and a wonderful day trip, not to mention a wonderful alternative to Disney. (Parents: Put the kids in one of the day-long camp programs—see chapter 2—and take a day to yourselves.) Mount Dora, established in 1874, has the genuine feel of an old Florida town with an authentic Main Street—like the one Disney tries to re-create. The 19th-century buildings still lining the streets are a perfect postcard picture leading up to the calm dark-green waters of Lake Dora. Unlike most of Florida, this town actually has rolling hills, adding to the charm.

Stroll through the dozens of shops featuring crafts, art, antiques, and collectibles and then take a break with lunch at the Beauclair Dining Room at the historic Lake-side Inn. Enjoy lemonade and cookies while rocking on the front porch overlooking the lake.

For information call the Mount Dora Area Chamber of Commerce ☎ **352/383-2165.**

To get there, take I-4 to U.S. 441 and go west. Take Old U.S. 441 or Route 44B into town. Look for signs directing you to the "business district."

SPORTS STORES

Magic FanAttic. 301 W. Colonial Dr. ☎ **407/649-2222.** Take I-4 east to exit 41 (Amelia St.). Stay to the right as the road goes around the bend. At the next light, turn left. Go under the freeway overpass.

Sports fans aching to add to their collection can tackle that shopping obsession at several stores specializing in merchandise for the Orlando Magic, the University of Florida Gators, and the Florida State University Seminoles.

There are four locations of the Magic FanAttic, which sells every conceivable item embossed with the logo of the NBA's Orlando Magic. From lamps to alarm clocks to jerseys from the Magic's most popular player, "Penny" Hardaway, the FanAttic delivers. There are even talking "Lil Penny" dolls made famous in Nike television commercials. (The store also carries merchandise featuring the cool images of the shades-wearing polar-bear mascot of Orlando's ice-hockey team, the Solar Bears. (Yes, I said ice hockey.)

The large silver building is on the right. The store is open daily from 10am to 6pm. Other locations are in the Renaissance Center near the Altamonte Mall (described earlier), at the Orlando International Airport, and in the West Oaks Mall in Ocoee.

Gatorstuff. 1021 E. Colonial Dr., Orlando. ☎ **407/898-2129.**

The name gives you a strong hint as to what is sold here.

University Store. 1406 N. Mills Ave. ☎ **407/896-9391.** Take I-4 to Princeton St. (exit 43). Turn right on Orange Ave. Turn left at Virginia Ave. The store is on the left at the corner of Mills and Virginia aves. There is a Seminole Indian rasslin' a gator painted on the wall. Open from Mon–Fri 10am–6pm; Sat 10am–4pm.

It's a wonder they can keep the peace among the rabid University of Florida and Florida State University fans at this location. But there is a selection of merchandise from both schools in addition to some stuff from the up-and-coming University of Florida Golden Knights. (They have had their first player arrested in the scandal, so they've officially made the big time.)

10

Walt Disney World & Orlando After Dark

The opening of Universal's nighttime entertainment complex, **City-Walk,** shows that people in charge seem to feel visitors need more places to go after a long day of schlepping around the theme parks.

Disney also expanded its nighttime options this year by opening a second set of restaurants and clubs called **Disney's West Side.** Together with Pleasure Island, Disney is promoting this area as Downtown Disney. But, don't be fooled, this is not Orlando's downtown. It is 25 miles or so up the road and has its own collection of bars, clubs, and restaurants.

My hat's off to those of you who after a long day traipsing around amusement parks still have the energy to venture out at night in search of entertainment. You'll find plenty to do. And this being a kid's world, many of the theme-park evening shows are geared to families. There is, however, plenty of adults-only entertainment both at the parks and beyond in downtown Orlando.

Check the "Calendar" section of Friday's *Orlando Sentinel* for up-to-the-minute details on local clubs, visiting performers, concerts, and events. Also check out the *Orlando Sentinel Online* at **www.oso@aol.com**. It has hundreds of listings. The *Orlando Weekly* is a free magazine circulated in boxes throughout Central Florida that highlights more offbeat and often more up-to-date performers and performances.

Tickets to many performances are handled by **TicketMaster** (☎ **407/839-3900** to charge tickets for a fee).

1 What's New in 1999 (& What's in the Works)

This figures to be a big year for nightlife in Orlando as Disney and Universal begin to compete head-to-head, with Disney adding Disney's West Side to the bars and clubs at Pleasure Island and Universal opening CityWalk. Plus, bars and clubs in downtown Orlando continue to flourish, offering locals and tourists something to do in addition to Church Street Station.

The **House of Blues,** which opened in late 1997, has attracted an eclectic mix of artists to perform. Groups as diverse as KC and the Sunshine Band and rappers have held forth here. That's good news for tourists who want to see a rockin' live act in a reasonably intimate setting. The barnlike building is filled with colorful funky folk art (who knew there were so many uses for bottle caps?), and features a restaurant next door with a New Orleans–style menu. Just down the Disney block is **Bongo's Cuban Cafe,** created by Gloria Estefan and her husband Emilio, which, like its popular Miami Beach sister club, features sizzling Latin American rhythms. There is also a massive, 24-screen multiplex **AMC Theatres,** the largest such complex in the state. Also coming is **Cirque Du Soleil,** a 1,650-seat theater in the Pleasure Island entertainment district. The unique venue will feature circus-style performances that have been very popular in Montréal, New York City, Las Vegas, and Berlin. The **Wildhorse Saloon,** styled on the one featured on cable television, is also scheduled to come to Disney's West Side.

In late 1998 Universal Studios Florida opens a multibillion-dollar expansion that will include a dynamic, high-energy 12-acre entertainment complex called **CityWalk.** Occupying a two-tiered promenade with authentic streetscapes, a 4-acre lagoon, waterfalls, and lush landscaping, CityWalk could easily be renamed theme-restaurant heaven. Not only is it home to the world's largest **Hard Rock Cafe**—the grande dame of all theme restaurants—but also the **NASCAR Cafe,** the **Motown Cafe,** and **Marvel Mania,** a theme send-up to villains and superheroes. CityWalk will also contain a hearty dose of Cajun spice with **Pat O'Brien's,** a re-creation of the joint in New Orleans, and **Emeril's of New Orleans,** featuring the Creole-based cuisine of chef Emeril Lagasse. If that's not enough to keep you busy, there is the **Down Beat Jazz Hall of Fame,** a tribute to *reggae mon* Bob Marley, and a 16-screen, 5,000-seat **Cineplex Odeon Megaplex** with a cutting-edge projection and sound system. Finally, there will be a floating outdoor theater to be used for special shows and concerts.

2 Walt Disney World Dinner Shows

Two distinctly different dinner shows are hosted by Walt Disney World: Hoop-Dee-Doo Musical Revue and Polynesian Luau Dinner Show. These two shows are located on the map "Dining in Walt Disney World & Lake Buena Vista" in chapter 6. However, there are other nighttime park shows if a dinner show isn't in your evening intinerary. These include SpectroMagic, fireworks, and IllumiNations (details in chapter 7).

Hoop-Dee-Doo Musical Revue. 3520 N. Fort Wilderness Trail (at Disney's Fort Wilderness Resort and Campground). ☎ **407/WDW-DINE** (939-3463). Reservations required. Adults $37, children 3–11 $19.50. Taxes and gratuities extra. Show times at 5, 7:15, and 9:30pm nightly. Free self-parking.

Fort Wilderness's rustic log-beamed Pioneer Hall is the setting for this 2-hour foot-stompin', hand-clappin', down-home musical revue. It's a high-energy show, with 1890s costumes, corny vaudeville jokes, rousing songs, and lots of good-natured audience participation.

During the show, the audience chows down on an all-you-can-eat barbecue dinner, including chips and salsa, salad, smoked ribs, country-fried chicken, corn on the cob, baked beans, loaves of fresh-baked bread with honey butter, and a big slab of strawberry shortcake for dessert. Beverages (coffee, tea, beer, sangria, and soda) are included.

Reservations are required. If you catch an early show, stick around for the Electrical Water Pageant at 9:45pm, which can be viewed from the Fort Wilderness Beach.

Polynesian Luau Dinner Show. 1600 Seven Seas Dr. (at Disney's Polynesian Resort). ☎ **407/WDW-DINE** (939-3463). Reservations required. Adults $37, children 3–11 $19.50. Taxes and gratuities are extra. Show times 6:45 and 9:30pm nightly. Free self- and valet parking.

This delightful 2-hour dinner show is a big favorite with kids, who are all invited up on the stage. It features a colorfully costumed cast of entertainers from New Zealand, Tahiti, Hawaii, and Samoa performing authentic hula, warrior, ceremonial, love, and fire dances on a flower-bedecked stage. The show also includes a Hawaiian/Polynesian fashion show.

It all takes place in an open-air theater (dress for nighttime weather) with candlelit tables, red-flame lanterns suggesting torches, and tapa-bark paintings adorning the walls. Arrive early; there's a preshow highlighting Polynesian crafts and culture (lei making, hula lessons, and more).

The all-you-can-eat meal includes a big platter of fresh island fruits, barbecued chicken, corn on the cob, other vegetables, roasted red potatoes and sweet potatoes, pull-apart cinnamon bread, beverages, and a tropical ice-cream sundae.

Reservations are required. There's also a 4:30pm version daily called **Mickey's Tropical Luau** (see character-meal listings in chapter 6).

3 More Dinner Shows

American Gladiators Orlando Live!. Gladiator Arena, 5515 W. Irlo Bronson Memorial Hwy. (U.S. 192, between I-4 and Fla. 535), Kissimmee. ☎ **800/BATTLE-4** or 407/390-0000. Reservations recommended. Adults $19.95, children 2–12 $14.50. Daily 7:30pm (doors open at 6:30pm). Free parking.

This 90-minute, action-packed dinner show features qualified contenders battling in areas such as assault, breakthrough and conquer, joust, powerball, the wall, and whiplash. If you don't know what all that means, watch it on TV before you decide whether or not it's your thing.

Arabian Nights. 6225 W. Irlo Bronson Memorial Hwy. (or U.S. Hwy. 192, just east of I-4 at exit 25A), Kissimmee. ☎ **800/553-6116** or 407/239-9223. Reservations recommended. Admission $36.95 adults, $23.95 children 3–11. Shows nightly at 7:30pm. Free parking.

Entering its 11th year, Arabian Nights offers a little bit of everything from prancing Royal Lipizzaner Stallions to chariot races. The 2-hour show claims to have more characters, costumes, and lights than any show on Broadway. You certainly won't find the "land of the mythical unicorn" on the Great White Way.

The menu includes salad, prime rib, vegetables, new potatoes, dinner rolls, dessert, and beer, wine, and soft drinks. The price of admission covers the cost of the dinner and the show.

King Henry's Feast. 8984 International Dr. ☎ **800/883-8181** or **407/351-5151**. Admission $36.95 adults, $22.50 children 3–11, under 3 free. Free Parking.

This jousting festival takes place in a 14,000-square-foot replica of a 16th-century English Tudor castle. Long wooden tables are set with pewter plates, and you drink out of heavy goblets and tankards. The 2-hour feast includes an all-you-can-eat four-course meal with beer, wine, or soda. A cast of 12 performers entertains with fire-breathing and even trapeze acts, while strolling minstrels perform throughout the evening. It's a fun frolic, although the food is nothing to write home about, and the show is not as big and dramatic as the one at Medieval Times. But then again how often, in these politically correct days, can you get away with calling someone a wench?

Medieval Times. 4510 W. Irlo Bronson Memorial Hwy. (or U.S. Hwy. 192, 11 miles east of the main Disney entrance, next to Super Wal-Mart) in Kissimmee. ☎ **800/229-8300** or 407/239-0214. Reservations recommended. Admission $36.95 adults, $22.95 children 3–12. Daily at 8pm. Free parking.

Blazing Pianos: A Perfect Hell for the Shy

A rambunctious crowd of all ages hangs out at this popular sing-along club, where talented singers and musicians—on fire-engine–red grand pianos—perform classic rock tunes, do a bit of comedy, and try to embarrass audience members. Most of the songs they select are on the lively side—"Great Balls of Fire," "The Twist," "Jailhouse Rock," and the like, as well as TV theme songs.

Audience members occasionally get up on the stage—or are dragooned there—to dance. And probably once a night everyone stands up to perform "Hand Jive." Blazing Pianos promotes audience participation to the max; it's an exhibitionist's paradise, and perhaps unbearable for the sensitive (you might be spotlighted if they see you're not singing!). The ambience is slick and upscale; special effects include smoke, mirror balls, and strobe lights. A fairly extensive bar menu has items such as fried calamari and buffalo wings, plus gourmet desserts.

Blazing Pianos is located in the **Mercado** at 8445 International Blvd., just south of Sand Lake Road (☎ **407/363-5104**).

Admission is $5. Though it opens earlier, the action begins about 9:30pm and continues until 2am nightly. No one under 21 is admitted weekend nights. Sunday through Thursday, children are welcome, and it makes for a fun family outing.

Jim Carrey fans know that the Cable Guy went to a California branch of Medieval Times to duel with his hapless friend. A longtime favorite for Orlando visitors, the Kissimmee-based show is billed as "dinner and tournament." Living up to its name, it includes jousting contests, armored clashes, and 80 Andalusian stallions performing with military precision. It's all put on for you and 1,000 of the "special" guests of the castle, who eat off heavy metal plates while watching the tournament contestants tumble about before them. Dark and cavernous, Medieval Times has an ambeance all its own. The menu includes a wine cocktail, fresh-vegetable soup, a whole roasted chicken, spare ribs, herb-basted potatoes, and dessert. The price includes dinner, beverages, and the show. The castle is air-conditioned and accessible to guests with disabilities. Medieval Times is very popular, so reservations are suggested.

Wild Bill's Wild West Dinner Extravaganza. 5260 U.S. 192 (just east of I-4). ☎ **800/883-8181** or 407/351-5151. Reservations recommended. Admission $36.92 adults, $22.50 children 3–11, under 3 free. Nightly at 7pm, with 9:30pm shows on selected nights. Free parking.

Located at Fort Liberty, a 22-acre western-themed shopping/dining/entertainment complex, this rambunctious dinner show takes place in a big, barnlike wooden building. You'll be given a cardboard cowboy hat when you sit down, which identifies you as a shepherd or cowherd for audience-participation activities (there are a lot of these). The show includes rousing song-and-dance numbers ("Annie Get Your Gun," "Oklahoma," "Back in the Saddle Again"); rodeo roping, knife-throwing, and archery demonstrations; sing-alongs; a cancan; and Comanche ceremonial and war dances. All the children in the audience get to go up on the stage.

Dinner—served on pewterware—is a hearty four-course meal consisting of salad, soup, beef stew, fried chicken, barbecued pork ribs, biscuits with honey butter, corn, beans, a baked potato, and hot apple pie. Beer, wine, and Coca-Cola are included.

4 At Walt Disney World

The places described in this section can be located on the map "Dining in Walt Disney World & Lake Buena Vista" in chapter 6.

A PAY-ONE-PRICE ENTERTAINMENT COMPLEX

Pleasure Island

In Downtown Disney, adjacent to Walt Disney World Village Marketplace. ☎ **407/ 934-7781.** Free admission before 7pm, $18.95 after 7pm. Admission included in the All-In-One-Hopper Pass. Clubs open daily 7pm–2am; shops 11am–2am. Free self-parking; valet parking $5.

This Walt Disney World theme park is a rollicking 6-acre complex of nightclubs, restaurants, shops, and movie theaters where, for a single admission price, you can enjoy a night of club-hopping until the wee hours.

Pleasure Island is designed to evoke an abandoned waterfront industrial district with clubs in "converted" ramshackle lofts, factories, and warehouses, but the streets are festive with brightly colored lights and balloons. Dozens of searchlights play overhead, and rock music emanates from the bushes. You'll be given a map and show schedule when you enter the park; take a look at it, and plan your evening around shows that interest you.

The mood here is always festive. For one thing, every night at Pleasure Island is New Year's Eve, celebrated on the stroke of midnight with a high-energy street party, live entertainment, a barrage of fireworks, and showers of confetti.

Although this is Disney, it is essentially a bar district where liquor is served, so when sending out your older children, use the same rules that you use at home. (This is the place at which the singer Bobby Brown got arrested for fighting.) They must be 18 to get in unless accompanied by a parent or legal guardian.

Pleasure Island has seven clubs:

Pleasure Island Jazz Company: This big, barnlike club—purported to be an abandoned waterfront carousel factory—features contemporary and traditional live jazz. Performers are mostly locals, but about once a month there are big names such as Kenny Rankin, Lionel Hampton, Maynard Ferguson, the Rippingtons, and Billy Taylor. Light fare, international coffees, and a variety of foreign and domestic wines are available.

Mannequins Dance Palace: Housed in a vast dance hall with a small-town moviehouse facade, Mannequins is supposed to be a converted theatrical mannequin warehouse (remember, you're still in Disney World). It's a high-energy club with a large rotating dance floor and is a favorite of locals. Three levels of bars and hangout space are festooned with elaborately costumed mannequins and moving scenery suspended from overhead rigging. A DJ plays contemporary tunes at ear-splitting decibel levels, and there are high-tech lighting effects. You must be 21 to get in, and they're very serious about it. Have your ID ready, even if you learned to dance to the Platters.

Neon Armadillo Music Saloon: You guessed it: This trilevel club is country—with neon beer signs, rustic tables mounted on beer barrels, walls hung with spurs and saddles, and a spur-shaped neon chandelier. Live country bands play nightly, and dancers whirl around the floor doing the Texas Two-Step or Cotton-Eyed Joe (lessons are given Sunday from 7 to 8pm). Name stars sometimes come in and take the stage. The staff is in cowboy/cowgirl garb. A bar specialty is Jell-O shooters—Jell-O cubes laced with rum, vodka, and other alcoholic beverages. You can also order Southwestern fare here such as chili and fajitas.

Adventurers Club: The most unique—and my personal favorite—of Pleasure Island's clubs occupies a multistory building that, according to Disney legend, was designed to house the vast library and archaeological trophy collection of island founder and compulsive explorer Merriweather Adam Pleasure. It's also headquarters for the Adventures Club, which Pleasure headed up until he vanished at sea in 1941. The plushly furnished club is chock-full of artifacts—early aviation photos, hunting trophies, shrunken heads, Buddhas, Indian goddesses, spears, and a mounted "yakoose" (half yak, half moose) who occasionally speaks. He's not the only one. In the eerie Mask Room, strange sounds are often heard, and more than 100 masks move their eyes, jeer, and make odd pronouncements. Also on hand are Pleasure's zany band of globe-trotting friends and club servants, played by skilled actors who interact with guests and always stay in character. Improvisational comedy shows take place throughout the evening in the main salon, diverse 20-minute cabaret shows/events in the library (during which "volunteers" are dragooned from the audience). You could easily hang out here all night imbibing potent tropical drinks in the library and at the bar—where elephant-foot barstools rise and sink mysteriously.

Comedy Warehouse: Housed in the island's former power plant, the Comedy Warehouse—another favorite of mine—has a rustic interior with tiered seating. A very talented troupe performs 45-minute improvisational comedy shows based on audience suggestions. There are five shows a night, and bar drinks are available. Arrive early.

Rock & Roll Beach Club: Once the laboratory in which Pleasure developed a unique flying machine, this three-story structure today houses a dance club where live bands play "classic rock from the 60s through the 90s." There are bars on all three floors, including one serving international beers. The first level contains the dance floor. The second and third levels offer air hockey, pool tables, basketball machines, pinball, video games, darts, and a pizza and beer stand.

8 Trax: This 1970s-style club, with about 50 TV monitors airing diverse shows and videos over the dance floor, occupies three levels, all with bars. Period movie posters (*Bananas, Star Wars*) adorn the walls, and the top-floor lounge is vaguely psychedelic in decor. A DJ plays disco music, and guests engage in games of Twister.

In addition, live bands—including occasional big-name groups—play the **West End Plaza** outdoor stage and the **Hub Stage;** check your schedule for show times. You can star in your own music video at **SuperStar Studios.** And there are carnival games, a video-game arcade, virtual-reality games, a Velcro wall (don a jumpsuit over your clothes, bounce on a trampoline, and stick yourself on), and an Orbitron (a "21st-century workout machine," originally developed for NASA, that lets you experience weightlessness). Shops and eateries (with outdoor umbrella tables) are found throughout the park. **Planet Hollywood** (see chapter 6 for details) is adjacent and does not require an admission charge.

DISNEY'S WEST SIDE

In Downtown Disney, this area of clubs and restaurants is located next to Pleasure Island. The following could be considered "night sports," though they also serve food.

Bongo's Cuban Cafe. In Disney's West Side. ☎ **407/828-0999**. No reservations. AE, DISC, DC, V, MC. Wed–Sun after 10am.

Created by Cuban-American songstress Gloria Estefan and her husband, Emilio, the cafe is Disney's version of old Havana. There are leopard spotted chairs and mosaic bar stools shaped like bongo drums. A Desi Arnaz look-alike might even show up to sing a few tunes. There is no dance floor to speak of, although you could cha-cha on the patio. This upstairs patio, which overlooks the rest of the West Side, is a great place to sit back and enjoy a good (faux) Cuban cigar while basking in the Latin rhythms.

House of Blues. In Disney's West Side, under the old-fashioned water tower. ☎ **407/934-2583.** AE, DISC, MC, V.

Cover charges vary here in proportion to the stature of the artist. A variety of top names popped up during the first year. The barnlike building, with three tiers, may be a little difficult for those with disabilities to maneuver, but there is not a bad seat in the house. The atmosphere is dark and boozy, perfect for the bluesy sounds. The sound system rocks to the rafters, and the dance floor is big enough to boogie without doing the bump with a stranger. You can eat in the adjoining restaurant, which is described in chapter 6.

5 Hot Spots in Downtown Orlando

Dozens of clubs and restaurants line Orange Avenue, the main street in downtown Orlando. A free public transportation system called **Lymmo** runs in a designated lane that connects many of these clubs, but since Lymmo stops running about 11pm, it may stop moving before you do. Keep enough money for a taxi. These places can be located on the map "Downtown Orlando Nightlife" in this section.

Church Street Station. 129 W. Church St. (off I-4, between Garland and Orange aves. in downtown Orlando). ☎ **407/422-2434.** Free admission prior to 5pm, after which you have to pay $16.95. Clubs open nightly until 2am; shops until 11pm. There are several parking lots nearby (call for specifics). Take I-4 east to Exit 38 (Anderson St.), stay in the left lane, and follow the signs.

Though not part of Walt Disney World, Church Street Station in downtown Orlando operates on a similar principle to Pleasure Island (in fact, it started the concept). Occupying a cobblestoned city block lined with turn-of-the-century buildings (real ones), it, too, is a shopping/dining/nightclub complex offering a diverse evening of entertainment for a single admission price. There are 20 live shows nightly (consult your show schedule upon entering), plus an array of street performers. Major blow-out celebrations are held for special events such as St. Patrick's Day and the Super Bowl.

Stunning interiors are the rule here. It's worth coming by just to check out the magnificent woodwork, stained glass, and thousands of authentic antiques. And capitalizing on the traffic that Church Street generates, many other clubs have opened in the immediate area, further enlarging your bar-hopping potential.

Entry to restaurants, the Exchange Shopping Emporium, and the Midway game area are all free. Check out the following highlights.

Rosie O'Grady's Good Time Emporium: This 1890s-style gambling hall–cum-saloon, with beveled- and leaded-glass panels, etched mirrors, and vast globe chandeliers suspended from a high pressed-tin ceiling, is filled with interesting antiques. The band here, a collection of seasoned professionals, really jams, and their collaborative efforts reflect the long time they've played together. The train benches came from an old Florida rail station, back-bar mirrors from a Glasgow pub, and bank tellers' cages from a 19th-century Pittsburgh bank. Dixieland bands, banjo players, singing waiters, and cancan dancers entertain nightly. Light fare (deli sandwiches, chili dogs) is available. The house specialty drink is a rum and fruit concoction called the Flaming Hurricane (served in a souvenir glass). The "Good Time Piano Man" plays at 1:30, 2:30, 3:30, and 4:30pm; visitors are encouraged to sing along.

Apple Annie's Courtyard: Adjoining Rosie's, this brick-floored establishment, domed by arched trusses from an early 19th-century New Orleans church, evokes a

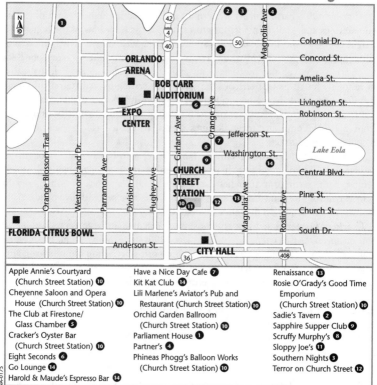

Apple Annie's Courtyard
(Church Street Station) **10**

Cheyenne Saloon and Opera
House (Church Street Station) **10**

The Club at Firestone/
Glass Chamber **5**

Cracker's Oyster Bar
(Church Street Station) **10**

Eight Seconds **6**

Go Lounge **14**

Harold & Maude's Espresso Bar **14**

Have a Nice Day Cafe **7**

Kit Kat Club **14**

Lili Marlene's Aviator's Pub and
Restaurant (Church Street Station) **10**

Orchid Garden Ballroom
(Church Street Station) **10**

Parliament House **1**

Partner's **4**

Phineas Phogg's Balloon Works
(Church Street Station) **10**

Renaissance **13**

Rosie O'Grady's Good Time
Emporium
(Church Street Station) **10**

Sadie's Tavern **2**

Sapphire Supper Club **9**

Scruffy Murphy's **8**

Sloppy Joe's **11**

Southern Nights **3**

Terror on Church Street **12**

NA-0175

Victorian tropical garden. The room is further embellished by 12-foot, hand-carved filigree mirrors created in Vienna circa 1740 and magnificent 1,000-pound chandeliers suspended from an ornate, vaulted cherry-wood ceiling. An 18th-century French communion rail serves as the front bar. Seating is in wicker peacock chairs at English pub tables. Patrons sip potent tropical fresh fruit and ice-cream drinks while listening to folk and bluegrass music.

Lili Marlene's Aviator's Pub & Restaurant: Its plush, oak-paneled interior is embellished with World War I memorabilia, stained-glass transoms, and accoutrements from an 1850 Rothschild town house in Paris, the latter including a walnut fireplace and wine cabinets. Eclectic seating ranges from hand-carved oak pews that came from a French church to a place at a large drop-leaf mahogany table where Al Capone once dined. Model airplanes and marvelous Victorian chandeliers are suspended from a beamed pine ceiling with a stained-glass skylight. The menu features premium aged steaks, prime rib, and fresh seafood.

Phineas Phogg's Balloon Works: This whimsical bar, with hot-air balloons and airplanes over the dance floor, is a high-energy club playing loud, pulsating music. (This is where the NBA's Charles Barkley threw a fellow patron through a plate glass window.) It doubles as a virtual ballooning museum housing photographs and artifacts from historic flights, including Orlando native Joe Kittinger—the first man to cross the Atlantic in a gas balloon. Every Wednesday from 6:30 to 7:30pm, beers cost just 5¢ here. No one under 21 is admitted.

Cheyenne Saloon and Opera House: This stunning trilevel balconied saloon, crowned by a lofty stained-glass skylight, is constructed of golden oak lumber from a century-old Ohio barn. Quality western art is displayed throughout, including many oil paintings and 11 Remington sculptures. This is the best show of the bunch, with a tight country band that really knows how to kick. Well-known artists do occasionally drop by to join in. If you know how to line dance or do the two-step, you'll love this place. If not, you can always take advantage of those slow songs. Balcony seating, in restored church pews, overlooks the stage—the setting for entertainment ranging from country bands (some big names) to clogging exhibitions—and the dance floor. There are free country-dance lessons in the saloon on Friday, Saturday, and Sunday from 2 to 5:30pm. The menu features steaks, barbecued chicken and ribs, and hickory-smoked brisket.

Orchid Garden Ballroom: This stunning space, with ornate white wrought-iron arches and Victorian lighting fixtures suspended from an elaborate oak-paneled ceiling, is the setting for an oldies dance club. A DJ plays rock 'n' roll classics like "Great Balls of Fire" and "Let's Go to the Hop," interspersed with live bands. As the evening progresses, so do the musical decades.

Crackers Oyster Bar: Brick columns, oak paneling, and a gorgeous antique oak and mahogany bar characterize this cozy, late 1800s–style dining room. Fresh Florida seafood is featured, along with more than 50 imported beers. You can nibble on appetizers such as oysters Rockefeller, smoked fish dip, and steamed mussels. Or opt for more serious entrees ranging from crab cakes rémoulade to paella.

In addition, the 87,000-square-foot Exchange houses the carnival-like **Commander Ragtime's Midway of Fun, Food, and Games** (including an enormous video-game arcade), a food court, and more than 50 specialty shops. You can rent a horse-drawn carriage out front for a drive around the downtown area and Lake Eola. And hot-air balloon flights can be arranged (☎ **407/841-8787**).

Note: Most hotels offer transportation to and from Church Street, and, since you'll probably be drinking, I advise it. As long as I'm giving advice, if you have disabilities or are in a wheelchair prepare to arrive early for each show so you can get a floor seat. Although my husband's Nana, who is her late 70s, tromped right to the top, the steps in the multitiered theaters are steep and can be difficult for those with physical limitations to navigate. Also, it's difficult to get around inside the theaters with a baby stroller.

Eight Seconds. 100 W. Livingston Ave., Orlando. ☎ **407/839-4800.** Cover charge varies.

What used to be the hottest concert spot in downtown has been transformed into a honky-tonk. There's not a whole lot to distinguish the dark cavernous interior, except a huge dance floor. (Ask about free line-dancing lessons early in the evenings.) Outside is what really sets this place apart. Just next to the parking lot is a rodeo pen where there are "Buckin' Bull Nights," with live bulls. There are also monster-truck pulls in the back lot. This place has really gone country; the managers even carry walkie-talkies painted white and black like cowhides. Just say "Yeeehaaaawww" and hang on. (In order to score, a cowboy or cowgirl needs to stay atop his or her steer for 8 seconds.) Country stars rising up the charts occasionally hold concerts here.

Jani Lane's Sunset Strip. 25 S. Orange Ave. (corner of Orange and Pine), Orlando. ☎ **407/649-4803.** Cover charge varies but is usually between $5 and $10.

Big hair, leather, and heavy-metal music are the standards at this large, loud downtown favorite. Local acts predominate, and you'll find occasional special concerts by hard-rocking bands. A balcony overlooks busy Orange Avenue. At press time there was a huge following for "swinger night." It features the kind of music that would make Sinatra bored, performed by a live band underneath a mirrored ball. There are even free swing dancing lessons early in the evening. If you've got that swing, call for information. It's Money, Baby.

Have a Nice Day Cafe. 120 N. Orange Ave., ☎ **407/839-1939.** No cover.

If you had a Brady Bunch lunch box or a crush on Keith (or Laurie) Patridge, this place will send you skipping down memory lane in wide-legged bell bottoms. Although there are some folks over 30, there are a lot of younger regulars who view all the seventies memorabilia as strictly retro. A large lighted disco floor in the back will give you Saturday night fever.

Kit Kat Club/Go Lounge/Harold & Maude's. 23 Wall St. Plaza (off Orange Ave.), Orlando. ☎ **407/422-6990.** No cover for the Kit Kat. The cover varies, usually under $10 for Go Lounge. Harold & Maude's cover varies.

Plush red-velvet couches, pool tables, and the feel of a swinging joint of a different era—complete with a cigarette girl—this is a magnet for Generation-X types who dig the Tony Bennett on the jukebox. The Kit Kat Club is attached to the coffeehouse Harold & Maude's, which features delicious javas—mostly of the spiked Irish variety—and a variety of sandwiches, and the Go Lounge, a small alternative dance club.

Renaissance. 22 S. Magnolia Ave. (1 block off Orange Ave.), Orlando. ☎ **407/422-3595.** Cover charge $5.

One of the newer arrivals to downtown, this is a large, popular dance club with bars on three levels. You'll find lots of seventies retro-clothes and kids trying to look older than their age. Reggae is played on an open-air rooftop on the weekends.

Sapphire Supper Club. 54 N. Orange Ave., Orlando. ☎ **407/246-1419.** Cover charge varies.

Local and national acts both perform at this laid-back club with vintage brick walls. Jazz legend and transplanted Orlando resident Sam Rivers is a regular. This place is as cool and jazzy as the music it often features and offers specials like "Martini and Cigar" nights. It's popular with young professionals and music lovers of all ages.

Scruffy Murphy's. 9 W. Washington St. (off Orange Ave.). ☎ **407/648-8233.** No cover.

Here you'll find Irish beers, special events like the "Celtic Throw Down," and bartenders with authentic Irish brogues saying there is "no, never" a cover charge. A good place to hang out and enjoy some unusual—for Florida at least—entertainment. But it's more watering hole than wild dance palace.

Sloppy Joe's. 41 W. Church St. (between Church Street Station and Orange Ave.). ☎ **407/843-5825.** No cover Sun–Thurs; $3 Fri–Sat.

Based loosely, very loosely, on the Key West bar where Papa Hemingway liked to hang, this place caters mainly to a college and tourist crowd. The live music is always loud, the lines are always long, and the drink specials help give a different meaning to the "sloppy" in the name. Everybody rushes to get in so they can sit on the patio and watch the Church Street traffic stream before them. Go figure.

Terror on Church Street. 135 S. Orange Ave. (at Church St. in downtown Orlando, a block from Church Street Station). ☎ **407/649-FEAR** or 407/649-1912. Admission $12 adults, $10 children under 17. Sun–Thurs 7pm–midnight; Fri–Sat 7pm–1am. Most hotels offer transportation to the area. There are several lots nearby (call for specifics). Take I-4 east to Exit 38 (Anderson St.), stay in the left lane, and follow the signs to Church Street Station parking.

Terror on Church Street is a multimedia, high-tech house of horrors incorporating innovative special effects and 23 highly theatrical sets on two floors. On a labyrinthine

25-minute tour of the darkened premises, guests are menaced by cleaver- and chain-saw–wielding maniacs, ghoulish monks, assorted cadavers, vicious dogs, Freddie Kreuger, and Dracula, among others—all convincingly portrayed by actors. Children under 10 are not admitted without an adult. A gift shop on the premises sells stick-on warts and burn scars, coffin banks, and the like.

Zuma Beach. 46 N. Orange Ave. ☎ **407/648-8363.** Open to those 18 and over. Under 21, generally a $5 cover. Over 21, no cover charge.

The bouncers are well muscled, and servers wear G-strings. One local newspaper dubbed Zuma Beach the "Best Pickup Place"; that is, if you are hot, hot, hot like the pumping dance music. Located in the former Becham Theater, this is still the site of occasional special live performances.

6 Gay & Lesbian Nightspots

Same-sex dancing is not expressly forbidden anywhere in Orlando—even in WDW—but although there is a lot of pixie dust floating around, we are still in Dixieland. Travelers interested in sampling some of the gay and lesbian hot spots might check out the following places.

The Club at Firestone. 578 N. Orange Ave. (at Concord St., in a converted garage still bearing the Firestone sign). ☎ **407/426-0005** for information and a weekly schedule. Cover varies.

Go-go boys dance on lifts converted into raised platforms, and a diverse group boogies on the large, concrete dance floor. This is a serious dance club with dark lighting and cavernous rooms.

In 1998 the upper floors were transformed into a separate, more low-key martini bar—The Glass Chamber. Completely enclosed in glass, you can get a good look at the dance floor below while sipping your drink shaken, not stirred.

Parliament House. 410 N. Orange Blossom Trace (just west of downtown Orlando). ☎ **407/425-7571.** Drag shows, 10 and 12pm Fri–Sun. Cover $5 Fri–Sat; $2 Sun.

Attached, conveniently, to a hotel, this is one of Orlando's wilder, and most popular, gay spots. Not a fancy place, the Parliament House shows the wear and tear of years of hard partying. This is a place to drink, dance, and watch as the infamous "Miss P" holds bawdy court in the packed drag shows. (There is also a weekly amateur night on Tuesdays.) The dance floor is relatively good sized, but it gets small quickly as the crowd swells. There is also a small piano lounge. The show is a big draw and seats go fast.

Partners. 916 N. Mills Ave. (about 5 miles from downtown, next to a dry cleaners). ☎ **407/896-4348.** No cover.

Low-key and laid-back, this place has the feel of a neighborhood bar rather than a pickup spot. Located in a nondescript concrete-block building, you have to be looking for the Partners sign. This is the place for a relaxing evening.

Sadie's Tavern. 415 S. Orlando Ave. (in Winter Park). ☎ **407/628-4562.** Cover varies.

This is your local, neighborhood lesbian bar. There is a laid-back crowd in this small club. Weekend entertainment is usually a local artist playing an acoustic guitar.

Southern Nights. 375 S. Bumby Ave. (between Anderson St. and Colonial Dr.). ☎ **407/898-0424.** No cover.

Voted "Best Gay Bar" by the readers of a local alternative weekly paper, theme nights pack in women on Saturdays and men on Sundays. On Friday night there are three female-impersonator shows.

7 More Entertainment

SPORTS BARS

All-Star Cafe. At Walt Disney World's Wide World of Sports Complex. ☎ **407/WDW-DINE** (939-3463). No cover.

Well, not a sports bar per se, this ninth entry in the themed restaurant chain opened at Disney in late 1998. Just a line-drive away from the entrance to the main stadium, the interior is packed with sports memorabilia and television monitors. One of the major investors, Tiger Woods, actually lives in the area. Who knows, you might catch a glimpse of him away from the links.

Champions. In Marriott's Orlando World Center, 8701 World Center Dr. ☎ **407/239-4200.** Open nightly until 2am. Free self-parking; valet parking $7. No cover.

Champions is a sports-bar chain—one so appealing, it's easy to see why the concept has succeeded. Its interior is chockablock with $25,000 worth of signed sports photos, posters, and artifacts such as Lou Gehrig's baseball bat, a golf bag autographed by Dallas Cowboys coach Jimmy Johnson, and (of local interest) a wet suit belonging to Cypress Gardens' famed barefoot waterskiing star, Banana George. Some nights a DJ plays music (mostly Motown and oldies) for dancing. Otherwise, entertainment includes three pool tables, video games, Foosball, darts, coin-op football and basketball, and blackjack tables. In addition, sporting events are aired on large-screen TVs and on smaller monitors around the room (a calendar at the entrance lists all game times). Champions offers a fairly extensive bar-food menu.

Note to single women: Men outnumber women about five to one, so this is a good place to meet guys—if you can distract them from the sports action on the screen.

ESPN Sports. In Walt Disney World at Disney's Boardwalk. ☎ **407/WDW-DINE** (939-3463). No cover.

Seventy-one monitors. Need I say more? If you are jonesing for a sports fix, this is the place. There is an full-service bar, but there is also a restaurant, so you have an excuse to drag your family along.

AN ALCOHOL-FREE ALTERNATIVE

Club Soda. 6341 N. Orange Blossom Trail (about 35 miles from the heart of tourist central, near the intersection of Clarcona–Ocoee Rd. and Orange Blossom Trail), Orlando. ☎ **407/523-1556.**

Those looking to party away from the (at times) alcohol-drenched tourist areas can have an alcohol-free night at Club Soda. Sunday and Tuesday are karaoke nights. There's live music with a house band on Wednesdays and a DJ and dancing on the weekends. Weekend dances are sometimes sponsored by various local 12-step groups. This place is very laid-back, very low-key. Crowds are small.

MOVIE THEATERS

Downtown Disney AMC Theater

In Walt Disney World adjacent to the Pleasure Island nightclub complex. ☎ **407/827-1300.** Matinees $4.50 adults, $3.75 seniors and children 2–13, under 2 free; twilight shows (4:30–6pm) $3.25 for all seats; evening shows $6.50 adults, $4.50 students, $3.75 seniors (over 55) and children 2–13, under 2 free.

This 24-screen AMC theater complex—equipped with state-of-the-art Dolby-digital sound systems and 70mm projection capability—extends the variety of nighttime entertainment available to Disney World guests and will soon extend it further. It's adding 14 new screens to become Florida's largest multiplex! A bridge connects the theater complex with Pleasure Island clubs. New Disney films premiere here, and first-run films are shown; check the *Orlando Sentinel* for show times.

8 Major Concert Halls & Auditoriums

Three large entertainment facilities, administered by the Orlando Centroplex, host the majority of big-name performers playing the Orlando area.

The **Florida Citrus Bowl,** 1610 W. Church St., at Tampa Street (☎ **407/ 849-2020** for information, 407/839-3900 to charge tickets), with 70,000 seats, is the largest. This is the setting for major rock concerts and headliners like Billy Joel, Elton John, The Eagles, Guns 'n' Roses, Paul McCartney, Metallica, and the Rolling Stones. To reach the Citrus Bowl, take I-4 east to the East-West Expressway and head west to Highway 441; make a left on Church Street and follow the signs. Parking is $5.

The 17,500-seat **Orlando Arena** at 600 W. Amelia St., between I-4 and Parramore Avenue (☎ **407/849-2020** for information, 407/839-3900 to charge tickets), also hosts major performers (Elton John, Bruce Springsteen, Billy Joel, Bette Midler) in addition to an array of family-oriented entertainment: Ringling Bros. Barnum & Bailey Circus every January, Discover Card Stars on Ice in February, Tour of World Figure-Skating Champions in April or May, and Walt Disney's World on Ice in September. To reach the arena, take I-4 east to Amelia Avenue, turn left at the traffic light at the bottom of the off-ramp, and follow the signs. Parking is $5.

The area's major cultural venue is the **Bob Carr Performing Arts Centre,** 401 W. Livingston St., between I-4 and Parramore Avenue (☎ **407/849-2020** for information, 407/839-3900 to charge tickets). Concert prices vary with performers: ballet tickets are $15 to $35, opera tickets $12 to $45, Broadway Series $24.50 to $46.50. This 2,500-seat facility is home to the Orlando Opera Company and the Southern Ballet Theater, both of which have October-to-May seasons. The Orlando Broadway Series (September to May) features original-cast Broadway shows such as *Carousel, The Who's Tommy, Damn Yankees,* and *Cats.* Also featured at the Bob Carr are concerts and comedy shows; a recent year's performers included Patti LaBelle, Lyle Lovett, Julio Iglesias, and Crosby, Stills, and Nash. To get here, take I-4 east to Amelia Avenue, turn left at the traffic light at the bottom of the off-ramp, and follow the signs. Parking is $5.

Short Trips in the Orlando Area

Get away from the glitter and glitz that characterize most Orlando attractions. Stroll through Cypress Gardens—a serene botanical paradise that was central Florida's first major tourist draw—or head to Winter Park, a charming upscale town with some exquisite attractions.

1 Cypress Gardens

40 miles southwest of Walt Disney World, 45 miles southwest of Orlando.

Founded in 1936, when Dick and Julie Pope hired a crew of laborers to dig canals and drain swamps, Cypress Gardens, located on Fla. 540 at Cypress Gardens Boulevard in Winter Haven (☎ **800/282-2123** or 941/324-2111), came into being as a 16-acre public garden along the banks of Lake Eloise with cypress-wood–block pathways and thousands of tropical and subtropical plants. Today it has grown to over 200 acres, with ponds and lagoons, waterfalls, classic Italian fountains, topiary, bronze sculptures, and manicured lawns. Ancient cypress trees shrouded in Spanish moss form a backdrop to ever-changing floral displays of 8,000 varieties of plants from more than 90 countries. Southern belles in Scarlett O'Hara costumes stroll the grounds or sit on benches under parasols in idyllic, tree-shaded nooks. They symbolize Florida's old-fashioned Southern hospitality.

In 1995, the park, once owned by Anheuser-Busch, was sold to a collection of one-time park managers. Little has changed, but the new team seems to be working hard to lure tourists to their little piece of paradise. New additions include a small tropical zoo, a nighttime show projecting animated characters onto a 35-by-70-foot water screen, and "Biblical Gardens," which features more than 25 plants, fruits, and spices mentioned in the Bible. (Now that's something you don't find at WDW.)

In the late winter and early spring, more than 20 varieties of bougainvillea, 40 of azalea, and hundreds of roses burst into bloom. Crape myrtles, magnolias, and gardenias perfume the late-spring air, while brilliant birds of paradise, hibiscus, and jasmine brighten the summer landscape. And in winter, the goldenrain trees, floss silk trees, and camellias of autumn give way to millions of colorful chrysanthemums and red, white, and pink poinsettias. *Tip for allergy sufferers:* Be sure to bring along your medicine; this place, though beautiful, can wreck your sinuses, especially on a windy day.

ESSENTIALS

GETTING THERE   Take I-4 west to U.S. 27 south and proceed west to Fla. 540. If you don't have a car, inquire about public transportation at your hotel. This is more than an hour drive from Orlando, so you will likely have to rent a car. Parking is free.

ADMISSION   Admission is $29.50 for ages 10 and over, $24.50 for seniors, $19.50 for children 3 to 9, and free for children 2 and under.

HOURS   Cypress Gardens is open 365 days a year, from 9:30am to 5:30pm, with extended hours during peak seasons.

EXPLORING THE GARDENS

Strolling the grounds is, of course, the main attraction (there are over 2 miles of winding botanical paths, and half of the park's acreage is devoted to floral displays), but this being central Florida, it's not the only one.

Shows are scheduled several times each day. The world-famous **Greatest American Ski Team** performs daring freestyle jumps, swivel skiing, barefooting, ski ballet, and slalom exhibitions on Lake Eloise in a show augmented by an awesome hang-gliding display. **Moscow on Ice Live!** is the Russian answer to America's Ice Capades. And **Variété Internationale** features specialty acts from all over the world.

And there's still more. An enchanting exhibit called **Wings of Wonder** surrounds visitors with more than 1,000 brightly colored free-flying butterflies (representing more than 50 species) in a 5,500-square-foot Victorian-style glass conservatory filled with tropical plantings, orchids, and waterfalls.

Electric boats navigate a maze of lushly landscaped canals in the original botanical gardens area. You can ascend 153 feet to the **Island in the Sky** for a panoramic vista of the gardens and a beautiful chain of central Florida lakes.

Carousel Cove, with eight kiddie rides and arcade games, centers on an ornate turn-of-the-century–style carousel. It adjoins another kid pleaser, **Cypress Junction,** an elaborately landscaped model railroad (scenery includes everything from a burning house to Mount Rushmore) that travels 1,100 feet of track with up to 20 trains moving at one time.

Cypress Roots, a museum of park memorabilia, displays photographs of famous visitors (Elvis on water skis, Tiny Tim tiptoeing through the roses) and airs ongoing showings of *Easy to Love* starring Esther Williams (it was filmed here). Another museum commemorates the age of radio, with a display of hundreds of vintage radios, radio memorabilia, and recordings of radio shows and music from the 1920s to the 1950s.

Wind up your visit with a relaxing 30-minute narrated **pontoon cruise** on scenic Lake Eloise, past virgin forest, bulrush, and beautiful shoreline homes. En route, you're likely to spot cormorants, osprey, ducks—maybe even an alligator or two. Don't forget to bring your binoculars. In recent years bald eagles have been spotted. This is very relaxing on calm days during the winter, spring, and fall. It can however get a little warm during the summer. There's an additional $4-per-person charge for this attraction.

WHERE TO DINE

Your options range from a **food court** to the **Crossroads Restaurant,** a cheerful full-service facility serving American fare and offering alfresco seating at umbrella tables on a terrace. I also like the more casual **Lakeview Terrace,** with covered outdoor seating overlooking Lake Eloise; it offers great views of the ski show.

Fresh strawberries are sold throughout the park in season. And if you care to pack a basket, there are picnic tables. Over a dozen shops sell everything from quaint country-store merchandise to gardening books and paraphernalia.

2 Winter Park

20 miles north of Walt Disney World, 5 miles north of Orlando.

The beautiful lakefront community of Winter Park was created in the early 1880s as "a first-class place" for "men and women of intelligence, culture, character, taste and means." Developers Loring A. Chase and Oliver E. Chapman priced their lots accordingly. The town was incorporated in 1887. To this day it remains an affluent haven—Florida's answer to Greenwich, Connecticut. You can visit on a day trip, or you can spend a relaxing night or two here away from theme-park hubbub.

Its attractions include a lovely Beverly Hills–like shopping strip (Park Avenue) lined with posh boutiques and art galleries; golf courses; fine old homes along winding, tree-shaded streets; shimmering lakes and canals (Winter Park has been called the "Venice of America"); Central Park, a large village green with lush lawns, stately moss-draped live oaks, and rose gardens; and a museum housing a treasure trove of Tiffany windows, lamps, and objets d'art. And though (actually, because) refined Winter Park takes no official notice of the fact, the town attracts numerous celebrities looking for a quaint and quiet retreat.

ESSENTIALS

GETTING THERE   Take I-4 east to Fairbanks Avenue (exit 45). Exit right and proceed east for about a mile, turn left on Park Avenue, and follow the signs to public parking.

Amtrak service (☎ **800/USA-RAIL**) is available from Orlando and Kissimmee (see chapter 2 for locations). The Winter Park station is located in the center of town at 150 W. Morse Blvd. (☎ **407/645-5055**).

Take **LYNX** bus no. 4 from the Osceola Square Mall at Columbia Street and Hoagland Avenue in Kissimmee. It will take you to the Orlando downtown terminal where you can transfer to bus no. 1 or 9, either of which makes several stops along Park Avenue in Winter Park. Call ☎ **407/841-8240** for a schedule.

VISITOR INFORMATION   For further information about Winter Park, contact the **Chamber of Commerce,** 150 N. New York Ave., just north of Morse Boulevard (P.O. Box 280), Winter Park, FL 32790 (☎ **407/644-8281**). Hours are 9am to 4pm Monday through Friday.

PARKING   Street parking is sometimes difficult. There are convenient and free municipal lots on South New York Avenue on either side of Morse Boulevard.

SEEING THE SIGHTS

Stroll Winter Park's main street, browse its boutiques, visit its museums, play a few rounds of golf, and take a leisurely lake cruise. Do note that most of the town's museums are closed on Monday.

✪ **Charles Hosmer Morse Museum of American Art.** 445 Park Ave. (between Canton and Cole aves.). ☎ **407/645-5311.** Admission $3 adults, $1 students of any age. Tues–Sat 9:30am–4pm; Sun 1–4pm. Closed Mon, Memorial Day, July 4, Labor Day, Thanksgiving, Christmas, and New Year's Day.

Anyone who loves the sinuous, nature-inspired art-nouveau genre (and who doesn't?) will be amazed and thrilled by this gem of a gallery. Even those who aren't usually big fans of art will be intrigued by the mammoth scale of these works marked by the intricate detail and brilliant colors of the individual panes. This gallery alone justifies a trip to Winter Park.

It was founded by Hugh and Jeannette McKean in 1942 to display their peerless collection (more than 4,000 pieces), including 40 magnificent windows and 21 paintings created by Louis Comfort Tiffany. Some of the treasures had in fact languished, unseen, in storage for years after a fire destroyed the Tiffany home.

But Tiffany is not the only artist displayed here. There are non-Tiffany windows by William Morris, Frank Lloyd Wright, Frederick Stymetz Lamb, and 15th- and 16th-century German masters; leaded lamps by Tiffany and Gallé; paintings by John Singer Sargent, Samuel F.B. Morse, Maxfield Parrish, Thomas Hart Benton, and Arthur B. Davies; jewelry designed by Tiffany, Lalique, and Fabergé; sculptures by Hiram Powers and Daniel Chester French (of Lincoln Memorial fame); prints by Cézanne, Childe Hassam, Rembrandt, Whistler, Winslow Homer, Mary Cassatt, and Grant Wood; photographic works by Tiffany and other 19th-century artists; and art-nouveau furnishings by Tiffany, Gallé, and others. The collection, which is shown on a rotating basis, also includes Tiffany memorabilia—letters, furnishings, personal effects, and photographs used by his studio as source materials.

Furniture and accessories by Gustav Stickley and his contemporaries—plus a major collection of American art pottery—make the Morse arts and crafts collection one of the most important in the Southeast.

Be sure to peek into the gift shop, where unique items include art-nouveau gift wrap, Maxfield Parrish stationery, and much more.

Cornell Fine Arts Museum. At the eastern end of Holt Ave., on the campus of Rollins College at Lake Virginia. ☎ **407/646-2526.** Free admission. Tues–Fri 10am–5pm; Sat–Sun 1–5pm. Closed Mon, July 4, Thanksgiving, Christmas Eve, Christmas Day, New Year's Eve, and New Year's Day. Free parking in adjacent lot "H."

Rollins College was the first home of Hugh and Jeannette McKean's (see the preceding listing) Tiffany glass. Today, with close to 4,000 square feet of exhibition space, it houses an impressive century-spanning collection that includes works by Hiram Powers, Childe Hassam, Tiffany, Thomas Sully, William Glackens, Reginald Marsh, Leonard Baskin, and the studio of Peter Paul Rubens. Also displayed here: 19th-century silver, 17th-century Dutch Delftware, French rococo decorative panels, and Chippendale furniture. Traveling exhibits supplement the collection.

A SCENIC BOAT TOUR

Since 1938, tourists have been boarding pontoons at the eastern end of Morse Boulevard for leisurely hour-long cruises on Winter Park's beautiful chain of natural lakes. The ride traverses Lake Osceola (which flows north into the St. John's River), Lake Virginia, and Lake Maitland, winding through canals built by loggers at the turn of the century and tree-shaded fern gullies lined with bamboo and lush tropical foliage.

You'll view magnificent lakeside mansions and villas (Margaret Mitchell used to winter on Lake Maitland), pristine beaches, cypress swamps, ancient trees draped with Spanish moss, and dozens of marsh birds—white herons, grackle, cormorants, osprey, and gallinule, possibly even an American bald eagle. The captain regales passengers with local lore. It's a delightful trip.

For information, call ☎ **407/644-4056.** The price is $6 for adults, $3 for children ages 2 to 11 (children under 2 ride free). Weather permitting, tours depart daily between 10am and 4pm, every hour on the hour, except on Christmas.

WHERE TO STAY

Though you could visit Winter Park on a day excursion from Orlando, you might also consider an overnight stay at one of the following properties.

Langford Resort Hotel. 300 E. New England Ave. (at Interlachen Ave.), Winter Park, FL 32789. ☎ **407/644-3400.** Fax 407/628-1952. 218 units. A/C TV TEL. $75–$115 double; $200 suite. Children 17 and under stay free in parents' room. Room with kitchenette $10 extra. AE, DC, MC, V. Free self-parking.

In pre-Disney days, Winter Park was one of central Florida's most-visited resorts, and the Langford was the place to stay. Vaughn Monroe entertained in the lounge, and the guest roster boasted people like Eleanor Roosevelt, Mamie Eisenhower, Lillian Gish, Vincent Price, and Dina Merrill. Ronald and Nancy Reagan celebrated their 25th wedding anniversary here.

Today, though it's no longer glamorous, this friendly, family-run resort does offer extensive resort facilities at very reasonable rates. Most notably, its on-premises spa offers sauna, steam, massage (shiatsu, Swedish, and deep athletic), body wraps, seaweed wraps, salt glows, facials, manicures, pedicures, and day-of-beauty packages. Its central location, on a lovely street shaded by tall oaks draped with Spanish moss, is another plus. Room decor varies and is notably eclectic. Many rooms have balconies and/or fully equipped kitchenettes with two-burner stoves and small refrigerators.

Dining/Diversions: The nautical/tropical Bamboo Room serves reasonably priced American fare; steak and seafood are featured at dinner. The adjoining Del Prado bar/lounge provides piano-bar entertainment and complimentary hors d'oeuvres from 5 to 8pm nightly. Tuesday through Saturday there's dancing to live band music from 8pm to midnight. The elegant Empire Room offers a lavish buffet champagne Sunday brunch and Saturday-night mystery dinner theater.

Amenities: Concierge (sells tickets, many of them discounted, to Walt Disney World and other Orlando attractions), room service, *Orlando Sentinel* delivered to your room Monday through Friday, baby-sitters. Olympic-size heated swimming pool, kiddie pool, car-rental service, small video-game arcade, unisex hair salon. Golf and tennis are close by.

Park Plaza Hotel. 307 Park Ave. S. (at New England Ave.), Winter Park, FL 32789. ☎ **800/228-7220** or 407/647-1072. Fax 407/647-4081. 27 units. A/C TV TEL. $80–$135 double; $150–$185 suite. During special events, rates may be higher. Rates include continental breakfast. AE, DC, MC, V. Free self- and valet parking.

Centrally located in the heart of the Park Avenue shopping and restaurant district, this small, elegant hotel dates to 1921. Owners John and Sandra Spang bought the property in 1975 and did an exquisite renovation, fitting out the rooms bed-and-breakfast–style with antique furnishings, Persian rugs, patchwork quilts, and beautiful floral-print bedspreads. Wide wooden Bermuda shutters on the windows and wood-bladed ceiling fans add tropical ambience. Homey touches include live plants in white wicker baskets and magazines in the rooms.

Most rooms open onto a wicker-furnished, plant-filled balcony, and many have cozy parlor areas. Especially lovely is the Balcony Suite, which has Victorian-reproduction wallpaper and a brass bed made up with a Ralph Lauren spread, throw pillows, and white dust ruffle. There are also four luxurious honeymoon suites with oversized oak beds and private balconies. In-room amenities include complimentary fruit baskets at check-in.

The hotel's Park Plaza Gardens restaurant (see "Where to Dine," next) adjoins. The front desk offers concierge-like service. Other amenities here include room service, complimentary daily newspaper, and nightly bed turndown. Transport to/from Disney parks and the Orlando airport can be arranged. A beauty shop is just behind the property, and, for a fee, guests can use the nearby Winter Park Wellness Center, an extensively equipped health club. A complimentary continental breakfast with fresh-squeezed orange juice and fresh-baked muffins is served daily in the European-style lobby (or in your room). Golf and tennis are close by.

WHERE TO DINE

There are so many fine restaurants in Winter Park that Orlandoans often drive over just to dine and stroll the tree-lined streets or enjoy an ice cream in the park while window shopping.

VERY EXPENSIVE

Park Plaza Gardens. 319 Park Ave. S. (between Lyman and New England aves.). ☎ **407/645-2475.** Reservations recommended. Main courses $7.95–$12.95 at lunch (sandwiches and salads $5.95–$8.95), $19.95–$26.95 at dinner. AE, CB, DC, DISC, MC, V. Mon–Sat 11:30am–3pm; Mon–Thurs 6–10pm, Fri–Sat 6–11pm; Sun 11am–3pm and 6–9pm. Free parking at city lot at New England and S. New York aves. CONTEMPORARY AMERICAN/ FLORIDIAN SEAFOOD.

This charming patio garden restaurant—with tables shaded by a striped canvas awning and seating amid a small forest of ficus trees—offers the feeling of outdoor dining in air-conditioned comfort. During the day, sunlight streams in through a skylit ceiling; at night, tables are romantically candlelit. Exposed-brick walls hung with changing exhibits serve as gallery space for local artists. There are also cafe tables on Park Avenue.

The culinary creations here—served on large, white platters—are as exquisitely presented as they are delicious. Good beginnings here include smoked duck pâté drizzled with goat-cheese cream and velvety lobster bisque beautifully marbleized with crème fraîche. Entrees include broiled sea bass wrapped in banana leaves, served with bulgur-wheat pilaf and wild-berry preserves. Also excellent are the rack of lamb dijonnaise with rosemary-thyme sauce and crisp, cherry-wood–smoked Muscovy duck served with sweet-potato haystack. For dessert, ebony and ivory is a sweet dream—espresso chocolate mousse and thin, semisweet chocolate leaves on a mirror of marbleized white chocolate sauce with blackberry garnish. The well-chosen wine list offers many by-the-glass selections, and there's page after page of after-dinner cordials, cognacs, ports, sherries, and brandies.

The lunch menu adds pasta, sandwich, and salad options. Brunch—including complimentary champagne, mimosa, or Kir royale—includes an appetizer, soup or salad, and entrees ranging from a seafood frittata topped with creamy velouté and caviar to sesame-seared Maui snapper glazed with Hawaiian fruit chutney and served on a bed of rice.

MODERATE

✪ **La Venezia Cafe.** 142 Park Ave. S. (between Morse Blvd. and Welbourne Ave.). ☎ **407/647-7557.** Reservations not accepted. Breakfast pastries $1.75; main courses $5.95–$9 lunch/brunch, $5.95–$18.50 at dinner; prix-fixe afternoon teas $7, $10, and $15. AE, DISC, MC, V. Mon–Thurs 8am–9:30pm; Fri–Sat 8am–10pm; Sun 8am–9:30pm. Parking on street only. ITALIAN/COSMOPOLITAN COFFEEHOUSE.

La Venezia Cafe is the highlight of a Winter Park visit, for continental breakfast, British-style afternoon tea, or a full meal. It's a charming place, with flower-bedecked tables (white-linen cloth and candlelit at night) and cream stucco walls hung with photographs of Italy. There's an open-air patio overlooking Central Park here, but the pièce de résistance is inside: a collection of six authentic Tiffany windows.

La Venezia fresh-brews 52 different kinds of coffee and offers an extensive choice of gourmet teas. Come by in the morning for a steaming pot of fragrant Ethiopian Yrgacheffe with a fresh-baked croissant, jalapeño corn bread, or brown-sugar–topped streusel coffee cake. At lunch and dinner, menu options include delicious salads (I love the chicken curry tossed with greens, mango chutney, raisins, coconut, and peanuts), sandwiches, pizzas, pastas, quesadillas, and quiches. The evening meal also features more serious entrees, such as pistachio-crusted baked salmon served with wild mushrooms in pink-champagne butter sauce.

Other enticements here are coffee/ice-cream drinks and frappés and a wide selection of liqueurs, aperitifs, and international beers. And save some room for oven-fresh desserts like buttered rum apple pie and amaretto-praline butter-cream torte. A $15 afternoon tea includes finger sandwiches, freshly baked scones and pastries, berries, tea, and champagne.

INEXPENSIVE

The Briarpatch. 252 Park Ave. N. (at Garfield Ave.). ☎ **407/628-8651.** Reservations not accepted. Breakfast $2.95–$6.95; lunch and dinner main courses and sandwiches $4.95–$8.95. AE, MC, V. Mon–Thurs 7am–9pm; Fri–Sat 7am–10pm; Sun 8am–5pm. Street parking only. AMERICAN.

A delightful way to start your day in Winter Park is with breakfast on the Briarpatch's open-air patio overlooking Central Park. If it's raining or chilly, the rustic garden-like interior is also alluring. Breakfast fare includes great coffee and fresh-baked biscuits, muffins, and cinnamon buns. Other options are buttermilk pancakes, a Brie and parsley omelet, a bagel with Nova and cream cheese, or hot oatmeal with berries and bananas.

Later in the day, come by for sandwiches, salads, stuffed baked potatoes, burgers, or pasta dishes—or for cappuccino with fresh-baked desserts such as Kahlua praline cream squares and mile-high chocolate-layer or carrot cake.

12

Beach Vacations in Central Florida

by Bill Goodwin

Bill Goodwin began his career as an award-winning newspaper reporter before becoming legal counsel and speechwriter for two U.S. senators. Now based in Virginia, he is also the author of *Frommer's Florida, Frommer's USA, Frommer's South Pacific,* and *Frommer's Virginia.*

1 Daytona Beach

54 miles northeast of Orlando, 251 miles north of Miami, 78 miles south of Jacksonville.

Daytona Beach is a town with many personalities. It is at once the "World's Most Famous Beach," the "World Center of Racing," and a mecca for spring break. It has been a destination for racing enthusiasts since the days when cars were called horseless carriages and raced on the hard-packed sand beach. One thing is for sure: Daytonans still love their cars. Recent debate over the environmental impact of unrestricted driving on the beach caused an uproar from citizens who couldn't imagine it any other way. As it worked out, they can still drive on the sand, but not in areas where sea turtles are nesting.

Today, hundreds of thousands of race enthusiasts come to the home of the National Association for Stock Car Auto Racing (NASCAR) for the Daytona 500, the Pepsi 400, and other races throughout the year. The Speedway is home to Daytona USA, a state-of-the-art motorsports entertainment attraction worth a visit even by nonracing fans.

Daytona Beach Shores even provides a drive-in church where a dedicated following can flock to hear Sunday morning sermons from speakers hooked to their car windows.

But you don't have to be a car aficionado to enjoy Daytona. It has 23 miles of sandy beach, an active nightlife, surprisingly good museums, and good shopping options. Be sure to check the "Orlando Calendar of Events" in chapter 2 to know when the town belongs to college students during spring break, when hundreds of thousands of leather-clad motorcycle buffs will be arriving for Bike Week, or when racing enthusiasts will be encamped for big competitions. Don't bother trying to find a hotel room, drive the highways, or enjoy a peaceful vacation at those times. You won't be able to.

ESSENTIALS
GETTING THERE If you're driving from north or south, take I-95 and head east on International Speedway Boulevard (U.S. 92). From

Daytona Beach

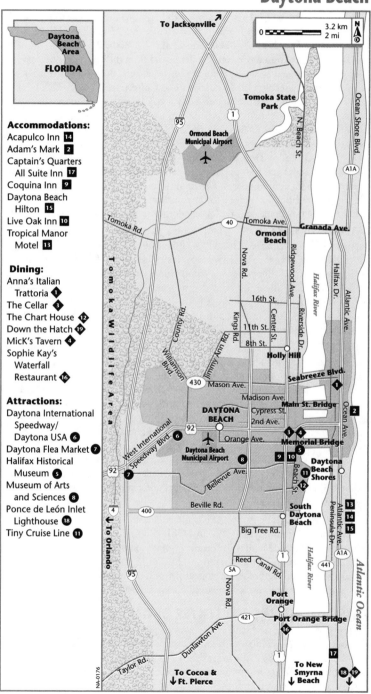

Accommodations:
Acapulco Inn **14**
Adam's Mark **2**
Captain's Quarters
 All Suite Inn **17**
Coquina Inn **9**
Daytona Beach
 Hilton **15**
Live Oak Inn **10**
Tropical Manor
 Motel **13**

Dining:
Anna's Italian
 Trattoria **1**
The Cellar **3**
The Chart House **12**
Down the Hatch **19**
Mick's Tavern **4**
Sophie Kay's
 Waterfall
 Restaurant **16**

Attractions:
Daytona International
 Speedway/
 Daytona USA **6**
Daytona Flea Market **7**
Halifax Historical
 Museum **5**
Museum of Arts
 and Sciences **8**
Ponce de León Inlet
 Lighthouse **18**
Tiny Cruise Line **11**

Tampa or Orlando, take I-4 east and follow the Daytona Beach signs to I-95 north to U.S. 92. From northwestern Florida, take I-10 east to I-95 south to U.S. 92.

Continental (☎ 800/525-0280) and **Delta** (☎ 800/221-1212) fly into **Daytona Beach International Airport,** 4 miles inland from the beach near the Speedway.

All major car-rental agencies operate from the airport. But why not rent a Harley? This is Daytona, after all. Call **American Road Collection** (☎ 888-RENT-HD3 or 904/238-1999). Rates start at about $100 a day, twice that amount during biker events.

Call **Yellow Cab Co.** (☎ 904/255-5555). The ride from the airport to most beach hotels runs between $10 and $15.

Daytona–Orlando Transit Service (DOTS) (☎ 800/231-1965 or 904/ 257-5411) provides van transportation to or from **Orlando International Airport.** The fare is $26 for adults one-way, $46 round-trip; children 11 and under are charged half. The service brings passengers to the company's terminal at 1598 N. Nova Rd., at 11th Street (LPGA Boulevard) or, for an additional fee, to beach hotels.

VISITOR INFORMATION The **Daytona Beach Area Convention & Visitors Bureau,** 126 E. Orange Ave. (P.O. Box 910), Daytona Beach, FL 32115 (☎ 800/854-1234 or 904/255-0415; fax 904/255-5478; www.daytonabeach-tourism.com), can help you with information on attractions, accommodations, dining, and events. The office is on the mainland just west of the Memorial Bridge. The information area of the lobby is open daily from 9am to 7pm; office hours are Monday to Friday from 9am to 5pm. The bureau also maintains a branch at Daytona USA, 1801 W. International Speedway Blvd.

CITY LAYOUT The Halifax River flows north to south through the middle of the city, separating the mainland from the beaches, which sit along a skinny, barrier island-like peninsula. From north to south, the **Seabreeze, Main Street, Charlton Blank** (International Speedway Blvd./U.S. 92), and **Memorial bridges** lead from downtown Daytona over to the beach. **Atlantic Avenue (Fla. A1A)** runs north-to-south along the beach through the towns of Ormond Beach, Daytona Beach, and Daytona Beach Shores. Fla. A1A returns to the mainland at Port Orange, but Atlantic Avenue continues south to Ponce Inlet, where it dead-ends.

On the mainland, **Ridgewood Avenue (U.S. 1)** runs inland paralleling the west side of the Halifax River, and I-95 vaguely parallels the river still farther west. **International Speedway Boulevard (U.S. 92)** is the main east-west artery from I-95 to downtown and the beach.

GETTING AROUND Although it's primarily a driver's town, VOTRAN, Volusia County's public transit system (☎ 904/761-7700), runs a **trolley** along Atlantic Avenue on the beach, Monday to Saturday from noon to midnight. Fares are 75¢ for adults, 35¢ for seniors and children 6–17, free for kids under 6 riding with an adult. Votran also runs **buses** throughout downtown and the beaches Monday through Saturday until 7:30pm and on Sunday until 7pm.

A VISIT TO THE WORLD CENTER OF RACING

Opened in 1959 with the first Daytona 500, the 480-acre ✪ **Daytona International Speedway complex,** at 1801 W. International Speedway Blvd. (U.S. 92 at Bill France Boulevard; P.O. Box 2801), Daytona Beach, FL 32120-2801 (☎ 904/253-RACE for tickets, 904/254-2700 for information), is certainly the keynote of the city's fame. It presents about nine weekends of major racing events usually, featuring stock cars, sports cars, motorcycles, and Go-Karts, and is also used for automobile testing. Its grandstands seat over 120,000.

Big events sell out months in advance (tickets to the Daytona 500 in February are gone as early as a year ahead of time), so get yours—and reserve your accommodations—well before your trip.

To learn more about racing, head for the **World Center of Racing Visitors' Center** at the east end of the Speedway and NASCAR office complex. Open daily from 9am to 5pm, the center is also the departure site for entertaining 25-minute guided tram tours of the facility. Admission is $5, free for children 6 and under. Tours depart daily every 30 minutes between 9:30am and 4pm, except during races and special events.

On the Speedway grounds, the phenomenally popular 50,000-square-foot ✪ **Daytona USA** (☎ **904/947-6800**) is a state-of-the-art interactive motor-sports entertainment attraction presenting the history, color, and excitement of stock-car, Go-Kart, and motorcycle racing in Daytona. Bring your video camera. There are lots of colorful photo-ops here. Visitors can participate in a pit stop on a NASCAR Winston Cup stock car, see the actual winning Daytona 500 car still covered in track dust, talk via video with favorite competitors, and play radio or television announcer by calling the finish of a race. The highlight of the attraction is the action-packed IMAX film that puts you in the winner's seat of a Daytona 500 race. Allow at least 3½ hours to enjoy this new theme attraction, which is open daily except Christmas from 9am to 6pm. Admission for adults is $12, seniors pay $10, children 6–12 pay $6, and children 5 and under are free. Discounted combination tickets are available for those who also want to take the tour of the facilities.

HITTING THE BEACH

The beach near the **Adam's Mark** and **Main Street Pier,** popular with families, is the hub of activity, with concessions, the city's famous **Boardwalk,** and a small amusement park. Couples seeking greater privacy usually prefer the northern or southern extremities of the beach. Especially peaceful is **Ponce Inlet** at the very southern tip of the island where there is precious little commerce or traffic to disturb the silence. Surfers and bikers congregate near the **Main Street** and **Sun Glow piers.**

You can drive and park directly on the sand along most of Daytona Beach's 500-foot-wide beaches, but watch for signs warning of sea turtles nesting. There's a $5 access fee, although in some areas like Ponce Inlet, the fee is waived in winter.

If Daytona's beaches aren't enough, you can venture south. New Smyrna Beach has 7 miles of hard-packed white sand, a quiet historic downtown, an active arts community, and excellent accommodations. Flagler Beach to the north is another pristine beach for those looking for solitude and natural beauty away from the condos and hotels.

OUTDOOR PURSUITS

CRUISES   Take a leisurely cruise on the Halifax River aboard the 14-passenger, 25-foot *Fancy,* a replica of the old fantail launches used at the turn of the century. It's operated by **A Tiny Cruise Line River Excursions,** 425 S. Beach St., at Halifax Harbor (☎ **904/226-2343**). Captain Jim regales passengers with river lore and points out dolphins, manatees, herons, diving cormorants, pelicans, egrets, osprey, oyster beds, and other natural phenomena during the morning cruise. Cruises are $8.75 to $14 for adults, $5.50 to $7.50 for children 4 to 12, free for children 3 and under. Weather permitting, cruises depart year-round (with a brief hiatus during the holidays), Monday through Saturday at 11:30am. A 1-hour tour of riverfront homes is at 2pm and of historic downtown at 3:30pm; there are no Monday cruises in winter months. Call for reservations. Romantic sunset cruises are also available.

Water Wheels of Daytona (☎ 407/255-2400) uses one vehicle for combined land-and-river tours: it's an amphibious "duck" which crawls into the river at the Riverfront Parking Lot, International Speedway Boulevard and Beach Street. Call for schedule and prices.

FISHING   The easiest and least expensive way to fish offshore for marlin, sailfish, king mackerel, grouper, red snapper, and more is with the **Critter Fleet,** 4950 S. Peninsula Dr., Ponce Inlet (☎ 800/338-0850 or 904/767-7676), which operates two party boats. One goes on all-day trips ($50 adults, $30 kids under 12), while the other makes morning and afternoon voyages ($30 adults, $20 kids under 12). The fares include rod, reel, and bait.

Deep-sea charter fishing boats dock at **Sea Love Marina,** 4884 Front St., Ponce Inlet (☎ 904/767-3406).

Save the cost of a boat, and fish with the locals from the **Main Street Pier,** at the ocean end of Main Street near the Adam's Mark (☎ 904/253-1212). Admission to the pier is $1 for adults, 50¢ for kids. Bait and fishing gear are available, and no license is required.

GOLF   There are more than a dozen excellent courses within 25 minutes of the beach, and most hotels can arrange starting times for you. **Golf Daytona Beach,** 126 E. Orange Ave., Daytona Beach, FL 32114 (☎ 800/881-7065 or 904/239-7065; fax 904/239-0064; www.golf-daytona.com), publishes an annual brochure describing the major courses. It's available at the tourist information offices (see "Essentials," earlier in this chapter).

Daytona's best known course is the **LPGA International,** 300 Championship Dr. (☎ 904/274-5742), one of the nation's top-rated links for women golfers. Designed by Rees Jones, the 7,088-yard, 18-hole course boasts five sets of tees and a number of challenging holes. A second 18-hole course designed by Lloyd Clifton is due to be on line by 1999. Just down the street from the Ladies Professional Golf Association headquarters, this center for professional and amateur women golfers has workshops and teaching programs, and the pro shop carries a great selection of ladies' equipment and clothing. Green fees with a cart are usually about $75, less in summer.

Another Lloyd Clifton–designed course, the centrally located 18-hole, par-72 **Indigo Lakes Golf Course,** 2620 W. International Speedway Blvd. (☎ 904/254-3607), has flat fairways and large bunkered Bermuda greens. Fees here are about $55 in winter, including a cart, less in summer.

The semiprivate South Course at **Pelican Bay Country Club,** 550 Sea Duck Dr. (☎ 904/788-6494), is one of the area's favorites, with fast greens to test your putting skills. With-cart fees are $40 in winter, less in summer (no walking allowed). The North Course here is for members only.

The city's prime municipal course is the **Daytona Beach Country Club,** 600 Wilder Blvd. (☎ 904/258-3119), which has 36 holes. Winter fees here are $18 to walk, $26.50 to share a cart. They drop $3 in summer.

HORSEBACK RIDING   Shenandoah Stables, 1759 Tomoka Farms Rd., off U.S. 92 (☎ 904/257-1444), offers daily trail rides and lessons. Call for prices and schedules.

WATER SPORTS   For jet-ski rentals, contact **Daytona High Performance—MBI,** 925 Sickler Dr., at the Seabreeze Bridge (☎ 904/257-5276). Additional water-sports equipment, as well as bicycles, beach buggies, and mopeds, can be rented along the beach in front of major hotels. A good place to look is in front of the **Adam's Mark,** on the beach at 100 N. Atlantic Ave.

MUSEUMS

✪ **Halifax Historical Museum.** 252 S. Beach St. (just north of Orange Ave.). ☎ **904/255-6976.** Admission $3 adults, $1 children 11 and under; free for everyone on Sat. Tues–Sat 10am–4pm.

This local history museum is housed in a former bank and is worth seeing just for the 1912 neoclassical architectural details. A mural of Old Florida wildlife graces one wall, the stained-glass ceiling reflects the sunlight, and across the room an old gold metal teller's window still stands. The musem's eclectic collection includes Native American artifacts, more than 10,000 historic photographs, possessions of past residents (such as a ball gown worn at Lincoln's inauguration), and, of course, model cars.

Mark Martin's Klassix Auto Museum. 2909 W. International Speedway Blvd., at Tomoka Farms Rd., just west of I-95. ☎ **904/252-3800.** Admission $8.50 adults, $4.25 children 7–12, free for children under 7. Daily 9am–6pm.

This museum showcases Corvettes—a model from every year since 1953. Also on display are collector cars (including cars from the movie *Days of Thunder*), and historic Daytona vehicles from all motor sports. A 1950s-style soda shop and gift shop are on the premises.

Museum of Arts and Sciences. 1040 Museum Blvd. (off Nova Rd./Fla. 5A). ☎ **904/255-0285.** Museum, $4 adults, $1 children and students with ID, free for children 5 and under; planetarium shows, $2. Tues–Fri 9am–4pm; Sat–Sun noon–5pm. Take International Speedway Blvd. west, make a left on Nova Rd. (Fla. 5A), and look for a sign on your right.

Impressive in this eclectic collection are the Cuban works—mostly paintings acquired in 1956, when Cuban dictator Fulgencio Batista donated his private collection to the city. One highlight is a portrait of Eva ("Evita") Perón, said to be the only existing painting completed while she was alive. Other exhibits include "Masterworks of American Art," a gallery dedicated to the prehistory of Florida, and "Africa: Life and Ritual."

Ponce de León Inlet Lighthouse & Museum. 4931 S. Peninsula Dr., Ponce Inlet. ☎ **904/761-1821.** Admission $4 adults, $1 children 11 and under. May–Aug daily 10am–8pm; Sept–Apr daily 10am–4pm (last admission an hour before closing). Follow Atlantic Ave. south, make a right on Beach St., and follow the signs.

If you are in the area, this 175-foot lighthouse—the second tallest in the United States—is worth a quick stop. Built in the 1880s, and restored in the 1970s, this brick-and-granite sentinel's beacon is visible for 16 nautical miles. The head lighthouse keeper's cottage now houses a museum of exhibits of maritime artifacts. The first-assistant keeper's house is furnished to reflect turn-of-the-century occupancy. A concise 12-minute video details the structure's history. Outside, you can walk around the tugboat *F.D. Russell*, now sitting high-and-dry in the sand.

SHOPPING

Daytona Beach's main riverside drag, Beach Street, is one of the only areas in town where people actually stroll. The street is wide and inviting, with decorative wrought-iron archways and fancy brickwork overlooking the Halifax River.

Today, between Bay Street and Orange Avenue, Beach Street offers more than a dozen antique shops, a magic shop, an excellent historical museum (see "Museums" earlier in this chapter), several good cafes, and the world famous **Dunn Toys & Hobbies**, which has an antiques mall upstairs.

Cycle fans should stop at the **Harley Davidson Store**, 290 Beach St., at Dr. Mary McLeod Bethune Boulevard, a 20,000-square-foot retail store and new diner serving breakfast and lunch (☎ **904/253-2453**). It's one of the largest dealerships in the country. In addition to hundreds of gleaming new and used Hogs, you'll find as much fringy leather as you've ever seen in one place.

The **Daytona Flea Market,** on Tomoka Farms Road at the junction of I-95 and U.S. 92, a mile west of the Speedway (☎ **904/252-1999**), is huge, with 1,000 covered outdoor booths plus 100 antique vendors in an air-conditioned building. Open year-round Friday through Sunday from 8am to 5pm. Admission and parking are free.

WHERE TO STAY

Room rates in Daytona are highest from the day after Christmas all the way to Labor Day, and they skyrocket during major events at the Speedway, during bikers' gatherings, and whenever college students are on break (see "Orlando Calendar of Events" in chapter 2). Daytona Beach hotels fill to the bursting point during these periods, and even if you can find a room, there's often a minimum-stay requirement.

In addition to the listings that follow, there are dozens of hotels and motels along Atlantic Avenue, many of them family owned and operated. The Daytona Beach Area Convention & Visitors Bureau (see "Essentials," earlier in this chapter) distributes a list of Superior Small Lodgings. None of these properties has more than 75 rooms, and all have been inspected for cleanliness, quality, comfort, privacy, and safety.

Among the other chain motels here, one of the better options is the **Days Inn,** 1909 S. Atlantic Ave., at Flamingo Avenue, in Daytona Beach (☎ **800/224-5056** or 904/255-4492), a nine-story beachfront hotel with a swimming pool/kiddie pool and a sundeck overlooking the beach. The **Ramada Inn Surfside,** 3125 S. Atlantic Ave. (☎ **800/255-3838** or 904/788-1000), also boasts a prime beachfront location. Families will appreciate its efficiency units with fully equipped eat-in kitchens and, in summer, free children's activities. Facilities include a large swimming pool, oceanfront picnic tables, and more. All rooms at these two properties have ocean views and balconies. In addition, there are three oceanfront **Howard Johnsons** to choose from (☎ **800/446-4656**).

Note: Along with the 6% state sales tax, Daytona levies a 4% tax on hotel bills.

AT THE BEACHES

Adam's Mark Daytona Beach Resort. 100 N. Atlantic Ave. (between Earl St. and Auditorium Blvd.), Daytona Beach, FL 32118. ☎ **800/872-9269** or 904/254-8200. Fax 904/253-0275. 413 units. A/C MINIBAR TV TEL. $99–$179 double; $159–$400 suite. AE, DC, DISC, MC, V. Free self-parking in lot across the street; valet parking $8.

This is Daytona's most central beachfront hotel—and one of its most luxurious—designed so that every room has an ocean view. Although the lobby and common areas are more elegantly detailed, guest rooms are not as spacious or well-laid-out as the less expensive and quieter Hilton (also described in this section) further south. It's right at the band shell, and, in season, its beach and boardwalk concessions offer parasailing, bicycle rentals, motorized four-wheelers, surfboards, boogie boards, cabanas, and umbrellas.

Dining: The hotel's premier dining room features steak and seafood dinners. Another facility, with picture windows overlooking the beach and umbrella tables outside, serves all meals. There's also a complex of small beachfront restaurants and bars with outdoor cafe seating. The sophisticated lounge offers piano bar or other live music nightly.

Amenities: Concierge, room service, dry cleaning and laundry, self-service laundry, free newspapers in executive-level rooms, baby-sitting, secretarial services, express checkout, indoor/outdoor heated swimming pool and kiddie pool, beach, health club, two whirlpools, steam and sauna, bicycle rental, children's center, business center, conference rooms, sundeck, water-sports equipment, sand volleyball court, playground, gift shops.

✪ **Acapulco Inn.** 2505 S. Atlantic Ave. (between Dundee Rd. and Seaspray St.), Daytona Beach, FL 32118. ☎ **800/874-7420,** 800/245-3580, or 904/761-2210. Fax 904/253-9935 or 904/761-2216. 133 units. A/C TV TEL. $50–$100 double; $54–$124 efficiency. Monthly rates and packages available. AE, DC, DISC, MC, V.

This Mayan-themed, mid-rise hotel is one of five beachfront hostelries managed by Oceans Eleven Resorts (the first toll-free and fax numbers given above go to Oceans Eleven's central reservations desk) and is a great choice for families. It's especially popular with Canadian snowbirds, who return year after year for the warm hospitality, clean ocean-view rooms with balconies, and organized activities like Bingo, bridge, and mah-jongg. All of the 42 hotel rooms have small refrigerators, and 91 efficiencies have fully equipped eat-in kitchens.

A large dining room overlooks the ocean, serving American fare at breakfast and lunch; a comfortable lounge adjoins. Facilities include a heated oceanfront swimming pool, two whirlpools, a kiddie pool, a picnic area, a coin-op laundry, and a video-game room. An on-staff PGA pro helps guests plan golf vacations and will arrange lessons and tee times.

Captain's Quarters All Suite Inn. 3711 S. Atlantic Ave. (½ mile south of Dunlawton Ave.), Daytona Beach, FL 32127. ☎ **800/332-3119** or 904/767-3119. Fax 904/767-0883. 27 units. A/C TV TEL. $85–$100 double; $140–$165 oceanfront penthouse suite. Lower rates available for extended stays. AE, DISC, MC, V.

A great choice down on the quiet southern part of Daytona Beach, this five-story beachfront inn has spacious suites, all with ocean or river views and large living/dining-room areas, balconies, and fully equipped kitchens. The country-look bedrooms have French doors that open onto balconies or patios with wooden rockers. Each is equipped with two cable TVs and VCRs (movies can be rented). The penthouse suite has a fireplace, a spa tub, and a big picture window overlooking the ocean. On-premises facilities include a heated swimming pool, a sundeck with love-seat swings and barbecue grills, and coin-op washer/dryers. The restaurant, which has an outdoor deck overlooking the ocean, is open for breakfast and lunch except on Tuesday. Newspapers are complimentary.

✪ **Daytona Beach Hilton Oceanfront Resort.** 2637 S. Atlantic Ave. (between Florida Shores Blvd. and Richard's Lane), Daytona Beach, FL 32118. ☎ **800/525-7350** or 904/767-7350. Fax 904/760-3651. 218 units. A/C TV TEL. $89–$150 river-view double; $124–$189 oceanfront double; from $250 suite. AE, DC, DISC, MC, V.

The best hotel choice here, the Hilton welcomes guests in an elegant terra-cotta–tiled lobby with comfortable seating areas, a fountain, and potted palms. The large guest rooms are grouped in pairs and can be joined to form a suite; one of each pair has a balcony. All have ocean and/or river views and major convenient extras like safes, coffeemakers, irons, full-size ironing boards, hair dryers, and small refrigerators. The hotel also has a small fitness room, unisex hair salon, and gift shop. Daily newspapers are complimentary. Kids appreciate the video-game room with pool table and the kiddie pool on the beautiful oceanfront sundeck where you can often see seagulls drinking from the large heated pool. A surprisingly good lobby restaurant—one of Daytona's most beautiful—serves all meals; patio dining is an option. A comfy bar/lounge with game tables adjoins; it's the setting for nightly entertainment. In summer, reggae bands play near the poolside bar.

Tropical Manor Motel. 2237 S. Atlantic Ave. (at Bonner Ave.), Daytona Beach, FL. ☎ **800/253-4920** or 904/252-4920. 71 units. A/C TV TEL. Winter, $33–$43 double; $34–$100 efficiency/suite; $95–$135 three-bedroom suite. High-season, $52–$63 double; $54–$127 efficiency/suite; $165–$237 three-bedroom suite. AE, DC, DISC, MC, V.

This Caribbean-tinted beachfront motel wins points for its unique and colorful murals, pleasant staff/owners, and meticulous upkeep. Located square in the middle of Daytona's nicest beach, these funky accommodations also offer sundecks, umbrella-covered tables, lounge areas, a large heated pool, water slide, shuffleboard court, cookout area, heated kiddie pool, and two gazebos—all surrounded by lush tropical foliage. The rooms are not large or particularly fancy, but many come with cable TV, kitchens, and ocean views. Especially good for families are the two- and three-bedroom suites.

BED-AND-BREAKFASTS ON THE MAINLAND

✪ **Coquina Inn.** 544 S. Palmetto Ave. (at Cedar St.), Daytona Beach, FL 32114. ☎ **800/805-7533** or 904/254-4969. Fax 904/254-4969. 4 units. A/C TV. $80–$110 double ($175–$200 double during special events). Rates include full breakfast. AE, MC, V. Free parking.

This charming coquina and cream-stucco house was built in 1912 in the Old Daytona historic section, just south of the Beach Street business district. It sits on a tranquil shady street half a block west of the Halifax River, about a 5-minute drive to the beaches. Innkeepers Joe Witek and Craig Heidel serve breakfast on fine china in their crystal-chandeliered dining room, and complimentary tea and sherry are available in the parlor throughout the day. A sitting room outfitted in a mishmash of antiques is a tranquil spot to enjoy the fireplace and a selection of books and magazines. Each of the guest rooms is decorated differently. In the sunny Hibiscus Room, French doors lead to a private plant-filled balcony (with Jacuzzi) overlooking an ancient live oak draped with Spanish moss. It and the next door Jasmine Room (it has a fireplace) can be combined to create a two-bedroom/two-bathroom suite. All rooms have cable TVs. Beach cruiser bikes are available at no charge. New in 1997 were two octagonal wooden decks, one with a large whirlpool under a Victorian gazebo, and a gift shop. There is no smoking inside, and children 11 and under are not accepted.

Live Oak Inn. 444-448 S. Beach St. (at Loomis Ave.), Daytona Beach, FL 32114. ☎ **888/881-4664** or 904/252-4667. Fax 904/239-0068. 12 units. A/C TV TEL. $80–$150 double. Rates include extended continental breakfast. AE, MC, V. Free parking.

Facing the river and occupying two adjoining restored 19th-century houses with a front lawn enclosed by a white picket fence, this B&B is surrounded by centuries-old live oaks. An inviting front porch with white wicker rocking chairs faces the street and a marina beyond. The guest rooms—seven with private sun porches or balconies—are delightfully decorated, with area rugs strewn on polished oak floors and wood-bladed fans whirring slowly overhead. Yours might be furnished with an Eastlake bed, or perhaps you'll get a Victorian sleigh bed with a patchwork quilt and a private plant-filled sun porch furnished with Adirondack chairs. The rooms overlook the Halifax Harbor Marina or a garden, and all are equipped with remote-control cable TVs, VCRs, and Victorian soaking tubs or Jacuzzis. Breakfast is served on an enclosed porch with lace-curtained windows. No smoking is permitted in the house, and children 9 and under are not accepted.

WHERE TO DINE

Perhaps as a concession to the spring-break crowd, Daytona Beach has a profusion of fast-food places that line the major thoroughfares, especially along International Speedway Boulevard, near the racetrack. You'll find many old and new restaurants on and around Beach Street. An old favorite is the little diner inside **Dunn's Toy Store.** Also check out the **Main Street Pier,** where a casual oceanfront restaurant serves burgers and chicken wings and lots of beer.

AT THE BEACHES

✪ Anna's Italian Trattoria. 304 Seabreeze Blvd. (at Peninsula Dr.). ☎ **904/239-9624.** Reservations recommended. Main courses $9–$17. AE, DISC, MC, V. Mon–Sat 5–10pm. ITALIAN.

The Triani family lends a warm, friendly air to this simple yet comfortable trattoria. Many of the pastas are homemade, but a star here is risotto alla Anna, an Italian version of Spanish paella. Portions are hearty; main courses come with soup or salad and a side dish of angel-hair pasta or a vegetable. There's a good selection of Italian wines to complement your meal. Everything is cooked to order, so allow plenty of time. Free parking is available in a lot on Seabreeze Boulevard across Peninsula Drive.

Down the Hatch. 4894 Front St., Ponce Inlet. ☎ **904/761-4831.** Reservations not accepted; call ahead for priority seating. Breakfast $2–$5; main courses $8–$15; early-bird menu (served 11:30am–5pm) $5–$7. Kids' menu. AE, MC, V. Daily 7am–10pm. Take Atlantic Ave. south, make a right on Beach St., and follow the signs. SEAFOOD.

Occupying a half-century-old fish camp on the Halifax River, Down the Hatch serves up fresh fish and seafood (note its shrimp boat docked outside). You can start your day here with a bagel or a country-style breakfast while taking in the scenic views of boats and shorebirds through the big picture windows—you might even see dolphins frolicking. At night, arrive early to catch the sunset over the river, and also to beat the crowd at this very popular place. In summer, light fare is served outside on an awninged wooden deck. Portions are large.

Sophie Kay's Waterfall Restaurant. 3516 S. Atlantic Ave. (at Raymond Ave.). ☎ **904/756-4444.** Reservations recommended. Main courses $7–$24; early-bird menu served 4–6:30pm, $8–$10. AE, DC, DISC, MC, V. Mon–Thurs 4–10pm; Fri–Sat 4–11pm; Sun noon–10pm. (Bar serves light fare Sun–Thurs until midnight, Fri–Sat until 1am.) CONTINENTAL.

Longtime Daytona restaurateur, cookbook author, and local television personality Sophie Kay has created a faux-tropical atmosphere with romantic details like a rock waterfall that cascades into a goldfish pond, full-size palm trees, candles, and soft piano music. Oysters Rockefeller (bubbling with cheese) or shrimp scampi make excellent starters. Sophie's chef has a great hand with pasta, and the primavera linguine in delicate white-wine sauce is perfection. Also very good is the baked seafood served en papillote in a creamy lobster béchamel sauce. Many people come here for filet mignon, roast prime rib au jus with creamy horseradish sauce, or surf-and-turf combinations. For dessert, don't pass up Sophie's delicious twice-baked cheesecake on a buttery graham-cracker crust. After dinner, adjourn to the piano bar for cocktails.

ON THE MAINLAND

The Cellar. 220 Magnolia Ave. (between Palmetto and Ridgewood aves.). ☎ **904/258-0011.** Reservations accepted only for large parties. Soups, salads, sandwiches $6–$7. AE, DC, DISC, MC, V. Mon–Fri 11am–3pm. AMERICAN.

An excellent place for lunch while you're touring downtown, this tea room occupies the basement of a National Historic Register Victorian home built in 1907 for President Warren G. Harding. It couldn't be more charming, with low-ceilings, fresh flowers on every table, and backlit stained-glass windows. In the warm months, there's outdoor seating at umbrella tables on a covered garden patio. A small but varied menu includes soups, salads, sandwiches, fresh seafood, chicken, and pastas.

● **The Chart House.** 1100 Marina Point Dr. (off Beach St. south of business district). ☎ **904/255-9022.** Reservations recommended. Main courses $16–$25. AE, DC, DISC, MC, V. Sun–Thurs 5–9:30pm; Fri–Sat 5–10:30pm. SEAFOOD/STEAKS/PRIME RIB.

This member of the up-scale chain offers some of the area's finest dining. The setting—under a soaring teepee roof and with big windows overlooking water views on three sides—is stunning. The menu is led by gargantuan cuts of tender prime rib, but the daily fresh-catch dishes and perfectly grilled steaks also draw the locals for special-occasion dinners. Caviar stars over on the bountiful salad bar.

Mick's Tavern. 218 S. Beach St. (between Magnolia St. and Ivy Lane). ☎ **904/238-3321.** Reservations not accepted. Main courses $8–$14; salads and sandwiches $4–$7. AE, MC, V. Mon–Sat 11am–3am; Sun 4pm–3am. IRISH/AMERICAN.

Especially worth knowing about because it serves food until 3am, this upscale Irish tavern has a highly eclectic menu. The pub fare includes vegetarian burritos and a few main courses of steaks, chicken, and "Mumzy's" meatloaf. Club sandwiches and burgers round out the large and reasonably priced selection. The food is not exceptional, but it's perfectly acceptable, especially once you've had a few Bass ales. The service is sometimes rushed but usually pleasant.

DAYTONA BEACH AFTER DARK

THE PERFORMING ARTS   Check the Friday edition of the Daytona Beach *News-Journal* for weekly listings of upcoming events, or call the **Peabody Auditorium,** 600 Auditorium Blvd., between Noble Street and Wild Olive Avenue (☎ **904/255-1314**), the city's major venue for high-brow performances.

They may look like them, but that's not Elvis Presley, Elton John, or Dolly Parton making music at **Legends in Concert,** in the Coliseum Theater, 176 N. Beach St. on the downtown waterfront (☎ **904/258-1500**). No, these are look-alikes doing very close imitations of a host of music's big names. The curtain rises on this Las Vegas–style revue Tuesday to Thursday at 8pm, Friday and Saturday at 6 and 9pm, and Sunday at 6pm, with matinees Tuesday, Wednesday, and Sunday at 2pm. Tickets are $19.95 adults, $16.95 seniors, and $9.95 kids under 15, plus tax. Not all of the "stars" appear at once, so call to see who'll be on stage.

You might just see a real country music star at the **Daytona Opry,** 2400 Ridgewood Ave., South Daytona (☎ **904/756-6779**), whose shows usually are Monday to Saturday at 7pm, with a matinee Sunday at 2pm (but call to make sure). Tickets are $17.95 adults, $10.95 kids under 12.

Sponsored by the city, the **Oceanfront Bandshell** (☎ **904/258-3169**), on the boardwalk next to the Adam's Mark Hotel, hosts a series of free big-band concerts at the band shell every Sunday night from early June to Labor Day. It's also the scene of raucous spring-break concerts.

THE CLUB & BAR SCENE   In addition to the following, the piano bar at **Sophie Kay's Waterfall Restaurant** (see the preceding "Where to Dine,") is worth a visit. Especially during biker festivities, Main Street is a happening area where dozens of bars and restaurants catering to the leather set are in full swing.

A popular beachfront bar for more than 40 years, **Ocean Deck,** 127 S. Ocean Ave., next to the Mayan Inn (☎ **904/253-5224**), is packed with a mix of locals and tourists, young and old, who come for live music and cheap drinks. Often reggae or ska bands will play after 9:30pm. Park across Ocean Avenue at the beach and surf shop, Reggae Republic (under the same ownership).

A typical spring-break party spot, **Razzles,** 611 Seabreeze Blvd., between Grandview and South Atlantic avenues (☎ **904/257-6236**), plays Top 40 tunes and high-energy music until 3am nightly. There's plenty to keep you occupied if you're not dancing—10 pool tables, a blackjack table, air hockey, electronic darts, pinball, and video games. The crowd is young—18 and up—and the scene is wild.

2 Cocoa Beach, Cape Canaveral & the Kennedy Space Center

46 miles southeast of Orlando, 186 miles north of Miami, 65 miles south of Daytona.

Known as "The Space Coast" after its most famous occupant—the NASA space program—the area around Cape Canaveral was once a sleepy place where city dwellers escaped the crowds from the exploding urban centers of Miami and Jacksonville. Now, the region has grown to accommodate its own crowds, especially hordes of tourists who come to visit the Kennedy Space Center and enjoy 72 miles of beaches, plus fishing, surfing, golfing, and tennis.

"I Dream of Jeanie" fans will recognize this as the home of television's most famous astronaut, Major Anthony Nelson, who lived with his bottle-dwelling Jeannie in Cocoa Beach.

Thanks to NASA, this also is a prime destination for nature lovers. The space agency originally took over much more land that it has needed to launch rockets. Rather than sell off the unused portions, it turned them over to the Cape Canaveral National Seashore and the Merritt Island National Wildlife Refuge, which have preserved them in their pristine natural states.

ESSENTIALS

GETTING THERE   Most people who visit the Space Center stay in nearby Cocoa Beach; dozens of beachfront hotels and restaurants make it a convenient home base. If you're driving from north or south, take I-95 to Fla. 520 east (the Merritt Island Causeway). You'll cross the Indian River and Banana River before hitting Fla. A1A, the north-south artery running along the Atlantic Ocean and connecting the beach towns from Sebastian Inlet to Port Canaveral.

The nearest airport is **Melbourne International Airport,** 22 miles south of Cocoa Beach, which is served by **Continental** (☎ 800/525-0280), **Delta** (☎ 800/221-1212), and **US Airways** (☎ 800/428-4322). **Melbourne Airport Shuttle** (☎ **407/724-1600**) takes passengers to the Cocoa Beach hotels, about a 45-minute ride, for $20 for the first person, $10 for each additional person. The shuttle desk is located in the baggage claim area. **Orlando International Airport,** about 35 miles to the southwest, is a larger hub with more flight options (see "Essentials" at the beginning of this chapter). From there, **Cocoa Beach Shuttle** (☎ 407/784-3831) will take you to the beach for about $20 per person.

VISITOR INFORMATION   For information about the area, contact the **Florida Space Coast Office of Tourism,** 8810 Astronaut Blvd., Suite 102, Cape Canaveral, FL 32920 (☎ **800/872-1969** or 407/868-1126; fax 407/868-1193; www.space-coast.com). The office is on Fla. A1A at Central Boulevard and is open Monday to Friday from 8am to 5pm.

You can also get specific information from the **Cocoa Beach Chamber of Commerce,** 400 Fortenberry Rd., Merritt Island, FL 32952 (☎ **407/459-2200,** fax 407/459-2232). The Chamber is between Plumosa Street and Merritt Square Mall. Open Monday to Friday from 9am to 5pm.

CITY LAYOUT   Fla. A1A joins nearly a dozen towns along this 72-mile coast. Three major causeways lead from the mainland across Merritt Island to the barrier island beaches. The **Bennett Memorial Causeway** (Fla. 528) to the north is nearest to Port Canaveral and the space center; **Merritt Island Causeway** (Fla. 520) in the center is a direct link to Cocoa Beach; and **Melbourne Causeway** is the southernmost access.

GETTING AROUND   A car is essential in this area. The **Space Coast Area Transit** (☎ **407/633-1878**) does operate buses, but routes tend to be circuitous and therefore extremely time-consuming. The fare for riders aged 18 to 60 is $1. All others pay 50¢.

TOURING THE KENNEDY SPACE CENTER

Nearly 60 million people have visited NASA's ✪ **John F. Kennedy Space Center** since it opened to the public in 1963. Whether you're a space buff or not, you're sure to appreciate the sheer grandeur of the facilities and the achievement of technology displayed here. Astronauts departed Earth at this site in 1969 en route to the most famous "small step" in history—humankind's first voyage to the moon.

All visitors must stop at the privately operated **Kennedy Space Center Visitors Center,** on NASA Parkway one-half mile west of Fla. 3 (☎ **407/452-2121; www.kscvisitor. com**). You can get there from Titusville on the mainland via the NASA Parkway Causeway (Fla. 405), or from Cape Canaveral and Cocoa Beach via Fla. 3. All other Space Center roads are closed to the public. From Orlando, take the Bee Line Expressway (Fla. 528) east, and where the road divides, go left on Fla. 407, make a right on Fla. 405, and follow the signs. Parking is free.

The center is open from 9am to dusk every day except Christmas and some launch days, but arrive early and pick up a schedule of events and a map to help plan your day. The offerings can be confusing, but a knowledgeable and helpful staff is on duty to answer questions and give advice. You'll need at least a full day to see and do everything.

The best way to get an overview of the area, and the only way to see actual working facilities, is by taking a **bus tour.** Two main tours are offered; each departs from the Visitors Center every 15 minutes starting at 9:45am, with the last tour leaving late in the afternoon (call for details). The tours will take at least 2 hours, depending on how interested you are in hanging out at the stops along the way. Buses run continuously, so you can reboard as you wish.

The better of the two is the **Kennedy Space Center Tour,** which visits facilities now in use, including the Complex 39 Space Shuttle launch pads and the massive Vehicle Assembly Building where shuttles are prepared for launch. The tour includes the impressive **Apollo/Saturn V Center,** a $37-million, 100,000-square-foot exhibit, which displays the most powerful rocket ever launched by the United States—the 363-foot-tall *Saturn V.* Videos, artifacts, photos, and interactive exhibits bring the history of the Apollo program to life.

The **Cape Canaveral Tour** is more historical and stops at the Cape Canaveral Air Station, where America's first satellites and astronauts were launched into space. Other stops include the launch pads currently used for unmanned launches, the original site of Mission Control, and the Air Force Space Museum.

For the same price as the longer tours, you can take the **Saturn Express Tour.** This scenic 15-minute drive to the new Apollo/Saturn V Center (described above) is a worthwhile abbreviated trip if you are short of time or have no patience for lengthy bus tours.

Back at the Visitors Center, rockets, interactive exhibits, and IMAX movies will both inform you and keep you entertained. Not-to-be-missed, the 3-D IMAX movie *L-5: First City in Space* depicts future life among the stars. Two other IMAX films

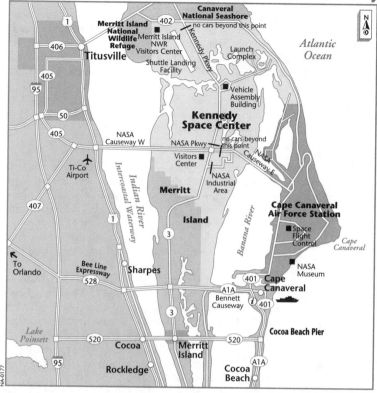

are also shown daily on the five-and-one-half-story-high screens: the 37-minute *Dream Is Alive,* giving an insider's view of the Space Shuttle program with in-flight footage shot by astronauts on various missions; and *Destiny in Space,* a Leonard Nimoy–narrated odyssey of the universe with exterior shots of shuttle flights.

Several dining venues in the Visitors Center will keep you fed and refreshed during your day here.

Admission to the Visitors Center is free, but tickets for the **bus tours** cost $10 for adults, $7 for children 3 to 11, free for children 2 and under. The regular **IMAX films** cost $6 for adults, $4 for children 3 to 11, free for children under 3. The 3-D IMAX movie costs $7 for adults and $5 for children. If you have a full day here, a **Mission Pass** is a better deal. It includes a bus tour and any two IMAX movies. These cost $23 for adults, $16 for kids 3 to 11, free for children under 3.

If you'd like to **see a launch,** call ☎ **407/867-4636** for a schedule of upcoming take-offs and ☎ **407/452-2121** for ticket information. At press time, tickets cost $10 to see the launch, $15 for the launch and an IMAX movie; you are required to buy them in person at the Visitors Center up to 5 days before a launch. They are sold on a first-come, first-served basis.

OTHER ASTRONAUT ATTRACTIONS

In addition to honoring our space voyagers, the **Astronaut Hall of Fame,** 6225 Vectorspace Blvd., Titusville (☎ **407/269-6100**), at the mainland end of NASA Causeway (Fla. 405), has artifacts from the space program and has several interactive exhibits, such as a flight simulator and a G Force Trainer that subjects you to four times the pull of gravity. A full-size replica of a space shuttle holds a theater with a multimedia presentation. Admission is $13.95 for adults, $9.95 for children 6 to 12, free for kids under 6. Open daily from 9am to 5pm.

The **Astronaut Memorial Planetarium and Observatory,** 1519 Clearlake Rd., Cocoa (☎ **407/634-3732**), south of Fla. 528, has its own International Hall of Space Explorers, but its big attractions are sound and light shows in the planetarium. The building is open Tuesday, Friday, and Saturday from 6:30 to 9pm on a regular basis, but call for the show schedule. Admission to the building is free; shows cost $4 for adults, $3 for seniors and students, and $2 for kids 12 and under.

BEACHES & WILDLIFE REFUGES

To the north of the Kennedy Space Center, ✪ **Canaveral National Seashore** is a protected 13-mile stretch of barrier island beach backed by cabbage palms, sea grapes, palmettos, marshes, and Mosquito Lagoon. This is a great area for watching herons, egrets, ibis, willets, sanderlings, turnstones, terns, and other birds. Giant sea turtles nest here from May to August. You might also glimpse dolphins and manatees in Mosquito Lagoon. Canoeists can paddle along a marked trail through the marshes of Shipyard Island, and you can go back-country camping from November through April (permits required).

The southern access gate and ranger station are east of Titusville on Fla. 402, just east of Fla. 3. A paved road leads from there to undeveloped ✪ **Playalinda Beach,** one of Florida's most beautiful. It's now officially illegal, but nude sunbathing has long been a tradition here (at least for those willing to walk a few miles to the more deserted areas). The main visitor center is at **Apollo Beach,** at the north end of the island, via Fla. A1A south from New Smyrna Beach. Admission fees are $5 per motor vehicle, $1 for pedestrians or bicyclists. For more information, contact the seashore at 308 Julia St., Titusville, FL 32796 (☎ **407/267-1110**).

Its neighbor to the south and west is the 140,000-acre **Merritt Island National Wildlife Refuge,** home to hundreds of species of shorebirds, waterfowl, reptiles, alligators, and mammals, many of them endangered. Pick up a map and other information at the **Visitors Center,** on Fla. 402 about 4 miles east of Titusville (it's on the way to Playalinda Beach). You can see some of nature's creatures from the 6-mile-long **Black Point Wildlife Drive,** or you can hike one of three nature trails through the hammocks and marshes. The Visitors Center is open Monday to Friday from 8:30am to 4:30pm, Saturday and Sunday from 9am to 5pm (closed Sunday from May through October). Admission is free. For more information, contact the Refuge at P.O. Box 6504, Titusville, FL 32782 (☎ **407/861-0667**).

Other beach areas here include **Port Canaveral Beach,** which boasts bike paths, campsites, wide beaches, parks, and dozens of shops and restaurants.

The beach at ✪ **Cocoa Beach Pier,** on Meade Avenue east of Fla. A1A (☎ **407/ 783-7549**), is also a popular spot, especially for surfers. Appearing rustic and slapped-together, the Pier was built in 1962 and shortly thereafter became the East Coast's surfing capital. It has 842 feet of fishing, shopping, and food and drinks overlooking a wide, sandy beach (see "Where to Dine," following).

OUTDOOR PURSUITS

CRUISES **Port Canaveral** is where a handful of the major Caribbean-bound cruise ships depart, including the *Disney Magic* and *Disney Wonder*. You can go on day trips under sail with **Tradewinds Sail Charters,** at the Port Canaveral Seaport (☎ **888/635-1895** or 407/635-1898; fax 407/456-5770; www.yourlink.net/ tradewinds). Many cruises are offered, from a 2-hour port excursion ($35 per person) to weekend getaways to Daytona Beach ($275 per person) to a week-long cruise to the Bahamas ($500 per person).

ECOTOURS   Call **Funday Discovery Tours** (☎ **407/725-0796**) to arrange back-country kayaking, airboat rides, horseback tours, and bird-watching expeditions. Prices range from $39 to $69 for adults, $19 to $49 for children 6 to 12.

FISHING   Whether you choose freshwater, shore, or deep-sea fishing, Brevard County has endless opportunities to cast a line. **Mosquito Lagoon** and **Eddy Creek** to the north are where you'll find trout and redfish. The **Indian River** and **Banana River** also yield trout and redfish, as well as snook, ladyfish, and black drum. Bass fishers enjoy a region in the west called **Farm 13/Stick Marsh** with more than 20,000 acres of freshwater angling. Head to Port Canaveral for offshore catches like snapper and grouper. Many beachside accommodations arrange fishing charters, and the port is lined with charter boats. For private outings, call **Dominics Guide Service** (☎ **800/BASS-909** or 407/242-892), one of the oldest licensed guides in the area.

You can go deep-sea fishing on the *Miss Cape Canaveral,* an 85-foot party boat docked at 670 Glen Cheek Dr., on the south dock in Port Canaveral (☎ **407/783-5274** or 407/648-2211 in Orlando). The day-long voyages leave daily at 8am and cost $55 per person, including breakfast, lunch, unlimited beer and soft drinks, gear, bait, and license.

GOLF   You can read about Northeast Florida's best courses in the free *Golfer's Guide,* available at tourist information offices and in many hotel lobbies.

In Cocoa Beach, the municipal **Cocoa Beach Country Club,** 500 Tom Warringer Blvd. (☎ **407/868-3351**), has 27 holes of championship golf and 10 lighted tennis courts set on acres of natural woodland, rivers, and lakes. Greens fees are about $38 in winter, dropping to about $32 in summer, including cart.

On Merritt Island south of the Kennedy Space Center, **The Savannahs at Sykes Creek,** 3915 Savannahs Trail (☎ **407/455-1377**), has 18 holes over 6,636 yards bordered by hardwood forests, lakes, and savannahs inhabited by a host of wildlife. You'll have to hit over a lake to reach the seventh hole. Fees with cart are $35 in winter, less in summer.

The best nearby course is the Gary Player–designed **Baytree National Golf Club,** 8010 N. Wickham Rd., one-half mile east of I-95 in Melbourne (☎ **407/259-9060**). Challenging marshy holes are flanked by towering palms. This par-72 course has 7,043 yards with a unique red-shale waste area. Fees are $85 in winter, dropping to about $50 in summer, including cart.

In Melbourne Beach, the expanded executive course at **Spessard Holland Golf Club,** 2374 Oak St. (☎ **407/952-4530**), lies between the Atlantic and the bays, making it one of the area's most scenic. The par-67 course covers 5,130 yards, with six holes of no more than 191 yards—presenting opportunities for holes-in-one. Winter fees here are $32 with cart, less in summer.

SURFING   Rip through some totally awesome waves at the **Cocoa Beach Pier** area or down south at the **Sebastian Inlet.** Get outfitted at **Ron Jon Surf Shop** (see "Shopping," next), or call **Cocoa Beach Surfing School,** 301 N. Atlantic Ave., at Desperados Restaurant (☎ **407/452-0854**). They offer equipment and lessons for beginners or pros at area beaches. Be sure to bring along a towel, flip-flops, sunscreen, and a lot of nerve.

SPECTATOR SPORTS   The Boys of Spring here take the form of Miami's **Florida Marlins,** who play their spring training baseball games from mid-Febraury through March at the Space Coast Stadium, 5800 Stadium Pkwy., off I-95 exit 73 in Melbourne (☎ **407/633-9200**). Tickets range from $5 to $12.

SHOPPING

If you haven't already been lured by the hundreds of billboards along the highway beckoning you to this 24-hour surf shop, once you drive through Cocoa Beach, you'll definitely notice the glaringly original building that houses the **Ron Jon Surf Shop,** at 4151 N. Atlantic Ave. (☎ **407/799-8888**), set beside Fla. A1A a block from the beach. It's a Hollywood version of art deco gone wild with tropical colors, lights, and towering sand sculptures of famous sports heroes. Inside you'll find souvenirs of every description and everything you need to make you look like a surfer. The shop also rents beach bikes, boogie boards, surfboards, scuba diving gear, and in-line skates by the hour, day, or week. The shop offers scuba lessons, and there is even a cafe (more like a fast-food burger joint).

The **Merritt Square Mall,** at 777 E. Merritt Island Causeway, has over 100 stores, including Florida's own department store, Burdine's, and many specialty shops, as well as a 12-screen movie theater.

Bargain hunters can dig through the wares of hundreds of merchants at **Frontenac Flea Market,** open Friday through Sunday from 8am until 4pm. It's located at 5605 U.S. 1, midway between Cocoa and Titusville.

WHERE TO STAY

If you want to combine your Space Center visit with some beaching, your best bet is to locate in Cocoa Beach, about a half-hour drive south.

The area has a plethora of rental condominiums and cottages. **King Rentals Inc.,** 320 N. Atlantic Ave., Cocoa Beach, FL 32930 (☎ **888/295-0934** or 407/784-5046; www.kingrentals.com), has a wide selection in its inventory.

Given the proximity of Orlando and the generally warm weather all year, there is little if any seasonal fluctuation in room rates here.

Note: You'll pay a 4% hotel tax on top of the Florida sales tax here.

COCOA BEACH

Cocoa Beach Hilton. 1550 N. Atlantic Ave., Cocoa Beach, FL 32931. ☎ **800/526-2609** or 407/799-0003. Fax 407/799-0344. 298 units. A/C TV TEL. Winter $129–$149 double; from $300 suite. Off-season $119–$129 double; from $200 suite. AE, DC, DISC, MC, V. Free parking.

True, there isn't much competition, but a recent upgrading has made this Hilton more upscale than the other chains represented here. No doubt you will run into a crew of name-tagged conventioneers, since it's especially popular with large groups. Rooms are a decent size, most have at least some view of the ocean, and all have coffeemakers, irons and ironing boards, and hairdryers. The best part is that you're right on the beach and can rent water and sports equipment. Other diversions include a game room, weight room, and a modestly sized outdoor heated pool surrounded by a sundeck. An oceanside restaurant/bar serves food and drinks, and room service is available until 10pm. Laundry, dry cleaning, and complimentary weekday newspaper delivery are convenient extras.

Comfort Inn & Suite Resort. 3901 N. Atlantic Ave. (Fla. A1A, at Brevard Lane), Cocoa Beach, FL 32931. ☎ **800/247-2221** or 407/783-2221. Fax 407/783-0461. 144 units. A/C TV TEL. $55–$87 double; $61–$135 suite. AE, DC, DISC, MC, V.

Half a block from the beach and a block from the congestion around Ron Jon Surf Shop (see the preceding section, "Shopping,"), this resort was born in the 1960s as a one-story motel enclosing a courtyard, which today sports a pool, whirlpool, bar with snacks, and volleyball and shuffleboard courts. Long since updated, the older rooms are medium-size and have doors opening to the courtyard and to the surrounding parking lots. Those in the south wing have cathedral ceilings which lend an almost cottagelike ambience. Newer one-bedroom suites are in their own mid-rise building at the beach end of the courtyard. The resort has a lounge but no restaurant (fast-food outlets sit across Atlantic Avenue).

Econo Lodge. 1275 N. Atlantic Ave. (Fla. A1A, at Holiday Lane), Cocoa Beach, FL 32931. ☎ **800/553-2666** or 407/783-2252. Fax 407/783-4485. 128 units. A/C TV TEL. $39–$75 double. AE, DC, DISC, MC, V. Pets accepted.

Across the avenue from the Holiday Inn Cocoa Beach (described next), this Econo Lodge is more charming than most members of this budget-priced chain. About half of its spacious rooms face a tropical courtyard with an L-shaped swimming pool whose bottom displays the names of the seven original astronauts. A poolside tiki hut serves libations and other refreshments, and there's a Chinese restaurant on the premises. Some units have kitchenettes.

Holiday Inn Cocoa Beach. 1300 N. Atlantic Ave. (Fla. A1A, at Holiday Lane), Cocoa Beach, FL 32931. ☎ **800/226-6587** or 407/783-2271. Fax 407/783-8878. 515 units. A/C TV TEL. $69–$99 double. AE, DC, DISC, MC, V.

Set on 30 beachside acres, this sprawling complex offers a wide variety of hotel rooms, efficiencies, and cottagelike villas in several buildings flanking a central courtyard with tropical foliage and eight tennis courts. A large heated pool sits to one side, and guests can use sports equipment at the beach. Dining outlets include Willard's Restaurant, specializing in buffets, and the Oceanside Cafe by the beach. There's a volleyball court, whirlpool, concierge desk, beauty salon, coin-op laundry, and gift shop. A convention center draws groups here.

CAPE CANAVERAL

Radisson Resort at the Port. 8701 Astronaut Blvd. (Fla. A1A, at Central Blvd.), Cape Canaveral, FL 32920. ☎ **800/333-3333** or 407/784-0000. Fax 407/784-3737. 200 units. A/C TV TEL. $119 double. AE, DC, DISC, MC, V. Free parking.

Although it's not on the beach, this resort complex is the closest major hotel to Port Canaveral, making it a handy base if you're visiting the Space Center or waiting to board one of the cruise ships based here. If you don't feel like driving a mile to the beach, relax at the lushly landscaped deck area where there's an outdoor heated pool (with a waterfall cascading over fake rocks) and a separate kids' pool. A large health club, whirlpool, and night-lit tennis courts are also on the premises. The hotel caters to a business crowd, which means lots of convenient services and facilities such as room service, laundry and dry cleaning, baby-sitting, express checkout, courtesy van to Port Canaveral, a conference desk, car-rental desk, and beauty salon.

WHERE TO DINE

On the **Cocoa Beach Pier,** at the beach end of Meade Avenue, the view down the coast overwhelms the seafood offerings at **The Pier House Restaurant** (☎ **407/783-7549**), a favorite haunt of astronauts on break (open daily from 5 to 10pm). So is the adjacent **Marlins Good Times Bar & Grill** (same phone), where inexpensive pub fare is offered daily from 11am until the last patron crawls home. Even if you don't dine on the Pier, the outdoor, tin-roofed **Mai Tiki Bar** is a fine place to have a drink while watching the surfers or a sunset.

Cocoa Beach has more fast-food chains than you could ask for along Fla. A1A and Fla. 520, plus a profusion of bars (serving bar snacks), Chinese restaurants, and barbecue joints. The best dining choices here, however, are on Cocoa Beach about 3 miles south of the Fla. 520 causeway.

Bernard's Surf. 2 South Atlantic Ave. (at Minuteman Causeway Rd.), Cocoa Beach. ☎ **407/783-2401.** Main courses $15–$25. Early-bird specials (4–6:30pm) $8–$11. AE, DC, DISC, MC, V. Mon–Sat 11am–11pm; Sun 5–10pm. SEAFOOD/STEAKS.

This Florida institution has been serving standard steak and seafood fare in a large and elegant setting since 1948. Photos on the wall testify to the claim that many astronauts come here to celebrate their landings. House specials like the filet mignon served with sautéed mushrooms and bernaise sauce are their best bets—and yours. Grilled swordfish and other fish are always good choices, too. A warm loaf of fresh bread is irresistible served with roasted whole garlic.

✪ **The Mango Tree.** 118 N. Atlantic Ave. (Fla. A1A, between N. 1st and N. 2nd sts.), Cocoa Beach. ☎ **407/799-0513.** Reservations recommended. Main courses $13–$29. AE, MC, V. Tues–Sun 6–9pm. CONTINENTAL.

Gourmet seafood, pastas, and chicken are served in a plantation-home atmosphere with elegant furnishings in this stucco house, now the finest dining venue here. A waterfall spashing into a Japanese koi pond provides a pleasing backdrop out in the lush tropical gardens. The chef does his daily spin on fresh tuna filets, but you can chose from roast Long Island duckling, tournedos with peppercorn mushroom sauce, and other excellent offerings drawing their inspiration from the continent.

Rusty's Seafood & Oyster Bar. 2 S. Atlantic Ave. (Fla. A1A, at Minuteman Causeway Rd.), Cocoa Beach. ☎ **407/783-2401.** Reservations not accepted. Sandwiches and salads $3–$8; main courses $5–$15. AE, DC, DISC, MC, V. Daily 11am–2am. SEAFOOD/PUB FARE.

Adjacent to and part of Bernard's Surf (see the earlier description), this lively sports bar with indoor and outdoor seating offers inexpensive chow ranging from very spicy seafood gumbo to a pot of seafood that will give two normal persons their fill of steamed oysters, clams, shrimp, crab legs, potatoes, and corn on the cob. Daily happy hour is from 3 to 6pm; oysters (raw or steamed) and spicy Buffalo wings go for 25¢ each.

THE SPACE COAST AFTER DARK

For a rundown of current performances and exhibits, call the **Brevard Cultural Alliance's Arts Line** (☎ 407/690-6819). For live music, walk out on the **Cocoa Beach Pier,** on Meade Avenue at the beach, where **Marlins Good Times Bar & Grill** (☎ 407/783-7549) has bands on weekends, more often during the winter season, and the al fresco **Mai Tiki Bar** is a great place to hang out over a cold beer.

3 The Tampa Bay Area

Tampa: 74 miles southwest of Orlando. St. Petersburg: 84 miles southwest of Orlando. Clearwater: 94 miles southwest of Orlando.

Many families visiting Orlando's theme parks eventually drive an hour west on I-4 to another major kiddie attraction, Busch Gardens Tampa Bay. But this area shouldn't be a mere side trip from Disney World, for Florida's central west coast is an exciting destination unto itself.

At the head of the bay, the city of Tampa is the commercial center of Florida's west coast—the country's eleventh busiest seaport and a center of banking, hi-tech manufacturing, and cigar-making (half a billion drugstore stogies a year). Downtown Tampa may roll up its sidewalks after dark, but you can come here during the day to see the sea life at the Florida Aquarium and stroll through the Henry B. Plant Museum, housed in an ornate, Moorish-style hotel built a century ago to lure tourists to Tampa. A trolley will take you on a short ride to Ybor City, the historic Cuban enclave, which is now an exciting entertainment and dining venue. And out in the suburbs, Busch Gardens may be best known for its scintillating rides, but it's also one of the world's largest zoos.

Two bridges and a causeway will whisk you westward across the bay to the Pinellas Peninsula, one of Florida's most densely packed urban areas. Over here on the bayfront, lovely downtown St. Petersburg is famous for wintering seniors, a shopping and dining complex built way out on a pier, and the world's largest collection of Salvador Dalí's surrealist paintings.

Keep driving west and you'll come to a line of barrier islands where St. Pete Beach, Treasure Island, Clearwater Beach, and other gulfside communities boast 28 miles of sunshine, surf, and white sand. Yes, they're lined with resorts and condos of every description and price, but parks on each end preserve two of the nation's finest beaches.

Drive north up the coast and you'll go back in time at the old Greek sponge enclave of Tarpon Springs, one of Florida's most attractive small towns, and at Weeki Wachee Springs, a tourist attraction where "mermaids" have been entertaining underwater for half a century.

Heading south, the Sunshine Skyway will take you soaring 175 feet above the bay to Bradenton, Sarasota, and another chain of barrier islands. One of Florida's cultural centers, affluent Sarasota is the gateway to St. Armands and Longboat keys, two playgrounds of the rich and famous, and to Lido and Siesta keys, attractive to families of more modest means. Even more reasonably priced is Anna Maria Island, off the riverfront town of Bradenton. You might say the bridge from Longboat to Anna Maria goes from one price range to another.

TAMPA

Even if you stay at the beaches 20 miles to the west, you should consider driving into Tampa to see its sights. If you have children in tow, they will *demand* that you come into the city so that they can ride the rides and see the animals at Busch Gardens. While here, you can educate them at the Florida Aquarium and the city's fine museums. And if you don't have kids, historic Ybor City has the bay area's liveliest nightlife.

Tampa was a sleepy little port when Cuban immigrants founded Ybor City's cigar industry in the 1880s. A few years later Henry B. Plant put Tampa on the tourist map by building a railroad to town and the bulbous minarets over his garish Tampa Bay Hotel. During the Spanish American War, Teddy Roosevelt trained his Rough Riders here and walked the Ybor City streets with Cuban Revolutionary José Marti. A land boom in the 1920s gave the city its charming, Victorian-style Hyde Park suburb, just across the Hillsborough River from downtown, now a gentrified redoubt of the baby boomers.

The downtown skyline we see today, however, is the product of a 1980s and early 1990s boom, when banks built skyscrapers and the city put up an expansive convention center, a performing arts center, and the Ice Palace, a 20,000-seat bayfront arena that is home to professional hockey's Tampa Bay Lightning. Alongside the new Florida Aquarium, the Garrison Seaport Center is a major home port for cruise ships bound for Mexico and the Caribbean. Baseball's New York Yankees helped things along by building their spring training complex here, including a scaled-down replica of Yankee Stadium. And although the project has been plagued by controversy, the city fathers also hope to build a new stadium to satisfy the owners of pro football's resurgent Tampa Bay Buccaneers.

Tampa Bay Area

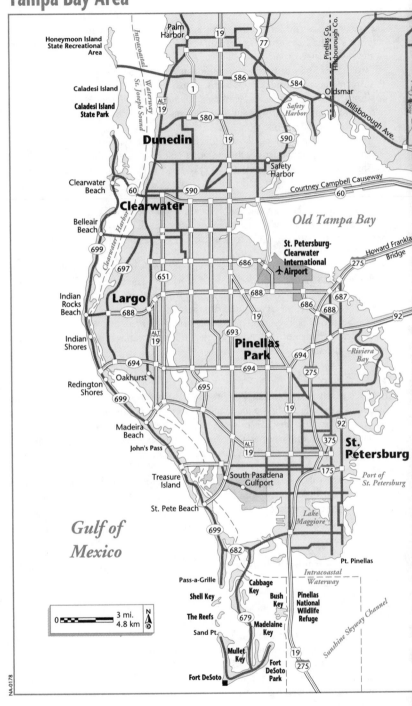

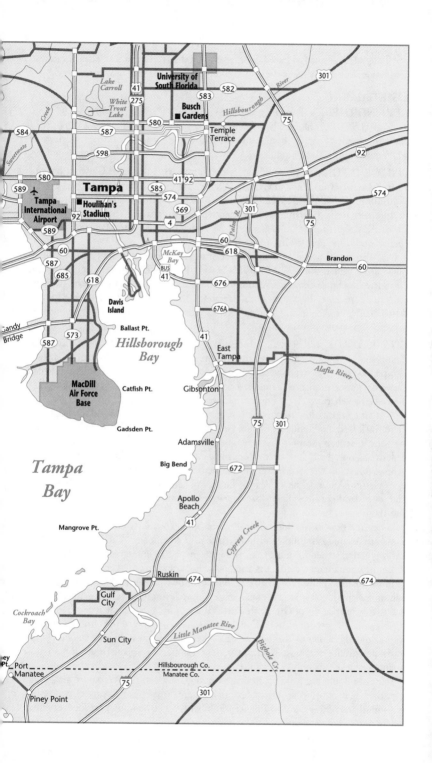

All this adds up to a fast-paced, modern city on the go. Tampa isn't a beach vacation destination, but there's plenty here to keep both adults and kids busy for a few days.

ESSENTIALS

GETTING THERE Tampa is accessible via I-275, I-75, I-4, U.S. 19, U.S. 41, U.S. 92, and U.S. 301. The Busch Gardens area lies between I-75 and I-275 north of downtown; exit at Busch Boulevard and follow the signs. Downtown is south of I-275; take exit 26 and go south on Ashley Street.

VISITOR INFORMATION Contact the **Tampa/Hillsborough Convention and Visitors Association, Inc. (THCVA),** 400 N. Tampa St., Tampa, FL 33602-4706 (☎ **800/44-TAMPA** or 813/223-2752; fax 813/229-6616) for advance information. Its Internet site is at **http://www.thcva.com**. Once you're downtown, head to the THCVA's Visitors Information Center at the corner of Ashley and Madison streets. It's open Monday to Saturday from 9am to 5pm.

Near Busch Gardens, the **Tampa Bay Visitor Information Center,** 3601 E. Busch Blvd., at N. Ednam Place (☎ **813/985-3601**), is a privately owned operation, but it offers free brochures about attractions in Tampa and sells discounted tickets to many attractions. You may be able to both save about $2 a head and avoid waiting in long Busch Gardens ticket lines by buying here, and the staff gives expert advice about how to get the most out of your visit.

CITY LAYOUT Other than business travelers and sports fans, most visitors to Tampa head 7 miles north of downtown to the suburban area around **Busch Gardens Tampa Bay,** the city's major attraction. The main drag here is Busch Boulevard, which passes the park entrance as it runs east-west between I-75 and I-275. It's a busy commercial strip where you'll find dozens of restaurants and hotels.

Tampa's compact **downtown** area is primarily a daytime business and financial hub. Here you'll find the Florida Aquarium (see "What to See & Do," later in this chapter) and the Garrison Seaport Center. The grid streets are all one-way except for pedestrians-only Franklin Street. From the southern tip of Franklin, you can ride the people mover, an elevated tram that automatically shuttles over to **Harbour Island** (see "Getting Around," next). Across the narrow Garrison Channel from downtown, Harbour Island is a struggling urban development project where spaces for restaurants and shops stand vacant.

When the downtown sidewalks roll up at 5pm, **Ybor City** comes alive. Centered along 7th Avenue East on the northeastern edge of downtown, "Ybor" is Tampa's lively Latin Quarter, settled for more than 100 years by Cuban immigrants. Today it's home to hot new restaurants, clubs, arts and crafts shops, and hand-rolled cigars.

Just across the Hillsborough River from downtown, **Hyde Park** is the city's oldest and once again its poshest residential neighborhood, complete with the upscale shops and trendy restaurants of **Old Hyde Park Village.** This Victorian neighborhood is on the National Register of Historic Districts. **Bayshore Boulevard** runs from Hyde Park south along the shores of Hillsborough Bay. With a view across the water to the downtown skyline, it's the most beautiful part of Tampa, a gorgeous route for driving, biking, or in-line skating.

Kennedy Boulevard is the main drag from downtown to the **Westshore** area, lying near the bay west of Hyde Park and south of Tampa International Airport. Westshore is a suburban commercial and financial hub, with office buildings, business-oriented hotels, and a shopping mall.

GETTING AROUND Like most other Florida destinations, it's virtually impossible to see Tampa's major sights and enjoy the best restaurants without a car. Nevertheless, the **Tampa-Ybor Trolley** connects downtown, Harbour Island, the Florida Aquarium, the Garrison Seaport Center, and Ybor City. It runs daily from 9am to 4pm, with additional service between downtown and the Florida Aquarium daily from 7:30 to 9am and from 4 to 5:30pm. The fare is 25¢ per person. Get a route map at the Visitor Information Center (see "Visitor Information, earlier in this chapter), or call HARTline at ☎ **813/224-4278** for information. The 18 stops are marked with green and orange signs.

There's little reason to go to Harbour Island unless you're staying there, but the **Harbour Island People Mover,** an automated tram on elevated tracks, runs between the third level of the Fort Brooke Parking Garage, on Whiting Street at Franklin Street, and Harbour Island continuously Monday to Saturday from 7am to midnight and Sunday from 8am to midnight (there's a shuttle bus off-hours). The fare is 25¢ each way.

The **Hillsborough Area Regional Transit/HARTline** (☎ 813/254-HART) provides regularly scheduled bus service between downtown Tampa and the suburbs. Fares are $1.15 for local rides, $1.50 for express routes; correct change is required. Pick up a route map at the Visitor Information Center (see "Visitor Information," earlier in this section).

Taxis in Tampa don't normally cruise the streets for fares, but they do line up at public loading places, such as hotels, the Tampa Bay Performing Arts Center, and bus and train depots. If you need a taxi, call **Tampa Bay Cab** (☎ 813/251-5555), **Yellow Cab** (☎ 813/253-0121), or **United Cab** (☎ 813/253-2424). Fares are 95¢ at flag fall plus $1.50 for each mile.

WHAT TO SEE & DO

Adventure Island. 10001 McKinley Dr. (between Busch Blvd. and Bougainvillea Ave.). ☎ 813/987-5600. Admission $22.95 adults, $20.95 children 3–9, plus tax. Free for children 2 and under. *Note:* Prices keep increasing, so expect to pay slightly more. Seasonal passes available. Mid-Feb–Labor Day, daily 10am–5pm; Sept–Oct, Fri–Sun 10am–5pm (extended hours in summer and on holidays). Closed Nov–mid-Feb. Take exit 33 off I-275, go east on Busch Blvd. for 2 miles, turn left onto McKinley Dr. (N. 40th St.), and entry is on right.

If the summer heat gets to you before one of Tampa's famous thunderstorms brings late afternoon relief, you can take a water-logged break at this 36-acre outdoor water theme park near Busch Gardens Tampa Bay (described next). In fact, you can frolick here even during the cooler days of spring and fall, when the water is heated. The Key West Rapids, Tampa Typhoon, Gulf Scream, and other exciting water rides will drench the teens, while other calmer rides are geared for kids. There are places to picnic and sunbathe, a games arcade, a volleyball complex, and an outdoor cafe. If you forget to bring your own, a surf shop sells bathing suits, towels, and suntan lotion.

✪ **Busch Gardens Tampa Bay.** 3000 E. Busch Blvd. (at McKinley Drive/N. 40th St.). ☎ 813/987-5283. Admission $37.95 adults, $31.95 children 3 to 9, plus tax. Free for children 2 and under. *Note:* Prices keep increasing, so expect to pay slightly more. Seasonal passes available. Parking $4 cars, $3 motorbikes, $5 campers and trailers. Take I-275 north of downtown to Busch Blvd. (Exit 33), and go east 2 miles. From I-75, take Exit 54 and follow Fowler Ave. and the signs west.

Although its thrill rides, live entertainment, shops, restaurants, and games get most of the ink, this venerable theme park (it predates Disney World) ranks among the top zoos in the country. This is a great place for the kids to see in person all those wild beasts they've watched on the Discovery Channel. The animals—several thousand of them—live in naturalistic environments and help carry out an overall "Dark Continent" of Africa theme.

The park is divided into several areas, each with its own theme, animals, live entertainment, thrill rides, kiddie attractions, dining, and shopping. A monorail train will take you from one to another. A Skyride cable car soars over the park, offering a bird's eye view of the beasts (but not much else).

Allow at least a day here, and arrive early—but try not to come when it's raining, since some rides may not operate and you won't get a rain check for admission on another day. You can avoid waiting in long lines—and save a few dollars—by buying your tickets in advance at the **Tampa Bay Visitor Information Center** (see "Essentials," earlier in this chapter). Bring comfortable shoes, and remember, you can get wet on some of the rides, so wear appropriate clothing. You can exchange foreign currency in the park, and interpreters are available.

As soon as you're through the turnstiles, pick up a copy of a park map and the day's activity schedule, which tells you what's showing and when at the park's 14 entertainment venues. Then take a few minutes to carefully plan your time.

Just past the main gate you'll come to **Morocco,** a walled city with exotic architecture, craft demonstrations, a sultan's tent with snake charmers, and an exhibit featuring alligators and turtles. The **Moroccan Palace Theater** features **Hollywood Live on Ice,** which many families consider to be the park's best entertainment. Here you can also attend **American Jukebox,** a song and dance show, in the **Marrakesh Theater,** or a **live TV show** in the **Tangiers Theater.**

After watching the snake charmers in Morocco, walk eastward to the main Skyride and monorail station and **Crown Colony,** home of a team of Anheuser-Busch's big-footed Clydesdale horses, the park's hospitality center, and **Questor,** a flight-simulator adventure ride.

From here, take the monorail train to **Egypt,** which mirrors that country's culture and history, including a replica of King Tutankhamen's tomb. Adults and older kids can ride **Montu,** the tallest and longest inverted roller coaster in the world with seven upside-down loops, one of them barely missing a crocodile pit. Youngsters can dig for their own ancient treasures in a sand area. Everyone can join comedian Martin Short, who plays a shady Egyptian tour guide in **Akbar's Adventure Tours,** a whacky simulator that transports one and all across Egypt via camel, biplane, and mine car.

From Egypt, walk under the monorail and out onto the **Serengeti Plain,** where glass walls separate you from lions, hippos, crocodiles, hyenas, meerkats, and vultures—among more than 500 African animals roaming freely on an 80-acre natural grassy veldt.

After you've seen them close-up, get back on the monorail and ride across the plain and around the park to **Nairobi,** where you can see gorillas and chimpanzees in the **Myombe Reserve,** replicating their natural tropical habitat. Nairobi also has a baby animal nursery, a petting zoo, turtle and reptile displays, an elephant exhibit, and **Nocturnal Mountain,** a simulated environment that allows you to observe animals that are active in the dark.

From Nairobi, walk into **Timbuktu,** evoking an ancient desert trading center with African craftspeople at work. Here you'll find several rides, including a train for kids, one through a sandstorm, another on swinging boats, and **Scorpion,** a 360° roller coaster. Plan to have lunch here at **Das Festhaus,** a 1,000-seat, air-conditioned German festival hall featuring a lively musical show (be sure to arrive at least 15 minutes before showtime). The kids will enjoy the **Dolphin Theater,** with performing porpoises, otters, and sea lions.

After lunch, head to **The Congo,** highlighted by rare white Bengal tigers living on **Claw Island.** The Congo also is home to **Kumba,** the largest and fastest roller coaster in the southeastern United States, and the **Python,** which twists and turns for 1,200 feet. You will get drenched (and refreshed on a hot day) by riding the **Congo River Rapids.** There are bumper cars and kiddie rides here, too.

From The Congo, walk south into **Stanleyville,** a prototype African village, with a shopping bazaar, orangutans living on an island, and the **Stanleyville Theater,** featuring a troupe of Russian acrobats. Two more water rides are here: the **Tanganyika Tidal Wave** and **Stanley Falls.** Serving ribs and chicken, the **Stanleyville Smokehouse** has some of the best chow here. This also is a good place to board the monorail for a sightseeing ride all the way around the park and back, since you'll avoid the crowds waiting to board elsewhere.

From Stanleyville, the next stop is **Land of the Dragons,** where the younger set can easily spend an entire day enjoying a variety of play elements in a fairy-tale setting, plus just-for-kids rides. The area is dominated by Dumphrey, a whimsical dragon who interacts with visitors and guides children around a three-story tree house with winding stairways, tall towers, stepping stones, illuminated water geysers, and an echo chamber.

The last stop is **Bird Gardens,** the park's original core, offering rich foliage, lagoons, and a free-flight aviary for hundreds of exotic birds, including golden and American bald eagles. Catch the **Bird Show** here.

You can finish your visit back at the hospitality center in **Crown Colony,** where adults can imbibe some of Anheuser-Busch's famous beers (there's a limit of two free mugs per seating).

✪ **Florida Aquarium.** 701 Channelside Dr. ☎ **813/273-4000.** Admission $10.95 adults, $9.95 seniors, $5.95 children 3–12, free for children under 3. Daily 9:30am–5pm. Closed Thanksgiving and Christmas. Parking $3.

Visitors here are introduced to more than 5,300 aquatic animals and plants that call Florida home. Various exhibits allow you to follow the pristine springs of the Florida Wetlands Gallery, go through a mangrove forest in the Bays and Beaches Gallery, and stand amazed at the Coral Reefs. The most impressive display is a 43-foot-wide, 14-foot-tall panoramic window with schools of fish and lots of sharks and stingrays. You can watch a diver twice a day. There's a half-million-dollar "Explore a Shore" playground to educate the kids, a deep water exhibit, and a tank housing moray eels. The Cafe Ray serves snacks and light meals.

Henry B. Plant Museum. 401 W. Kennedy Blvd. (between Hyde Park and Magnolia aves.). ☎ **813/254-1891.** Free admission; suggested donation, $3 adults, $1 children 12 and under. Tues–Sat 10am–4pm; Sun noon–4pm. Take Fla. 60 west of downtown.

You can't miss the 13 silver minarets and distinctive Moorish architecture—it's modeled after the Alhambra in Spain—that make this National Historic Landmark a focal point of the Tampa skyline. Originally built in 1891 as the 511-room Tampa Bay Hotel by railroad tycoon Henry B. Plant, it's filled with art and furnishings from Europe and the Orient. Other exhibits focus on the history of the original railroad resort, Florida's early tourist industry, and the hotel's role as a staging point for Teddy Roosevelt's Rough Riders during the Spanish-American War.

✪ **Museum of African-American Art.** 1308 N. Marion St. (entry and parking lot face N. Florida Ave. between Scott and Laurel sts.), downtown. ☎ **813/272-2466.** Admission $3 adults, $2 seniors and children grades K–12. Tues–Fri 10am–4:30pm; Sat 10am–5pm. Take Exit 26 off I-275.

Recently renovated to the tune of $200,000, the museum is touted as the first of its kind in Florida and one of four in the United States. It's the home of the Barnett-Aden collection, considered the state's foremost collection of African-American art. More

Tampa Accommodations, Dining & Attractions

Accommodations:

Best Western Resort Tampa **2**
Budgetel Inn **3**
Courtyard by Marriott **17**
Days Inn Maingate **4**
DoubleTree Guest Suites **15**
Holiday Inn Select Downtown **31**
Hyatt Regency Westshore **14**
Quality Suites Hotel–
    USF/Busch Gardens **6**
Saddlebrook Resort **1**
Sheraton Grand Hotel **16**
Wyndham Harbour
    Island Hotel **36**

Dining:

Bern's Steak House **20**
Cactus Club **22**
Cafe Creole & Oyster Bar **26**
Carmine's Restaurant & Bar **24**
The Colonnade **21**
The Columbia **28**
Lauro Ristorante Italiano **18**
Mel's Hot Dogs **5**
Mise en Place **23**
Ovo Cafe **25**
Shells **7**
SideBern's **19**

Attractions:

Adventure Island **9**
Busch Gardens **8**
Florida Aquarium/Garrison
    Seaport Center **35**
Houlihan's Stadium **12**
Museum of African-
    American Art **32**
Museum of Science
    and Industry **10**
N.Y. Yankee Spring
    Training Complex **13**
Seminole Indian Casino **11**
Tampa Museum of Art **33**
University of Tampa **30**
Visitor Information
    Center **34**
Ybor City Brewing Co. **29**
Ybor City State Museum **27**

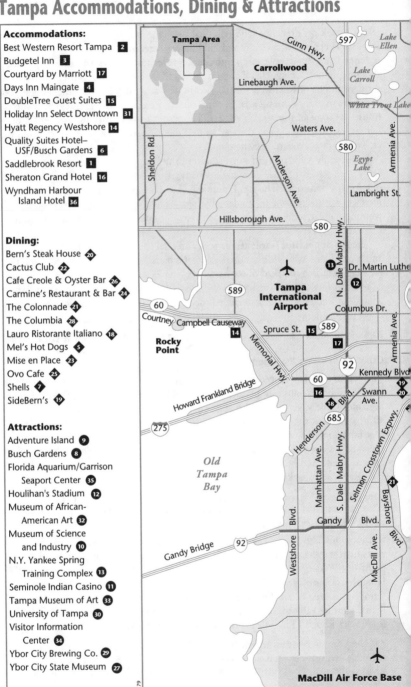

NA-0179

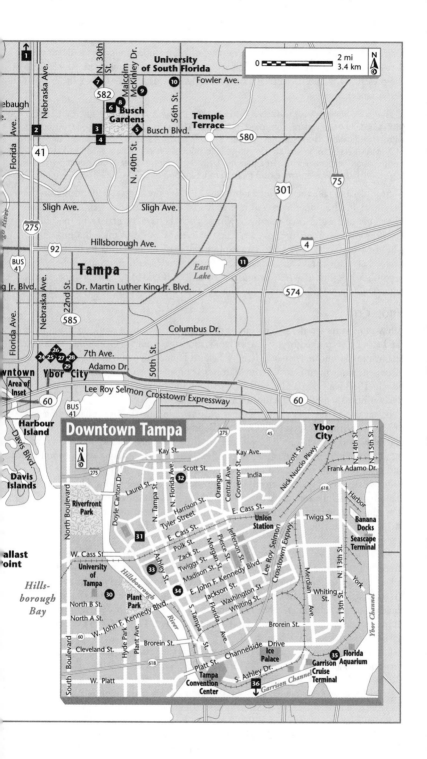

than 80 artists are represented in the display, which includes sculptures and paintings that depict the history, culture, and lifestyle of African-Americans from the 1800s to the present, with special emphasis on the works of artists active during the Harlem Renaissance.

Museum of Science and Industry (MOSI). 4801 E. Fowler Ave. (at N. 50th St.). ☎ **813/ 987-6300.** www.tampatrib.com/mosi. Admission $11 adults; $9 seniors, college students with identification, and children 13–18; $7 children 2–12; free for children under 2. MOSIMAX tickets $6 adults; $5 seniors, college students, and children 3–18; $4 kids 2–12. Combination tickets available. Free parking. Daily 9am–5pm or later. From downtown, take I-275 north, then Fowler Ave. east 2 miles to museum on right.

A great place to take the kids on a rainy day, MOSI is the largest science center in the Southeast and has more than 450 interactive exhibits. Guests can step into the Gulf Hurricane and experience gale-force winds, defy the laws of gravity in the unique *Challenger* space experience, or cruise the mysterious world of microbes in LifeLab. The Amazing You allows visitors to explore the body, Our Florida focuses on environmental factors, and Our Place in the Universe introduces them to space, flight, and beyond. You can also watch stunning movies in MOSIMAX, Florida's first IMAX dome theater.

YBOR CITY

A few short years ago the part of Tampa northeast of downtown was known simply as the Latin Quarter, the historic district famous for cigars and for Columbia, the largest Spanish restaurant in the world (see "Where to Dine," later in this chapter). It takes its present name from Don Vicente Martinez Ybor, a Spanish cigar maker who arrived here in 1886 via Cuba and Key West. Soon his and other Tampa factories were producing more than 300,000 hand-rolled stogies a day.

It may not be the cigar capital of the world anymore, but Ybor is the happening part of Tampa, a cross between New Orleans's Bourbon Street, Washington's Georgetown, and New York's SoHo. By day, you can stroll past the art galleries, boutiques, and trendy new restaurants and cafes that line 7th Avenue East. At night, when good food and great music dominate the scene, streets will be bustling until 4am. Shops offer a wide assortment of goodies, from silk boxer shorts to unique tattoos. Dozens of outstanding nightclubs and dance clubs have waiting lines out the door. Live-music offerings run the gamut from jazz and blues to indie rock. There are lots of police around in the wee hours, but be as cautious here as you would be exploring any big city at night.

✪ **Ybor City Walking Tours** are an ideal way to check out the the highlights of this historic district. Free 1½-hour tours are sponsored by the Ybor City State Museum (see below) and are led by enthusiastic local volunteers. Tours start at the information desk in Ybor Square shopping center, on 13th Street between 8th and 9th avenues, and cover over three dozen points of interest before ending at the Ybor City State Museum. January to April the tours depart on Tuesday, Thursday, and Saturday at 11am; May to December only on Thursday and Saturday.

Cigar smokers will enjoy a stroll through the **Ybor City State Museum,** 1818 9th Ave., between 18th and 19th streets (☎ **813/247-6323**), housed in the former Ferlita Bakery (1896–1973). You can take a self-guided tour around the museum to see a collection of cigar labels, cigar memorabilia, and works by local artisans. Admission is $2 per person. The museum is open Tuesday to Saturday from 9am to noon and 1 to 5pm.

Another interesting stop here is the **Ybor City Brewing Company,** 2205 N. 20th St., facing Palm Avenue (☎ **813/242-9222**). Housed in a 100-year-old, three-story former cigar factory, this microbrewery produces Ybor Gold and other brews, none with preservatives.

Admission of $2 per person includes a tour of the brewery and taste of the end result. Open Tuesday to Saturday from 11am to 3pm.

OUTDOOR PURSUITS & SPECTATOR SPORTS

BIKING, IN-LINE SKATING & JOGGING   Bayshore Boulevard, a 7-mile promenade, is famous for its sidewalk right on the shores of Hillsborough Bay. Reputed to be the world's longest continuous sidewalk, it's a favorite for runners, joggers, walkers, and in-line skaters. The route goes from the western edge of downtown in a southward direction, passing stately old homes of Hyde Park, a few high-rise condos, retirement communities, and houses of worship, ending at Ballast Point Park. The view from the promenade across the bay to the downtown skyline is unmatched here (Bayshore Boulevard also is great for a drive).

Rent bicycles and in-line skates at **Blades & Bikes,** in a pink-and-blue shop at 201-A W. Platt St., at South Parker Street (☎ 813/251-0780), a block west of the northern end of Bayshore Boulevard. Prices for both bikes and blades range from $8 for 1 hour to $20 for all day. Hours are Monday to Friday from 10am to 7pm, Saturday from 9am to 7pm, and Sunday from 10am to 5pm.

GOLF   Tampa has three municipal golf courses where you can play for a relative pittance—just $26 to $34—when compared to the privately owned courses here and elsewhere in Florida. The **Babe Zaharias Municipal Golf Course,** 11412 Forest Hills Dr., north of Lowry Park (☎ 813/631-4374), is an 18-hole, par-70 course with a pro shop, putting greens, and a driving range. It's the shortest of the municipal courses, but small greens and narrow fairways present ample challenges. Water presents the challenges and obstacles on 12 of the 18 holes at **Rocky Point Municipal Golf Course,** 4151 Dana Shores Dr. (☎ 813/673-4316), located between the airport and the bay. It's a par-71 course with a pro shop, practice range, and putting greens. On the Hillsborough River in north Tampa, the **Rogers Park Municipal Golf Course,** 7910 N. 30th St. (☎ 813/673-4396), is an 18-hole, par-72 championship course with a lighted driving and practice range. They all are open daily from 7am to dusk, and lessons and club rentals are available.

Another inexpensive place to play is the **University of South Florida Golf Course,** Fletcher Avenue and 46th Street (☎ 813/632-6893), just north of the USF campus. This 18-hole, par-71 course is nicknamed "The Claw" because of its challenging layout. It offers lessons and club rentals. Greens fees range from about $19 to $25, or $25 to $35 with a cart, depending on the season and time of day. It's open daily from 7am to dusk.

You can book starting times and get information about these and the area's other courses by calling **Tee Times USA** (☎ 800/374-8633).

If you want to do some serious work on your game, the **Arnold Palmer Golf Academy World Headquarters** is at the renowned Saddlebrook Resort, 5700 Saddlebrook Way, Wesley Chapel, 12 miles north of Tampa (☎ 800/729-8383 or 813/973-1111). There are 2-, 3-, and 5-day programs available for adults and juniors, ranging from $248 to $320 per person per night, double occupancy, including accommodations, breakfast, daily instruction, 18 holes of golf daily, cart and greens fees, and nightly club storage and cleaning. You have to stay at the resort or enroll in the golf program to play at Saddlebrook. See "Where to Stay," later in this chapter, for more information about the resort.

SPECTATOR SPORTS   National Football League fans can catch the improving **Tampa Bay Buccaneers** at Houlihan's Stadium, 4201 N. Dale Mabry Hwy., at Dr. Martin Luther King, Jr. Boulevard (☎ 813/872-BUCS). Their season runs from September through December, and tickets range from $20 to $30.

New York Yankees fans can watch the Boys in Blue during baseball spring training from mid-February through March at Legends Field, opposite Houlihan's Stadium (☎ 813/875-7753). A scaled-down replica of Yankee Stadium, it's the largest spring-training facility in Florida, with a 10,000-seat capacity. Tickets range from $6 to $10. The club's minor league team, the **Tampa Yankees** (same phone), plays at Legends Field from April to September. Tickets are $3 for adults, $2 for kids.

TENNIS   The **City of Tampa Tennis Complex,** at the Hillsborough Community College, 3901 Tampa Bay Blvd. (☎ 813/348-1173), across from Houlihan's Stadium, is the largest public complex in Tampa, with 16 hard courts and 12 clay courts. It also has four racquetball courts, a pro shop, locker rooms, showers, and lessons. Reservations are recommended. Prices range from $2.50 to $5 per person per hour. It's open Monday to Thursday from 8am to 9pm, Friday from 8am to 7pm, and Saturday and Sunday from 8am to 6pm.

On the water and overlooking Harbour Island, the **Sandra W. Freedman Tennis Complex,** in Marjorie Park, 59 Columbia Dr., Davis Island (☎ 813/259-1664), has eight clay courts. Reservations are required. The price is $5 per person per hour. Hours are Monday to Friday from 8am to 9pm and Saturday and Sunday from 8am to 6pm.

SHOPPING

Hyde Park and Ybor City are two areas of Tampa worth some window shopping, perhaps combined with lunch at one of their fine restaurants (see "Where to Dine," later in this chapter). ✪ **Old Hyde Park Village,** 1507 W. Swann Ave., at South Dakoka Avenue (☎ 813/251-3500), is a terrific alternative to cookie-cutter suburban malls. **Ybor City,** along East 7th Avenue, between 14th and 22nd streets, has several shops worth browsing. You can watch an artisan rolling stogies at **Tampa Rico Cigar Co.,** one of the shops in **Ybor Square,** 1901 13th St., at 8th Avenue (☎ 813/247-4497), a shopping complex that is listed on the National Register of Historic Places. Today it's primarily notable for several small shops selling an amazing variety of collectibles. If you want to stock up on fresh Florida fruits and vegetables, head to **Whaley's Markets,** 533 S. Howard Ave., at DeLeon, northwest of Hyde Park (☎ 813/254-2904).

WHERE TO STAY

If you're going to Busch Gardens, Adventure Island, and the Museum of Science and Industry (MOSI), the motels near Busch Gardens are much more convenient than those downtown, about 7 miles to the south. The downtown hotels are geared to business travelers, but staying there will put you near the Florida Aquarium, the Museum of African-American Art, the Henry B. Plant Museum, the Tampa Bay Performing Arts Center, scenic Bayshore Boulevard, the dining and shopping opportunities in the Hyde Park historic district, and Ybor City's restaurants and nightlife.

The Westshore area, near the bay west of downtown and south of Tampa International Airport, is another commercial center, with a wide range of national chain hotels catering to business travelers and conventioneers. It's convenient to Houlihan's Stadium and the New York Yankees' spring training complex. Here you'll find the Spanish-style **Doubletree Guest Suites,** 4400 W. Cypress St., at Manhattan Avenue (☎ 800/222-TREE or 813/873-8675); **Courtyard by Marriott,** 3805 W. Cypress St., at Dale Mabry Highway (☎ 800/321-2211 or 813/874-0555); the **Hyatt Regency Westshore,** 6200 Courtney Campbell Causeway (☎ 800/233-1234 or 813/874-1234), nestled on a 35-acre bayside nature preserve; the **Sheraton Grand Hotel,** 4860 W. Kennedy Blvd., at Shore Boulevard (☎ 800/325-3535 or 813/286-4400), across the street from Westshore Plaza mall and home to one of former Miami Dolphins Coach Don Shula's steak houses; and the **Tampa Marriott Westshore,** 1001 N. Westshore Blvd. (☎ 800/228-9290 or 813/287-2555).

The high season in Tampa generally runs from January to April, but you won't find as large an increase here as at the beach resorts. Most hotels offer discounted package rates in the summer and weekend specials all year, dropping their rates by as much as 50%. Hotels often combine tickets to major attractions like Busch Gardens in their packages, so always ask about special deals.

Near Busch Gardens

In addition to the listings that follow, there's the **Red Roof Inn,** 2307 E. Busch Blvd., between 22nd and 26th streets (☎ **800/THE-ROOF** or 813/932-0073), a pleasant property on landscaped grounds where doubles are $69 in high-season, $45 off-season. **Days Inn Maingate,** 2901 E. Busch Blvd., at 30th Street (☎ **800/ DAYS-INN** or 813/933-6471), charging $64 double in winter, $42 to $52 double off-season, is less appealing than the Budgetel Inn across the street (see below), but it's convenient for families on a budget since you can walk to Busch Gardens from here (there're also two more Days Inns within a short drive of Busch Gardens. Both motels have outdoor pools.)

Best Western Resort Tampa at Busch Gardens. 820 E. Busch Blvd. (at I-275), Tampa, FL 33612. ☎ **800/288-4011** or 813/933-4011. Fax 813/932-1784. 255 units. A/C TV TEL. Winter $99 double; off-season $59 double. AE, DC, DISC, MC, V.

Right at the Busch Boulevard exit off I-275, this motel is fine for families on a budget. The lobby leads to an enclosed skylit atrium-style courtyard with fountains, streetlights, benches, a pool, and tropical foliage. Guest rooms in this wing open to walkways facing the indoor atrium or the parking lots. Newer units are in a four-story annex. They all have standard furnishings and coffeemakers.

The Palm Grill Restaurant off the lobby features a variety of dishes, while the Bull Pen Sports Bar offers pub fare and libations until 11pm nightly. Services include a concierge desk, secretarial services, valet laundry, limited room service, and courtesy transport to Busch Gardens. There are indoor and outdoor heated swimming pools, two whirlpools, a sauna, four lighted tennis courts, exercise and game rooms, a coin-operated laundry, and a gift shop.

Budgetel Inn. 9202 N. 30th St. (at Busch Blvd.), Tampa, FL 33612. ☎ **800/428-3438** or 813/930-6900. Fax 813/930-0563. 150 units. A/C TV TEL. Winter $77 double; off-season $57 double. Rates include continental breakfast. AE, DC, DISC, MC, V.

Fake banana trees and a parrot cage welcome guests to the terra-cotta–floored lobby of this comfortable and convenient member of a fine chain of budget-conscious motels. All rooms are spacious and have ceiling fans, bright wood furniture with tropical trim, desks, phones with long cords, and coffeemakers (Danish pastries or a blueberry muffin and juice are hung on your doorknob before dawn). Rooms with king beds also have recliners. Outside, a courtyard with an unheated swimming pool has plenty of space for sunning. There's a game room and coin laundry, and local telephone calls are free. There's no restaurant on the premises, but plenty are nearby.

✪ **Quality Suites Hotel—USF Near Busch Gardens.** 3001 University Center Dr., Tampa, FL 33612. ☎ **800/786-7446** or 813/971-8930. Fax 813/971-8935. 150 suites. A/C TV TEL. Winter $99–$159 suite for 2; off-season $89–$139 suite for 2. Rates include full breakfast buffet and evening cocktail reception. AE, DC, DISC, MC, V.

Actually on North 30th Street, between Busch Boulevard and Fletcher Avenue, this hacienda-style all-suite hotel sits about a mile from the Busch Gardens entrance and is the pick of the hotels in this area. The complex encloses a lushly tropical courtyard surrounding a heated pool, hot tub, covered games area, and outdoor seating for Ruzik's Roost, a beach-bar type grill serving a complimentary breakfast buffet plus lunch and dinner (it can get noisy on this end of the courtyard, so ask for a suite away from the action). Opening to this pleasant vista, each suite has two TVs and a separate bedroom with built-in armoire and well-lit mirrored vanity area. Living/dining rooms have a sofa bed, La-Z-Boy recliner, wet bar, coffeemaker, microwave, and stereo/VCR unit. Facilities also include a 24-hour gift shop/food store, VCR rentals, whirlpool, meeting rooms, and coin-operated laundry.

Downtown Tampa

Holiday Inn Select Downtown. 111 W. Fortune St. (at Ashley St.), Tampa, FL 33602. ☎ **800/513-8940** or 813/223-1351. Fax 813/221-2000. 312 units. A/C TV TEL. Winter $105–$150 double; off-season $89–$125 double. AE, DC, DISC, MC, V. Take Ashley St. (Exit 25) off I-275; turn right at bottom of ramp to hotel.

This modern 14-story hotel is adjacent to the Tampa Bay Performing Arts Center and within walking distance of the Tampa Museum of Art. The guest rooms are spacious, with dark-wood furnishings, full-length wall mirrors, coffeemakers, irons and ironing boards. Most rooms on the upper floors have views of the Hillsborough River, and rooms on the 11th floor come equipped with microwave ovens and refrigerators. The lobby level offers three dining choices: a restaurant for moderately priced meals, a deli for light fare, and lounge for drinks and occasional live music. There's limited room service, airport courtesy shuttle, an outdoor heated swimming pool, whirlpool, fitness room, gift shop, and both laundry service and a coin-operated Laundromat.

✪ **Wyndham Harbour Island Hotel.** 725 S. Harbour Island Blvd., Harbour Island, Tampa, FL 33602. ☎ **800/WYNDHAM** or 813/229-5000. Fax 813/229-5322. 299 units. A/C MINIBAR TV TEL. Winter $139–$219 double; off-season $99–$169 double. AE, DC, DISC, MC, V.

With the shops closed, there's not much action on this little island, but you'll enjoy quiet elegance at this 12-story luxury property. It has great views of the surrounding channels that link the Hillsborough River and the bay. The bedrooms, all with views of the water, are furnished in dark woods and floral fabrics, and each has a well-lit marble-trimmed bathroom, executive desk, and work area, plus in-room conveniences such as a coffeemaker, iron, and ironing board.

Dining: Watch the yachts drift by as you dine at the Harbourview Room, or enjoy your favorite drink in the Bar, a clubby room with equally good views. Snacks and drinks are available during the day at the Pool Bar.

Amenities: Outdoor heated swimming pool and deck, newsstand/gift shop, guest privileges at the Harbour Island Athletic Club. Concierge, room service, secretarial services, notary public, evening turndown, valet laundry, courtesy airport shuttle.

WHERE TO DINE

Near Busch Gardens

You'll find the national fast-food and family restaurants located east of I-275 on Busch Boulevard and along Fletcher Avenue near University Mall.

✪ **Mel's Hot Dogs.** 4136 E. Busch Blvd., at 42nd St. ☎ **813/985-8000.** Main courses $3–$6.50. No credit cards. Daily 11am–9pm. AMERICAN.

Catering to everyone from businesspeople on a lunch break to hungry families craving inexpensive all-beef hot dogs, this red-and-white cottage offers everything from "bagel-dogs" and corndogs to a bacon/cheddar Reuben. All choices are served on a poppyseed bun, and most come with french fries and a choice of cole slaw or baked beans. Even the decor is dedicated to wieners: The walls and windows are lined with hot-dog memorabilia. And just in case hot-dog mania hasn't won you over, there are a few alternative choices (sausages, chicken breast, and beef and veggie burgers).

Shells. 11010 N. 30th St. (between Busch Blvd. and Fowler Ave.). ☎ **813/977-8456.** Reservations not accepted. Main courses $6–$17. AE, DISC, MC, V. Mon–Thurs 11:30am–10pm; Fri–Sat 11:30am–11pm; Sun noon–10pm. SEAFOOD.

You'll see Shells restaurants in many parts of Florida, and with good reason, for this casual, award-winning chain consistently provides excellent value, especially if you have a family to feed. They all have the same menu and prices, and are particularly known for their spicy Jack Daniel's buffalo shrimp and scallop appetizers. Main courses range from the usual fried seafood platters to pastas and chargrilled shrimp, fish, steaks, and chicken. I counted 21 tender, bite-size shrimp in a light, garlic-tinged cream sauce and served over linguine—a bargain for $9.50—and 30 of them perfectly char-grilled on a skewer and served with saffron rice and steamed vegetables for $11. There's a children's menu.

HYDE PARK

An appropriately dark atmosphere for meat lovers, for here you order and pay for char-grilled steaks (beef or buffalo) according to the thickness and weight. They come with onion soup, salad, baked potato, garlic toast, onion rings, and vegetables grown in Bern's own organic garden. The phone book–size wine list offers more than 7,000 selections.

Cactus Club. In Old Hyde Park shopping complex, 1601 Snow Ave. (south of Swan St.). ☎ **813/251-4089.** Reservations not accepted. Main courses $6.50–$15. AE, DC, MC, V. Mon–Thurs 11am–11pm; Fri–Sat 11am–midnight; Sun 11am–10:30pm. AMERICAN SOUTHWEST.

Watch all the shoppers go by at Old Hyde Park from this fun and casual cafe with a Southwestern accent. Dine inside or outside on tacos, enchiladas, chili, sizzling fajitas, hickory-smoked baby-back ribs, Jamaican jerk chicken, guacamole/green-chili burgers, fajitas, quesadillas, sandwiches, smoked chicken salad, and more. It's always packed at lunchtime—get here early.

The Colonnade. 3401 Bayshore Blvd. (at W. Julia St.). ☎ **813/839-7558.** Reservations accepted only for large parties. Main courses $8–$18. AE, DC, DISC, MC, V. Sun–Thurs 11am–10pm; Fri–Sat 11am–11pm. AMERICAN/SEAFOOD.

Locals have been flocking to this rough-hewn, shiplap place since 1935, primarily for the great view of Hillsborough Bay across Bayshore Boulevard. The food is a bit on the Red Lobsterish side, but get here early or wait for a windowside table; the vista is worth it. Fresh seafood is the specialty: grouper prepared seven ways, crab-stuffed flounder, Maryland-style crab cakes, even wild Florida alligator as an appetizer. Prime rib, steaks, and chicken are also available.

✪ **Lauro Ristorante Italiano.** 3915 Henderson Blvd. (2 blocks west of Dale Mabry Hwy., between Watrous and Neptune aves.). ☎ **813/281-2100.** Reservations recommended. Main courses $10–$25. AE, DC, DISC, MC, V. Mon–Fri 11:30am–2pm and 5:30–10pm; Sat 5:30–11pm. ITALIAN.

Known for extraordinary sauces and pastas, chef/owner Lauro Medeglia is a native Italian who cooks his home fare with love. Though his restaurant is off the beaten track, it's worth the detour. Classical decor and soft music have made it one of Tampa's favorite places to "pop the question," and smartly attired waiters render efficient yet friendly and unobtrusive service. Try the caprese, putanesca, gnocchi, or agnolotti.

✪ **Mise en Place.** In Grand Central Place, 442 W. Kennedy Blvd. (at S. Magnolia Ave., opposite the University of Tampa). ☎ **813/254-5373.** Reservations accepted only for parties of 6 or more. Main courses $13–$21. AE, DC, DISC, MC, V. Mon–Fri 11am–3pm; Tues–Thurs 5:30–10pm; Fri–Sat 5:30–11pm. INTERNATIONAL.

Look around at all those happy, stylish people soaking up the trendy ambience, and you'll know why chef Marty Blitz and his wife, Marianne, are the culinary darlings of Tampa. They continue to present the freshest of ingredients, with a creative international menu that changes daily. Main courses often include such choices as roast duck with Jamaica wild-strawberry sauce, grilled swordfish with tri-melon mint salsa, or Ethopian lentil stew served with steamed *injera* bread. There's valet parking at the rear of the building on Grand Central Place.

After dinner you can wander next door into **442,** an upscale bar with live jazz and blues.

Selena's. In Old Hyde Park shopping complex, 1623 Snow Ave. (south of Swan St.). ☎ **813/251-2116.** Reservations recommended. Main courses $10–$18. AE, MC, V. Mon–Thurs 11am–10pm; Fri–Sat 11am–11pm; Sun 11am–9pm. LOUISIANA.

This charming restaurant seems straight out of New Orleans. Sit in the plant-filled Patio Room, in the eclectic Queen Anne Room, or at the outdoor cafe where you can watch the world go by. Local seafoods, especially grouper and shrimp, top the menu at dinner, with many of the dishes served Louisiana style (to exercise your taste buds, try the rustic crab cakes with Cajun spices or the "voodoo" shrimp Creole). The vegetarian broccoli, cauliflower, and mushrooms over linguini has justifiably won awards. Other choices include pastas, chicken, steaks, and apricot-glazed quail. At night, jazz enlivens the proceedings as musical groups perform in the upstairs lounge.

Ybor City

✪ **Cafe Creole and Oyster Bar.** 1330 9th Ave. (at Avenida de Republica de Cuba/14th St.). ☎ **813/247-6283.** Reservations not accepted but call for perferred seating. Main courses $9–$17. AE, DC, DISC, MC, V. Mon–Thurs 11:30am–10pm; Fri 11:30am–11:30pm; Sat 5–11:30pm. CREOLE/CAJUN.

Resembling a turn-of-the-century railway station, this brick building dates from 1896 and was originally known as El Pasaje, the home of the Cherokee Club, a gentlemen's hotel and private club with a casino and a decor rich in stained-glass windows, wrought-iron balconies, Spanish murals, and marble bathrooms. Specialties include exceptionally prepared Louisiana crab cakes, oysters, blackened grouper, and jambalaya. If you're new to cuisine of the bayou, try the Creole sampler. Dine inside or out.

✪ **Carmine's Restaurant & Bar.** 1802 E. 7th Ave. (at 18th St.). ☎ **813/248-3834.** Reservations not accepted. Sandwiches $4–$7; main courses $5–$16 (most $7–$8). No credit cards. Mon–Tues 9am–10pm; Wed–Thurs 9am–midnight; Fri–Sat 9am–3am; Sun 9am–6pm. CUBAN/ITALIAN/AMERICAN.

Bright blue poles hold up an ancient pressed-tin ceiling above this noisy corner cafe, one of Ybor's most popular hangouts. A great variety of patrons gather at a stainless steel-topped bar or sit at an eclectic collection of chairs and tables that appear to have been gathered at a long series of yard sales. For lunch or dinner, you can order a genuine Cuban sandwich—smoked ham, roast pork, Genoa salami, Swiss cheese, pickles, salad dressing, mustard, lettuce, and tomato on a crispy, submarine roll. There's a vegetarian version, too, and the combination half sandwich and bowl of Spanish soup made with sausages, potatoes, and garbanzo beans makes a hearty meal for just $4. Main courses are led by Cuban-style roast pork, thin-cut pork chops with mushroom sauce, spaghetti with a blue crab tomato sauce, and a few seafood and chicken platters.

✪ **Columbia.** 2117 E. 7th Ave. (between 21st and 22nd sts). ☎ **813/248-4961.** Reservations recommended. Main courses $12–$23. AE, DC, DISC, MC, V. Mon–Thurs 11am–10pm; Fri–Sat 11am–11pm; Sun noon–9pm. SPANISH.

Dating back to 1905, this hand-painted tile building occupies an entire city block in the heart of Ybor City. Tourists flock here to soak up the ambience and so do the locals because it's so much fun to clap along during fire-belching floor shows in the main dining room. You can't help coming back time after time for the famous Spanish bean soup and original "1905" salad. The paella à la valenciana is outstanding, with more than a dozen ingredients from gulf grouper and gulf pink shrimp to calamari, mussels, clams, chicken, and pork. The decor throughout is graced with hand-painted tiles, wrought-iron chandeliers, dark woods, rich red fabrics, and stained-glass windows. You can breathe your own fumes in the Cigar Bar.

Ovo Cafe. 1901 E. 7th Ave. (at 19th St.). ☎ **813/248-6979.** Reservations not accepted. Main courses $8–$15. AE, MC, V. Mon–Tues 11am–4pm; Wed–Sat 11am–2am; Sun 11am–10pm. INTERNATIONAL.

This cafe, popular with the business set by day and the club crowd at night, is Tampa's answer to SoHo. You'll find a blend of good food, eclectic art, and pleasing surroundings. Locals love the "ménage à trois" omelets at breakfast. The fresh Ovo's chicken feta salad is a great lunch choice. An eclectic menu includes pierogies, smoked tuna sandwiches, and shrimp bisque soup. The big surprise is finding Dom Perignon on the menu, as well as root-beer floats made with Absolut vodka.

TAMPA AFTER DARK

The Tampa/Hillsborough Arts Council maintains an **Artsline** (☎ 813/229-ARTS), a 24-hour information service providing the latest on current and upcoming cultural events. Racks in many restaurants and bars have copies of *Weekly Planet, Focus,* and *Accent on Tampa Bay,* three free publications detailing what's going on in the entire bay area. And you can check the "Baylife" and "Friday Extra" sections of the *Tampa Tribune* and the Friday "Weekend" section of the *St. Petersburg Times.* The visitors center usually has copies of the week's newspaper sections (see "Essentials," earlier in the chapter). And be on the lookout for the slick bimonthly magazine *Event Guide Tampa Bay,* which gives a rundown on what's going on.

THE CLUB & MUSIC SCENE   Ybor City is Tampa's favorite nighttime venue by far. All you have to do is stroll along 7th Avenue East between 15th and 20th streets to find a club or bar to your liking. The avenue is packed with people of every possible age and description on Friday and Saturday from 9pm to 3am, but you'll also find something going on from Tuesday to Thursday and even on Sunday. You don't need addresses or phone numbers; your ears will guide you along 7th Avenue East.

Starting at 15th Street and heading east, you'll come first to **The Masquerade,** with retro and old wave bands on Friday to Sunday. The body-pierced 20-something crowd gets primed at **Club Hedo** and **Cherry's** before dancing at **The Rubb** across the avenue. Between 16th and 17th streets, the **Blue Shark** features the blues (and refuses to sell alcholic beverages to anyone who appears to be intoxicated).

Between 17th and 18th streets, you'll smell the cigar smoke coming from the sidewalk tables of the **Green Iguana Bar & Grill,** a refined establishment frequented by young professionals. The **Irish Pub** is just that, while **Fat Tuesday** has a large dance floor and long bar. Between 18th and 19th streets, you'll see **Harpo's** and **The Polyester Patio,** which don't extract a cover charge. Keep going across 19th Street to **The Beach Club,** the kind of noisy joint that advertises "no panties" on Thursday. Upstairs over Bubba's is one of Ybor's best clubs, **Blues Ship Café on Top,** which features live blues, jazz, and reggae. And last but not least is the warehouselike ✪ **Frankie's Patio Bar & Grill,** known for its reasonably priced food as well as its outstanding musical acts. Across the avenue, country meets city at **Spurs in Ybor,** a country-and-western joint.

Lastly, comedy lovers can get their laughs at **Key West on 7th,** between 20th and 21st streets.

Although not in the heart of Ybor's bar scene, the ✪ **Jazz Cellar,** on 9th Avenue East between 13th Street and Avenida de Republica de Cuba (14th Street), features comtemporary jazz, rhythm and blues, and just plain blues. This basement establishment is on the north side of Ybor Square. Call ☎ **813/248-1862** for reservations.

Elsewhere in town, you can lose your life savings playing bingo, poker, and the video slot machines at the **Seminole Indian Casino,** 5223 N. Orient Rd., at Hillsborough Road east of the city (☎ **800/282-7016** or 813/621-1302). It's open 24 hours every day of the year.

THE PERFORMING ARTS   With a prime downtown location on 9 acres along the east bank of the Hillsborough River, the huge **Tampa Bay Performing Arts Center,** 1010 N. MacInnes Place (☎ **800/955-1045** or 813/229-STAR), is the largest performing arts venue south of the Kennedy Center in Washington, D.C. Accordingly, this four-theater complex is the focal point of Tampa's performing arts scene, presenting a wide range of Broadway plays, classical and pop concerts, operas, cabarets, improv, and special events.

A sightseeing attraction in its own right, the restored ✪ **Tampa Theatre,** 711 Franklin St. (☎ **813/223-8981**), dates from 1926 and is on the National Register of Historic Places. It presents a varied program of classic, foreign, and alternative films, as well as concerts and special events.

ST. PETERSBURG

On the western shore of the bay, St. Petersburg stands in contrast to Tampa, much like San Francisco compares to Oakland in California. While Tampa is the area's business, industrial, and shipping center, St. Petersburg was conceived and built almost a century ago primarily for tourists and wintering snowbirds. Here you'll find one of the most picturesque and pleasant downtowns of any city in Florida, with a waterfront promenade and the famous pyramid-shaped Pier offering great views across the bay, plus quality museums, interesting shops, and fine restaurants.

Away from downtown, the city pretty much consists of strip malls dividing residential neighborhoods, but plan at least to have a look around the charming bayfront area. If you don't do anything else, go out on The Pier and take a pleasant stroll along Bayshore Drive.

All is not completely happy in this urban paradise, however, for St. Petersburg was rocked by riots after a white police officer shot and killed a black motorist in late 1996. Although all was calm at press time, you should avoid the area south of I-175 and east of I-275.

ESSENTIALS

GETTING THERE   To reach downtown from Tampa, take I-275 or the Gandy Causeway (U.S. 92) across the bay, and then I-275 south to I-375 east to the waterfront. From Sarasota and Bradenton, take I-275 north across the towering Sunshine Skyway ($2 toll) to I-175 or I-375 east. From points north, take congested U.S. 19 straight to downtown.

VISITOR INFORMATION   For advance information about both St. Petersburg and the beaches, contact the **St. Petersburg/Clearwater Area Convention & Visitors Bureau,** 14450 46th St. N., Clearwater, FL 34622 (☎ **800/345-6710,** or 813/464-7200 for advance hotel reservations; fax 813/464-7222; **www.stpete-clearwater.com**). The office is south of Roosevelt Boulevard (Fla. 686) opposite St. Petersburg–Clearwater International Airport.

A wealth of information is also available from the **St. Petersburg Area Chamber of Commerce,** 100 2nd Ave. N. (at 1st Street), St. Petersburg, FL 33701 (☎ 813/821-4069; fax 813/895-6326; **www.stpete.com**). This downtown main office and visitors center is open Monday to Friday from 8am to 5pm. Ask for a copy of the chamber's visitors guide, which lists hotels, motels, condominiums, and other accommodations.

The Chamber also operates the **Suncoast Welcome Center,** on Ulmerton Road at exit 18 southbound off I-275 (there's no exit here for northbound traffic).

Also downtown, there are **walk-in information centers** on the first level of The Pier and in the lobby of the Florida International Museum (see "Seeing the Top Attractions" later in this chapter).

CITY LAYOUT   St. Petersburg's **downtown** is laid out according to a grid system, with streets running north-south and avenues running east-west. **Central Avenue** is the dividing line for north and south addresses. "Northeast" avenues—those designated NE—lie east of 1st Street North. With the exception of Central Avenue, most streets and avenues downtown are one way.

GETTING AROUND   You can see everything on the free **Looper: The Downtown Trolley** (☎ 813/571-3440), which runs to the end of The Pier and past all of the downtown attractions every 30 minutes from 11am to 5pm daily except Thanksgiving and Christmas.

The **Pinellas Suncoast Transit Authority/PSTA** (☎ 813/530-9911) operates regular bus service throughout Pinellas County. The fare is $1.

If you need a cab, call Yellow Cab (☎ 813/821-7777) or Independent Cab (☎ 813/327-3444).

Pierside Rentals, on The Pier (☎ 822-8697), rents bicycles for $5 an hour, $20 a day, or $50 a week.

SEEING THE TOP ATTRACTIONS

Florida International Museum. 100 2nd St. N. (between 1st and 2nd aves. N.). ☎ **800/777-9882** or 813/822-3693. www.floridamuseum.org. Admission $13.95 adults, $12.95 seniors, $5.95 children. Daily 9am–6pm (or later depending on special exhibits).

This facility attracted 600,000 visitors from around the world in 1995 when it opened its first exhibition called "Treasures of the Czars," and the success has continued (its recent exhibit on the *Titanic* was a smash hit). Call to see what's scheduled during your visit. The museum is housed in the former Maas Brothers Department Store, long an area landmark. Tickets should be reserved and purchased in advance to be sure of a specific time. Each visitor is equipped with an audio guide as part of the admission price; allow at least 2 hours to tour a major exhibition.

Great Explorations: The Hands-On Museum. 1120 4th St. S. (at 11th Ave. S.). ☎ **813/821-8885.** Admission $5, free for children 2 and under. Mon–Sat 10am–5pm; Sun noon–5pm.

With a variety of hands-on exhibits, this museum is great for a rainy day or for kids who've overdosed on the sun and need to cool off inside. They can explore a long, dark tunnel; measure their strength, flexibility, and fitness; paint a work of art with sunlight; and play a melody with a sweep of the hand.

Museum of Fine Arts. 255 Beach Dr. NE (at 3rd Ave. N.). ☎ **813/896-2667.** Admission Mon–Sat $6 adults, $5 seniors, $2 students. Free admission on Sun. Tues–Sat 10am–5pm; Sun 1–5pm; in winter, the third Thurs of each month 10am–9pm.

Resembling a Mediterranean villa on the waterfront, this museum houses a permanent collection of European, American, pre-Colombian, and Far Eastern art, with works by such artists as Fragonard, Monet, Renoir, Cézanne, and Gauguin. Other highlights include period rooms with antiques and historical furnishings, plus a gallery of Steuben crystal, a new decorative-arts gallery, and world-class rotating exhibits.

The Pier. 800 2nd Ave. NE. ☎ **813/821-6164.** www.stpete-pier.com. Free admission to all the public areas and decks; donations welcome at the aquarium. Valet parking $5, self-parking $3. Pier, Mon–Sat 10am–9pm; Sun 11am–6pm. Aquarium, Mon–Sat 10am–8pm; Sun noon–6pm. Restaurant hours vary.

Walk out or ride out on The Pier and enjoy this festive waterfront dining and shopping complex overlooking Tampa Bay. Originally built as a railroad pier in 1889, today it's capped by a spaceship-like inverted pyramid offering five levels of shops and restaurants, plus an aquarium, tourist information desk, observation deck, catwalks for fishing, boat docks, a small bayside beach, miniature golf, boat and water-sports rentals, sightseeing boats, and a food court. You can rent boats and go on cruises from here (see "Outdoor Activities & Spectators Sports," next), and from November to April climb aboard the *H.M.S. Bounty,* a replica of the famous vessel built in 1960 for the Marlon Brando version of *Mutiny on the Bounty* (30-minute tours of the ship cost $5 for adults, $4 for seniors, and $3 for kids 5 to 17; call ☎ **813/896-5668** for more information). A free trolley service operates between The Pier and the parking lots on shore.

✪ **Salvador Dalí Museum.** 1000 3rd St. S. (near 11th Ave. S.). ☎ **813/823-3767.** Admission $8 adults, $7 seniors, $4 students, free for children 9 and under. Mon–Wed 9:30am–5:30pm; Thurs 9:30am–8pm; Fri–Sat 9:30am–5:30pm; Sun noon–5pm. Closed Thanksgiving and Christmas.

Located on Tampa Bay south of The Pier, this starkly modern museum houses the world's largest collection of works by the renowned Spanish surrealist. Valued at over $150 million, it includes 94 oil paintings, more than 100 watercolors and drawings, and 1,300 graphics, plus posters, photos, sculptures, objets d'art, and a 5,000-volume library on Dalí and surrealism. There also are special exhibits of works by other famous artists.

Sunken Gardens. 1825 4th St. N. (between 18th and 19th aves. NE). ☎ **813/896-3186.** Admission $14 adults, $8 children 3–11, free for children 2 and under. Daily 9:30am–5pm.

One of the city's oldest attractions, this 7-acre tropical garden park dating back to 1935 is a holdover from Florida's early tourist days. It contains a vast array of 5,000 plants, flowers, and trees, and there are bird and alligator shows.

Outdoor Activities & Spectator Sports

You can get up-to-the-minute recorded information about the city's sports and recreational activities by calling the **Leisure Line** (☎ 813/893-7500).

BOAT RENTALS On The Pier, **Pierside Rentals** (☎ 813/363-0000) rents Wave Runners and jet boats. Prices for Wave Runners begin at $45 for an hour; for jet boats, from $55 per hour. Open daily from 9am to dusk.

CRUISES The *Caribbean Queen* (☎ 813/895-BOAT) departs from The Pier and offers 1-hour sightseeing and dolphin-watching cruises around Tampa Bay. Sailings are daily at 1, 3, and 5pm; they cost $10 for adults, $8 for seniors and juniors 12 to 17, $5 for children 3 to 11, and free for children 2 and under.

GOLF One of the nation's top 50 municipal courses, the **Mangrove Bay Golf Course,** 875 62nd Ave. NE (☎ 813/893-7797), hugs the inlets of Old Tampa Bay and offers 18-hole, par-72 play. Facilities include a driving range; lessons and golf-club

Downtown St. Petersburg

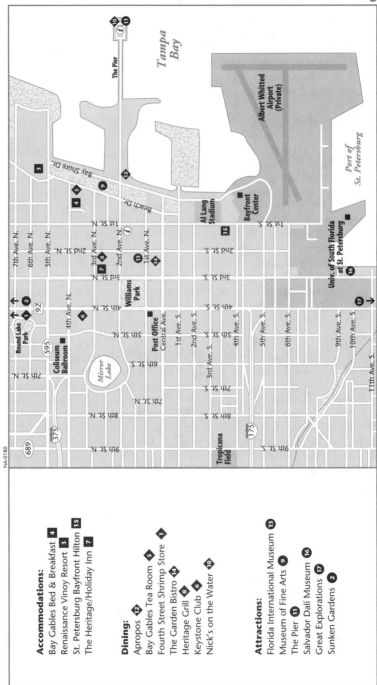

Accommodations:

Bay Gables Bed & Breakfast **4**
Renaissance Vinoy Resort **3**
St. Petersburg Bayfront Hilton **15**
The Heritage/Holiday Inn **7**

Dining:

Apropos **12**
Bay Gables Tea Room **5**
Fourth Street Shrimp Store **1**
The Garden Bistro **14**
Heritage Grill **8**
Keystone Club **6**
Nick's on the Water **10**

Attractions:

Florida International Museum **13**
Museum of Fine Arts **9**
The Pier **11**
Salvador Dali Museum **16**
Great Explorations **17**
Sunken Gardens **2**

NA-0180

rental are also available. Fees are about $22, $32 including a cart in winter, slightly lower off-season. Open daily from 6:30am to 6pm.

In Largo, the **Bardmoor Golf Club,** 7919 Bardmoor Blvd. (☎ **813/397-0483**), is often the venue for major tournaments. Lakes punctuate 17 of the 18 holes on this par-72 championship course. Lessons and rental clubs are available, as is a Tom Fazio–designed practice range. Call the clubhouse for seasonal greens fees. Open daily from 7am to dusk.

Call **Tee Times USA** (☎ **800/374-8633**) to reserve times at these and other area courses.

SPECTATOR SPORTS   St. Petersburg has always been a baseball town, and **Tropicana Field,** a 45,000-seat domed stadium alongside I-175 between 9th and 16th streets south, is the home of the **Tampa Bay Devil Rays,** the area's expansion team, which began American League play in 1998. The season runs from April through September. Call ☎ **813/898-RAYS** for schedule and ticket information. The Devil Rays move outdoors to Al Lang Stadium, on 2nd Avenue South at 1st Street South (☎ **813/822-3384**), for their spring training games from mid-February through March. Tickets to the spring games range from $3 to $12.

The **Philadelphia Phillies** play their spring-training season at Jack Russell Stadium, 800 Phillies Dr., in nearby Clearwater (☎ **813/442-8496**). Admission is $8 to $9. Their minor league **Clearwater Phillies** play in the stadium from April to September. Grant Field, 373 Douglas Ave. in Dunedin (☎ **813/733-0429**), is the winter home of the **Toronto Blue Jays.**

SHOPPING

The Pier, at the end of 2nd Avenue NE (☎ **813/821-6164**), houses more than a dozen boutiques and craft shops, but nearby **Beach Drive,** running along the waterfront, is one of the most fashionable downtown strolling and shopping venues. **Central Avenue** is another shopping area, featuring the **Gas Plant Antique Arcade,** between 12th and 13th streets (☎ **813/895-0368**), the largest antique mall on Florida's west coast, with over 100 dealers displaying their wares. In the suburbs, outlet shoppers can browse at the air-conditioned **Bay Area Outlet Mall,** at the intersection of U.S. 19 and East Bay Drive (☎ **813/535-2337**), west of St. Petersburg–Clearwater International Airport.

WHERE TO STAY

Ask the **St. Petersburg Area Chamber of Commerce** (see "Essentials," earlier in this section) for a copy of its visitors guide, which lists a wide range of hotels, motels, condominiums, and other accommodations. In addition, the St. Petersburg/Clearwater Convention & Visitors Bureau has a free **reservations service** (☎ **800/345-6710**).

You'll find plenty of chain motels along U.S. 19.

The high season—and higher prices—is from January to April. The hotel tax rate in Pinellas County is 11%.

Very Expensive

✪ **Renaissance Vinoy Resort.** 501 5th Ave. NE (at Beach Dr.), St. Petersburg, FL 33701. ☎ **800/HOTELS-1** or 813/894-1000. Fax 813/822-2785. 360 units. A/C MINIBAR TV TEL. Winter $265–$365 double; off-season $145–$235 double. Valet parking $12, self-parking $8. AE, DC, DISC, MC, V.

Built as the Vinoy Park in 1925 during Florida's heyday of grand hotels, this elegant Spanish-style establishment reopened in 1992 after a total and meticulous $93-million restoration that has made it more luxurious than ever. Dominating the northern part of downtown, it overlooks Tampa Bay and is within walking distance of The Pier, Central Avenue, museums, and other attractions. All the guest rooms, many of which enjoy lovely views of the bayfront, are designed to offer the utmost in comfort and include three phones, an additional TV in the bathroom, hair dryer, bath scales, and more. Some units in the new wing also have whirlpools and private patios/balconies.

Dining: Marchand's Grille, an elegant room overlooking the bay, specializes in steaks, seafood, and chops. The Terrace Room is the main dining room for breakfast, lunch, and dinner. Casual lunches and dinners are available at the indoor-outdoor Alfresco, near the pool deck, and at the Clubhouse, at the golf course on Snell Isle. There are also two bar/lounges.

Amenities: Two swimming pools (connected by a roaring waterfall), 14-court tennis complex (9 lighted), 18-hole private championship golf course on nearby Snell Isle, private 74-slip marina. Two croquet courts, fitness center (with sauna, steam room, spa, massage, and exercise equipment), hair salon, gift shop. Access to two bay-side beaches, shuttle service to gulf beaches. Concierge, room service (24 hours), laundry service, tour desk, child care, complimentary coffee and newspaper with wake-up call.

Moderate

St. Petersburg Bayfront Hilton. 333 1st St. S. (between 3rd and 4th aves. S., opposite Al Lang Field), St. Petersburg, FL 33701. ☎ **800/HILTONS** or 813/894-5000. Fax 813/823-4797. 333 units. A/C TV TEL. Winter $159 double; off-season $119 double. Packages available. AE, DC, MC, V.

This 15-story convention hotel has a spacious lobby with a rich decor of marble, crystal, tile, antiques, artwork, and potted trees and plants. The bedrooms are furnished with traditional dark woods, floral fabrics, a king-size bed or two double beds, and an executive desk; many have views of the bay. Cafe 333 is a full-service restaurant specializing in continental cuisine. The First Street Deli provides light fare, and Brandi's Lobby Bar has piano entertainment. Amenities include an outdoor heated swimming pool, whirlpool, health club with a sauna, and gift shop.

Inexpensive

Bay Gables Bed & Breakfast. 136 4th Ave. NE (between Beach Dr. and 1st St. N), St. Petersburg, FL 33701. ☎ **800/822-8803** or 813/822-8855. Fax 813/824-7223. 9 units. A/C. $85–$135 double. Rates include continental breakfast. MC, V.

You can walk to The Pier from this charming B&B, which was built in the 1930s. It overlooks a flower-filled garden with a gazebo and faces a fanciful Victorian-style house whose first floor is a tearoom/restaurant. The guest rooms have been furnished with ceiling fans and Victorian pieces, including some canopy beds. All units have bathrooms with clawfoot tubs and modern showers. Half of the rooms have a porch; the rest have a separate sitting room and kitchenette. Continental breakfast is served in the common room, on the garden deck, or in the gazebo. This is a professionally managed operation; the owners don't live on the premises.

✪ **Heritage/Holiday Inn.** 234 3rd Ave. N. (between 2nd and 3rd sts.), St. Petersburg, FL 33701. ☎ **800/283-7829** or 813/822-4814. Fax 813/823-1644. 71 units. A/C TV TEL. Winter $86–$107 double; off-season $58–$74 double. Rates include continental breakfast. AE, DC, DISC, MC, V.

No ordinary Holiday Inn, the Heritage dates to the early 1920s and is the closest thing to a Southern mansion you'll find in the heart of downtown. With a sweeping veranda, French doors, and tropical courtyard, it attracts an eclectic clientele, from young families to seniors. The furnishings include period antiques. There's a heated swimming pool and a whirlpool in a small tropical courtyard between the main building and the Heritage Grill next door, one of the area's most popular restaurants (see "Where to Dine," next).

WHERE TO DINE

Don't overlook the food court at **The Pier,** where the inexpensive chow is accompanied by a very rich—but quite free—view of the bay. Among the stalls, **Alessi Deli** is a good bet for salads, pastries, and coffee. Upstairs there's a branch of Tampa's famous **Columbia Restaurant** (see "Where to Dine" in the earlier Tampa section).

Moderate

Apropos. 300 2nd Ave. NE (at Bayshore Dr.). ☎ **813/823-8934.** Reservations accepted only for dinner. Breakfast $3.50–$6; lunch $5–$9; dinner main courses $9–$16. DC, MC, V. Tues–Sat 7:30–10:30am and 11am–3pm; Thurs–Sun 6–10pm; Sun brunch 8:30am–2pm. AMERICAN.

Sitting at the foot of The Pier, Apropros is a fine place to breakfast before your tour of downtown, perhaps with a brie and bacon omelet, or a seasonal fruit plate, or just plain eggs. At lunch, the view through the masts in the adjacent marina sets the scene for the likes of shrimp and artichoke salad with a sherry mayonnaise dressing. And at dinner, you can choose from a blackboard offering the chef's nightly nouveau cuisine selections. You'll find as many locals here as tourists.

Garden Bistro. 217 Central Ave. ☎ **813/896-3800.** Reservations recommended for dinner. Main courses $10–$16. AE, MC, V. Daily noon–2pm and 5pm–2am. MEDITERANEAN.

A popular hot spot with those in the know, this lively restaurant combines European ambience with Moroccan cuisine. Choice seats are under huge shade trees in the garden, screened from the street by a trellis fence. Inside, the decor blends the American Southwest with the Mediterranean, with arches, a 19th-century tiled floor, modern local art, and lots of flowers and plants. The creative menu features couscous, a daily *tajin* (a traditional Moroccan stew), pastas such as wild mushrooms with strips of roast duck, and smoked salmon in a light cream sauce. On Friday and Saturday, live jazz adds to the ambience from 9pm to 1am.

Heritage Grill. 256 2nd St. N. (at 3rd Ave. N.). ☎ **813/823-6382.** Reservations recommended. Main courses $17–$20. AE, DC, DISC, MC, V. Mon–Fri 11:30am–2pm and 5:30–10pm; Sat 5:30–10pm. AMERICAN.

Next door to the Heritage/Holiday Inn (see "Where to Stay," earlier in this section), this 1920s-vintage house has been transformed into a restaurant cum modern art gallery, with the walls displaying for-sale works by local artists. The colorful placemats are hand-painted once a week, and even the waiters are part of the art scene—their tuxedo shirts also are hand-painted. For something old, look behind the bar as you enter: The ornate mahogany liquor and wine cabinet reportedly came from the Mississippi home of Confederate President Jefferson Davis. When you're ready to dine, the menu offers dishes like sautéed macadamia-nut–crusted chicken breast stuffed with prosciutto and sun-dried tomatoes and New Zealand lamb chops with a roasted garlic and rosemary demiglaze.

Keystone Club. 320 4th St. N. (between 3rd and 4th aves. N.). ☎ **813/822-6600.** Reservations recommended. Main courses $11–$23; early-bird specials $7.50–$12. AE, DC, DISC, MC, V. Mon–Fri 11am–2:30pm and 5–10pm; Sat 4–10pm; Sun 4–9pm. Early-bird specials, winter only Mon–Fri 4:30–5:30pm, Sat–Sun 4–5:30pm. STEAKS/PRIME RIB.

Resembling an exclusive men's club, this cozy restuarant's forest-green walls accented by dark wood and etched glass create an atmosphere that's reminiscent of a Manhattan-style chophouse. But women are also welcome to partake of the beef, which is king here. Specialties include roast prime rib, New York strip steak, and filet mignon. Seafood also makes an appearance, with fresh lobster and grouper at market price. During winter, "sunset" early-bird specials include lunch-size portions, a beverage, and dessert.

Inexpensive

⭐ **Fourth Street Shrimp Store.** 1006 4th St. N. (at 10th Ave. N.). ☎ **813/822-0325.** Reservations not accepted. Sandwiches $2.50–$6; main courses $4–$12. MC, V. Sun–Thurs 11am–9pm; Fri–Sat 11am–10pm. SEAFOOD.

If you're anywhere in the area, don't miss at least driving by to see the colorful, cartoonlike mural on the outside of this eclectic establishment just north of downtown. On first impression it looks like graffiti, but it's actually a gigantic drawing of people eating. Inside, it gets even better, with paraphernalia and murals on two walls making the dining room seem like a warehouse with windows looking out on an early 19th-century seaport (one painted sailor permanently peers in to see what you're eating). You'll pass a seafood market counter when you enter, from which comes the fresh namesake shrimp, the star here. You can also pick from grouper, clam strips, catfish, or oysters fried, broiled, or steamed, all served in heaping portions. This is the best and certainly the most interesting bargain in town.

Nick's on the Water. On The Pier, east end of 2nd Ave. NE. ☎ **813/898-5800.** Reservations recommended for dinner. Main courses $8–$18. AE, DC, MC, V. Sun–Thurs 11:30am–10pm; Fri–Sat 11:30am–11pm. ITALIAN/SEAFOOD.

Located on the main level of The Pier, this informal restaurant offers expansive views of downtown St. Petersburg and the bayfront marina. The menu features a variety of Italian choices, including Nick's tortellini, but the specialty of the house is wood-fired fish, meats, and pizza. The veal dishes also are a big hit, especially the française, with sautéed medaillons.

ST. PETERSBURG AFTER DARK

Good sources of nightlife information are the the Friday "Weekend" section of the *St. Petersburg Times,* the "Baylife" and "Friday Extra" sections of the *Tampa Tribune,* and the *Weekly Planet,* a tabloid available at visitor information offices and in many hotel and restaurant lobbies. The bimonthly magazine *Event Guide Tampa Bay* gives a rundown on what's going on.

THE CLUB & MUSIC SCENE   A historic attraction as well as an entertainment venue, the Moorish-style **Coliseum Ballroom,** 535 4th Ave. N. (☎ **813/892-5202**), has been hosting dancing, big bands, boxing, and other events since 1924 (it even made an appearance in the 1985 movie *Cocoon*). An acquaintance of mine said it's fun to watch the town's many seniors doing the jitterbug just like it was 1945 again! Call for the schedule and prices.

A much younger set heads to the casual, downtown **Big Catch,** 9 1st St. NE (☎ **813/821-6444**), featuring live and danceable rock and Top 40 hits, as well as darts, pool, and hoops. North of downtown, the **Ringside Cafe,** 2742 4th St. N. (☎ **813/894-8465**), in a renovated boxing gymnasium, is an informal neighborhood cafe with a decided sports motif. The music focuses on jazz and blues (and sometimes reggae).

THE ST. PETE & CLEARWATER BEACHES

If you're looking for sun and sand, you'll find plenty of both on the 28 miles of slim barrier islands that skirt the gulf shore of the Pinellas Peninsula. With some 1 million visitors coming here every year, don't be surprised if you have lots of company. But you'll also discover quieter neighborhoods geared to families, and this area has some of the nation's finest beaches, which are protected from development by parks and nature preserves.

At the southern end of the strip, St. Pete Beach is the granddaddy of the area's resorts. In fact, visitors started coming here nearly a century ago, and they haven't quit. Today St. Pete Beach is heavily developed and often overcrowded during the winter season. If you like high-rises and mile-a-minute action, St. Pete Beach is for you. But even here, Pass-a-Grille, on the island's southern end, is a quiet residential enclave with eclectic shops and a fine public beach.

A more gentle lifestyle begins just to the north on 3½-mile-long Treasure Island. From there, you cross famous John's Pass to Sand Key, a 12-mile island occupied by primarily residential Madeira Beach, Redington Beach, North Redington Beach, Redington Shores, Indian Shores, Indian Rocks Beach, and Belleair Beach. Finally the road crosses a soaring bridge to Clearwater Beach, whose silky sands attract active families and couples.

If you like your great outdoors unfettered by development, the jewels here are Fort Desoto Park, down below St. Pete Beach at the mouth of Tampa Bay, and Caladesi Island State Park, north of Clearwater Beach. They are consistently rated among America's top beaches. And Sand Key Park, looking at Clearwater Beach from the southern shores of Little Pass, is one of Florida's finest local beach parks.

ESSENTIALS

GETTING THERE   To reach St. Pete Beach and Treasure Island from I-275, take exit 4 and follow the Pinellas Bayway (Fla. 682) west (50¢ toll). For Indian Rocks Beach, take exit 18 and follow Ulmerton Road due west to the gulf. For the Redington beaches, take exit 15 and follow Gandy and Park boulevards (Fla. 694) due west (Park Boulevard also is known as 74th Avenue North). For Clearwater Beach, take the Courtney Campbell Causeway (Fla. 60) west from Tampa; the causeway becomes Gulf-to-Bay Boulevard (also Fla. 60), which leads straight west into Clearwater.

VISITOR INFORMATION   See "Essentials," earlier, in the St. Petersburg section for the St. Petersburg/Clearwater Area Convention & Visitors Bureau and the St. Petersburg Area Chamber of Commerce. You can get information specific to the beaches from the **Gulf Beaches of Tampa Bay Chamber of Commerce,** 6990 Gulf Blvd. (at 70th Avenue), St. Pete Beach, FL 33706 (☎ **800/944-1847** or 813/ 360-6957; fax 813/360-2233). The main office is open Monday to Friday from 9am to 5pm. The Chamber also has welcome centers at 501 150th Ave. in Madeira Beach (☎ **813/391-7373**); at 105 5th Ave. in Indian Rocks Beach (☎ **813/595-4575**); and at 152 108th Ave. in Treasure Island (☎ **813/367-4529**).

For advance information about Clearwater Beach, contact the **Greater Clearwater Chamber of Commerce,** 128 N. Osceola Ave. (P.O. Box 2457), Clearwater, FL 34615 (☎ **813/461-0011**).

CITY LAYOUT   These barrier islands are barely wide enough to accommodate **Gulf Boulevard,** the main drag that runs all the way from St. Pete Beach north to the top of Sand Key. Once you cross Little Pass into Clearwater Beach, **Gulfview Boulevard** and **Mandalay Avenue** become the central north-south arteries.

Street addresses are geared to the short, numbered avenues crossing the main drags; they increase as you go north from 1st Avenue in Pass-a-Grille to 200th Avenue in Indian Rocks Beach, where the numbering begins all over again with another 1st Avenue. The Pinellas Byway comes onto St. Pete Beach at 34th Avenue, so turn right and head north on Gulf Boulevard to reach street addresses above 3400; left, or south, for lower numbers. Street numbers in Clearwater Beach start at Little Pass and increase as you go north.

St. Pete & Clearwater Beaches

St. Pete & Clearwater Beaches

Accommodations:
Beach Haven 13
Belleview Biltmore
   Resort & Spa 1
Best Western Sea
   Stone Resort 24
Captain's Quarters Inn 6
Clearwater Beach Hotel 18
Colonial Gateway Inn 7
Days Inn Island
   Beach Resort 8
Don CeSar Beach
   Resort and Spa 14
Great Heron Inn 4
Island's End Resort 16
Palm Pavilion Inn 17
Pelican—East & West 2
Radisson Sandpiper
   Beach Resort 10
Radisson Suite Resort
   on Sand Key 26
Sheraton Sand Key
   Resort 25
Sun West Beach Motel 23
TradeWinds Resort 12

Dining:
Bob Heilman's
   Beachcomber 20
Bubby's Bistro
   & Wine Bar 21
Crabby Billls 11
Frenchy's Cafe 19
Guppy's 3
Hurricane 15
Lobster Pot 5
Seafood & Sunsets
   at Julie's 22
Skidder's 9

Honeymoon Island
State Recreational
Area
Palm
Harbor
19
77
Intracoastal
586
Caladesi Island
1
590
St. Joseph Sound
Caladesi Island
State Park
ALT
19
580
19
Dunedin
Safety
Harbor
**Clearwater
Beach**
Area
of
Inset
590
60
Clearwater
Belleair
Beach
1
St. Petersburg-
Clearwater
International
Airport
699
Four
Corners
High
Point
686
2
Clearwater Harbor
697
651
3
688
Largo
Indian
Rocks
Beach
688
4
ALT
19
693
Indian
Shores
694
**Pinellas
Park**
Oakhurst
694
Redington
Shores
5
695
699
Madeira
Beach
ALT
19
*Gulf of
Mexico*
John's Pass
6
Treasure
Island
South Pasadena
Gulfport
0   3 mi.
4.8 km
N
St. Pete
Beach
7
9
8
10
12
11
682
13
14
Kipling
Plaza
*Clearwater
Harbor*
17
18
Bay Esplanade
15
16
Cabbage
Key
Bush
Key
19
Pass-a-Grille
Gulfview
Blvd.
20
21
Shell Key
The Reefs
679
Madelaine
Key
19
22
Hamden
Dr.
Clearwater Marine
Aquarium
23
24
Devon Dr.
Bayside Dr.
Sand Pt.
Mullet
Key
275
Sand Key
Park
Bayway Blvd.
Memorial
Causeway
25
26
Clearwater
Pass
Fort DeSoto
Fort
DeSoto
Park
NA-0181
Clearwater Beach

GETTING AROUND   BATS City Transit (☎ 813/367-3086) offers bus service along the St. Pete Beach strip. The fare is $1.

Treasure Island Transit System (☎ 813/547-4575) runs buses along the Treasure Island strip. The fare is $1.

The **Jolley Trolley** (☎ 813/445-1200), operated in conjunction with the City of Clearwater, provides service in the Clearwater Beach area, from downtown to the beaches as far south as Sand Key. It also goes to the Belleview Mido resort (see "Where to Stay," below). The ride costs 25¢.

Along the beach, the major cab company is **BATS Taxi** (☎ 813/367-3702).

Water Taxis operate along the bay side of the islands Tuesday to Sunday from 11am to 1am (☎ 813/323-8294). It's best to call for reservations. Rides cost $5 per person one-way, or you can buy an all-day pass for $15 per person.

You can rent bicycles and scooters in St. Pete Beach from **Beach Cyclist Sports Center,** 7517 Blind Pass Rd. (☎ 813/367-5001), and **Cycle & Scooter Services,** 7116-A Gulf Blvd. (☎ 813/367-3882). In Clearwater Beach, contact **Transportation Station,** 652 Gulfview Blvd. (☎ 813/443-3188). See "Outdoor Activities," below, for more information.

HITTING THE BEACH

This entire stretch of coast is one long beach, but since hotels, condominiums, and private homes occupy much of it, you may want to sun and swim at one of the area's public parks. The very best are described next, but there's also the fine **Pass-a-Grille Public Beach,** on the southern end of St. Pete Beach, where you can watch the boats going in and out of Pass-a-Grille Channel. This and all other Pinellas County public beaches have metered parking lots, so bring a supply of quarters.

Clearwater Public Beach has beach volleyball, water-sports rentals, lifeguards, restrooms, showers, and concessions. The swimming is excellent, and there's a children's playground and a pier for fishing. Gated municipal parking lots here cost $1 per hour or $7 a day. The lots are right across the street from Clearwater Beach Marina, a prime base for boating, cruises, and other waterborne activities (see "Outdoor Activities," below).

CALADESI ISLAND STATE PARK   Occupying a 3½-mile island north of Clearwater Beach, ✪ **Caladesi Island State Park** boasts a lovely, relatively secluded beach with fine soft sand edged in sea grass and palmettos. Dolphins cavort in the waters offshore. In the park itself, there's a nature trail, and you might see one of the rattlesnakes, black racers, raccoons, armadillos, or rabbits that live here. A concession stand, ranger station, and bathhouses (with rest rooms and showers) are available. Caladesi Island is accessible only by ferry from **Honeymoon Island State Recreation Area,** which is connected by Causeway Boulevard to Dunedin, north of Clearwater. (Honeymoon Island isn't great for swimming, but it has its own rugged beauty and a fascinating nature trail.) You'll first have to pay the admission to Honeymoon Island: $4 per vehicle with 2 to 8 occupants, $2 per single-occupant vehicle, $1 for pedestrians and bicyclists. Beginning daily at 10am, the ferry departs Honeymoon Island every hour on winter weekdays, every 30 minutes on summer weekdays, and every 30 minutes on weekends year-round. Rides cost $6 for adults and $3.50 for kids. The two parks are open daily from 8am to sunset. The two islands are administered by **Gulf Islands Geopark,** #1 Causeway Blvd., Dunedin, FL 34698 (☎ 813/469-5942).

FORT DESOTO PARK   South of St. Pete Beach at the very mouth of Tampa Bay, this group of five connected barrier islands has been set aside by Pinellas County as a 900-acre bird, animal, and plant sanctuary. Besides the stunning white-sugar sand beach (where you can watch the manatees and dolphins play offshore), there's a Spanish-American War–era fort, great fishing from piers, a large playground for kids, and 4 miles of trails winding through the park for in-line skaters, bicyclists, and joggers.

Sitting on an island by themselves, the park's 230 camp sites all have water and electricity hookups, but they usually are sold out, especially on weekends. Sites cost $18.76 a night. To make reservations, you must appear *in person* and pay for your site no more than 30 days in advance at the campground office, at 631 Chestnut St. in Clearwater, or at 150 5th St. N. in downtown St. Petersburg. You must camp here at least 2 nights, but you can stay no more than 14 nights. The park is open from 8am to dusk, although campers and persons fishing from the piers can stay later. Admission is free. To get here, take the Pinellas Byway (50¢ toll) east from St. Pete Beach and follow Fla. 679 (35¢ toll) and the signs south to the park. For more information, contact the park at 3500 Pinellas Bayway, Tierra Verde, FL 33715 (☎ **813/866-2662**).

SAND KEY PARK This fine county park on the northern tip of Sand Key facing Clearwater Beach sports a wide beach and gentle surf and is relatively off the beaten path in this commercial area. It's great to get out of the hotel for a morning walk or jog here. Open 8am to dark. Admission is free, but the parking lot has meters. For more information, call ☎ **813/464-3347.**

OUTDOOR ACTIVITIES

BICYCLING & IN-LINE SKATING With miles of flat terrain and paved roads, the beach area is ideal for bikers and in-line skaters. In St. Pete Beach, you can rent bicycles, skates, and scooters from **Beach Cyclist Sports Center,** 7517 Blind Pass Rd. (☎ **813/367-5001**), and **Cycle & Scooter Services,** 7116-A Gulf Blvd [tel] **813/367-3882**). In Clearwater Beach, contact **Transportation Station,** 652 Gulfview Blvd. (☎ **813/443-3188).** Bikes at all three range from about $5 per hour to $20 a day; scooters, about $13 a hour to $40 per day.

BOATING, FISHING & OTHER WATER SPORTS You can indulge in parasailing, boating, deep-sea fishing, wave running, sightseeing, dolphin-watching, water skiing, and just about any other waterborne diversion your heart could desire here. All you have to do is head to one of two beach locations: **Hubbard's Marina,** at John's Pass Village and Boardwalk (☎ **813/393-1947**), in Madeira Beach on the southern tip of Sand Key; or **Clearwater Beach Marina,** at Coronado Drive and Causeway Boulevard (☎ **800/772-4479** or 813/461-3133), which is at the beach end of the causeway leading to downtown Clearwater. Agents in booths there will give you the schedules and prices, answer any questions you have, and make reservations if necessary. Go in the early morning to set up today's activities, or in the afternoon to book tomorrow's.

CRUISES The **Shell Key Shuttle,** Merry Pier, 801 Pass-a-Grille Way in southern St. Pete Beach (☎ **813/360-1348**), uses a 57-passenger catamaran to shuttle out to Shell Island, one of Florida's last completely undeveloped barrier islands. It's great for bird-watchers, who could spot a remarkable 88 different species, including some of North America's rarest shorebirds. Boats leave daily at 10am, noon, and 2pm, plus 4pm in summer. Prices are $10 for adults, $5 for children 12 and under. The ride takes 15 minutes, and you can return on any shuttle you wish. Departing Hubbard's Marina at John's Pass Village and Boardwalk in Madeira Beach, **Shell Island Adventure** (☎ **813/399-9633**) has a 5-hour daily trip to the island, including a barbecue lunch, for $27 adults, $15 for kids, and you can rent beach chairs, umbrellas, snorkeling gear, and other equipment once you get there.

Captain Memo's Pirate Cruise, at Clearwater Beach Marina (☎ 813/446-2587), sails the *Pirate's Ransom,* an authentic reproduction of a pirate ship, on 2-hour daytime "pirate cruises" as well as sunset and evening champagne cruises. Cruises operate year-round, daily at 10am and at 2, 4:30, and 7pm. For adults, daytime or sunset cruises cost $27; evening cruises, $30; both daytime and evening cruises cost $20 for seniors and juniors 13 to 17, $17 for children 2 to 12, free for children under 2.

ATTRACTIONS ON LAND

Clearwater Marine Aquarium. 249 Windward Passage, Clearwater. ☎ **813/447-0980.** Admission $6.75 adults, $4.25 children 3–11, free for children 2 and under. Mon–Fri 9am–5pm; Sat 9am–4pm; Sun 11am–4pm. The aquarium is off the causeway between Clearwater and Clearwater Beach; follow the signs.

This little jewel of an aquarium on Clearwater Harbor is very low-key and friendly; it's dedicated to the rescue and rehabilitation of marine mammals and sea turtles. Exhibits include dolphins, otters, sea turtles, sharks, stingrays, mangroves, and sea grass.

✪ **John's Pass Village and Boardwalk.** 12901 Gulf Blvd. (at John's Pass), Madeira Beach. ☎ **800/944-1847** or 813/397-1511. Free admission. Shops and activities, daily 9am–6pm or later.

Casual and charming, this Old Florida fishing village on John's Pass consists of a string of simple wooden structures topped by tin roofs and connected by a 1,000-foot boardwalk. Most of the buildings have been converted into shops, art galleries, restaurants, and saloons. The focal point is the boardwalk and marina, where many water sports are available for visitors (see "Outdoor Activities," earlier).

✪ **Suncoast Seabird Sanctuary.** 18328 Gulf Blvd., Indian Shores. ☎ **813/391-6211.** Free admission, donations welcome. Daily 9am–dusk. Free tours Wed and Sun 2pm.

At any one time there are usually more than 500 sea and land birds living at the sanctuary, from cormorants, white herons, and birds of prey to the ubiquitous brown pelican. The nation's largest wild-bird hospital, dedicated to the rescue, repair, recuperation, and release of sick and injured wild birds, is also here.

The Tampa Bay Holocaust Memorial and Educational Research Center. 55 5th St. S., at Duhme Road (113th Street N.), Madeira Beach. ☎ **813/821-8261.** Admission by $6 donation adults, $5 seniors. Mon–Fri 10am–4pm; Sun noon–4pm.

Situated on the mainland grounds of the Jewish Community Center of Pinellas County, this thought-provoking museum has exhibits about the Holocaust, including a boxcar used to transport human cargo to the Auschwitz death camp in Poland. Its main focus, however, is to promote tolerance and understanding in the present. It was founded by Walter P. Loebenberg, a local businessman who escaped Nazi Germany in 1939 and fought with the U.S. Army in World War II.

SHOPPING

In addition to being a sightseeing attraction here, **John's Pass Village and Boardwalk,** on John's Pass in Madeira Beach, just north of Treasure Island (☎ 813/391-7373), is the key shopping venue on the beaches. You'll find the **Bronze Lady,** the world's largest single dealer of works—especially paintings of circus clowns—by the late comedian-artist Red Skelton. On the mainland in Clearwater, the ✪ **Senior Citizen Craft Center Gift Shop,** 940 Court St. (☎ 813/442-4266), is one of the area's most unique gift shops—an outlet for the work of some 400 local senior citizens.

WHERE TO STAY

St. Pete Beach has national chain hotels and motels of every name and description along Gulf Boulevard. For even more choices, the **St. Petersburg Area Chamber of**

Commerce lists a wide range of hotels, motels, condominiums, and other accommodations in its annual visitors guide (see "Essentials," earlier, in the St. Petersburg section). You can also use the St. Petersburg/Clearwater Convention & Visitors Bureau's free **reservations service** (☎ 800/345-6710).

As is the case throughout Florida, there are at least as many rental condominums here as there are hotel rooms. Many of them are in high-rise buildings right on the beach. Among several local rental agents, **Excell Vacation Condos,** 14955 Gulf Blvd., Madeira Beach, FL 33708 (☎ **800/733-4004** or 813/391-5512; fax 813/393-8885; **www.islandtime.com/vacation**), and **JC Resort Management,** 17200 Gulf Blvd., North Redington Beach, FL 33708 (☎ **800/535-7776** or 813/397-0441; fax 813/397-8894; **www.jcresort.com**), have many from which to choose.

High season—and higher prices—runs from January to April. Ask about special discounted packages in the summer. Any time of year, though, it's wise to make reservations early. The hotel tax in Pinellas County is 11%.

St. Pete Beach Area

✪ Beach Haven. 4980 Gulf Blvd. (at 50th Ave.), St. Pete Beach, FL 33706. ☎ **813/367-8642.** Fax 813/360-8202. 18 units. A/C TV TEL. Winter $75–$125 double; off-season $50–$108 double. MC, V.

Nestled on the beach between two high-rise condos, these low-slung, pink-with-white-trim structures look from the outside like the early-1950s motel they once were. But Jone and Millard Gamble (they also own the charming Island's End Resort, described later) have replaced the innards and installed bright tile floors, vertical blinds, pastel tropical furniture, and many modern amenities, including TVs, VCRs, refrigerators, and coffeemakers. Five of the original quarters remain as motel rooms (with shower-only bathrooms), but the Gambles linked the others to make 12 one-bedroom units and 1 two-bedroom. The choice is the one-bedroom unit with sliding glass doors opening to a deck shaded by a sprawling Brazilian pepper tree. There's an outdoor heated pool surrounded by a white picket fence, plus a sunning deck with lounge furniture by the beach. You don't get maid service on Sunday or holidays, and the rooms and bathrooms are 1950s smallish, but every unit here is bright, airy, and comfortable. Complimentary coffee and tea are served to all guests two days a week, and they can use barbecue grills and a coin laundry. This is the heart of the hotel district, so lots of restaurants are just steps away.

Captain's Quarters Inn. 10035 Gulf Blvd. (between 100th and 101st aves.), Treasure Island, FL 33706. ☎ **800/526-9547** or 813/360-1659. Fax 813/363-3074. 6 efficiencies, 2 suites, 1 cottage. A/C TV TEL. Winter $70–$100 double; off-season $55–$75 double. Weekly rates available. MC, V.

This nautically themed property is a real find, offering well-kept accommodations on the gulf at inland rates. All but one of the units sit on 100 yards of beach, an ideal vantage point for sunset-watching. Six units are efficiencies (two of them on the beach) with minikitchens including microwave oven, coffeemaker, and wet bar or sink. There's also a bayside cottage with separate bedroom and a full kitchen. Facilities include an outdoor solar-heated freshwater swimming pool, a sundeck, guest barbecues, and a library. Small pets are accepted.

Colonial Gateway Inn. 6300 Gulf Blvd. (at 63rd Ave.), St. Pete Beach, FL 33706. ☎ **800/237-8918** or 813/367-2711. Fax 813/367-7068. 100 units, 100 efficiencies. A/C TV TEL. Winter $97–$123 double; off-season $73–$115 double. Efficiencies $10 more. AE, DC, DISC, MC, V.

On the beachfront, this U-shaped complex of one- and two-story units is a favorite with families. The rooms, most of which face the pool and a central landscaped courtyard, are contemporary, with light woods and beach tones. About half the units are efficiencies with kitchenettes.

On the premises is a branch of the very good Shells seafood restaurant (see "Where to Dine" in Tampa). Bambooz Lounge and the Swigwam beach bar offer light refreshments. Facilities include an outdoor heated swimming pool with an expansive concrete deck, a kiddie pool, shuffleboard, and a games room. The water-sports shack here offers parasailing equipment rentals and also services the Days Inn Island Beach Resort next door (see below).

Days Inn Island Beach Resort. 6200 Gulf Blvd. (at 62nd Ave.), St. Pete Beach, FL 33706. ☎ **800/544-4222** or 813/367-1902. Fax 813/367-4422. 51 units, 51 efficiencies. A/C TV TEL. Winter $118–$148 double; off-season $78–$108 double. AE, DC, DISC, MC, V.

Two long, gray buildings flank a courtyard with heated swimming pool at this beachside property popular with young families. Furnished in dark woods and rich tones, guest rooms have picture-window views, and exterior walkways are set back far enough to provide sitting areas. All units have refrigerators and coffeemakers, and about half have kitchenettes. Inside the building, Players Bar & Grille has sports TVs, pizzas, pub fare, and free hot snacks from noon to 7pm daily. Outside, Jimmy B.'s beach bar is a fine place for a sunset cocktail (happy hour runs from noon to 7:30pm) and for evening entertainment, including beachside bonfires on Saturdays in winter. Amenities include two outdoor heated swimming pools, volleyball, horseshoes, shuffleboard, and a games room.

✪ **Don CeSar Beach Resort and Spa.** 3400 Gulf Blvd. (at 34th Ave./Pinellas Byway), St. Pete Beach, FL 33706. ☎ **800/282-1116,** 800/637-7200, or 813/360-1881. Fax 813/367-3609. www.media.don-cesar.com. 275 units, 70 suites. A/C MINIBAR TV TEL. Winter $275–$350 double; $340–$745 suite. Off-season $175–$300 double; $230–$670 suite. Valet parking $10, free self-parking. AE, DC, MC, V.

Dating back to 1928 and listed on the National Register of Historic Places, this Moorish-style "Pink Palace" tropical getaway is so romantic you may bump into six or seven honeymooning couples in one weekend. Sitting majestically on 7½ acres of beachfront, the landmark sports a lobby of classic high windows and archways, crystal chandeliers, marble floors, and original artworks. Most rooms have high ceilings and offer views of the gulf or Boca Ciega Bay. In addition to the 275 rooms under the minarets of the original building, the resort has 70 luxury condos in The Don Cesar Beach House, a mid-rise building several blocks to the north (there's complimentary transportation between the two). The service is good, although the front desk can get a bit overwhelmed when groups are checking in.

Dining: The pricey but intimate Maritana Grille can't be beat for fresh gourmet seafood—and caviar, if your budget can afford a serious splurge. Other outlets include the King Charles Restaurant (offering a sumptuous Sunday brunch), the Sea Porch Cafe for indoor or outdoor dining by the pool and beach, the Lobby Bar, two beachside bars, and an ice cream parlor.

Amenities: Concierge, 24-hour room service, valet parking, laundry, newspaper delivery, in-room massage, business services, complimentary coffee in lobby, babysitting, children's program. Beach, two outdoor heated swimming pools, whirlpool, exercise room, sauna, steam room, volleyball, gift shops, rentals for water-sports equipment, hair dresser, shopping arcade with upscale jewelers and men's and women's resort wear.

✪ **Island's End Resort.** 1 Pass-a-Grille Way (at 1st Ave.), St. Pete Beach, FL 33706. ☎ **813/360-5023.** Fax 813/367-7890. 6 cottages. A/C TV TEL. Dec 15 to June 1, $82–$175; off-season $61–$175. Weekly rates available. MC, V.

A wonderful respite from the maddening crowd, and a great bargain to boot, this little all-cottage hideaway sits right on the southern tip of St. Pete Beach, smack-dab on Pass-a-Grille, where the Gulf of Mexico meets Tampa Bay. You can step from the six contemporary cottages right onto the beach. And since the island curves sharply here, nothing blocks your view of the emerald bay. If you prefer to swim directly in the gulf or grab a brilliant sunset, the Pass-a-Grille public beach is virtually next door. Linked to each other by boardwalks, the comfortable one- or three-bedroom cottages have dining areas, living rooms, VCRs, and kitchens; the one three-bedroom unit also has its own private pool. Facilities include a fishing dock, patios, decks, barbecues, and hammocks. Owners Jone and Millard Gamble are no fools: they live at this shady, idyllic setting.

Radisson Sandpiper Beach Resort. 6000 Gulf Blvd. (at 60th Ave.), St. Pete Beach, FL 33706. ☎ **800/333-3333,** 813/562-1222, or 813/360-5551. Fax 813/562-1222. 36 units, 123 suites. A/C TV TEL. Winter $149–$197 double; $227–$267 suite. Off-season $115–$147 double; $157–$199 suite. AE, DC, DISC, MC, V.

Right on the beach, this employee-owned sister of the TradeWinds (see below) has a well-landscaped, tropical courtyard separating its two six-story wings, both set back from the main road. Decorated with light woods, pastel tones, and touches of rattan, most units here have coffeemakers, toasters, small refrigerators, dishwashers, and wet bars. Suites also have a living area with sofa bed.

Dining: Piper's Patio is a casual cafe with indoor/outdoor seating; and the Sand Bar offers frozen drinks, snacks, and fine sunsets by the pool. There's a Chili Peppers Mexican restaurant on the premises.

Amenities: Concierge, room service, valet laundry, newspaper delivery, in-room massage, baby-sitting, child care. Beachfront heated swimming pool and another heated swimming pool in its own greenhouse. Two air-conditioned sports courts (for racquetball, handball, and squash), exercise room, volleyball, shuffleboard, games room, gift shop/general store.

TradeWinds Resort. 5500 Gulf Blvd. (at 55th Ave.), St. Pete Beach, FL 33706. ☎ **800/237-0707** or 813/367-6461. Fax 813/360-3848. 377 units. A/C TV TEL. Winter $195–$221 double; off-season $135–$180 double. Discount packages available in summer and fall. Valet parking $3–$6; free self-parking. AE, DC, DISC, MC, V.

Don't be dismayed by the outward appearance of this six- and seven-story, concrete-and-steel monstrosity, for underneath and beside it runs a maze of brick walkways, patios, and lily ponds connected by a quarter-mile of streams. It all gives surprising charm to this employee-owned hotel. The guest units, which overlook the gulf or the 18 acres of grounds, have up-to-date kitchens or kitchenettes, contemporary furnishings, and private balconies. The children's program and summer packages are a big hit with families from around the world, attracting lots of Europeans.

Dining/Diversions: The top spot for lunch or dinner is the Palm Court, with an Italian-bistro atmosphere; for dinner, there's also Bermudas, a casual family spot. Other food outlets include the Fountain Square Deli, Pizza Hut, and Tropic Treats. Bars include Reflections piano lounge; B. R. Cuda's, with live entertainment and dancing; and the Flying Bridge, a Florida cracker-house–style beachside bar floating on one of the lily ponds.

Amenities: With the employees having a stake in the profits as well as the tips, you should get good service here. Room service, valet parking, laundry, baby-sitting, children's program. Four heated swimming pools, whirlpools, sauna, fitness center, four tennis courts, racquetball, croquet, water-sports rentals. Gas grills, guest laundry, video-game room, gift shops, full-service hair salon with massage and tanning.

Indian Rocks Beach Area

Great Heron Inn. 68 Gulf Blvd. (south of 1st Ave.), Indian Rocks Beach, FL 33785. ☎ **813/595-2589.** Fax 813/596-7309. 16 apts. A/C TV TEL. Winter $85–$88 double; off-season $59–$63 double. Weekly and monthly rates available. DISC, MC, V. Hotel is 4 blocks south of Fla. 688.

Formerly known as Alpaugh's Gulf Beach Apartments but now owned and operated by transplanted Michiganders Ralph and Teena Hickerson, this family-oriented motel sits at the narrowest section of Indian Rocks Beach, facing the gulf on one side and its own Intracoastal Waterway dock on the other. The buildings flank a central courtyard with a heated pool. The rooms offer modern furnishings, and each unit has a full kitchen and dining area. Facilities include coin-operated laundry and picnic tables. There's a boat dock across the boulevard.

✪ **Pelican–East & West.** 108 21st Ave. (at Gulf Blvd.), Indian Rocks Beach, FL 33785. ☎ **813/595-9741.** 4 suites, 4 apts. A/C TV. Winter $50–$75 double;. off-season $40–$60 double. Weekly rates available. MC, V.

"P.D.I.P." (Perfect Day in Paradise) is the motto at Mike and Carol McGlaughlin's motel complex, which offers a choice of two settings. Their lowest rates are at Pelican East, in a residential setting 500 feet from the beach, where four suites each have a bedroom and a separate kitchen. You'll pay more at Pelican West, but it's directly on the beachfront. The four beachside apartments each have a living room, bedroom, kitchen, patio, and unbeatable views of the gulf. You don't get phones in your rooms here or a swimming pool to splash around in, but it's clean and modern in all other respects.

Clearwater Beach

Best Western Sea Stone Resort. 445 Hamden Dr. (at Coronado Dr.), Clearwater Beach, FL 33767. ☎ **800/444-1919,** 800/528-1234, or 813/441-1722. Fax 813/449-1580. 65 units, 43 suites. A/C TV TEL. Winter $103–$201 double; off-season $72–$140 double. AE, DC, DISC, MC, V.

Located just across the street from the beach in Clearwater's busy south end, the Sea Stone Suites is a six-story building of classic Key West–style architecture containing 43 one-bedroom suites, each with a kitchenette and a living room. Their living room windows look across external walkways to the harbor. A few steps away, the older five-story Gulfview Wing offers 65 bedrooms. The furnishings are bright and airy, with pastel tones, light woods, and sea scenes on the walls. The on-site Marker 5 Restaurant serves breakfast only. There's valet laundry service, newspaper delivery, and complimentary coffee in the lobby. Facilities include a heated outdoor swimming pool, whirlpool, boat dock, coin-operated laundry, and meeting rooms.

✪ **Clearwater Beach Hotel.** 500 Mandalay Ave. (at Belmont St.), Clearwater Beach, FL 33767. ☎ **800/292-2295** or 813/441-2425. Fax 813/449-2083. 157 units. A/C TV TEL. Winter $105–$185 double; off-season $98–$118 double. AE, DC, MC, V.

Besides the great beach location, you'll enjoy easy access to many nearby shops and restaurants from this Old Florida–style hotel. It's been owned and operated by the same family for more than 40 years and attracts an older clientele. Directly on the gulf, the complex consists of a six-story main building and two- and three-story wings. Rooms and rates vary according to location—bay view or gulf view, poolside or beachfront. Some rooms have balconies. The dining room is romantic at sunset and offers great views of the gulf, while the nautically themed lounge has entertainment nightly. A bar provides snacks and libations beside an outdoor heated swimming pool. There's valet laundry and parking, and limited room service.

Palm Pavilion Inn. 18 Bay Esplanade (at Mandalay Ave.), Clearwater Beach, FL 33767. ☎ **800/433-PALM** or 813/446-6777. 24 units, 4 efficiencies. A/C TV TEL. Winter $82–$117 double; off-season $56–$81 double. AE, DISC, MC, V.

Just north of the tourist area, this quiet beachfront spot is removed from the bustle yet within easy walking distance of all the action. The three-story art deco building is artfully trimmed in pink and blue. The lobby area and guest rooms, also art deco in design, feature rounded light-wood and rattan furnishings, bright sea-toned fabrics, photographs from the 1920s to 1950s era, and vertical blinds. Rooms in the front of the house face the gulf; those in back face the bay. Four efficiencies have kitchenettes. Facilities include a rooftop sundeck, beach access, heated swimming pool, complimentary coffee, and beach chair and umbrella rentals. By the beach, the Palm Pavilion Grill & Bar is a fine place to catch the sunset and some live entertainment Tuesday to Sunday nights during winter, on weekends off-season. Lighted tennis courts and an athletic center are across the street.

✪ **Radisson Suite Resort on Sand Key.** 1201 Gulf Blvd., Clearwater Beach, FL 33767. ☎ **800/333-3333** or 813/596-1100. Fax 813/595-4292. 220 suites. A/C MINIBAR TV TEL. Winter $179–$279 suite for 2; off-season $135–$219 suite for 2. AE, DC, DISC, MC, V. From Clearwater Beach, go south across Clearwater Pass Bridge; hotel is on left.

You'll see the beauty of Sand Key from the suites in this boomerang-shaped, 10-story hotel overlooking Clearwater Bay. The gulf is just beyond the Sheraton Sand Key Resort across the street, and beautiful Sand Key Park is a few steps away. The whole family will enjoy exploring the adjacent boardwalk with 25 shops and restaurants. Each suite has a bedroom with a balcony offering water views, as well as a complete living room with a sofa bed, wet bar, entertainment unit, coffeemaker, and microwave oven.

Dining/Diversions: The Harbor Grille offers fresh seafood, steaks, and grand bay views. The Harbor Lounge has live entertainment, while Kokomo's serves light fare and tropical drinks.

Amenities: Room service, laundry, free trolley to the beach, year-round children's activities program at "Lisa's Klubhouse," free valet parking, masseuse. Bayside outdoor heated swimming pool with waterfall, sundeck, sauna, exercise room, guest laundry. Waterfront boardwalk with a variety of shops and restaurants.

Sheraton Sand Key Resort. 1160 Gulf Blvd., Clearwater Beach, FL 33767. ☎ **800/325-3535** or 813/595-1611. Fax 813/596-8488. 390 units. A/C TV TEL. Winter $150–$220 double; off-season $140–$200 double. AE, DC, DISC, MC, V. From Clearwater Beach, go south across Clearwater Pass Bridge; hotel is on right.

Away from the honky-tonk of Clearwater, this hotel on 10 acres right next door to Sand Key Park is a big favorite with water-sports enthusiasts. It also gets lots of European guests year-round, which explains why the room rates don't drop much during the off-season. The guest rooms have coffeemakers, hair dryers, and a balcony or patio with views of the gulf or the bay.

Dining: Rusty's Restaurant serves breakfast and dinner; for lighter fare, try the Island Café, the Sundeck, or Fast Johnny's Poolside Snack Bar. The Snack Store is open 24 hours.

Amenities: Limited room service, newspaper delivery, in-room massage, valet parking and laundry, baby-sitting, children's program (summer only). Beachside outdoor heated swimming pool, fitness center, whirlpool, three lighted tennis courts, beach volleyball, newsstand, games room, children's pool, playground, water-sports rentals, 24-hour general store.

✪ **Sun West Beach Motel.** 409 Hamden Dr. (at Bayside Dr.), Clearwater Beach, FL 33767.
☎ **813/442-5008.** Fax 813/461-1395. www.clearwaterbeach.com/SUNWEST/sunwest.
E-mail: sunwest@mail.gte.net. 4 units, 10 efficiencies. A/C TV TEL. $40–$61 double; $48–$79
efficiency. MC, V.

Overlooking the bay and yet only a two-block walk from the beach, this well-maintained one-story motel has a heated pool, fishing/boating dock, sundeck, shuffle-board court, and guest laundry. All units, which face either the bay, the pool, or the sundeck, have contemporary resort-style furnishings. The four motel rooms have small refrigerators and the 10 efficiencies have kitchens.

A Historic Hotel on the Mainland

Belleview Biltmore Resort & Spa. 25 Belleview Blvd. (P.O. Box 2317), Clearwater, FL
33757. ☎ **800/237-8947** or 813/442-6171. Fax 813/441-4173 or 813/443-6361. 200 nits,
40 suites. A/C MINIBAR TV TEL. Winter $190–$210 double; $260–$450 suite. Off-season
$150–$190 double; $220–$430 suite. AE, DC, DISC, MC, V. Resort is 1 mile south of down-town on Belleview Rd., off Alt. U.S. 19.

The Gulf Coast's oldest operating luxury tourist hotel, this gabled clapboard structure was built in 1896 by Henry B. Plant as the Hotel Belleview to attract customers to his Orange Belt Railroad. On a bluff overlooking the bay, it's the largest occupied wooden structure in the world. Today it attracts mostly groups and serious golfers (guests can play at the adjoining Belleview Biltmore Country Club, an 18-hole par-72 champi-onship course), but there's no denying its Victorian charm and old-fashioned ambi-ence—once you get past the out-of-place, glass-and-steel foyer added by more recent owners. The creaky hallways lead to several shops and a museum explaining the hotel's history. Large, high-ceilinged guest rooms are decorated in Queen Anne style, with dark-wood period furniture.

   Dining: The informal indoor/outdoor Terrace Café provides breakfast, lunch, or dinner. There's also a pub in the basement, a lounge, and a poolside bar.

   Amenities: Room service, dry cleaning and valet laundry, nightly turndown on request, currency exchange, baby-sitting. Four red-clay tennis courts; indoor and out-door heated swimming pools (one with a waterfall); whirlpool. Spa with sauna, Swiss showers, workout gym. Jogging and walking trails, bicycle rentals, yacht charters, gift shops, newsstand, golf privileges at the country club.

WHERE TO DINE

St. Pete Beach and Clearwater Beach both have a wide selection of national chain fast-food and family restaurants along their main drags.

St. Pete Beach Area

✪ **Crabby Bill's.** 5100 Gulf Blvd. (at 51st Ave.), St. Pete Beach. (☎ 813/360-8858). Reser-vations not accepted. Sandwiches $4–$6; main courses $6–$18. AE, MC, V. Mon–Thurs
11am–10pm; Fri–Sat 11am–11pm; Sun noon–10pm. SEAFOOD.

The least expensive gulfside dining here, this member of a small local chain sits right on the beach in the heart of the hotel district. It's a great place to bring the kids—especially after 5:30pm Tuesday, when they eat free and are entertained by games and contests. There's a small al fresco area off one of the two bars here, but big glass windows enclose the large dining room. They offer fine water views from picnic tables equipped with rolls of paper towels and buckets of saltine crackers, the better to eat the Alaskan, snow, golden, and stone crabs which are the big draws here. The crustaceans fall into the moderate price category, but most other main courses, such as fried clam strips or a combo broiled fish platter, are inexpensive. The creamy smoked fish spread is a delicious appetizer, and you'll get enough to whet the appetites of at least two persons for just $4.

Hurricane. 807 Gulf Way (at 9th Ave.), Pass-a-Grille. ☎ **813/360-9558.** Reservations not accepted. Salads and sandwiches $2.50–$9; main courses $7–$17. MC, V. Daily 8am–1am (breakfast Mon–Fri 8–11am, Sat–Sun 8am–noon). SEAFOOD.

A longtime institution across the street from Pass-a-Grille Public Beach, this three-level gray Victorian building with white gingerbread trim is a great place to toast the sunset, especially on the rooftop. It's more beach bar than fine restaurant, but the grouper sandwiches are a big hit, and there's always fresh fish to be broiled or fried, and shrimp and crab to be steamed. You can dine inside the knotty-pine–paneled dining room or on the sidewalk terrace, where bathers from across Gulf Way are welcome (there's a walk-up bar for beach libations). The joint jumps at night when one level turns into a virtual dance hall.

Skidder's Restaurant. 5799 Gulf Blvd. (at 60th Ave.), St. Pete Beach. ☎ **813/360-1029.** Reservations not accepted. Breakfast $3–$6; sandwiches and burgers $3–$7; pizza $5.50–$15; main courses $8–$15. AE, DC, DISC, MC, V. Daily 7am–9pm. ITALIAN/GREEK/AMERICAN.

A local favorite, this inexpensive family restaurant in the hotel district offers a full range of breakfast fare plus pizzas (available to eat here or carry out), burgers and sandwiches, big salads, gyro and *souvlaki* platters, and Italian-style veal and chicken dishes (sautéed in wine with artichokes is a house specialty). Divided by cut glass panels, the dining room has ceiling fans rotating over gray tables and booths.

Indian Rocks Beach Area

You'll find a bayfront edition of **Shells,** the fine and inexpensive local seafood chain, opposite the Lobster Pot on Gulf Boulevard at 178th Avenue in Redington Shores (☎ **813/393-8990**). See "Where to Dine" in Tampa for more information about Shells's menu and prices, which are the same at all branches.

✪ **Guppy's.** 1701 Gulf Blvd. (at 17th Ave.), Indian Rocks Beach. ☎ **813/593-2032.** Reservations not accepted. Sandwiches $5–$7; main courses $9–$20. AE, DC, DISC, MC, V. Sun–Thurs 11:30am–10:30pm; Fri–Sat 11:30am–11:30pm. SEAFOOD.

Locals love this small bar and grill across from Indian Rocks Public Beach because they know they'll always get terrific chow (it's associated with the excellent Lobster Pot, mentioned next). You won't soon forget the salmon coated with potatoes and lightly fried to brown, and then baked with a creamy leek and garlic sauce; it's fattening, yes, but also a bargain at $9. Another good choice is lightly cooked tuna (only slightly more done than sushi) finished with a peppercorn sauce. The atmosphere is casual beach friendly, with a fun bar in the rear. Scotty's famous upside-down apple-walnut pie topped with ice cream will require a little extra work on the weights tomorrow. You can dine outside on a patio beside the main road.

✪ **Lobster Pot.** 17814 Gulf Blvd. (at 178th Ave.), Redington Shores. ☎ **813/391-8592.** www.beachdirectory.com. Reservations recommended. Main courses $14.50–$29.50. AE, DC, MC, V. Mon–Thurs 4:30–10pm; Fri–Sat 4:30–11pm; Sun 4–10pm. SEAFOOD.

Step into this weathered-looking restaurant near the beach and owner Eugen Fuhrmann will tell you to get ready to experience the finest seafood in the area. The prices are high, but the variety of lobster dishes is amazing. The lobster américaine is flambéed in brandy with garlic, and the bouillabaisse is as authentic as any you'd find in the south of France. In addition to lobster, there's a wide selection of grouper, snapper, salmon, swordfish, shrimp, scallops, crab, and Dover sole, prepared simply or with elaborate sauces. There's no ordinary children's menu here: it features half a main lobster and a petite filet mignon.

❖ **Wine Cellar.** 17307 Gulf Blvd. (at 173rd Ave.), North Redington Beach. ☎ **813/ 393-3491.** Reservations recommended. Main courses $13–$30. AE, DC, MC, V. Tues–Sat 4:30–11pm; Sun 4–11pm. CONTINENTAL.

Every evening during the high season and on weekends all year, the cars pack the parking lot at this restaurant, which is highly popular with locals and visitors alike. You'll find an assortment of divided dining rooms, and the cuisine offers the best of Europe and the States. Start off with caviar, move on to a fresh North Carolina rainbow trout or chateaubriand, and top it all off with chocolate velvet torte. There's jazz in the lounge on Thursday, Friday, and Saturday evenings; Dixieland jazz on Sunday. You'll often find noisy private parties going on.

Clearwater Beach

❖ **Bob Heilman's Beachcomber.** 447 Mandalay Ave. (at Papaya St.). ☎ **813/442-4144.** Reservations recommended. Main courses $12–$24. AE, DC, DISC, MC, V. Mon–Sat 11:30am–11pm; Sun noon–10pm. AMERICAN.

In a restaurant row opposite the beach, this nautically attired establishment has been popular for more than 45 years. It's a classy bistro, with a pianist adding to an elegant but relaxed ambience. The menu presents a variety of fresh seafood, beef, veal, and lamb selections. The "back-to-the-farm" fried chicken—from an original 1910 Heilman family recipe—is incredible.

Bubby's Bistro & Wine Bar. 447 Mandalay Ave. (at Papaya St., behind Bob Heilman's Beachcomber). ☎ **813/446-9463.** Reservations not accepted. Sandwiches and pizzas $6–$12; main courses $10–$17. AE, DC, DISC, MC, V. Daily 5pm–midnight. AMERICAN.

Bob and Sherri Heilman opened this dark, very urban bistro behind their popular restaurant in 1993, and it's been a local hit ever since. The wine-cellar theme is amply justified by the real thing: a walk-in closet with several thousand bottles kept at a constant 55°F. Walk through and pick your vintage; then listen to jazz while you dine inside at tall, bar-height tables or outside on a covered patio. The chef specializes in gourmet pizzas on homemade focaccia crust (as a tasty appetizer), plus char-grilled veal chops, filet mignon, fresh fish, and monstrous pork chops with carmelized Granny Smith apples and a Mount Vernon mustard sauce. Everything's served à la carte here, so watch your credit card. On the other hand, there's an affordable sandwich menu featuring bronzed grouper and chicken with a spicy Jack cheese.

Frenchy's Cafe. 41 Baymont St. ☎ **813/446-3607.** Reservations not accepted. Main courses $5–$15. AE, MC, V. Mon–Thurs 11:30am–11pm; Fri–Sat 11:30am–midnight; Sun noon–11pm. SEAFOOD.

Always popular with locals and visitors in the know, this casual cafe makes the best grouper sandwiches in the area—and has all the awards to prove it. They're fresh, thick, juicy, and always delicious. The atmosphere is pure Florida casual style, and there's always a wait.

For more casual fare directly on the beach, **Frenchy's Rockaway Grill,** at 7 Rockaway St. (☎ **813/446-4844**), has a wonderful outdoor setting.

❖ **Seafood & Sunsets at Julie's.** 351 S. Gulfview Blvd. (at 5th St.), Clearwater Beach. ☎ **813/441-2548.** Reservations recommended. Main courses $8–$15. AE, MC, V. Daily 11am–10pm. SEAFOOD.

A Key West–style tradition takes over Julie Nichols' place at dusk as both locals and visitors gather to toast the sunset over the beach across the street. The best seats are in the tiny upstairs dining room. Check out the seafood menu featuring mahi mahi, charcoal-broiled with sour cream, or fresh Florida grouper and Mike Macy's stuffed flounder.

The Beaches After Dark

If you haven't already found it during your sightseeing and shopping excursions, the restored fishing community of **John's Pass Village and Boardwalk,** on Gulf Boulevard at John's Pass in Madeira Beach, has plenty of restaurants, bars, and shops to keep you occupied after the sun sets. Elsewhere, the nightlife scene at the beach revolves around rocking bars that pump out the music until 2am.

Down south in Pass-a-Grille, there's the popular, always lively **Hurricane,** on Gulf Way at 9th Avenue opposite the public beach (see "Where to Dine," earlier).

On Treasure Island, **Beach Nutts,** on West Gulf Boulevard at 96th Ave. (☎ 813/367-7427), is perched atop a stilt foundation like a wooden beach cottage on the Gulf of Mexico. The music ranges from Top 40 to reggae and rock. **Manhattans,** Gulf Boulevard at 116th Avenue (☎ 813/363-1500), offers a variety of live music, from country to contemporary and classic rock. Up on the northern tip of Treasure Island, **Gators on the Pass** (☎ 813/367-8951) claims to have the world's longest waterfront bar, with a huge deck overlooking the waters of John's Pass. The complex also includes a no-smoking sports bar and a three-story tower with a top-level observation deck for panoramic views of the Gulf of Mexico. There's live music, from acoustic and blues to rock, most nights.

In Clearwater Beach, the **Palm Pavilion Grill & Bar,** on the beach at 18 Bay Esplanade (☎ 813/446-6777), has live music Tuesday through Sunday nights during winter, on weekends off-season. Nearby, **Frenchy's Rockaway Grill,** at 7 Rockaway St. (☎ 813/446-4844), is another popular hangout.

If you're into laughs, **Coconuts Comedy Club,** at the Howard Johnson motel, Gulf Boulevard at 61st Avenue in St. Pete Beach (☎ 813/360-5653), has an ever-changing program of live stand-up funny men and women. Call for the schedule, performers, and prices.

Index

See also separate Accommodations and Restaurant indexes below.
Page numbers in italics refer to maps.

ACCOMMODATIONS INDEX

Medieval Times®

DINNER & TOURNAMENT

**4510 W. Irlo Bronson Mem. Hwy.
Kissimmee, FL 34746
(407) 396-1518 • (407) 239-0214**

**Must present this coupon at time of purchase.
Not valid with any other offers or discounts.
Valid for up to 6 people. Valid at the
Medieval Times Florida Castle only.**

**Located on Highway 192 just 6 miles east of I-4
Between guide markers 14 & 15**

Expires 9/30/99   Code: Frommer

VOTED #1 DINNER ATTRACTION™

Coupon valid for up to six admissions. Not valid
with any other discounts, coupons,
or special events.

Nightly Performances!

For reservations and show times, call:
407/237-9223 or 1-800-553-6116

Hwy. 192 at the Osceola Square Mall in Kissimmee
(407) 870-2222

King Henry's Feast
8984 International Drive
Orlando, FL 32819

Retail Price
$36.95 + tax & tip for adults
$22.95 + tax & tip for children 3-11 years old

Celebrating 10 Years!
King Henry the XIII's Birthday Celebration
Singing Wenches
Fighting Knights in Action!
16th Century Music
Spectacular Aerial Ballerina
Comedy, Action and Thrills!
Amazing Death Defying Specialty Acts
Audience Participation
Family Oriented
Free Parking

Wild Bill's Wild West Dinner Extravaganza
5260 W. Highway 192 (East of 1-4)
Kissimmee, FL 34741

Retail Price:
$35.95 + tax & tip for adults
$22.95 + tax & tip for children 3-11 years old

20 Great Shops
Professional Trick Roper
Native American Indian Dancers
Amazing Specialty Acts
Dance Hall Girls
Lots of Country Music
Comedy, Action Thrills!
Audience Participation
Family Oriented
Free Parking

Blazing Pianos
8445 International Drive
(In the Mercado Shopping Center)
Orlando, FL 32819
407-363-5104

Open Nightly at 7:00pm

All ages welcome Sunday through Thursday

21 Years and Over Friday and Saturday

Full Service Kitchen & Bar

Laughing Required!

Fun For All Ages!

$4.00 off each person

Take advantage of our $24 Value and enjoy 36 fun acres of stimulating slides, adventurous pools and a splashin' wave pool. Bring your own lunch and retreat to 3 acres of beautifully landscaped picnic area.

There's something for the whole family at Water Mania!

Good for up to 6 people.
$24.00 value

407/396-2626

Save $2
admission to

INTERNATIONAL DRIVE, ORLANDO

Offer good for up to six people.
Not to be used with any other offer or afternoon pricing.

Expires 12/31/99

Macmillian Travel PLU 1671A 1672C

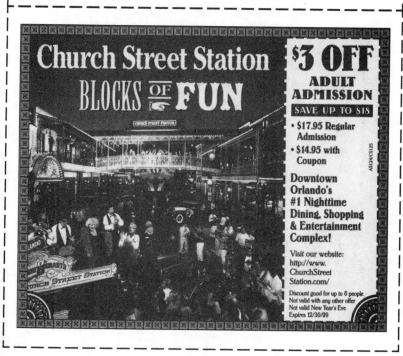

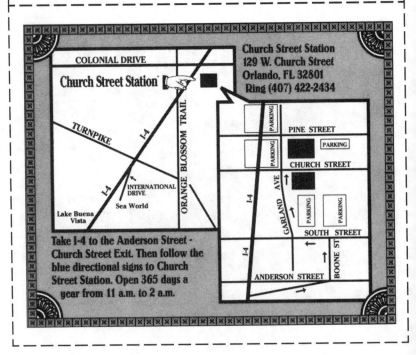

DAYS INN

Follow the Sun

- Available at participating properties.

- This coupon cannot be combined with any other special discount offer.

- Limit one coupon per room, per stay.

- Expires December 31, 1999.

1-800-DAYS INN

Save $15 on a Weekly Rental

Terms and Conditions:

Offer valid on an Intermediate (Group C) through a Full Size 4-Door (Group E) car. Dollars off applies to the cost of the total rental with a minimum of 5 days. Coupon must be surrendered at time of rental; one per rental. An advance reservation is required. May not be used in conjunction with any other coupon, promotion or offer. Coupon valid at participating Avis locations in the contiguous U.S. Offer may not be available on all rates at all times. Cars subject to availability. Taxes, local government surcharges, vehicle licensing fee no higher than $1.85/day in CA, airport recoupment fee up to 12% at some locations and optional items, such as LDW, additional driver fee and fuel service are extra. Renter must meet Avis age, driver and credit requirements. Minimum age is 25 but may vary by location. Rental must begin by 12/31/99.

Rental Sales Agent Instructions
At checkout:
In CPN, enter **MUFA877.**
Complete this information:

RA #: _____

Rental location: _____
Attach to coupon tape.

AVIS

We try harder.

COUPON # MUFA877

©1998 Wizard Co., Inc.   7/98 DTPV/

DISCOUNT AIRLINE TICKETS ARE ALL WE DO

Offer valid on major U.S. airlines. No charters.
Discounts vary depending on which airline you use.
Valid on one-way tickets both domestically and internationally.

PIN Number: 7110111

FROMMER'S® COMPLETE TRAVEL GUIDES

(Comprehensive guides with selections in all price ranges—from deluxe to budget)

Alaska
Amsterdam
Arizona
Atlanta
Australia
Austria
Bahamas
Barcelona, Madrid & Seville
Belgium, Holland & Luxembourg
Bermuda
Boston
Budapest & the Best of Hungary
California
Canada
Cancún, Cozumel & the Yucatán
Cape Cod, Nantucket & Martha's Vineyard
Caribbean
Caribbean Cruises & Ports of Call
Caribbean Ports of Call
Carolinas & Georgia
Chicago
China
Colorado
Costa Rica
Denver, Boulder & Colorado Springs
England
Europe
Florida

France
Germany
Greece
Hawaii
Hong Kong
Honolulu, Waikiki & Oahu
Ireland
Israel
Italy
Jamaica & Barbados
Japan
Las Vegas
London
Los Angeles
Maryland & Delaware
Maui
Mexico
Miami & the Keys
Montana & Wyoming
Montréal & Québec City
Munich & the Bavarian Alps
Nashville & Memphis
Nepal
New England
New Mexico
New Orleans
New York City
Nova Scotia, New Brunswick & Prince Edward Island
Oregon
Paris
Philadelphia & the Amish Country

Portugal
Prague & the Best of the Czech Republic
Provence & the Riviera
Puerto Rico
Rome
San Antonio & Austin
San Diego
San Francisco
Santa Fe, Taos & Albuquerque
Scandinavia
Scotland
Seattle & Portland
Singapore & Malaysia
South Pacific
Spain
Switzerland
Thailand
Tokyo
Toronto
Tuscany & Umbria
USA
Utah
Vancouver & Victoria
Vermont, New Hampshire & Maine
Vienna & the Danube Valley
Virgin Islands
Virginia
Walt Disney World & Orlando
Washington, D.C.
Washington State

FROMMER'S® DOLLAR-A-DAY GUIDES

(The ultimate guides to comfortable low-cost travel)

Australia from $50 a Day
California from $60 a Day
Caribbean from $60 a Day
England from $60 a Day
Europe from $50 a Day
Florida from $60 a Day
Greece from $50 a Day
Hawaii from $60 a Day
Ireland from $50 a Day

Israel from $45 a Day
Italy from $50 a Day
London from $70 a Day
New York from $75 a Day
New Zealand from $50 a Day
Paris from $70 a Day
San Francisco from $60 a Day
Washington, D.C., from $60 a Day

FROMMER'S® MEMORABLE WALKS

Chicago
London

New York
Paris

San Francisco

YOU TRAVEL,
*H*ELP IS NEVER
FAR AWAY.

From planning your trip to providing travel assistance
along the way, American Express® Travel Service Offices
are always there to help you do more.

Disney

American Express Travel Service
Epcot Center
Walt Disney World® Resort
Lake Buena Vista
407/827-7500

American Express Travel Service
2 West Church Street, Suite 1
Sun Bank Center
Orlando
407/843-0004

Travel

http://www.americanexpress.com/travel

For the office nearest you, call 1-800-AXP-3429.